THE

WHIZ

KIDS

Books by John A. Byrne

The Whiz Kids
Odyssey by John Sculley with John A. Byrne
The Headhunters
Business Week's Guide to the Best Business Schools
Business Week's Guide to the Best Executive Education Programs
with Cynthia Green

THE

WHIZ

KIDS

·

The Founding Fathers
of American Business
—and the Legacy
They Left Us

John A. Byrne

CURRENCY

DOUBLEDAY

NEW YORK · LONDON · TORONTO · SYDNEY · AUCKLAND

To Mom and Dad

Contents

Introduction WHAT IT TAKES TO CHANGE THE WORLD 5

Part One

FRIENDS & DREAMS

1 INDUSTRIAL PRINCE *13*

2 "YOUNG NAPOLEON" *23*

3 OF RULERS & MEASURING STICKS *39*

4 CARNIVAL MAN *53*

5 GENTLE GEORGE *65*

6 THE TELEGRAM *77*

7 QUIZ KIDS *91*

8 ALL THAT GLITTERS *111*

9 CLASH OF AMBITION *123*

10 WASHOUT *143*

Part Two

PAYING DUES

11 ANOTHER CHANCE *155*

12 THE CIRCUMFERENCE OF A BERRY *167*

13 MR. BLANDINGS' DREAM HOUSE *185*

14 AN AMERICAN IN PARIS *197*

15 "GARY COOPER ON WHEELS" *213*

16 SHOWDOWN AT CULVER CITY   *231*

17 UNSAFE AT ANY SPEED   *247*

18 STEEL CARTOONS   *267*

19 THE BIRTH OF A NEW ERA   *285*

20 THE IMPOSSIBLE TAKES A LITTLE LONGER   *299*

21 THE INDY 500   *309*

22 THE EDSEL FIASCO   *335*

23 A BIRTHDAY   *347*

24 PRINCIPLE VERSUS EXPEDIENCY   *361*

Part Three

■

TWILIGHT OF HONOR

25 SYNERGY?   *379*

26 "ADDING MACHINE WARRIORS"   *393*

27 FRIDEN BRAINS   *411*

28 MCNAMARA'S WAR   *437*

29 DEATH OF A WHIZ KID   *465*

30 THE SHATTERED IMAGE   *483*

31 A REUNION   *501*

32 THE IMPERFECT WORLD THEY LEFT US   *515*

Epilogue   *521*

Notes & Sources   *537*

Bibliography   *563*

Acknowledgements   *567*

Index   *569*

CHARLES "TEX" THORNTON: The man everyone underestimated had surprises for all. Born in a dusty Texas farm town, a product of a poor and broken home, Tex made a name for himself in Washington during World War Two, when sheer bravado helped him sell a business ideology to win the war from the back office. For Tex, war was management strategy—a method of counting out planes, supplies, bullets and bombs and delivering them to the theater of war on budget and on time. With his war buddies, rechristened the Whiz Kids, he brought his skills to Ford. Years later he founded Litton Industries, one of the fastest-growing enterprises in history, building it into a multi-billion dollar conglomerate—the first of its kind. Ten years later, already a millionaire forty times over, he legitimized the notion that a professional manager could manage and control eveything without knowing anything about the products a company produces.

ROBERT S. MCNAMARA: "The leading specimen of *homo mathematicus*" he was called by an enemy; "the human computer" he was called by a friend. Everyone saw in Bob a fierce intellect almost devoid of emotion, a man so work-obsessed that he brought his business notes to study at the funeral of a friend. Though he had little personal interest in cars, McNamara rose quickly at Ford to become president at age forty-four in 1960, only to answer just weeks later President John F. Kennedy's call to become Secretary of Defense. His early, controversial role in the Vietnam War led one senator to dub the conflict "McNamara's War," and his search for rational answers in an often irrational world ultimately made him a tragic figure.

FRANCIS C. REITH: Numbers and metal were always at war for Jack Reith's affections. When he finally broke free of the Whiz Kids' reliance on numbers and had the chance to create a car of his own, he created a "Gary Cooper on wheels, a car with hair on its chest." The Mercury Turnpike Cruiser, launched with the fanfare of a marketing visionary in 1956, was Jack's baby and a precursor to the Edsel in many ways. The Cruiser became one of the car industry's biggest disasters, from which Jack never recovered.

GEORGE E. MOORE: Baby-faced George came of age under Thornton in the dark and desperate days of World War Two. Everyone's good son, people loved to protect him, to ease his path, save him from his weaknesses. Breaking away from his Whiz Kid friends and their unrelenting pace and standards, George left to begin a business of his own, but never realized a comparable success to his buddies.

J. EDWARD LUNDY: People say he had two loves in his life: the Ford Motor Company and the Roman Catholic Church. Ford managers knew that when they couldn't find Lundy at the office, they could always drop work off for him with the parish priest. Ed Lundy was the quiet man who gave the Whiz Kids their legacy. He recruited followers by the thousands and rotated them through the company like prized crops. They spread the Whiz Kids' gospel to companies far beyond Ford.

ARJAY R. MILLER: Indecisive except when it came to saying yes to Henry Ford, Miller rose high in Ford's ranks. He proved to be a bright, though, ineffectual president of the company. Of all of Ford's second-in-commands, Arjay is perhaps the most forgettable because, unlike Bob or Lee Iacocca, he never created a car he could call his own. Shortly after being fired by Henry, he became dean of the Stanford School of Business, a post he served in with high distinction.

BEN D. MILLS: At Ford, he moved up through a variety of line jobs to become a vice president with the thankless task of cleaning up the Edsel mess—a clean-up equivalent to the Exxon Valdez incident. A highly dramatic failure for Ford and American business, the Edsel was the first sign that Detroit didn't really have its act together.

JAMES O. WRIGHT: The ultimate corporate bureaucrat, Wright followed McNamara's footsteps all the way up the corporate ladder until being passed over for the presidency by Whiz Kid colleague Miller. He resigned, later becoming the president of a major auto supplier to Ford.

CHARLES E. BOSWORTH: The only Whiz Kid who stayed at Ford and failed to achieve the rank of vice president. Bosworth quit in disgust, even retiring in 1966, a few months shy of his 51st birthday. He never worked again.

WILBUR R. ANDRESON: The first dropout. Andy grew disenchanted with the competition at Ford and left within eight months. He went west to California, joining the Bekins Moving & Storage Co., where he reached the presidency in 1969.

WHAT IT
TAKES TO
CHANGE THE
WORLD

———————
■

*B*usiness is the crudest science, the coldest art. It teaches endless lessons in performance measurements, quality checks,
profit and loss, but next to nothing about why people give their lives to
their jobs, and what it means to do so. You wake up in the morning to
devote yourself to your ambition, to the daily climb onto the high wire of
power. Where does this routine leave you by the end of the day or a year,
much less over the course of a career? Is too much ambition harmful,
like too much sun, or booze, or sleep?

In reporting on business for fifteen years—most of that time with
Business Week—I've unscrambled most of the obvious stories of how
companies produce billions of dollars in goods and services. But I've
always wanted to pursue the mysteries of the human side of business.
I've wanted to learn how the same practices that organize societies into
economies and markets can disorganize individual lives.

So I set out to study ten men possessed by some of the biggest dreams in recent corporate history. These ten friends came to be called the Whiz Kids. They were like no group before or since in business—a team whose members were as coldly and rationally driven as the men of the Manhattan Project. They were sometimes compared to the Apollo astronauts, full of daring and drive—a potent mix of the Right Stuff and the Wise Men. The Whiz Kids believed—and convinced others—that they could create a perfect world, and that business was the means to do it. Their story takes place in the center of American industrial power in the 1950s and 1960s. But the most interesting part of it unfolds just beyond the spotlight of success, in the place deep in the soul where, as F. Scott Fitzgerald said, it's always three in the morning. The story of this book always returns there.

One of the most intriguing things about the Whiz Kids is that they were friends, loyalists to the cause of one another. They were war buddies first, partners at Ford later. They showed one another respect and support in quantities I rarely witness in the business people I cover. Then at some point, they changed allegiances and forged closer, Faustian ties, to their individual careers. As success became more important, their isolation became more pronounced: obsession plunged a few of them headlong into despair; petty jealousies transformed friends into rivals; pride derailed brilliance. The shortcuts they took to success gave me a new map for understanding why people can be so smart, yet create organizations that are tragically foolish.

Researching the lives of the Whiz Kids, I came to understand that there is a series of natural laws in business, the most important of which is balance. The gyro embedded in every driven person and every ambitious organization is a sensitive instrument. At some point the spin turns into an imbalanced wobble. When and how do organizations lose their sense of balance? To what extent is institutional balance dependent on the equilibrium of the people within it? When does ambition help us achieve our desires and passions, and when is the successful person better off destroying what he creates rather than taking it or himself too seriously? By becoming more aware of the balance between institutions and individuals, we can craft saner, more successful lives. The Whiz Kids are a portrait of the near success of this. Perhaps they would have created something like a perfect America, or at least perfect companies. But each of them failed in simple human ways.

THEY WERE THE best men of the last big generation to come to power, as big in size and promise as the boomers who are coming to power in

American business and politics today. They were smart, brazen Army Air Force officers who devised a new means of competitive might. Back office heroes, they'd figured out the math necessary to outnumber and overpower the enemy and so helped the GIs win World War Two. The grunts fought the war with their lives; the Whiz Kids' revolutionary new answer was printouts. They could deliver the planes, the troops, the K-rations it took to rout the enemy. For them, every problem had a number as its answer, not a rah-rah let's-storm-the-beachhead emotion, not a secret bit of wisdom. They thought that if they stuck it out together after the war, they could do for business what they'd done for the Allies: bring the skills of control and scientific management to an industry as troubled then as it is today: the car business. It was poised to become the powerhouse American industry, and the Whiz Kids could smell the potential several miles off. Henry Ford II hired all of them in 1945. It turned out to be one of the best deals Henry ever made. The Whiz Kids rescued Ford from the doldrums and helped the company soar.

Ten guys, even smart guys, who are young, green, totally naive, love-struck on ideals, and suddenly in over their heads should by rights have done their jobs, then disappeared from history. But these ten were determined to change the world. That mission would ultimately tear apart their friendship, drive one of them to suicide, and eventually force us, their heirs, into business systems and rituals that in the last twenty years have brought us to the jumping-off point of economic ruin. America's economic struggles—our relentless belief in the numbers, our insistence that corporate strength is equated with corporate size—can be traced to their ideals.

Just how remarkable they were is captured on the cover of this book, in their "class picture" taken in 1946, in their first month at Ford. They were in their mid-twenties and early thirties. Already Tex Thornton's gaze was focused like a gunsight on his target, impatient almost to the point of self-destruction. Robert McNamara was a portrait of intellectual coolness, a quality that would lead others to brand him the "human computer" more out of fear than respect. Jack Reith's cocked head announced his swagger and determination before he ever opened his mouth. George Moore, who was almost too human and vulnerable for so hell-bent a group, is the picture of baby-faced fragility. Standing shoulder to shoulder were the future leaders of American business in the 1960s and 70s. What made these leaders different from others is that they were also ideologues.

Together at Ford, Thornton's group refined and built a mystique for the methods of rational management they invented during the war—a system of tight financial controls that made quantitative analysis of every business problem essential. They sold the rest of the world solutions that drew on hard numbers and cold facts. Some would say they lobotomized business, and in truth, they drove emotion and intuition and chaos out of decision making. They persuaded themselves and others that a professional manager can and must control everything without knowing anything about the products the company produces.

Numbers became the one true moral compass, the deciding point in every decision. This methodology unbalanced business and unbalanced their lives.

That explains how Tex Thornton, one of the world's first conglomerateurs, built Litton Industries—an empire of disparate businesses that had won Wall Street's approval but that also sowed the early seeds of the country's decline in competitiveness. That is the reason why McNamara's fame rests with turning more soldiers into body bags when he managed the Vietnam War than any modern military strategist. That may be why the perfect world the Whiz Kids longed to build could at its best be no more than a phantom and at its worst a trap.

The Whiz Kids dragged Ford and all of American industry into the modern world but not without some dire consequences. Their belief in the numbers gave us systems that promoted efficiency at the expense of responsiveness. A postwar generation of managers became slaves to numbers, taught to squeeze out costs in every part and every product while building looming hierarchies of white-collar staffs that centralized authority and decision making. For the efficiencies of cutting costs and gaining control, we sacrificed all notions of product quality and customer satisfaction, and we obliterated individual initiative.

Their point of view also created a cult of management and number worship, of hubris and arrogance. The Whiz Kids brought to bear a supreme confidence in their own abilities, a confidence flawed because it was derived not from any real knowledge of markets or experience with products, but from a system of empirical data that made them and other professional managers nearly godlike. Ultimately, these systems taught managers to trust numbers more than people.

For a time, however, their ideas worked brilliantly. American business needed discipline, order, and control. They provided the model to manage growth and build business empires. Traditional histories say that entrepreneurs like J.P. Morgan and Henry Ford created the businesses that gave Americans the highest standard of living in the world. Those histories are half wrong. Morgan, Ford and their like were glorious but also anomalous. A new generation of professional managers hit the American scene in the postwar years with a bronco rider's sense of how to push vast, complicated enterprises through untold challenges, making American institutions respected and feared throughout the world. The Whiz Kids were simply the first of this new industrial elite.

THROUGH THE FIVE years I spent reporting and writing this book, Jack Reith became the flash point for the best and the worst of the Whiz Kids. The extremes met in his character.

Reith was the Whiz Kid closest to a shooting star. He could have been as crucial a figure in American history as McNamara, who went on to Washington to serve two presidents as Secretary of Defense, or Thornton, who worked for two of America's most famous capitalists—Henry Ford II and Howard Hughes—only to become one himself. Reith could have accomplished every bit as much as they did. He turned around Ford of France, and came back to the U.S. a legitimate hero with a medal from the French government pinned to his chest.

Boldly confident, Jack put together the strategic plan for Ford to confront head-on its larger, stronger nemesis—General Motors. He convinced himself that he could win this confrontation by building bigger, flashier, better cars, the true American Dream Machines. His vision was to create "Gary Cooper on wheels, a car with hair on its chest." His prototype became the 1957 Mercury Turnpike Cruiser. Jack poured himself into the creation of that car. He was totally unprepared for anything other than total success. And when the car bombed, along with Jack's ambitious plan for Ford to take on GM, he couldn't recover. The failure cost him the job he loved, and that destroyed him. The Cincinnati coroner ruled his death by a .38-caliber gunshot wound a suicide.

Had his friends known the depth of Jack's despair, they might have helped him get through this crisis. But Jack's isolation was total. Of course, business often gets in the way of friendship. But there are times when friendship moves in the way of business. To what extent did the Whiz Kids collude in Jack's demise? One of the revelations I came upon is the behind-the-scenes tale of how Ford launched its infamous Edsel plan—regarded to this day as one of the biggest commercial product disasters of all time. It will shock many to learn that the friendship among the Whiz Kids was instrumental in leading to the disaster. Several of the men were opposed to the huge investment from the start. One even predicted, with chilling accuracy, that it would be suicidal to take on GM; the assumptions behind the numbers were foolish; they verged on fiction. Yet, the Whiz Kids failed to assert their opposition because the plan was hatched and promoted by their colleague, Jack Reith. As Arjay Miller put it, "We didn't want to rain on Jack's parade." Friendship and ambition do not always mix.

WITH REITH, I hit the pay dirt of my own fears and ambitions. I know the times that work has reduced me to a fortress of my own making. I could imagine how easily his success would put him out of touch with his strength, when he'd begin to mistake the vigor of the organization for his own. I needed to immerse myself in Jack's story to get a feeling for how far one could go. When I found an ad for Jack's gaudy creation —the 1957 Mercury Turnpike Cruiser—I rushed to see the clunker up on cinder blocks in the grimy garage of an antique car collector, looking for all the world like one of those dinosaur skeletons you see in museums, the kind held together by nothing but pins. I had to buy it— extravagantly ugly though it was. It was Whiz Kid Jack Reith in steel. His personality. His mania. To get into the Cruiser, to ride it down the street, to feel its tank-like power, gave me a new understanding of who he was and what he wanted.

Near the end of their lives, each of the Whiz Kids found that business was no science and even less of an art. The ways in which McNamara, Reith, Thornton, and their buddies finally did change the world were not the ways they had anticipated.

The Whiz Kids are our business ancestors. They may well have been too smart, too eager, too sure of themselves and their methods. As their work-obsessed heirs, we have much to learn from them.

Part One

FRIENDS & DREAMS

When the Whiz Kids first glimpsed the tremendous expanse of Ford Motor's River Rouge plant—the world's largest industrial complex—they were overwhelmed by the vast opportunity it represented.

INDUSTRIAL
PRINCE

■

"Look ahead! Those carefree
days will return. And with them
will come a smart new motorcar
. . . Then head for heights that
put the clouds at your fingertips.
Go where the winter roads are
bright with sun. Or drop down
at dusk to where the breeze
trembles that hidden lake."
—A FORD ADVERTISEMENT IN 1945

*I*n the war's glorious aftermath, anything seemed possible.

Bob McNamara and Charlie Bosworth were rumbling their
way up I-75, bound for Detroit in McNamara's weathered Ford Model
A Roadster. The heart of Industrial America was a good four- or five-
hour drive from the Army Air Force base in Dayton. They'd left before
sunrise that Wednesday in early November 1945. There was a crispness
in the air, a harbinger of another unbearable Detroit winter, and the chill
seeped through the car as they drove toward their destination, two cogs
in a machine that smelt of engine oil and gas. But they were heroes, too.
Like so many men at the end of World War Two, they had just helped a
nation win a colossal war. Back-office heroes, but heroes no less than the
guys who died for the Great Cause. What set them apart was that they
held an even higher dream now. If any dream could be bigger than
winning the war, theirs was. It all hinged on the collusion of one of the
most important men in America, Henry Ford II.

They joked about how unfathomable this interview with Ford II would have been before the war. Now, at the dawn of the postwar world, when everyone was hungry or a job out of uniform, it should have been impossible. Henry had the jobs they wanted in the most desirable American industry of the era. And now they were to meet the Industrial Prince himself thanks to Colonel Charles "Tex" Thornton, their gutsy, imperious boss.

Tex had hatched the quirky idea: to offer young Henry the best of his elite Air Force team in a package deal. It was crazy but brilliant. Why wouldn't a giant company hire ten men—war buddies that a common enemy and set of ambitions had brought close—in one fell swoop, even if the vast majority of returning servicemen faced the future with worry and uncertainty. Even if a postwar economy meant fewer, lesser jobs.

Only the war had lifted the country out of the Great Depression. Many feared that the war's end would bring about another period of unemployment, resignation and despair as millions of men overwhelmed the job market. But things that would have been beyond the horizons of most people, Tex saw plainly within his reach. The war had given him a new life and new expectations, just as it had given America a new sense of dignity and pride. And unlike many of the sons of the Depression, Tex possessed the bravado and optimism to think that he could write his own ticket to the history of the American Century.

To Colonel Thornton, the war had not been an interruption in his men's lives. It was part of their climb. Their years in uniform represented invaluable experience to be sold at a premium. The ten of them had been soldiers who didn't carry rifles or commandeer tanks. Yet they made the air war devastatingly effective against the enemy in World War Two. Tex had lured the sharpest minds of the day to soldier under his command, educated them at Harvard in "advanced management techniques" and installed them in far-flung outposts throughout the world. Once in the field, they gathered the facts and the numbers of modern warfare. Tex had fought to establish systems in the War Department to track how many bombers and fighters the Army Air Force could launch into combat every day. They matched planes to airfields, crews to planes, armament to aircraft. They compared the relative benefits of the B-17 to the B-24. They were the professionals who transformed battle into science, helping to organize, manage and run America's deadly air war.

If anyone could sell Henry Ford on this wacky idea, it was him. Thornton was all of thirty-two years old in 1945, but in appearance and in speech he radiated authority. When Tex sat face to face with you, it was like a sunlamp coming on—a warming flood of energy, as one admirer put it. He could charm anyone with his resonant Texas twang. Tex was ruggedly handsome, medium height and solidly built, with the kind of features that welcomed people: a round face, warm hazel eyes and a dazzlingly disarming smile. Clamped between his teeth was invariably a short cigarette holder smoldering tobacco, a splendid affectation of the late President Roosevelt. Like FDR, he was breezy and direct, and full of bile when he didn't get his way.

Since war's end, America had been drawing new maps for the world, etching new borders in Europe and elsewhere. Tex and his buddies were out to do the same in business. For the war was as much a triumph of American management as it was a victory for democracy. In the new postwar America, Tex foresaw an unprecedented opportunity ahead for a new generation of leaders. He understood that industry was waiting for new ideas and new leaders who would determine what peacetime goods would be produced by the same factories that had turned out the instruments of war. These leaders would set the economic agenda for the country's future. Nine of those leaders were right there, still under his command. To maneuver his way in this upcoming session with young Ford, all Tex had to do was persuade him that he and his colleagues could tune up Ford's company just the way they shook awake a dormant Army Air Force and made it super efficient and strong enough to become the decisive factor in winning the war. If anything, they had rallied around efficiency and proved its potency in a war. They made efficiency their religion—a faith based on strength, not like most religions' foundation in weakness. It was an ideal standpoint for an era that would be dominated by machine worship and Darwinian notions that only the stronger and faster survive. They were ten professional soldiers marching out to a different battleground and a new war. It was the beginning of an American era when ambition was both bold and impudent, what Gore Vidal would call "The Brazen Age." Tex and his crew were in synch with the times. When McNamara wheeled his dark blue roadster closer to the land of Ford, with Charlie Bosworth sitting there next to him, they knew Tex had got it right.

THE TWO WIRY officers caught their first glimpse of the looming smokestacks of the great River Rouge plant. He and Bosworth were left breathless by the sight. Rising from the flat terrain was a huge belching empire of factory, an unrelenting expanse of industrial brick buildings, steel mills and rail yards. They had seen pictures of this muscular man-made world in magazines before, but its grand size could hardly be appreciated by a black-and-white photograph.

If there was a single place to witness an industrial miracle, this was it —the first time they had seen the plant, and it was really all they noticed of Detroit, all they could remember for a long time of this initial visit. Since the late 1920s, the Ford Motor Company facility stood as an industrial icon, some ninety buildings in all, the world's largest manufacturing plant. The sun barely penetrated many of the 330 acres of soot-covered windows. It was the only plant in the world where iron ore arrived by ship from the ports on the Great Lakes, was smelted into iron, converted into steel and in a matter of days transformed into thousands of parts that become an automobile.

They rode past the plant and onto the company's headquarters on Schaefer Road where they would rendezvous with Tex and the others who had taken the overnight train from Washington. Carved into the granite above the front entrance was the vision of what Henry Ford had accomplished: "Industrious application of inventive genius to the natural resources of the earth is the groundwork of prosperous civilization." No poetry could have touched them more deeply.

Young Henry's office was to the right of the marble foyer at the end of the hall, with a private entrance just off a small circular driveway. It had belonged to his grandfather, and a large window afforded a movie screen's broad view of the River Rouge complex the men had just passed. From here, old Henry could gaze out across dozens of railroad sidings to the awesome plant and admire all that he created.

McNamara and Bosworth met Tex and the others in the building's lobby on November 7. Amid the sea of dark suits flowing through the foyer, they were a funny sight in their military dress, with their dark green jackets and pinkish trousers then worn by Army Air Force officers. All they knew of Henry was what they had read in a recent *Life* magazine cover story on his assumption of the presidency of the world's largest privately owned Industrial empire. Henry's rise to power was made premature by the untimely death of his father two years ago in 1943. Edsel Ford, the company's president and the only logical heir to its throne, died at age forty-nine of complications from an operation for stomach ulcers. Shortly after Edsel's death, Henry was released by the Navy to work alongside his frail grandfather and to learn the automobile business. In Detroit, he became known simply as "Young Henry" or "Henry the Second" to distinguish him from his grandfather.

A year before he had confessed, "I am green and reaching for answers." The company's record since the late 1920s proved it sorely needed them. Ford Motor emerged from World War One with about 60 percent of the nation's auto business, but entered the second war with less than 20 percent of it. Ford's delay at bringing out new and different models beyond his once immensely successful Model T had brought his company to near collapse. During the same period, a revitalized General Motors rose to about 50 percent of the market from only 12 percent, while the Chrysler Corporation went from nothing to capture about 20 percent of the business.

Worse, Ford losses nearly canceled out all the company's profits from 1927 to 1941. *Life* magazine, describing all this in detail, noted that "U.S. industrial history can show no other example of corporate recession on so prolonged and grand a scale." If Ford were a public company, subject to the pressures of Wall Street and its shareholders, old man Henry would have lost control of the enterprise long ago. Because Ford made huge sums of money early and bought out his partners, the company was completely owned by the Ford family. It needed only to make enough money to satisfy the family's needs.

Tex's men could not have arrived at a better time. Henry was desperately trying to free himself from the old-time power brokers who had ruled Ford for his senile grandfather. He had surrounded himself with a small cluster of loyal managers, but outside the group he didn't know whom he could trust. How would Tex and his military friends fit in?

They were met by a Ford intermediary who escorted them across the street to a queer gear-shaped building with rectangular wings on two sides, an oddity left over from the 1934 World's Fair in Chicago. At the height of the Depression, old man Henry had spent $2.6 million to build a steel and limestone pavilion to house the Ford exhibit. After the fair, he demanded that the Rotunda, as it was called, be moved to Dearborn. Ford encircled it with sculptured gardens and used the building as overflow office space for his growing enterprise.

They came to a nondescript meeting room and took seats around a long walnut conference table: Charles Thornton, Robert McNamara, Francis Reith, George Moore, Charles Bosworth, Arjay Miller, J. Edward Lundy and James Wright. Two others from Tex's group, Ben Mills and Wilbur Andreson, waited anxiously in California for word of the outcome.

This was their moment. They were an exceptional team, but would Ford dare to hire all of them? None was brighter than McNamara, a former Harvard Business School assistant professor. A cool rationalist, he formed the intellectual core of the group. His sheer brainpower and analytic acumen allowed Tex's outfit to make the transition from little more than a fact-gathering center to one that analyzed the numbers and boldly urged action. Yet, Lieutenant Colonel McNamara was the only member of the group who wasn't so sure he wanted to be there. He had planned to return to Harvard to pursue his academic career when Tex had dangled this unusual opportunity before him.

McNamara's indecision was more than offset by Jack Reith, a tightly-wound bundle of energy and big ideas, for whom the possibility of working for Ford was a dream come true. As a kid growing up in Des Moines, he would sit for hours on the front stoop of his parents' home, identifying the make and model of every auto that sped down the road. His passion for cars was exceeded only by his ambition to succeed. He had watched his father lose much of what he had during the Depression and vowed that he would never fall into the same sorry trap. He despised uncertainty and loved control, and by war's end his belief in systems control had saved the Army Air Force more than $1 billion. The other six present could fill a pantheon of abilities: symbols of leadership and judgment, precision and order, smarts and perseverance.

In minutes, the Industrial Prince strolled into the room as if he had come off the pages of *Life* magazine. The men studied him. Henry Ford was handsome, all 190 pounds and six feet of him. He had a large head topped by a crew cut, blue eyes, a Roman nose and a small mouth, and he spoke with a soft and husky voice. He was slightly overweight as he always had been, even as a young man when some classmates called him "Lard-ass." But there was his unmistakable presence. Maybe it was his position, his money, his power. Whatever, it made them hover over each princely gesture. They were accustomed to reporting to military brass, the top brass. But in Henry's aura, some of them felt small. Henry was the closest you came in America to royalty. They felt the presence of real wealth and respected it more than they anticipated they would.

But there were no pretensions. It was all business. Henry walked around the table, shaking each man's hand as Tex introduced the lineup. He welcomed them to Ford, exchanged some pleasantries and then slumped into an armchair off to the side.

He was one of their generation. At twenty-eight years of age he was younger than any of them except George Moore, who was two months shy of his twenty-sixth birthday. Henry began by speaking about the goals and ambitions he had for the company, and his words made clear that both circumstances and time made Ford a lavish opportunity, a time when a new order was rising after an old one had collapsed. Only seven weeks had passed since Ford succeeded his eighty-two-year-old grandfather. "We need to make a fresh start, to do things differently," said Henry. "Maybe the company will have to be reorganized. We will certainly need to rebuild it. I want to make the company first again.

"How do you men think you could help?"

THAT STOPPED THEM. Not even Bob McNamara knew how to answer the question. Tex could talk about the past with authority. He could tell Henry how his elite group helped to systemize and analyze the largest air force ever known, with the biggest and fastest aircraft. He could boast how those planes dumped 2,057,244 tons of bombs and shot 459,750,000 rounds of ammunition on Germany, Italy and Japan in the most destructive air campaigns of all time. He knew all the numbers and all the facts. It was his business to know them.

But even at this golden moment, Tex could not foresee the future. None of them could. Even if Henry Ford could trust them, there was no clear picture of how they would fit into his automotive empire. How many old-timers would resent them, view them as a threat, try to destroy them? Would Ford give them enough power so they could make a difference? Would he let them work together as a team? Throughout the war, they marvelled at how easily the right answers came to them. Suddenly, they had none.

But Henry was undeterred. What Ford and the world hungered for in this new business frontier were decisions based on fact. He was looking at the guys who were the architects of fact for what had been the most unwieldy machine of all—the Pentagon. Before Tex arrived, the Army Air Force had been a jumble of confusion. Decisions were made on guesswork. No one seemed to know with any certainty how many airplanes were on hand, where they were and whether they could even fly. The business of America was not just steel and grain, it would be numbers and control. These guys had a lock on systems. They had it down cold. That's why Henry Ford had bothered to invite them in.

Facts and more facts. Decisions were to be based on numbers, properly analyzed and interpreted statistics, on historical "truths" and empirical evidence. Not intuition, not gut feel, not even experience, but on the disciplines of reason, logic and science—all based on facts. As a group, they would become the very model of the modern professional manager, a prototype to a generation: brilliant, tough, systematic and coldly rational.

Eventually they would unwittingly become ministers of a management theology that dominated American business and social culture. The numbers-only mentality they began would lead to an emphasis on cost control rather than quality, on finance instead of manufacturing and on paper rather than people. The nation's graduate schools of business became its shrine. It helped to build the great companies of the U.S., but did it build them right? At its worst, the model informed a generation of American managers that every human being was little more than a factor of production and every business a nugget of value to be bought, sold or closed down based on its return on investment. Much of what is inexplicable about American business today is rooted in the story of the men sitting around Henry's table on that brisk November day.

"We ran our operations in the Army Air Force," Ted told Ford, "on the basis that it was efficient to standardize, organize and systematize. If it wasn't done, each command would have done its own thing, and the Army Air Force would have wound up in a state of confusion. It would have been like trying to take one piece from fifty-six different jigsaw puzzles and trying to fit them all into one puzzle. Your eyes would cross, and you would go nuts."

The comment drew a knowing chuckle from Ford who seemed ready to hire the men on the spot until one of his top aides, John Bugas, interrupted the session's flow with some caution.

"Well, Mr. Ford," Bugas finally said, "if you subsequently feel you want to employ these people . . ."

Young Henry wouldn't let him finish. He had made up his mind. The sudden appearance of the men, patriots in uniform daring enough to even ask for employment as a package, obviously appealed to his fancy.

"John, stop giving me this 'if stuff,'" snapped Ford. "I am going to hire these men and that's all I want to hear about it."

They were hired. And why not? They were ten unusual men, brought together at the height of the American Century, a period when the nation enjoyed the economic, political and military leadership of the world. The country's fortunes were in their hands. "The most gifted management team of the century, purveyors of a new managerial art in American industry," as Pulitzer Prize-winning author David Halberstam called them—"the Whiz Kids." Together these ten friends would achieve a degree of power and influence that none of them could have gained alone.

ON THE WAY home to Dayton, the young officers chatted endlessly. Charlie Bosworth was grinning like crazy. For once, even Bob McNamara seemed excited, like a kid, by the prospect of working for Henry Ford. What he saw and heard on this trip convinced him that there was great promise at the company, great opportunity amid the company's horrendous problems. It looked good. He was aroused by the intellectual challenge—even though his old Ford coupe was giving them trouble, fluttering and sputtering with some problem in the carburetor or the fuel pump. Neither of them knew a damn thing about cars. They were both mechanically hopeless. So Bob pulled the choke all the way out, pumped down on the accelerator and kept the bomb moving down the dark highway.

"Hell," laughed McNamara, "we've got to go to Ford and do something about these damn cars!"

It was as if they were moving through a dream. There was nothing they couldn't do now if they put their minds to it. When Bosworth wrote to his mother, he described the opportunity as ". . . almost breathtaking —both as to the immediate income and position and as to the future possibilities."

McNamara could not have resisted an opportunity like this. Could anyone, for that matter? They were going to work for Henry Ford, all ten of them. And they even got to tell Henry how much money they thought they should be paid. It was extraordinary—even in an extraordinary time like this.

Tex Thornton, the brazen son-of-a-gun, had pulled it off.

Tex and Flora Thornton outside their apartment in Virginia during World War Two.

Abandoned by his father when he was not yet five years old, Tex on the lap of his young mother.

A dapper teenager, Thornton during his high school years.

Chapter 2

"YOUNG NAPOLEON"

■

"Knowledge is power. And in this chaos, we're going to be the only people with knowledge. Everyone else will be guessing."

—Tex Thornton

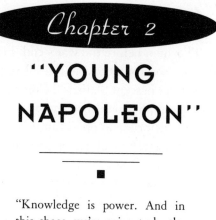

*B*ut then Tex had been pulling it off for years.

In Washington, behind his back, always out of earshot, they had a name for him: Young Napoleon. It seemed to conjure up all of the War Department's dislike for a man who had little awe of authority and who badly needed to gain control over everything in his life.

When Tex uncovered a high-ranking officer fudging the numbers on aircraft production, he did not hesitate to bring him down—even though Major General Bennett E. Meyers heavily outranked Lieutenant Colonel Thornton. "Those figures of yours are wrong," Tex challenged in his West Texas drawl. "They're wronger than any you can grab out of thin air!"

Incensed, the general shot back: "If you ever come under my command, Thornton, I'll court-martial your ass!"

"If I ever permitted myself to serve under you, General, I'd deserve a court-martial," retorted Tex in a level voice.

Meyers joined the growing list of military bureaucrats who vowed to get Thornton before the war's end. He never got the chance. A few days after the confrontation, he lost all responsibility for aircraft reporting to Thornton's nascent Statistical Control group in Washington. His bureaucratic triumph would become one of the young Texan's most dramatic wartime victories, an opportunity not only to help to build the largest air force in history—but an opportunity to build his own base of power within it.

Young Napoleon's military empire had begun as little more than an esoteric division of eggheads and business types inside the Army Air Force. By the end of World War Two, Thornton would command three thousand of the country's brightest officers trained by the Harvard Business School and a fifteen thousand personnel complement. Through sixty-six far-flung units around the world, the operation could boast that it had the largest centrally controlled installation of mechanical accounting equipment and the largest private-wire teletype in the world. The group functioned as a giant analytical thinking machine that helped to organize, manage and run America's air war.

And over it all was the unlikely Tex Thornton. In the primitive world of the early 1940s, a world without televisions or computers or satellites, where information traveled ever so slowly, Thornton's command of the group was an astonishing achievement made possible by a naiveté as indomitable as his will and by an overpowering urge to seize control over his destiny. In the military, the means of control was the hierarchy. Tex set out to define his own sense of order, to create his own framework to exercise power.

No sane soldier dared to challenge the military chain of command as Tex did with Meyer and other officers. But Thornton overflowed with such confidence that he failed to understand how vulnerable he had made himself. His assurance seemed unbreakable. Many years later, after many more conquests, one of Tex's colleagues would be reminded of him when on a trip to London he heard author Ian Fleming describe what it took to be an outstanding Shakespearean actor. "He said, 'At least 90 percent of success is confidence. When you walk out on that stage you know it. You feel in your soul that you can do well.' That was Tex. He exuded self-assurance and it inspired the same in everyone who worked for him."

In those early days, he was a hungry young man with no other original aim than to make his way in the world, to sort out for himself a future that would allow him to forget part of his past. His years in uniform convinced him of the invincibility of logic. It was how he beat Meyers and so many others with the facts; it was how he acquired the influence that put greater distance between the Tex Thornton who emerged in Washington and the Bates Thornton who grew up in the backwoods of Texas.

WASHINGTON IN 1941 was the perfect place for a man with ambition and not much money. War made it the perfect time. Japan's surprise attack on Pearl Harbor woke up the slumberous Southern town, giving it an urgency and importance it had lacked. Washington was about to realize its potential, its great power, the same as Tex was about to and so many who were drawn there. The city would give America an identity as the great democratic empire, remake the world and create a new Europe. The men who made their pilgrimage to the city would play key roles in the drama.

President Roosevelt's New Deal had transformed the city into the New Jerusalem, a converging point for the country's drifters and dreamers. After all, the Depression ended early in Washington. New Dealers had taken over the city, running parts of government that had not existed before FDR. Washington had always been home to many strangers. Now, as the new agencies lured tens of thousands of civil servants, it became a magnet for anyone escaping a disenchanted life. They arrived from the Midwest and the South, from Oklahoma and Texas, from everywhere, wandering out of a noisy, crowded Union Station.

Tex was another one of them, seeking a future in Washington's promise and escaping a background in the flat plains of northwestern Texas. In 1934, he stepped off the bus in a rumpled black suit, white shirt and a pair of shoes that badly needed a shine. The newcomers worked mainly as clerks at government-issue desks arranged in long rows in vast offices. It was a town, as one so aptly described it, "of people who spend their time sitting at desks, writing little things on little pieces of paper, dictating letters into machines, talking on the telephone to people they never see." To Tex, single, twenty-one years old and full of himself, a cocky braggart, Washington seemed small and conquerable.

IF HE HAD a controlling personality, a need to make tidy all the elements of his life, it was because his childhood had been made messy by a father who abandoned him and his mother. Born in flat and dusty Haskell,

Texas, on July 22, 1913, Charles Bates Thornton had no expectations of a grand future in his destiny. He grew up as the only child of a dirt-poor broken family. Tex's formative years were spent in West Texas, where the dirt roads were lined with mules and chickens, where the cotton wore out the black land. Farmers, ranchers and small town merchants dominated the economy. Doctors delivered babies for a watermelon and two chickens.

Tex's father was a tough old nut, an uneducated man from the down-and-dirty, tobacco-spittin' Texas where the old-timers spun tall tales and swilled booze by the gallon. W.A. "Tex" Thornton couldn't read or write, but he made a living by donning an asbestos suit and helmet and walking into a blazing oil well fire to snuff it out with nitroglycerin. Whatever Tex learned from this, the image of his father—wild and remote—always seemed to dog him.

Tex was not yet five years old, a small, scrawny kid who ran around barefoot during the hot summer months, when the man walked out on him and his mother. Though he would rarely speak of his father's abandonment, it dealt him a devastating blow. For years, he was resentful of his father for leaving his mother. It was one of the reasons his friends called him Bates when he was a boy. He shunned his father's nickname, Tex, acquiring it much later in Washington, when he seemed to come closer in his actions to his father's memory.

His father had walked out on his family shortly after the stillborn birth of a brother, only to remarry and move to Amarillo. Over the years, he drifted in and out of Tex's life. Cash or clothing would sporadically arrive in packages, even his first bicycle and cowboy boots, from a father whose presence was rare. On occasion, Tex would be summoned to the Hotel Haskell to meet his dad when he passed through town. Once, he handed Tex and a friend three five-dollar bills.

The senior Tex was more interested in being a hell-raiser than a father. His oil well fighting exploits made him a storied character of the New West, a romantic, rough-and-tumble figure whose raw courage and recklessness set him apart from other men. It took a gutsy—some said half-crazed—individual with no fear of death to walk into a blazing fire with nitroglycerin. He was to the oil fields what Wyatt Earp, who made himself famous in the fight at the OK Corral, was to the hell-roaring mining towns of Arizona. Years later, in 1949, he died just as recklessly as he led his life—bludgeoned to death with his own pistol in an Amarillo motel room by a hitchhiker who claimed he found him in bed naked with his twenty-two-year-old wife. Blood was splattered on the walls four feet above the double bed where Tex's fifty-seven-year-old father was found nude in a pool of blood. His shirt and towel were knotted tightly about his neck. His killer, who was tried for murder, was acquitted after a lengthy trial.

His father's absence virtually denied Tex his childhood, though it provided him with a compensating degree of strength and confidence. It made him older, more willing to stand up to authority, knowing that the first authority figure in his life—his father—was a man ridden with faults. To help out his divorced mother, Tex worked at odd jobs. "Even before the Depression," he said, "I had to work on Saturdays, picking cotton, making deliveries, working in a store. It didn't matter what other kids were doing, I was expected to work and put aside the money."

Sometimes, he and his mother would arrive in a town with little more than ten cents between them. His mother, the former Sarah Alice Bates, was a religious woman, a domineering taskmaster with a third-grade education. She could not control Tex's father, but she would be the controlling influence on Tex. Short and plump, with black hair and blue eyes, she wouldn't hesitate to take a strap out and beat the hell out of him.

Yet, Tex revered her. She instilled in him self-reliance and the drive to succeed, and she drilled in him simple, country values that would become the foundation of his life. "Your word is your bond," she'd say. "You never tell someone something you're not going to do. Your credit is the most important thing in the world." He heard the same lessons over and over. When he was eleven, she married again, this time to Dr. Alan J. Lewis, a veterinarian who worked for the state, treating cattle and horses and testing for TB on the big ranches. Tex became a stepson in a family that would include two boys and a girl—and always their mother would talk about her first son.

Tex developed his sense of self not from his distant father, but from his overbearing mother. She forced him to be the antithesis of his wayward father and hoped to realize her own unrealized ambitions through him. Tex was going to be someone; he was going to do something big. She told him this herself as much as she demanded success of him. And later in his life when he began to fulfill her dreams, her first son would be the role model for everyone else in the family. She pounded it into them so incessantly that none of her other three children could ever hope to meet her expectations. Her youngest son, Allan, would become distraught, alienated from the family, and would eventually commit suicide by drinking cyanide. In an unsuccessful effort to stop him, his wife shot him in the hand with a .357-caliber handgun.

Home was nothing fancy, an old-fashioned, two-story clapboard house. They never did without a meal, but money always seemed tight. Yet, Thornton—even in these adolescent days—displayed the diligence and self-reliance that would push him toward the top in his later years. During the summers, Tex scrambled out of bed at 4 a.m., tossed down a quick breakfast and then hiked five miles to work a farm for ten cents an hour. His mother would send him off with a biscuit stuffed with a couple slices of bacon and a can of beans for lunch. He'd made the trip with John Kimbrough, a friend whose father owned the farm. To cool off, they'd wade through knee-high mud to a stock tank for the hogs and chickens and doggie-paddle in their birthday suits. They would return home by sundown. "Bates wasn't any angel," remembers Kimbrough. "On Halloween, he'd turn over the outhouses. If a boy and girl were riding around in a car, we might throw a rotten egg at them or let the air out of the tires if they parked." It was typical country mischief.

At Haskell High School, he was a so-so student but one with a lot of fortitude, always defying any expectations that someone might pin on him. He endured a merciless pounding as the undersized center for the Haskell Indians, having earned his way onto the football team on pure grit and tenacity. His small stature lent courage to others who would continually taunt him with cruel remarks and jokes about his absent dad. "It made him mad as hell," recalls Wallace Sanders, a boyhood friend. "He wouldn't hesitate to fight them off."

Indeed, he proved handy with his fists, beating the living bejesus out of one guy who tried to horn in on a date. Scrappy Tex simply refused to allow anyone to gain an advantage over him, no matter that the odds were hardly in his favor. It served him well in defending girlfriends' honor and in plying his trade as a little hustler, who raised chickens in the backyard, sold eggs and even tried to home-brew booze with a friend.

To anyone with ambition, Haskell seemed like prison. Life revolved around an unpaved square marked by the typical county courthouse with a towering steeple and a broad-faced clock. Along the square's perimeter were a bunch of ramshackle stores, selling dry goods, hardware and groceries. His mother would have a recurring dream, though, one that she would repeat to her other children who came to realize how ambitious her expectations were for Tex. In it, her son was riding in a big, dark open car, slowly moving down a wide boulevard lined with hundreds, maybe thousands, of people. From the sidewalks, they smiled and waved and shouted encouragement to a beaming Tex. The dream did not place him in a little dirt town, scrambling for a job.

When Tex graduated from Haskell High with forty-six other boys and girls in 1931, the country was in the midst of the Depression. Haskell's two banks were closed. Its farmers were selling out to meet their debts. His stepfather moved the family to Lubbock where Tex enrolled as an engineering student at Texas Technological College, later changing his major to business. His mother took in a couple of boarders to send him to school. But he dropped out at the end of his second year and moved back to Haskell where he opened up a small Plymouth dealership with a friend, Buford Cox. Tex hit on the idea of selling farmers cars on promissory notes payable when their harvests came in. He hadn't figured out that the farmers already were heavily in hock to the banks. Tex was a marvelous salesman, but his customers were less than creditworthy, causing the dealership to collapse after only a brief spell. His father eventually bailed him out of the business. That's when Tex decided to get out of town.

WITH $50 BORROWED from a Haskell bank, a few more bucks from friends, he hopped aboard a Greyhound bus bound for Washington, D.C., and Roosevelt's New Deal. To a poor kid from a backwater town, Washington was a symbol of power and progress. The news that filtered back to places like Haskell and Lubbock was of an ever-enlarging government of new agencies, departments and commissions, each one offering hundreds of jobs for the city's newcomers.

Even then, however, Washington was a town of connections. To land a lousy job in some agency, you often had to know somebody. To his credit, Tex had figured that out. Before coming to Washington, he had shown up on the doorstep of Representative George H. Mahon, a freshman congressman from his district. One day, he strutted into Mahon's Colorado City office, introduced himself and requested a letter of introduction he might bring to Washington with him. Mahon obliged with a note to the Works Progress Administration. The agency, however, had no immediate openings.

He faced enough turndowns to wonder if he should have remained in Texas. The surprise was how many people gravitated to Washington to look for work. Newspapers reported that fifty thousand new people were flowing into the city each year. The $50 Tex had borrowed before his departure had dwindled to only a few bucks. He arranged an interview with a man at the Agricultural Adjustment Administration, another of those dull bureaucratic agencies, for November 1, 1934.

It was quiet and cold outside, the street noise muffled by falling snow. The man sat with his back to a window open on a little park and more white buildings beyond it. The winter-stripped trees made the scene seem bleak. A few homeless people sat on a bench munching sandwiches out of brown bags. An old man was feeding the pigeons. A couple of squirrels scampered across a path, making tracks in the white stuff.

It wasn't bitter cold. Washington seldom gets bitter cold. It was that damp cold that invaded the bones. If Tex's mother could see him now, not in some White House anteroom or at a Georgetown cocktail party, but nearly pleading for work as a junior clerk, she might have cried.

"See that bench out there?" Tex said, motioning to the window. "If I don't land this job, that's where I'll be sleeping tonight."

He got the $1,260-a-year job with the title of "Under Clerk," but left two months later when another one of Roosevelt's alphabet agencies offered him a similar job with a 15 percent pay increase. He worked like a madman, gaining a promotion to "Junior Statistical Clerk," moving again to still another government agency until ending up at the U.S. Housing Authority with the title of "Statistician" in 1941. From 1935 until 1941, he was a workmonger with one goal: getting ahead. Whatever he did, however, he did with the intention of gaining control over all the pieces of his life, including his emerging courtship of Flora Laney.

IT WAS A time when American women were a distantly second gender in a world completely dominated by men. It was often thought that the most attractive women were the would-be wives willing to become full-time mothers. If they did not find joy in the dreams of their husbands, they nonetheless shared their husbands' hopes to the exclusion of their own. The war, of course, would draw millions of women into the economy where for the first time in their lives, they realized they were capable of doing something more than cleaning house or cooking meals. But when the war would end, they would quickly assume more traditional roles in the home as partners and confidants to hardworking men.

Tex Thornton had no other expectations for the woman he would someday marry. He desired, like so many unattached men of his day, a wife around which a family and a home could be built. Thornton had met a woman like this, Flora, at a small dinner party arranged by her sister, Elizabeth, who worked with him at the Housing Authority. Flora was slender, deep-voiced, with long legs and blue-gray eyes. She had gone to Texas Tech, but was a year ahead of Tex so they never formally met on campus. Besides, she would never have dated an underclassman. No one did in those days, not least of all Flora, as self-possessed and cocky as Tex. But he remembered her because Flora knew some of his older fraternity brothers and also sang in the First Methodist Church Choir. His mother's prodding forced him into the church youth group and made him a regular at Sunday services.

That night of their first meeting, she saw in him something unique. It wasn't that she thought he was going to be a great success. Not at all. But Flora felt secure with Tex because of his sense of loyalty and character. "I saw this integrity," she said. "I saw a turn of mind that was unorthodox. There was a freshness about him." He was, well, different. One evening, Tex somehow latched onto the subject of science. He talked and talked about the potential of overcoming gravity and what it might mean. It was an odd conversation on a date, something few of the men she had ever met would talk about. But that was Tex, always surprising you.

He hardly approved of the theater or her New York lifestyle. Her goal was to be an opera singer, and as she grew more serious, she came to New York to study voice with a private coach in the early 1930s. She landed a principal part in Oscar Hammerstein's and Sigmund Romberg's *May Wine*, a small operetta staged at the St. James Theatre on West Forty-fourth Street. This was too frivolous a life for him to either understand or appreciate. He told her it was not the kind of life for a woman he wanted to marry—even then trying to exert control where he had no right to do so.

"Who said anything about marriage?" she laughed.

"Of course, I'm going to marry you," he said. "But not until we can afford it."

"Thanks for the compliment," she replied. "But I have no intention of keeping myself in storage for you or any other man to accommodate your timetable."

Yet Tex had no doubts at all. They would continue to spar over the issue, but Tex would still ride the train up to New York on Saturdays and return Sunday nights. He would pick her up at the stage door of the Center Theatre on Forty-ninth Street and Sixth Avenue after the show on Saturday evening, and they would wander around New York. He was earning only about $1,800 a year, so there wasn't much money for lavish entertaining. Still, he knew he was expected to come to New York and entertain her and once he even splurged on a night of dancing at Rockefeller Center's Rainbow Room.

It got serious quickly. She cut a last-minute rehearsal in order to see

Tex in Washington. A week later, she was dropped from the show, and Tex got his way again. She and Tex were married on April 10, 1937, roughly a year after their first meeting over dinner. A long weekend drive through Virginia's Shenandoah Valley in Tex's old Chevy served as the honeymoon. On Monday morning, Tex was back to work at his desk in the Housing Authority.

They lived in a one-bedroom upstairs apartment on Gerard Street. Flora got a job in the wedding department at Woodward & Lathrop and also had a paying job to sing in the choir of the Lutheran Church on Capitol Hill. At night, Tex would go off to class at George Washington University with all the other clerks and typists who no longer wanted to be clerks and typists in Washington agencies.

At the Housing Authority, Tex worked his way up by being adept with figures. He drew attention by compiling what his superiors considered a lucid and thoughtful study on low-cost housing. Tex befriended a George Washington University economics professor who urged him to call up a Mr. Robert A. Lovett in the War Department. The teacher admired Tex, knew Lovett and thought the two Texans could link up.

IT WAS THE break Tex badly needed. The winds of war were blowing through the city. Hitler had invaded Poland. The British entered the war. France had been conquered and Paris captured. The Luftwaffe rained tons of bombs on London and the English countryside in massive air raids. FDR held a fireside chat calling for aid to Britain. Legislators branded him a warmonger. Storefronts hung Bundles for Britain signs under their windows, seeking clothing and other sorely needed items. Congress renewed the draft by a single vote.

Tex already had earned an Army reserve commission. If there was a war, he would be in it from day one. Lovett, who would come as close as anyone to the father Tex never really had, was already a principal character on Washington's stage those days, ready to assume a large and more visible role when war would break out. A bomber pilot in the last war, he was a tall, suave man looking for new ideas to help him make his own mark as Assistant Secretary of War. Tex followed up on the connection, meeting the urbane Lovett in his office in the old Munitions Building on Constitution Avenue. He waited for a full half hour before Lovett showed up for the appointment, dressed in a blue double-breasted linen suit, a monogrammed white shirt and a Yale-blue tie.

Like Tex, Lovett came from a small, rural town in Texas, but not the

Texas that Thornton understood. Lovett's cool elegance, his courtly manner, suggested that he was bred from the very beginning into a world of privilege and power. His father was a lawyer, a judge and chairman of the powerful Union Pacific Railroad. Lovett zipped through prep school and on to Yale, Phi Beta Kappa, Skull & Bones and a Wall Street partnership at Brown Brothers Harriman & Co. He was recruited to Washington after writing a critical report on the ability of aircraft factories to prepare for war.

Tex was surprised at Lovett's candor. He told Tex that the organization chart of the Army Air Force was enough to make you dizzy. "It resembles nothing in the world so much as a bowl of spaghetti," he laughed. Lovett foresaw a massive expansion of the Air Force and a need to keep track of it all. He was essentially a businessman and he was amazed at the paucity of accurate information to manage what would become the largest air force in the world. What immediately impressed Lovett about Tex was that he wasn't intimidated by authority. They talked statistics and numbers, and Lovett saw a man who had a naturally analytical mind and spoke the language of figures.

"Mr. Secretary," he said, "we're putting a tremendous effort into enemy intelligence. But how are we doing at friendly intelligence—reliable information about us?"

The question struck a sympathetic chord with Lovett who was trying to find out from the Air Staff what it had in planes, parts, pilots and mechanics and what it would need to mount a war if the U.S. were to become involved in the hostilities in Europe. Lovett arranged for a transfer for the civilian statistical planner to the plans division of the Air Force, putting Tex in charge of a small group of men, mainly National Guard types, who furnished support for all staff sections in early March of 1941. It was not a critical job, but it would give him a window on the incredible chaos and confusion within the Army Air Force and teach him how valuable facts and numbers were to efficiency.

Almost every day, someone would walk into the office and ask to see the air corp's program and its airplane requirements. The answer would be different every day because no real plans existed. Tex eventually found someone in an obscure section of the War Department who had a program that called for the training of twelve thousand pilots a month.

"Now how did we arrive at that number?" Tex asked.

"It was pulled out of thin air," came the reply.

Amused, Tex pressed on. "Well, does it have any relationship to our airplane procurement program or our expansion plans?"

"None at all," he said. "If there is a relation, it's purely coincidental."

The truth was that each staff section willy-nilly made up its own plans, routinely grabbing numbers out of the air. Nothing matched; nothing came together. You could start an uprising like this, but not a war.

Headquarters boasted over a dozen number-gathering organizations in it and the majority of time they would argue over whose figures were correct. Commanding General of the Army Air Force Henry "Hap" Arnold would typically ask four different staff sections for the same information and then took as the most nearly correct any two sets of figures that came close to each other. One Air Force commander contended that he didn't need information anyway, that he ran his air force by personal contact. "That's absurd," Tex barked. "You're a $500 million investment and not even a single combat group can operate on that basis, much less a complete air force."

What was missing was an urgency to do anything about it. It came on December 7, 1941, when Tex was away on military business in Florida and radios crackled with the first reports of the Japanese attack on Pearl Harbor. Flora, then pregnant with their first child, was having lunch in a restaurant near their new apartment in Arlington Village when she heard about the attack. Someone burst through the place and shouted out the news. Tex rushed home, like so many others, in the panic and bedlam of a nation that was now vulnerable.

From then on, work escalated immensely. He always had a penchant for working long hours, but now Flora saw even less of him. All around Washington, life changed swiftly. Anti-aircraft guns were mounted on top of the government buildings. Outside the Munitions Building, the creaky wooden headquarters for the War Department, men stood guard with bayonets fixed on antiquated Springfields. Inside, the guys who had worn only brown tweed jackets and gray trousers now showed up in uniform, swarming the dilapidated building.

IN OFFICIAL WASHINGTON, a new ethic took hold because new heroes were being made and unmade every day in the chaotic dash to prepare for a big war. No one knew for sure who was going to be tapped or tossed out on his ear. As one observer put it, "The town is as full of Richelieus as a masked ball, and below the level of the Richelieus the hundreds of No. 2, 3 and 4 men spend a fair share of their time running around trying to find out just who the real Richelieu is and who will take his place when his star begins to wane."

Thornton spent considerable time figuring out which general to avoid and which one to embrace, but thanks to Lovett, he often was able to get a glimpse of the man behind the mask and to know in advance how to approach him. Lovett was becoming his protector and his mentor amid the chaos of the early days of the war.

For Tex, the work pace became nearly hysterical. He was under constant stress, often breaking out in little pimples. The frenzy was fed by the pressure of having more work than anyone could possibly do and by the need to keep track of more projects at different stages of development than possible. But it also was turned up by all the bickering, back-biting and horse trading in the War Department. Tex had to worry about all the people who were less than anxious to allow him to seize what power or authority they had over information.

The only chance Tex had to sit and think was late at night in a cubbyhole of an office. The room, with its water-stained ceiling, opened onto a pair of rooms crowded with tables where statisticians tallied figures for the planners. In the evenings, he would gather a few of his men together and spend hours thinking out loud. Always, he kept his hands busy, unscrewing the charcoal cylinder inside his cigarette holder, cleaning the filthy thing out with a pipe cleaner. He would sit at the window that looked out on a courtyard to the wings and fiddle with the venetian blind cord.

"Knowledge," he would tell them, "is power. And in this chaos, we're going to be the only people with knowledge. Everyone else will be guessing."

They knew he was right, but it seemed nearly impossible to gather the information up and know that you could trust it and make decisions on it. Tex had seen and heard men invent facts on demand. And what they got was chaos.

After the Pearl Harbor attack, officers raced up and down the crooked halls of the Munitions Building, saying, "Something has to be done." Some frankly hoped to gain transfers out of the hopeless mess and into the field. Tex would later say that he would have sold out the country's chances of winning the war pretty cheaply then, but he kept his doubts to himself. Still, the outbreak of war created a compelling urgency to organize and correct the deficiencies.

Thornton moved into the vacuum. He urged Lovett to endorse a crash program to get a handle on the Air Force before it destroyed itself in a sea of assumptions and half truths. By March of 1942, General Arnold announced a major reorganization of AAF headquarters. Tex was made head of "Statistical Control," a tiny box on an organization chart under

Colonel Byron E. Gates's office of Management Control. Gates, an old-timer and West Pointer who got the nickname of "Hungry" because of his gaunt, wiry frame, could provide essential protection and support to Tex who, after all, was only a twenty-eight-year-old major with no more than one year's service and not a day of real military training.

"Statistical Control" sounded innocuous enough, far less threatening than "Management Control," and few of the Air Staff had any idea about Lovett's intentions. In the military, you didn't bandy the word "control" around without putting a modifier in front of it. Who could argue with statisticians? The recruiting notices posted on base bulletin boards for Stat Control generated a flood of jokes. "What the hell would a stat officer do?" went one. "He'd be counting bottle caps at the PX!"

Tex, however, had something else in mind. Lovett's vision, confidence and backing would make it possible. Assigned to each Air Force command around the world, they foresaw a network of statistical officers who could collect, organize and interpret facts and figures on personnel and equipment. They would serve the role of corporate controllers, their reports flowing up to Air Force headquarters through a parallel and largely independent command structure headed by Tex.

And he, the college dropout from Texas, would be calling the shots, exercising the control and the power, doing something big for the first time in his life. The job held a mesmerizing appeal to someone who had so little control over his formative years at home. At this moment of urgency, information would become power. Thornton stood apart from his peers in recognizing the need for it. As an outsider, he saw it more clearly than so many of the insiders who wanted to protect the status quo.

It was an incredibly ambitious and imposing idea. But Tex was in the grip of his mother's desire that he be someone and do something. What kind of men would staff such an organization? His answer proved nothing less than a stroke of genius. To run a system as large as Tex envisioned, he needed men with enough rank to be noticed. Not sergeants or corporals. They had to have special training and they had to have status and authority. Lovett, who so thoroughly understood the value of connections and the power of elitism, suggested to Tex that he go to the Harvard Business School to sound the dean out on a program to train an elite corps of officers. With Lovett's advice and backing, Thornton boarded a train in April of 1942 and visited the great university he had only read about in Texas. On that train ride, he hatched one of the best schemes of his career.

THE

WHIZ

KIDS

Tex is front row, center,
where he always wanted to
be, in this 1944 picture of the
Stat Control Staff in Washington. A young Bob McNa-
mara is at the extreme left
of the top row, while Whiz
Kid James Wright is second
from left in the second row.

Cigarette in hand, Tex listens intently to a Stat Control colleague at an officer's
club in Washington, D.C.

A young, tweedy version of
Bob McNamara as an in-
structor at the Harvard Business School.

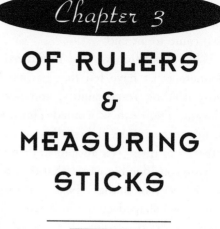

Chapter 3

OF RULERS
&
MEASURING
STICKS

■

"To count is a modern practice,
the ancient method was to guess;
and when numbers are guessed
they are always magnified."
—SAMUEL JOHNSON

ex Thornton arrived on the doorstep of Harvard Business School four months after the attack on Pearl Harbor, with a deal he felt sure no dean could resist: to turn tony Harvard into a military bunker, a breeding ground for officers who would fight the war not with weapons but with facts. When Tex finished up his pitch, the dean would think it was the greatest deal he'd ever heard, too.

Thornton badly needed Harvard's imprimatur to gain credibility in the military. Ivy League-branded officers would command instant attention. Tex couldn't have known how much Dean Wallace D. Donham needed him and the U.S. military to keep his school alive for as many years as this depleting war would last. In the autumn of 1939, Harvard Business School was an institution with an uncertain future. During World War One, it had nearly disappeared as students marched off to war and the professors fled to Washington to assume the brainy jobs. Dean Donham was determined that the school would survive this new crisis without the need to rebuild his entire faculty when World War Two came to an end.

When Thornton walked into the dean's cozy office in Morgan Hall, Donham must have felt that he met his Sugar Daddy. Here was Tex badly needing respectability; and here was a school desperate to stay relevant. The dean welcomed Thornton and arranged for his youngest faculty to assemble in his office. The assistant professors who quickly gathered to meet Tex all had draft numbers, some of them low enough to cause considerable worry that they could be sucked into the war at any moment as foot soldiers. Nearly a dozen teachers assembled around the dean's oval-shaped conference table. They were an impressive, though largely untried, group that included a young, brilliant accounting teacher, Robert S. McNamara. Not one of them had ever flown in an airplane before, much less seen an air force training base.

Thornton began his animated pitch, waving his cigarette holder through the air and chatting about this great opportunity for all of them in Washington. He told them how the idea for a Stat Control group began when General Arnold held a staff meeting and asked a simple question: How many people do we have in the air force? The general, Tex told them, got a different answer from each of the military chiefs in charge of personnel, operations, intelligence and materiel. This was too much to take in peacetime, much less in the every-man-counts fever of war. "General Arnold said, 'I'm going to have no more of this,'" Tex recalled. "'When I ask how many people we have in the air force and how many airplanes we have, I want one answer. I don't care if it's right or not. I want just one answer.'"

Tex allowed the words to penetrate. Unaware of the widespread disorganization in the War Department, the academicians expressed surprise at how badly prepared the military was to wage a war. But here was Thornton coming to the rescue. He explained how Stat Control was a new venture that required new thinking from new, young men. He talked about how crucial Stat Control would become to the overall war effort. "The more Tex talked, the more intrigued we were with the idea," recalls Myles Mace, an assistant professor. "He was a hell of a salesman and he had the ability to verbally seduce you."

The men hashed over the proposal of a school to train Tex's Stat Control officers. Harvard was to prepare second lieutenants who would tell the majors and colonels how to run their air force. They *had* to be good or it would never work. It took a couple of hours, but Tex convinced a dozen of the faculty, including Bob McNamara, to come with him to

Washington to begin the military education that would be necessary for them to design the courses and workload for Tex's Stat Control students.

TEX LANDED HIS first jackpot. The Harvard Business School, founded in 1908, a depression year, the same year as Ford's Model T appeared on the scene, was an institution waiting for change to happen. It had been established on a simple, though, pioneering idea: that the administration of business enterprises needed to be and could be a professional matter worthy of the time and attention of learned, thoughtful, responsible men.

In these adolescent years of American business enterprise, the days before legions of professionals came to populate the corporation, it was the brutally aggressive tycoon and the crass speculator who were the most colorful figures in business mythology. More often than not, the managers of America's factories were illiterate foremen. Business's heroes, like Henry Ford and Andrew Carnegie, were self-made men who built their companies on grit and determination. They were not educated professionals with advanced degrees in, of all things, business. They did not plot points on graphs, draw lines on charts or adjust numbers on balance sheets. You didn't *study* business, you *did* business.

Harvard Business School, an institution aching to give business greater legitimacy, was as one writer exuberantly put it, a place where "new muscles of thought overcome the old muscles of habit." Its faculty was teaching the early language of business professionalism, the cycles of production and the systems of accounting. By today's standards, Harvard's early notions were elemental if not crude, not unlike the discovery by a cave man that a stone ax was a decided improvement over a pointed stick.

Yet, the school was charting the birth and evolution of an idea with profound consequences: that measurement, through numbers and facts, could make America a mighty power, a global empire built on the ability to hold a yardstick up to nature. In his own way, Thornton was among the first to discover this fragile worm of an idea that had already been advanced by Frederick Taylor, the father of scientific management.

Dean Donham, in a 1919 memo, sounding more like a scientist than a profiteer, stated that the school's missions should be to train students in the practice of "1) ascertaining facts; 2) appraising and sorting facts; 3) stating business problems in a business way; 4) analyzing business problems; 5) reaching definite conclusions; 6) presenting such conclusions orally and in writing." They were Tex's goals exactly.

SPURRED BY THORNTON'S enthusiastic appeal and the urgency of a war, the professors, only hours after their meeting with Tex, packed overnight suitcases and boarded a New Haven Railroad train bound for Washington. Arriving full of hopes and anticipation the next morning, they discovered there were no Stat Control students. Moreover, there was no such thing as Stat Control. Tex had sold them nothing but an idea in his head.

But they were needed. In place of the centralized group Thornton was dead set on creating, headquarters had as many as thirteen statistics-gathering fiefdoms under its jurisdiction. Each staff section collected data in isolation from the other, sometimes sending out soldiers to manually count aircraft in hangars and depots. It was said by Thornton himself that nearly 75 percent of a given meeting would be consumed by arguments over the accuracy of the figures at hand. But how could Thornton have neglected to tell them there was no real program? They had been carried to Washington on his moxie and salesmanship and quickly realized how much work lay ahead.

Not only would they have to research and create a bevy of courses to fill a school, they also had to help Thornton build part of the foundation of his systems for Stat Control. The job's challenge—and the professors' low draft numbers—prevented any reconsideration, so they decided to roll up their sleeves and give it a go. Tex wanted to send his first class to Soldiers Field, where the business school was located in Boston, in only three weeks. A contract was hurriedly drafted with Harvard, and the faculty divvied up the work and canvassed the Army Air Force operations to figure out what to do.

At the forefront of the effort was Professor Edmund P. Learned, who redesigned the most loathed class on campus: Business Statistics, a dull and tedious course, dominated by mundane calculations of averages and regressions. Learned had transformed the subject into a course that focused on the use of figures in decision making. He urged students to aggressively use numbers to gain control over their operations. Simply knowing accounting and statistics, thought Learned, was not equal to practicing managerial control. So the change, though subtle, was a way to give management power over its organizations.

This new thinking was critical to Thornton's group. The job of a Stat Control officer required "the presenting of facts from . . . reports and from special studies of other staff officers in such form as to emphasize the meaning of the data and to bring out the significance of the facts." The emphasis was on action, not calculation.

By June, nearly six weeks to the day since his pitch, more than one hundred men reported to Soldiers Field for the school's first session. Learned and his associates cobbled together a five-week course which was later expanded into eight weeks of training. In the first half, cadets learned elementary statistics, including statistical lingo and its uses from ratios and percentages to measures of dispersion and correlation. In the second half, they were assigned a series of case studies drawn from actual air force data to apply the basic knowledge to decision-making. Because little formal authority went along with the job, Harvard also ran the new officers through human relations cases to sensitize them to the politics of power and control.

The cadets Tex recruited would report to Harvard after spending six weeks at the Army Air Forces' Officer Candidate School in Miami where they were to acquire the spit and polish of the military, learning to bounce a coin off a well-made bed, how to carry and shoot a rifle and identify an enemy aircraft. At the half-way mark, Thornton would go down to pluck off the best and brightest men to work on his pipe-dream, dangling before them the chance to complete the remainder of their OCS training at Harvard. Tex had carte blanche because other commanders never imagined that many top officers would be interested in as boring a subject as statistics, not when they could go out to the battlefield and gain all the glamour of combat.

Everyone underestimated him. If he did not come off as a hayseed, he was still young and a bit green, especially next to the military's career men. But his offer appealed to the accountants, bankers, business executives and college professors who found their way into OCS. For them, Harvard was a desirable posting. In Cambridge, unlike Miami Beach, there were no dawn drills. The weather was cool, and the discipline not nearly as strict. The Stat School was housed in ivy-covered Mellon Hall and instructed in Baker Library classrooms. Cadets would graduate as second lieutenants and then help Tex build an organization that would wield considerable power within the military.

The newly mobilized Harvard Business School took on all the appearances of a military academy. Uniformed soldiers marched in formation past the white pillars of Baker Library. Salutes were exchanged, flags were waved and catchy ditties sung by the men who became known as the "Singing Statisticians." During drills, rifles were stacked in tepee shapes on the manicured grounds. Behind the red-brick dormitories, cadets lined up in rows for practical introductions to sidearms. Within a year, Harvard suspended all civilian instruction. Dean Donham succeeded in keeping the Harvard Business School alive during the war years—but it was less a school of business than a military outpost hung with ivy, though one that would play a part in the managerial revolution Thornton and his select group would lead.

THE GENERALS WHO ran the U.S. war effort had been groping for instantaneous decisions based on something they could trust, calculations and facts that had some meaning. Tex began building an empire that would provide them what they wanted. The foundation of his growing power was a simple, though insightful, idea: All intelligent decisions, Tex believed, were based on three ingredients: 1) bright, experienced people with solid educational backgrounds, 2) judgment and common sense, and 3) the facts.

Most people read words better than numbers. It was a keen observation made decades later by Harold S. Geneen, the corporate autocrat who, as ruler of ITT, would one day compete with Tex. "They may understand the complex novels of Henry James or James Joyce or Marcel Proust," he said, "but they read columns of numbers as they would a vocabulary list of strange, esoteric words."

In Tex's nascent empire, however, figures were as integral a part of the vocabulary as words. He built an organization that saw the gathering and analysis of facts as a new theology. There was truth in it, or at least it had the perception of absolute truth. Numbers were facts, not to be grasped out of the air, not dependent on hopes or whims. They were precise symbols of what was real and palpable, gathered by men on the firing lines who were close enough to the action to insure their authenticity. They brought fine-grain detail to what was an impossibly large and complex operation. They knew what Geneen would put into practice many years later—that numbers synthesize the mass effects of many individual items which make up the whole. They were the tools of decision-making.

Stat Control's true source of power had little to do with the actual gathering of numbers. On their own, the numbers and facts did not tell you what to do. But Tex's officers would search for the trends and patterns revealed by the numbers. They would probe for the variations and the changes and consider what they meant. They could use the numbers to win compliance and submission, which was not all that different from holding up a totem before primitive people and announcing a new godhead. In the confusion and fear generated by war, people believed Thornton's numbers spoke the truth. Everyone wanted to believe someone had the answers, whatever those answers might be.

Tex was not only building a staff, he was increasing his own presence in the form of project papers, program reports, memoranda on contingency plans, objectives, alternatives, dissents and appraisals of situations that gave him access to nearly every crucial source of information about the air war. "Staff policies and commands are only as good as the information upon which they are based," he argued. When the war ended, he would describe the operation in a final military report with unabashed hyperbole, calling his outfit "a super brain with nerve ganglia extending to the very tips of the air force command, from squadron level to headquarters, absorbing, analyzing, summarizing the vast flow of information deluging headquarters daily."

Within the Army Air Force, the system forged a class of elites with rulers and measuring sticks, Friden calculators and IBM tabulators. It would be a massive human computer with all the functional elements that would characterize the machine: potent processors, dynamic memory and input and output devices. The machine would bring order to the chaos of planning war.

TEX UNDERSTOOD THE link between knowledge and power. But his newfound friends from the Harvard Business School actually forged the connection for him. Thornton had failed to complete his college education because he was a doer, lacking the discipline to sit in a classroom and absorb an education. Of all the junior faculty assigned to the Stat Control school, none more impressed Tex than Robert Strange McNamara, who was among the first to rush down to Washington after Tex's trip to Harvard. He could not have invented a better alter-ego for himself.

Bob at twenty-five was lean and tall, with a passion for cerebral pursuits. He relished the academic life. McNamara would come to fill a critical void for Thornton, providing the analytical powers that made Tex and his operation all the more formidable. Today, someone would be tempted to call it a whole-brain partnership: McNamara, the left-brainer, comfortable in the technical and numerical, and Thornton, the right-brainer, able to charm and disarm.

Tex was fascinated by the way Bob worked single-mindedly. He could assign him anywhere to any job, and he just took it and did it well, never complaining, never bucking for a promotion or more pay. But there was something else about him, too, that Thornton greatly admired: McNamara always had ideas and lots of them. He knew how to get things done, but he also knew how to subordinate his own thinking. Bob would always give you his opinion, and it would be given without personal attachment or emotion. But whatever Tex decided was final. McNamara accepted it and carried the order out, never looking back, always the loyal soldier.

When it came to personal ambition, however, Thornton had it all over McNamara. Bob's ambitions in these early days, took him only so far as the paper in front of him. Gathering the numbers and making those symbols mean something became a personal test, a brain teaser that somehow captivated him. While others might have looked upon such work as monotonous, McNamara genuinely took pleasure in the puzzles the task presented.

Like Thornton, McNamara had a mother who pushed him hard—so hard that she had once conceded to one of his teacher's that her expectations of Bob were too high. The teacher agreed. His mother read David Copperfield aloud to him at the dinner table and drilled him relentlessly when his report card showed anything but an A. Bob's father was a "stiff, dignified businesslike man" who had no education beyond the eighth grade. A sales manager for a wholesale shoe company, Robert J. McNamara was Catholic, twenty-five years older than Bob's mother and was fifty when Bob was born in San Francisco on June 9, 1916. Bob's unusual middle name came from his Protestant mother, Claranell Strange. Both parents doted on their first and only son. A second child, Margaret, was born three years later.

They were brought up across the bay in a comfortable middle class area of Oakland at 1036 Annerly Road. As a youngster, Bob was an early reader, a voracious reader, fast with figures but sickly—always seeming to come down with this or that. He was fifteen before he showed signs of wanting to break out of the protective parental eggshell. He did, going to sea as an ordinary hand, traveling once through the Panama Canal, once to the Orient and four times to Hawaii.

At Piedmont High School, he came close to always pleasing his mother—virtually a straight A student, garnering a record of twenty-six A's and seven B's in three years. (Four of the B's were in French and two were in physical education.) While impressing Piedmont's teachers, Bob —the eagle boy scout—also handled a full load of student activities as editor of the 1933 *Clan-O-Log* yearbook, president of the French club, a member of the glee club and of the board of student control. "He was so painfully good," recalls a high school friend. "He was so neat, so clean; he was the kind of boy you'd trust with either your money or your sick kittens. But when I say that, I make him sound like a square. Yet he wasn't, he wasn't—a square is an object of ridicule, and Bob was a great talker, a good dancer; it was always fun to have him around. He was never left out of anything."

Early in the spring of 1933 as McNamara completed his senior year at Piedmont, Franklin D. Roosevelt was inaugurated as president. On the same day, March 4, banks throughout the nation were closed; the New York Stock Exchange was shuttered; there was not enough money in the U.S. Treasury to meet the federal payroll. Retiring President Herbert Hoover announced that the nation was "on the verge of chaos."

McNamara entered the University of California at Berkeley during the very depths of the Depression. It was a grim time. One of every four adult males was unemployed. More than five thousand banks had failed. Over 270,000 families had been evicted from their homes. "Parents of my classmates were committing suicide because they couldn't provide food for their families," McNamara would recall years later. "Now I grew up in that environment, of a very liberal university, a very liberal environment, and I absorbed the values and the social objectives of many of my classmates and professors and others at the time, and I've held them ever since."

He did not allow the Depression nor its complications to distract him from his economics studies. He made Phi Beta Kappa at the end of his sophomore year and proved to be a popular student. He spent his summers mining gold, learning to ski and cultivating what would become a lifelong passion for climbing mountains. When he graduated in 1937, he had accumulated a spectacularly high grade of 288 points on his courses out of a possible 315.

He gained an interview for a Rhodes scholarship at Oxford, but was rejected so he continued his education at the Harvard Business School. In those days, it was common for 12 percent of the entering class to flunk out in the first year. McNamara wouldn't be one of them. He was the kind of student whose hand was constantly in the air, who gained more air time in class than anyone. "He liked to be in the spotlight," says A. Reynolds Morse, a Harvard classmate. "But he was smart. He was eloquent. He knew his stuff. He wasn't a phony." McNamara's comments always seemed on the mark, and he impressed classmates with an ability to synthesize problems. "He started taking off for the higher altitudes when we were still at the foothills," recalls Walter Haas, who was in the same study group with him at Harvard and would return to his family business in San Francisco to run Levi Strauss.

More than ever, McNamara set himself apart. Focused on little more than his studies, he grew aloof, even impersonal. He roomed alone, in a single hole in Gallatin C-39, while most students shared rooms. His yearbook photo showed him with the same wire-rimmed glasses and slicked-back hair that would forever define him. As expected, McNamara graduated in the spring of 1939 with distinction and accepted a job as an accountant in the San Francisco office of Price Waterhouse.

To celebrate, he and five classmates shipped off for a three-month fling in Europe. Each of the guys chipped in $20 apiece for a beat-up Ford station wagon that they took with them on an Italian freighter to Genoa from Boston. True to form, Bob insisted on making the most of the trip. He played guide and organizer, deciding what churches, chapels and castles they would see, dragging his friends to some of the more cultural attractions of Europe, including the medieval Chartres Cathedral. It was one of those whirlwind student tours on the cheap, six American men gleefully roving through Italy, Scandinavia, France, Algiers, Gibraltar, England, Scotland and Germany.

The group separated in Copenhagen, with Bob and friend Richard Hodgson, who also had a job waiting for him in San Francisco, going on to Berlin. Hitler marched into Poland on Sept. 1, 1939. Two days later, France and England declared war on Germany—unbeknownst to either Bob or Hodgson who strolled up to a ticket window in Berlin's crowded train station to buy tickets for the journey back to Genoa and home.

"Don't you know there's a war on?" they were told.

Neither of them had the foggiest notion of it. Years later, they would laugh that a future Secretary of Defense for the U.S. was in the middle of what would become the greatest war ever and hadn't even known that it started. Yet it was an omen, perhaps an inability to see the big picture. They eventually squeezed onto the train, standing all the way to Italy, and arrived in Genoa with about $5 left between them and more bad news. The Italian freighter they had booked for their return to the U.S. was no longer sailing. They found a room over a bar near the harbor, borrowing money from a few elderly American tourists to pay for the rent, until Bob spotted an American President line freighter in the harbor. He had been on the same line two years earlier from San Francisco and managed to talk his way onto the boat packed with American tourists scrambling to escape the turmoil in Europe. For the next fourteen days, Bob and Hodgson waited tables for fourteen hours a day to pay for their fare home.

After a brief and disillusioning stint as an accountant for Price Water-house & Co., he returned to Harvard in 1940 to become an assistant professor of accounting. When America entered the war, McNamara couldn't help but get involved. Tex provided the perfect opportunity: McNamara's first job was to set up the systems that told the Air Force how many planes it had. McNamara and his Harvard colleague Myles Mace spent three days holed up in a small room in the Munitions Build-ing, writing out by hand the report that would go with it. Later, they learned that the Stat Control officer who volunteered to type up their intricate, lengthy, detailed draft would get a Legion of Merit for creating the report. It seemed like military justice at its best.

The 110 report, as it was called, would form the foundation for the Army Air Force's decisions on how to allocate airplanes and crews, how to distribute equipment, plan training schedules and the movement of troops. It mandated a daily inventory of the number, disposition, location and use of all aircraft—down to type, model and serial number. Though a rudimentary document, a passive tool, the "facts" it helped to collect allowed Thornton to turn it radioactive. For the first time Tex saw the power numbers could afford them.

Both men itched to play a more crucial role than principally teach recruits at Harvard, so in March of 1943, Tex arranged for McNamara and Mace to be commissioned as Stat Control captains in the Army Air Force. The commissioning took place in England where Bob and Mace were billeted with a family in Teddington. They shared a front room on the second floor of a brick rowhouse. These were modest living quarters —no central heating or hot water, and the Luftwaffe's ferocious bomb-ing of the area had left a wide crack in their room where the cold air rushed through. Air-raid sirens wailed the first night they arrived. McNamara naively rushed out to catch a glimpse of the attack until being urged back into the house.

Each morning, McNamara and Mace rode their bicycles the 20 min-utes to Bushey Park where the Supreme Command feverishly worked on plans for D-Day. An observer watching the pair tunnel their way through the rubble of London's streets could have easily mistaken McNamara for an English bank clerk eager to tally the day's receipts. He seemed completely oblivious to the danger around him, focusing on little more than the work ahead of him. Mace rushed to the mess hall for the breakfast of powdered eggs, spam, brussel sprouts and coffee—the same miserable menu every day. But McNamara hungered only for the numbers, always skipping the meal and going directly to his desk by 7 a.m.

They were a crackerjack team. On one occasion, they were sent to a major supply and maintenance depot in Burtonwood where hundreds of British workers overhauled B-17 engines in a cavernous hangar. Airplane parts were strewn all over the cement floors, without rhyme or reason. McNamara and Mace set up an inventory system so each airplane part could be drawn down by number.

McNamara and others like him who crunched the numbers came up with the answers in what would be the early beginnings of a managerial revolution. His genuis lay in an ability to extract from numbers unusual efficiency in one project after another. Stat Control determined the most efficient way to transport 100,000 tons of military equipment from San Francisco to Australia. They found it would take 10,022 planes and 120,765 Army Air Force men to duplicate the job already being performed by forty-four surface vessels and 3,200 sailors.

Years later, General Curtis LeMay recalled how McNamara was able to squeeze 30 percent more flying hours out of his B-29 bombers than he had been getting, simply by bringing operations analysis into the field. McNamara had analyzed the numbers of crews and planes and rescheduled them more efficiently than any of LeMay's military staff. Like other military leaders, however, LeMay did not kindly accept all of Stat Control's suggestions. When one Stat Control officer concluded that it was inefficient and costly in both men and machines to use fighter planes as escorts for bombers, LeMay scrawled an expletive across the report before discarding it in a trash can.

It was analysis that led Tex to fight a major battle in favor of the B-17 bomber, a graceful and beautiful angel of destruction. On paper, the B-24 was superb, a low-slung, mean-looking hunk of metal that could wreck havoc from the air. The so-called Liberator was supposedly more deadly than the "17" because it carried 50 percent more bombs; moreover, relatively few B-24s incurred much damage in battle. But Thornton's team discovered that the only reason the plane held up so well in battle was because it was given shorter and less dangerous missions to heighten crew morale and keep crew losses equal. Once the bomber was damaged, its chance of getting home was much smaller than that of the B-17, whose all-around performance was greater. The numbers proved it. Stat Control's analysis discovered that the B-17 could deliver more bombs to its targets than the B-24. The B-24 was also ridden with defects. Once Thornton was on a transatlantic flight in a B-24 and it was leaking fuel so badly that it would have blown up if anyone had lit a cigarette. Tex won the battle, gaining priorities for the B-17 and scaling down production on the B-24.

Later, toward the end of the war when Washington was preparing to mount its final assault on Japan, Thornton's group delivered another shocking analysis. The Army Air Force had begun to redeploy heavy bomb groups of B-17s and B-24s from Europe to the Pacific to crush Japan. But Stat Control's beancounters disagreed with the plan, arguing that the U.S. should use the newer B-29 bombers instead. Stat Control proved that B-29s could drop 28,000 tons of bombs per month in only 15,000 combat hours. It would have taken the B-17 and B-24 groups more than 90,000 hours to accomplish the same goal. The study found that by using B-29s 70 percent of combat crews killed, missing and wounded would be saved along with a quarter of a billion gallons of gasoline a year. The upshot: the Army Air Force halted the redeployment of its heavy bomber groups from Europe.

THORNTON'S MEN ACQUIRED influence and lots of it, thanks to three critical decisions Tex made early on when he created Stat Control: he engineered it so that he could pick his men from among the top 10 percent of those going through OCS; next, he sent them to Harvard for an education and an elite aura that few would challenge; and finally, he required that every Stat Control officer graduate from the Harvard program. This meant that Tex narrowed down the numbers of men in Stat Control, tightly closing entry into his exclusive fraternity. That way, no commanding generals in the field could sneak people into his organization. He both controlled who could get into the club and then ran it with an iron-fist. All its members had passed through the same fine screen, had the same training, could speak the same stylized patter. All shared a mission.

That mission went beyond ratios and percentages. The stat controllers forged close relationships with each other, conforming to a distinct style of casual bravado in the knowledge that they belonged to an exclusive club. At the officers' clubs, they would light one another's cigarettes, fetch each other's drinks and laugh at one another's jokes. And over it all stood Tex Thornton. He took an active interest in so many of the men. Why, Tex wouldn't even hesitate to intervene in a man's love life.

In 1945 Charlie Bosworth and Maxine and Jack Reith (right) crowd around a tiny table at La Martinique, a New York City nightclub.

Chapter 4

CARNIVAL
MAN

■

"Business is the very soul of an
American: he pursues it, not as a
means of procuring for himself
and his family the necessary com-
forts of life, but as the foundation
of all human felicity; and shows
as much enthusiastic ardor in his
application to it as any crusader
has ever evinced for the conquest
of the Holy Land . . ."

—Francis J. Grund

She had been refusing to answer the telephone for days. The
engagement was off, ended after a fight about something she
wouldn't even be able to recall years later. What the fight was about
really didn't matter, anyway. Maxine Minton had already lost one husband in the war. She had seen enough pregnant women saying good-bye
to their husbands, often for the last time. It was perfectly reasonable for
her to feel it was too soon to be tied to another soldier and the possibility
of another tragedy.

Lieutenant Colonel Francis "Jack" Reith, however, had become so
unaccountably despondent over her refusal to take his calls that Tex
couldn't help but notice. If anyone equalled his own drive and ambition,
it was Jack. He tumbled toward a goal with a will and a momentum that
few could sustain. Whatever Reith's other merits, it was his obsession
that made him unequal and unstoppable, a terrier who latched onto
things and refused to let go. It was that way with his work in Tex's 15th

Stat Control Unit, in Dayton, Ohio, and that way with this latest infatuation with Maxine.

Her rejection was forcing Reith into a complete funk. The airmen
would have called him "flak happy" given his slightly muddled mental
state. Alarmed by Jack's moody behavior, Tex pried the details loose
from him and decided to call Maxine up himself. They had never met,
but she knew who he was and surmised why he was calling. Still, Maxine refused to come to the phone.

Undaunted, Tex had one of his secretaries dial again and again until
Maxine's boss insisted that she accept the call. She had to take it: Tex was
tying up the only telephone line at work. Within seconds, he came on the
line, introduced himself and then went to work.

"Now, please don't hang up on me, Maxine," he pleaded. "The truth
is that my office is grinding to a halt because Jack Reith can't reach you.
He's just plain come apart at the seams. Do you realize you're jeopardiz-
ing my whole operation and impeding the war effort? For God's sake at
least let him come down and see you—it can't hurt."

"But Colonel," Maxine said, "I don't really think it can change anything."

"This is one of the finest guys we have in the Air Force. You've got to
take his phone call."

"Please . . ."

"I'll get him aboard an airplane tonight," Tex interrupted. "There's
some official business in Oklahoma he can take care of for me."

"But I have no intention of seeing him."

"At least talk to him. Better still, marry him and give me some peace.
Any girl that wouldn't grab this wonderful guy is probably in need of
professional help."

Tex hung up, satisfied with himself. Reith would owe him big after
this.

Whatever Reith became involved in, he got in deep. Sometimes it was
so bad he had to have someone haul him out, or settle him in. The things
that haunted him most were the things he couldn't immediately possess.
He tended to pour all his emotion and all his energy into one objective at
a time, never quite striking a balance. Before Reith had fallen for Maxine, he had been obsessed with nothing more than his war-time work for
Tex Thornton.

Tex QUICKLY DIALED Jack in Dayton and asked him to phone Maxine
again. She was a striking blonde of twenty-nine, with the looks and

figure that could have graced many a GI's barracks locker. Maxine was fetching and fresh, with a bubbling-over personality. Jack was standing in line when he first saw the Braniff Airline hostess only a few weeks earlier in her tailored beige suit and white blouse. She was apologizing to each of the twenty-one Dayton passengers about a landing delay and helping them arrange new plans.

"Colonel," she asked Jack, "what can I do for you?"

"Well, you can let me take you to dinner tonight," he answered, flashing a boyish, almost mischievous, grin.

"No, I don't date passengers. What else can we do for you?"

Jack shrugged. He was boyishly good-looking with hazel eyes, six-foot-one-inch tall and a slim 130-pounds. She noticed how confident he looked in his well-pressed Army Air Force uniform. His tag indicated he was with Stat Control.

"Do you know Major Ed Searles out at the base?" she asked, trying to be polite.

"He's the person I've been out here to see."

"Well, he and his wife are old friends of mine."

Less than two hours later, she got a call from Major Searles.

"Maxine," he playfully teased, "you've got to do me a favor. You've got to go to dinner with my boss."

The next night Jack brought her to a banquet and dinner dance at Tinker Field in Oklahoma City. Everyone came up to him to congratulate him on a speech he had made the day before. It was an impressive show. Jack put on the charm and laid the groundwork for another date in the future.

They hit it off well and suddenly Stat Control developed an unusual number of problems in Oklahoma City, the sort of things that would require him to fly out and straighten them up. The next trip, he proposed marriage and shortly after that came the fallout and now Tex's intervention. Not content to simply get back together, he quickly began his campaign to convince her to marry him. Failure just wasn't in his vocabulary.

REITH SAT ATOP the epicenter of Thornton's entire operation. His office was on the second floor of a massive two-story block of cinder-block and concrete, amid the military sprawl of hangars, warehouses and barracks at Patterson Field in Dayton. Beneath his feet lay the noisiest and largest installation of IBM equipment in the world, wall after wall of huge cold machines, lined up like vast institutional refrigerators in the basement of a world-class hotel. There were sixty-five black 405 IBM machines in a windowless bay that stretched longer than a football field. Each night, the Stat Control reports would clatter into the massive room via teletype from Army Air Force depots and bases around the country.

On one side, operators would convert the teletype tape into punched cards on clamorous keypunch machines. On the other side, the cards were sorted at four hundred a minute. They were slipped into the tabulators that would spit out the calculations and printouts. The soldiers would rush the raw numbers upstairs to Jack and his men who spent the night converting them into charts and graphs, making the figures a meaningful foundation for decisions on where the air force's strength was greatest or most vulnerable at any given moment. No matter how beautiful a certain regression equation appeared to a statistician, it made no difference to a commanding general. Jack helped Tex keep the tools of the trade hidden in a black box. The next morning, a complete report pinpointing the number and location of many thousands of aircraft and support personnel, hundreds of thousands of parts and billions of gallons of gasoline would be sitting on the general's desk. This was the lifeblood of Tex's operation.

Each morning, Reith had to account for how many B-17s, B-24s and B-29s were grounded for repairs within the continental U.S. He could say why they were grounded and what parts or assemblies would be needed to get them in the air again, and where the needed parts were. He could rattle off the Army Air Force's monthly inventory of some six hundred thousand parts, from three-bladed propellers to an intricate piece of cylindrical fuselage—a feat that alone required the tabulation of more than 10 million punch cards every thirty days. It was more than five times the number of items listed in the Sears Roebuck catalog. He could pinpoint how many military and civilian personnel were on each air force base in the world, how many were AWOL or in sick bay, and whether they were trained to fly a four-engine bomber, strip a .50-caliber machine gun, fill out a weather map or rig a parachute. Jack had an eagle eye view of the war that was unique.

The whole department was an extraordinary triumph of control over a huge, rapidly expanding bureaucracy, and Jack virtually built it from scratch into the largest and most important of Tex's Stat Control units. At war's end, Jack would be told that he was directly responsible for its achievement, that he had singlehandedly saved the Air Force more than $1 billion on the procurement of parts. Some 5,600 people, directly or indirectly under Jack's command, fed the mammoth system.

Jack's work did more than save money; it got whole fleets back up into the air to help rout the Axis forces. At one base B-17s were grounded for spare parts. Just fifty miles away, another air field had stockpiled ten years' worth of the same sorely needed item, unbeknown to anyone who could put them into service. When a plane was grounded overseas, it could take up to six months to get a required part to put it back into the sky. At one point, 12 percent of the air force's airplanes were grounded for lack of parts. Jack managed to squeeze this down to only 3 percent, freeing five thousand more aircraft in the critical spring of 1943 for training and overseas missions. Before the war the Air Force not only failed to keep track of its use of spare parts, it also had no inventory information for 250 major Army Air Force bases or fifty-six specialized depots.

Everywhere you looked, there was disorder and mis-management. Of the more than half a million items of supply, Jack found that nearly one-third were useless. Some forty-five thousand items on the Air Force's critical list for procurement were given priority for materials, money and facilities by manufacturers who were told to produce them. Yet, no one was using the parts. Tex could claim that his group cut the procurement of bombs and ammunition by a total of $3.6 billion in 1943 alone. It was the salary equivalent of one million people working in industry for a full year.

The same chaos existed in the way the Army Air Force kept track of personnel. Before the war, the AAF had maintained manual records. The system couldn't keep pace with the rapid mobilization that occurred after the attack on Pearl Harbor. The Air Force didn't know how many enlisted men and officers it had on hand, neither did it know the specialty in which each soldier was trained. The only hard figure available was the number of pilots on hand, and these records existed only to keep tabs on "flying pay."

It was virtually impossible to balance crews with planes because there were no accurate figures anyone could use to base planning decisions. In the fall of 1942, the Air Force had more pilots than it had airplanes for them to fly. The military could only give them the minimum flying time necessary to qualify for flight pay. Four months later, the service suffered from a drastic shortage of pilots. Similar imbalances with spare parts, gasoline, oil, bombs and ammunition threatened the Allied operation. Jack and his team were to gather all this data and feed it to others throughout Tex's empire who would use it to control the flow of graduates from the technical and flying training schools. Jack had the fix on exactly how many bombardiers, navigators, gunners and co-pilots had to be trained each month to meet the air force's needs in each overseas theater.

These feats were made all the more impressive because the Air Force kept mushrooming. Temporary buildings went up overnight. A pre-war work force of under five thousand mushroomed to nearly fifty thousand military and civilian employees. Three shifts worked around the clock, drawing up engineering specs for fighters and bombers, inspecting aircraft and buying parts from the military contractors. Reith worked as if he were possessed, at one point suffering a nervous breakdown. But instead of taking time off, Jack had a doctor prescribe some medication so he could continue to work.

HE WAS OFTEN going through the night, pouring over the numbers. But Jack's war was one a grunt in the trenches would have eagerly traded for in an instant. While most recruits were holed up in "Wood City," a maze of monotonous, nondescript wooden barracks, Jack lived in "Little Woods," a lush estate belonging to paper baron George H. Mead. Little Woods was an Old English style mansion of stone with a slate roof set in the rolling southern Ohio countryside, as distant and detached from the wretched battlefields of Europe as a place could be. Mead, who rescued a small family concern and built it into a formidable paper company, had left the house for Washington where he served on the President's National Defense Mediation Board. He was only too proud to turn it over to AAF officers. It was a lavish place, with a servants' house, stables for fifteen horses, dog kennels, squash and tennis courts, and a swimming pool, all surrounded by large expanses of lawn, trees, hedges and flowers. During Christmas, the Meads would decorate trees for the horses in the stable yard, hanging carrots, sugar and apples from the branches.

About ten officers had the run of the estate plus two meals a day for all of $125 a month. Jack shared a large bedroom upstairs with Stat Control's number-two man at the base, Charlie Bosworth, an engaging, rakish sport from Denver. They claimed a comfortable room with two twin beds and a private bathroom as large as Charlie's kitchen back in Denver. On Sunday mornings, they would pair up as partners and try to beat some of the other guests on the tennis court.

It was the only time off Reith allowed himself. Jack was always the first to rise and shower, rousing Charlie from his sleep. The two of them would rush down to the long, ornate dining room where the servants would place their eggs before them in egg cups. Neither of them had ever seen an egg served in a cup. As a joke, they each tried to outdo the other in the neatest topping-off of the egg, though they both lacked the delicate steady hand of the rich to win the competition. It was as close as they got to ever using their target training.

War seemed to be the best thing for men who tended toward the obsessive: it brought their inner world and outer life into a frantic symmetry. Jack was never so overwhelmed with his work or Maxine or the Mead lifestyle that he couldn't pore over the car he and Charlie drove to the base. The romantic in Jack worshiped this elegant machine, his gold Lincoln Zephyr. It was a classy, dark sedan that packed amazing power in a V-12 under the hood. Oh yes, that hood—it was shaped like the head of an alligator, with a massive ornament at its peak. Its headlamps were nestled snugly in the front fenders, a unique feature that only added to the pure romance of the machine. Jack forever raved about the car's rounded body contours with as much fervor as the typical GI who studied the curves of Lana Turner. Charlie hardly shared Jack's gusto for the car, often complaining that on those frigid mornings in Dayton it took far too long for the jalopy to warm up.

Jack's war, of course, was not *the* war. Far removed from the front lines, he was distant from the action, assuming a detached role like virtually all of Stat Control's hands, never really serving time, seldom if ever a witness to war's brutal realities.

THE MEAD ESTATE, the tennis games and the martinis sipped before dinner made it a luxurious world that bore little resemblance to the world Reith had known for most of his life. Born September 4, 1914, in Des Moines, Iowa, Jack was the only child of older parents. His mother, Emma, was a mysterious woman, so introverted that she would shy away from the door when friends came by, disappearing as rapidly as a faint shadow. His father, Frank, was a victim of the Depression. He was interested in money and real estate, but lost much of both when the bad times hit and reduced him to selling bread and other groceries from a window in the house. Mostly his son saw a beaten man, with a shock of white hair, lying about the house. Deep in debt, he had given up on life. He lost everything, including his will, his vigor and his determination. "If my dad had spent as much time trying to make money as he had trying to save it," Jack said later, "things would have been much easier for my mother."

If there was one thing he was going to do in life it was to make damn sure that he would never fall into the same trap. You cheated not only yourself, he thought, but everyone who depended on you. He came to almost despise people who simply gave up. Reith saved his greatest contempt for the indolent.

He went to nearby Drake University, graduated in 1936 and sweet-talked his way into General Electric's management trainee program in Schenectady, New York. Shortly after the attack at Pearl Harbor, Reith quit GE to enlist and found himself stuck with an outfit in Mississippi likely to serve real battle time. Then he glimpsed the Stat Control notice on a bulletin board. Harvard, that educational playground of the favored, the famous and the rich, sounded pretty good to him. He applied, was accepted and passed up the chance to go home one Christmas so he could directly report to Patterson Field and press his way into a slot as the executive officer to the Stat Control Unit head Reau Barringer.

One day, Major Barringer called Jim Wright, one of Thornton's top men in Washington, requesting an overseas posting for himself in North Africa.

"Reau," Wright said with his Virginia drawl, "I'm sure you're qualified. But who the hell is going to run that unit if you leave? It's our biggest one."

"I think Jack Reith can do it," Barringer replied.

"Reau, are you out of your mind? He's a captain, right out of school. How old is he anyhow?"

"He's twenty-eight, but I'm certain he can run it. He has done sensational things around here."

With Tex's okay, the change was made. The line of authority directly tied him to Jack, and Jack and he would run the show pretty much as they wished.

You couldn't accomplish all that Reith did at Patterson and not get into a conflict with someone else—especially if you were Jack. Conflicts were endemic. The second lieutenants turned out at Harvard would have to go out and tell majors and colonels how to run their business. Each new victory gained by Tex or his men often had its offsetting fallout. Jack succeeded in developing a couple of key antagonists.

One of these helped to inspire him to eventually try to go abroad. Just to be overseas in a war zone made a man a hero in at least a minor degree back home. So Tex arranged for Jack to switch jobs with Bob McNamara, who was ready to leave an assignment in the Pacific. He had been working on improving the logistics connected with the immense B-29 Superfortress bombers. Now Jack would take up a similar task.

Jack's dream of an overseas posting, however, ended abruptly when news arrived that Japan had surrendered. It happened while he was in San Francisco, awaiting a flight that would take him closer to the front. He returned to Dayton to gather his things and then went straight to Oklahoma and Maxine. Under his persistence, Maxine had relented. She agreed to marry Jack when the war was over.

When she told her parents about her engagement, they were skeptical. Reith had no land or money beyond the cash he got for selling his Zephyr, and Jack's pre-war credentials seemed unimpressive.

"What did he do before the war?" asked her father, a moderately prosperous doctor.

Maxine hadn't known he worked for General Electric.

"I know he had an orchestra at one time," she said, recalling his stories of playing the drums in a band while in college.

"Well, we've never had a carnival man in the family before. But if that's what you want, I guess it's okay."

It was a small, wartime wedding in Holdenville, Oklahoma, on September 20, 1945, without a best man at the groom's side. Their honeymoon was the drive from Oklahoma to Washington in Maxine's old Chevy. Good news awaited their return. Tex had arranged for Jack to receive the Legion of Merit for his Stat Control work at Patterson. Tex brought him and Maxine into Gen. Hap Arnold's office in the Pentagon one day for the ceremony. Arnold read through the densely-worded commendation while Jack beamed at the a fat paragraph of military-styled praise. It told how he was directly responsible for developing and operating the inventory control system; how crucial it was to the war effort.

Suddenly, it hit Maxine. She had married the same Reith she had cursed only years earlier in the course of an early wartime job. Before her job with Braniff, she had worked as a civilian clerk for an air force depot in San Angelo, Texas, while her first husband was away at war. She worked the 3 to 11 p.m. shift in a room full of women whose husbands were also in uniform. During the hours they were together, they shared one thing: a deep contempt for men who were able to hang around in the states while their husbands were directly in the fight, or as came to be Maxine's case, recently buried. While everyone typed away, Maxine's independence and her spirit, bruised by the loss of someone she loved, made her angry.

Every day, she would type this tortuously long inventory report to an "F.C. Reith, Chief of Statistical Control, at Patterson Field." "Why in the world would this guy need all these figures every day," she complained to her boss. "If they took some of these people and sent them overseas to fight, we might end the war a lot quicker!"

It wasn't until Arnold read the commendation that she finally made the connection. Maxine had written his name hundreds of times, but it was always F.C. Reith. Jack, of course, was F.C. Reith; the officer she had so often denounced and despised was the man she had now fallen in love with. My goodness, she thought, this is the guy who made me do that consolidation report every day!

THROUGH THESE DIFFICULT years, Tex had pulled the strings, prompted the players from the wings and given purpose and direction to the cast that was Stat Control. At war's end, Thornton was collecting the characters to mount a new great drama. It was less a plan than a lucky accident, but it was all coming together nonetheless. Every man in Stat Control was a part of a greater whole. The best of them could be broken off into a crackerjack team to stage another offensive when the war was over. To a handful of his very best men, Thornton talked vaguely about getting together in some business venture when they were out of uniform. But he did not know exactly what it might be.

Tex was forming a team with combustible properties. Bob and Jack were a great balance. But he needed others, too. Like the most potent chemicals, his team would have to have the potential of a commanding combination, even if it also had the chance of turning a bit unstable. His friendship brought together the kind of characters that could lead a revolution, or stop one.

THE
WHIZ
KIDS

.

A matchbook portrait of George and Mimi Moore.

Whiz Kids George Moore (second from left) and J. Edward Lundy (third from left) at an officer's club in Washington, D.C., in 1945.

Chapter 5

GENTLE GEORGE

■

"I'm a very gentle man; even-tempered and good-natured, whom you never hear complain; who has the milk of human kindness by the quart in every vein."

—ALAN JAY LERNER

*I*nto Tex's world of facts and precision tumbled one George Moore who was all emotion, a person who wore his heart on his sleeve.

In so many ways, he was a figure drawn out of the ideals of America's own innocence—that time in history when the United States was a prosperous land blessed by the natural boundaries of geography that protected it from its enemies. Everything about the American myth suggested a girl-meets-boy, Horatio Alger success lay within the reach of many. It was a world where the cold tools of Tex's power had a place only at the fringes of society.

The whole country seemed to be George's age, a high-spirited twenty-one, just before a sense of horror, uncertainty and purpose shot into people's lives. On December 7, 1941, when Pearl Harbor was attacked innocence only got you so far. If anything, innocence had left the innocent defenseless. Thornton, McNamara and Reith hurried to shed any vestige of these trappings—the carefree naivete that Moore fought to preserve.

If all this made George the most tenuous member of Tex's group, it also made him an extraordinarily appealing human being. He had traveled the globe for Tex as a trouble-shooter, through Australia and New Guinea, India and China, North Africa and Saudi Arabia. Everywhere he went, his job was to either set up a new Stat Control unit, often having to convince a skeptical commanding officer, or to rejuvenate a tired, underperforming Stat Control staff. He could set even the worst skeptics at ease, winning them over without trying.

One of Tex's early favorites, he had been in the very first Stat Control class at Harvard, graduating in early July, 1942. But when he arrived in Australia with thirty-seven other second lieutenants fresh from Harvard, he became a pawn in a power play between General Douglas MacArthur and Tex.

His orders specified that he and his classmates could only be used for Stat Control work. Those were the early days, when no one in the field knew what the hell Stat Control was, and when a theater commander assumed absolute control over all his resources. General MacArthur and his officers, enraged that some Washington colonel would dictate how he could use the men, assigned all of them to field units as mess officers, dead last in the military pecking order.

Tex hatched a strategy to rescue his men, but before he could put it into effect, George had talked himself out of the mess hall by convincing his commander in Brisbane that he was indispensable in the other, more sorely-needed job of organizing a Stat Control outfit to collect the data Thornton wanted back in Washington. It was Tex's first glimpse of Moore as a self-starter, someone who conquered with elan the seemingly impossible assignments.

George had the natural charm of a smooth salesman and a terrific sense of humor. He was good company, a happy-go-lucky fellow. What everyone most remembers is his unselfishness, always wanting to please, almost to a fault—as if to cover up some personal insecurity or misgiving. And he loved the part: a short, pudgy guy, five-foot-eight and one-half, with a round cherubic face, fine blond hair, blue eyes and a light complexion. When the guys would venture out for a few drinks, George was the first to pick up the tab.

And he was fun to be with. George seemed to be in the middle of wild parties in Washington, drinking bouts in his room with burlesque queens from Brisbane, carousing with the guys through the streets always looking for a good time. He would lead a bunch of them to Officers' Leave Clubs on Springfield Avenue or Elizabeth Bay Road in Sydney, lustily singing "Waltzing Matilda" at the top of his lungs in the middle of King Street.

His Australian compatriots jokingly awarded him the "Lavender Heart." The June 14, 1943, citation read: "For hopping on and off street cars above and beyond the call of duty. In the course of his mission, Lieutenant Moore became separated from his companions. In spite of a heavy load aboard and in very foggy weather, Lieutenant Moore made a severe attack upon the pavement. He skillfully maneuvered himself into a position from which to carry out his foray, but, as he made his approach and reached terminal velocity, he discovered his flaps were not working. Nothing daunted, he made his release, causing great damage to the pavement. As a result of his intrepidity, he suffered grievous personal injuries and a not so temporary black-out. His skill, courage and determination were in accord with the finest traditions of the Army Air Corps."

It was a commendation that Thornton or McNamara or Reith would never have won. But it set him apart from the rest, as much as the tender letters he wrote to his wife, Marika, during the months of his final assignment for Stat Control in the Philippines. Somehow, you could not imagine that Tex or Bob or Jack would expose themselves so thoroughly. They were too sensible, too restrained. But Moore's letters movingly caught the glow and the pathos of his character. They were full of his fears and his hopes.

May 1, 1945
Dearest Mims:

Exactly five months and two hours ago the happiest day of my entire life began. I can still picture that entire day. As you came down the aisle, to the strains of one of the world's most moving marches, you looked so utterly beautiful and real, and then we joined and went on up to the altar, your faltering voice but firm hand. . . . The whole night—reception, champagne, the sincere congratulations I received from our many friends, our own dinner and wine together alone after such a long day. The day was beautiful from five o'clock on—I shall never forget it. So Mims, my dearest, a happy fifth anniversary to you from a long way off.

There are now about ten of us living in a house that was but a couple of months ago the home of Japanese officers. Next door was the post brothel. War's havoc is readily visible hereabouts—the destruction has been very thorough. I have a room to myself—your pictures are already on the wall, my cot

and air mattress set, my clothes hung and all. Have a houseboy who takes care
of about nine of us—shines shoes, makes beds, cleans up, etc. . . .
    Goodnight dearest one. George.

His role was to help the Stat Control offices in the Far East prepare for the invasion of Japan. It was a tough and thankless job, made worse because he would have to recommend the sacking of his commanding officer, Lieutenant Colonel Harold Suttle.

Spent and tired, Suttle simply wasn't up to the task of analyzing numbers as Tex demanded, spending much of his time reading *Time* magazine. Yet, Moore counted him as a friend. "He's the kind of a guy that makes me feel like a bastard for writing this letter," conceded George to Tex, in urging him to bring Suttle back to Washington on temporary leave and take him out of action.

It was so difficult for George to do in his friend that he would write Mimi and ask her to invite him over for dinner when he returned to Washington. Sitting around with a handful of other officers, George even cooked up a suggested menu: fruit cocktail, smoked salmon, steak or beef, chef's salad, browned potatoes and Suttle's favorite vegetable, cauliflower. George recalled that Suttle loved jello and asked that Mimi fix up a bowl for the dessert. "Harold and I served together for a long time," he wrote Mimi. "It was never too easy for reasons you know, but he has always been extremely loyal and good to me. At this minute, I am in a position in which I cannot return that loyalty and be honest to either Tex or myself."

If Tex saw in George's softness a value that none of his other men had, he was canny indeed. Tex called him in to talk about their plans after the war. He told George that he and Jack Reith and possibly a few other men in Stat Control might stay together and do something as a group. Ideally, Tex wanted to buy into a business, gain a controlling interest in some company that they all could run. But none of them had much money for that.

George was immediately taken by the idea, and he was flattered, too, that Tex would want him in on the deal. He enjoyed not only Tex's company, but the company of most of the men who gravitated to Stat Control. They were people who talked about politics and education, economics and music, books and art. They were different from many of the people he knew during his school years in Detroit or the three years he spent at Colgate University. In his enthusiasm, George even suggested that maybe they could convince his father to become an investor with them. His father, Lyford, was an insurance broker in Detroit whose biggest account was the Ford Motor Company.

"If he were sold on the idea," said George, "he might be willing to mortgage his oil interests in Michigan and lend us the sixty or seventy thousand we need."

Tex would hear none of it.

"I like your family too well to see them, at their age, take any risk that might endanger their future security. That's out," said Tex.

It made George admire Tex even more. During his weeks in the Pacific, Moore kept thinking about what they might do, especially since receiving news of the victory in Europe. The men sat around all night, drowsy from the cheap booze and talk, listening to the radio, hearing the celebrations in London, Paris, New York and Washington. And they sat around chatting about things that men seldom discussed, like post-war plans to build homes and families, even guessing how many children each man would someday like to have (George hoped for three or four).

May 20, 1945

I believe, Mims, I am accomplishing the job I was sent out here to do, which is by no means an easy one. So I do get a mental lift out of that. A guy's job means a great deal to him. It is the limiting factor in so many things, some important, some not. What he can do for his wife and family, his own peace of mind, his ego, the future of his family and himself. In justice to the man himself, it requires the best that is in him. That is about the most a man can do for those to whom he is responsible and for his family—produce to the limit of his abilities. That, Mims, is what I shall always do for you, and for myself, and I trust we may have a fairly comfortable life.

Almost constantly, without letup, since August of '42, I have been under real pressure. At times, I hate it. Yet at times, I'm lost without it. Tonight the hours of toil seem to have all caught up and I feel physically and mentally aged.

Despite the pressure, the intrigue, the politics and the absorbing influence Stat Control is, it is that type of thing that gives one a warm feeling of being part of something human, not just a machine. When you figure Tex, out of his jammed and busy day, finds time to try to make you a little happier, you see why there is a loyalty to Stat Control—really a loyalty to Tex himself.

Few people will ever understand the age in experience and maturity the war has brought (us) in Stat Control. After the war, when I tell someone I'm twenty-seven, or Tex says he's thirty-three, people will say "my young fellow" when in actuality, we've crowded ten years into four. . . .

Through it all, Thornton didn't fail him. When his wife was rushed to the hospital to have her appendix removed, he did the kind of small though endearing favors that set people apart. Tex sent Mimi a lavish arrangement of flowers, telephoned to see how she was progressing and visited her in the hospital. He also arranged for a bouquet of flowers to be sent in George's name. And during the worst of it Thornton employed Stat Control's vast teletype network to keep George informed of her progress, using the word "Bootie" as a code for Mimi:

"PROGRESS ON BOOTIE PROJECT WELL ABOVE PROGRAM. ALL FACTORS FAVORABLE."

"RECOVERY VERY RAPID AND NOW AT HOME."

"PROJECT BOOTIE COMING ALONG GREAT BUT YOUR PERSONAL DIRECTIVES DEFINITELY MISSED."

Tex would slip the notes in among the official communiques. The teletype messages helped to ease George's worry because there were no telephones and it would take eleven painful days for a personal letter to travel the distance. Three weeks would pass before either one of them could respond to a query in any given letter. That's why George and Mimi would number each letter in sequence so they could keep track of their correspondence. Her illness, however, brought him down into a deep funk. He had never wanted to be out of uniform until Japan was defeated. It would have been, he told her, like leaving a football game in the third quarter. But God, did he wish he could be back in Washington with her.

He was war-worn. He was away too long. He had been feverishly sick with dengue fever during an earlier stint on Guadalcanal. From a bombing raid early in the war, he suffered some hearing loss in one ear. Then he shrugged the injury off, joking that the raid put an end to a poker game when he was down $35. Now it seemed to become more bothersome. And his weight added to his depression. In February of 1944 when he was en route from Miami to Karachi his air transport command ticket showed he weighed in at 213 pounds. A month later, en route to Delhi from Karachi, he tipped the scales at 233. Flying from Calcutta to Colombo in June he had slimmed down to 175 pounds. Now his weight had soared above 200 again, and he could barely squeeze into his uniform. Upon seeing him in the communal shower, a friend joked, "Tell your wife I didn't know she married a Buddhist!" What a bastard, thought George. He tried to disguise his depression by writing Mimi eloquent

love letters that would avoid any mention of the troubles he was laboring
under at work.

July 15, 1945
   I miss my adorable wife more than anyone can imagine. I need the zest and
spark of life that only your presence makes possible, the happiness so complete,
attainable only at the sight of your beauty, the music of your laughter and
voice, the calm and security of your love and the warmth of your body. This
letter could be one page or twenty pages, but it would all amount to the same
thing. I miss you, I need you and I adore you.
   Good night, my darling, Mims. George.

He'd stare at her snapshot, scribbling pages and pages of his thoughts
to her on paper until he fell asleep from exhaustion to the pounding of
what seemed a constant rain. It gushed so relentlessly that it wasn't
possible to hear one another without shouting.

July 16, 1945
Dear Mims:
   I'm tired of maneuvering, operating, politicking, having all your effort
depend on one or two vital factors, tired of the long hours, of rain and heat and
sweat, of sitting on a hard wooden chair in an office for endless hours and days,
of hiring, firing, arguing, selling, hoping, losing hope, gaining hope—all I
want is you, Mims, and the peace of mind and love that only you can give me.
Obviously, my dearest, the mood is low, the pressure heavy, and the heart
homesick for you. . . .

Everywhere George would see first hand the destruction, the flattened
villages, the evidence of Japanese torture and the tragic disruption to so
many lives. For many of Stat Control's officers, the war was statistics—a
job, a sense of control, the exercise of a dazzling intellect reinforced by
steely ambitions. For Moore, it was blood and gore and broken hopes. In
Manila, after its liberation by MacArthur, he saw the bodies of Filipino
women, children, even babies who had been bayoneted for sport by the
Japanese. There was no glory in war. Numbers had no power here. He
was so repulsed by the devastation that he wondered if man had shown
himself qualified for the privilege of life.
   Yet, he saw good things, too, things that made his eyes brim with
happiness. He had been among the American forces who helped to free
the prisoners of war at a battered camp in Manila. For years, George
would recall how a group of captured soldiers, living in one of those

awful hellholes, had constructed an American flag out of tiny pieces of cloth picked up here and there, and hid it from their captors. As George and others came into the camp, they waved the clever bit of patchwork in the air. The end was within sight.

Aug. 11, 1945
My Dearest Mims:

Shortly after lunch, I was sitting in a B-25 headed for Leyte on a rush and unexpected trip. I returned from there this morning.

Of course, the thing we're all sweating out is the same the world as a whole intensely awaits. The glorious news that indicates final victory may be in the immediate offing reached us last night. We were at a show at Leyte when suddenly someone shouted "the war is over." I don't believe I have ever heard such a deafening din as suddenly broke loose. Ack ack, carbines, pistols, everything was being fired to an extent that made a normal 4th of July seem infinitesimal in contrast. We immediately left the show and went over to the 13th Officers Club right on the beach. The harbor with its ships was a spectacle I shall never forget. All the pent-up' feelings of four and one-half years of war broke loose—multi-colored rockets and flares filled the skies, searchlights pierced the dark of night in constant movement. The roar of guns was tremendous—it is absolutely indescribable.

Generals, Colonels, Lieutenants dropped all bars, and drinks, song, laughter and honest unrestrained joy became the order of the evening. I stayed with it until three a.m. and then finally turned in still awaiting confirmation. Still today we wait and probably shall for a few more—still men go out in planes to die if necessary to keep the course set as it is. Now there is no longer gaiety, now there is almost within vision and overall prayer—'God, let it be true. Give us all peace at last!"

Imagine what it means, Mims. I thought considerably about it last night. So long as we do not compromise future security. I hope to God it's true. If we may have peace and control the horrible power of the atomic bomb I shall be ever grateful. Personally it naturally means much—at long last I can look forward to the freedom I left back in '41–42. I can count on some real time with you—personally that probably means most. A Saturday is a day with you, at five or so I forget work and have the wonderful pleasure of you.

It also means the future becomes fairly immediate. I'd guess it will be about another eight or ten months before I'm out after it's all over. But then comes a permanent position, a decision as to Tex and Jack or something on my own, probably a move to some city—possibly Detroit. Whatever the future holds, with your faith and support, it will be good I'm certain. I'm confidant we'll do alright Mims—financially and in terms of happiness.

I love you beyond all measure of sanity Mims, and how I'd like to be with you at this great time in history, sharing the joys of it together as well as the anxieties. But in spirit, we are. Goodnight dearest beauty. George.

In Washington, Tex Thornton and his men were as surprised as George and nearly everyone else to hear about an atomic bomb. Thornton had noticed on the wall-sized maps in Stat Control's war room a tactical air squadron training at Los Alamos. One day, the button representing the squadron moved alone to one of the islands. It seemed like a wild card floating through the system. But he had no idea that it was a B-29 group being trained to drop the most devastating weapon ever developed. When the President announced that the United States had successfully detonated an atomic bomb over Hiroshima, Tex came rushing out of his office.

"What do you know about a special bomb that has just been dropped?" he asked one of his top men.

Nothing, came the reply. So Tex scampered around the Pentagon to get the press release to find out the details of the bomb's impact. In its aftermath, he tensely waited like everyone else for final word of Japan's surrender. For days, George hugged the office radio but only soft music drifted out as they hoped and prayed to hear an announcer cut in with a news flash and the words, "It's over!" He had voluntarily flown some fifty thousand miles to the front line and to active combat zones to gather intelligence for Tex. He had spent a total of twenty-six months overseas during his three separate tours of duty outside Washington. Now he could hardly concentrate on anything except going home. George mechanically went through the paces, rushing through changes in the unit's plans, toting up war summaries for the general who needed them for release to the press, until finally word came on August 14. The place went berserk. Nearly everyone got drunk. George began tapping into the second-rate Philippine gin at five in the afternoon, staying with it until the bitter end at one in the morning.

Even in a mind with a jackhammer ache, by the next day George could see the future so well. The scene had played in his mind over and over—arriving at National Airport, Mimi waiting on the tarmac in a gorgeous tan and a white dress. He could see them together, with some of the other guys and their gals, on a brisk November Sunday, watching the Redskins, sipping Scotch from a flask in the stands. Beer and oysters at the Shoreham. Dinner at the Parrott. His favorite maroon chair, a beer in his hand, Dorsey on the record player and Mimi in his lap. He could see himself in a gray chalk stripe suit huddled with Tex and Jack doing something important. He didn't know what it might be and neither did they. But George knew it would be compelling and forceful. His new business partners and friends wouldn't accept anything else.

Soon he sat down to write his last letter home, his ninety-sixth letter to Mimi since he left her more than four months ago.

Aug. 19, 1945

My darling Mims:

Yes, Mimi, the great day has finally come, my request for air transportation to Hawaii is in and my departure awaits only the easing of the strain on air transportation due to Japan's capitulation—just how long that will be is hard to know just yet but I'm sure the bottleneck will not exist for long. I shall stop only at Hawaii and then proceed on into the states.

My work was completed here last night and today was indeed lazy. I read a ton of magazines last night—Colliers, Reader's Digest, Time and News-week. This morning I came into the office for a last conference.

WHOA! Mims the phone just rang. I leave for you & America tonight! I bet I'll talk to you before you get this! I love you! I'll soon be with you. Thank God it's over at long last! George.

THE
WHIZ
KIDS

On October 19, 1945, Col. Charles B. Thornton sent this telegram in typical Western Union shorthand to Henry Ford II. The message not only attracted immediate attention from Ford, it started off a journey for ten men who would become known as the Whiz Kids.

Gen. "Hap" Arnold presents the Legion of Merit award to Colonel Thornton at war's end.

This cartoon-like portrait of Tex, the world balanced on a single finger, was signed by his fellow Stat Control officers and given to him at a club in Washington at the end of the war.

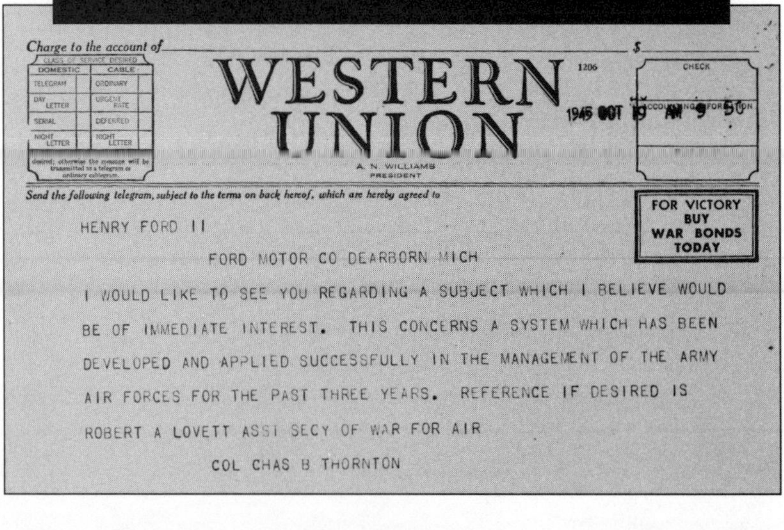

Charge to the account of _____

WESTERN UNION

1206

$ _____

CHECK

CLASS OF SERVICE DESIRED	
DOMESTIC	CABLE
TELEGRAM	ORDINARY
DAY LETTER	URGENT RATE
SERIAL	DEFERRED
NIGHT LETTER	NIGHT LETTER

1945 OCT 19 AM 9 50

desired, otherwise the message will be transmitted as a telegram or ordinary cablegram.

A. N. WILLIAMS
PRESIDENT

Send the following telegram, subject to the terms on back hereof, which are hereby agreed to

FOR VICTORY
BUY
WAR BONDS
TODAY

HENRY FORD II

FORD MOTOR CO DEARBORN MICH

I WOULD LIKE TO SEE YOU REGARDING A SUBJECT WHICH I BELIEVE WOULD
BE OF IMMEDIATE INTEREST. THIS CONCERNS A SYSTEM WHICH HAS BEEN
DEVELOPED AND APPLIED SUCCESSFULLY IN THE MANAGEMENT OF THE ARMY
AIR FORCES FOR THE PAST THREE YEARS. REFERENCE IF DESIRED IS
ROBERT A LOVETT ASST SECY OF WAR FOR AIR

COL CHAS B THORNTON

Chapter 6

THE
TELEGRAM

■

"There's a Ford in your future!
When America's biggest job is
done, a smart new Ford will
point the way to pleasures now
denied you. And you will want to
share them."

—A Ford Advertisement in 1945

Washington went delirious just after 7 p.m. People streamed out of offices and houses into the street, tearing telephone books into confetti, tossing the paper into the air. They drummed pots and pans. They cheered at the top of their lungs. They hollered. They sang. You could barely hear the car horns, church bells and firecrackers. They were all part of the melee. Washington, the city of endless cross purposes, had a single-minded drive that night for NOISE.

Probably the first conga line ever to rush up Pennsylvania Avenue chanted, "We want Harry! We want Harry! We want Harry!" The wavering line of MPs struggled to keep merrymakers from breaking onto the grounds of the White House. Shouts brought President Truman onto the front lawn where he reached through the iron fence to shake the hands of well-wishers. August 14, 1945: The war was finally over.

In the midst of the celebration, Tex Thornton, the arch pragmatist, went on fast-forward. He had to get serious about the plans he'd begun hatching months earlier with a few of his men. Why not stick together through this postwar transition? A team had more impact and would make more of an impression. No matter how brilliant, a single man could be swallowed whole by a corporation, rendered impotent by its bureaucracy and its politics. But not a group working as a team to control the destiny of a great institution. "If you went in with one or two people," Thornton would later say, "you could get lost or chewed up; if you were going to convert a relatively large company quickly you needed a group."

Could it work? Only the war had lifted the nation out of its decade-long depression. Was it possible that the war's end could dump the country into another downward spiral? Some pundits feared the worst as hundreds of thousands of returning soldiers swamped the economy.

The fears intertwined with fast-paced change everywhere. At the Pentagon, demobilization hit like a raging hurricane, twisting and snafuing everything in its path. Plans didn't change daily. They changed hourly. With amazing swiftness, departments and sections disappeared overnight. They were merged or consolidated or reorganized or simply eliminated. Thousands of desk officers were being transferred or discharged. Far greater numbers of men, once fresh-faced and naive, were returning from overseas.

BEFORE THE WAR had disturbed the pattern of his life, Thornton had thought about returning to Texas, looking up one of his old pals and getting into some kind of business together. But the war had changed him. He had come to Washington for the opportunity and a different life. Tex found that and more—lots more. Unlike the tens of thousands of others who believed the war had stolen some of their best years, Thornton held a dramatically different point of view. To him, the war wasn't a wasted detour that only delayed or halted careers and ambitions. It was his coming of age. It was a few steps up on a ladder, and it should count in the climb.

Many men had little if any idea what they would now do; most of them felt the war was an unavoidable wrench thrown into their dreams. But Thornton and his men could hear the inevitable question from an employer even before it was posed: "What did you do before the war?" "Hell," Tex said, "we weren't going to let anyone take four years out of our life and throw it away. If we were carrying rifles on our shoulders, it might have been legitimate. But, hell, we were in business. We were doing the same things in the military that we thought were needed in business. It had direct application."

INCLUDING HIMSELF, TEX already had assembled a four-man team. Jack and George were on board and so was Ben Mills, another of Thornton's bright young recruits Tex had first met at the old Housing Authority. Mills was twenty-seven, disciplined, well-built with a stomach ridged like a washboard. He was drawn to Washington from Oklahoma, deeply wanting to be, in his own words, "a big frog in a big pond." Even he didn't quite understand what that meant. But whatever it was, he knew he would be hard pressed to find it in his hometown of Stillwater. Now, at war's end, it was possible the "big pond" was no longer Washington.

For Tex's post-war team, he was the perfect complement. Ben could not match the intellectual strength of a McNamara nor the force of leadership that Tex brought to the team. He was not a smooth salesman like George, nor was he the obsessive workaholic like Jack Reith. Instead, Mills was a little bit like all of them: strong, yet not pretentious; systematic, though not narrowly; bright, yet not quite cerebral. He could be all things to all people, the kind of person every alliance badly needs.

Tex gave him the team's first job: to put together a brochure that would sell the group to industry, by highlighting their military work and its applicability to the business world. The basic theme: "No decision is better than the facts upon which it is based." On the left side, he listed their wartime record. On the right, a possible business use of the their methods. He wrote up about eight or ten examples, with a few charts. Tex had them printed up, and mailed them to more than a hundred companies. The idea was to maximize their chance of landing good jobs as a group. The brochure boasted their collective years of experience in planning, managing and controlling what Thornton called the largest global operation ever undertaken by man. To recoup the cost of printing them, Tex even offered to sell the document for a buck a copy to others in the Stat Control office so they could use it on their own to move into business.

The mailing drew some promising replies from at least ten companies. Arthur D. Little, U.S. Steel, Eastman Kodak, and Nash Motor were among the bigger names that expressed at least some interest. The most aggressive response, however, came from a railroad holding company in Cleveland called Allegheny Corporation. It was run by a dynamic go-getter named Robert R. Young.

After receiving the brochure, Young directly called Tex and asked to see him in person. Young was a compact, dapper Texan in his late forties who had a penchant for flourish and the grand gesture. Hiring a package of men seemed a unique enough idea to have immediate appeal to him. Ever since he acquired control of the Chesapeake & Ohio Railway in 1937, he had garnered a reputation as a railroad man interested in empire building. Though Allegheny was a public company, Young completely dominated it, treating the firm as his personal property. His postwar visions were grand, and the idea of hiring a group of Air Force men in a package tickled his fancy. Young had been advocating a transcontinental railroad system and he would shortly come to the attention of the public by running newspaper advertisements under the headline: "A Hog Can Cross the Country without Changing Trains—But You Can't." (After acquiring in 1954 the New York Central Railroad in one of the first major takeover battles, Young grew despondent when the stock took a nose-dive. He killed himself with a 20-gauge shotgun in the billiard room of his Palm Beach mansion.) Tex agreed on a date to see him and to talk about the possibility of bringing a team to Allegheny.

Still, the men were trying a bit of everything, not sure whether to stake a claim in an established company or go completely on their own. Tex thought that one possibility was to do for the civilian world exactly what Stat Control did in the military: market research and analysis. The men would gather facts on different markets for companies wishing to sell products in them. A nationwide market research company would have been the most natural outgrowth of their service experience. Jack had even flown out to Chicago to visit with A.C. Nielsen Co., the large research firm that was one of the pioneers in the field.

It would cost about $3 million to launch such a company, and none of them had anything approaching that. The luckier ones had a few hundred dollars put away. Tex talked to one of his contacts, a banker in Philadelphia, who was ready to commit $1 million to the start-up. Lovett, too, told Tex the start-up seemed a good idea. But the competition of Nielsen and their own doubts kept them exploring other possibilities.

To a man, they were drawn to the car business. It was the place to be. The automobile market was not only America's biggest industry, it was also one of the country's most desirable and romantic. Where else does a hero go? He doesn't go into real estate. He doesn't sell clothes. He sells dreams and power and speed. Every homecoming GI dreamed of cruising the roads in a brand new automobile. No product was more glamorous.

The fever for new cars was about to hit. More than a third of the 24 million cars on the road then had a value of $100 or less and would have been consigned to junk yards if not for the unavailability of new models. Automakers had converted their plant capacity to increase the nation's military might, and hadn't made cars for the civilian market since early 1942. Detroit estimated that roughly 10 million Americans were in the market for postwar cars off its reconverted assembly lines.

The group considered buying a dealership with Nash Motor Company, a prominent automaker that would later merge with Hudson to form American Motors Corporation. It didn't have the broader marketplace coverage of General Motors, Chrysler or Ford, but it was one of the biggest of the other major independents, which included Hudson, Kaiser-Fraser, Willys, Packard and Studebaker.

Ben and Jack were deployed to study the Washington car market as if they were preparing a Stat Control paper for Lovett. Jack snooped around existing Ford, Buick and Nash dealers, snapping black-and-white pictures of storefronts and showrooms for the group to study. He and Ben interviewed the owners, finding out details about the size of their order backlogs as well as their contractual arrangements with Nash. They even calculated the sales potential for Nash cars in Washington. But after discovering a third and new Nash dealer in the city, Safford-Chandler Motor on H Street, Ben and Jack advised against a regular dealership.

"We cased the joint and found that it is primarily a former service garage which has been specializing in Nashes," the pair wrote in a letter to Tex and George. "They have a pretty poor location but a good showroom: This is their first effort at selling automobiles, and they just got the Nash agency. This revelation puts a new emphasis on the picture and brings the contractual coverage of Nash to an estimated 1,150 cars. We certainly don't want to go in as a fourth dealer."

For the first time in years, they were floundering. They had facts, lots of them, but no clear direction. If they didn't quite search their souls, presumably they were looking for a sign. Then, good old George Moore got a lead. On a vacation trip home to Detroit, he'd been advised by his father that vast changes were occurring at the Ford Motor Company. His dad had an inside friend, Treasurer Burt J. Craig, who told him that Henry was looking for new blood. Craig was one of three men who was closest to old man Ford, and he was the one who read old Henry's resignation into the minutes of the board meeting at which young Henry took over as president on September 21, 1945. Returning to Washington, George told Tex it was a long shot but worth a try. What could they lose?

Tex and George debated over how to approach Henry. Should they just send him another brochure? They had already dispatched one and hadn't heard a word from Ford. What good would it do to send another? George initially suggested that he go to Detroit and see Craig himself. Or maybe George's dad should make the first contact with Craig. But Tex wanted to go straight to the top.

"Phooey," he said, "we'll just wire Henry Ford directly. Why beat around the bush, George?"

What would they possibly say to Henry in a telegram to grab his attention? It had to be brief and succinct, right to the point without sounding too cheeky. For it to be received seriously, they had to mention Lovett who had become well known for his efforts during the war. Tex had checked with him to make sure that was okay. Of course it was. Tex and George carefully went over the wording, drafting it late into the night. The next morning, on October 19, 1945, George took the note to the local Western Union office in Washington. The operator typed out the message on flimsy, newspaper print that still contained the wartime slogan: "For Victory, Buy War Bonds today!" It clattered over the teletype machine at exactly 9:50 a.m. It was both formal and direct, or as Ben would say, it "bordered on impudence":

> *Henry Ford II, Ford Motor Co., Dearborn, Mich.*
>
> *"I would like to see you regarding a subject which I believe would be of immediate interest. This concerns a system which has been developed and applied successfully in the management of the Army Air Forces for the past three years. Reference, if desired, is Robert A. Lovett, assistant secretary of war for air. Colonel Chas Thornton."*

The telegram arrived on young Henry's desk and he was hardly impressed. He was getting lots of letters from people hungry to get on with their lives now that the war was over. "Cripes," he said, "colonels were like pebbles on a beach at that time." Still, the name Lovett commanded attention. He was well known in Washington circles, and it didn't hurt that he owned a home not far from Henry's mother's house in Hobe Sound, Florida. The very next day, Tex got a call from a functionary in Ford's Washington office.

"Could you come to Dearborn?" he was asked. "Mr. Ford is very much interested."

Tex and George arranged to drive out first to meet Allegheny's CEO in Cleveland. Then they'd swing up to Detroit. Young made an offer on the spot, giving Tex and his men ten days for a final decision. Armed with at least one solid offer, the pair then drove to Ford. No meeting with Henry had been planned. Tex was understandably let down when he was met by George Coulton, who held the uninspiring title of office manager. But Tex insisted that he meet Henry himself. Coulton excused himself and made his way to Henry's office, shaking his head.

"This Colonel Thornton is too hot for me to handle," he told Ford. "You've got to see him."

Surprisingly, Henry did. He had already spoken on the telephone about the men to Lovett, who assured him that they were trustworthy and talented. It was a brief meeting. Tex outlined what his men might be able to contribute to modernizing Ford management, and he described the skills some of his men had in planning, finance and organization. Before the session was over, Henry not only seemed ready to hire the four men, but invited Tex to include others.

"Why don't we all sleep on it and talk again tomorrow?" Tex smoothly suggested. "There's not that much of a rush."

Tex asked Ford to call him at the Statler Hotel the next day. He left for his hotel and excitably told George the news. The next morning, Tex informed the hotel bell captain his name and said, "I'll be having breakfast in the coffee shop across the street. If I get a phone call that I'm expecting from Henry Ford, please send a bellboy over."

The bell captain's smile hardly disguised the incredulous look on his face. He agreed to send for them, and Tex and George crossed the street to take advantage of the cheaper meal available there instead of the hotel's dining room. They were halfway through the meal when an excited bellboy appeared at their table with word that Ford was on the phone. They raced back to the hotel lobby, and heard the great news that Henry still thought it a wonderful idea.

Now all they needed was to deliver Henry a bona fide group. Ford asked them to send a telegram to him listing the names of all the officers he planned to bring with him. As for the salaries, "Why don't you fill in the spaces and send them on to me?" Ford asked.

Tex was beside himself. The deal wasn't yet solid, but it was getting that way quickly. On their drive back to Washington, Tex and George began thinking what it might be like to work at Ford. Back in Washington, they huddled one day in George and Mimi's Park Fairfax apartment, mulling over who else they might pick to come into the group.

"We've got to have Bob McNamara in the group," urged George, "and we've got to have Ed Lundy." Ed, a former economics instructor at Princeton University, had instantly impressed Moore as a quick study in Washington's Stat Control group.

Jack suggested his old Dayton companion, Charlie Bosworth. They had maintained a firm friendship together, even though Charlie left Patterson Field in February of 1944 for a special mission in England. They corresponded frequently, exchanging gossip and news of the latest personnel changes. Ever since their early days together, Charlie had considered Jack his closest friend in the service. Here was a chance to rekindle their friendship.

At Tex's request, Ben had secretly perused the files of personnel records to come up with a few more names. Sifting through the records, Mills could gain a sense of a man's intelligence because each file contained his IQ scores. Every new military recruit had to take the test. As it turned out, the exams showed that nearly half of all American recruits could be classified as morons. But in Thornton's branch there was hardly a soul whose intelligence quotient wasn't well above 100. And Mills made sure the digits of his chosen few were as high as could be.

He rifled through hundreds of files, making up a long list, and lining across the top the characteristics of the ideal person. He read through the commendations, ratings and evaluations by superiors. "We were looking not only for competent people," recalls Mills, "we were looking for diversification: a couple of finance guys, an attorney or two. We were trying to get a group together with broad appeal rather than have everyone in the same mold. We gave serious consideration to what would be the most salable kind of package, whatever would maximize our chances to get jobs."

Tex wanted him to consider every quality one could imagine: personal appearance, education, stamina, loyalty, intelligence and ambition. These men had to look the part as well as play it. Ben's search of the confidential files turned up the names of perhaps twenty-five final candidates. He scribbled their names down the side of the list, methodically rating them, one by one.

They poured through the candidates, narrowing them down to little more than a dozen. Tex personally knew them all and would do the calling to persuade them to come aboard. Charlie, Jack's good friend from Dayton days, eagerly signed on. Ed Lundy, George's old Stat Control pal from the Progress Analysis Branch, agreed to come along. He brought with him Arjay Miller, a folksy intellectual off a Nebraska farm. Jim Wright, one of Tex's earliest Stat Control hires, was talked out of returning to Norfolk to practice law. Andy Andreson, the only other full colonel in the group other than Tex, was persuaded into leaving a job he already had in California. Slowly, the loosely-organized team was becoming an alliance.

Virtually everyone Tex spoke to leaped at the chance. Only a few Stat Control officers turned him down. Myles Mace, an attorney and Harvard pal of Bob, returned to the academic life at Harvard; John F. Symms, one of Tex's sharpest analysts, resumed his law practice in Albuquerque and would later become governor of New Mexico; and Dusty Porterfield, Tex's former executive officer, bowed out when he learned that Tex was trying to get Bob to join the group; the two of them didn't get along.

Tex's only major holdout was Bob McNamara. Still officially on leave from Harvard, Bob had an attractive offer to return as a full professor and to teach virtually any course he wished from the business school dean, who badly wanted him back. It is what Bob wanted more than anything. He had little interest in business, especially the politics of it. But he loved teaching and he loved the academic life.

With the Ford offer in hand, however, Tex kept badgering him about joining the group, calling him on the phone at Patterson Field, refusing to take no for an answer. There was at least one very good reason for him not to return to Harvard. His wife, Margy, had been in the hospital with polio for close to nine months. The disease was the scourge of the 1940s, a constant source of dread. Bob caught it first, coming down with a high fever shortly after his arrival at Dayton. At first, the doctors thought it was a recurrence of malaria which he had caught earlier in India. A week later, however, his wife checked into the Air Force hospital with a high fever, too. Margy was quickly diagnosed as having infantile paralysis, and Bob was rediagnosed as having polio as well. When V-J Day arrived, they were both in hospital beds.

Bob had only a mild case and was out of the hospital in less than six weeks with few aftereffects. Margy, though, was seriously ill. Flat on her back, she was paralyzed with the disease, unable to even lift an arm or leg off the bed. The doctors doubted that she would ever walk again. It was clear that Bob would have great difficulty paying the mounting medical bills for Margy on a professor's salary.

"Didn't you tell me you're broke?" asked Tex.

Bob nodded.

"Come with us then," Tex prevailed. "You owe it to your wife."

Bob resisted.

"Look," said Tex, "you could go back to business school. You'll make

$4,000 or $5,000 a year. At Ford, you'll make double that and there will be plenty more. We're going to be very successful out there, and we're going to be amply rewarded. You can bet the pay scale at Ford is a lot better than the one at Harvard."

In the end, Bob reluctantly agreed to consider it. He realized Tex was right: he could never meet Margy's bills on a professor's salary, and it forced him to look at his finances and at his life, to reassess his plans at least for now. He called Tex again, saying yes, maybe I'll do it. But Bob laid down conditions. It would depend on where the group would go, who would go and how much money he could make. The money mattered only in order to meet Margy's doctor bills. When Tex told him that Ford was ready to hire them, sight unseen, Bob dragged his feet, saying he wasn't ready. He insisted he had to go to Dearborn with the others to meet Henry and look over the place. Tex agreed, surmising that once he got Bob in Detroit, he would never want to leave. The opportunity was just too great to pass up.

If Bob would go, that would make ten of them, a nice round number Tex thought. No one knows exactly why Tex settled on ten officers. It was doubtful he knew that in Biblical law ten people are required to band together to constitute a religious quorum. The Hebrew word for ten also means center because once you gathered ten men who could pray you possessed a center for human life. The number ten seemed magical. Behind it lay a powerful evolutionary justification, for researchers have theorized that ten was the optimal size of a hunting group in the first several million years of human existence. A group of ten could provide nourishment for a total band of perhaps forty dependents, tapping into some primal force to achieve the greatest efficiencies in the hunt. Whatever impulse caused Tex to settle on a tribe of ten, it was the right one.

BEFORE ARRANGING THE group's first hunting expedition—their trip to meet Henry in the flesh—there was one last remaining detail to settle: How each of them should be compensated.

"For God's sake, Tex," laughed Jack. "You know I'm worth more than that!"

A few of the guys were sprawled out in Tex's living room in Arlington deciding how much each of them was worth. It was an uproariously boisterous session. They had put together an elite group of colleagues, sold themselves to Henry Ford II, and then gained Ford's invitation to set their own pay scales. Salary was an emblem of prestige, and Henry was allowing them to design their own badges. It was no time for modesty.

"Well," said Tex, "we already have this much on the table from Young at Allegheny."

"Let's boost it," said Jack. "Why the hell not? If we're worth that much to him, Ford should pay us the sky."

"Tex, how much do you think we're really worth?" asked George.

"What do you mean we?" quipped Ben. "I know I'm worth a helluva lot more than you guys. Hell, how many of you dodged bombs in London."

"Ben," laughed Jack, "I didn't party at the Savoy."

Tex figured he would throw out some numbers based not necessarily on anyone's ability to do the job, but on potential earnings or on other offers some received before the Ford deal came up. He didn't want to scare Henry away by demanding scandalously high salaries, but he wasn't about to sell any of them short, either.

"Ben, how about $11,000," asked Tex.

Ben was elated. Hell, the highest pay he had ever pulled down before the war was $4,800. He didn't make much more than that as a major in the Air Force. That was good, solid American money. The autoworkers in Ford's Rouge complex made little more than $1.10 an hour. The New York *Times* then sold for a mere three pennies, and a ride on a city street car in Detroit cost all of a dime. It certainly beat what someone like McNamara would have gotten if he returned to Harvard as a professor for the going rate of $5,000 a year.

"Can you imagine what Hap Arnold would say?" joked Ben. "Tex that sounds fine to me."

Tex put Bob among those at the top of his salary list, partly because he had already promised to at least double the Harvard Business School offer and partly because he saw so much potential in him. The same was true of Jack, whose GE experience before the war was invaluable and who ran the largest single operation in Stat Control. For his sheer intellect, Ed Lundy was worth $12,000, too.

Even if you ended up at the bottom of the scale, at $8,000 a year, it was a handsome sum.

"Arjay," asked Tex, "how 'bout eight for you?"

"Hell," he laughed, "I'll never have to work again after this. I made $2,600 a year at the bank."

Before the war, his first job as a junior socio-economic planner at the

Federal Reserve Bank of San Francisco paid all of $135 a month. Arjay and his wife Frances lived on $65 and banked the rest. For that matter, George and Mimi lived on a monthly budget of $58—enough to pay for their apartment, food, transportation, laundry and cigarettes.

"Hell, Tex, we'll never have to worry about money again," joked Arjay.

In a notebook on his lap, Tex jotted down each person's starting pay, next to his age:

> Lieutenant Colonel Robert S. McNamara, 29, $12,000.
> Lieutenant Colonel F.C. "Jack" Reith, 31, $12,000.
> Major J. Edward Lundy, 31, $12,000.
> Major Ben Mills, 30, $11,000.
> Lieutenant Colonel James Wright, 33, $10,000.
> Lieutenant Colonel George Moore, 25, $9,000.
> Colonel W.R. "Andy" Andreson, 30, $9,000.
> First Lieutenant Arjay Miller, 29, $8,000.
> Lieutenant Colonel Charles Bosworth, 30, $8,000.

Tex, free to negotiate his own deal with Henry, demanded exactly $16,000 a year—twice as much as the lowest paid on the list. Crossing his fingers, he sent off the telegram on November 5, 1945; and all of the men anxiously awaited their meeting with the Industrial Prince.

When Henry said yes, as he did only days later when the group first met him, they knew they'd met their destiny.

THE

WHIZ

KIDS

The classic early picture of the group taken in 1946 shortly after the men joined Ford Motor (left to right, front row): Arjay Miller, Jack Reith, George Moore, James Wright, Tex Thornton, Andy Andreson, Charlie Bosworth, Ben Mills, Ed Lundy, Bob McNamara.

QUIZ KIDS

■

"They were pretty obnoxious."
—A FORD VETERAN ON
TEX'S GROUP

*T*hough they barely had a single suitcase of civilian clothes between them, ten anxious men arrived in Detroit with their families on January 29, 1946 to start a new life. They came by car and by train, checking into a couple of hotels in downtown Detroit, a brief walk from the Union Guardian Building in the financial district. Tex Thornton had scheduled their first meeting together for 2 p.m. in a small room in this building, where George's dad kept his own office.

Tex likened their journey to a hunting expedition. Armed with a rifle and ammo, you began your march through the woods, not really knowing what you'll find, what you'll bring home. But you know there'll be something; you know it will be an adventure.

It was, curiously enough, the first occasion when all ten of them would meet together in a single room. They seemed so earnest, so intent, so deadly serious. Tex sliced through the chit-chat, and then launched into the discussion they'd come to hear. Heady stuff, serious stuff. Big ideas and cautious warnings: Tex sounded as if he was laying the groundwork for some kind of invasion. Jack had typed up a fourteen-page agenda for the meeting. It was an audacious document that reflected both a chillingly disciplined approach and a love of power shared by all of them. He had already reviewed the agenda informally with Ben, George and Jim before handing it over to Tex.

"Fellas," Thornton said, "we've been given an exceptional opportunity to work for Mr. Ford. You know we're part of an effort by him to bring young men with proven ability into the company. We have to be willing to work hard, and we must do everything possible to produce good results quickly."

The men nodded approvingly.

"We'll no doubt be under some suspicion and attack. Some people may even resent us. So we have to use extreme tact and diplomacy. There can't be any big-shot complexes in the group. We have to be confident and assured, but courteous, friendly and open-minded. We can't be overbearing or supercilious.

"The group," Tex continued, "must function as a group. Eventually, we'll all be placed in other positions with the company, but for now we have to work as a team. The first six months may bring disappointment and disillusionment. We have to get over it, work with the ultimate future in our minds."

Tex told the men that none of the company's executive privileges were to be requested by them. Those things would come to them in time. If they were offered, it would be okay to accept them. But Tex didn't want to ask for any special favors. As for salaries, he noted that the group average was $10,000—when the average employee in the United States was making less than $2,500 a year.

"Four of you will get salaries above $10,000 and a few will get less," said Tex. "The salaries are based on potential earnings or on other offers you received before deciding to go with Ford. They aren't based on ability to do the job or your potential. So let's not have any critical discussion about the money, All of us are being well paid."

This had already become something of a sore point. Jim Wright, the lawyer in the group, privately complained to Tex about being paid less money than some of the other guys with less experience. He felt so unhappy about it that he almost left Ford. Tex grew flush with anger, explaining that he set Wright's salary on how much he'd likely earn practicing law in Norfolk, Virginia, Wright's hometown, which was about a third less. Even though there were disagreements over some money, the group wouldn't allow that to divide them or distract them from their mission.

The men would focus, not on the day-to-day operations, Tex explained, but only on the "highest policy level" decisions. As Tex and his men defined it, they would become an overall "control" group reporting only to Henry and responsible only to him. Tex would lead this "super staff," an executive agency attached personally to Henry to act as his corporate filter, screening and passing judgment on the flow of information to him. They would decide what reports, summaries and proposals he would need, and then they would interpret and analyze them for him —just as they did for Bob Lovett and Hap Arnold in the Air Force. The goal, it was agreed, would be to establish Ford cars as leaders in their respective price fields and to make the entire company as effective and efficient as humanly possible.

For a bunch of guys who knew nothing about the car business, they mapped out for themselves an incredibly brazen agenda that betrayed how little they knew about business. They weren't going to master Ford the way they mastered the Army Air Force. Business wasn't government. It was less principled, less democratic—especially big business and especially Ford. In the 1940s, many companies were run like fiefdoms by strong-willed managers who crushed all dissent. These were often crude, uneducated men who thought nothing of using force to accomplish their goals. Business could be lawless. And many large companies were often run out of shoeboxes, with the most primitive accounting systems imaginable. They weren't managed according to the simple principles Stat Control officers articulated during the war.

If Tex thought that ten former officers could lead a revolution at Ford, he was either naive or badly mistaken. Sure, the Army Air Force had been ungovernable, messy and almost reliant on fraud. If they were a success in World War Two, when they clearly knew nothing about war, why couldn't they succeed at Ford, knowing zip about the automobile? A victory in business, however, is less certain than one in war in which you always fight for closure. In business, there's never an end: it's the art of getting from today to tomorrow, every day. Moreover, Ford was full of people who weren't about to welcome a group of outsiders who thought they knew better. Even ten of Stat Control's best weren't going to be enough. They probably needed over a thousand Army Air Force officers or more. Their preparation for this new arena only revealed how unprepared they truly were. Yet, here they assembled, conspirators plotting the takeover of a huge organization.

Jack Reith had even jotted down a list of "typically offensive or dangerous words or phrases" that they would agree not to utter: efficiency, expense reduction, sales leadership, programming, planning, control and investigation. They were code words for death, used by those so-called efficiency experts who would comb through a company to chop out the dead wood. Even if that's what the group eventually would urge, they weren't going to let anyone in on it, not now.

That was not all. The men began to define the persona they would adopt as a group, creating an identification for themselves that would be non-threatening, yet would convey a good measure of the power they believed they had. "Obviously," Jack had written, "many people in the Ford organization and some outside of it will be anxious to know why we are here, what we are going to do." If they answered with vague replies that they didn't yet know or they wanted to learn more about the company, it could cause resentment and suspicion. Their answers had to be somewhat cautious and consistent, they agreed. What to say? Tex believed they should identify themselves as "a group responsible to the President to work on special projects" as part of an Office of the President. The title conjured up the power and prestige they so eagerly desired, without sounding as if they were a form of secret police.

They agreed to take the initiative to convert what could be a tedious and pedestrian orientation tour into a springboard for influence with Young Henry. They would reshape the entire program. If one session explored dealer operations, it would hardly help them to have a single manager deliver a lecture to the group for two weeks. Jack thought the better approach would be to break the men up in teams of two each, spend a pair of days immersed in reading materials followed by team visits to five different dealers in five different parts of the country. Each team would spend five days with the dealer, and each day would be devoted to a single department: new car sales, used car sales, service, accounting and finance and overall management. Then, the teams would hustle back to Detroit for a five-day forum at which each team would present its findings to the group for discussion. The men didn't simply want to learn the business; they wanted to be able to run it immediately.

They demanded mountains of reading materials and background before each session, and they gained authority to obtain all data and records on each department—however random and scattered out these records were—so they could use these as a basis for action. They even requested day-to-day stenographic recordings of statements by Young Henry to insure they were on the same wavelength. They asked for a secretary, a conference room and, appropriately enough, a Friden calculator.

They spent all that January afternoon readying themselves, finally breaking up at 6 p.m., agreeing to meet again the next day at 10 a.m. Tex wasn't able to make this meeting because he was waiting in his hotel room at the Statler for a call from Young Henry. They talked for nearly three hours about what duties they might perform for Ford until finally going over to see Thornton at 1 p.m. Henry hadn't yet called. So the men hung around Tex's room, plotting and dreaming their future at Ford. They agreed to something Tex felt was important: that there would be no "peeling off" by individual members of the group unless by and with the consent of the majority—not, at least, for one and one-half to two years or until the group had really become productive. They arrived as a package for a reason: to wield far greater influence than any single individual possibly could and they didn't want to lose the magic that a team could bring.

They wanted to make a difference. They didn't just come to Ford for paychecks and some perks. They had bigger plans that only a big company with huge resources could satisfy. Bob McNamara, for one, believed that management was responsible for many of Detroit's labor problems. The auto companies, he thought, treated their employees as if they were disposable, summoning them into the plants during good times but just as quickly laying them off when times were bad. For years, the prevailing management technique to deal with unions was to beat up on their leaders.

The phone finally rang in Tex's room. It was Henry. He and Tex exchanged greetings. Ford told him to report to the aircraft engine building in the Rouge complex at 8:30 a.m. the next day for their first day of work—January 31. They could take care of some final paperwork, receive their employee badges and begin an orientation program that the company was planning.

A MAJOR SHOCK was waiting for them the moment they walked into the brick building in the Rouge. Examinations—a battery of them.

"We're here, Goddammit!" Tex protested. "Our IQs are a matter of record. We don't have to prove our intelligence or our emotional security."

Jim objected strenuously. As the lawyer in the group he wondered whether the company had the legal right to subject them like guinea pigs to tests. They considered walking out on the spot, but didn't, partly because their military training had accustomed them to these invasive indignities, partly because, well, they were here and had had cut their ties with the world beyond Dearborn.

"Jim," Tex finally said, "I don't think we have much of an alternative. Let's just go in and do the best we can."

Robert Dunham, a former FBI agent hired by Ford to create a personnel department for Ford white collars, had his office here along with the dozen or so psychologists employed by the company. Dunham, with Ford less than two months himself, greeted the unhappy men. They must have felt as if they were joining the military again: each was issued an employee badge, numbering from 966 to 975, with Tex getting the first number and the others receiving their own in alphabetical order. No sooner did they get their badges than they were filed into a sterile testing room.

They settled into wooden armchair desks in a bare whitewashed room, and Dunham passed out the papers. For the entire day until 5:30 p.m. they took the tests under the watchful eyes of a pair of monitors. After each exam, there would be another and another and another— eleven in all, tests of ability and practical judgment, achievement exams challenging their knowledge of current social problems, science and mathematics, psychological profiles and mental stability exams. They even got ranked against the general population on such factors as masculinity and depression. Then there were the individual interviews with a Ford psychologist in the next room. Either Ford wanted to check out the merchandise he just purchased or his right-hand man John Bugas, resentful of these ten characters coming in at fancy salaries, wanted to be damn sure they were worth it. Or maybe, he wanted to show them up or see if there was a screwball in the bunch.

The exams were a rude slap, a complete comedown after spending two days discussing how to seize control of their fate at Ford. They were above this sort of thing. They could scarcely believe how juvenile it seemed. Some of the tests were on a high school level. Bob, Arjay and Ed, who had respectively done graduate work at Harvard, Berkeley and Princeton, had taken plenty of exams through the years, had even written tests for students. But this was just too much. Wacky questions, hundreds of them, allowed the psychologists to play their games:

"Are you inclined to be moody?"

"Are your feelings rather easily hurt?"

"Can you usually let yourself go and have a hilariously good time at a gay party?"

Each question required a yes or no answer on a standard form that would be scored by benefit of a stencil, the kind you answer with a number two pencil. The men wondered what it was all about, whether any dark and hidden secrets about themselves might be revealed by the silly tests. As they read through the next list of questions, they must have wondered. . . .

"Do you feel sorry for a mistreated horse?"

"Can you go into a dark cellar or basement alone without even the slightest trembly feeling?

"Do loud noises tend to upset you?"

"Are you inclined to be thinking about yourself much of the time?"

"Are most people thoughtless of the rights of others?"

"Are there times when it seems that everyone is against you?"

As farcical as some of these queries seemed, years later Bob would recall one question more than any other and laugh over the foolishness of it. "If you had the choice, would you rather be a big-game hunter or a florist?" Bob couldn't see the significance of it, unless some psychologist thought it was supposed to offer a clue to a man's sexual preferences. He knew what he wanted to be; he had come here to work for Ford. They all did. What had this to do with their plans? Was it possible to fail these exams and be shown the door?

More than the others, Ed Lundy, who once designed and graded exams as a Princeton instructor, zipped through the tests, almost seeming to enjoy them. He was consistently the first to complete an exam, only to leave the room or walk about until the group was ready to start the next one. George worried his way through them. Maybe it was just his age, at twenty-six he was seven years younger than Jim and three years short of Bob and Arjay. Maybe it was his lack of experience.

If anything, however, the examinations only bolstered their reputation, confirming to Ford what he had been led to believe by Lovett: that these men were extraordinarily bright, rare specimens of intellect, balance and emotional maturity. Compared against the general population, they tipped the scales toward elite superiority. The group ranked above the ninetieth percentile in general mental ability, practical judgment, business practice, cooperation, self-reliance, objectivity and masculinity. So impressed was the Ford psychologist who interviewed the men and studied the test results that he commented on how personable they appeared. "To pass among them or to talk with them individually, one can detect nothing in air or manner that would indicate arrogance or conceit," he wrote. "They appear completely unspoiled. Also outstanding is the group tolerance, often not found among a group of 'intellectuals.'"

Still, the tests showed that Ford hadn't hired Renaissance Men. They rated in the lower half of the population for their interest in art, music and social activity. Ford obviously didn't employ them to paint a canvas or play an instrument. And for a group that used numbers almost exclusively to quantify and analyze life, they scored surprisingly low in mathematics and science.

What the tests also demonstrated—and what the men secretly feared—is how they stacked up against each other in brainpower, reason and ambition. Out of any group of ten, half of them would be graded in the lower ratings by definition. If Henry could have forced such tests on Jesus and his disciples, half of them wouldn't have made it either. That's what really made it seem so unfair and humiliating.

Each of them was ranked by graph on thirty test factors, from general mental level of ability to a tendency toward depression. In brainpower, Bob, Ben, Ed and Andy all scored in the hundredth percentile for their ability to think and reason. Bob was as close as you could get to being an organic computer, achieving the highest scores in the group in both verbal and non-verbal abilities. All ten men scored in the hundredth percentile on another key section of the exam that measured practical judgment, though Charlie and Ben broke the scale. Charlie's grade was thirty-six points above the highest score recorded in the test manual while Ben's was twenty-one points over the record.

It was revealing to Ford, however, to look over the results of Tex's exams. The tests showed him to be dead last in mental ability and among the lower half of the group in knowledge. Tex, though, topped the others in outstanding leadership qualities. The evaluator noted that the results showed "exceptional understanding of human nature and ability to evaluate others" as well as the "presence of strong motivation and drive." Only Bob, the exams showed, equaled Tex in drive and ambition.

The exams would not be the only indignity forced upon the men. They were told that they would not only have to wear their employee badges but would also have to punch a clock, like everyone else. Tex was incensed. They were used to keeping their own hours, working twelve to fourteen hours a day. They were conscientious professionals. It seemed absurd that Ford would want them to punch time cards, like mere laborers in a plant. The tests were enough. Now Tex rebelled, and he won. It was a small victory in a world that allowed few victories. In war, heroics were expected. In business, you had to be careful of how you tried to stand out.

EXECUTIVE LIFE AT Ford was often described in terms of the Indian rope trick: the performer climbs to the top and then disappears. In the days before H.F.II took over, only one man seemed able to pull off the trick and remain. He was Harry H. Bennett, who ran Ford's private police for more than twenty years. A short, stocky man with scars on his ruddy cheeks, Bennett was universally feared within the company. Ford hired him in 1919 in after having met him in one of his plants building submarine chasers for World War One. A former prizefighter, Bennett was part of a Navy intelligence unit combatting sabotage in U.S. plants.

He immediately fired 1,500 men in the Ford "service department," a euphemism for the company's internal police department, and he replaced them with boorish ex-athletes and ex-convicts. Ford quickly came to rely on the man who several times risked his life for him. At one point, in 1932, Bennett's neck was broken and he was knocked unconscious by a concrete block while trying to quell a riot that culminated in a hunger march against the Ford property. Four men were shot dead in the melee, including one who fell on top of him.

In some queer way, Bennett resembled the domineering master who presided over the mechanized empire that dehumanized the workers in Fritz Lang's classic 1926 movie *Metropolis*. Like Master John Fredersen of the movie, Bennett's office boasted a large control board about six feet square, covered with signal lights, switch keys and buttons. The board linked him with all the stations of his plant police force and was able to receive and transmit radio messages to cars owned by key Ford executives. The door to his office, in the basement of the company's administration building, could not be opened unless Bennett pressed a button underneath his plain oak desk.

Bennett's influence with Henry Ford had only increased as the old man grew more indecisive and forgetful. Some family members feared that Ford would turn the company over to him. But young Henry's claim as crown prince won the support of other executives and of his grandmother and mother who were both major stockholders in the family-owned business. The company's official biographers, in fact, had reported that his mother told the ailing Ford that unless her son were made president, she would sell her sizable block of shares.

It was on September 20, 1945, that Henry Ford bowed to the ultimatum, telling his grandson at a meeting at his Fair Lane estate that he was ready to step aside and allow young Henry to take over. The very next day, the new president of the Ford Motor Company walked down to the basement of the administration building and informed Bennett that his services were no longer needed. An angry Bennett told him: "You're

taking over a billion dollar organization here that you haven't contributed a thing to!"

Entering Ford at this fragile point, Tex and his cohorts were for the
first time entering the infantry. They were headed for the frontlines of
alien terrain: an organization populated by smiling vipers. The company
hadn't employed managers before but rather "strong men" without defined responsibilities or authority who called the shots based on their
own ambition and success in acting like mobsters. A man in the Rouge
told Arjay what it meant to be a good manager: "I can make a man pee
in his pants just by standing next to him," he bragged. "That's all I have
to do." They were leftovers from the rule of Old Man Ford and Bennett,
whose policy it was to play one man against the other to insure that none
of them became too powerful.

Tex and his team became strangers in a strange land, with no real
titles and no fixed assignments. Many of the men treated them as if they
were lepers. Few dared to get close to them because they didn't really
know what the group was up to. If someone asked who they were, they
would reply with the agreed-upon phrase: "A group responsible to the
President to work on special projects." People assumed it was a lie. It
wasn't simply that the group fell outside the corporate chain of command. There was no command, no vehicle for moving Ford ahead. No
organization charts. Nothing.

Older company bosses viewed them with great skepticism and fear.
Thornton's group were educated men in a city that valued the grease
monkey, the mechanic. It was one of the reasons why Bob McNamara
and Arjay Miller would later opt to live among the eggheads in Ann
Arbor where the University of Michigan carved out its home. In Detroit,
as in much of industry, there was prejudice against a formally schooled
businessman. Education made a man "impractical," people said. It kept
him from doing "honest work." Bugas didn't have a degree. Neither did
old Harry Bennett who as personnel director ruled over Ford with billy
clubs and brass knuckles for years. And young Henry was tossed out of
Yale for turning in a paper written by someone else. Among the several
hundred top executives at Ford, there may have been two with college
degrees—a fact that would still amaze McNamara more than four decades later.

Ford was not alone in its disdain of education. While General Motors
had a heavily credentialed chief financial officer at the time, the company
actually tried to hide his educational background. As GM's vice chairman then told managing consultant Peter F. Drucker who was having

difficulty obtaining the man's biography, "Don't you see that he not only went to college but worse, got a Ph.D. in economics from Michigan and worst, taught at the university for a few years. . . ."

They were so unlike the men around them, not bound by industry tradition or practice. As outsiders and non-auto men, Tex's group could more easily challenge and question. Indeed, some of their observations would have been heretical to the old guard and even to the young Ford. Bob, for one, strongly believed that Ford's serious difficulties with labor were partly its own fault. Ford had been hobbled by more than 750 strikes in the previous four and one-half years. Minor grievances often blew up into slowdowns or wildcat strikes. It wasn't unusual for some disgruntled employees to forget a bolt, leave a nut off or a part unwelded or even to put live rats or soda bottles into the door panels of Lincolns. Young Henry moved cautiously with the labor unions, but basically felt they needed to bear responsibility for the troubled relations.

"There is much that labor may be blamed for," wrote Bob McNamara in an early letter to his friend Ed Learned at Harvard. "However, at present I feel sure that a major part of the fault in Detroit lies with management. Detroit management, because of the easy money and boom-time atmosphere which existed here for so many years, appears to me to be far behind the rest of the country in its recognition of its social responsibilities. For the eleven-year period, 1927 through 1937, General Motors' profits were the equivalent of a 25 percent annual return on investment, and yet GM continued to foster a production and marketing program which place a disproportionate share of the risk of the business on the worker. . . ." GM treated its employees as if they were disposable. When demand for cars fell, they were laid off. When volume rose, they were hired back. McNamara believed the company had a social responsibility to better manage its business so workers could enjoy greater security for themselves. If Bennett had been around to intercept McNamara's mail, he would have branded the newcomer a communist.

For now, their headquarters would be an assigned wedge of space in the Rotunda, across the street from Henry's office in the Administration Building. Bob and Tex were closeted in an office, while the rest of them sat in the open bull pen. It was an odd place. There were no room numbers, no way to describe anything here. You would just point and mumble, almost having to describe the positions of the desks by degrees. The setup didn't allow for much privacy. Indeed, the domed shape of the Rotunda's ceiling was such that you could pick up words, conversations, clear across the Rotunda. The men even tested it, moving around the floor to different spots, speaking in a whisper, then a normal tone of voice, while another would stake out a spot across the open room to discover whether the voice would carry that far. If you stood in the right place, the words would bounce up and down across the floor layout and the conversation would be as clear as if you were sitting in the same room.

Much to Tex's chagrin, smoking in the offices was not only considered a breach of etiquette; it also was a matter for discipline. Old Henry, who forbade smoking at Ford, was said to have been delighted to hear once that Bennett had shot a cigar out of the mouth of a union official with a single blast from his .45 pistol. Whenever Tex wanted to light up, he'd run down to the rest room which always seemed to be blue and hazy with the odious fumes. Being a heavy smoker, Tex spent more time there than normal bladder function would require. Later in the year, when Henry would lift his grandfather's ban on smoking in the company, Ford would still refuse to permit women that liberty.

But there were many things to notice and to see and to learn and to criticize, too. During the day, the men would completely smother a function or operation, absorbing everything about it. Superintendents giving them facts about their work perspired from tension, and as they read from papers their hands shook. For everywhere they went, the men were preceded by the rumor: they were "hatchet men" gathering information to be used to fire people. Within days of visiting a key area of the company, one department head lost his job. The ouster had been pending for some time yet only occurred after their orientation visit. Word spread like a brush fire that Tex and his men had gotten rid of this poor soul. To the men, it was almost comical. They had no power and no authority. They had nothing to do with it, of course, didn't even know about it at the time. But it only set off more fear and loathing among the goons and morons at Ford and envy and dislike among the rest.

They would march into and through offices and plants, a mass of dark suits with the exception of Ed Lundy, who for the first few weeks toured the place in military uniform. Even if they weren't a threat, they certainly looked threatening. And at the end of the orientation, each of them would be assigned a different area for a week, to soak in everything, asking still more questions and feverishly taking more notes. Dispatched to the most hellish place of all by Tex was Jim Wright. He was sent to the blast furnaces in the Rouge. It was like Dante's *Inferno,* like being in the bowels of a living hell. Fires blazed everywhere. The heat was unbearable. Hundreds of men were stripped to their waists, pouring molten steel out of huge containers. Jim took his suit jacket off, and sweated with the rest of them, watching all of it, feeling more out of place than the workers felt spied upon.

Every afternoon or night, they huddled together to review the day's events, discuss where they were going and what they had seen. More often than not, these sessions took place in either Charlie or Ben's room at the Dearborn Inn, a red-brick, neo-Georgian hotel originally built for old Henry's guests. The men piled into one of the small hotel rooms, filling it to capacity, utilizing the bed and every stick of furniture they could put their hands on. Meeting together in the security of their own bedrooms, they could speak freely. Still, they often spoke in hushed tones, paranoid perhaps or fretful that if an eavesdropper heard that they were too critical of what they saw—the sheer incompetence, the corruption—they could lose their jobs.

These freewheeling discussions dealt with delicate stuff, judgment and opinion that the men were too reticent to express in public. No one could accuse them of acting out of school. So Jim Wright's wife, Alice, would type up the longhand notes her husband took as secretary for the group because there was no one at Ford they could trust. The stories of Ford craziness amazed them. They often shook their heads at each other, incredulous at what they found. Was this for real?

Arjay told the group how he'd spotted a man who seemed to be endlessly watching contractors build an annex on the aircraft building, day after day. Curious, he went over to him.

"Say, fella, who do you work for?" he asked.

"Well, I work for the Ford Motor Company."

"Yes," persisted Arjay, "but who's your boss?"

"The Ford Motor Company's my boss," he retorted.

"Well, what if I told you you were fired right now?" Miller went on.

"I guess I'd go over and pick up my paycheck," he said.

That was the state of things then; the hierarchy wasn't even clear to people. The company was in total disarray as Tex saw for himself when he prevailed on a secretary in an adjoining department to type a few letters for him. She did so on two or three occasions. Then, one day, the man who was in charge of her department stopped by to see him.

"Mr. Thornton," he asked, "do you mind if I take the afternoon off. I've had trouble with my heart and I have to see my doctor."

"No," said a bewildered Thornton. "No, I don't mind but why in the hell are you asking me?"

"Well, I saw you giving my secretary orders, so I figured you must be my boss, too."

Tex laughed as he told the men the story, saving the best for last. He said the man who didn't even know who his superior was had assumed authority over a part of the company with seven thousand employees.

THE MEN WERE baffled at what they found. All corporations are run by the numbers, and there are tens of thousands of numbers if not more in every corporation. They tell you how much it costs to make a part or how much it costs to buy it from the outside. They tell you how many parts to build, how many to stock and how many to sell. They tell you how much profit each one should make. For every minute part, from the bolt that fastens the bumper to a car to the spring under the upholstery, there might be dozens of numbers to trace and to track. And with them, management manages through control and planning.

But at Ford, if the numbers were available, they couldn't be trusted. Tex used to go around telling the military types that the Air Force had to be run like a business. And here was Ford, nothing but a complete mess. It reminded them of those early days in the Army Air Force when there was no truth in any numbers and pure chaos reigned. McNamara was astounded at what he saw. In his letter to Learned at Soldiers Field, he wrote: "Our work here continues to be hectic, but stimulating. In many ways it reminds me of those early days in the Air Force when there was no information on which to base decisions, no organization pattern, and when it seemed as if everyone was running round like chickens with their heads cut off. Ford must be rebuilt from the ground up. The extent of the decay which existed throughout the organization defies description. Channels of communication are poor, controls are lacking, organization is non-existent, planning is unheard of, and the personnel problem is serious beyond belief."

Many of the numbers at Ford were just plain phony. Sometimes because supervisors and managers were lying; sometimes because there was no control over the figures; sometimes because people didn't know what they were doing. The monthly and annual profit and loss statements landing on Young Henry's desk—the documents that were supposed to be a valid overall measure of corporate well-being—failed to show the results of the company's different businesses, from the steel mill to the basic Ford car operations. Ford Motor had never had an audit in its forty-four-year history. When outside auditors came into the company to sift through its records for an audit for 1945, they labored over the accounts an entire year, only to quit in despair. It was hopeless. They had a wartime term for it in Stat Control. They called it FUBAR: "Fucked Up Beyond All Recognition."

The accounting department was slapped together only because the tax laws and the Internal Revenue Service forced the company to do so for tax purposes. It functioned for no other purpose, and certainly not as a tool of management. Ford wouldn't know until the end of the year what his automobiles cost to produce nor how much money his company would make. No one had yet made profit or loss projections for either the current year or 1947; no one knew how the profit picture would vary depending on how many cars Ford could sell, and no one bothered to relate the company's plans to the general economy. It made no difference what the economists were predicting because they wouldn't affect Ford's plans either way.

When numbers were available they often were slapped together so haphazardly that they were meaningless. At Ford, the numbers told you one thing: that the company was out of control. Tex jokingly called it "GIGO," meaning Garbage In, Garbage Out. Costs were so illogically allocated that studies of costs and profits by activity or by department were useless. The expense of reconverting plants from war contracts to auto production was offset against January car costs instead of the government payments for reconversion. The cost of by-product sales, such as coke, bore part of the cost of car advertising.

Near their desks in the Rotunda was what amounted to the Accounts Payable department. Every invoice the company received was piled in alphabetical order on wooden sleds. On the other side of the stacks were the receipts. When the company received a bill, it would look for the receipt, pin the two together and mail out the check—always months late. To find out how much money was owed at any time, they'd stack the bills up and measure them by the foot.

Arjay, assigned to come up with a profit forecast, was amazed at how hopeless it was. Searching for some data, he went to one of the controllers to squeeze some numbers out of him.

"What do you think the profit will be for this month?" Arjay asked.

"What do you want it to be?" he replied.

"Well, how do you mean that?" Arjay asked, a puzzled look on his face.

"I can make the profit anything you want it to be."

The man then began to explain how he would shift funds around to get whatever results were needed at the time. The company's finances were kept so secret that nobody inside knew what the company was worth. The policy was a holdover from Old Man Ford who had been satisfied with a balance sheet he could scribble on the back of an envelope.

The same held true for organization. In the first forty years of its history, it was Ford policy that anyone found with an organization chart, regardless of how sketchily it was drawn up, was automatically fired. Ford loathed organization charts because he believed they spawned red tape and delay. Tex believed that a good organization formed a pattern, a blueprint, for conducting the affairs of business. It made operations more definite and orderly. Without it, he said, objectives become aimless and confused. Organization avoids duplication of effort, wasted motion and purposelessness. And it affords a workable means for allocating and controlling costs, for budgeting expenses and for measuring results in terms of profit and loss. "It helps every employee to know what his job is, how much authority he has, who his superior is and what his relationship is to the whole enterprise."

There was neither understanding nor agreement among the company's divisions. The sales division, seeing a sellers' market for cars, was eager to take as many cars as possible. Manufacturing, proceeding with major tooling and construction to pump up capacity, didn't believe the purchasing division's warning that there would be severe shortages of key parts such as cylinder blocks and cold-rolled steel. Nonetheless, purchasing continued to make commitments based on a manufacturing schedule it had not agreed upon and could not meet.

The engineering division barely functioned without a schedule of deadlines for engineering releases. There were large sheets of "promise dates," but the vast majority of these were already months overdue. The company's new engine for its 1947 model, moreover, was not completely tested before being released by engineering. The upshot: a major problem emerged with the engine's lubrication. The lead time on the engine for manufacturing and procurement already was too short for it to be available for the 1947 model. Tex quipped that engineering spent half its time trying to match specifications to the cars that manufacturing was already producing.

If there was one area of the company that seemed in good shape, it was sales. Maybe because sales didn't require much sophistication in those days, just a few go-getters willing to slap the right backs. It was during their orientation sessions with the salesmen that *the* picture was taken outside the Rotunda, the only extant shot of Tex's group. All of them were down in front of the sales guys lined up in a row in their postwar suits, except for Bob—a portrait of intellectual coolness—who was standing in the January cold wearing brown gabardine. Arjay was so busy that he had only found time to buy a suit, yet not have it altered. So his pants drooped around his ankles, over the tops of his shoes. Jack and Charlie wore the clothes they bought on a quick trip to New York just before coming to Ford.

All of them looked so deadly serious and formal in their suits and white shirts with the middle coat buttons fastened, just a slight trace of a smile on their faces. Tex was smack in the middle, his hair pushed back, in a gray double-breasted suit with wide lapels. Ed Lundy stood in the background, as he always would, erect as a statue, a fountain pen jutting from his breast pocket. George, short, chubby, seemed uncomfortably out of place, squeezed between Jim and Jack, his head tilted slightly to the left, a wisp of hair dangling over his forehead. Jack was the only one leaning forward, as if ready to charge ahead.

Their faces wore confidence, determination and a certain smugness, too. For despite the shocking disarray, Ford seemed perfect—all opportunity, all challenge. There was so much to do that each of them could have a piece of the world for his own. Yet, they had to know that they were now in a jungle, and they couldn't know who the enemy was: Was it Bennett's surviving cronies, or perhaps his ghost, who would undermine anything they did? Was it John Bugas, who wanted to accept them but also wanted them to fall flat on their faces? Was it Henry himself who buys a man and then humiliates him with a batch of exams?

Amid all the chaos and confusion they found at Ford, however, there was opportunity, for their arrangement led to an unusual degree of latitude and direct access to the boss. There was an informality about the place in those days. Tex like everyone else would always call him Mr. Ford, but he could walk into Young Henry's office at will and chat for long stretches of time about what his group had found. So pleased was Henry at their insights that he was even willing to step aside and share the spotlight with the group. Ford told Tex he was interested in getting some national publicity for the group at some point. Maybe a cover story in *Time* magazine. Imagine, Tex thought, that Henry could pull something like that off. Henry had a good feel for PR and was eager to cultivate the thinking that Ford was an up-and-coming company with new management and new ideas.

For three straight months, every day, they talked to a department supervisor—one a day. All of them asking questions, tons of questions, reversing their first-day roles in the testing room. This earned them the nickname of Quiz Kids, then a popular radio show that hit the airwaves just before the war. It's what most people tuned into every Sunday night immediately after Jack Benny. The show featured a panel of kids, some as young as six, who competed for cash prizes by answering difficult questions on everything from astronomy to history. It was a sardonic tag. These men were young, yet hardly kids, and they performed the role of quizmasters, not precocious panelists, asking all the delicate and sticky questions themselves, seldom venturing the answers.

Nobody told them to perform this role, nor did any one tell them what to do. They did it themselves, marching in early in the morning, sitting down across the old-timers, firing questions and taking notes. They asked questions no one around Ford was supposed to ask—and they got answers. Young Henry backed them all the way. At the end of that time they knew more about the company than anyone else—and perhaps more than anyone had ever known.

THE
WHIZ
KIDS

Whiz Kid "Andy" Andreson—the first to drop out of the group at Ford—during the war.

Andy and Jane Andreson with their daughter, Sally, in 1946.

Chapter 8

ALL THAT
GLITTERS

■

"Just wait till the Joneses see you!
You—and that new Mercury. It'll
be a car to make you enthuse.
Big. Sturdy. Beautiful! Smart
company anywhere . . . How
you'll love to take folks out in it.
Luxurious appointments. Plenty
of room. Relax. You won't feel
crowded . . . Wait for it! It's
due to arrive soon! New car production—starting fast—will be
quick to hit its stride."
——A Ford Advertisement in 1945

Jhe news of the last day in January of 1946 focused on a bitter
strike at General Motors, a stabbing on a downtown bus and
a liquor graft conspiracy. Spanning four columns on the front page was
the dramatic picture of a seven-year-old child who had been raped then
slashed across the throat.

Detroit was a harsh and intractable place after Washington which had
been the center of the world during the war. If Washington was a rare
colony where people of myriad interests worked, Detroit was just the
opposite: oddly provincial. You either worked for a company that made
cars or one that supplied parts to the industry. Industrial smokestacks
replaced the elegant dome of the Capitol Building as the city landmark.
Local crime, not news of the world or of national policy, dominated the
newspapers. During the war, Detroit had staged its own war—race riots.

"In this part of the country, we're pretty well isolated," Tex wrote a
friend on March 20, 1947. "Even the newspapers carry local news, except

for the fourth page of the sports section that sort of briefs down the foreign and nationwide news for the few in this city who might be interested. Thank goodness a group of us came together out here, otherwise it would really be a lonely place."

If Thornton and his men didn't exactly feel at home, it may have been because most of them had little attachment to the machines Detroit produced. With the exception of Jack Reith, it wouldn't have made the slightest difference if the group were working for a company that made refrigerators or airplanes, railroad cars or steel. Their skills and talents were generic and dispassionate. Their ambitions and desires were propelled not by product so much as the need to make a good living and to make their mark.

Yet, in Detroit, only one thing mattered: the automobile. In the postwar period, Detroit rivaled Hollywood as the capital of pop culture, with the car as celebrated as any movie star or film of the time. When in 1946 the city commemorated the industry's golden jubilee, the pavement of Woodward Avenue was sprayed with hundreds of gallons of gold paint. Businesses closed down. People danced in the streets. Nearly three million spectators cheered a three-hour parade of old and new cars, floats and bands down the broad avenue. It even made the cover of *Business Week* magazine.

The event's theme, "Hats off to the past, coats off to the future," summed up Detroit's own ambitions. Not only did the city generate much of the country's great wealth. Its cars defined wealth and status in an ever socially conscious society. The automobile had become a key symbol of self-expression. If you could buy the new Ford Deluxe "6," the lowest priced standard coupe at $1,088 in 1947, you were making it—but not nearly as much as someone who could park a new and shiny Buick or Oldsmobile in his driveway at a price of $1,500.

Nearly everywhere you went, whether a department store or a coffee shop, you overheard car talk. Cars were becoming an intricate part of the nation's social fabric, the symbol for the good and the bad in these times. This hunk of metal provided freedom, escape, isolation. The car's importance turned up the pressure on Tex. He knew the eyes of the world would be on Detroit. If the group could help restore Ford, their exploits would almost surely win them prominence and acclaim. They had the chance to seize advantage of the all-consuming interest in the machine that would change the world.

The label of outsiders to both Detroit and the emerging car culture cut both ways. They resented the "Quiz Kids" tag, preferring to refer to themselves as "the group." But they saw the advantage in creating their own community, insulated from the city's parochial interests. They became as inseparable outside of work as they were at Ford. The uniqueness of their circumstances made the quality of their friendship different and special in many ways. They gave to each other support, both in and outside the workplace. And like all families after the war, they were trying to establish new lives, new patterns and new beginnings.

Most of them lacked the money to buy houses straight off—not that they could be completely confident that they were here to stay for good. For a time they holed up in the Dearborn Inn, or in the other Detroit hotels. In these days just after the war, there were many restrictions on life: one prevented you from remaining a hotel guest for too long. Jack and Maxine, along with George and Mimi, moved into the Statler for the maximum five-day period. Then they packed up and moved into the luxurious apartments at the Detroit Country Club thanks to George's dad. One week later, they got their first bill and realized they could hardly afford to stay there. So it was on to the Tuller Hotel which agreed to give the two couples a permanent residence. It was a shabby, rundown place, just one room with a double bed that came out of the wall. Unless you sat down gently on one of the upholstered chairs or the overstuffed couch, the dust would rise up in a cloud and choke you. Jack worked at the small desk in their room every night, drawing organization charts and reading over his notes so Maxine could type up a report or two for the group.

Jack and George were stuck in the place, partly because both their wives, Maxine and Mimi, were pregnant. When the guys went to work, the women met for breakfast in the grim cafeteria downstairs—both in black tent-like maternity dresses that they would try to dress up with different scarves and pins. During the day, they would stroll to Hudson's to shop. Once a week, they'd hop aboard a bus and take in a movie and stage show.

Both women were due about the same time in June. For Maxine, it brought endless teasing from the guys because she had only married Jack in late September. She eventually gave birth to a daughter, Donna, exactly nine months and one day after her marriage to Jack. For weeks before, though, as their bellys grew in size, the two new friends spent hours together wondering exactly what sign would tell them it was time to rush off to the hospital. Neither of them had the slightest idea what to expect. After Donna's birth, Maxine told Jack to relay the message to Mimi that the pains began in the lower back. Five days later, when Mimi went into labor, George had a terrible time bringing her into the hospital because she was waiting for the back pains to start. They never did, and Mimi didn't get to the hospital until late in the labor. She, too, had a girl, and they named her Marika. George tapped Ed Lundy to be his first child's godfather.

Early on, Ed and Arjay Miller shared the Edgar Allan Poe cottage at the Dearborn Inn. Miller, the Nebraska farm boy turned folksy intellectual who graduated from UCLA with the highest honors, struck up an immediate friendship with Lundy, an Iowa-born intellectual who had become an instructor at Princeton. Miller's wife, Frances, stayed in California with her folks until Arjay got a more permanent place to stay. But after a few weeks, Ed got all his civilian wardrobe and shoes back and there just wasn't enough room for Arjay anymore. So he moved into Ben's suite at the Inn because Ben's wife, Helen, hadn't yet come out either. Ben was the athlete in the group, wanting fresh air every night. Arjay got to calling it "the treatment." Ben would open up all the windows and the frigid air would gust through the room, sending a shivering Arjay under the covers. Arjay finally escaped to a room in the Sheraton, until Henry arranged for more comfortable quarters for him and most of the others.

Charlie moved into an apartment on the north side of Detroit. Tex, Jim and Andy bought homes. Borrowing some money from his mother, Tex bought sight unseen by Flora a tidy English Tudor with a pitched roof in nearby Huntington Woods. There just wasn't time for her to rush out to Detroit with the boys and scour the real estate market for a new home, even if it was to be their first house together. Enthused by the purchase, Tex described the home at 26640 Huntington Road in baronial terms, though Flora, returning from Texas with the boys, would find many deficiencies, a lack of closet space and other amenities that a man in a hurry would hardly notice. Their arrival was memorable because the boys moved into the new home with a case of chicken pox so bad that even Tex came down with it and stayed home for two-and-one-half weeks. It was the first time in fifteen years that he had any illness other than a bad cold, and of course, it had to be a "child's illness."

Jim, borrowing $470 from Tex, moved into a place in Lathrop Park on San Jose Boulevard in Birmingham, while Andy and Jane went into a two-story house on Plainview Avenue and 17 Mile Road. The rest of the families all moved into Springswells Park, a cluster of cozy red brick rowhouses owned by the Ford Foundation. Old Henry and his son Edsel opened the development back in 1940. There was a quaint New England quality to the place, with curving streets, cul-de-sacs, slate roofs and cupolas with copper weathervanes. Compared to hotel living, these were spacious abodes, with a pair of bedrooms upstairs and a common back-yard. They didn't only work together; most of them lived together, too, either across the street or down the street or just the next door over.

They converged on each other's apartments or homes almost weekly. When they first got together in Bob and Margy's apartment, they sat on the floor using wooden orange crates as tables to eat a potluck dinner. Bob didn't yet have any furniture, except for his Harvard chair and a bed for themselves and one for the kids. Margy was still recovering from polio, yet she was a gracious, charming host.

It was a well-mixed and well-balanced group, a mutual admiration society in which everyone displayed a great deal of respect for each other. They were warm, friendly and embracing. They blended together, en-joying each other's company, seldom drifting off into the corners as couples. Sometimes, they'd play charades or word games, contests that either teased or challenged the mind, never cards. Tex was the social leader, too, leading a discussion or suggesting the games they might play at their get-togethers. Like families everywhere, they were turning more inward and insulated.

To lubricate an evening's conversation, they drank Scotch and Bour-bon, martinis and manhattans from stemmed glasses. "Now, I know what you all like, but tonight we're having martinis," Tex announced. All he needed to know was gin or vodka, rocks or straight up. That's what he mixed, and that's what they had.

Business discussion was virtually verboten. They talked business all day long. It crowded their days and often troubled their nights. The hours were brutal. The wives seldom knew when their husbands would get home for dinner, if they got home for dinner, and they were gone again at the crack of dawn. The pressure on them, or rather the pressure they put on themselves, was enormous. Tex wanted to prove that Ford didn't make a mistake when he hired them, and he wanted to prove it quickly.

So when they got together in their homes, they did so to relax and to escape. They liked to chat about national and world affairs, the latest movies and books, and music. Oh yes, music. Sometimes, Ben, Charlie and Jack formed a little trio at their parties: Ben at the piano, Charlie on clarinet and Jack on the traps. If a drum kit wasn't available, Jack would make do with a pair of spoons. They'd sing to everything from Maurice Chevalier's "Louise" to Al Jolson's "California Here We Come."

Several were real fans of swing—despite the Ford tests that showed the group had little interest in music. Like the car, it was music that symbolized escape. It brought you away from the numbing routine of life, easing the transition from the highly charged moment of war to normality. A new swing record was as desirable as a piece of gold. On Saturday afternoons in Washington, Jim and Alice had gone down to the Earl Theater or the Fox on F Street to see one of the big bands come through—Benny Goodman, Tommy or Jimmy Dorsey, Artie Shaw, Jimmie Lunceford. Jim laughed that he could identify any band around by listening to just three bars of their music, though no one could tell him that there was a better big band than Glenn Gray and The Casa Loma Orchestra. They were the early pioneers of big band jazz, the forerunners of Dorsey and Goodman, he reminded them.

Jack had even booked a number of big bands during his days in Schenectady working for General Electric. He'd tell them all about the time he booked Glenn Miller into a local ballroom and almost lost his shirt. A freak storm broke out on the day of the concert, covering the roads with ice. He had borrowed money to put up the guarantee, and now Jack feared no one would show up and he'd be wiped out. But Miller could always draw the crowds, and enough people came to allow Jack to just barely break even on the concert. Miller, said Jack, was a stinker because he held out for full pay despite the poor turnout.

Jack loved Louis Armstrong and Nat King Cole, having seen both of them in cocktail lounges back in Washington. But there was one song that really sent him: Bunny Berigan's hypnotic "I Can't Get Started With You." Jack recalled that when he saw Bunny play the emotional trumpet solo, tears rolled down his face.

More than music even, they loved talk. Most of them could leap from a debate over Secretary of State George C. Marshall's proposals of aid to Europe to Jackie Robinson's Brooklyn Dodgers debut that broke the color barrier in major league baseball. Ed had informed opinions on nearly any subject, from Irish linen to porcelain. But no one was as well read as Bob. He'd turn to a book for an evening's entertainment just as readily as Jack would flip a Nat King Cole number on the record player. Bob gave Charlie his Modern Library copy of *War and Peace*. It was the only book Charlie Bosworth ever tackled that he couldn't finish. Not that he didn't relish a good book. His bookshelves were lined with Marcel Proust and D.H. Lawrence, Plato and Thomas Wolfe.

Then there were the women, whom their husbands alternately worshipped and ignored. Sometimes it was difficult to tell who they'd married: Ford or their wives. Jack's Maxine was the blonde bombshell of the crowd. In a black gown, she was a knockout, and probably the prettiest of them all and an outgoing person, too. Model-pretty Mimi was the most sensuous of them, though a little more reticent partly because of her youth. But she carried herself with grace. It was hard not to gaze at her from across the room because she lent a great deal of radiance to a social gathering.

Helen, Ben's wife, seemed to be everyone's favorite. It was something that Ben had noticed about her when they first met in Washington. She stood out among the twenty-seven typists in the typing pool he took over, and he got into the habit of walking her home at night. He married her on July 17, 1937.

Jim, like Ben, had also met his wife in Washington where, like Helen, she was a government agency employee. One day, Jim arranged for some desks to be placed in the hall for some new file clerks. Among the trio of new clerks was Alice, an attractive young lady from Alabama, who caught Jim's eyes and ears with her Southern courtesy, manners and hospitality. He married her on October 22, 1938, shortly after finishing law school and passing the bar exam.

Fran was the best educated, cultured and with a great deal of savvy in academic matters, just like her husband. Arjay met her at UCLA where she was a teaching assistant on a course in labor economics that he was taking. Fran had just graded one of his papers, giving him a B for the work. Arjay went storming into the room where she shared a desk with other teaching assistants.

"I am not a B student," he told her. "Don't you know I don't get Bs. I get As."

Fran didn't budge.

"You might be an A student," she retorted, "but this is B work." Arjay ended up with an A in the course, later becoming a teaching assistant himself and sharing both a desk and a relationship with her. He graduated from UCLA with highest honors in 1937. Three years later, on August 18, he married Frances Marion Fearing.

Margy was lovely and gracious—the best hula dancer among the group, they joked. She once taught biology and physical education in California high schools. She met Bob at the University of California at Berkeley, though they didn't date until after he earned his Harvard M.B.A. and returned to California to work as an accountant for Price Waterhouse. They dated for four months and then married on August 13, 1940.

Flora, towering and regal with almost an aristocratic air about her, had taken up singing again, volunteering for the choir at the Presbyterian Church in Huntington Woods. Most of the other wives felt some distance to her, because she was a forceful woman with a strong will, hardly shy or retiring. And like some colonels' wives, she could, at times, wear her husband's leaves.

Although the wives organized all the social gatherings, they felt largely out of the picture of the men's lives.

THE WIVES WEREN'T the only casualty.

Andy knew before any of the others that Tex and the guys weren't going to take control of Ford as they had planned. In his gut, he seemed to realize that whatever the group would have to do to survive wasn't worth the price in time or frustration. Nor was it worth the price of friendship. If these doubts surfaced in Andy's mind, he didn't share them with the others.

Andy was at the furthest end of their circle, one of the few men sifted from the personnel files by Ben. Unlike the vast numbers of officers who passed through Harvard and Washington, Andy did neither. But he'd made his mark: he was the youngest non-flying full colonel in the Air Force, second-in-command of the Stat Control group for the China-Burma-India front. George worked with him briefly and became immediately impressed with him. He told Tex that Andy worked so hard that he was wearing him out.

Six months after moving to Detroit, he wasn't so sure he'd made the right move. Andy who had been a full colonel in the Asian theater now found himself well subordinated in the group. Unlike the others who had a department, he was one of three with George and Charlie who reported to Jim Wright as head of the administration planning department. Jim tried to make the best of the arrangement, treating it as if Andy had been temporarily assigned to him to help on the organization project. But Jim sensed that Andy felt a bit put out by the pecking order, that he didn't like what he saw he would have to do to progress at Ford.

Jane felt no love of Detroit. Years later, she would remember the bad weather. In the summer, she'd go down to the nursery to buy a slew of flowers, plant them in June and then lose them all because of a late frost. "By gosh," she'd tell Andy, "you should be able to plant flowers by June!" By July it would get so hot and humid that she and Andy would be up and down all night, unable to sleep, until they finally carried the mattresses clear down to the basement where it was cool enough to get an undisturbed rest.

She missed California as much as she disliked Michigan. Her family was there and so was her life. It was the same for Andy.

"What would you think about moving back to California?" he asked her.

"What do you mean by that?" asked Jane, completely surprised by the question. She was aware of his frustrations at Ford. One time he had worked furiously on a report, spending weekends and nights on it, submitted it and someone else took the credit for it. It seemed to him that there was less honor in business than in war, that you could bring your emotions to war to do a business-like job, but you couldn't bring your emotions to business.

"I've just been thinking. . . . it's absolutely ridiculous to spend all of our lives back here with the idea that we're saving money to go to retire in California. We could go now if we really want to. Besides, I think I'd rather be a big frog in a little pond than a little frog in a big one."

"I'll do whatever you decide to do," she said. "You spend so many hours of your time working and you have to enjoy it."

They talked about what he could do. He had been approached by The Bekins Company, a major moving and storage firm based in Los Angeles. A friend had told him they needed someone to take over the controller's office.

Soon after the conversation, Andy had made his decision. He would quit and head west, having received a solid offer from Bekins to assume a job that would become a stepping stone to the position of comptroller. No one in the group was surprised when they heard of Andy's decision.

He typed up a short, formal, note of resignation on August 15, 1946— less than two hundred days after joining the company—and handed it to Tex.

Dear Mr. Thornton:
This is to advise the Ford Motor Company that I wish to resign, effective Aug. 31, 1946. Resignation is prompted by the offer of a very attractive position with a company in Los Angeles, California, and by the desire on the part of my family to return to that city in which we resided for many years.
"I appreciate the consideration that has been shown me during my employment with the Ford Motor Company.

Very truly yours,
Andy Andreson
(Badge No. Adm.76)

The excitement Andy once felt about working for Henry faded as quickly as a suntan. He had gotten out because he wanted a better life,

not a better job. Despite Tex's efforts to create a sense of community in
Detroit for the group, it just wasn't enough. The group saw Andy and
Jane off with a gala farewell dinner at one of Detroit's swank hotels.
That night, Jane strolled up to the bandstand to request her favorite song
maybe a half dozen times. It didn't matter that her friends had had
enough of it. One song seemed to sum up Detroit and Ford so perfectly.
And when they drove home that evening in Jim's coupe, they sang it
again at the top of their lungs.

"Never be foolish and naive,
when someone wants you to believe,
His life without you is so dull,
do not need to go at all.

All that glitters is not gold,
All that glitters is not gold.
That's the story often told.
All that glitters is not gold."

THE
WHIZ
KIDS

Henry Ford II (left) and Ernest Breech, the man who got the job Tex wanted, in the dining room at Ford headquarters.

Tex Thornton thought he would report directly to Henry Ford II, and he did—until Ernest Breech and Lewis Crusoe were recruited from General Motors. Part of a Ford Motor organization chart shows how Thornton's group was quickly put in little boxes beneath the GM duo and far from Henry. Tex's planning office reported to Crusoe.

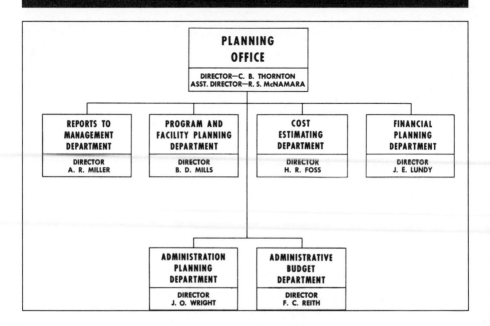

PLANNING OFFICE

DIRECTOR—C. B. THORNTON
ASST. DIRECTOR—R. S. McNAMARA

REPORTS TO MANAGEMENT DEPARTMENT	PROGRAM AND FACILITY PLANNING DEPARTMENT	COST ESTIMATING DEPARTMENT	FINANCIAL PLANNING DEPARTMENT
DIRECTOR A. R. MILLER	DIRECTOR B. D. MILLS	DIRECTOR H. R. FOSS	DIRECTOR J. E. LUNDY

ADMINISTRATION PLANNING DEPARTMENT	ADMINISTRATIVE BUDGET DEPARTMENT
DIRECTOR J. O. WRIGHT	DIRECTOR F. C. REITH

CLASH OF
AMBITION

■

"Pyramids being what they are in
the professional world, most men
will have to adjust their dream
downward to some degree."

—Gail Sheehy

*T*he rumors had begun within months of their arrival. Henry
was about to bring in a new right hand man, and Tex took
it like a bullet to the heart. He wanted to rule Ford. As Jack Davis, one
of Ford's trusted aides, put it, Thornton "wanted to be president practically the first day." Unknown to Tex, even before the group arrived in
Dearborn, however, Henry had made the first of his overtures to bring
Ernie Breech to Ford. Henry wanted as a possible successor someone
who lived to make cars, as Thornton and his buddies never would.

Ernest R. Breech was the kind of executive that Detroiters said had
gasoline coarsing through his veins. Short and stocky with a thin mustache and an accountant by training, he had spent nearly his entire career
in the car business until being put in charge of General Motor's multi-
million-dollar Bendix Aviation Corp. Breech had just been passed over
for the presidency of General Motors, losing out to Charles E. "Engine
Charlie" Wilson.

Breech initially thought Henry was calling to do business with Bendix because a few weeks earlier he had made a sales call on the company's purchasing department. Within minutes of the conversation, however, it was clear that Henry had something else in mind. He said he was interested in installing a GM type of management at Ford, one based on organization, discipline and deliberateness. Ford asked if Breech would take the job to do it. He'd run the company as executive vice president and could write his own ticket. Breech declined, saying he was honored to be offered the post but that he had a fine job at Bendix and had no intention to leave.

Henry countered, asking him at least to study his company's situation. Breech agreed, thinking that it couldn't hurt to get Ford as a big customer. But once he saw some of what Tex and his group had already absorbed—the wholesale inefficiencies of a badly disorganized empire—Breech was hooked. He saw the vast opportunity and challenge awaiting him, just as the group recognized it after touring the Rouge on the day they first met Ford. Henry renewed his offer, and Breech accepted.

Breech's peek into Ford's finances and its postwar car, however, tipped Tex off. Breech posed a severe threat. For one thing, Tex would no longer report directly to Henry, but to this new man from GM. Upset by the prospect, he went to see Henry, asking him to sign a letter that would empower Tex and his group with responsibility for overall company planning. The directive would give Tex virtual veto power over everything.

Henry seemed cool to the idea. It was little more than an undisguised power play, an attempt to capture authority and influence before Breech came aboard. Yet Henry showed signs of diplomacy, asking Tex to meet with Breech and to show him the letter. Why turn over this role to Tex when Breech was only a few months away from joining Ford?

In May, some five weeks before Breech's expected arrival on July 1, the two met at Breech's home on Manor Road in Birmingham. It was awkward from the start. They chatted about Ford, GM, the severe shortage of materials holding back the industry. And then the letter. Henry had called Breech, told him about Tex and his Quiz Kids and forwarded Tex's directive. Breech had the piece of paper in his hand, as if introducing a piece of evidence.

"Why can't you wait till I get there?" Breech demanded of Tex.

"Every month means money that doesn't have to be lost," Tex grumbled. He felt that his team was beginning to provide the intelligence and knew what had to be done. The company was losing millions of dollars each month, and Ford lacked an effective executive team to do something about it. Tex and his men could move in *now* and begin the long process. Breech wouldn't budge.

"All right, fine, if that's the way it has to be, we'll wait," Tex said. "But it's going to cost us millions."

If it was a disagreeable meeting and a disappointment to Tex, it was not a bitter session. The pair discussed their ideas, talked about organization, top management's role in policy formation, the delegation of authority, measuring results and weeding out waste. Breech asked Tex to pick up and read Peter Drucker's *Concept of the Corporation,* a book on GM published a year earlier. Not to be outdone, a day later, Tex suggested that Breech read a research study put together by Stanford University's graduate school of business. Tex's impatience was obviously getting in his way because he was clearly in a losing situation.

Bruised and disillusioned, Tex wrote his old mentor Lovett, who had returned to Wall Street at Brown Brothers Harriman & Co. Tex had kept in constant contact with him since his departure from Washington. Even before he joined Ford, Tex promised Lovett in a letter that he "will do my best to live up to the recommendation which you gave Mr. Ford." Five months later, in an unusually candid assessment on June 20, 1946, he wrote:

> *As you can imagine, his coming has changed the complexion of our assignment quite a bit. We were hired with the understanding that we would perform certain management functions for Mr. Ford, and since Mr. Breech will evidently become the operating head of the company, those functions will, no doubt, be performed under his direction. Moreover, I understand that he is bringing certain assistants with him. While our jobs are apparently secure, and there are many opportunities to do constructive work in the Company, it is questionable whether I would have come with Ford had I been able to anticipate developments here. In other words, the opportunity and the job will not be what they were originally represented to be, and I must confess that I am disappointed, especially since we haven't had the chance to show what we could do.*

Lovett, assuming the role of a substitute father, wrote back, asking to see Tex in New York to talk over the situation and then tried hard to cheer him up. "I can understand the element of uncertainty which has recently been injected into the picture," wrote Lovett, "but I am not at all sure that it may not work out to your advantage."

Perhaps Lovett was right. In the past five months, Tex and his men had deftly moved to fill the vacuum of power in the company. His group kept control of over-all planning for the company, including all its plans for car programs, finances, investments and facilities, along with the power to oversee the company's budgets, cost estimating, economic analysis and administration and organizational planning. It was an immense responsibility and a great challenge. So Tex plowed back into the work, wondering what Breech's arrival would ultimately mean.

MEANTIME, TEX'S TROOPS, exploring the bowels of the company, were scoring a lot of firsts. Ben put together the first coordinated production schedule; Arjay delivered the first cash forecast; Jack, the first capital budgets, and Jim, the first organization charts.

One of Arjay's first assignments was to work up a twelve-month cash and profit forecast for Henry and the company's Policy Committee. He was assigned two old-timers, one an alcoholic, the other dying of bone cancer. The only solid figure at Ford was cash and that was because the banks gave the company the number. So Arjay and his cohorts had to wade through bills of material for rubber, copper and other things, find out how many cars, trucks and tractors they were producing, how much they were selling for. Then an avalanche of numbers were plugged into a Friden to come up with the forecasts. The company's disorganization and the less than reliable facts made it nearly an impossible task. So Ed and Bob ended up pitching in to help.

The night before September 27, 1946, when Arjay would present the numbers to the Policy Committee, they were still putting the report together. Arjay and Bob asked the group's newly hired secretary, Nora B. Elliot, if she would return after dinner to type the huge financial statement. She agreed after Bob told her they would drive her home and pick her up on their return. She had fit in the group well, in part because she had spent nearly six years working for the Ministry of Aircraft Production in England.

The car zipped down Rotunda Drive, with Arjay and Bob completely absorbed by the pile of numbers they gathered. When they reached the Foundation Apartments—where several of the men lived—Bob turned around to ask Miss Elliot, as Tex always called her, if she could drive. As soon as she answered yes, they abruptly hopped out of the car and walked to their apartments, leaving her to figure out how to drive home on a completely unfamiliar route. She didn't have a U.S. driver's license nor had she ever driven a car on the right side of the road. She drove away in the darkness terrified. By the time she found her way back to the office, Miss Elliot was quite unnerved.

She had never typed statistical tables before and this one was a bear. Besides, Arjay and Bob—returning in Arjay's car—stood over her shoulder making sure she typed in the right numbers on a huge twelve-by-seventeen sheet of paper. Ed, who also was enough of an expert at shorthand to terrify his secretaries later on, came to the rescue and finished the job. The next morning Arjay, consulting handwritten notes on three-by-five file cards, delivered a cash forecast that predicted a net deficit of $17 million. The company had lost $60 million in the first eight months of 1946, he said, and might have to go to the banks to ask for money just to complete the work in hand over the next few months.

The company's inability to generate profit hardly surprised the men because, as Ben discovered, Ford even lacked a single, coordinated production schedule. Engineering had one; purchasing had one, and manufacturing had one—but they weren't the same. The company churned out cars in a chaotic frenzy, lurching from one set of plans to the next. Ben was trying to force a single, coordinated schedule together so that the entire company would work toward one result. Engineering had to complete blueprints for parts in time to allow Ford and its suppliers adequate time to make them. Purchasing had to order and buy enough parts for manufacturing to produce enough cars. Any well-organized production program pulled all the company's sectors together so they all aimed at the same target. At Ford, the engineers were either too late or too early or they would release prints that weren't yet ready, forcing revisions along the line. If a delay wasn't engineering's fault, it might be the fault of purchasing or manufacturing.

It fell to Ben Mills to tell the Policy Committee that a product they were counting on wasn't going to meet the set deadline for it. Its delay would ripple through the organization, forcing further interruptions in the plan to produce a new car.

"The part's not going to be there," he told the committee.

"How do you know that?" asked someone.

"The people who are going to produce it do not think it's going to be there. Each one of them says they can't make it. It can't be ready on time. I've got enough people saying it that I know it's not going to happen."

"Well, when do you think it will be ready?"

"I've put together a schedule and it is going to have to be six months late."

"We can't wait six months. We've got all these plans dependent on it."

"Well," countered Mills, "I don't think you're going to have it."

And they didn't get the product because there was so little coordination among the different groups. But to insure that they would have it within six months, Ben went to the head of each department—from engineering to purchasing to manufacturing—with a timetable. Each was asked whether they could make it. If so, Ben had them sign a commitment to get the job done on time.

"Now don't you sign this just because you think the next guy is going to fail," he told them. "It's not going to work that way. If you're worried about getting in trouble, you'll sign something knowing you can't do it and then you're the one that fails. So don't sign something you're not sure of."

It worked handsomely, though one time he had one department head claim that his signature was not his own.

"Look, I sat right here and you signed it. I watched you sign it," protested Ben.

"No sir," he said, "that's not my signature."

With some notable exceptions, Ford was a reflection of the chaotic and messy state of management at many other large industrial empires just after the war. The management systems that would suffocate so many American companies decades later were largely non-existent and sorely in need.

AT FORD, THERE were loose ends dangling all over the place. One of the most notorious was Ray Dahlinger. Once a company test driver, he married a Ford secretary who had supposedly carried on a long affair with old man Henry. Eventually, the Dahlingers' son would claim that Henry Ford was his natural father. Under Ford, Dahlinger had accumulated a fiefdom in the engineering building of the Rouge with his own barber and valet. Some 112 people on the Ford payroll worked under him on the 1,200 acres of farmland across from Ford Road. His private paradise was draining half a million dollars a year from the company budget.

Over the years, someone would try to clamp down on him but to no avail. He had a solid link with old Henry who protected him, and he was a favorite of his wife, Clara, because she could always count on him to do whatever she asked. One day, Arjay unwittingly found himself put in a position to end it.

"We finally solved the Dahlinger problem," Henry told him. "He's going to work with you. I want you to take care of him."

Arjay was ashen, silent for a moment at the horrible news.

"Well, does he know this?"

"Not yet, but you write him a letter and I'll sign it."

Arjay turned and walked out of the office, wondering what he was in for. He wrote the letter that informed Dahlinger he would work for him and that he would be in his office on 10 a.m. the following Monday.

When he finally went over to confront Dahlinger, Arjay summoned as much force as possible.

"You're going to have to tighten things up," he told him.

Dahlinger shot him a good, drop-dead look and laughed.

"I've seen accountants come and go here, and I'll see you go, too. And if you don't like the way things are run over here, you can kiss my ass."

"Look, it's not just me, it's the IRS," Arjay said, trying to divert his anger. "You're not supposed to give income to people and not declare it. We can get in a helluva lot of trouble here."

"Well, if the IRS doesn't like it, they can stick their nose up my ass."

"All right," Miller replied, more sternly. "Fine, Mr. Dahlinger, but in the morning there's going to be a man outside your office, and he's going to sign for every penny you spend."

Arjay picked out the biggest, toughest guy he could find and installed him in Dahlinger's outer office. Then, he nervously awaited what would happen. Less than a year later, Mrs. Ford, Henry's grandmother, died and Henry called within a few hours of her death from New York with the order to fire Dahlinger immediately.

At Arjay's request, the man came to his office and Arjay told him he had forty-eight hours to get out.

"Get all of your property off the Ford grounds and after that we don't ever want to see you on the Ford property again," Arjay told him.

Dahlinger stalked off and moved out, even taking with him the cows that grazed on the vast Ford property. And Arjay thought he had finally gotten rid of him for good. But then a year or two later, one of his men asked him if Ford should continue to service Dahlinger's fire extinguishers at his home. Apparently, he was still sending personal bills into Ford.

As SOON AS Breech arrived, moving into an adjoining office next to Henry's, trouble began. Tex had been right: their jobs were secure. Both Henry and Breech reassured him on that score. He also was right in thinking that Breech would bring a number of his own lieutenants with him. In fact, one of the conditions Henry met upon hiring Breech was that he could bring in three or four key men from the outside. The day after accepting the job, Breech hired his chief engineer and old friend, Harold Youngren, on the telephone. He also won over Del Harder, a former GM manufacturing man who had coined the word automation, as well as Lewis Crusoe, who was a principal aide at Bendix.

In the old Administration Building on Schaefer Road, Tex's office was six doors down from Henry's. But even with Breech there, Henry would summon Tex to his office on the "buzz box." Tex thought, "Oh no, here it comes." Breech and Henry even shared a private bathroom between their offices, so Breech could plainly see the visits by Tex to Henry. It annoyed him, made him feel a twinge of jealousy. After all, Breech had an agreement with Henry that everything would flow through him. Henry would sometimes ignore it. Either he was simply naive, or he wanted to keep Breech off balance.

So Tex would go in, somewhat embarrassed, and sit with Henry and talk. Often, it would be over some trifling matter, something of so little significance that if Breech knew he could not have minded. One time, for instance, Henry wanted Tex to put Benson Ford in his planning group which Tex did. Another time he asked him to put James McDonnell, Henry's father-in-law, into the group.

"Would you take him in?" Henry asked.

"What can he do?"

"Well, he's been an investment banker," Henry said.

Tex said he'd give it some thought and two weeks later Henry had him in his office again.

"Would you please find some place for Jimmy," he told Tex. "Anne won't leave me alone about it."

So Tex put Henry's father-in-law in the planning group. It always seemed to be something inconsequential. Still, when Breech saw Tex emerge from the man's office, he would glower. Shrugging his shoulders, Tex would try to explain that it was Henry who called him in. It did little to change things, however. Breech knew, as Tex did, that Henry had an unsettling habit of agreeing with the last person he saw in his office. So it made the threat seem very real.

Even worse, another time Henry asked Tex to do some work with Earl Newsom, a slick public relations flack whom Henry had recruited from New York. Breech had no love for the man, thought he was a shyster, too polished and smooth for his taste. And yet Tex would have to huddle with Newsom in his office, watching for Breech and thinking, "This is just what I need! When Ernie sees this, it's all over."

More than that, however, Tex violently disagreed with Henry and

Breech that he and his men knew nothing about the car business and therefore couldn't expect to run it. Hell, he had seen that you didn't have to pilot a B-27 or boast the rank of a major to run an air force. Certainly, they had proven that; even helping to create, in a handful of months, daring flyers out of "pimply faced Willy at the drugstore," as Tex would put it. He would especially grow incensed when the other men seemed to accept the argument.

"I don't need to know how to put the damn things together," Tex told Jim.

"Hell, Billy Durant (the ebullient founder of General Motors) knew nothing about the automobile, either."

THORNTON'S IMMENSE DISAPPOINTMENT turned nearly to dismay, however, when Breech recruited his own second-in-command who like him knew the auto business inside and out: Lewis D. Crusoe. Another General Motors alum, Crusoe came to Detroit from Minnesota in 1913 at the age of eighteen and took a job as a 30-cents-an-hour clerk in the sheet metal and power hammer department of Fisher Body Company. Crusoe climbed to the post of a divisional controller at GM's Fisher before retiring in 1945 to his real love—his 920-acre Golden River Ranch near Cheboygan, Michigan, where he raised purebred cattle.

Breech coaxed Crusoe off his ranch and out of retirement in order to use his knowledge of finance and accounting. Unlike Tex's men, Crusoe knew the auto industry cold, having spent thirty-two years in the business. He also was a man who loved to hear his own voice. Crusoe could dismantle a business operation as if it were his own car up on a block. And he enjoyed doing it for an audience, giving his men little tutorials on what the auto business was all about. Crusoe liked to teach, even taking classes to keep his mind sharp. He had a yacht, navigating it not with a compass but by the stars which he had studied in an astronomy class.

Like Breech, Crusoe was to Tex just another body, another hurdle standing in his way, another person who came to steal his ambitions. Tex thought of him as a bookkeeper. He was cut in a bookkeeper's image: small, nondescript, with a high forehead, thinning gray hair, blue owlish eyes and gold circular spectacles with thick lenses that looked like a pair of magnifying glasses. He didn't smoke or drink, going out of his way to decry both vices with a high pitched voice.

But Thornton, perhaps because of his own disappointment at the arrival of the guys from GM, couldn't see past Crusoe's meager appearance. More than Tex, Crusoe had his heart handwired to cars. He loved the business of making cars as much as he loved the end product. And he knew the business in ways that Thornton could never fathom.

With Crusoe on board, Breech committed the ultimate humiliation. He assigned Crusoe Tex and his men. Crusoe would come in as a vice president and director of finance with three major offices below reporting to him: the controller, the treasurer and finally the planning office run by Tex. But Tex had lost what he most wanted: his direct access to influence Henry.

Tex still headed up what was clearly the glamour job at Ford, the group that held the power to dramatically change and reshape the company. Decisions that came out of planning would ripple through the organization, altering the way it functioned. With Thornton as director of planning and Bob as his assistant, five of the other Quiz Kids also got to run their own growing fiefdoms under Tex, all with bureaucratic-sounding titles. Arjay headed up a "Reports to Management Department" that would screen, summarize and clear all proposals to the executive staff. Ben was placed in charge of a "Program and Facility Planning Department" that was to develop a master production program. Ed stood on top of a "Financial Planning Department" that prepared cash and profit forecasts and put together studies on pricing. Jack ran the "Administrative Budget Department" that would develop the company's overall budget. And finally, Jim rode herd over an "Administration Planning Department" whose task it was to completely reorganize the company. George and Charlie were all assigned to help Jim with the project to establish a clear-cut organization.

In the early days, Crusoe seemed nervous, unsure of himself—not the all-powerful manager he would soon become, the executive who would befriend several of Tex's men. He'd line Tex and his men up inside his office like school children and lecture them, carrying on about this or that while they fidgeted and rolled their eyes. All of them were impatient of it, but especially Tex. It bored him to listen to the man. If you heard him for three hours, Tex thought, you knew everything he had to tell you. Tex would concede he was good at what he did, but that he had no range. He was a cold and pompous accountant, a little old lady with a repetitive harangue. Sure, he spent thirty-two years at General Motors, Tex said. But it was like the same year thirty-two times over. He never progressed. For Tex, Crusoe was a maddening irritation. Sometimes he would even come to Tex's home and Flora, sitting in the living room knitting, would have to endure him as well.

One day, Crusoe collected them, lined the entire group up in his office and with a sense of self-importance told the men how he had been selected for a special mission. He would have to address a group of middle management being assembled to understand the new company. Henry would speak on human relations; Breech would talk about the cars and he, Crusoe, would have to explain the Quiz Kids' function. He said it was a critical moment for himself and for all of them; their future lay in the balance. So he needed their help in drafting the critical speech. When the men walked out, they asked themselves, "What's the big deal?" Tex shrugged and told Jim, "You're it." And Jim would put the report for Crusoe together with Bob's help.

Crusoe had an odd, almost peculiar way of putting things that amused the people who worked for him. It was deliberate, to make sure things he decreed were remembered by others. The maxims gushed from what seemed a treasure chest of folk wisdom. "This is worse than shooting six ducks in the head with one bullet," he'd say when having trouble getting everyone in a meeting to agree on something. "We'd cut your throat for a nickel," he'd tell his men, coaxing them to shave a few extra pennies off a part provided by an outside supplier. And when his staffers would bring him financial projections that would make it hard to sell a proposal to Breech or Henry, he'd snap: "You've got these numbers out of a phone book. Now go back and do them right!"

Many of his dictums would have the force of commandments from God, sending people scampering off like frightened mice. His most famous aphorism, though, would become his oft-repeated phrase, "Don't nickel plate a crow bar!," a commandment that instructed his men not to spend extra money on parts of a car that customers would never see. Indeed, later in his career, Ford would ceremoniously present him with a nickel-plated crow bar as a memento of his career there.

Most of his managers would grow to respect and admire him, if only for his know-how of the car business. But few could ever like the man. He was too cold, too aloof. One of his assistants, delivering his mail to him in the morning, once tried to explain an important item to him. "I don't have time to talk to you," he shrieked. "Don't talk to me! Don't talk to me!" His words chased the assistant from the office.

Like Jack, he generated megabolts of nervous energy. His head would turn with quick, sharp movements and his eyes would cast about a room, taking every inch of it in. He was a suspicious man, keeping records on everyone around him, including transcripts of private conferences with Breech and others. Benson Ford, Henry's younger brother, would later say that Crusoe quietly came to his office to play the conversations back to him. But Benson never wanted to intervene.

TEX CAME TO loathe Crusoe more than he loathed Breech. They would argue over everything, sometimes becoming cruelly sarcastic to each other: how the company should be organized; who was able and who wasn't; how different functions should be staffed. Someone else might have bided his time or shown greater patience, if not political savvy. Thornton's bitter disappointment with things at Ford made him throw caution to the wind. It was almost as if he were battling some force inside himself—a fatal flaw in every truly ambitious person. Thornton was drawn to action, even self-destructive behavior, rather than simply waiting the situation out. With each gambit to regain Henry's attention, he only seemed to get in deeper—from his earliest attempt to get Ford to agree to his letter giving Tex power over planning to his initial session with Breech and his continual conflicts with Crusoe.

Tex believed that Crusoe wanted to organize Ford into another General Motors. At best, he thought that such an objective would only make Ford second rate. Imitation didn't lead to success. Innovative differences would pave the way. To copy GM, thought Tex, was suicide. Crusoe vehemently disagreed. GM was successful; Ford was not. To him, the solution was simple: emulate the GM model.

"It's trying to be like somebody else," Tex protested. "It just doesn't seem to be inspiring to the people inside a company when its objective is to be number two. Ford's objective should be to build the kind of company that other automobile companies would want to be like."

The debate raged on and on, and they argued over every little item. Tex made his position untenable by bucking Crusoe at every turn. And he warned his mates to watch out for the untrustworthy Crusoe. Tex couldn't trust someone he so vehemently disliked or someone who abusedly spoke of any member in his group. In the beginning, Tex and Jim would sometimes ride to work with Crusoe who would always refer to Jim in the backseat as "the fella who talks so slow." It irked Wright for years.

Just as Breech lured Crusoe to Ford with him, Crusoe enticed others from GM to Dearborn, the recruitment of each GM man bringing scores of others trained in GM's style and culture. Some Detroiters jokingly dubbed the company the "Ford Division of GM." Ford, of course, desperately needed good people then, but it also became something of a contest over who would recruit them: Tex and his men widened their own circle by recruiting a fair share of other Stat Control-types into Ford. Crusoe brought in his old friends from GM, including Mervin E. Sheppard from Fisher Body, who would assume control of the controller's office. Predictably, rivalries developed between the two groups. Crusoe also began criticizing Tex's men, accusing them of holding back financial results and numbers from the different divisions. In truth, what few numbers were available were so unreliable that Tex didn't believe they were worth passing on.

When Crusoe eventually wanted someone to keep the peace between the factions, he tapped Arjay to go to work directly for him. It was an impossible job because Crusoe would force him to do things that would rub Tex the wrong way. Arjay respected the man, but he really wasn't his kind of ballplayer. He would remember how Crusoe would even bully and insult his own wife. One day, Crusoe called home to tell her what time to expect him for dinner. Suddenly, Crusoe gruffly barked into the receiver, "I didn't call you up to get balled out!" and slammed the phone down. Arjay shifted in his chair, feeling discomfort at Crusoe's behavior. Besides, Arjay felt unquestionable allegiance to Tex. Eventually, he convinced Crusoe of the awkwardness of the job and pleaded to be moved into the assistant treasurer's post, a request that Crusoe granted.

CHANGE THORNTON WAS ALLOWING himself to be eaten away by the pressure. Indeed, it grew so bad that he jumped at the chance to escape the increasing friction between himself and Crusoe by going to Washington to work on an assignment for Lovett, who had just become General Marshall's under secretary. If anything, however, his return to Washington may have convinced him that he could never be happy in Detroit. It would only come to remind Thornton how different he was next to Ford or Breech.

Lovett wanted Tex to help him straighten out and overhaul the organization of the Department of State. Tex welcomed the break. His patriotism was important to him and he believed that the struggle hadn't ended with the bomb, but only changed. Tex was a man who gravely considered the state of the world and who believed with a fervor that American business had an obligation to keep the armed forces in readiness. He spoke with Henry about this many times, though Tex felt that Henry didn't really want to listen to his argument. Having seen first hand how unprepared America was for the war, Tex believed that government and business should never let it happen again. For in the next war, there might be no time for the kind of military buildup they had all sweated through. But, no, Henry wouldn't hear of it. He told Tex that Ford had done its share during the war, that "we were never going to touch another government contract." Henry's attitude amazed him. "There is a definite lack of feeling of public responsibility in industry today," he griped to a Stat Control buddy in a letter. "Honestly, they seem to look upon the government almost as an adversary. When you observe attitudes of this type, it makes you admire someone like Lovett, yourself, and others even more."

While on his leave, Tex worked in a small office between Lovett on one side and Marshall on the other. Bob and Ed Lundy would keep him informed of the goings-on in Dearborn. The friction with Crusoe continued. "At the moment I feel just as if I had been shot from the mouth of a cannon," wrote McNamara, "nothing but stars in front of my eyes! Yesterday afternoon Mr. Crusoe was in one of his periodic flaps . . . in a vile mood when he called me in." Crusoe, unable to keep up with his own paperwork, pushed an eight-inch pile onto Bob, forcing him to go through it. Having worked it down to the last half-inch, he found everything in there from a request from one manager to send a man to a two-day course in gas meter reading to another request to move a print shop. At least Tex knew it was business as usual back in Dearborn.

One day, Henry came to town and called him.

"What are you doing tonight, Tex? Are you free for dinner?" asked Ford.

Tex agreed to go out for seafood that night because it was difficult to get fresh fish in Detroit. And the two conversed about Washington and Ford, Henry telling Tex that Breech had only let him come to Washington reluctantly; that he felt it was a useless thing for Tex to waste his time here, but they couldn't really turn down Lovett. Tex asked Henry if he'd like to come by the State Department to meet Lovett for lunch.

Before Henry arrived, Tex told Lovett about Henry's lack of interest in Washington and in foreign affairs. Early on, Tex had urged Henry to accept President Truman's invitation to serve as a member of the Air Policy Commission. Ford accepted the post, despite the counsel of others that he should devote all his time to the company. Later, however, he told Tex he wanted to resign. Disappointed, Thornton spent considerable time talking him out of it. The following day Henry went through with the resignation anyway. He had no interest in broader affairs and felt no great obligation to his country.

If anyone could turn around Henry, thought Thornton, it would be Lovett. Few men in Washington could speak with as much authority as Lovett on the need for public service. When Henry arrived for his lunch, Lovett sat him down, explaining Marshall's plan, the condition of Europe, the Russian threat, and what could happen to business if there was no foreign market for American producers. To Tex's delight, Ford seemed to understand, to finally feel some empathy for his position.

"Yes," Henry said, "people have to understand this. When I get back I'm going to organize something with Tex, a program to at least spread the word around Detroit."

When Thornton returned to Detroit he waited and waited. Three weeks passed and still there was no word from Henry. Finally, he cornered him and reminded Ford of his promise to Lovett.

"When are we going to get started on it?" asked Tex.

Henry's response was a laugh.

"Oh, that!" he said. "I talked with Ernie about it and he said, 'Forget it. It's just politics.' "

Tex, let down and disappointed, sulked off. It simmered in him for days. Tex, of course, was judging young Henry against the exceptional role model of Lovett, a man who would time after time demonstrate unselfishness in his service to the country.

Lovett was also savvy. Aware of the growing friction between Tex and Crusoe, he was sure to drop a letter to Crusoe on his friend's behalf. "By now Tex Thornton ought to be back on the job with you, having completed a very excellent survey of the State Department organization," he wrote. "It will be most helpful in our efforts to improve management control and I am writing to thank you again for your courtesy in lending Thornton to us and for your generous help."

To Tex, Ford's refusal to help his country only reinforced his sense that Detroit was a small-minded and insular community. Even then, it was a closed society, waiting for Japan to happen. All it cared about were its cars and what it took to make them. Detroit's fear of anything non-Detroit would made Japan's later incursions into the auto market possible.

WHILE TEX AND Breech would one day confide to each other that they were too alike to work at Ford, they also were vastly different men. The profit motive seemed a stronger motivator for Ernie Breech. Tex felt a sense of responsibility for his country that he brought with him on the job.

Breech was more ruthless where Thornton was warm, more passionate. Tex would see what was right, what was good but also what was expedient and aim for it directly. Breech would see things the way an auto man would. He would perceive a world of power blocs, full of dangers and threats to be evaded. That's how you survived at a place like General Motors or Ford. Tex may have been a power broker and a hustler, but he also was more innocent in the world of Detroit. He was the ambitious outsider, the patriot. And Lovett was no longer able to protect him, like some ever-watchful guardian angel.

His feuding with Crusoe was coming to a fever pitch. Tex would do almost anything he could to undercut Crusoe, hardly disguising it from him or anyone else. He would go in to see board director William T. Gossett, an august figure brought in to build a legal department, and sit there for hours, complaining about things that Crusoe had done. Gossett would try to little avail to calm him, seek out compromises and maintain some kind of truce.

Tex would walk into Crusoe's office, explain how he disagreed with him over an issue and then proceed to convince Crusoe that his position would be detrimental to his career at Ford, as if trying to protect Crusoe from himself. Their eyes would flash like swords in such meetings. Ben once overheard Crusoe shout, "I think Tex would be wiser to look out after himself than to try to look out after me."

IT WAS BECOMING clear that Ford wasn't all that Tex expected. The same was true for his friend, the younger Quiz Kid, George Moore. In Detroit, there wasn't enough distance between his childhood, when the kids would taunt him because of his heft, and his new-found maturity and accomplishments. After traveling throughout the world for Stat Control, Detroit seemed pretty parochial. He was back in his hometown, living not all that far from his parents and old chums. He was no longer in charge of an operation as he was in the Pacific. He was part of Jim's organization planning group. Jim thought the world of George, but it was apparent that George had lost some of his momentum.

There was, of course, resistance everywhere. Ford managers were still suspicious of them. All of the men were trying to get organized as a group and also to plan for specific individual assignments in a fluid organization, complicated by the inflow of GM people under Breech. There were so many personal uncertainties that it was a tough period for any of them to adjust to. Andy had left. Tex was having problems with Crusoe. Moore now had his doubts.

Jim would try to pump him up.

"George," he'd say, "we've got to organize the sales department."

"Ah hell, Jim, they won't pay any attention to me," George said. "They just do what the hell they want to do."

His youthfulness and his appearance could not have helped nor could the fact that he was among such elite company. Indeed, the early examinations showed that if there was a laggard in the group, it would have been George. He had fallen within the lower half of the men in ability and knowledge and was the lowest in what the psychologists termed "total adjustment." After conducting his personal interview with George, the examiner wrote that "conversation is not easy. Mr. Moore is somewhat reticent. He seems to be struggling with feelings of inferiority. A sense of humor is evident, though his witticisms are directed chiefly toward himself."

The inferiority, if that's what it was, had begun to take second place to George's discovery that he had more to offer than a large organization could value. Henry also had asked his employees to make political contributions to Republican party candidates. It didn't really sit well with him. He was a loyal Democrat, an avid FDR supporter during the war. He saw no reason why a company should tell him to contribute to any political campaign. That was a personal decision, not a company decision.

The issue only fueled his disenchantment. He wanted to build something he could call his own, something that he would have more control over. That was one reason why he grew so enthusiastic about the possibility of buying a Nash dealership with Tex, Jack and Ben. He was fond of Washington, had forged connections and made friends there and liked the idea of returning to the city.

"I want to be on my own," he told Mimi. "I want to be my own boss. I want to live life the way I want to live it, without anyone looking over my shoulder."

Mimi agreed. She had no great attachment to Detroit, and if George could move the family to Washington that would suit her fine. Her mother still lived in the city that she enjoyed as much as George. He began to fix on a solution: if he could wrangle a Ford dealership in Washington, he'd be able to run his own show while also returning to a city he loved. George bumped into Mark Day, an old friend, at the Detroit Athletic Club. Day and he were boyhood friends, and after the war, Day returned to Detroit to work for his father, a manufacturing rep who sold piston rings. Day agreed to put up most of the money for the dealership if George could get one.

When George talked to Tex about it, Thornton completely understood. Tex even suggested that his mother had squirreled away some money and might be willing to invest in George's business. George's father had also agreed to contribute some cash as well. Tex told George he would mention it to Henry and grease the skids for him.

George lined up an appointment with the Lincoln-Mercury district manager in Washington to explore the possibility of becoming a dealer. Then he went to Jim with a worried expression. He told Jim of his plans.

"If that's what you want to do, George, I think it's great," Jim said.

"Well, I don't really know this fellow and he may not approve it. Will you go with me to meet him?"

Jim was actually flattered that George asked him. A few days later, the two of them flew to Washington on a DC-3 to meet the man. It was a horrible flight. The plane jumped around in a sky full of thunder and lightning. But they made it, had lunch with the district manager and secured a Lincoln-Mercury dealership for George.

In February of 1947, George, Mimi and their eight-month-old daughter, Marika, left the group and returned to Washington. They rented another apartment in Park Fairfax, getting more spacious accommodations with two bedrooms, and George rolled up his sleeves and went to work as a Lincoln-Mercury dealer.

Suddenly, Tex Thornton, still battling Crusoe and still stung by Henry's rejection of him, had lost two of his hand-picked comrades. And in George's quick departure, he might have seen a bit of himself. He had to see that his opportunities were being cut short, that his role at Ford was less meaningful than he wanted. For someone who always kept his eye on the future, Tex had to sense that the further down at Ford he was forced to go, the further away from Henry, the more limited were his own horizons.

WASHINGTON, THE TOWN that manufactures nothing but gossip, had picked up word that Tex's team was floundering in Detroit. As early as March, 1947, Tex's friends in the Pentagon began hearing rumors that all was not going well for the group in Detroit. George's return to Washington may have prompted the talk, along with Andy's decision to go back to California. One friend relayed the rumor, asking Tex if it were true. "I'll keep it under my hat," he assured Tex, "but I'm interested in knowing how this experiment works out. I've been reading *Business Week* regularly and haven't seen anything yet about any new techniques in management at the Ford concern." Tex Thornton was clearly irked. He shot off a letter immediately, demanding to know the source of the rumor. His response was both defensive and candid:

> The Ford Motor Company is a billion dollar corporation and has 123,000 people in it. You do not radically change a way of thinking or operating in something that large over night. Sure, there are a lot of things that we would like to do here at Ford which we have not been able to do to date. Personalities and traditions are the main obstacles, and I can't say we're too surprised in finding them in existence here. However, we're not discouraged and most of us have received pay raises since joining the company. You'll do me a favor if you will spike any rumors that you hear to the contrary. I don't mean to say that everything is perfect. The work is right down our alley, but we are proceeding at a much slower pace in accomplishing it than is absolutely necessary. Maybe we're impatient; probably so, but I think we will successfully overcome our obstacles in time.

But it wasn't to be. In a corporation, rumors feed on facts that tend to confirm them. This rumor was hardly malnourished.

Lewis Crusoe, here on the cover of *Business Week*, had numerous run-ins with Tex that ultimately led to Thornton's being dismissed from Ford.

Tex Thornton in a pensive mood.

Chapter 10

WASHOUT

■

"Well it is known that ambition
can creep as well as soar."

—Burke

*I*t was one of those hellish Fridays. Tex had spent this early January day racing from one project to another in a total blur. His conflicts with Crusoe were growing worse by the day, to the point where even minor issues were sparking friction. Today the break had come. Now, after everyone else had gone home, Tex realized how late the hour was. He was determined not to miss dinner at Bob and Margy's place in Springwells Park. He had to see his friends.

McNamara's home was a modestly decorated place, though furniture had long replaced the orange crates. Bob was spare and frugal, the last of the group to get a television set. His dining room boasted a white enamel freezer chest which he and Margy proudly bought on sale from an appliance wholesaler in Detroit. They had a hell of a time getting it in the back door of their townhouse, only to discover it couldn't be squeezed through the inside door and down into the basement. So it sat in the dining room against the wall, covered by a white tablecloth and a lit candelabra.

The gang had gathered at the house not much after 6 p.m., drinks in hand. Bob poured himself a little Canadian Club and water. Finally, a weary Thornton arrived straight from work at a quarter to seven, looking as if he'd finally crossed the finish line.

"Hi, Tex," said Bob, "how about a drink?"

Bob mixed a martini for him as Tex made the rounds, greeting his men and their wives.

"I've got some news for you," Tex announced before Bob could place a drink in his hand. "I've just been fired."

"Oh God!" someone moaned. There were a few gasps and a few incredulous looks around the room.

"Breech called me into his office today and said, 'Tex, I've got something that I've got to take care of. I don't like to do it but it's the best thing to do. You know, you've been running around here acting like you're the executive vice president of this company and you're not. I am. And there's only room for one, so you're going to have to leave.'"

Tex said he put up a protest, but he knew it was over. Breech obviously cleared the decision with Henry, and Tex himself had become so disenchanted he wondered aloud if he really cared. Still, it hurt his pride.

"As I was going out of his office," Tex continued, "he called me and said, 'Tex you don't realize it now, but someday you're going to thank me for this.' That sonofabitch!" Tex said.

Things hadn't been going smoothly, but few expected a blow-up like this. Tex had received a raise only a few weeks earlier. And just before Christmas, Crusoe had sent Tex a note assigning him parking space "#15" in the Administration Building's garage. Earlier in the year, he had informed Tex that he could eat in the executive dining room on the fourth floor. Breech had put Tex in for several Detroit club memberships and had enrolled him in an executive book club. All the trappings and perks, the corporate symbols of power and success, were being given to him. They were just formalities that only disguised his problems with Crusoe.

And now this! Thornton was supposed to end up president of the place, and then Bob if anything ever happened to Tex. There was no competition between them. They'd come to think of themselves as royalty, aspiring in succession to the throne. That Henry had chosen Breech, and his pals from GM had arrived to take control, seemed a temporary complication. But sometimes Tex's best quality, his relentless drive, seemed his worst. Ben would joke that whenever Tex died and was lying in his casket in a funeral home, he would somehow manage to get up long enough to tell the director how to run his business. You just couldn't stop him from butting heads with Crusoe, who groused that Tex's ambition was way ahead of his ability. Crusoe called Tex shallow and accused him of being an empire builder, which was certainly true. The tension between them continued to build and build. It had to explode.

After more than a year, Crusoe had had enough. His feuds with Tex over everything forced him to declare to Ford and Breech that "it's either him or me." Crusoe not only disliked Tex, he distrusted him. Crusoe believed that "if you want your bite out of the apple too quick, that's the end." So it was, he would later say, with Thornton. "Tex wanted his bite out of the apple too soon. That's why he's no longer here."

Tex, too, had delivered a similar ultimatum to Breech, trying to squeeze Crusoe out. In the end, it was not a difficult decision for Breech, who had to let Tex go. Over lunch with one of his GM recruits, Gerry Lynch, he let it be known that Tex was as good as gone. "I've had it up to my eyeballs with Tex," Lynch recalls Crusoe saying. "I'm going to take him out of here."

"Lewie, how are you going to do that?" Lynch asked.

"I've cleared it with Henry. I just can't take the guy anymore."

Lynch remembers seeing Thornton walk out that day. "He looked pretty beaten up."

For the men who looked up to Tex, it was a the worst crisis they'd faced together. What did it mean for them? Would they go to work on Monday morning and be told they were out of the company as well? Would Breech or Crusoe cut all of them loose?

"I can't believe it, Tex," said Jack. "We'll all resign, we'll all leave, if that's the way they want it."

"It may come to that," interrupted Bob, "but we're not going to do that. We're going to handle this quietly and in a businesslike manner."

It was hardly a good time for any of them to quit. They were glad just to have a job. They were relieved that Tex didn't ask them to walk out together. Yet, over the weekend, McNamara seriously considered leaving the company out of loyalty. He discussed the idea with a visiting friend, who recalls that McNamara was torn over what, if anything, to do. Bob, however, concluded that quitting wouldn't prove much of anything.

Still, it was a tremendous blow to their futures. Tex would be alone, orphaned from the group he created. Ironically, he who cared most about friendship would be one of the first to be cut off. For Tex, with his grand ambitions and imperious ego, it was a humbling defeat. Worse, it had to be suffered in front of his friends.

Tex had staked his life, his future on Henry Ford II, and Ford had bitterly disappointed him. When push came to shove, Ford abandoned him with no more diplomacy than Tex's father had done when Tex was a child. Later, Bob felt so concerned about Tex's state of mind that he asked Ed Learned, the old Harvard B-School professor who helped to set up the Stat Control school in the early days, to telephone Tex and offer him some encouragement. Learned gladly complied.

That Monday Tex met with Breech again. The GM executive seemed more conciliatory, offering to lend Tex whatever help he could to get him another job. Breech joked that the day he met Tex, he went home to tell his wife that "I've run into a guy who's just like me."

"You ought to be running your own company," Breech told him. "But you're just not ready to run Ford."

They spoke about the miscues and the misunderstandings, how and why things didn't work out. Breech knew of some possibilities in Detroit and asked if Tex might be interested in them. That afternoon, he jotted a thank you note to Breech that would pave the way for more cordial relations in the future:

> *I would again like to express my appreciation to you for the time you spent with me this morning, and for your interest in my future. I will do my best not to let you down.*
>
> *I am sorry it was not possible to have had a session of this nature with you some time ago. However, I sincerely believe that if my present predicament was necessary in order to occasion an opportunity to have a discussion with you, it is worth the price I am paying.*
>
> *Please accept my sincere thanks. Yours truly, Tex.*

The very next day, Breech began contacting several of his friends on Tex's behalf. He wrote the president of the Manufacturers National Bank in Detroit, letting him know that "due to certain complications, Tex was looking for a connection other than the Ford Motor Co." Breech called him "one of the most competent young men, being thirty-four years of age, that I have had the privilege of meeting in many years." He arranged for Tex to see the president of the Great Lakes Steel Corporation in Detroit.

Tex spent the next few months looking for a new job. Breech kept getting him interviews. He explored the possibilities and turned down a couple of offers in Detroit after he and Flora realized that neither of them liked the city nor the society that coalesced around it. Shortly after Crusoe had arrived, his new boss invited them to his wedding anniversary party at the country club along with all of Crusoe's old buddies from Detroit. Lacking dinner clothes, Tex had to rent a black-tie for the occasion. To Tex, it proved a dull, stodgy night, a peek into the closed, clubby world of Detroit where the conversation tended to drone on about cars. Driving home to Huntington Woods that evening, Tex felt numbed by the experience. After a long silence, he turned to Flora and said, "If that's what I have to look forward to at that stage in my life, that's not what I want." Detroit lacked sophistication and civility. It was too isolated a place, too provincial for them. He had gone a long way from Texas, hungry for something more, something bigger to fit his aspirations. In every corner he looked, from banking to steel, Motor City could never match his desires.

ON MONDAY MORNING, after the long weekend following his firing, the group had also gathered in Tex's office. Like all the offices in the Administration Building, with the exception of Henry's and Breech's, it was an austere room with a glass-topped mahogany desk, a matching table and four standard issue visitors' chairs. Above a large credenza was a small framed picture, an aerial shot of the Rotunda and the Administration Building with the Rouge plant in the background. The venetian blinds were pulled. This was a private meeting.

The men filed into the room, taking over the available chairs and leaning against the off-white walls. Tex sat at his desk. Several of them cursed Crusoe for handing it to Tex. But Thornton wasn't about to advise them to leave, nor did he tell them they should stay. He had no idea what he would do himself and couldn't even offer to draft them if they wanted to leave. It was clearly their decision. He tried to assure them that they would be unaffected by his ouster, that it was a personal thing between him and Crusoe.

"I'll take the stigma of any of this with me," Tex said. "So I leave you fellows free and clear. You're not to blame for any of this. I'm the one. There won't be any ruboff on you fellows. I'm taking the full shot here."

What comfort his words could provide had to be limited. The meeting wasn't only about Tex's sudden departure. It was about the breaking apart of the group. For each of them, it would now be a new ball game.

Tex told them that Bob would take over as leader of the group. McNamara had been Tex's assistant from the very start, and all of them were in awe of him. Jim Wright privately thought Bob was the only one among them, other than Tex, whom he would gladly work under.

Yet, how could McNamara fill Tex's shoes? He was smart, but he wasn't charismatic. He didn't have that charming warmth that filled the room as Thornton did. Tex had a way of aligning himself to his men, articulating a bigger vision—and it always boosted them. They admired Bob's analytical acumen, but they also knew that people always came second to McNamara. Tex was taking something away that was irreplaceable. With his departure, they lost some faith, some trust, even a part of the dream. And McNamara, however brilliant, could never make things the same.

One thing seemed sure, Tex joked, his trademark smile finally reemerging across his face. "I don't want a staff job again. I have to get a line job. I'm convinced that a staff job cannot be strong and peaceful at the same time."

They knew exactly what he meant. Working for Crusoe meant that you had only so much responsibility, and even less power. Still, the sentiment of the group was that all of them started something here and owed it to themselves and to Henry to finish it. Tex couldn't offer them anything now. But he could foresee a time when the group might come together again under his leadership. If it didn't work out as he had planned at Ford, perhaps it could work somewhere else.

Tex looked around the room, more uncertain than he had ever appeared.

"Would you join me again if I needed you?" he asked, almost out of the blue.

His question was met with a long silence. It was one of those awkward moments that seem to last forever. Maybe they admired Tex too much to make a promise they couldn't fulfill. Maybe they didn't trust a future that could unseat someone they admired so much. Or maybe they wanted to be free of the group to test their individual mettle. They could showcase each of themselves now, with their king dead.

Tex felt hurt, even betrayed by the absence of a quick, positive response. After all, hadn't he brought them to Ford as a group? Wasn't he their leader? He hadn't expected them to up and quit. But wasn't he right to assume that someday the group might join forces again? Was their friendship so fragile?

Tex had always wanted work to embody friendship. You'd want to trust your colleagues, much as you'd trust the guy next to you in the foxhole. You'd treat both of them as if they held your life in their hands, because they did. It was true enough that he had told Flora not to get too close to the other wives. Tex wanted both of them to stand a little higher, as if he were in uniform outranking the rest. Still, Tex tried hard to establish a fraternity of work and achievement among the group that went beyond a professional relationship. They could all accomplish so much more if they worked together in support of each other as friends not just colleagues. From the very first, in his hotel room at the Statler, they had agreed to stick it out together; there would be no "peeling off" of individual members. Little did he know that someday he would be among the first to peel off.

But that silence would haunt the men for months to come. They felt as uncomfortable and as embarrassed by it as Tex, shuffling out of his office after each of them shook his hand to exchange best wishes for the future. Loyalty meant so much to Tex, maybe even more than skill or talent. For him, it was the foundation of every relationship. He demanded it from his people; and they gave it to him in return for his respect and dedication to them.

Ben Mills struggled with that silence for the next five months, wondering over what it meant and how he might tell Tex what he and the others really felt. Straining somehow to explain it, Ben finally summoned the nerve to write Tex about it. He began the letter, by recalling how Tex had backed him, stroked him when he felt completely defeated in Washington. It was his very first assignment for Tex: to devise the master plan for the expansion of the Air Force.

Mills rushed into the challenge only days after the Pearl Harbor attack. For the next three months, exactly ninety days, he worked fourteen hours a day, seven days a week, sometimes going without sleep for three days straight. Many nights he would sleep on a desk in an office in the Munitions Building. He had to account for everything on hand at each air base—men, planes, spare parts, ammunition, bombs, just everything —and then he had to project what they would need for the war and how long it would take industry to produce it. Half the Air Force lacked simple tables of organization, or T/Os, plans for every type of Army Air Force unit showing just how many soldiers it should have, down to the number of cooks required in a battalion, and the job and rating of each man. Ben literally had to invent them from scratch.

Finally the day came when he had to deliver the plan to the military brass. It was an elaborate presentation, with thousands of numbers and dozens of charts, an exhaustive program to build a large and destructive air force. Ben had rehearsed it with Tex, and now his boss watched as he sketched out his ideas before General George Stratemeyer, Chief of Air Staff.

When Ben was through, emotionally fatigued and mentally spent, Stratemeyer, a cigarette dangling from his lips, motioned to a handful of the charts.

"Mmmm, yes," he said, "all this sounds good. But I don't really like this, and I don't agree with that. Now take it back and do it all over again."

Ben was at the end of his string. He hadn't had a wink of sleep for three days. All he could think was, "You bastard! And you've had a full night's sleep."

"General Stratemeyer," he said in a voice that quivered, "maybe it's going to be done over again, but I ain't going to do it! I'm going home and going to bed!"

Ben stomped out, hearing the general yell over his shoulder, "Now you come back!" Tex chased him, but had no intention of bringing him back into the room for Stratemeyer to dress him down. He put his arm around him, and Ben broke down from the strain. Tex hustled him down the corridor, protected him and sent him home for a week of rest. There were no consequences to Ben's remark. Tex made sure of it because he stood with him, taking the flak himself. That was Tex, always allying himself to his men, never permitting any of them to fall out.

Ben mulled over the event as he thought about Tex's farewell session with the men. He wrote his letter to Tex on June 8, 1948, little more than a month after Tex had finally landed a new job.

> For two or three days I tried to analyze why in the hell nobody spoke up. I don't know what went on in the other fellows' minds, but to me your question required the almost instantaneous consideration of numerous factors, the evaluation of these factors, and the application of judgment. Perhaps typical of the way all of us think, we began a thought process considering the pros and cons of the situation. Such questions as "what would be the circumstances both on your side and ours," and "what kind of situation might be created by our leaving the Company." It only took one such thought to use up that split second after which a spontaneous response to your question was too late.
>
> In any case, Tex, we were all a pretty confused lot. One thing is sure, however, Tex, and that is that in our eyes your stature improved by virtue of your conduct. I seriously doubt that I would have done anywhere near as well.

None of us entertained the idea that you had failed in any manner whatsoever. As a group, we made some mistakes. There is no doubt of that. And, true to one of your strongest characteristics, you again stuck out your neck for us. How foolish we would be if all of us failed to realize that we would not have been with Ford in the first place if it hadn't been for your efforts. How inadequate we would all be if we even considered discarding our loyalty to you. One thing that seems extremely important, however, and that is that a blind loyalty and sound judgment are not compatible.

I don't think there is any question whatsoever, Tex, but that all of us considered it a privilege to be associated with you. Our loyalty to you as a person I don't believe has ever been questioned in any or our minds. When you left the Company, however, we were all faced with a split loyalty—a personal loyalty to you and an ethical loyalty to our jobs . . .

I think if you will consider, Tex, the things that you and I went through together, the times when I cried on your shoulder, and the times when you stuck your neck out a mile for me, I believe you will know that I could not possibly have forgotten these things in so short a time. . . . It is unfortunate that things happened the way they did, but it would be far more unfortunate I think if, as a result of the role you were forced to play and which commanded the admiration and respect of all of us, there should be a weakening of ties of friendship and understanding which were forged under great pressure and over a long period of time. If such a thing even tended to happen, then I am sure I (would) fail to understand your reactions or to appreciate the extent of the strain you were under.

If Tex felt betrayed by the group he brought together, it could only help him make a clean break with Ford. And, in Detroit, those who regard transients as nonpersons quickly spoke of him in the past tense.

Part Two

PAYING

DUES

Tex soon found a job with Howard Hughes, the nutty billionaire. Here is Hughes at the controls of his giant wooden flying boat dubbed the "Spruce Goose"—a $25 million disaster—in the 1940s.

Chapter 11

ANOTHER
CHANCE

■

"Fortune does not stoop often to take anyone up. Favorable opportunities will not happen precisely in the way that you have imagined. Nothing does."

—Sir Arthur Helps

*J*ane had just stepped out of the shower and slipped into a bathrobe when the phone rang. It was Friday morning. Her daughter Sally had left for school. Andy was out of town on business in San Francisco for the week.

"Jane," said the familiar voice, "It's Tex! I'm in L.A. I had an appointment to see Howard Hughes and he just postponed it. I thought I'd hop in a cab and come out and see you."

"Where are you Tex?" Jane asked, her hair still sopping wet. He was a fifteen-minute drive from their home at the Beverly Hills Hotel on Sunset Boulevard. Hughes, like many of Hollywood's movie stars at the time, hid out in one of the hotel's bungalows by the pool. "Tex, you have to give me an hour. My hair is dripping wet."

"I don't have that much time. Just put a bandana on your head."

"Tex, I'm not going to do it," she protested. "You've got to give me an hour to get ready."

Tex charmed and cajoled and before she knew it he was at the doorstep giving her a kiss on the cheek. Andy and Jane lived in her parents'
home, a tiny Truesdale tract house. Her hair wasn't quite dry, but she
offered him a cup of coffee as she tidied up and dressed. They chatted
about their friends in Detroit, his leaving Ford and the surprise meeting
with Hughes. Tex was planning to meet with the mysterious billionaire
to explore the chance to work for him. He had never been to L.A. so
Jane suggested they take a ride through Beverly Hills until his 11 a.m.
appointment with Hughes.

No sooner had Jane dropped him off, returned home and rolled back
her hair when Tex called again. Now Hughes wasn't going to see him
until 3:30 p.m. So down came the hair and Jane drove over to pick Tex
up for lunch at McHenry's, a popular hangout ever since the end of the
war. They arranged to meet for dinner at the Beverly Hills Hotel later
that night when Andy would return. And by the time they saw Tex
again, he still hadn't met with Hughes. His 3:30 appointment passed by;
4:00 went by; so did 4:30, 5:00, 5:30 and 6:00 with no sight nor word of
Hughes. Tex gave up, and met Andy and Jane for dinner in the hotel's
lush dining room.

Andy had only been with Bekins for a few months but was high on
the job and his new life in California. He'd acquired season tickets to
UCLA's football games on Saturday, spent Sundays at the Jonathan Club
on the beach and bought a beautiful lot in West Los Angeles where they
were building a new home. His boss, Bekins's comptroller, was an alcoholic so if there were any questions Andy had for him, he'd have to pose
them before noon. After lunch, a coherent conversation with him was
virtually impossible. Andy was clearly on the track to assume the man's
job. He and Jane had already been to supper at the Beverly Hills mansion of Milo W. Bekins, Sr., president and owner of the company and the
founder's son. They'd been ushered into the book-lined library for
chilled wine and then into the huge dining room for an elaborate dinner
for just the four of them (Bekins's wife rounded out the party), hovered
over by two servants. Andy clearly wasn't suffering from having left the
group. If Tex took special notice of this, he didn't say. But clearly Tex
was delighted.

Jane joked that their four-day drive across country from Detroit was
noteworthy for one major reason: the Mercury they bought from Ford
was a bear to steer. As soon as you lifted your hands from the wheel, the
car would careen off the road. They severed any connection to Ford by
ditching the car as soon as they arrived in L.A.

The three of them talked about Ford and how Tex had landed his appointment with the elusive Howard Hughes. In early January, 1948, just after Tex's confrontation with Crusoe, he'd gone to Houston to make a speech before the Junior Chamber of Commerce. At the session, he met an old wartime friend, General Ira Eaker, who was then working for Hughes. Tex had spent his last few days in Washington in January of 1946 working on a special project under Eaker for the Secretaries of War and Navy. Tex told Eaker he was leaving Ford, and Eaker asked him to come to California to speak with Hughes.

So here he was, summoned by America's famous rich playboy. But whether to meet him, or simply to wait in some strange test of wills Hughes concocted, Tex didn't know. Thornton continued to wait. He would wait one more day for Hughes to call. Then, having grown miserably impatient, he called up a Hughes aide and insisted that the appointment take place.

"Look, I've really got to meet him," Tex protested. "I've been sitting around here for two days!"

"We'll give you a call, don't worry," the aide said. "Mr. Hughes has been extremely busy. Just stay put, and we'll give you a call."

"No, listen, I've got to meet him now. Either you check this out, or I'm going to leave tomorrow."

Tex sat and steamed, sometimes leaving his room to sit and nurse a drink in the Polo Lounge, meeting out-of-work actors and actresses. He struck up a conversation and a friendship with actor Dale Robertson, who Tex had admired for his western cowboy roles on television and in the movies. The two of them spent hours drinking and chatting together. Finally, Tex was called at the bar by a Hughes intermediary who told him to meet the enigmatic man at the hotel's entrance in twenty minutes, at exactly midnight. "He'll be driving a Chevrolet," the voice said, before hanging up.

At the appointed time, a battered Chevy rambled up the hotel's driveway and stopped next to Tex. The driver reached over to the passenger door and pushed it open, motioning for Tex to jump into the car.

"Hi," he said, "I'm Howard Hughes."

Tex would have recognized him even without this bizarre hello, having seen enough pictures of him with some fashionable Hollywood beauty on his arm. He was gaunt, with a pencil-thin mustache and severely brushed-back hair. In his well-pressed suit, Tex seemed overdressed for the clandestine meeting. Hughes sported neither jacket or tie, but an open-necked shirt and a pair of light beige trousers. The two men drove off in the night in silence.

Hughes brought him to his office on the backlot of RKO Studios, where Astaire and Rogers had for years danced with grace and charm into the hearts of Thornton's generation. The multi-millionaire had recently become the controlling stockholder of the film studio. Hughes told Tex of his love of movies and women. He boasted about approving all the stories for RKO films, selecting each cast, each director and then painstakingly editing each picture. Tex had little interest in Hughes's movie or airline businesses. Instead, he zeroed in on the Hughes Tool Company. It was the gem among Hughes's holdings, a nuts-and-bolts business that lacked the glamour of RKO or TWA but was the heart of Hughes's empire. He'd built his fortune and his fame in tools to extract oil out of the ground.

As the two men sat in Hughes's modest back office, what impressed Tex more than anything else was that, unlike young Henry, Hughes seemed a true patriot. The pair spoke about their mutual concern that America remain militarily strong for its new position of world leadership. Tex, obviously putting his departure from Ford in different terms, told him he was leaving Detroit because it had no sense of responsibility to the country. Hughes understood, saying he considered communism a dangerous threat for which the country should be prepared.

They talked for three hours, and Hughes finally drove Tex back to the hotel around 3 a.m. Though a firm offer to join Hughes was lacking, Tex felt a certain rapport with the man. Hughes arranged a brief meeting for Tex with his chief aide, Noah Dietrich, and Tex returned to Detroit, wondering if something would come of his strange visit.

He carried on discussions with Dietrich and Eaker by telephone and letter before agreeing to join Hughes Tool as a vice president in Houston on May 1—nearly four months after he was fired from Ford. Tex took a pay cut from his lofty salary at Ford, but this time he didn't have the luxury of setting his own salary. Still, he and Flora were pleased with the turn of events. Since the war days, Tex had thought about returning to Texas. He sensed that the postwar years would be good ones there. And both he and Flora would be closer to home and to family. Hughes Tool would be their ticket back and there was even the possibility of becoming Hughes's right-hand man, succeeding Dietrich who was getting on in age.

Dietrich had joined Hughes in 1925, helping him transform an inheritance of about $1.3 million into a vast fortune. Hughes had told the small-statured accountant, "I want you to make me the richest man in the world." He very nearly succeeded, and now Tex envisioned the chance to replace him should all go well. The two men were a generation apart: Tex in his mid-thirties and Dietrich, sixty. And Hughes Tool, through its dominant position in manufacturing drilling tools for the oil industry, was a pretty nice empire on its own, earning about $15 million a year after taxes. If he couldn't run the show for Henry, he might very well be able to direct it for Hughes.

But during lunch with Dietrich on his first day with Hughes, Tex got surprise orders to take a temporary assignment at a small subsidiary of Hughes Tool in Culver City, California. Hughes wanted him to study the operation, Hughes Aircraft, and to recommend what should be done about it. The subsidiary was started in 1934, mainly to build private racing airplanes for Hughes, but it was so disorganized that the operation had never put a model into production. Instead, it quickly earned the reputation of being something of a hobby shop for Howard.

Hughes had installed and discarded half a dozen general managers in the division in as many years. The subsidiary was still reeling under the blow it suffered when an experimental Navy reconnaissance test plane crashed with the eccentric Hughes at the controls. It was now in the midst of working on a huge plywood flying boat that Hughes had begun early in the war. Tex had read about the two-hundred-ton plane with a wingspan of 319 feet and eight propeller engines. It had flown only once, lifting into the air for just forty seconds. About four hundred of the company's one thousand employees were still working on the Spruce Goose, as it was called. The only revenue the company booked was by making such mundane things as ammunition belts, ammunition feed chutes and even television cabinets.

Fed up, Dietrich asked Tex to cut the company's losses and suggested that perhaps he should shut the entire operation down, once and for all. It lost $750,000 on sales of only $1.9 million in 1947.

"I've been trying for years to persuade Howard to get rid of the Culver City division," Dietrich told him. "It's always been a loser and the money has to come out of our hide at Tool."

THORNTON MAY HAVE been disappointed at having to go to California instead of Texas, but his new assignment soon revealed possibilities and traps. Culver City is one of those towns that take the generic name of Hollywood. On the outskirts of Los Angeles, just two miles from the ocean, it is a place of well-to-do squalor, gas stations and oil derricks. The Hughes operation here was a small cluster of light green buildings. An elongated grass runway stretched through the 1,200 acre site. It was

Hughes's private airport to test fly the racing planes he used to break speed records around the world. A colossal wooden hangar that housed the construction of the flying boat stood on the property along with a compact manufacturing plant, a research laboratory and a small office building.

What Tex found here was a bleak company with immense promise. In the electronics lab, he discovered two brilliant scientists who were working on a group of Air Force research contracts with about 150 employees. Simon Ramo and Dean Wooldridge had been classmates together at the California Institute of Technology but then separated: Ramo went to General Electric and Wooldridge to Bell Laboratories. Now reunited at Hughes, the pair was working on two Air Force studies: one, to put together an airborne search radar and a gunsight fitted with an electronic computer; the other was a study to explore the making of a guidance system for an air-to-air missile.

They were hardly urgent projects. In fact, the Air Force had only committed a few hundred thousand dollars to both contracts. But after sitting down with both Ramo and Wooldridge, Tex was convinced that they had huge potential. "My God," he told Arjay, "those guys are geniuses." Hughes got them to his hobby shop by paying them hefty salaries and letting them dream about future technologies. Jet airplanes had made their debut during the war, and they immediately brought with them a major problem. The aircraft flew so fast that a crew could no longer use its eyes, ears and hands to shoot down another plane. Their speed required sophisticated sensing equipment and computers that would allow a crew to lock on a target plane, extrapolate its course and fire at a place where you'd be more likely to hit your target. If the two scientists could pull off this trick, these fire-control systems could become the launching pad for a major turnaround in the company's operations.

Tex decided to ditch the worthless projects at Culver City and transform the company into a military electronics concern. After the end of the war, most companies had abandoned the military market. No one anticipated another war so the competition significantly lessened. General Electric and Westinghouse, in common with most other firms, rushed back into consumer products to take advantage of what was expected to become a booming market for white goods. Hughes Aircraft could make its mark by going in a contrarian direction, and it held emotional appeal for Thornton. Why not press this new frontier of electronics to help keep America strong?

Dietrich, however, was none too pleased to get Tex's recommendation.

Thornton had been on the job only a few weeks when he and Eaker were called to Dietrich's Hollywood office on 7000 Romaine to discuss the plan. Dietrich had hoped that Tex would close Culver City down, or at the very least shrink it. Now his new manager was already contradicting him and proposing that Hughes invest millions in a major expansion program to help the scientists further along in their research. At once Dietrich had to realize that he had a new ambitious pretender to his throne.

Dietrich told the men that the company never made money in its history, that it was nothing more than a financial drain and that he opposed any plan that would cost still more money. Tex must have wondered if he had left Ford only to find another Crusoe at Hughes.

"That's not what I hired you to do," he told Tex. "I thought you were my man!"

"I thought I should go in there and study the place with a constructive attitude, not a destructive one," retorted Tex.

"If it were up to me, I would close the place down. There's no future in it. It's just a nuisance."

After the session ended, however, Eaker called Hughes to gain approval despite Dietrich's objections. Hughes was already being lobbied by Dietrich to turn the men down. Dietrich told Hughes that if he approved the plan he would assume no responsibility for its outcome and predicted that it would materialize into a financial disaster. Hughes, though, saw the recommendations as an opportunity to vindicate himself from his company's poor record with the military. So he approved the plan and directed Dietrich to advance the cash Tex and Eaker would need to fund the expansion.

Hughes insisted that Eaker serve as the liaison between the parent company and the subsidiary, and with Tex's approval, Eaker recruited Lieutenant General Harold L. George to be general manager of the aircraft division with Tex as his assistant general manager. Tex had known the cigar-chewing George during the war because he had been commander of the famous wartime Air Transport Command. Hughes promised the new management team the resources of his highly profitable tool company and also pledged not to interfere with the aircraft division's operations.

Tex got his way. But there were vast differences between this job and the one he had held at Ford, differences that could only humble a driven man. Tex had moved from one of the world's largest companies to a playboy's hobby shop. Now he was virtually alone, without a team he knew and could trust. His domain was a fraction of the empire at Ford:

barely $2 million in sales instead of nearly $1 billion; one thousand employees instead of 130,000; a few wooden hangars instead of the imposing Rouge. While the Ford job at least held up the prospect of directly reporting to the CEO, there was no chance of that here. Virtually no one saw the whimsical and elusive Hughes, except a handful of his top lieutenants and Dietrich.

Yet, just as he had seen great promise in the chaos and confusion at Ford, Tex envisioned the same here. For one thing, Tex had Hughes's considerable money to play with. And despite his skimpy assistant general manager's title, Tex found he had the authority to run the company's day-to-day operations. General George seemed content, as he was during the war, to rely on someone else to run the business. In none of the obvious ways, it seemed an ideal situation for an empire builder.

Tex and Flora had shipped their belongings from Detroit to Houston, assuming that Tex would work in Texas. Now they had to move to California instead. Hughes, having no idea of the extent of the assignment, told Thornton it would only take him six months, so they kept their furniture in storage in Houston. Tex leased a furnished home in Cheviot Hills, Los Angeles, while Flora stayed in Detroit to sell their home before coming west to settle the family in.

Immediately, Tex began to build a new team around him. He stole two men from Ford, including George Fenimore, a Harvard-trained lawyer and Stat Control hand who was told by Bob that he would be sorry for leaving Ford. Tex didn't attempt to persuade any of his original Ford group to follow him. Perhaps he was still hurt by their silence, or didn't want any reminders of his failure at Ford. Instead, Tex again sifted through his records to lure other Stat Control officers to Hughes. Ramo and Wooldridge did the same in their area of expertise, enticing scientific brainpower to their growing laboratory in Culver City.

That fall, in 1948, the group got their first breakthrough: a small $8 million contract for two-hundred fire-control devices to be installed in the Lockheed F-94 fighter. The company had run a few of the devices through the laboratory, but had no production line. But with Hughes's money, Tex bid on the fixed-price contract and promised delivery within eleven months—a bold timetable because other manufacturers estimated it would take them three to five years to develop and produce the same device.

As caught up as he was in his new job, Tex kept in touch with his friends at Ford. When an item appeared in the Detroit papers suggesting that Howard Hughes might invest in a fledgling auto company run by a zany entrepreneur named Preston Tucker, Arjay dashed off a letter suggesting that "here is one you ought to be able to scotch in a hurry." Tex wrote back that Hughes never seriously considered investing in the Tucker, that he had the car for a few days and ran some tests on it. "That was one project that individually and collectively Mr. Hughes's whole organization would have gone up in arms had he seriously considered making an investment."

AT FORD, THE remaining seven Quiz Kids were surviving better without Tex and the conflicts he had caused. Reorganizations and reshuffling remained the order of the day. Bob, Arjay and Ed were gaining more of Breech's direct attention for their work in finance. Jack was putting through a budget reduction program that Breech considered essential to the company's survival. Jim and Charlie had just gotten pay raises. Ben moved on to a new assignment in sales and advertising. In sending a progress report to Tex, Arjay apologized for his disjointed letter, blaming Bob who had interrupted him three times on the "buzz" box during the last fifteen minutes. Arjay used the occasion to read Bob the last line of Tex's most recent letter asking that Bob and Ed write him if they have a little time. "Tell Tex to write," joked Bob. "He knows I have always had the reputation of being a poor correspondent, and I don't want him to gain a similar one."

When the men heard of Tex's promotion to chairman of the executive committee of Hughes Aircraft, letters of congratulations crossed the country. And Tex, feeling a little more secure and a little more distant from Ford, began to say what was on his mind. Invited by the University of Notre Dame to deliver a speech on "The Organization of Business Management," he took the occasion to synthesize the lessons he learned at Ford.

The seminar's audience didn't know it at the time, but they were hearing Tex tell the story of his own disappointment at Ford. He regaled them with a few quips about old Henry and the sorry state of the company when he arrived after the war, noting that Ford made money in its first twenty years partly because its only competitor was the horse. But the bulk of his talk was deadly serious. "Unless an entrepreneur operates a one-man business, he must decentralize some of his responsibilities to assistants," he told the group. "Too often in a business enterprise, the responsibilities delegated are indefinite, vague and inconclusive. Responsibilities of each individual, at the various management levels, should be clearly defined in order that he and his associates clearly understand them. Care should be taken that there be no duplication of effort or 'gaps' in the assignment of duties which are necessary to the conduct of the business.

"A second principle which is necessary to good organization, and which is probably the least recognized in modern day business enterprises, is the one that authority must be commensurate with the responsibility delegated.

"An individual cannot be required to assume responsibility without the authority necessary to accomplish the task assigned to him. As important as this principle is to good organization, more than one-half the companies with which I am familiar violate it. You will hear, time and time again, in a large company that so-and-so is responsible for the performance of such-and-such work. In most instances a little investigation will reveal the fact that the necessary authority to accomplish the task is vested elsewhere. This breeds frustration in an organization and stifles efficient operation.

"When an executive has the authority and his subordinate has the responsibility, the executive automatically assumes the responsibility when he approves the action taken by the subordinate. The subordinate in effect, then, is only a glorified clerk. . . ."

If at his low points at Ford he felt merely a "glorified clerk," Tex was sailing the heights now. He was proud of landing on his feet at Hughes and wanted those in his past to know how well he was doing. He innocently dispatched copies of the speech to his friends at Ford, including young Henry who apparently read the document and reacted as if Tex had danced on his grandfather's grave. So outraged was Henry that he sent Tex a letter on November 9, 1948, that hardly disguised his displeasure:

> *I do feel that you were a bit indiscreet in several of the anecdotes that you used. However, it is not my intention to go into any detail on the anecdotes, but I do think that one example you used when you said that my grandfather's only competitor was the horse is one that deserves an answer. Obviously, you didn't spend enough time in the automobile business to be qualified to make such a remark, because I am quite sure that anyone who is a student of this industry would challenge that statement as being untrue.*

When Tex received Ford's letter, on its slim Office-of-the-President stationery, he could barely believe Henry's reply. Tex foolishly didn't think his remarks would anger Henry, and he didn't believe his comments about his grandfather were derogatory in the least. Tex replied immediately on November 18, seeking to preserve some semblance of friendship. It was still what Tex valued most in life.

> *Henry, contrary to the implication of your letter, I bear no resentment toward the Ford Motor Co. . . . Even though you and I had an agreement which was the deciding factor in my decision to go with the Ford Motor Co., and which agreement was shelved soon after I joined the company, I do not bear ill will toward the company or to you personally. At the time of my departure, I did not tell you any of the circumstances surrounding the condition which existed, nor do I now intend to do so. I think in time you may see the whole thing more clearly. . . .*
>
> *Please remember me always as a friend. . . .*

Henry Ford was a simple man with simple beliefs. He would have despised everything the Whiz Kids stood for. The founder of Ford banned organization charts and titles from his company—a fine strategy when Ford was smaller, but one that led to chaos and disorganization everywhere as the company became a giant.

Chapter 12

THE
CIRCUMFERENCE
OF A BERRY

■

"Most men can swing a job, but
they are floored by a title. The
effect of a title is very peculiar. It
is almost equivalent to a badge
bearing the legend: This man has
nothing to do but regard himself
as important and all others as inferior."

—HENRY FORD

Upwards of two thousand people were getting soaked to
the bones as they queued up in the rain around New
York's Waldorf-Astoria Hotel, hours before the ballroom doors opened.
It was June 10, 1948, a year when America was gripped by spy mania
and politicians argued the merits of the Marshall Plan, but everything
seemed to stop in that moment when Henry himself drove a spanking
new Ford a dozen blocks from the Carlton House to the Waldorf. There
New York Mayor Paul O'Dwyer formally opened the exhibition with a
flick of a switch, lighting the hotel's grand ballroom like a carnival.

The crowd wet but happy overflowed the gold-and-white ballroom,
where the new models had been parked, overtaking the east and west
foyers, the Basildon and Jade rooms and the Astor Gallery. From a seat
in the balcony of the ballroom, Mrs. Henry Ford peered down at the
crowds who sought a peek of her grandson as much as they wanted to
see the new cars. More than forty years ago she had attended the first

auto show in which her husband took part, describing it, like P.T. Bar-
num, as the "greatest show on earth."

Some 250,000 people came over six days to see the results of Breech's
crash program to beat GM at releasing cars that attracted rave reviews
from the press. After six months of hellish work and endless politicking,
he'd met his goal. Now he was throwing himself a party fit for a conquering Caesar.

This was Breech's event. The 1949 model was the most dramatically
different Ford since the Model A had replaced the Model T a generation
earlier. It was his baby. The familiar fenders hanging from a boxy body
were discarded in favor of a more compact car with smooth fenders,
hood and rear deck and minimal ornamentation. It was an immediate
hit. More than 100,000 people placed orders for the car the first day it
was unveiled in dealer showrooms.

Yet, for the seven men in Tex's group who remained at the company,
the new model was something of an abstraction. They were not oblivious
to it as much as they were removed from it. Ford claimed it took ten
million man hours and $72 million to get the car into production. Very
little of that time or money was expended by the Quiz Kids. They
weren't consumed with the making of the cars, but rather with the
remaking of the company. Financial controls, budgets, production schedules, organization charts, cost and pricing studies, economic analysis and
competitive surveys preoccupied them.

They considered the new car not a styling or engineering achievement
but a unit of production. None of them, with perhaps the exception of
Jack, could hop into a car and like Breech or Crusoe, render an instant
analysis. Breech could ride in an auto for fifteen minutes and tell you by
instinct that it was too heavy or too light, that its roadability was heaven
or hell. Touch and feel weren't useful concepts to the Quiz Kids. They
weren't quantifiable concepts. They weren't concepts at all. Touch and
feel were not the building blocks of a revolution or a way station to the
perfectibility of business.

But they were to Breech who lived in the moment. He or Crusoe
could pop open the hood of a stalled car and diagnose the source of
engine trouble within moments. They could be heard to sigh at the
sound of an engine revving. They were gourmands of gears and oil.

Breech had succeeded in making the car he wanted, but he hadn't
really won the war. Behind his differences with the Whiz Kids lay a
struggle for the future of American business. On one side, were the car
guys who lived for the beauty, the noise, the sensuality and the freedom

of the car. Detailed talk about a V8 engine thrilled them. On the other side, you had Tex's team and growing numbers of support staff who got their kicks from exerting control over the organization, not from seeing a new shiny model roll off an assembly line.

This split, which earlier appeared in the great railroad empires of the late 1800s, grew more apparent and pervasive in all of American business in the late 1940s and early 1950s as tens of thousands of professionals flooded the fast growing companies of the postwar boom. They came out of uniform, many of them educated under the GI Bill, and they were badly needed to control growth and make large enterprise more efficient. At one company after another, these educated newcomers engaged in a battle for control of the American corporation: the numbers guys versus the product guys. The odds favored people like Tex if only because America's postwar prosperity fueled the galloping growth of the American corporation, making it more vast and complicated and more difficult to manage.

At Ford, this shaped up to be less a fight than a forgone conclusion. The company's troubles and Ford's attempt to solve them assumed greater importance. The car guys had their glory days numbered.

AT FORD, THE Quiz Kids became *the* professionals. Like a surgeon in an operating room with no emotion invested in the patient on the table, each of the Quiz Kids was cool, dispassionate and detached. Yet it was the 1949 car that would ironically allow them to play a role in a monumental decision at Ford. Though Breech's hastily designed and engineered car garnered an enthusiastic reception from the public, it was a quality nightmare. The cars leaked water. Doors popped open unexpectedly. There were dents in the metal. The engine would conk out in the middle of a ride. The suspension would fall out of the car when it rumbled over a tough railroad crossing. The engineers blamed the manufacturing people, and the manufacturing people blamed the engineers. Someone needed to assume responsibility for the complete product.

Early on, Tex Thornton had assigned Jim, Charlie, George and Andy to the project of getting the company better organized with clearer lines of authority and responsibility. Jim had done the original T/O's—the tables of organization—for Stat Control. Ford had adopted some of their suggestions, but had not followed through completely. The task of building a new postwar car took precedence over organizational matters. Still, Breech understood its importance when at his first meeting with Tex he recommended that Tex and his followers read Drucker's *Concept of the Corporation.*

The book would eventually be recognized as a landmark study, adopted as the universal blueprint for the modern corporation. There was a paucity of books on the subject of management then, and none of them seemed written for the management public. Most managers hardly realized they were practicing management.

In 1943, just as Tex was gaining great power in Washington, GM invited Drucker to study the company's policies and structure. A generation of the corporation's pioneers had already departed or would soon retire. Pierre DuPont, who first introduced GM's decentralized structure when he took over a virtually-bankrupt GM in 1920, had been gone for twenty years. Alfred Sloan, the professional manager whom DuPont installed as president, had been GM's architect and chief executive for two decades. Sloan was past retirement age and intended to call it quits at the end of the war. Donaldson Brown, who designed the financial and statistical controls that held GM together, planned to depart with Sloan. The company wanted the next generation of its managers to have a written document to which they could refer as a map.

The private study turned into a book that helped to transform management into a discipline. As Drucker himself would boast, the book dissected all the main concerns of management, many of them for the first time: organization and social responsibility; the relationship between individual and organization; the function of top management and the decision-making process; the development of managers; labor relations, community relations, and customer relations.

It was esoteric stuff, a new "quantum mechanics" of business that old Henry had had little use for. At the time Sloan began to build the GM organization, when Ford had 55 percent of the market and GM only 11 percent, old man Ford virtually laughed aloud at the changes. In his autobiography, he wrote:

> To my mind there is no bent of mind more dangerous than that which sometimes is described as the "genius for organization." This usually results in the birth of a great big chart showing, after the fashion of a family tree, how authority ramifies. The tree is heavy with nice round berries, each of which bears the name of a man or an office. Each man has a title and certain duties which are strictly limited by the circumference of his berry. . . . It takes about six weeks for a message from a man living in one berry at the lower left-hand corner of the chart to reach the president

or chairman of the board, and if it ever does reach one of these august officials, it has by that time gathered to itself about a pound of criticisms, suggestions, and comments.

If the old man didn't need organization, it was because he saw every piece of the company go up himself, piece by piece. But the company had grown like an untended garden, berries everywhere. The organization chart Ford referred to was precisely that for the rebuilt General Motors, the tree that made the company's performance more than the sum of its parts. By 1940, GM would have 45 percent of the car market while Ford was down to only 16 percent. Tex's analysis had shown that from 1927 to 1939, Ford wound up close to break even. General Motors made more than a billion dollars. Chrysler, organized along the same pattern as GM, made over $700 million.

The ideas Drucker analyzed and publicized would come to dominate organizational thinking for decades to come. Large companies were organized into smaller, sub-businesses, known as divisions, and headed by operating executives with the authority to manage their own affairs with less interference. Profit held them accountable to the corporation. The product divisions focused on the existing businesses of the company, while the corporate level supposedly took the longer view. Sloan was not alone in popularizing these ideas. Ralph Cordiner of General Electric also was in the forefront of the movement, and by 1945 many large companies, including Standard Oil and AT&T, had overhauled their organizations to adhere to this decentralized model. But the problems with living in berries would always be much as Ford described.

THE REMAINING QUIZ Kids at Ford devoured the information in Drucker's book because it addressed and confirmed all the problems they had turned up during their orientation. They had agreed that their first objective would be to establish a clear-cut organization with well understood lines of responsibility and authority. As they wound their way through the ponderous mass of inefficiency at Ford, what struck them most was the complete lack of staff above the divisional level. Most large corporations were divided into two camps, those who worked on staff and those who worked on line. The staff people planned and plotted the company's strategy, measuring its progress and making the decisions that would flow downward. The men in line jobs would implement those decisions. No such distinction existed at Ford. If it did, everyone's job would have been more clearly defined and understood. What staff men existed often made line decisions. The severe quality problems with the 1949 car reflected the confusion.

At one point, Tex sent Jim Wright to the Dearborn Inn to stay in Charlie's room and work on a plan to completely reorganize Ford without distraction. It was a mission explicitly given to them by Henry. "Stay there until you get it fixed," Tex told him. Jim left the Rotunda, remained in Charlie's room for over a week and came back with a mammoth report called "Organizational Problems of the Ford Motor Co." They dubbed it the "Blue Book" because of the covers of the report. It was a weighty and impressive work, some fifty-seven pages of text and charts, that clearly articulated the need for decentralized operations and centralized control at Ford. It was written with such clarity and simplicity that it almost seemed as if Jim knew that young Henry, even with Breech beside him, needed as complete and thorough a business education as possible. Indeed, Arjay Miller would later say that he always preferred to separately brief Breech and Ford. "Breech was a real pro," he recalls. "You could shorthand a lot of stuff for him. But with Henry in those early days, well, you'd lay a background you would try to fill in."

Jim maintained in his report that organization

forms a pattern, a blueprint, for conducting the affairs of the business. It adds definiteness, orderliness, and objectivity to operations that without it become aimless and confused.

It helps every employee to know what his job is, how much authority he has, who his supervisor is, and what his relation is to the whole enterprise.

It avoids duplication of effort, wasted motion, and purposeless endeavor.

It affords a workable means for allocating and controlling costs, for budgeting expenses, and for measuring results in terms of profit and loss.

Similarly, Jim laid out the case for decentralizing every operation at the company, including the creation of a Ford Division.

Each decentralized operation is primarily responsible for the design, production, and sale of its product, having all the aspects of a separate business; it can consequently be held completely accountable on a profit and loss basis.

When applied to decentralized operations, financial records become realistic. Costs can be readily isolated and determined, unprofitable activities can be easily detected, and management decisions, such as the making of capital expenditures and the changing of products, can be based on reliable figures.

Top management is relieved of the burden of routine operations and is left free to concentrate upon its fundamental jobs—planning, policy-making, and controlling.

Better all-round executives are developed; broader experience is afforded at operating levels and the qualities of self-reliance, initiative, and leadership are fostered.

Wright made decentralization sound so liberating. But it would actually imprison thousands in Ford. The practice of decentralization allowed professional managers to gain more clout and influence in large organizations. Yet, decentralization is business double–talk. Executives think of decentralization as a way to empower greater numbers of managers down the corporate ladder. In fact, under decentralization, managers often have less authority, because it makes the large corporation run itself, permitting central staffs to assume greater control. In the 1950s, staff-driven, over-populated corporate headquarters grew like topsy, allowing those removed from the making of products to drift still further away yet more effectively control operations. Decentralization was largely the invention of ambitious executives like Wright and his pals who lacked the nuts-and-bolts knowledge of business but sought control over it.

At Ford, their ideas won immediate acceptance, and the men rushed about implementing them. Jim Wright, Charlie Bosworth and Jack Reith wrote detailed job descriptions, separated line and staff positions, deciphered reporting relationships, defined the flow of information and money in the company, forced agreement on each box in each chart in the corporation. No department could exist without being officially listed and accounted for by Jim and Charlie's organization department. They even designed the paper on which Henry and Breech would set down the rules for the company. A "policy letter"—any memo establishing corporate policy—was on green paper, while an "executive communication"—any memo from a company vice president—was blue to make them stand out from the tons of paperwork the corporation generated. No detail seemed too small for their appetite.

IN THORNTON'S ABSENCE, however, one man in the team quickly distanced himself from the others. The Quiz Kids quickly discovered, just as everyone else would much later on, that in any group where Bob McNamara was present, he soon emerged as the dominant voice. It did not surprise Charlie Bosworth, who had first met McNamara when he was lying on his back in a hospital bed. Just as the war was winding down, Bosworth had returned from England to a reprocessing center in Santa Ana, California, when Thornton sent him a cable ordering him to relieve McNamara, stricken with polio, of his command at Patterson Field.

Bosworth booked himself on the next flight to Dayton and immediately reported to McNamara's room, and there was Bob, as exuberant as ever, sitting up in the hospital bed with a bunch of Air Force papers scattered over the covers. Most people would have given you a rundown of what was wrong and how they were feeling. Not Bob. He was so intense, set on only one speed: fast forward.

"Oh, I'm fine, fine," he said hurriedly when Bosworth asked how he was doing. There was no talk of his illness. Charlie had come for a briefing from Bob so he could assume command, but McNamara had no intention of turning it over. Even from a hospital bed, he would remain in charge. He ran through a number of things he insisted that Bosworth do at the office. Ten days later, McNamara checked out of the hospital and was back in action again.

That was the indefatigable, take-charge Bob McNamara, quickly conquering a mild case of polio, refusing to yield any control—just as the men found him at Ford, untiring, unbending, leading the charge toward a more rational style of management. A calculating genius, he whizzed through the financial statements of Ford competitors, deciphering them for Henry, Breech and Crusoe. He dug into the long lost numbers of the company, isolating costs to unveil the true profit of a given business. He was determined to put Ford in the forefront of management in the late 1940s.

What he, Ed and Arjay did was not unlike what occurred in Stat Control. They put systems in place that brought to the surface "facts" that would permit financial control. Then they seized greater and greater power by virtue of their interpretation of those figures. In the past, the controller basically recorded what happened—he performed an accounting function and kept the financial records. But Bob would carve out a new and critical role for the controller just as Thornton had done in the Air Force. The position, as they redefined it, permitted the controller to plan and to forecast the future, to do quantitative analysis.

The new approach was greatly influenced by such Harvard professors as Tom Sanders, Russ Walker and Ed Learned. Walker had used the terms "cost centers" and "budget centers" from which the phrase "profit center" emerged as a natural derivative. And Bob McNamara was behind the effort to install profit centers throughout the corporation so they could take the pulse of each operation. The men went beyond the traditional control of manufacturing costs to include control over everything, from marketing to purchasing. They would figure out what Ford "ought to pay" for products, rather than simply taking the best price possible.

Slowly but surely, Bob was evolving a new lingo and new rules for corporate America. His numerical wizardry so impressed both Breech and Crusoe that they named him controller in 1949. His quick rise was abetted by the two other Quiz Kids who together with Bob formed the intellectual core of the group. Miller and Lundy brought the same discipline and beliefs to the job that McNamara did. Their rise signalled a major shift: brains were becoming more important to business than cunning.

Amidst the disarray they inherited, what most struck them was the lack of quality people. By and large, Ford's old-timers weren't up to the job. Lacking in formal education, they were intellectually incapable of moving the company forward, and they were suspicious of change. "We couldn't retrain the people in finance," recalled Miller. "The old-timers had been so set in their former ways that they were incapable of changing. They just didn't have it in them to adapt."

The financial staff of the company, thought Miller, was a victim of what he termed "adverse selection." Always, the wrong people were recruited for the wrong reasons. They emigrated to Ford's finance staff because they knew the henchman Bennett or someone else, not because they could boast any expertise. There was never an effort to lure to the company what Miller called "smart kids" who had been first in their college classes. Indeed, there was no recruiting at all on college campuses.

McNamara, Miller and Lundy—who studied business and economics at Harvard, UCLA and Princeton—reorganized the old-timers out of their jobs, replacing them with young, like-minded, degreed people. Finance was becoming an intellectual sanctuary inside Ford. Lundy more than any of them made recruiting new blood his project and his concern.

The former Princeton economics instructor would personally go out and recruit the sharpest graduates from the important MBA factories— Harvard, Stanford, Chicago, Wharton, Berkeley and Carnegie Mellon. When he recruited at the lesser-known universities, he would reach no lower than the number one or number two person in the graduating class. Lundy figured they were just as good as hires from the elite schools and were only there because they didn't know any better. He recruited MBAs to Ford long before they became popular in American industry— when they were mostly lured into management consulting jobs. Lundy was so intent on recruiting the best that each finance man had a quota to bring to Ford a certain number of fellow MBAs each year.

The way Lundy and his deputies drew the talent into the company was phenomenal. There was a speech that the men would deliver to the best prospects, recalled Tom Lilly, who came to Ford from the Harvard Business School faculty with the Lundy immigration wave. "You'll start your day with ten things on a pad," he would tell his quarry. "And you'll be so busy, running from one meeting, one appointment to the next, that you might get to nibble at one of those things, and you'll add another ten to the list as the day goes on. You'll work fifteen-hour days. You'll be married to your telephone. It's all chaos. And at the end of the day, you'll probably lean back in your chair and say, 'shit.' But if you smile after that, just a little, you're the right man for it." Lilly agreed it was corny, cheap theater, a huckster's pitch. But it brought the best of them in year after year, not only from the top business schools but also from the best corporations, such as Eastman Kodak. It worked because other corporations, said Lilly, offered them nothing but a routine progression. But at Ford you never knew where you could go because the company was growing so rapidly.

Through the years, greater numbers of MBAs came to work as financial analysts and more work was thrown their way. And after Ford moved its headquarters into the Glass House on American Road, Lundy's MBAs—toiling amid a sea of battleship gray desks—occupied several floors and wielded greater power. One of his deputies would carry a small card in his pocket that kept track of the number of Harvard Business School graduates at Ford. Dozens of new MBAs would swell the ranks of finance each year until the key finance staff numbered as many as four hundred people, with many more given critical assignments in the field.

THE SWELLING RANKS of financial bureaucrats who owed their allegiance to McNamara, Miller and Lundy would soon spark a civil war between those who produced product and those who didn't. It was a war between those who believed Detroit was in the car business and those new technocrats who wanted to create a transportation business built on economical production. The war has only intensified over the years, and it might be said that the major casualty so far is Detroit itself. Each side had its constituency: the car guys cared about the American public's desire to have a new car every year. The numbers guys cared about the bankers and shareholders. Each had nowhere to go but to opposite corners and, every now and then, duke it out.

But in the early skirmishes of 1949, Crusoe won the job that Tex so badly desired. His elevation came, ironically, with the final implementation of Jim Wright's decentralization plans. A separate Ford division was the result, and it immediately became the company's most important profit center, with its own engineering, styling, finance and sales staffs. It could fight for lower costs from the other divisions—or by getting work done cheaper outside. This second most important job at Ford, now Crusoe's, was a job dreamed up by the man he got fired, and designed by Tex's followers. Henry spotted him in the hall. "Well, Lewis," he said, "you'll be running practically the whole Ford Motor Company." Tex had sold the man short.

After his appointment, Crusoe moved out of the Administration Building and set himself up in an old warehouse, the company's parts and accessories depot on Middlebelt Road. GM's Chevrolet had once done a similar thing, moving from the GM building into the company gymnasium in order to get costs down. And that was Crusoe's intention as well. Jack Reith was one of his first recruits. He also tapped Jim Wright as his personal assistant, and then Charlie took over the organization department.

When Crusoe first joined the company, Tex would pick up Jim and then Crusoe on his way to work. Tex and Crusoe would dominate their drive time, talking business, occasionally Crusoe would refer to Jim in the back seat as "the fella who talks too slow"—a derogatory comment about Wright's southern background. He hated the implication that he didn't know what he was doing. When Jim finished his term studying accounting at night, he took his report card in to Crusoe. "Now you don't have to be worried about sending me into accounting."

Crusoe was meticulous, requiring that Wright prepare detailed biographies of the men who directly reported to him. The histories were to include the ages of a man's dependents. If he had a legal separation or a divorce from his wife, that too was noted, perhaps because Crusoe considered it a sign of instability. He was the perfect corporate politician, even lecturing his men on how to write a memo so that you always had an out. "You don't say it's so and so," Crusoe maintained. "You say it appears that it is possible that such a situation can occur."

Jim found him a compelling teacher. Charlie, too, was fascinated by Crusoe's knowledge of the auto business. He could always relate a problem at Ford back to a similar experience at GM or Fisher Body. As his assistant in the newly formed Ford division, Jim walked the assembly line with him, as Crusoe pointed out things to look for: a poor welding, wrinkles and sags in the ceiling headlining. He understood the proper use of gunk, the tar-like soundproofing material which the assembly men slapped into a car's joints to silence the squeaks and rattles, insulating one metal from another. The men who troweled gunk were specimens beyond belief, encrusted like pre-historic creatures with the horrible stuff. If gunk wasn't applied with precision, a car could be noisy as hell, dust would creep in, and water would leak through the car frame.

In later years, when Tex called and asked how things were, Jim would inevitably mention Crusoe and the good job he was doing. "Oh, for God's sake, Jim," Tex would reply. He could never stand the idea.

ALWAYS, THEY KEPT in touch with Tex. Sometimes by telephone, sometimes by letter. In July of 1949, Jack jotted a quick letter to him.

> *Dear Tex:*
>
> *We have wondered many times how you are getting along out there in sunny California. We heard about your new house. I imagine it will be a wonderful home—know you are anxious to get it finished.*
>
> *Say, weren't you the great advocate of having boys instead of girls! I'd like you to know that FCR Jr. arrived last month, weighing nine lbs., ten ounces— a real All-American candidate.*
>
> *Maxine is feeling fine—recovered very quickly. So we feel we have a complete family now.*
>
> *I have been very busy the last three months with the creation of the Ford Division. Remember that big block on our first organization chart? I'm doing very interesting work and getting a big kick out of it.*
>
> *Would sure like to hear from you once in awhile. Hope that maybe you and Flora will be back this way sometime soon.*
>
> *Best wishes,*
Jack

Crusoe must have sensed just how big a kick Jack was getting out of the job because he became very fond of him. While Jim learned to respect Crusoe, to Tex's never-ending chagrin, no one seemed to grow closer to him than Jack. Indeed, when the Reiths' second son was born years later they would name him after Crusoe because of their fondness for the man. A few days after the Ford division was formed, Crusoe recruited him as his manager of programming and product planning. The job entailed monitoring every step of how a car gets styled, tooled up and created. Until then, Reith had been dabbling in both organization and planning after helping set up some of the company's first budgets. The new job could put Reith in conflict with Bob McNamara, who as controller would watch every new cost that could creep into a car and seek every old cost he could squeeze out of one.

It set up Jack as a traffic cop for everything that went into Crusoe's office and everything that came out. He participated in all the important meetings, read all the important reports, formulating what would get done and what would get ignored. It was a central role in the biggest part of Ford's business, and Jack would shine in it.

Crusoe and Jack immediately went to work improving the quality of the 1949 car. Their men would tear down a Ford and a Chevy and mount each of its parts on huge boards for close inspection, figuring out how much each cost, which one was better and why and whether it needed to be improved or replaced. New assembly plants had to be campaigned for and built. New sales programs had to be invented. New cars designed and put into production.

What also became increasingly apparent was that the organization that Jim and Charlie put in place created inherent conflicts between line and staff people. Whenever Crusoe and Jack needed money to change the tooling in a plant to repair a fault in the 1949 models, whenever they needed money to build a new plant, they would have to appeal to the finance staff and face Bob, Ed and Arjay. They were expected to come up with the programs that would consume cash, but the central staff was expected to challenge and question those requests. It was a corporate check-and-balance game.

They worked well in such situations—Crusoe's precision and thoroughness combined with Jack's ability to give an idea wings, to promote and to market it, seemed unbeatable. Together they would build an identity of interests against the conservatism that financial controls often dictate.

Within weeks of taking over the job, Jack inherited the plan for the next Ford car. It had already been approved and it contained startling news. The company proposed to eliminate the eight-cylinder engine in favor of the cheaper six-cylinder model already in the Chevrolet. The estimates from central finance showed that the V-8 engine cost an extra $100 to produce as well as additional charges in extra tooling in the plants because Ford then offered two engines. Finance, engineering and marketing had already concurred in the change.

But when one of Jack's men, Chase Morsey, who had worked for Reith in Stat Control at Patterson Field, raised questions about it, Jack immediately took up the challenge. Chevrolet had switched to a six-cylinder engine in 1929 when the Ford Model A carried only four cylinders. "So they like cylinders?" Ford exclaimed. "I'll give 'em eight!" It scored an immediate hit, the favorite of youngsters, gangsters and police departments for the extra kick it gave the Ford. Bonnie Parker and Clyde Barrow left the police in the dust with their V-8; so did Ma Barker and her boys as well as John Dillinger, who wrote to old Henry thanking him for the car.

They marched into Crusoe's office.

"Mr. Crusoe," Jack said, "you know the automobile business better than I do. But we think it would be a mistake to lose the V-8 in the Ford."

"I've always owned a Ford car," chimed in Morsey, "and I love automobiles. My first car was a V-8 and everyone loved the feel of that engine. It gave them a sense of being in command as they went down the road. Ford and the V-8 go together. They go to bed at night and wake up the next morning. You can't separate them."

"You've seen the cost estimates," said Crusoe. "It costs too much money."

"If we lose the V-8," said Jack, "we'll never catch Chevrolet. We could get more money for it as an option. I can't believe that two cylinders cost that much more."

"Well," said Crusoe, arching his eyebrows, "when I was over at GM I always thought we were crazy to only put a six in the Chevy. I think it makes sense. Let me go and see Mr. Breech."

Breech didn't like the idea at all, but reluctantly agreed to give Crusoe's men ninety days to get their facts together to support a decision in favor of the V-8 engine. So Jack was sent out to gather the facts to fight the figures. He and Morsey interviewed key dealers about the change. No one had ever bothered to talk to the dealers about this issue. Overwhelmingly they wanted to retain the higher-powered engine. Jack and Morsey then examined the financial data more closely, tracing the estimates back up through the different departments—sales, product planning, engineering and manufacturing. They discovered that the $100 estimate came from some of the new GM recruits. The actual cost of the engine was only $16 more than a six, yet Ford could charge an extra $100 for the eight as an option. That would bring the base model down in price, yet preserve the company's point of differentiation. Jack moved the new position through the organization, and 90 percent of the customers who bought Fords took them with the bigger engine. The extra profits on the V-8 were phenomenal.

They fought similar battles to get automatic transmission, then a feature exclusive to luxury cars only, in the Ford car. Jack lobbied for the change, gaining huge investments for a new plant that would build cars with automatic transmission, forcing engineering to come up with procedures a year before they claimed they could. Each month Jack would argue persuasively for higher production and higher inventories to catch Chevy, and each month he won many of the battles over a questioning and hesitant financial staff. Crusoe made the Ford car, and Jack helped make Crusoe. To many, it seemed that Jack was rising above his Whiz Kid colleagues.

NOVEMBER, 1952. BEN Mills was sitting in Crusoe's office, back home from one of his marathon country-wide trips for Ford, conducting studies on the steel and glass plants. He had recently taken a job as assistant manager of Ford's new aircraft plant in Kansas City. Crusoe had urged him to assume the post: "If I were you I'd take this job for nothing." Ben had just come into Dearborn to talk with Crusoe about the operation when the phone rang.

It was Breech, calling from Paris. He was there with Henry and other top Ford executives looking over the company's struggling Ford of France operations in Poissy, just outside Paris. Severely underfinanced and in the red, the company was on its way toward reporting a $2.9 million loss for 1952.

For the past four years, the business had been headed by Francois Lehideux, an elegant and polished Frenchman. Breech, later recalling the conversation in his autobiography, told Crusoe he wanted Jim Wright to come to Paris to succeed Lehideux as general manager of Ford of France. Breech liked Jim, thought him an able man and would see him and his family every Sunday at the Christ Church Cranbrook in Bloomfield Hills. But Crusoe recommended Jack for the post. He told Breech Jack was the ablest man he had.

"Can he handle the job?" asked Breech.

"Yes, he can handle it. He's just about the best man you could get."

Overhearing Crusoe's end of the telephone conversation, Ben detected an undertone in Crusoe's endorsing Jack for the job. He felt that Crusoe sincerely didn't want to lose Jack at Ford, but liked him so well he wouldn't stand in his way.

"All right," said Breech, "it doesn't make any difference to me. Put him on a plane and have him here this weekend. He can make it by Saturday or Sunday. It's only Wednesday today."

THE GROUP WAS losing its identity. At Ford, there were still seven original survivors. But Bob, Arjay and Ed split off into their own team in finance; Jim and Charlie remained in the Ford Division with Crusoe. Ben was doing a variety of jobs, here and there, carving out a reputation as a troubleshooter. And now Jack was going off to Paris. Tex, Andy and George had gone their own very separate ways. The friendships were a fragile glue. As each of the men entered his mid to late thirties, each increasingly lived for himself, for success and power. The past, and the partnerships, seemed to be unnecessary baggage. Quaint. Immature. What mattered now was to be in a hurry. Speed required few attachments.

THE

WHIZ

KIDS

George and Mimi Moore.

When George's new dealership building was erected on 4400 Connecticut Avenue in Washington, D.C., it was the flashiest and biggest ever—and it cost some $150,000 to construct.

Apart from his friends in Detroit, George Moore stands with partner Marcus Day Jr. at the site of their new dealership.

MR. BLANDINGS' DREAM HOUSE

■

"A man is known by the company he organizes."

—Ambrose Bierce

For most of the guys, the group had been a flying wedge, a case of strength in numbers. For George Moore, it was security, layers thick, against the reality of having to do more, be more. As long as he was one of a great up-and-coming group, he could do what he did best: be everyone's favorite son.

But as the demands on the team and each of its members increased, George's deficiencies rushed to the surface. He could work as hard as any of the others, but he couldn't match the best of them in intelligence or ambition. Within this high-powered group of friends, George could only play a subsidiary role. And Breech's arrival at Ford made it clear that he might not even have been able to do this if the group was forced to split up. Who could protect him if he had to work for one of the GM transplants that Breech and Crusoe recruited to Ford?

In early 1947, he hatched the idea of starting a new venture. He had to see if he could make it on his own.

George Moore didn't have his eye on just another car dealership in Washington, D.C. It had to be the biggest, best and most prestigious. It was as if each of the friends' ambitions stoked each other's fire. In 1948, George realized his ambition in a handsome new building at 4400 Connecticut Avenue, with some 14,500 square feet of floor space. He made sure it was the flashiest-looking automobile showroom in Washington. A modern glass-and-concrete structure, with a stone wall that curved round the front, it won an architectural award for its smart design.

Right from the beginning, the cars raced out of the showroom. You couldn't fail in postwar America. Crammed inside the pages of *Life* magazine were ads for Old Gold cigarettes, Norge electric ranges, Maytag washers, and cars, plentiful ads for cars: Packards, Studebakers, Fords, Mercurys, Buicks and Chevrolets. Corporate America hardly needed to advertise for customers. They came in droves to the car lots. They lined up and were put on waiting lists for new cars. The demand for cars, built up and unsatisfied during the war, far outstripped the supply. George found that he didn't have to sell cars so much as deliver them. Ford couldn't make them fast enough. It arranged a priority system where doctors, nurses, public health officials and rural mail carriers got their cars before anyone else.

Abuses were endemic. Immediately after the war, Ford's recommended resale prices were well below what buyers were willing to pay for a car because of the pentup demand. When a customer drove off the lot with his new car, he often would get no further than the first stop light before someone would drive up and offer to take the car off his hands at a hefty premium over the price he had paid for it. The situation led to widespread "bootlegging" in which dealers would quickly turn over their new cars to their own used-car lots where they could more easily be sold at higher prices. Within days after the 1949 Ford was introduced, the cars showed up on used-car lots at premiums averaging more than $1,100. New car models sometimes were in the bootleg market even before there was sufficient production to supply dealers with showroom models. Ford canceled the franchises of twenty-four dealers because of "gray-market" transactions in the first three years after the end of the war.

Price packing, the practice of adding costs to the manufacturer's suggested retail price, was another popular practice. Dealers could tack on all sorts of additional charges to raise the price of the car. It wasn't until 1958 that Congress forced companies to place the now-ubiquitous label of all charges on the window glass of each new car.

If anything, George sorely wanted to change that. He sought to carve out a different image. He ran radio ads with the slogan, "Honesty is the best policy"—something that only angered his competitors in Washington because the ads obviously implied they weren't honest. While some of his Washington competitors were hauled into a Congressional hearing room and accused of wrongdoing, George was out suggesting that people buy the 1949 Lincoln Cosmopolitan as a "fabulous Christmas gift for a fortunate few." Drafting the advertising copy himself, he wrote about his ability to present the car on Christmas Day "delivered gift wrapped in glittering crystal cellophane, crisscrossed with a wide red sash, culminating in a beautiful bow."

Before George constructed his enormous showroom, he had set up shop as Moore-Day Motors in mid-June of 1947, converting an old service station on 6503 Georgia Avenue into a Lincoln-Mercury dealership. From the start, it was to be a temporary location until he and his partner Mark Day could build a more lavish home for the business. He sealed up the pumps, erected a canopy outside the small building and had it glassed-in for a display room. For his service department, he had hired a couple of mechanics and lubrication men, a porter and some office help.

He and Day had capitalized the business at $250,000, most of it Day's cash though even Tex's mother bought thirty-five shares of stock with cash she scrapped together from old homes she and her husband rehabilitated and sold. More importantly, though, it showed that the entanglements among the men were getting deeper and more complex, extending to Thornton's mother back in Texas.

When George sent his first progress report to Tex in June, he joked: "This seems of particular importance since your mother by now is probably fully convinced that her money is down the drain." But George was not only concerned about Tex's mother, he was concerned about Tex's opinion. He didn't want to fail either Thornton or the group. Tex's mother had a 5 percent stake in his firm. George's dad sunk enough money into the dealership to own 9 percent of it. The rest was divided equally between George and Day.

George was following Tex's lead, modeling himself slavishly on his friend and mentor. He sought to surround himself with bright, ambitious, young people—tapping into the same talent pool of Stat Control refugees, including Lynn Bartlett, a wartime buddy he had met at Keesler Field in Biloxi, and Myles Mace, the Harvard B-school instructor. Mace joined a small board of directors George formed for the partnership. Mace was one of the few men who originally turned Tex down, preferring to go back to Harvard where he had written his doctoral dissertation on boards of directors of small companies. But even this new team wouldn't be able to save him from disaster.

No ONE SAW it coming, least of all George. The postwar seller's market didn't last as long as everyone predicted. The automakers had reconverted their plants, pushed new cars out of them so quickly that by early 1949, Ford was publicly declaring the situation a buyer's market. Publicity generated by Congressional hearings into the greedy practices of dealers didn't help much either. "Detroit Iron," as dealers called the used cars they seized as trade-ins, was scattered all over the lots.

George was caught up in the bad news—though most of his troubles were self-inflicted. By late May, 1949, his dealership was in severe trouble, and he was appearing less and less the Whiz Kid many assumed he was. He was a great promoter, a flatterer and cajoler—and willing to spread the wealth this brought him. James R. Grear, a Stat Control buddy, had noticed this during the war. "He was a born salesman, charming and personable," says Grear. "But he was not cerebral, not a statistical-type person."

So when George needed someone handy with numbers he thought of Grear. He had moved to Chicago to work for the treasurer of a pots and pans company. But George told him he would pay his airplane ticket to Washington and back, and while he was in town he talked him into a job as the accountant for Moore-Day. The day Grear arrived for work he found a month's worth of paperwork piled on the desk. Already the finances were a mess.

Moore and Day routinely spent money on advertising that they could hardly afford. Both partners often wrote company checks for personal matters. Day had a maid on the company payroll. Grear eventually decided to take the company checkbook home every night so neither Moore nor Day could draw down the dealership's account without his knowledge. "That's the only way I can keep control," he told George who did not disagree with him. "You guys are doing a lot of stupid things."

Poring over the company's balance sheets and operating statements, he found to his dismay that the dealership was insolvent and close to bankruptcy. Grear borrowed $15,000 from his mother and put it in the business to keep it afloat. George had a hefty $4,000 weekly payroll to meet with only a few hundred dollars in the bank. His bankers were getting the jitters. Myles Mace, one of his directors, even offered him $5,000 of his own savings to help him out of the crisis, but George refused.

Finally he called together all his forty employees in the showroom. George delivered the bad news to them.

"Look," he bravely said, "I'm going to level with you. My accountant here, Jim Grear, told me this morning that it's doubtful we can make payroll this Friday. We're broke. Jim and I are flying out to Detroit today to see if Ford can help us through this. But I wouldn't blame any of you if you walked out today. If you're still here when we get back, thank you."

It was an extraordinary little speech. Most car dealers would have issued the checks and allowed them to bounce. They certainly wouldn't have called together the salesmen and mechanics to fess up to the fact that they were nearly bankrupt. But that wasn't George's way. He was honest, even if he was also less than competent to manage a small business.

DISHEARTENED, HE FLEW to Detroit, conceded to the company that he wasn't cutting it and intended to give the agency back to Ford. He had a long talk with Jack about his troubles, and Jack urged George to rejoin Ford again and work alongside him with Crusoe. George wasn't so sure. But on the same trip, he also met James K. Dobbs, one of the first mega-dealers who was there to address a group of Ford dealers. Jimmy was a dynamic southerner, a multi-millionaire auto dealer partial to loud ties and floppy hats. With a long-time business partner, he owned Hull-Dobbs Company in Memphis, then advertised as the "world's largest Ford dealer" with branches spread over thirty-five cities.

Over dinner at the Detroit Athletic Club, George bared his soul. Dobbs listened intently across the table to the man who was more than twenty years younger than him. The more he heard, the more he became intrigued, so much so that he volunteered to help George out. It was the same attraction that had cemented George's friendship with Tex: George was the kind of guy who attracted not just any help, but the help of smart and successful people. Maybe it was because George was a master at showing gratitude. Anyone who helped him out could easily see the difference he made in George's life. Whatever you did for George, however big or small, you could feel you were saving him.

"I'll tell you what I'll do," Dobbs told George. "I'll come down to Washington tomorrow and if you promise to do everything I tell you to do, I will show you how to run an auto agency."

The next day he accompanied George back home and began to coach him through the business. Dobbs, who his partner noted "could charm the buttons off your coat," stormed into George's dealership like a hurricane. He interviewed every person in the dealership, redefining each man's role in the company. He slashed overhead and put everyone left into sales, including Bartlett who ran the tire department. Dobbs's idea was to push as many cars as possible off the lot. It didn't make a difference if you sold a car for a profit of $13 or for a profit of $230, he said. Just keep the cars moving, keep the inventory turning over.

George had run the dealership as if it were a drugstore where a bottle of shampoo sold for 59 cents. If you wanted it, you paid the money. If not, you walked out. Dobbs coaxed George's salesmen into trading and dickering. A car that sits on the lot unsold costs a dealer money—the interest charges on the debt incurred to buy the inventory. He preached that you should never allow a trade-in to sit on the lot for more than ten days. In the 1940s, Dobbs's beliefs were heresy. Dealers seldom negotiated, preferring to quote a fixed price and preserve their profits, even if it meant a car would hang around the lot a little longer.

Above all, you were to treat the customer with respect. There were all sorts of games dealers would play. Some would take the customer's keys to appraise the trade-in value of his car, preventing a customer from shopping around. George adhered to Dobbs's ideas without deviation. Some nights, George would keep the place open all evening long to sell cars. People would pass by, see the lot ablaze in lights with some thirty salesmen hustling all over the place. They'd stop and come in out of curiosity. George would man the sales desk from 8 a.m., okaying the sales his men would bring in and running the parts and service department. These were new sales tactics for their time and they worked magic.

Within a few months, George had the business straightened out. So thankful was he to Dobbs that he arranged for a new Mercury convertible to be delivered to him as a surprise on Christmas Eve morning in 1949. The car was parked in the front of his home, a huge red ribbon neatly tied in a bow around it—just as George had advertised it a year earlier. Dobbs seemed to derive as much happiness as George in the turnaround. "The thing that thrills me more than anything else on earth is the wonderful job you are doing in Washington," he wrote him. "No one, not even your own father, gets any more kick out of seeing you make a monkey out of all of your competitors than I do."

The business took off. George opened another dealership, Yonkers Ford, in Yonkers, New York, and that started his expansion. He sponsored an extravagant testimonial dinner for Dobbs at the Mayflower

Hotel in Washington, flying in his key people from New York for the celebration. Dobbs had never even charged George a consulting fee for all his help. George gave a speech in his honor, handed him a bronze plaque and it all brought tears to the man's eyes. Each year, George would sponsor a big dealer meeting, often getting some of Ford's top officials to attend the event, including his old friend Bob McNamara.

George's ambitions to become a big dealer outgrew his partner Day, who disliked all the travel involved in managing so many dealerships. So Grear, George's accountant, became his primary partner in the business, and Moore-Day Motors became Moore-Grear Motors, still expanding and growing to new areas of the country. By 1953, the partnership earned pretax income of $89,000, or nearly half a million in 1993 dollars, by 1954 it earned over $100,000, and by 1955 the company took in $210,000—now worth $1.1 million. He owned dealerships or had management contracts with some twenty dealers in Connecticut, New York, Maryland, Massachusetts, Michigan, Missouri, Ohio and Pennsylvania. If he didn't own a dealership outright, he often was the major investor and installed one of his own men as general manager. In some cases, he signed management contracts under which George spread the Dobbs system as a consultant in exchange for 40 percent of a dealer's net profit.

OVER THIS EXPANDING empire, George played the role of his hero Tex Thornton, cultivating a network of followers and friends. The people who worked for George revered him. Certain people he made his projects. Philip Fitts was an eighth-grade dropout and an excellent mechanic. George was going to prove that he could make him an educated, successful gentleman. He moved him up in the dealership, training him, nurturing him, cultivating him so that one day he could take over his own show which he did very successfully to George's delight.

George knew what he wanted out of life. He told Mimi he wanted to be independently wealthy, to have several dealerships and to play golf and travel, to make people care more about him. If that is all George really wanted, his business seems to have delivered it to him by the mid-1950s.

George and Mimi moved out of the Park Fairfax apartment after only a few months and into a pretty home in Sumner, Maryland, a Washington suburb. The real estate developer called the place "Mr. Blandings' Dream House" after the famous Cary Grant movie of 1948, and George immediately embraced it as a private Shangri-La for Mimi and him. It was a small colonial on a corner lot modeled after the house in the movie. A couple of years later, they moved to a handsome home on a shady street in Washington at 5100 Lowell Lane. It was a beautiful house built in the 1930s, a white brick colonial with grand white pillars, and a strong, twisting oak tree right outside the front door. A small balcony was set just above the entrance. Every weekend, his children remembered, George would pull into the circular driveway with a brand new, highly polished car.

George not only lived in a dream house, he seemed to live in a dream. His thriving business provided him with the luxury to give generously to friends—generous to a fault. It was part of his nature, even when he was struggling in the early days. As soon as Grear joined his troubled dealership in 1949, George gave him a membership at the Congressional Country Club. The first time that Grear broke par on the golf course, George bought him a sterling silver platter engraved with Grear's scorecard. One day in 1950 Grear was surprised to see that the huge sign over the dealership had changed from Moore-Day to Moore-Grear. Not long after Day's departure, George made Grear his partner without a trace of a hint that it was coming.

One close companion, a frequent luncheon partner of George's, recalls the routine of flipping a coin for the check at such lavish restaurants as La Salle DuBois and Rîve Gauche. He won ten times in a row, but George didn't hesitate to pick up the tab. He would shower highly expensive gifts on his companions, dispatching new cars to his doctor, his minister, other friends and relatives. One morning Tex woke up to find in his driveway a new woody-look Ford Country Squire station wagon, wrapped up in a bow just like the one George had given Dobbs. Years later, Tex's sons would recall the gift and the excitement it stirred in the house on Christmas Eve day. It was George's thank you to Tex for all his years of friendship and advice. Tex was taken aback by the gift, immediately calling George on the telephone to convey his thanks and tell him he shouldn't have done it.

But that was George. Yet if his gifts seemed generous to a fault at first, they also seemed troubling, a way for George to buy good will, loyalty or friendship. It was as if George was determined to play Tex's role in life, without really understanding what Tex had done. George wanted his own group. He would invite friends on extravagant cruises and trips to foreign locales. He'd give them expensive jewelry and glass. It would end up embarrassing some of them because they felt awkward at not being able to reciprocate his generosity. One time he gave a set of sterling silver candlesticks to one of his best friends, Eugene M. Zuckert, who had taught at the Stat Control school at Harvard.

"George, it's beautiful," Zuckert told him after opening the Christmas gift. "But I wish you wouldn't give those gifts because we can't afford to give you anything similar in return."

George would open the bottle of booze Zuckert gave him and shrug the remark away. He never expected grandiose gifts in return. That would blunt the edge of his own excesses. So he continued to be embarrassingly generous, despite protestations from Mimi and friends. On Christmas Eve, he would go down to Erlbacher's and Camalier & Buckley, two of the priciest stores in Washington, to do his last-minute shopping. They would greet him at the door by name, waiting for his arrival because they knew he would walk out with a pile of beautifully wrapped gifts in his arms.

He'd buy dozens of small gifts at a time, stacking them in separate piles near the front door in case an acquaintance or business associate should pay a Christmas visit. The presents would be arranged in piles for men, women and children. Inside the boxes were expensive leather gloves, silk neckties, small leather purses and briefcases. "He lived like a millionaire, even though he never was one," recalls Grear.

The most extravagant presents, of course, were reserved for Mimi. He gave her the most beautiful jewelry he could buy, often designing pieces himself and then getting them made with sapphires and diamonds. George adored her, providing the lifestyle he promised in his letters during the war, treating her like a queen. When Mimi became pregnant with their third child, Jennifer, and the family moved into Lowell Lane, he insisted that she not lift a finger in the move. He arranged for moving men to pack everything, from the china to the books. And when they arrived at Lowell Lane, the movers served her tea and then unpacked everything, even hanging their clothes in the closets. "She was treated like a doll carried around on a pillow," says Virginia Peyton Unger, her sister.

George loved to pamper Mimi, outfitting her in beautiful clothes and furs. All done up for a party, she resembled actress Hedy Lamarr. It was a good relationship because she fitted the role George cast for her, both as a glamorous wife and as a good mother. He insisted that she always dress fashionably as if, recalled a friend, "she had stepped out of a bandbox." She fit the role as effortlessly as she slipped into a size six dress.

They traveled to Europe and South America, cruised the Atlantic and the Mediterranean, and gambled in Havana where George lost a good deal of money but didn't seem to mind. He loved to travel by sea, eating off fine china and crystal set on white linen tablecloths. They traveled to the south of France to see Picasso and buy a couple of his ceramic pieces; they went to fashionable French restaurants where the gypsy violinists strolled to the table to serenade him and Mimi with Smenna's "La Mer." In the summers, they would bring their children to the Homestead in Hot Springs, Va., where white-haired Negroes would do a tray dance and guests tossed coins at their feet.

George spoke of his marriage as a partnership: he provided the financial support, working outside the home; she added the emotional support, working the inside, tending to the children and to him. She was devoted to him. After the arrival of Marika in Dearborn, she gave birth to three more children in Washington: Douglas, Jennifer and Laura, the youngest born in 1953. Joyous over Laura's birth, George had left Mimi at the hospital and stumbled up to old Stat Control friend Zuckert to tell him the good news. George was smashed, having begun the celebration with a few martinis before meeting Zuckert, an indulgence that was becoming more of a habit. They sat and drank some more, debating what to name George's newborn girl. Sinatra's hauntingly smooth "Laura," the Johnny Mercer lyric, had been playing in Zuckert's mind for some reason. By coincidence, the tune flew out of the radio and Laura she became.

George loved the good life. He liked to live it completely, to enjoy it, to luxuriate whenever possible in fashionable places with important people. There were many parties and much entertaining. People were always coming and going through their home, gathering for dinner and drinks and fun. From Bob, George got the idea to put together a group of people who would meet every month to discuss the great books. He was a well-read man with eclectic tastes, enjoying the classics as much as a book on sports.

He assembled a core of good friends—Zuckert, Day, Grear and Jim Sharp, his attorney, and they would do everything together with George as the group's leader. Whatever George did, the rest of them did, too, going on vacation at the Homestead and at Virginia Beach. One time George decided to sign up for an expensive series of dancing lessons at Arthur Murray. So everyone signed on for weeks and weeks of lessons, learning to dance the conga, the rumba and the jitterbug. When it was all over, the only person who couldn't dance was George. He had no sense of rhythm.

Like the five-star general in the White House, President Eisenhower,

George relished a few rounds of golf and a game of bridge. He played the course at the Congressional Country Club in Bethesda, Maryland, often cursing about its 465-yard, par-four, eighteenth hole. After that, he would gladly retire with Zuckert or another friend to the grill room and the bar for a spate of drinks and a game of gin rummy. On a hot summer afternoon, George could go off and play thirty-six holes in a row.

Underneath the movie-like life in the dream house, however, George was vulnerable, never really sure of himself. That may have been the real reason he left the group in Detroit and returned to Washington, why he moved into Mr. Blandings' Dream House, and why he surrounded himself with people he knew and could trust. He was, in some odd way, the extreme part of the group, the member who still couldn't quite stand on his own. In Cary Grant's screwball comedy, Mr. Blandings quickly discovered that his fantasy and reality had come into conflict. George Moore would soon make the same discovery.

Sent to France to turn around Ford's operations there, Jack Reith ultimately returned a hero with a medal awarded to him by the French government. Here Reith is in Paris, giving a speech to Ford dealers.

AN
AMERICAN IN
PARIS

■

"Know your opportunity."
—PITTACUS

*J*ack Reith had waited years for his big break, and Lewis Crusoe was about to hand it to him.

Jack was vacationing on Sea Island, one of Georgia's barrier islands, a place where you felt protected from life's intrusions and nuisances. He had just slipped a driver out of his golf bag and was getting ready to tee off on the 414-yard seaside seventh when he spotted a young man making a mad dash toward him in a covered golf cart.

"Mr. Reith," the man called, "there's an urgent call for you." He rushed back to the clubhouse.

"Mr. Crusoe?" Jack tentatively said into the receiver.

"Have you ever been to Paris?" Crusoe asked, not waiting for Jack's reply. "I want you there as soon as possible."

"Why the rush?"

Crusoe explained that Henry and Breech, now in Paris, were appalled at the terrible state of the company's French subsidiary. They wanted someone to look over the state of the business and come up with a plan to get rid of the headache. Henry did not trust the French nor did he believe that Ford had the resources to feed all three of its European children: subsidiaries in England, France and Germany. "I will double the bonus of any son-of-a-bitch who gets me out of France," he said.

"Do you have a passport?" asked Crusoe.

Jack had never been abroad in his life. He didn't have a passport nor a clue as to what to expect. Crusoe said he would make the arrangements, and then asked to speak to Maxine. He apologized for disturbing them while on vacation.

"Look," said Crusoe, "since you've only been there for three days, we'll let you go along to Paris, too. Do you have a passport?"

She didn't even have a birth certificate. She was born in a tiny Oklahoma town delivered by her physician father who had never gotten around to getting the proper documents.

"Well, be in Washington by tomorrow, and we'll make sure you get your passports."

They raced back to the hotel to repack their bags and book a flight to Washington. Maxine wouldn't fly with Jack, fearful that if the plane ever crashed their two children would be without both parents. So he flew out in the morning, and she caught a flight later that night. She was too naive to know that Henry and Breech really wanted to look her over, too, to see whether she could cut it with Jack in Paris. Ford needed a gracious hostess as well as a consummate turnaround artist. The company would not be disappointed.

JACK QUICKLY DISCOVERED that Lehideux, a nephew of the carmaker Renault had had extensive experience in the automobile business, exercising control over the entire French motor vehicle industry during the German occupation. But he scorned any advice from Americans, feeling that he could run the company alone.

Renault, Citroen and Simca shot ahead in production and sales, while Ford SAF made no progress. The company introduced a good-looking car, the Vedette, in 1948, but it was far too expensive for the average Frenchman and it suffered from poor quality. The volume market and profits both lay in the small-car field, and in that area Ford of France had no entry.

By late 1952 things had deteriorated so badly that unless Henry and Breech were willing to guarantee loans, their French firm would go into bankruptcy or receivership. Ford made the concession, but it was obvious something would have to give. The factory was stuck with a three-month supply of unsold cars. Breech told Jack that he had offered to give the operation away for $1 to anyone who would assume its assets and liabilities. They knew the liabilities far exceeded the assets. All Henry wanted back were the Ford patents, trademarks and brand names. But all the major French automakers had turned the offer down. It looked like an impossible job to make something of it.

It seemed even more impossible for Jack who didn't know a word of French. Reith stayed for six weeks, combing through every detail of the operation, meeting with Lehideux, his key managers and major dealers. Ed Lundy sent over one of his finance men, Val Menger—another Stat Control officer recruited to Ford by the group—to get the books in order. The sight of the humorless though brilliant Menger poring over the financial records gave the French a chill. *"L'oiseau de mort,"* The Death Bird, they called him.

Jack returned to Dearborn in early December of 1952 to present the Ford's Executive Committee with its options. Decades later, his performance would still be remembered as a thing of beauty, the finest, most perfectly constructed presentation that Alan Gornick, the company's tax counsel, had ever seen in his sixteen years at Ford. Jack brilliantly laid out the situation, with charts, figures and pictures, keeping up a steady discourse without either a hint of optimism or gloom. He was smooth, objective, never betraying his personal preferences. Can Ford-France be saved? The answer, he said, is yes, it *probably* can, but here is what it will take. Can it be sold? Again the answer was *probably,* though no one was eager to buy it, not even the management of the company who had been offered the chance. The committee told Jack it would study the matter and that in the meantime he should return to France to work on bringing out a sorely needed new, more promising car.

He was in Dearborn for only three days, hustling through meetings with Crusoe and Breech, helping Maxine pack up for the move abroad. To return to France, he had assembled a team of three key men: Richard Hanel and William Grimes, two Stat Control alums whom Jack had lured to Ford and one cost accountant. All were American, and not one could speak a word of French. Jacques Maroni, a young financial analyst decided to use this linguistic opening. Maroni arranged to squeeze onto Jack's calendar for what he promised a secretary would be only one minute. He walked into Jack's office with an outstretched hand and a smile.

"Congratulations on your appointment," he said. "My only regret is that you've made a grievous error before even reaching your new post."

"What are you talking about?" Jack said. "Is this your way of wishing me well?"

"I know you have a tough assignment," Maroni said. "I hear you've already chosen your aides, but you still don't have the key assistant you really need: a young, unmarried engineer from MIT with a Harvard MBA, totally fluent in French and English and trained in the way Ford does things."

There was a moment of silence. Jack flashed a wide grin.

"I suppose you're here to help me find him?" he laughed.

"That's right. I'll be waiting for your call. Good luck in France."

Maroni shook Jack's hand and walked out, thanking the secretary on his way and saying, "I didn't use up the full minute, did I?" In the outer office, five other people were waiting to see Jack, who planned to fly back to Paris the next day. A few weeks later, Maroni was told to report to his native France, the country he fled in 1940 as the Nazis rolled in. Jack requested him for his team. It was just the kind of gutsy approach that Tex had taught them all to respect, and it made Jack take an immediate liking to Maroni.

WHILE JACK STRUGGLED with problems at work, Maxine dealt with the problems of putting together a home before she would have to enter the hospital to have her third baby. They moved into what Jack called "the ugliest house in Paris." It was a tall and narrow nineteenth century building of stone, concrete and stucco, three stories high, the kind of house that Charles Adams would have sketched for *The New Yorker*. But it was a home they could immediately move into.

Ford of France was hardly thrilled to see Jack again. The French operations had never had an American at the helm, and Jack was there to seize control from Francois Lehideux. A former minister of the Vichy government, Lehideux had surrounded himself with others like him who had collaborated with the Germans during their occupation of France. The leaders of the Communist-led union known as *La Confédération Générale du Travail* had in earlier years sabotaged production, captured and held hostage the plant's general manager, and refused to do anything that would increase the factory's productivity. Leaflets littered the factory grounds about the new *Monsieur Americain* and his family from Dearborn. Jack asked Maxine to keep the gas tank of their car filled to the brim constantly lest they need to make a quick getaway.

Politically, the 1950s were an unstable time for France. Before the reascendancy of de Gaulle, governments rose and fell with the swiftness of a souffle and with about as much substance, as songwriter Alan Jay Lerner aptly put it. French currency had about the same consistency, causing Henry's reluctance to invest dollars into the operation. Somehow, to get the business back in the black, Jack and his men would have to convince the French banks to loan them money.

Car sales were held back by a government anti-inflation program, thus limiting Jack's efforts to increase revenue. To become profitable, he had to drastically cut costs. He imposed a minimum 10 percent cutback in every department of the company. Then he went through a review of every part in each car, deciding whether it could be replaced by a less expensive item or could be eliminated. If neither was possible, Jack would attempt to renegotiate the purchase price with the company's outside suppliers.

It was a long, torturous process. Each manager was called to Jack's corner office on the second floor of the headquarters for a bilingual review of each item in his budget. Maroni would grope to translate Jack's American expressions into French. "Tell him he's way out in left field," Jack would say. A befuddled Maroni would wonder what to say in French. As Jack questioned the expenses, some men argued and fought back. Some broke down and cried. Some actually cheered, knowing that the business would finally benefit from strong leadership.

Many, however, were still loyal to Lehideux and engaged in either passive resistance or open hostility. When Jack told the controller to start clamping down on travel expenses, he was met with a smirk and an excuse.

"Ahh, monsieur, this is a bad season for travel expenses. Lovely weather. Flowers. Clamping down in the spring is very difficult."

"Do it!" barked Jack.

The man turned to Maroni and in French told him: "When the Americans wanted to destroy the bridge at Monte, they sent a hundred B-24s on Monday, a hundred more on Tuesday and a hundred more on Wednesday. They destroyed the whole town to get the bridge. You have to be more careful this time."

But Jack didn't have the resources or the patience to be careful. He had to act. Lehideux's top managers would have five-course luncheons in the company's elegant dining room. They were leisurely affairs, lasting as long as three hours. Not wanting to alienate the managers too quickly, Jack tried to overcome the midday break by asking the men to bring along this or that report so he could discuss it with them over lunch. It was unheard of. Lunch was the time to talk about leisure, women and wine, never work. Soon the men started scheduling appointments outside the office. They'd arrive at 9 a.m., leave at 11 for a "business appointment" in Paris and then disappear for the rest of the day.

Exasperated, Jack insisted upon their attendance, gradually cutting the lunch time down to an hour and focusing virtually all the talk on business. The men came to realize that Jack wasn't going to let them get away with it. If one of them didn't have an answer to his questions, Jack would demand he bring it with him to the next meeting.

IT WAS SOMETIMES difficult to figure out who posed a greater threat: Lehideux and his supporters or the Communist workers. When Jack met with the union leaders, they passed a motion of grief and condolences on the occasion of the death of Joseph Stalin. They had already arranged for the French flag to be flown at half-mast. Then they started to complain to Jack about the Marshall Plan. The union leaders demanded that Jack send a telegram to President Eisenhower urging him to free Ethel and Julius Rosenberg, the convicted atomic bomb spies.

Their union contract required, among other things, that the company supply red wine for the employees' cafeteria lunch to drink with their cold meats, cheese and bread. Jack, upset about the poor quality of the cars they produced, ordered that the wine be watered down. He put so much water in it, in fact, that labor leaders later made the quality of wine their main demand at the negotiating table. The Communist newspapers then began attacking Lehideux, whom they called a lackey of Hitler, and the "crooked American lawyers."

It became clear that Lehideux had to go. Jack discovered that Lehideux and his key aides had issued new cars without invoices to well over 100 dignitaries, friends, relatives and mistresses. He also had billed the company for what Jack believed were personal expenses, cocktail parties at his homes and trips abroad. The man signed contracts with other companies without getting the necessary approval of the board of directors. Going through the records, Jack calculated that Lehideux owed the company 9.5 million francs.

The company's board of directors, however, was stacked with Lehideux loyalists. To toss him out, Jack would have to engineer a shareholders' meeting where the parent company could vote its 54 percent stake against the current management. Lehideux, meantime, could appeal to the French shareholders. Rather than risk a nasty, public skirmish, Jack began to seize greater control of the place with Lehideux remaining in his job. As he did so, the Frenchman spent more and more time at home, until Jack got him to sign a letter of resignation on March 30. It was not an easy time. Lehideux considered all Americans vulgar. The American team, meantime, considered the highly-perfumed Frenchman pompous.

Soon after, the men would deal with their conflicts through attorneys and via a bitter correspondence. Jack told Lehideux he was going to debit him for a car to his son, another vehicle for his wife, the use of a Dodge truck, a tractor given to his doctor, a cash advance of two million francs, and on and on. Lehideux wrote back, arguing that some vehicles already were returned to the company and the advances were for company trips. Lehideux's letters were full of snide contempt. At one point, he even returned a cigarette lighter to Jack and groused about the quality of the Ford car. "Please find enclosed here a cigarette lighter that your company sent me without charge," he wrote with bitter humor. The bickering would go on for nearly a full year until Jack agreed to settle the dispute for five million francs.

Firmly in control, Jack sought to forge better working relationships with the company's managers and employees. Though it had been four months since he returned to France from Dearborn, he still hadn't been through the large factory. He decided to tour the plant, in part to show the flag. The French director of personnel, however, warned him against it.

"You must not go in the plant," he insisted in French. "It's not safe."

"What did you just say?" asked Maroni, before translating the warning to Jack.

"I said he must not go inside the plant because it isn't safe. You do know that Monsieur Lehideux had once been held prisoner by the union?"

"We can't follow your advice," Maroni said. "We're running this factory."

He translated the personnel director's words to Jack, who was shocked.

"We're going to go right in," Jack said. "We can't run this plant by staying out of it. We've got to know these people."

"Well, I cannot be held accountable for your safety," the director warned.

"We're not only going to walk through the plant," said Jack. "We're going to do it without any security personnel. Just the two of us. And if you want to come along, Monsieur Guiriec, why don't you?"

Jack and Maroni left the man's office and walked into the plant. The personnel director sheepishly trailed behind. They started to shake as they walked the plant floor, noticing the tremendous gulf between the plant's managers and its blue-coated workers, who stared with stern faces at their visitors. Maroni stepped up to the men and did the introductions.

"Bonjour, Monsieur. May I introduce you to Monsieur Reith, the new director general."

Some foremen backed away from Jack, unwilling to shake his hand or acknowledge him. But as they moved through the plant, people started to warm up to him. They were amazed that the new American boss would have the nerve to show his face inside the factory. The shock treatment was needed, demonstrating that the new American team intended to work with them.

It was a sizable plant, if nothing like the Rouge. The factory was the largest industrial complex along the River Seine, about a half-hour's drive from the center of Paris, built in the hopes of capturing a huge part of the European market. During the war, the factory was seized by the Germans to produce trucks for the eastern front. The sprawling factory was behind a three-story administration building, where Jack and his American team worked.

Jack assembled 180 senior managers to set the stage for more harmonious relations. He spoke in English, while Maroni repeated his words in French. "Many of you have worked here ten to fifteen years," Jack said. "You have a stake in the business. If I can't succeed, I can go back to the United States where a job is waiting for me. But if we work together as a team, we can solve our problems. You can carry out your plans of educating your children and providing a future for your families."

There was so much to do. Dealer morale was low. The bankers had to be convinced to ante up the money to help Jack get a new, more competitive car into the market. That car had to be engineered and styled, and the plant had to be retooled to put it into production. Quality had to be significantly improved. Managers and employees had to forge better working relationships.

A month after Jack toured the factory, the Communist labor union decided to test the American team. All work came to a halt for one hour when the delegates marched into the headquarters building with a list of demands. The next day, the work stoppage virtually shut the plant down. Jack posted notices on the bulletin boards: "No further discussion until work is resumed." He cleverly added a sweetener, a bonus of three thousand francs per worker if the plant met its production targets until the August vacation period. Jack mailed letters containing the offer to the homes of the workers so that their wives might pressure them to accept the deal and end the walkout. It worked like a charm.

To get rid of old inventory, Jack came up with the idea of painting the Vedettes in two-tone colors—something unheard of before in Europe. When he informed the French sales staff of his plan, they reacted in horror. "Oh, my God!" one said. "You can't do that! They'll never sell here." Surprisingly, though, they sold well enough.

JACK REITH AND his men harbored many doubts about their ability to make Ford in France a big success. So many things had to fall in place. One evening, Maroni and Jack were having yet another late dinner at the plant in Poissy when Maroni spoke aloud about the possibility of failing.

"What are you going to do if it fails, Jack?" he asked.

"I'm in this for the long-term," he said.

"If this thing doesn't succeed, you're not going back to Ford, are you?"

"Don't worry," Reith replied. "If we succeed, we'll be golden. They'll take care of us."

Faith didn't make the pressure any more bearable. Jack would chew down the ends of pencils as if they were lollipops. He would spit out pieces of eraser and lead. Soon the shape of his teeth began to change.

One night, he joined Maroni and another colleague for dinner at the plant. It was late, around 9 p.m., and the men were tired. They often worked until 11 p.m. and had arranged for the executive dining room to remain open for late dinners. Jack that night at first seemed his usual friendly self, relaxed and cool when he sat down at the table. But what then came out of his mouth made no sense. His sentences were disjointed and disconnected, as if he had just come out of anesthesia. After he left, the men looked at each other in amazement, not knowing what to make of it. They had never witnessed this high-strung fragility in Reith.

Jack was capable of approaching a manic state. He could reach and sustain a high degree of optimism and self-confidence. Someone whose mood could swing so high is often also capable of hitting depressive lows. Yet, the peculiar conversation at dinner that night was the only time Maroni had seen something amiss in Jack. Energy and enthusiasm seemed to carry him through the difficulties.

SLOWLY SIGNS OF progress in the company appeared. Reith had driven expenses down and persuaded the workers to improve quality and productivity; work on the new Vedette was also proceeding well. Henry already was publicly singing Jack's praise when a *Time* magazine article quoted him as saying that Jack "will put Ford of France in the black if anybody can." In July, 1953, eight months after he took the job, Reith gave Henry wonderful news: Ford of France's stock on the Paris Bourse had climbed to well over 300 francs, from 228 when Lehideux had resigned only three months earlier. By pruning nearly 350 people from the payroll and cutting expenses, Jack was able to move Ford SAF into a profitable position for the first time in well over two years. He explained how the 1955 model they were working on would permit much lower production costs and a leap in profitability.

Henry was delighted. So were Crusoe and Breech. "We would still prefer to come out of France," Henry told Reith on his next trip back to Dearborn. "We need you back here for bigger things. And you should be able to do it if you continue to do what you're doing in France."

Arjay took Jack to the Dearborn Inn for a drink and brought him up to date on news about his Whiz Kid colleagues. Maroni trailed along. Arjay told Jack how everyone at Ford admired him for what he was accomplishing in France. Jack beamed.

Arjay had some good news about the other guys, too. In less than a month, he was going to take over Bob's job as controller of the corporation. Bob, in turn, was moving out of finance and into an operating role as assistant general manager of the Ford Division under Crusoe. All of them were moving up into key slots, making their mark.

But Jack had won hands down. To head up the foreign subsidiary of a large American company was a posh and prestigious job. Jack and Maxine had a cook, a maid and a chauffeur. Before their dinner parties with government ministers, company presidents, the ambassador, Ford would dispatch a man to the house to help Maxine select the proper wines. Yet as elegant as it all sounded, she would laugh at spending so much time settling fights among the servants, each one jealous of each other, accusing one another of a petty theft in the house.

From Dearborn, engineers and stylists flowed through Poissy and Jack's home. Henry would come with his entourage, too. A foreign posting seemed to draw people to your front door. George called from Washington and arranged to visit Jack and Maxine with Mimi. Jack looked forward to the visit from George, anxious to renew their friendship. He had told Maroni about George and how he was "selling cars like you can't believe."

George had business to discuss as well. He wanted to import American cars into France to sell mainly to the American troops still stationed there. Jack and George talked for hours about the possibility of a Paris dealership for George and eventually George opened up a dealership in Pasison Quaide Grenelle near the River Seine.

For Jack, there was the opportunity to meet heads of state. When the company introduced the Comet, a sports car, in Monte Carlo, Jack was told that Prince Ranier would consent to have him and Maxine as his guests. They arranged to sit down with him for tea at the palace, after which Ranier's majordomo escorted Maxine through the castle to show her the Prince's collection of Napoleonic antiques.

On their way out, Jack said, "Do you know what he wanted? He wanted me to replace his Lincoln for free."

Meantime, some small failures jeopardized Jack's fragile recovery at Poissy. But his men worked feverishly to hide them from Dearborn so the miraculous turnaround would retain its shimmering quality. There was the contract that Lehideux had signed with a French body building firm to build sports cars, unbeknownst to Dearborn. Trouble was, the only engine they could put under the hood was a four-cylinder job that made the car literally crawl up a hill. The unsold cars started piling up. Jack stuck eight-cylinder truck engines in them, despite the disapproval of Dearborn engineers who argued that the bodies weren't engineered for the heavier engines. The cars finally sold.

At one point, when Jack and Maxine went off to Morocco for a brief vacation, the French car market fell apart with alarming speed. The inventory of cars continued to build in Jack's absence, while Maroni argued for a cut in production and a cut in car prices before they ran out of cash. No one wanted to do anything until consulting with Jack, who was difficult to reach in Morocco. By the time he returned, two thousand unsold new cars had piled up outside the plant.

Somehow, they figured out a way to convert the cars into taxi cabs, getting rid of one thousand of them that way in exchange not for cash but for a factory and property on the north side of Paris. Maroni hired an industrial broker who sold the plant to Citroen for 275 million francs, leaving Ford with a profit on the taxi deal and resolving the company's cash crunch. Of course, the company's bylaws didn't permit Jack to sell cars for real estate without going back to Dearborn for approval. But there was also no way that Jack was going to rush back to explain to Henry or Breech how they overproduced the cars and were going to convert them into taxis! The cars were repainted black and ivory; modifications were made in the doors and braking systems, and a year later Ford taxis rumbled along the Paris boulevards.

Still, the recovery went forward. On the strength of Jack's 1955 pro-

gram to come out with a completely new Vedette, he was able to persuade the bankers to make available a $2.1 billion credit line. Jack and
Maroni met for a long, three-hour dinner one night to talk about the
next key step. Henry and Breech still wanted out of France, and it was
Jack's job to make it possible.

"We don't want to stay in France forever," Jack told him. "There are
much bigger opportunities waiting for us back home. Do you think we
could arrange a merger?"

"I don't know," Maroni replied.

As they began to chat about the possibilities, however, it became clear
that the most likely merger partner was Simca, a leading French car
company. Both Ford and Simca were too small to compete in the long
run, much smaller than Renault, Peugeot or Citroen. What Simca desperately needed was more scale, and a merger with Ford was an easy
way to get it. Jack had met H. T. Pigozzi, director of Simca, at a dinner
in honor of U.S. Ambassador James C. Dunn, and they began to talk
about the difficulty of competing with the larger companies due to the
constraints of their size. Pigozzi was an Italian-born scrapdealer who had
bootstrapped himself into making cars in France with the backing of
Fiat. He spoke French with an Italian accent but could hardly utter a
word of English.

Pigozzi again met with Jack, Maroni at his side as his interpreter.
Pigozzi suggested they consider some kind of joint deal, such as a
foundry that both companies could own. Jack played it like an astute
poker player. He wanted Pigozzi to feel threatened by Ford, so he spoke
enthusiastically about the new car they were developing, trying to seduce
Simca into making a move. After all, the car would pose new and more
severe competition to Simca—at least that is what Jack wanted Pigozzi
to think and fear.

"I'm not interested in a joint venture," he told Pigozzi. "Our first
priority is to increase volume and marketshare."

The bluff worked. Pigozzi, perceiving a threat to his market position,
suggested that Simca was not for sale. And he knew that little Simca
could not swallow big Ford. Simca, however, was twice as large as Ford
of France and four times as profitable. Jack was delighted to see
Pigozzi's mind so quickly focused on combining the two companies.

"You know," Jack said, "Simca is not so little and French Ford is not
so big. Besides, we're Americans and we'd like to go back to Michigan.
Maybe Simca could acquire Ford."

Pigozzi seemed pleased and indicated his desire to talk to his friends in Turin, Italy. Jack urged complete secrecy, saying he had no authority to negotiate the sale of his company. In fact, he bluffed, Henry Ford might be shocked at the idea of lowering the Ford flag in France.

The talks grew serious in mid-May. Henry shipped out of Dearborn three men, including Menger, to watch over the delicate negotiations. Fearful that public knowledge of the deal would play havoc with Ford stock, the negotiations were conducted in great secrecy. They posed as tourists, secretly holed up at the Trian de Palace, the large ornate hotel at Versailles where Eisenhower had maintained his headquarters after beating back the Germans. When the Ford men wanted to communicate with Jack, they would call Maxine at the house and ask her to have Jack get in touch with them. After days of bleary-eyed discussions, Jack dubbed the negotiations with Simca, "Operation Martini." In the midst of the negotiations in June, Henry came to France to meet with Jack and congratulate him on his success in France. Assuming everything went well with the merger, Henry told him he would be coming back to Dearborn to head an operating division. He wasn't yet sure what it might be but told Jack that it was probably either international or Lincoln plus an exciting new car line that Henry called Edsel. It was the first time Reith heard the name.

The two sides were still far apart on the valuation of the two companies. Initially, Pigozzi had offered to buy Ford SAF for 200,000 shares of Simca stock. By the end of June, he had doubled his offer. When a last-minute hitch developed, Jack stood up, shoved his desk drawer shut and said: "Gentlemen, I give you the reason the French lost the war in three days." He turned and walked out of the room. It was audacious and dramatic, but Simca came around and the deal was consummated. Simca agreed to up the ante to 455,713 shares. Now they were all dead on their feet, but they had to call board meetings, sign documents, draft press releases, meet with employees, communicate with dealers and bankers. Big headlines splashed across the French newspapers. Big mergers were hardly what they would someday become. This was dramatic news. The final merger agreements were signed on August 27—a little more than a month before the debut of the new Vedette.

Once the deal was set, it was one climax after another for Jack and his American team. Simca rented the Eiffel Tower to stage a lavish party for business leaders, government ministers, embassy officials, actors and artists. It was the event of the fall, attended by some 3,500 people. Then came the debut of the new Vedette at the Paris Auto Show, complete with costumed horn players with authentic hunting horns. Jack was the featured speaker at an American Club luncheon. There were glowing profiles of him in the French press. Back in Detroit, the *Free Press* glowingly told the story under the headline: "Ford of France Stages Production Miracle." Reith dazzled Henry, Breech and Crusoe by delivering in French a speech to the Ford dealers who sponsored an enormous going-away banquet for Jack.

Indeed, the dealers, ecstatic about getting a car they could actually sell, had grown so fond of him that a representative called Maxine wanting her suggestion for a possible gift.

"Well," she said, "he needs a new golf bag."

"Oh no, no, Madame, we had something much bigger in mind than this."

"We could use a nice silver coffee service," she suggested.

In the end, at a lavish banquet for Jack, they presented him with a massive Louis Quatorze desk, a baroque dark-wooded antique, as well as an ornate mantel clock. But of all the events that closed out the most successful stage of his life, none could top the Legion of Honor that the government agreed to bestow on Jack.

The honor had originally been created by Napoleon to reward French citizens, primarily those who fought in Napoleon's campaigns. Over the years, however, it evolved into a prestigious accolade to recognize great accomplishments in the arts, business and politics. The government was told about Jack's efforts in Poissy—how he had arrived from America, saved the business and many jobs.

At an opulent luncheon in an elegant restaurant, Jack was presented the medal with all of the appropriate pomp and circumstance. After stringing it around Jack's neck, the country's Minister of Commerce gently kissed Jack's right and left cheeks, and Jack went home to Dearborn a hero with a medal to prove it.

THE
WHIZ
KIDS

In 1955, the Whiz Kids finally gained firm control of Ford: three became vice presidents and general managers, heading up the largest parts of the company: Ford, Mercury, and Lincoln. Another became corporate controller, and yet another was made a member of the Administration Committee—the politburo of Ford. At a party celebrating the batch of promotions, the friends hold a mock press conference complete with a boom mike. (Left to right are Ben Mills, Jack Reith, Bob McNamara, and Jim Wright.)

Bob and Margy McNamara. At the celebratory party, Margy dressed up in a French maid's outfit.

In 1959, Bob McNamara made the cover of *Business Week* in a story that detailed the achievements of the Whiz Kids. Under the headline, "Ford Hands the Wheel to Youth," the article outlined the group's rise to power. Precise, efficient and coldly serious, McNamara assumed the role as the prototype of the modern manager. He poses, rather awkwardly, outside Ford's new corporate headquarters' building, with the car next to him little more than a publicity prop.

Chapter 15

"GARY COOPER ON WHEELS"

■

"Logic never attracts men to the point of carrying them away."

—Alexis Carrel

The returning hero hardly savored his accomplishments before gambling on an ambitious new scheme. He set out to lead Ford's frontal attack on General Motors—a battle the dimensions of which Ford had never before taken on.

This was the time for head-to-head combat. In the mid-1950s, the auto industry was racing at high speeds. Henry's revamped Ford Motor Company had become a triumph of man and machine, the proof of what financial and managerial brilliance could achieve. The Whiz Kids and their allies had helped to organize chaos and to bring the power of measurement to business. Ford boasted the best financial controls in all of American business and the unsurpassed talent to watch over every penny of its wealth. Its lineup of cars beckoned unprecedented hordes of buyers.

The troubled company they had joined in 1946 was now a citadel of strength, the third largest industrial enterprise in the country after General Motors and Standard Oil of New Jersey. Since the day they walked through the Rouge gates, Ford's net worth had more than doubled to $1.8 billion and its assets had tripled to $2.6 billion. Profit before taxes hit a record $986 million in 1955, nearly double the previous year's $511 million total and more than triple the $289 million earned in 1952. Payroll alone was more than a billion dollars a year.

Yet, Ford still played second fiddle to bigger, stronger GM. For years, Henry wanted to redeem his grandfather and retake the industry lead GM had captured from him in the 1930s. Crusoe, feeling ever more confident over the company's fortune, wanted to extract a measure of revenge on his old employer, too. As Ford grew stronger, the competition with its larger rival had become fierce.

With the 1954 model year, Ford had just achieved its biggest postwar production, nearly overtaking GM's Chevy. Indeed, many at Ford felt they had beaten their nemesis, that GM cheated them. On the last day of the year, they were tipped off that there would be a flood of fictitious car registrations filed with the Secretary of State's office in Springfield, Ill. It would be just enough to put GM over the top again, to allow them to maintain their claim that Chevy was number one.

When the final numbers came in, they showed that a swing of less than 9,000 cars to Ford would have allowed Crusoe to declare the company's first victory over Chevy since 1935. Ford churned out 1,400,000 units to Chevy's 1,417,453. Crusoe didn't want to believe the story, couldn't believe that his alma mater would do that to him so he didn't touch it. Besides, there was enough to go around and Ford was well on its way to its most successful year in history, with sales, production and profits likely to reach all-time highs in 1955. But the story, whether true or not, underlined the no-holds-barred rivalry that existed between the two companies.

Increasingly, the battle cry became "Beat GM." Crusoe realized that Reith, full of ambition and fearless, was Ford's answer. Of all the Whiz Kids, Reith was never one of the naysayers. When he worked for Crusoe, he often made the case for bolder investments in new plant and equipment against his more cautious colleagues in finance. Reith had certainly proven himself in France. Who better to help develop and push through a risky plan to overtake GM for good?

BLACK AND WHITE images floated across the room from a bulky mahogany box in the corner. On the midget TV screen, Gale Sondergaard was

successfully outwitting Basil Rathbone in _Sherlock Holmes and the Spider
Woman._ A bound-and-gagged Sherlock Holmes had been lured behind
an image of Hitler in an arcade shooting gallery and was within seconds
of death. Jack was watching the mystery from an overstuffed sofa when
Maroni knocked on his door.

Jack had temporarily moved into this three-room suite in the Dearborn Inn until he could find a new home. Maxine and the children were
already asleep. Given the urgency of Jack's call, Maroni only thought it
appropriate to check in with him after his plane landed at Wayne-Major
Airport, even though it was near midnight.

"Hi Jacques," Jack intoned, "come on in."

The men shook hands, obviously pleased to see each other back in the
states.

"You look rested," Jacques said. "What's the big news? Why am I
here instead of enjoying my vacation?"

"Jacques, we're going to make a run at General Motors," he began.
"We're going to introduce a whole new set of divisions and a new car.
Ford can't compete with GM with only two car divisions. We've never
been able to beat them because their customers can buy a Chevy and then
upgrade to Pontiac, Buick, Oldsmobile and Cadillac without ever leaving
the GM family. The Ford buyer can only move up to Mercury. He has
no other choice. Can we change that? You bet. They have five divisions.
So can we. Ford, Lincoln, Mercury, Continental and a new one that
might be called Edsel."

Jack was pacing the room, clearly thrilled and excited by the huge risk
of the undertaking. His mind was reeling. He went on and on, piled
detail upon detail, as if rehearsing a presentation he might some day
make to the board of directors. Maroni had seen him like this before—
intense, almost possessed. He had been this way during the most pres-
sured moments of their experience in Paris.

"Now, wait a minute, Jack," interrupted Maroni. "The dealers that
are in business today selling Lincoln and Mercury are expected to gladly
give up one or the other and also face a new Edsel dealer with whom to
share customers? You've got to be kidding!"

"Some of them will have to be sold," said Jack. "But you'll see we'll
have a completely new line of Mercury cars, completely different from
the Ford line. That's exactly what the dealers have always wanted. Look,
we're going to bring out a Merc that you can't believe. It'll be bigger and
better than ever."

"Not bad, I guess, if you can pull it off," Maroni said. "But if the

Mercury line is so great, there's a fair chance you'll undermine the Ford dealer."

"No," Jack said, "they'll have a super Ford."

"Jack, by now you've convinced me I don't want to risk my money on an Edsel franchise with all the punch going into Mercury and Ford. But this country doesn't need another medium-priced car. It needs a small car, just like the car we launched in France."

"You just don't know the American market," Jack said, annoyed by his colleague's skepticism. "There's no demand for small cars here. This is a big country, with big people and big dogs. The American buyer wants a Gary Cooper on wheels, not a baby carriage. He wants a car with hair on its chest. A car a westerner would buy to take on long trips on wide-open highways.

"We'll match Buick dollar for dollar and top them feature by feature and then run them into the ground on performance. Buick has never really been up against competition like this. We're going to separate the men from the boys."

Maroni could see that Jack's mind was made up, but he tried one more time to inject reality into the rush of Jack's enthusiasms.

"It will take a lot of money. How do you pay for all this and how long does it take?"

"We'll pay for it with marketshare. That's the name of the game. Stealing it from GM. Last year they had 50% and we had 31%. We're going for 35%. We want to do some of this in the 1957 model year with the balance in '58."

Maroni said no more. He was awed and concerned by the boldness of the plan and by how passionate, resolute and self-sacrificing Jack was in assuming such great risk. It would cost hundreds of millions of dollars. New manufacturing plants would have to be built. Thousands of new automobile dealers would have to be recruited. New cars would have to be created, their names drummed into the public consciousness like a Top 40 song on a radio playlist. If it failed, it could cost all of them their jobs. Jack's courage and ambition was taking him into dangerous territory. To wager their futures so soon after a stunning success seemed insane.

Corporations extract from the people in them a strange, nearly impossible balance. People are asked to weigh the risk of danger against the demand for profit. Most pursue a strategy that seeks the most profit at the least risk. Bob McNamara, employing more logic and reason than most businessmen, was like that. So were Jim Wright and Ben Mills. As guardians of the company's purse strings, Arjay Miller and Ed Lundy had created vast hurdles against big investments, no matter what the risk. Yet for Jack, the scale tipped elsewhere. He was excited by the huge stakes, knowing, too, that it would probably put him at odds with his more conservative Whiz Kid friends.

"What do you want me to do?" Maroni asked. Jack explained that the program was largely pre-sold in the company. Bob didn't like it and some others favored a far more modest approach. But Crusoe, to whose office he would be formally assigned within a couple of days, would back it to the hilt. So would Ford and Breech. And those three had all the clout. "What I want you to do is to focus on the sales and marketing aspects. I know you can do finance. You've shown that skill in France. I need help there because that's where we might encounter resistance."

At headquarters, people got out of Jack's way. He and his team returned to Dearborn true heroes. There was a glorious welcome home dinner for Jack at the Dearborn Inn attended by nearly one hundred key executives and managers. Ernie Breech publicly held out Jack as the embodiment of the American dream, a testament to what American management could accomplish. Breech would walk down the halls, his arm around Jack or members of his French team. They felt anointed. Indeed, William Grimes figured Jack would someday make president and he would follow him up the ladder, gaining perhaps a vice presidency. It was an intoxicating tonic at a powerful time.

THE AMERICAN PUBLIC'S appetite for the car seemed insatiable. The 1950s auto was reshaping America, spawning new communities, turning the suburb into the habitat of choice for Americans. It made possible meals on trays delivered by carhops at drive-in restaurants, drive-in movies and drive-in banks. Spectacular new expressways plowed directly into the hearts of major cities, cutting wide swaths through densely packed areas. Shorter highways linked urban centers in half a dozen states and others were being built from Massachusetts to Texas. New high-speed thruways were opening across New York, New Jersey and Pennsylvania. A special presidential highway advisory committee urged spending $101 billion for new interstate highways over the next ten years.

Even the most optimistic auto company leaders had failed to predict how hungry the market had become for their products. In 1955, General Motors would emerge as the first corporation in the world to earn $1 billion in a single year. That same year would become the industry's

greatest selling year ever with nearly 7.2 million cars registered to owners. It would become the year of Jack Kerouac's *On the Road,* that riotous
celebration of the automobile as a symbol of freedom.

The automobile provided a cheap escape for the Beat Generation, both
a means of transportation and a home on wheels for a new generation of
nomads. High school kids saved up their money for fender skirts, new
grilles and coon tails, and talked about peeling out and laying rubber.
Their parents saw in the car an ostentatious symbol of status, a way to
one-up the guy next door.

Within the first half of the twentieth century, the standard of living
had doubled, spreading the fruits of productivity among the masses of
Americans. Arthur F. Burns, then chairman of President Eisenhower's
Council of Economic Advisers, called these years "one of the great social
revolutions in history." The revolution created a vast middle-income
market of people who were buying products on desire instead of on
need, on style instead of price. In early 1956, a *Business Week* writer
neatly summed up the transformation: "It is an age in which all the old
admonitions appear to have been outdated: 'Make do.' 'Neither a bor-
rower nor a lender be.' 'Penny-wise, pound-foolish.' 'Waste not, want
not.' 'A penny saved is a penny earned.' 'A fool and his money are soon
parted.' Just past the midmark of the 20th Century, it looks as though all
of our business forces are bent on getting everyone to do just the reverse:
Borrow. Spend. Buy. Waste. Want."

Against this backdrop, Crusoe saw in Jack a man who could lead the
company to even greater heights. Having so completely turned Ford
around, Crusoe felt he was within striking distance of GM and Jack
would help deliver the blow. "Jack can do anything now," he told people. "He has done a car from top to bottom, and he's ready for anything
this company can give him."

If Crusoe was ready to promote Jack in Dearborn, he was just as
willing to move McNamara along as well. Crusoe eventually recommended that Bob take his job as general manager of the Ford Division,
freeing himself for his work with Jack on the master plan. McNamara
took over the company's biggest division in January, just as Reith returned from abroad.

This would also mean, of course, that Reith and McNamara would be
in direct competition with each other. As the new head of the Ford
Division, Bob had the upper hand. But if Reith could pull off this plan to
make the company a player in the medium-priced and luxury-car business, he would be the obvious successor to Breech. The former GM

executive, who tutored Henry so well, would turn 60 in 1957. Ford was already showing some signs that he had learned enough from Breech, for he was beginning to openly disagree with him at meetings and conferences. So Crusoe, two years older than Breech, was putting in motion a competitive battle not only between Ford and GM, but between the two friends brought to the company by Tex Thornton nearly a decade earlier.

FOR YEARS, HENRY had talked about someday meeting or beating GM's hefty 50 percent share of the market. But that goal would be impossible without new entries in the medium-price field where Ford was obviously weak. GM had the benefit of three marquees—Buick, Oldsmobile and Pontiac. Even Chrysler offered three lines of mid-priced cars. Ford had only one: Mercury.

Through the early 1950s, medium-priced cars were taking half the market. Some 45 percent of new car registrations were in the mid-priced field at GM and 47 percent at Chrysler. Ford, however, only managed to capture 17 percent of the medium-priced registrations. While only half of GM's total volume rested on Chevy, eight out of every ten cars sold by the Ford Motor Company bore the Ford nameplate. It was too great an imbalance.

Three years earlier, Ford put together a group under Jack R. Davis, vice president of sales, to study whether the company should establish a new car line. The so-called Davis Committee urged in an April 30, 1952, report that the Lincoln and Mercury divisions be split and that a Special Products division be formed to create a new Continental. The group said a major study should also be done to consider a Mercury-Monterey that would combine Lincoln body parts with Mercury chassis components. If the car was successful, Ford could then spin it off as a separate Monterey line. But nothing ever really came of the proposal.

Reith and Crusoe felt that Ford should be more ambitious. The timing seemed perfect. Everything was moving in their favor. Neither of them wanted to hear of the more cautious line of adding a new nameplate under Mercury. Why not establish a new marquee from scratch with an entirely separate network of dealers? At the same time, why shouldn't they dramatically expand the reach of the Mercury, too? Why not take it all?

Behind the plan was a dream. Jack confessed as much to his friend Gene Bordinat, the flamboyant stylist who had come to Paris to help him create the new Vedette. Jack saw in Mercury the possibility that he could be the second coming of Harlow "Red" Curtice, then the president of General Motors. Curtice was a role model to Reith and a legendary figure in Detroit. Jack was beside himself when Curtice, in France for the Paris Automobile Salon, had sat next to him for Jack's American Club speech. Curtice told him something that he would remember for many years: "You don't drive by looking out the rear window at where you have just come from. You drive by looking ahead."

Curtice pulled off a near miracle by taking over Buick in 1933 at the young age of 39. Once GM's leading division, Buick was then fast fading into near oblivion with production at a low of only 40,621 units, less than one-sixth of Buick's 1926 peak of 266,753 cars. Like Jack, "Red" could claim a grounding in numbers yet was clearly a car buff and a super salesman. He loved big cars, the bigger the better. And he prodded GM stylist Harley Earl to design ever flashier models.

Red launched a new line of pace-setting cars, revamped the division's management and drove Buick to a string of successive wins. By 1941, he had pumped Buick production up to a record 377,428 cars and established it as the fourth best-selling car in the business, far from its slumping eighth spot in 1933. After the war, production soared to well over 500,000 units. Buick made "Red" just as "Red" made Buick.

Now, Reith envisioned the same possibilities for Mercury. Crusoe promised Jack the job of heading up the division if they could push through his expansion plan. Unlike Buick, Merc never realized Edsel Ford's promise to capture a large share of the mid-priced market. Edsel had championed the idea in the depths of the Great Depression, convincing his father of the need for a gap-bridging car. The idea was to move the buyers up in size, prestige, power and price. The line was named for the Roman god of commerce who also presided over wrestling, gymnastics and all sports requiring skill and dexterity. He was nicknamed, "The Messenger of the Gods" and his winged cap and shoes reflected his speed. The first 1939 Mercs off the line debuted on November 4, 1938.

Jack never owned a Merc himself. The cars really were little more than souped-up Fords for people who had enough money to buy a fancy version with extra trim and a few extra cubic inches. The Merc was built off the Ford shell. While this helped lower production costs, the Ford shell made it nearly impossible to derive any particular distinction for the Mercury.

Still, Mercury was an established nameplate with 5 percent of the car market. With a completely new line of Mercs on their own body shells and a big expansion of dealers, Jack believed he could pull off what old "Red" achieved for Buick years ago. Jack gambled that with a new 1957 line of Mercs, he would be able to pump up the division's sales by 45 percent in a single year and increase its share of the market to 6.5 percent. A year later, he figured on capturing 8 percent of the field. To sell that many cars, the division had to sign up one thousand extra dealers in eight months—nearly an unthinkable task. For Reith, the goal would become something of a battle cry: "Three thousand Mercury dealers by Christmas Eve."

To gain approval for his entire plan—including the launch of a new line of cars and the expansion of Mercury—he would have to make a major presentation on April 15, 1955, to the board of directors. There wasn't much time to get all the work done: just about ten weeks. Even before that, Reith had to get dozens of signoffs from all of Ford's key executives and departments for a plan that would spell out how many dealers would be added, by when, what marketshare would be achieved, what capital would be expended and what profit would be earned.

Within days, Maroni joined a small task force put together by Jack to help with the massive presentation. The men moved into the Administration Building, near Crusoe, and began a horrendous pace of work to meet the board deadline. Jack was an obsessive worker, routinely putting in fourteen hours a day, often working to near exhaustion. He would arrive home so tired that he would tell Maxine to forget dinner. He had to nap before he could eat. Years and many bosses later, his associates would recall him as the hardest working man they had ever met. Working for Jack was both mesmerizing and exhausting. People loved the challenge he threw at them, but many wilted under the daunting workload. "Reith, you bastard," at least one thought, "I want to scream at you."

His men arrived early in the morning, worked non-stop through the day, returned home for dinner with their families and then came back to work for three or four more hours before calling it quits. During one especially tough spell, Reith's team dragged itself into his office for their fourth consecutive Sunday, only to see him smiling at a desk with a big easel covered with a sheet.

"Well boys," he said, lifting his frame from his desk chair, "we're going to start with a little Sunday service. I want you all to bow your heads but keep looking up here."

They watched as he ripped the sheet off a presentation easel to reveal a painting of a cathedral.

"Ok. We get one minute of silence and then I want you to get your asses to work."

It was classic Jack. He could be an inspiration to work for, or pure torture. His charm and his wit could disarm a man's anger over having to come in for a 9 a.m. presentation on a Sunday. Outside his office, men would pile up, some of them waiting for more than an hour to see him. There was a constant flow of people, ready to show him the next piece of work on the presentation, the latest development, all hungering for his approval.

NOT EVERYONE, HOWEVER, shared Jack's enthusiasm for spending lots of money to take on General Motors. One day, Crusoe made a rare visit to Jim Wright's office. Wright was then director of purchasing, a big job, but without the stature and prestige of a divisional vice presidency. He told Jim about Reith's plan and asked him to attend one of Jack's upcoming overviews. Jim obliged, sitting in the back of a small room, watching Jack and what he called his "shock troops" with the charts. He had heard rumors about the plan, but left feeling shocked at how ambitious it all seemed.

Jim immediately went to see Bob McNamara to ask what he thought of the program.

"I've just spent the last three hours with Jack. Have you seen his presentation? I'm really concerned about it."

"Jim, stay away from what they're doing over there," McNamara said.

"How can I?" Jim asked. "I'm working with Lewis, and he wants to know what I think."

"You've got a head on your shoulders. You like what you're doing. I like what I'm doing. Just find a way to stay out of it and leave them alone."

McNamara, recalled Wright, believed the plan was doomed to fail. Not because he was intimately familiar with it. In fact, he was kept apart from the plan from the beginning because the new car division and the Mercury would overlap the upper level of the Ford line. So even though McNamara was a Ford director, argued Jack and Crusoe, he should not share in their decision to take on GM. Obviously, he had a vested interest in preserving the current Ford line-up. They even kept from him the critical documents.

Even before Jack's involvement, Bob had raised questions about a new middle-priced line of cars. "What is the new car intended to offer the car-buying public?" he asked at an executive committee session in May of 1954. McNamara thought he could expand his division's cars into the same market and argued against putting a lid on the specs for the Ford

car. He saw no reason to incur the huge risks and expense to create a
new division with new dealers while dramatically expanding the Mercury line as well. McNamara then got approval to upgrade the top-of-
the-line Ford with the 1957 Ford Fairlane.

But, like Jim, Bob must have felt he couldn't assume the role of either
a proponent or an obstructionist. It wasn't just because of their friendship
with Jack. Crusoe was completely supportive of the program, and they
both owed a large part of their success in the company to him. He was
both a friend and a supporter. How could they aggressively oppose something he completely encouraged? It would have been corporate treason, a
form of political suicide. Some believed McNamara felt sure that it
would have been a black mark against him to resist the plan. So he
stayed out of it. "Count me out," Arjay Miller remembers him saying.

Indeed, Wright's first thought upon seeing the presentation was, "Oh
God, I'm going to alienate Mr. Crusoe" if I tell him what I really think.
So when Crusoe bumped into Jim outside his office and asked for his
opinion, Jim hemmed and hawed before finally admitting how he felt.
Even then, he couched his opposition in the most delicate terms.

"Mr. Crusoe," Wright eventually said, "I've got to tell you, I think
you're biting off an awful lot to chew all at once."

As the words came out, he could see a cloud pass over Crusoe's face.

"Maybe it can be done," Jim quickly added, feeling the discomfort.
"But I would try to do it in smaller chunks."

His comment made Crusoe mad as hell. He turned and bolted down
the hall. "Oh God!" Jim thought.

April would be the make-or-break month for Reith. On the 15th, he
would finally present his plan to the board of directors. Typically, Jack
would have had to clear a key hurdle before pitching his plan to the
board. Every proposal costing more than $1 million had to be submitted
to finance for review before going to the board. Jack figured the price tag
for the entire plan would total $485 million—nearly equal the company's
total profit before taxes the previous year.

Finance had a habit of nitpicking figures, challenging assumptions,
and all around delaying the flow of things. While this was an important
check and a balance, it could also seem a nuisance to men with dreams.

Arjay assigned one of his young analysts, Warren Bergbom, to the
project. It fell to him to sit with Jack's group to insure that they followed
the company's accounting conventions and to discreetly report back to
Arjay and Ed. There wasn't anything that went on in the company that
Arjay, as controller, didn't know about—at least anything that cost

money, because he would ultimately have to sign the check. But the opinions of Arjay and Ed weren't sought. Crusoe was in tight with Henry who was just as eager as Jack to take on GM.

So the formal financial review would never occur. The logic was that every day of delay is a day lost.

Just as Bob and Jim backed away, half out of friendship and loyalty, half out of fear, Arjay and Ed would back away, too. None of them wanted "to rain on Jack's parade," as Miller put it. And while there were difficult times, Crusoe had treated Miller generously, once arranging for Arjay to get four pay raises in a single year. Miller's caution was the only obvious thing about this understated, unprepossessing guy. His boss would recall that when Arjay was first offered the controller's job, he was afraid to take it. He felt he wasn't yet prepared for the job, that he didn't have the background. "Nonsense, you'll learn." So Arjay had stepped onto the fast track, almost in spite of himself.

If anyone was to force the issue with Crusoe, Miller thought, it should have been his boss, Ted Yntema, vice president of finance. As a director on the board, he was Crusoe's equal in the company. But Yntema knew opposition would be useless. In the forty-three years of Arjay's association with the company, it would be the first and the last time anyone would sneak a proposal past Finance.

Later at a meeting with Bergbom and Maroni, Miller seemed willing to accept fate. "There comes a time in our lives when we have to become buccaneers," he said. Maroni remained quiet, but thought "riverboat gamblers" would have been more appropriate. Loyalty being what it is, he knew he owed his entire position in the company to Jack Reith and never contemplated turning against his mentor. He would rise or fall with this enormous undertaking even though it threatened to stretch the capability of the company beyond the breaking point.

Jack sold the plan as aggressively as a hustling dealer on a lot and as astutely as a politician on Capitol Hill. For weeks, he worked privately in the offices and corridors, quietly campaigning, selling his ideas until the vote was assumed in his favor. By force of will, Jack persevered. Leaving a meeting after having his goals or methods debated, Jack would say, "Okay, we're going to regroup and come up with another battle plan." There was always another plan, another way to get his way, never a surrender.

He knew something about the corporation that few completely understood or wished to admit. He knew that people were afraid, that corporations were often populated by cold and timid souls who felt great discomfort making big decisions. That is why a great idea has a lot of fathers in a big company, but a poor idea is a bastard. He knew that a man of confidence who could persevere in that atmosphere was the kind of person who should rise to the top.

In that climb, he could not take "no" for an answer. Those who said "no" got nowhere with Jack. The case was always closed. When the company's engineers protested that they sorely needed another year to develop an automatic transmission, Jack hammered the table, insisting that Ford must have the feature for the 1951 model. Chevy already had beaten Ford by a year with automatic transmission, and it was already cutting into sales. There could be no more delay. The haste paid off. Engineering came up with the feature a year ahead of its own timetable and it was of good quality.

"It is not the critic who counts," said one of Jack's heroes, Theodore Roosevelt, "not the man who points out how the strong man stumbles, or where the doer of deeds could have done them better. The credit belongs to the man who is actually in the arena, whose face is marred by dust and sweat and blood; who strives valiantly; who errs and comes short again and again, because there is no effort without error and shortcoming . . . the man who does nothing cuts the same sordid figure in the pages of history, whether he be cynic, or fop, or voluptuary. There is little use for the being whose tepid soul knows nothing of the great and generous emotion, of the high pride, the stern belief, the lofty enthusiasm, of the men who quell the storm and ride the thunder."

Jack rode the thunder, and if he had to cajole and disarm he would. And why not? How could big dreams hurt a company like Ford?

To justify the plan, his men had to serve up numbers and projections that violated the tenets of rationalism long held sacred by Tex Thornton, Bob McNamara and many of the group. They had built their reputations on the numbers and the facts. Yet, the numbers now had to capture fantasy, not reality. The sales projections grew and grew, not because of any rigorous analysis, but because they had to support the huge investments Jack was asking Ford to make. "The numbers were wild," remembers J. Emmett Judge, a key Lincoln-Mercury executive. "They were totally unrealistic. They had to be. It was the only way to justify the plans."

When Paul Lorenz, a finance man on Jack's own staff, objected to what Reith wanted him to do, Jack pushed him along like everyone else.

"Well, Paul, I'll tell you what," Jack would say, sitting on the edge of his chair. "Why don't you go back to your office and write the memo this way."

"You know, Jack, I don't agree with you," Lorenz recalled telling Reith.

"Yeah I do," Jack smiled, "but you know more about the project than anybody else so I know you'll do a good job."

The night before the April 15th presentation, Jack spent a restless night, perfecting in his mind every nuance of his presentation. He had already showered and shaved long before Maxine awakened, and had slipped on his conservative gray herringbone trousers, a fresh white shirt and a knit tie. He got to the boardroom by 7 a.m. to rehearse the key parts of his presentation.

Even for this, the most important presentation of his life, his men had worked well into the early morning hours, putting his last-minute changes on the nearly fifty charts he would use for the show, each forty-by-sixty-inch board painstakingly lettered and illustrated by hand. They would sit upon two wooden easels, each at the open end of the horseshoe table that dominated the boardroom.

From that end, a presenter couldn't help but feel reverence and awe. Facing him were the formal portraits of three Fords, old man Henry, Edsel and HFII, all prominently hung from the bleached mahogany walls. It made you feel that Henry's ghost was watching everything in this chamber. The old man's office was still intact in the front left corner of the building, where Henry used to gaze out and admire the great Rouge factory he created.

The boardroom began filling up just a few minutes before 9 a.m. with a close-knit group of insiders and friends. The only outside directors were Jimmy Webber, who headed up J.L. Hudson, the largest department store in Detroit and one of Henry's close friends, and Donald David, dean of the Harvard Business School. Ford executives might speak reverently of "the board," but they were really referring to only two men: Henry and Breech.

The session convened promptly at 9 a.m. Henry was at his usual spot at the end of the horseshoe. For hours, Jack paced between the two easels, laying out the attack. He spoke in a soft, reasoned voice that commanded respect.

He moved through the numbers first. Ford produced 43.1 percent of all popular low-priced car sales, he noted, but in the middle and upper-priced range, Mercury and Lincoln scratched and clawed for a mere 13.6 percent. In the top portion of the market, where the prices hovered between $2,400 and $3,100, Mercury and Lincoln had no entries at all to compete against three GM models and two Chrysler cars. The gap caused the company to be severely weak in the middle-priced field. "Too large a percentage of our business is in one car and one price bracket," Jack said.

His daring solution: Introduce an entire new line of cars in the middle and upper price range with a completely new network of dealers, and vastly expand the Mercury nameplate. Ford then built all its cars on two shells: some 97.7 percent of the company's total output under the Ford and Mercury nameplates. The remaining 2.3% were built on a Lincoln shell.

Under the plan, Ford cars would compete with the Chevy and the Plymouth. Mercury, in its own shell, would tackle the lowest-priced Buick but would also develop a super-Mercury to battle the high-priced Buick and the Chrysler. Different models in a new car line would challenge Pontiac and Dodge at the low end of the mid-priced range as well as challenge the De Soto, Oldsmobile and the middle-priced Buick. The Lincoln would square off against the Cadillac in the top prestige sweeps.

The time to seize this challenge was now, Jack explained. "The economy of the future will be based on the word 'more,' " he said. "More people, more families, more money to spend, more willingness to spend it, more wants and needs, more public construction of every kind— schools, roads, hospitals, libraries and parks. Success will smile on those who move aggressively and sell hard in what should be a tough, but profitable buyer's market."

It was rare for strong objections to be raised in this room. If there was significant opposition, a proposal simply wouldn't be able to gain a spot on the agenda. But a delay was almost as bad because that was the easy way to kill something in the corporation: put it out for further study and never get back to it. You could tell by the drift of the questions whether your ideas faced death or not. There were no hostile questions that day. The men around the table tossed at Jack a few questions of clarity now and then, but were generally impressed by the show. If anyone would register objections today, Arjay thought, it would be Breech. But he did not.

Jack and his entourage then left the room so the personnel part of the plan could be presented and the board could vote in private. Crusoe proposed that Jack be named a vice president and general manager of the Mercury division—the titles he coveted. Ben was named a vice president and general manager of the Lincoln division at Jack's request.

The vote was unanimous. The drive to be first became more than a slogan or a battle cry at Ford; it had now become a corporate mission.

IF TEX COULD see them now. Indeed, he would brag to his own associates and friends of the extraordinary accomplishment. Surely, it was unprecedented in business. It took his package deal nine years, but the seven of them remaining were now largely in control of the corporation.

The news was worth a party, at least, and Bob Dunham, who originally showed the men around the Ford plants, decided to throw one. To celebrate their achievement, Dunham put on a wild bash at his home in Ann Arbor. To put some magic into this delicious moment for them, each couple's arrival was announced in a loud stentorian voice by a college student decked out in long tails.

"Sir and Lady McNamara," boomed the announcer, as Bob and Margy climbed the stairs to Dunham's living room. The party applauded as Dunham draped a blue ribbon around Bob's neck and mock-kissed his cheeks. A black cardboard medal hung from it with the title VICE PRESIDENT scrolled in white ink. Arjay's medal simply read: EMPLOYEE. Margy who was in on the joke played a flirtatious French maid in a skimpy lace outfit with jet black stockings. As she flitted around the house, she carried with her a roll of toilet paper, stringing it around the guys, and puckering up her rouged lips for a kiss.

The evening's entertainment was a mock press conference with the new stars of the company. Topped by a fedora with a press card stuck in its band, Dunham played reporter. He rigged up a boom mike and a tape recorder over the sectional sofa where he lined up Ben, Jack, Bob and Jim.

"Ladies and gentlemen," joked Dunham, "I'd like to introduce the new men of Ford tonight. Our very own American in, or should I say from, Paris, Monsieur Reith . . . How does it feel to be a ninety-day wonder?"

"Why don't you tell me, Bob," joked Jack.

"Mr. McNamara, sir," mocked Dunham, "how can a Harvard professor justify making foul-smelling armchairs on wheels?" Khrushchev had recently been quoted in the news as ridiculing automobiles and Dunham picked up on it.

No one was spared, and no one wanted to be.

"Arjay, to you, I'd like to offer my condolences"—a barb directed at Miller because he failed so far to gain new ground in this latest round of promotions. Everyone roared their approval.

"Ed, even though you didn't get a promotion, you look much better since you've gotten out of uniform," laughed Dunham, recalling that for his first few weeks Ed ran around Ford in his Army Air Force uniform.

The evening's humor brought the new competition between them out in the open, where it was safer, rather than bottled up in their own fears and jealousies and machinations. So much had changed with Jack's meteoric rise. Suddenly they were less a team with a strong leader and more a clutch of rivalries. The friendships were starting to wear thin.

So quick was their rise at Ford that a new term had been coined to describe them: The Quiz Kids had now truly become the Whiz Kids. What had been a deprecating tag, one they once resented, had evolved into an accolade, a celebration of their brilliance, their youth, their achievement.

They broke corporate barriers by gaining so much power so quickly. As Harvard professor Abraham Zaleznik would later observe, "The Whiz Kids exercised clout to a degree unusual for young people, heralding the end of a tradition of business that correlated power with age. Their rapid advancement in the company also violated the tradition that for emotional as well as intellectual seasoning, a person should move through the levels before exercising a great deal of power. If the Whiz Kids accomplished little else, they helped bring to life the managerial mystique."

The group was fast becoming a part of the Detroit myth: that American carmakers ruled supreme not only because they created the world's best cars but also because they boasted the world's best industrial managers. In the boosterism of the fabulous fifties, the Whiz Kids had risen to celebrity status. A cover story in *Business Week* in September of 1959 featured Bob McNamara, posing on the lawn outside the company's headquarters in front of a Thunderbird. Under the headline "Ford Hands the Wheel to Youth," their story won international prominence. All ten men were pictured on the opening spread, even though four had left Ford. "They are not auto men in the old-time Detroit context," explained *Business Week*. "They are professional management men with an interest in sociology and philosophy unheard of in the hard-nosed auto business. They are more inclined to apply intelligence than instinct to anything they do—not a bad idea itself, but car customers notoriously buy by instinct rather than intelligence. . . . Over the next decade, at least, Ford Motor Co. largely will be the kind of company they make it."

At Hughes Aircraft, Tex Thornton became a well-known management star. He recruited a McNamara-like protege in Roy Ash (pictured on the right).

SHOWDOWN AT
CULVER CITY

■

"Failure is often that early morning hour of darkness which precedes the dawning of the day of
success."

—Leigh Mitchell Hodges

*T*ex, meanwhile, wasn't letting any moss grow under his feet.
He possessed a tremendous imagination, tempered with
the ability to peer into the future and see what lay ahead. It was not
because he knew technology the way the scientists at Hughes Aircraft
knew it. It was because, like Steve Jobs of Apple Computer decades later,
he inherently knew what would come of it. In the early 1950s he came to
believe that electronics would control and command everything in life.
Electronics would open new industries that would dwarf the car business.

The idea would one day make him a pioneering entrepreneur. Now
Thornton was busy reconstructing his own future, absorbing all he could
about technology from the scientists at Hughes, perhaps the best collection of talent in any research lab at the time with the exception of Bell
Laboratories. Yet, in Howard Hughes, he found himself working for a
flake and a menace.

In September 1948, Tex arrived at Wright-Patterson Air Force Base—
Jack's old stomping grounds as a Hughes vice president. A month earlier, the company's top scientists began work on a $150,000 Air Force
contract to study the chances of tying radar and computer together in jet
fighters. General Kenneth B. Wolfe, head of procurement for the Air
Force, was due in for a goodwill visit. Tex knew him from the war.

They were shooting the breeze when Wolfe's deputy rushed into his
office with an important message from Washington. Wolfe had gained
top priority for a project with the code name "Bow Legs." Tex had no
idea what the deputy was talking about, until he mentioned that Hughes
Aircraft had the only contract let out on Bow Legs. Washington had
approved the first all-weather jet aircraft to intercept and shoot down
enemy aircraft.

The winds of the Cold War were blowing fiercely through the nation.
And like World War Two, an event so instrumental in Thornton's life,
this new war would help further his own success. The Pentagon had
given the project its highest priority because it was vital to defend the
country from a nuclear air strike. In Culver City, scientists Ramo and
Wooldridge were studying the possibility of an electronic fire-control
system that would allow a crew to lock on a target and shoot with
accuracy even though both jets were flying at high speeds. Hearing the
news in Dayton, where he was making a sales call, Tex began to talk
with Wolfe about converting the small study contract into a major crash
program to build the systems.

Wolfe had his doubts that Hughes Aircraft could complete the entire
project. He was going to meet over the weekend with key Lockheed
executives in charge of producing the company's F-92 Starfire all-
weather jets. If they believed Hughes could design and produce the
system on a crash basis, he would go along with it.

Tex met the next day with Ramo and Wooldridge to come up with a
schedule to engineer, design, develop and produce the complex product.
It was mostly guesswork, but it was informed guessing. He agreed to
design and make the first fire-control system no later than September 1
of 1949—little more than eleven months away. More incredible, he convinced Wolfe to give Hughes a shot.

It was an unheard of schedule for a nonexistent product that, for all
Tex knew, could not even be made. He had no production line to build it
even if Ramo and Wooldridge could have provided it on the spot. But
Tex infused in his people a wartime urgency, and he got from his co-
directors of research and development the feeling that he could pull it

off. It was a gutsy move, placing at risk the company's reputation as a reliable defense contractor that could meet a tight deadline with a quality product.

The small $8 million contract that Tex captured proved crucial. People worked their asses off, even sleeping in their cars at night instead of going home. On occasion, Tex and his key people worked twenty, thirty, even forty hours straight without a break. They moved the Flying Boat out of the hangar at Culver City and set up their production factory in the huge wooden building.

Tex was recruiting people like mad, picking off top-level brass, managers and engineers from every blue-chip company in the country. He called a few of the guys at Ford. Jack talked it over with Maxine, but decided things were far too good for him to quit Ford. He called Andy who felt the same about his career at Bekins. Besides, his old friends thought, Howard Hughes was too flaky a guy to trust. He even tried to coax the Whiz Kids' secretary, Nora Elliot, to Hughes to no avail. Ramo and Wooldridge, meantime, lured great numbers of scientists and technicians to their R&D operation.

Tex met the tight deadline, and the product virtually transformed the company. It helped to restore the company's reputation with the military, and it led to a huge business for Hughes Aircraft propelled by two key events that few could have predicted. In 1949, President Truman announced that the Soviet Union had successfully tested a nuclear bomb. A year later, in June of 1950, the Korean War broke out. The onset of both a cold and a hot war sent military contracts and orders surging. The fire-control devices Tex delivered turned out to be, in General George's words, "the company's dress rehearsal for mobilization." Hughes Aircraft emerged the sole source of fire-control systems for the Air Force. Already proven successful in the Lockheed F-94, the systems now found a lucrative place on military aircraft being built by North American, Northrop and McDonnell.

Tex rapidly built on the success, capturing another key contract to develop the Air Force's Falcon missile to track and destroy Soviet bombers. The weapon, the world's first guided air-to-air missile, was to be part of a complete electronics package that could locate an enemy plane, automatically launch the missile, and then nearly guarantee through radar impulses that the missile would hit its target. The team scored its own direct hit in beating out some twenty companies, including GE and Westinghouse, for a design contract for an electronic fire and navigational control system to be used in a supersonic interceptor planned to be the mainstay of future air-defense strategy. Hughes Aircraft emerged with a virtual monopoly on the Air Force's advanced electronics needs.

A unique culture evolved at Culver City, with management and scientists working together as a team. It was a youthful group, with virtually everyone between the ages of twenty-eight and thirty-six. Tex spoke of "liberating" people to do outstanding work. "It was not a dictatorial management," one fascinated observer told a reporter. "It was permissive. Everybody spoke for the rest; it was quite a sight to see the longhairs sitting down with management on production problems, everybody pushing ahead together."

ALWAYS FASCINATED BY technology, to the point of making it the subject of his courtship chatter to Flora back when he first met her, Tex was now in the middle of this relatively unexplored frontier. Glen McDaniel became one of his teachers. President of the Radio-Television Manufacturers Association, a group of 320 technology-based companies, McDaniel met Tex on a recruiting mission to Hughes in 1951.

He had already heard about the young man at Hughes. Tex had lured many executives and engineers from General Electric and Western Electric. Industry executives had told him not to be fooled by the two levels of generals above Tex at Hughes Tool: "They were merely figureheads. It was Tex who really ran the business."

McDaniel would soon come to know Tex well. Whenever the group would meet in New York for a professional gathering, Tex would corner McDaniel, tag along with him up to McDaniel's apartment at Ninety-sixth and Fifth and talk about electronics and technology until 3 a.m. Tex pumped him for knowledge. Tex quizzed him for hours on who he thought were the industry's top technologists and gurus. Then, he would cross-examine him for their views. He wanted to know everything about their concepts and their perceptions about where the industry was heading. What were the emerging patterns and trends? What could the key electronic components really do for industry and consumers? How far could you push these technologies? What came next? He befriended Don Mitchell, president of Sylvania, and Bob Tait, president of Stromberg-Carlson; and he did the same with them, incessantly probing their passions and conflicts and sifting from the conversations his own vision for the future.

Every fact Tex hungrily absorbed. "He was a master brain-picker," recalls McDaniel. Years later, McDaniel would go to Cambridge, England, with his family to study Shakespeare and history. A guest lecturer, a navigation expert, made the point that readers of *The Tempest* would be convinced that Shakespeare had to be a sailor and had to have experienced a storm at sea during the Elizabethan era because his dialogue was so richly detailed with the techniques and procedures of navigation.

"Do you think Shakespeare was a sailor?" McDaniel asked his professor after the lecturer departed. He laughed. Others had thought Shakespeare must have been a doctor or a paid assassin or a land proprietor because of the magnificent detail he stitched into his plays. "Shakespeare was not only a genius but a brain-picker," the professor said. "He invited men into the tavern, plied them with ale until three in the morning, drawing out stories and ideas until he knew everything there was to know about navigating a ship at sea." Immediately, Tex popped into McDaniel's mind.

HOWARD HUGHES, OF course, was too busy chasing Hollywood starlets, remaining elusive only to emerge with some ridiculous demand. Hughes once sent one of Tex's men a five-page, single-spaced typed memo on how to escort people through the hangar that housed his Flying Boat. He told them what kind of seat covers to buy for the company-owned Chevrolets. He issued orders for an investigation of the sale of candy bars, cigarettes and soft drinks from the vending machines at Culver City.

It was a rare day when Hughes would show up himself. He kept an office next to Tex's in the A1 building, a plaster structure painted, like everything else at Culver City, in celadon green—a shade lighter than grass that Hughes insisted upon. But the reclusive billionaire used the office so rarely that Tex allowed Myles Mace, the Stat Control alum he hired as a consultant, to work from it. On occasion, Hughes would call Tex to arrange a midnight meeting at Sepulvada Drive at the top of a mountain. It was a little turnoff that afforded a view of the valley and Beverly Hills. Hughes would be there in his Chevy with the lights out. They'd sit in the front seat of the car and talk. Hughes would complain about the color of a new building or some minor construction detail at Culver City. Whenever Tex tried to bring up some serious concern, Hughes would cut the conversation short. He had somewhere to go in a hurry, he'd say. "Howard is interested only in girls and airplanes—in that order," explained a Hughes Tool executive.

He was getting stranger by the day. Flora had only met him once. He showed up at the house one day, unshaven, in his tennis shoes, his thin black hair plastered down on his head. He refused Flora's invitation to sit down, turned down her offer for a cup of coffee, then wandered over to a radio in the living room, one of those clunky old-fashioned jobs with lots of knobs and dials. He fiddled with it alone in silence, ignoring Flora, as he waited for Tex. About ten minutes later, he was gone.

It was too bad that Hughes owned the company. Tex kept in touch with the inaccessible man by memo. Each month, he would draft a report for the reclusive owner. Sometimes, it would take more than twenty-five hours to get it right. There were pages and pages of reports to Hughes, each one painstakingly put together by Tex and one of his Stat Control recruits, Roy Ash, whom he brought in as assistant controller in 1949. Ash was, like Bob McNamara, an absolute whiz at interpreting numbers. He was the only person to receive a Harvard MBA without a single day of undergraduate study. Ash had graduated first in his Stat Control class at Harvard and ran a research project for Tex there during the war. He joined Hughes after a brief stint at the Bank of America in San Francisco. Though they faithfully filed the detailed reports every month, neither Tex or Ash ever knew if Hughes read them.

If Hughes wasn't particularly interested in what happened at the company, however, his brusque majordomo, Noah Dietrich, was becoming more than intrigued with the place. He was amazed as he watched what was once a hobby shop for Hughes become a company that was overwhelming the parent in both size and risk, forcing it to borrow from the banks—all to his considerable chagrin. Years later, George Fenimore, one of Tex's aides would say: "When I think of evil, I think of Noah Dietrich. He was devious, self-seeking and dishonest."

Dietrich immediately resented Tex. Hughes had hired him without his involvement. At first, Dietrich tried to befriend Thornton, inviting him and Flora over to his home, seeing them on social occasions. He could be a charming raconteur, conversing about his young days as the son of a poor Wisconsin minister or as a semi-pro race car driver. But there was little chemistry between the pair, no matter how hard Dietrich tried to gain Tex's friendship and loyalty. Thornton had failed to heed his advice in recommending an expansion, instead of the closure, of Hughes Aircraft. When Hughes sided with his new management team rather than with Dietrich, Tex's win only embittered the man more, making him a far more threatening nemesis for Tex than Crusoe had been at Ford.

When Tex asked for a revolving credit of $35 million for working capital in late 1950, Dietrich deemed the sum excessive and refused it. He arbitrarily fixed it at $25 million, forcing Tex to pressure the Air Force into larger partial payments than were accepted. Dietrich eventually raised the credit to $35 million. When Ramo and Wooldridge proposed a major expansion of the company's laboratory, Dietrich told them that Hughes opposed any expansion at Culver City. Instead, he wanted the research laboratory built in the desert outside Las Vegas. The scientists warned that it would be a grave mistake to split R&D operations into two sites, and they eventually prevailed but not without great delays in their plans. So badly needed was additional space that Tex sent his men scrambling to look at leasing Sam Goldwyn's movie studios and the Pomona Fairgrounds.

Hughes Aircraft became one of the true wonders of the post-Korean War industrial buildup. When Tex arrived in 1948, the company was in the red on sales of only $1.9 million. Four years later, Tex was booking profits of $12 million on $153 million in sales, with an order backlog of $650 million. In 1952, the company's return on investment of 35 percent far exceeded that of any of the major electronics companies including RCA, Sylvania and Philco and of most airplane companies, too, including Lockheed and North American. Looking ahead to 1953, Tex was predicting that Hughes Aircraft would earn $18 million on more than $200 million in sales. The company, which employed only one thousand in 1948, boasted 17,000 employees and expected to grow to 21,000 over the next year alone.

His rosy outlook, however, would soon receive a jolt from Dietrich. Haskins and Sells, the company's accounting firm, had discovered a breakdown in the accounting of Hughes Aircraft and refused to give the company an audit for the 1951 year. Dietrich reported the news calmly at a meeting in his home, and it astounded Tex because none of the firm's precious audits ever gave cause for alarm. Then, Dietrich began to attack the company's controller, William McGee, arguing that he wasn't qualified for the job.

"I'm surprised you can sit here and say that because you selected him," said Tex.

Dietrich didn't answer Tex. He said, instead, that McGee, who originally hailed from Haskins and Sells, had only been an auditor, not a certified public accountant, and had handled only administrative work.

"You can keep him if you assign the contracts to someone else, but he can't be controller anymore," said Dietrich. "I'm going to appoint a new man to the job."

McGee sat in the room too dumbfounded to defend himself. Years later, Tex would say he would never forget Dietrich's brutality toward a man whom he had considered conscientious, dedicated and hard working. Dietrich insisted, however, that the accounts were so screwed up that they might jeopardize a crucial loan the company had with the Mellon Bank in Pittsburgh.

The Haskins and Sells partner, Malcolm DeVore, then explained why his firm refused to give the company a clean audit. They had found nearly $500,000 of finished parts inventory missing from the Culver City plant. He said some of the trouble began in 1949 and 1950.

"That's the first I've heard of it," said Tex. "We've had copies of the audit reports for those years and I've seen nothing in them to show we had any serious problem."

The meeting broke up in discord. The next day, Tex began an investigation of the accounting department. His study revealed that foremen on the assembly line, under intense pressure to meet tight delivery deadlines, often grabbed parts from the fabrication sections and released them to the assembly line without completing the paper work for the accounting department. Each month, the manufacturing organization alone had to handle more than a million pieces of paper for the company's accountants. Besides, things grew so fast that they had to put in all kinds of improvised control systems. Sometimes, they would send an accountant down to the factory floor at night to literally count what came off the end of the assembly line. No one had done anything dishonest, Tex insisted. In every case, the supposedly missing parts reappeared in the actual end items delivered to the Air Force. Dietrich refused to accept the explanation, suggesting that the alleged missing parts had been sold on the outside. He told some people there had been "midnight requisitions" of the unaccounted parts.

The conflicts between them continued, and by June of 1952, the management team at Culver City had just about had enough. Tex, George, Ramo and Wooldridge sent Hughes a memo accusing Dietrich of trying "to seize personal power without regard to the consequences" of the company and to the likely detriment of Air Force schedules. They demanded a meeting immediately, hoping to force Hughes to choose between them and Dietrich.

A week went by before Hughes's secretary acknowledged that he had received the memo. Still, there was no word and no meeting. Then one day Hughes made a rare appearance at Culver City, shepherding several executives from Westinghouse through the facilities. Tex heard of the visit from an associate because Hughes had come unannounced. Tracking down the visitors, whose names were signed on a visitors' registry, Tex discovered that Hughes had put the company up for sale.

Discussing the new development among themselves, Thornton and his colleagues decided to find a buyer to their own liking, one that would also agree to give them a stake in the company. Tex first met with Lovett in Washington, filling him in on the problems at Hughes and asking for advice. Lovett, now Secretary of Defense, gave him several contacts to help arrange for some financial backing to buy Hughes and sent him off to Wall Street. Tex even telephoned Breech at Ford to ask for his support as a reference for Wall Street investment bankers who would need to check Thornton out. With Lovett's connections, Tex gained the attention of Ben Pepper, head of Pennroad Corp., and of a syndicate including Lehman Brothers, Smith Barney, Bear, Stearns and the Rockefellers. The group agreed to give Tex and the key management team 20 percent of the company's equity if a deal could be arranged with Hughes. On August 21, 1952, Tex sought a meeting with Hughes to explore how willing he might be to sell the company to them.

He got word through Dietrich that Hughes would consider a deal. Then Pepper waited, as did everyone, for Howard to call him at the Beverly Hills Hotel. Four days passed. Pepper threatened to leave. Finally, he got a phone message that he would be picked up in half an hour at a street corner several miles away from the hotel. He took a cab to the spot, where a Chevy picked him up and drove him back to the same hotel from which Hughes now emerged to sit behind the wheel. The mysterious man said nothing to Pepper, only nodded and smiled and then drove off to a home in Brentwood. Outside the house, he pulled a yachting cap from a rumpled brown paper bag and left the car to get actress Mona Freeman, who had recently starred in *The Heiress*. The three then drove off in silence to a harbor. As Hughes and his blond starlet walked toward the moored boats, Dietrich introduced himself to Pepper, explaining that Hughes wasn't likely to return. Predictably, Tex's deal was over.

Angry, the group sent Hughes another memo, putting him on notice that they could no longer be held responsible for meeting the company's military commitments and that they planned to notify the Air Force accordingly. Hughes finally agreed to meet with them, some three months after they had requested their earlier meeting in June.

On September 20, Tex drove to the Beverly Hills Hotel with George, Ramo and Wooldridge to meet Hughes in one of the hotel's bungalows. They found him in a conciliatory mood.

"We really don't have a disagreement," he insisted. Internal squabbles for control in large corporations were common; Dietrich's job was to relate the aircraft company's affairs to the "whole picture." He told the men they were allowing emotion to cloud their judgment.

General George said they couldn't do their jobs if Dietrich continued to intervene in the company's affairs. They wanted him to get rid of Dietrich or to at least straighten out his attitude.

"Mr. Hughes," said Tex, "if we were making television sets, you would be right to tell us to go to hell. But you have to realize this isn't just another company. We're doing important work for the country's defense so it's a public trust."

Tex's remark immediately seemed to provoke Hughes. At first, he had fallen silent. Then he became defensive in his support for Dietrich. Now Hughes grew alarmed, perhaps feeling outnumbered in the discussion.

"Well, we're not living in a Communist state yet," Hughes told Tex. "And I'm the owner of the company!"

From there, the meeting degenerated, and nothing was accomplished. Hughes would later tell Ramo that he didn't like or trust Thornton, never quite forgiving him for his few comments at the meeting.

Several days later, Tex and his two top scientists flew to Washington to tell the Defense Department that the company's management was falling apart. But the government was at a loss to intervene in the dispute in the absence of a breakdown of production.

The fights between Thornton and Dietrich went on for months—until the spring of 1953 when rumors spread that Robert Gross, head of Lockheed, was planning to buy the company. Lockheed had done business with Hughes Aircraft for twenty years. After the military, the airplane maker was Hughes's second largest customer. Once confirmed, the rumors only disheartened Tex and his other managers. Hughes asked Tex to stay on with him and Gross in the event Gross was successful in buying the company. Tex, however, was uncertain about his plans. He had been approached by a few companies over the last several months and seriously planned to entertain the offers. He also had an idea for starting his own company.

On April 11, he wrote a long, rambling letter to Breech, also sending along a copy to Bob and the other Whiz Kids, relaying the entire story of Hughes that had absorbed all his time since joining the company in May of 1948:

> *I am disappointed, of course, that one of these deals was not successful but I am not discouraged. I could have spent fifty years in business and industry and*

not have had the experiences nor the opportunities which I have had here during the past five years.

Should I decide to leave this company I am in no hurry to make a move except for the fact that I will have to give Bob Gross an answer in the very near future. . . . My concern is primarily the fact that I believe the full potential of an electronics company cannot be realized either militarily or commercially if it is a division of an airframe company. We sell our products to airframe companies and at least some have already indicated to us that, to protect their own competitive position, they would prefer not to buy these products from an electronics division owned by a competitor.

When I started dictating this letter to you I did not know of Mr. Hughes's final decision to sell this company to Lockheed. Even though indications had been for several weeks that it would probably go that way, we thought it still possible that he might reconsider the other offer. I was told of his final decision by a telephone call in the middle of this letter to you.

The Lockheed deal never came off, but the problems with Dietrich still failed to disappear. If anything, they only intensified. Dietrich held back their 1952 bonuses. It became almost impossible to get around Dietrich to locate Hughes. He moved from one gaudy Las Vegas hotel to another, rotating through suites at the El Rancho Vegas, the Flamingo and the Desert Inn. George or Tex would call over to Romaine Street, like everyone else, and virtually beg a secretary to get a message to Hughes. Sometimes he would call, often days or weeks later. More often than not, Dietrich would get back to them.

As relations worsened between the senior management team and Dietrich, Ash was roused out of bed at 2 a.m. one night by the ringing of his telephone. The caller said only: "Howard Hughes wants to see you at noon tomorrow in Las Vegas."

"Well, where in Las Vegas?" asked Ash, who had now assumed the job of controller.

"Don't worry. We'll see you in Las Vegas at noon tomorrow."

Ash booked a seat on a plane, caught an early flight out of Los Angeles and checked into a hotel on the strip. As soon as he was being shown to his room, he heard his name being paged. Yet no one knew of his arrangements. A Hughes aide had to have been at the airport and followed his cab to the hotel.

Ash went to the lobby and met a man who told him to stick around in his room. "We'll call you when Mr. Hughes is ready," he said.

At 6 p.m., he finally got word to go down to the hotel's front door. He was picked up and driven to the Desert Inn. Ash was escorted down a long corridor on the main floor, through a bevy of bodyguards. Hughes had rented all the rooms to the very end of the wing, keeping them empty so he would be the only one on the floor. He met Ralph Dayton, head of TWA, who was also waiting to see Hughes.

"What are you here for?" Dayton asked.

"I don't know."

"Well, I've been in a holding pattern here for three days, waiting for him," Dayton said.

When Ash finally was called into the room, Hughes was sitting barefooted on an unmade bed. The controller from Hughes Tool was with him. Hughes brought up a financial matter, and Ash was immediately impressed by the detail. It was consistent with the belief that when Hughes worked on something he worked to the bottom of it, putting everything else in his mind aside. They discussed the issue for a few minutes. Hughes told Ash he wanted him to keep the financial books differently and then he dismissed him.

When Ash returned, he immediately went to see Tex.

"There's no way we can keep the books that way," Ash told him. "What do I do now? If I keep them the right way he'll fire me. If I keep them his way, I won't be able to live with myself."

Tex was still feuding with Dietrich over Ash's role as controller because Dietrich still wanted to put in his own man. If Ash disobeyed a direct order from Hughes, Dietrich could finally move to fire Ash. Tex came up with a Solomonic solution.

"Don't keep them at all," he told Ash. "For the next few months don't draw off any numbers. Keep all the books but don't create any statements." This frustrated Dietrich for a time. But eventually he was authorized by Hughes to take over management of Hughes Aircraft.

"I know that some people might resign because I've taken over things, but I don't care if they do," Dietrich said. "If half the people resign, I can still run this company."

That was it. The four vice presidents had talked about leaving together to form their own company. But they couldn't decide who would be the boss. Tex wanted to be on top of it. Ramo, whose ego was even larger than Tex's, preferred to be boss. But their ambitions differed greatly. Ramo and Wooldridge wanted to be involved in a high technology company in which science and engineering met to produce viable products. Tex was fascinated by technology, too, but only so far as it would help him build a huge, money-making corporation. For Tex, technology was merely a means to that end. For the scientists, technology came first.

"It doesn't make any difference what you make," Tex told them. "You could make fences if that's where there's money to be made."

"Tex, then I'd have to insist that we make wire fences since I'm interested in electronics," Wooldridge joked.

For all the talk, Wooldridge and Ramo never seriously considered setting up a company with Tex. Their discussions with him convinced them that it would not work. Tex would always insist that management was a profession in itself. If you were a good manager, you could manage anything. Ramo and Wooldridge were convinced that wasn't true. Companies that seized advantage of technology, they thought, demanded managers who had been brought up as engineers or scientists.

Besides, Wooldridge felt, Tex was too much of a promoter. At Hughes, he had promised the Air Force more than they could deliver on at least a couple of occasions. Tex might promise an unrealistic schedule for a product in order to get the job, forcing the scientists to go crawling back to the Air Force to change the promise.

On August 11, 1953, Ramo and Wooldridge sent Hughes a letter of resignation. The two scientists walked out a month later to put together the Ramo-Wooldridge Corp., which went on to supervise the development of intercontinental ballistic missiles for the Air Force and eventually became TRW, Inc. (the T coming from the Thompson Products Co., an auto parts maker which emerged as Ramo-Wooldridge's financial backer). Four days after the scientists left Culver City, Tex submitted his resignation to be effective October 1. Hughes called Tex, asking him to stay; but Tex refused.

Now the escape routes were all he had. He heard that an engineer named Charles V. Litton owned a small microwave tube company in San Carlos, near San Francisco and wanted to sell out. For years, Hughes had relied on Litton for its magnetron tubes, a vital component of the radar system in the fire-control technology. Tex had met Litton once before.

"If Charlie Litton is really serious about selling, maybe that would be a good place to start," Tex thought. A colleague was given the assignment of finding out how serious Charlie Litton was.

Within days Tex discovered that his Hughes office was locked up and sealed and he was told not to bother coming to work. His files were crated and stored in the basement of Dietrich's Hollywood office and would not be returned to Tex until more than a year later.

What shocked Tex even more, though, was an invitation he received from Dietrich himself to visit him at his office. Dietrich apparently had second thoughts, worried that he could not manage the place himself—especially when so many were bailing out.

"You're a young man with a future," Dietrich told Tex. "I'm getting older and will retire one day. If you stay, you'll be my logical replacement when I retire."

Tex couldn't believe what he was hearing.

"Look, I can control who my replacement will be and if you stay with the company I'll see to it that you're my replacement."

"Mr. Dietrich," Tex said, "I've made up my mind. I really have no interest in the possibility of such a future."

Tex never saw Dietrich again. The very last time Tex heard from Hughes was when he was preparing to leave for New York for a meeting with Lehman Brothers to gain the financing to buy Charlie Litton's business. Hughes phoned him.

"Tex," he said, "you know I really want you to stay."

Tex told Hughes his decision to resign was final. He had other plans for his life and they didn't include Hughes Aircraft.

"Howard, I have to go now because I have to catch a plane to New York," Tex said.

Howard kept right on talking as if he hadn't heard Tex at all. Losing Ramo and Wooldridge was bad enough, he said, urging Thornton to stay. He acknowledged that people thought him an eccentric.

"I really have to go," Tex insisted. "I'm going to miss the plane!"

Thornton's appeal didn't faze him.

"Howard, I'm running out of time."

"Look, don't worry about your plane. We'll hold it on the runway for you."

"I've never hung up on anybody in my life, Howard. Don't make me hang up on you. But I've got to catch this plane and I'm going to hang up on you unless you say good-bye."

Howard kept right on talking, and Tex Thornton put down the receiver and raced to catch his plane to New York.

THE
WHIZ
KIDS

Bob McNamara quickly proved he wasn't your typical Detroit executive. He lived in Ann Arbor, instead of Bloomfield Hills; he loved numbers, instead of cars; and he promoted safety, instead of speed, in an advertising campaign that nearly cost him his job. Here's one of his unusual advertisements heralding the safety features of Ford's 1956 car line.

Chapter 17

UNSAFE AT ANY SPEED

■

"At last! A car dedicated to 'Safety First' . . . the '56 Ford. More than two years ago, Ford determined to find the causes of accident injuries . . . so a safer car could be built. It was found that most serious injuries were caused by drivers being thrown against the steering post, riders being thrown forward against hard surfaces within the car, or being thrown from the car. See how new Lifeguard Design gives you added protection from these hazards."

—A FORD ADVERTISEMENT

They could hear Bob coming down the hall, his heavy, imperial wingtips pounding the floor in a quick, steady gait. At the sound of those shoes, executives would stiffen to attention. Soon enough, Bob would march into view, rimless spectacles and the glossy hair looking buttered onto his head, a determined stare that went with the thudding arrival and the severe cut of his jib.

It was not that Bob McNamara instilled fear in everyone who came in contact with him, though he did frighten a good many people at Ford. He was simply an imposing man with an important job. He would fire away, one question after another until people were overwhelmed, if not terrified. McNamara's personal style was to rush through everything at high speed, cowing subordinates and peers with how much he knew and how much they didn't. It was how he won their agreement.

247

■

Those who did not know Bob had no idea that he possessed a marvelous sense of humor. They didn't know he could be friendly or polite or that he was even a decent human being. The Whiz Kids knew that.

But McNamara was becoming a terror. The devout husband, the doting father and the engaging friend was, around the office, an intellectual bully. People feared him. He was so dominating at meetings that people were afraid to contradict him and tended not to say what they really thought. If you took issue with Bob, you had to be as ready as he was to do battle with a flurry of facts and numbers. Bob did not tolerate fools gladly, and on more than one occasion he asked that a man be fired because he failed to hold his own in a single meeting.

The people who worked for him had a habit of discreetly glancing under the conference table at Bob's legs. There they could spot the clues for how he was reacting in a meeting because it was virtually impossible to read his face. It was a serious, often grim, humorless face. Under the table, however, they could see his hands gathering the fabric of his trousers in bunches. The more impatient he became and the more likely he would explode, the more intensely he would tug on his pants, rising them higher and higher until he pulled them up to his knees.

"He didn't understand people well," recalls Ben Mills, who became one of Bob's closest friends in those days. Their friendship was so strong that both couples had made arrangements so that the Mills would care for Bob and Margy's children if anything happened to them, and if the Mills died, the McNamaras would take care of their children. "His relationship with co-workers would often scare people a little bit," Mills said, "quite a bit in some cases. He was aware of it, too. But it did not bother him. I don't think he ever attempted to change it. He just went on being himself. He couldn't be someone he didn't know or didn't understand."

Bob dreaded nothing so much as becoming emotionally involved, or losing control. Even those who admired McNamara had to concede this was true. Charles E. Beck, brought to Ford in 1949 as a cost analyst, was so awed by Bob's brilliance that he confessed to becoming weak-kneed when he entered McNamara's office. "He was one of the brightest men I've ever known," recalls Beck, who became one of the finance staff's leading lights in the 1950s. "But he also was one of the poorest managers of people I ever knew in my life. Bob never reached out to people. He felt that once he analyzed a problem and reached a logical conclusion, that was it. He forgot that it takes people to make a solution work."

Beck worked for McNamara on a number of special projects over the years, including one in which he had to go into the stamping plants to eliminate a critical bottleneck. The stamping division could not produce enough deck lids or fenders for McNamara's new Falcon and was holding up production of the car. With the help of the division, Beck reorganized the work in the plant, realigning press lines to clear the bottleneck in ten days.

The job complete, he reported back to McNamara and asked him to telephone the divisional manager to thank him and his people.

"No, Charlie," McNamara told him. "You really have done the job. Do you know how many millions it will save the company? You did it."

Beck insisted he had little to do with the solution, heaping the credit on the people in the plant whose improvements would allow Ford to produce sixty thousand more Falcons in a single year.

"These guys were busting their chops working fifteen to sixteen hours a day," Beck said. "You've got sixty thousand extra units of cars, and you're talking about millions. What's a call?"

"No!" McNamara said tersely, and that was that. Beck was so angry that he asked Arjay Miller to intervene. But if Bob thought the men in the plants didn't deserve a pat on the back, no word of thanks or praise would be forthcoming.

There were other admirers, of course, people Bob brought into the company, people who shared his outlook and his ideas. "Bob is so smart that I feel perfectly comfortable having him take me down like a book off a shelf in his library, open me up and take out what he wants and put me back," one of them told a friend. "And that would make me happy."

"Well, you're obviously a whore," he was told. Yet Bob attracted like people to his cause and they tended to stay supportive, eager to be in his intellectual company.

No ONE COULD ever accuse Bob of being a whore . . . or a politician. On the Whiz Kids' first Christmas together, when Ford's advertising agency sent each of them a gift, McNamara was the only one who indignantly returned it. Everyone else seemed pleased to receive the gifts, putting them under their trees with the other presents. Not Bob. He sent his gift back with a terse note reprimanding the agency for sending it in the first place.

He was beyond reproach, the very model if not the standard of business propriety. When he was controller, McNamara billed out over $2 million to corporate executives who made use of company facilities without compensating the company for them. He billed them for misuse of corporate resources, remembers a colleague, not so much to penalize them for misbehavior as to set a standard for expected behavior in the corporation.

Bob told those who worked for him that a boss had to be more Catholic than the Pope. Once, for a skiing vacation he planned in Aspen, McNamara needed a car with a ski rack. "No problem," a Ford colleague told him. "I'll put a rack on one of our company cars out in Denver, and you just pick it up." McNamara resolutely refused, even though Ford loaned out hundreds of courtesy cars to VIPs every weekend. He insisted that Ford rent him a car from Hertz, pay extra for the ski rack and send him the bill.

McNamara was always driving down the less-travelled road. Along with Arjay, he avoided the fashionable suburbs of Bloomfield Hills, Birmingham and Grosse Pointe where most of the auto moguls lived, including Jack, Ben and Jim. Instead, he and Arjay left their Ford Foundation apartments for the academic atmosphere of Ann Arbor, home of the University of Michigan and a distant thirty-eight miles away from Dearborn. When they moved to the university enclave, they were among the first auto people ever to live there. Dunham had also moved to Ann Arbor around the same time and was amused by the reception he and his wife received at one of the first cocktail parties they attended.

"Oh where does your husband work?" a professor's wife asked.

When Dunham's wife replied that her husband did not, like almost everyone else, work at the university but at the Ford Motor Company, the woman replied: "Oh, it's so nice to have factory people here." They all got a chuckle out of that one.

At home in Ann Arbor, McNamara led the life of a humane, family man. His wife, Margy, was an antidote—a humanizing influence some said—to straightlaced Bob. She didn't hide her emotions or her feelings. Indeed, when McNamara had been at Ford only a short time, Margy wrote an outraged letter of complaint to the company. She raised hell about Ford's practice of driving its test cars down the public highway at speeds of 120 miles per hour and braking in the middle of the road to find out how long it took to stop the car. She never told Bob about the letter; he only found out about it when someone who didn't connect him with the angry letter writer casually mentioned it to him at work.

Margy brought McNamara back to reality, tearing him away from the intensity he brought to his job. She loved to party all night, while her husband always wanted to go home early so he could begin his workday early also.

He led a life in Ann Arbor very different from the lives of the typical auto men. He and Margy became lively participants in the town's civic affairs. Bob was among the leaders of one movement to upgrade sub-marginal housing in the city, a proposal later turned down by the city council. He was a contributor to the NAACP and the American Civil Liberties Union. At the First Presbyterian Church, Bob and Margy were among the first to fix their signatures to a "Covenant of Open Occu-pancy," a church movement that advocated an end to racial discrimina-tion in real estate.

Unlike most auto men, he didn't play golf, though he once tried to learn the game. He went down to the bookstore one late fall, his friend Bob Dunham recalls, picked up half a dozen books on the game and began studying them over the winter. Bob bought some golf clubs and started swinging them in the basement over the cold months. When spring arrived, he went out by himself to try the sport. He thought anyone with any brains could read a few books and learn to play. But he was lousy and quit in a few weeks. Almost no part of McNamara's lifestyle fit the Detroit mold and Bob consciously wanted it that way, as if to remind himself and others that he was, indeed, not the typical, nar-row-minded executive in the car business.

The company itself acknowledged the difference. When McNamara later gained a key promotion to group executive over the vehicle divi-sions, his men in the Ford Division gave him a complete set of Arnold J. Toynbee's *A Study of History*. And at the celebratory luncheon at which he was given the gift, it was announced half way through the meal that everyone was dining on a rare treat: rattlesnake meat. Some joked that the menu was perfect, because wasn't Bob a snake. Others thought it just fit: let everyone else have steak; he would have snake. A few hardy souls with good nausea control continued eating, recalled Charlie Bosworth, but most of them firmly put down their forks and waited for dessert.

With the exception of their Whiz Kid get togethers, Bob largely shunned the automotive world cocktail party circuit. He belonged to an informal monthly dinner club comprised of seven other businessmen and five University of Michigan intellectuals, including university president Harlan Hatcher and economist Paul W. McCracken, to discuss matters of world import. He and Margy also co-founded an informal club of near neighbors in which eight couples would gather eight times a year to dissect a recent book all of them had read. The idea was to break their intellectual ruts, to link university people with powerful outsiders. It was an eclectic bunch, professors of astronomy, natural resources, public wel-fare and sociology, directors of the university's Museum of Art and the

Mental Health-Research Institute, a politician and a fellow Ford executive and Harvard professor, Tom Lilly.

Some confessed to feeling slightly self-conscious about the sessions, especially the wives, but not McNamara. He seemed sharper and quicker, sometimes displaying a touch of impatience with them. He always read the book, though most of the others couldn't say as much, recalled Robert Angell, a member and chairman of the university's sociology department.

They seldom picked a novel to discuss, preferring books that dealt with new ideas or public policy like *The Affluent Society, Irrational Man, To Be a Politician* and *Important Giant: Red China*. Bob would invariably pick such tomes as *The Western Mind in Transition* and *The Ugly American*. One time, he compelled them to read Camus's *The Rebel*.

He would never discuss his work even when he and Margy would have over Ben and Helen or Arjay and Fran. Long, involved discussions would take place instead. They'd get engaged in debates over politics and religion. They gathered books on the Bible and the history of religion, coming to the conclusion that the concept of Christianity was the most powerful single force in the world. Yet they also agreed that when Christianity became ritualistic and formalized, it began to detract from people's real needs. A Presbyterian, McNamara described his personal religion as a "doctrine of ethics, a belief in the relationship of man to man," rather than compliance to the rules of a church.

One time Bob got together copies of the Scholastic Aptitude Test so they could spend an entire evening taking the test, reading aloud their answers to the verbal and math questions posed to college-bound students.

Bob would weigh in with his answer, compare it to Ben's or Arjay's or one of the gals to see how they all fared. If all of them agreed on a specific answer, they moved on to the next one. If not, each person would explain why they chose A over B or C or D. By the end of the evening, Bob and Ben were virtually redesigning the college entrance exams because they concluded that the questions were too ambiguous, not nearly as precise as they needed to be to allow one to draw the proper conclusions.

If Bob could be said to have a passion, it was for precision. Statistical control was even applied to family camping trips for which he carefully analyzed the volume and weight of food, drink and equipment Margy and the kids would have to carry. All the Whiz Kids had a bit of it, in both their professional and personal lives. When he was still at the Dearborn Inn, Charlie would methodically place his shoehorn on his bedside table every morning. When he returned at night, the maid would put it on top of his bureau. It drove him crazy. Why the hell did she have to move it everyday? George put up little posters at his dealerships, eight simple and precise steps every salesman should take to sell a car, reducing everything down to a systematic procedure. Andy Andreson assembled meticulous lists for the family vacations, checking off each item before he left to make sure he brought them along. "1. Keys to boat _____ 2. Battery charger _____ 3. Extra motor _____ 4. Extra fuel line _____ 5. Gas tank for small motor _____." The list went on and on, through pocket wallets and travel clocks, habachis and binoculars, jiggers and knife sharpeners. Driving down the California Freeway with his wife, Jane, and their daughter, Sally, he could tell them to the exact minute the time they would pull in to their destination. Reith was no different. When he planned an outing, he would have a typewritten timetable that recorded by the minute where he and Maxine would be at any point in the day.

With Bob, organization was an even more intense matter. His mind was carved up into compartments, neat little havens for every thought and every number—just as he had compartmentalized his professional and personal lives. Nearly every problem or every solution had as many points to them as the fingers on his hand. He would tick them off in rapid order. One. Two. Three. Four. Five. Or A, B, C, D and E. With each number or letter, Bob would push one finger down after another, unfolding them in an orderly, methodical way. Sometimes, he would run out of fingers but never of numbers or letters. And his staffers would sit, stare and listen at how precise it all seemed.

No one was more punctual than Bob. One time, at one of his early morning meetings, Arjay jumped atop a chair and moved the hands of the wall clock ten minutes ahead. When Bob arrived in the room for his 9 a.m. meeting, the clock read 9:10.

"Bob," Arjay teased, "what happened? We've been waiting for you for ten minutes."

Bob glanced up at the clock, smiled and snapped: "The clock's wrong!" Then, he began the meeting as if nothing had happened.

He left the house early so he would arrive in Dearborn by 7:30 a.m., when many of the other executives were only getting out of bed. Bob would typically leave the office at 6:30 p.m. to return home. He seldom brought work home with the exception of a Sunday night when one of his men would come by the house and drop off a package of charts and tables for his Monday morning meeting. Like clockwork, his key reports would start off each week early in the morning in Bob's office in the Ford Division Administration Building at Plymouth and Middle Belt. The office, with the dull beige carpeting, was as utilitarian as a gas station, as one observer put it. The light green walls were decorated with black-and-white pictures of thirteen of Ford's seventeen models, and a promotion sign that read: "They're Delivering Our Ford." With his men, Bob would review the past week and plan the coming one.

He brought to the job tremendous discipline. It had to do with the way Bob thought through a problem, lusting for every detail, then assembling all the facts and coming up with as logical and rational a decision as possible, a decision based solely on the numbers. It was the same skill that Tex sorely needed in the early days when Stat Control was making the leap from a figures-gathering outfit into one that interpreted the data. It required dispassionate analysis, devoid of intuition or emotion or of that gut feel so many of the auto men often relied upon to base their decisions. And for McNamara, the outsider, it was the only way, for he had no gut feel for the business at all nor any true passion for the product. So he demanded the same rationality from those who worked for him. Those who "felt," those whose "gut" led them to a conclusion, were scorned and scolded, compelled to base their opinions on imperative fact.

One wag joked that Bob's brain cells had to be lined up in his head like the buttons on a calculator because he was so quick to access information from memory. "One must see McNamara's performance for what it really was: an athlete's feat," one admirer would write of him years later. "The mind is a large muscle, and its ability to grasp, sort and organize information can reach an artistry as perfect as an outfielder's leap for a backhand catch."

McNamara was most persuasive in committee discussions. He knew what to say and when to say it, and he was not averse to improvising some of the facts to create support for his position. One colleague noted that he had heard Bob talk for fourteen minutes straight, without having a single fact right. But he was so eloquent and so persuasive that his presentation overwhelmed the men in the room.

Bob thought that truth could be quantified. And if something could not be quantified, it couldn't be true. "Bob," one man argued with him, "you know that some of the greatest ideas in the history of man have nothing to do with numbers and some of the greatest truths have nothing to do with numbers." Bob would shake his head, and the manager would go down another notch in his estimation.

He wanted to measure everything, trying to bring quantification to even sales, marketing and advertising. Some of his men insisted it wasn't possible, that you couldn't measure everything the way you could measure and control costs. In the Ford Division, Bob was straining to apply rationalism to an irrational business. He demanded numbers for everything, from the capacity of Ford's network of dealers to the effectiveness of advertising.

"I know what the capacity of the assembly system is, but I don't know what our dealer capacity is," Bob complained.

"The dealer body doesn't have a capacity," one of his executives told him.

"Oh yes, it does," Bob would insist.

But Detroit could not explain exactly how a car was sold and why, measuring it so you could control the process. In the sale of a car, there was a mixture of persuasion and emotion, of impulse and irrationality, of a salesman's sincerity and a customer's enthusiasm, things that you could not count nor measure. To McNamara, however, the car was simply a product to transport a person from here to there. It provided transportation, not status, nor prestige or even fun. It was a product more complex than a hula-hoop, a television set or a tube of toothpaste, but really nothing more than just another consumer product. So he could never understand why his men couldn't break down the sale of the car to look at the process as a science.

"We don't know how to count sincerity," explained an executive ordered by Bob to figure it out.

"We don't have a sincerity meter. We don't have an enthusiasm meter."

The men who worked for him at Ford thought that he was most uncomfortable when dealing with something that he could not easily quantify—particularly styling and advertising. At one point, his men ran an experiment with *Reader's Digest,* publishing a major Ford ad in only half of the magazine's editions. Then the group researched the buying patterns of the half of the circulation area exposed to the advertising and of the half that wasn't. The relative buying patterns proved conclusively to McNamara that advertising sold cars. Ford was able to get an additional sale by spending $29 on advertising, while the profit on the added sale was about $180. His men could actually prove there was a large benefit from advertising in *Reader's Digest.* He was pleased. But some time later, Ford's market researchers tried to repeat the experiment and could never prove as strong a link as the first test. It unnerved him.

Though McNamara was tough and relentless in his pursuit of the rational, he was also surprisingly naive. When he came to Dearborn with the guys, he had been convinced that there didn't have to be a conflict between his own private goals and the objectives of a corporation. It was a genuine concern for someone who wanted to go back to academia, and it was something he shared with Tex. In a 1946 letter to Ed Learned, his old professorial friend at Harvard, Bob had written: "Detroit management, because of the easy money and boom-time atmosphere which existed here for so many years, appears to me to be far behind the rest of the country in its recognition of its social responsibilities."

McNamara felt business owed society something. Ford dealers were shocked when they received a letter from Bob asking them not to give any holiday gifts to the men in his division. "I think it would be even more in keeping with the Christmas spirit if you would use funds spent on Christmas gifts for Ford personnel—even token remembrances—to bolster your contributions to local organizations that can insure a more bountiful holiday for those less fortunate in your community," he wrote.

Back when the men gathered in Tex's hotel room to map out their strategy at Ford, Jack had urged the group to make its objective that of gaining sales leadership and making the entire Ford operation as effective and efficient as humanly possible. Bob, however, argued that it also was critical to help Young Henry put Ford in a leading position of public responsibility. That was a decade ago. Ed, Arjay and Jim strongly agreed with McNamara back in 1946. But Jack and Ben supported the idea only on the grounds that it would be complementary to achieving the main objectives.

Of course, the discussion was then mostly wishful thinking. Now, as head of the Ford Division, McNamara badly wanted to do something about safety. He had become alarmed by the rising number of fatalities in car crashes and shocked at Detroit's ambivalence toward them.

He had worried about safety as early as 1952, even before he moved out of his job as controller and into the Ford Division. He had been aware of some early research on safety being conducted by John O. Moore, director of an auto crash-injury research project at Cornell University. During McNamara's years with Tex Thornton, Cornell had been commissioned to study safety in aircraft in order to find some way of preserving the lives of air crews. But when the university began its studies, it found that the leading cause of death among pilots occurred not in planes but in their cars.

More than forty thousand people would lose their lives in auto accidents in 1956. Another 1.5 million people would be injured. Crashes had become the chief cause of death for Americans between the ages of fifteen and twenty-four and the second most frequent killer among twenty-five- to twenty-nine-year-olds. It was a horrible tragedy. Yet, Cornell's Moore convinced Bob that it was largely a question of packaging.

He told McNamara that when you package a dozen eggs, you don't put them in a shoebox. You pack them in individual cushions and that's how you cut the breakage to nothing. There was no reason that cars couldn't be built so that people in them could be cushioned for safety, too, because Cornell's early studies found that the leading cause of death was caused by ejection. One of the basic rules of physics suggested as much: you double the speed and square the force when something, like a body, that is moving hits a still object, like the ground. The university's data showed that a person's chance of a fatal injury increased by five-fold when they were thrown from their vehicle. After ejection, instrument panels and windshields caused the largest number of deaths and injuries in car crashes. So you had to keep the passenger in the car, which meant sealing the doors, and adding more protection on the inside: seat belts, a padded dashboard and safety glass.

They were simple things, things that looked entirely logical to Bob, who did not understand how volatile the subject was in Detroit. The auto men had little interest in safety partly because they were selling romance and beauty; they didn't want to call attention to death. It was not that GM couldn't be bothered about it all. The corporation was simply indifferent to it, unwilling to concede that a car maker had responsibility for the problem. The legendary Alfred Sloan, when presented with a new technological breakthrough in safety glass, dismissed the idea out of hand. "Accidents or no accidents," he groused in a letter to L. du Pont, "my concern in this problem is a matter of profit and loss. Somebody is always trying to add to the cost of the product."

GM's attitude would incite Bob and fuel a competitive spirit in him that might not have existed if not for the huge corporation's insensitivity and callousness. McNamara first glimpsed it during the Korean War when the government controlled the prices on cars. He had been in Washington—sent there to argue for an increase—and the regulators told the assembled car makers that if they wanted the price increase they would have to turn over their cost data to justify it. GM flatly refused. The company demanded the price hike, insisted the government had to give it to them, and demanded that the regulators take its word on it. GM didn't give its cost data to anyone.

The company's attitude appalled Bob, perhaps because GM was also becoming his own professional frustration. GM dominated him and his division, and set the terms by which he lived in the marketplace. McNamara was also angered because he held a reverence for the community, and felt that even General Motors had to give to the public interest.

In the mid-1950s, the Cornell lab was sorely in need of money to survive. In those early days, little information was available about accidents and casualties. Cornell desperately needed money to enhance its data collection which at one point had been limited to only one police department in the Carolinas. Bob persuaded Ford to contribute $200,000 to help fund the research, and Chrysler also kicked in some money. GM refused to help out at all. The company was spending millions on advertising but could not be bothered to make even a small contribution to help the academics study safety.

In the Fifties, Detroit sold cars by highlighting horsepower, compression ratios, torque, cubic-inch displacement, racing, and new and advanced styling. No one did this better than Ed Cole, chief engineer and later division manager of Chevrolet. He advertised speed and performance, putting in bigger engines under Chevy hoods and promoting race track victories. Bob hated Cole's approach because it was the antithesis to his concern over safety. If anything, it promoted recklessness on the road. There were people at Ford who inherently believed in the same things as Cole—people who were in fact doing the same things to sell cars, including Jack Reith. But Cole was setting the pace.

Bob arranged to meet with him and asked him, face to face, to give up speed and racing. It was foolish, wrong and immoral, McNamara told him. Winning races had nothing to do with what people bought on a car lot. The car companies, in pushing speed over safety, were creating a desire to rush out on the road in abandon instead of educating people in how to contain the danger of speed. Ford copywriters were taking the word "speed" out of advertisements altogether. Ford cars were hurrying down roads now, not speeding down them.

Predictably Cole laughed him off. He wasn't about to allow some oddball at Ford to tell him how to run his business. Yet, McNamara continued to make these pilgrimages to meet with GM executives and press his ideas. They would listen, but not give in. GM could face anyone down, the government, the consumer and certainly Ford. Though Bob would never publicly ridicule the company, it represented everything he despised.

On the issue of safety, McNamara believed he could change some of the rules. He pushed his marketing people to build a Ford advertising campaign about safety—an extraordinary thing in Detroit, a full decade before Nader, eleven years before passage of the federal auto safety act of 1966. But there were many doubts about the campaign, even within Ford. Henry Ford himself liked hot cars. Still, Bob had all of the division cars equipped with seat belts, and when he got into a car and put his on, the man driving, one of his executives, looked at him out of the corner of his eye and asked, "What's the matter, Bob, don't you trust my driving?" Fastening a seat belt seemed an act of downright hostility.

Some of his friends believe that Bob became highly interested in safety after Dunham's wife, Mary, was thrown from her car in an accident. She was badly injured, and McNamara told them it was a graphic illustration of what happened when you couldn't keep a person in the package. But years later, McNamara would not concede that this was true. It was the numbers of injuries and deaths, not the emotional trauma of a friend's wife being severely injured, that motivated him to move ahead with a safety effort.

Bob was able to talk Henry into the campaign. Breech, who had no interest in safety, required that Bob submit the text of his speeches to him in advance. (With the exception of Henry, no one at Ford spoke publicly unless Breech gave his okay.) Bob had worked on one of his earliest speeches with Holmes Brown, his personal public relations adviser, and Breech had ended up deleting a couple of paragraphs that had something to do with the profit motive not being enough. There had to be a higher calling for a businessman. Bob didn't object, but he steamed. "Damn it," he told friends, "I'm making more money for them than they've ever made before. Why can't they leave me alone." He said nothing to Breech, but when he delivered the address and came to the missing paragraphs, McNamara looked up and out they came, word by word from memory, with great conviction.

With just as much conviction, Bob eventually sold Ford on the idea that safety could even help sell more cars. It was the right thing, yes, but it could give them an extra boost in the marketplace for the 1956 model year. As standard equipment, he added a dished steering wheel, breakaway rearview mirror and crashproof door locks. A padded dash and sunvisors were priced as options costing $16 extra, while factory-installed seat belts were made available for $9. Somehow Bob was even able to convince Henry to price the options at a loss. Ford would lose a buck on every seat belt it sold, but would make up the loss in conscience and in advertising value. However, Bob not only wanted to make these modest improvements available; he also wanted to built an entire advertising campaign on them. Based on Moore's research at Cornell, Bob became convinced that if everyone wore seat belts in cars, fatalities would drop by half and injuries would fall to no more than 50,000 a year from 1.25 million.

Ford launched Bob's safety campaign as their major advertising theme in the fall of 1955 on a major television special featuring Mary Martin and Ethel Merman, and then followed it up with one-third of the advertisements selling safety. "Coming Friday, the first major contribution to your driving safety—Ford lifeguard design," the ads read. For the first time ever, Ford devoted more than twice as much advertising to its new safety features as it did to anything else, including acceleration, styling, racing, or horsepower.

If Jack Reith was fighting his war against GM, McNamara was taking on Detroit history. The war was on. In picking the safety issue, Bob was aiming not only at a mindset that disregarded the public. He was battling Detroit's insularity, the same inbred attitudes that would prevent the industry from taking foreign competitors more seriously in the 1960s and 1970s. While everyone else in Detroit was adding chrome and hawking speed, Bob was going hellbent workaholic against the grain, personally racing himself at unsafe speeds for the sake of some odd notion of public service.

At Chevy, Cole poured millions into advertising that sold frisky, sassy, bold cars with sweeping chrome, Chevies with new, higher horsepower, the car that smashed the Pikes Peak climb record. At Ford, Bob spent millions advertising safety and protection, anchored seat belts that were a third stronger than those in airplanes—seat belts that could hold back four thousand pounds of weight. Even Jack's Mercury Division joined the campaign, modifying nearly everything in the car with the word safety: "safety-beam head lamps," "safety-grip brakes" and "safety-surge" horsepower.

The ads suggested that when Ford cars got into crashes the new safety features not only would help diminish the owners' injuries but would do so in ways superior to their competitors' cars. Some of Bob's managers also prepared bimonthly brochures filled with comparable crash pictures of Fords and Chevrolets in which Ford came out significantly better. The pictures were sent to Ford dealers who were told to display them in their showroom windows to best advantage.

Chrysler had actually announced that it would offer seat belts as a dealer-installed option before the Ford announcement. GM, however, not only refused to offer belts; it tried to block its competitors' plans to offer them. As chairman of a vehicle safety committee for the Automobile Manufacturers Association, a GM official had drafted a report that flatly stated that "seat belts are not essential for safe driving." When Ford and Chrysler refused to accept the findings, the report was never issued to the public.

Even so, GM officials were publicly quoted stating that there was no conclusive evidence that seat belts were helpful in avoiding injury. Instead, they claimed that seat belts could cause internal injuries in auto crashes, a claim based on one test in which doped dogs were strapped into drop cages with window-washers' safety belts strapped across their stomachs. "A lot of people are hurt in bathtubs, too, aren't they?" said GM's vehicle safety engineer, Howard K. Gandelot. "Do you hear anybody demanding that they take the bathtubs out of homes? A lot of people fall on hardwood floors and hurt themselves, don't they? Should we take the hardwood floors out of houses?" When one Buick customer suggested to GM that it consider adding padding to the dashboard after his eight-year-old son was injured when he had to step quickly on his brake, Gandelot urged him to "train" his children to put their hands against the dash to protect themselves at a driver's command.

The cars Bob outfitted with seat belts, however, proved GM dead wrong. The early reports from the field upheld him, and bore out his promise that he could make money and serve a higher purpose. He repeated some of these reports to Henry and to Breech and to anyone who would listen. One from the West Coast concerned a man who had been driving a Thunderbird on Highway 395. He turned over at seventy-five miles an hour. But wearing a seat belt, he was able to walk away from the accident. It struck Bob with the force of holy truth.

But McNamara's safety ads sparked a nasty behind-the-scenes battle in Detroit. Two months into the campaign, someone from on high at GM called over to Dearborn to complain about Bob and his safety campaign. The call came not to Henry nor to Breech or Crusoe but to Walker Williams, Ford's vice president for sales. It was high enough to get the GM story across, yet it allowed them to deny they were putting pressure on Ford. Bob was taking the romance out of the business, GM said, injecting collisions and casualties into the customer's decision about which car to purchase. The campaign could cause irreparable harm to the industry, Williams was told.

It was enough to trap Bob in the nasty politics of Detroit. The pressure had been building on him, anyway, because sales of Ford product were well below expectations. While Bob was hammering away on the importance of seat belts, Chevy was highlighting its new V-8 engine, the engine Cole helped to create as chief engineer. Chevy was clearly and decisively beating Ford in the marketplace. Decades later, Bob would vividly recall a haunting headline in *Automotive News:* "McNamara sells safety. Chevy sells cars." In fact, no such headline ever appeared, but the myth that safety failed to sell cars would persist for years to come.

The pressure became intense. Margy noticed that in his sleep Bob was constantly grinding his teeth, wearing down the enamel until she forced him to go to a dentist who recapped his molars. Instead of getting the work done in Detroit where it might give rise to gossip, however, Bob snuck off to New York to find a dentist who could take care of the problem.

Soon it got ugly. Working on a tip from GM, a *Time* magazine correspondent called Holmes Brown, Bob's public relations chief.

"I understand that they've fired Bob," he said.

"No, I don't think you're right," replied Brown, shaken by the news.

"Yeah, well go on down the hall and look. You'll see that he's gone."

Brown hung the phone up and rushed to Bob's office, and he was still there, presiding over his desk littered with paper. Brown didn't go in. What could he possibly say, anyway. He couldn't tell him, "Bob, I understand that they got you."

Three days later, McNamara mysteriously disappeared. They hadn't fired Bob; they privately arranged for him to come down with a cold and to spend several weeks in Florida while the company put its safety campaign on the shelf. "I damned near got fired because of it," he later told someone. It was a low point for him and a low blow. He started thinking that he could not stay at Ford and he told Henry so. He had come with a notion that it would be indefinite, that you didn't play games or go half way. He had turned down an invitation to become an assistant secretary of the Navy one year, thinking it was necessary to stay at Ford and push ahead. But slowly it became clear that he could not function here. Tex was right: There was no social commitment in Detroit—not patriotism, and not respect for human life.

For an entire month while the heat was on, Crusoe came over to run the Ford Division and put it back the way it was. Jim Wright also was called in by Breech and told that Bob was ill. After being head of purchasing for one year, he was asked to go to the Ford Division as assistant general manager—a post that did not exist under McNamara. It was an awkward moment for Bob and for Jim. Was Wright being asked by

Breech to undermine his friend? Within an hour of his appointment, Jim was on the phone with Margy checking in to see how Bob was feeling and to make sure they knew of his new assignment.

"Tell Bob not to worry," Wright recalls telling Margy. "I'll do my best to keep things on an even keel. And I'll certainly do my best to support Bob. You know, I'd never do anything to undercut him."

"Jim, we know that," Margy said.

But while Bob was gone, J. Walter Thompson, Ford's advertising agency, was called in to revamp the advertising campaign, and safety was demoted to third in a three-point program. It was back to styling and performance. Ford cancelled the bimonthly dealer brochures with the crash pictures. Though the company continued to offer seat belts as an option, it didn't loudly trumpet the fact as it had for the first three months after the introduction of the 1956 model cars. Years later, McNamara is not entirely candid about the incident. In one interview, he admits he almost lost his job. In another, he denies it became that serious. Complete honesty about it would tend to invade his loyalty to the memory of Henry Ford.

Still, McNamara refused to turn his back on the issue. When a House of Representatives subcommittee on traffic safety came to Dearborn in August, Bob was there with Jack Reith and a few other Ford officials to testify. Henry didn't show up because, it was said, he could not rearrange his travel schedule. But Bob was again clearly in charge, making some of the more dramatic statements about car safety and its importance. At the hearing, held in the styling conference room at Ford, Bob told the legislators that Ford had lost $800,000 by pricing seat belts and other options below cost to educate the public and promote their use.

"The demand from the public far exceeded our expectations," McNamara told the panel. "The manufacturers of seat belt buckles up to that time were, of course, manufacturers who previously had directed their efforts toward supplying the aircraft market. All of a sudden, instead of supplying fifty belts a month, or fifty buckles a month, we demanded one thousand buckles a day. The result was that it was impossible for us to supply our dealers with stocks adequate to meet the demand at that time."

But that was not enough for Bob. He seemed eager to get on the record as a major auto executive with a prediction that GM and virtually everyone else avoided.

"I would give you my personal opinion that the application of seat belts and the use of seat belts in all cars on the American road today would reduce the thirty-eight thousand fatality figure to no more than nineteen thousand, and would reduce the 1.2 million injury figure to no more than five hundred thousand," Bob told the committee.

Still, thanks largely to GM, the idea lingered, as it would for years, that safety did not sell. In an unsuccessful effort to quiet the critics, Bob issued a press release in mid-November of 1956 that contained a section with the headline "Public Will Buy Safety":

> Since two of the five features—crash padding and seat belts—were optional with the customer, it was possible to measure demand by totaling up the number sold. The demand surprised even the optimistic Ford staff. No optional feature in Ford history caught on so fast in the first year. For example, 43% of all 1956 Fords were ordered with safety padding. When tinted glass was first introduced in 1952, only 6% of the customers wanted it. Even Fordomatic (automatic transmission), one of the most popular options, was ordered by only 23% of the customers when it was introduced in 1951. Power steering, introduced in 1953, was ordered by only 4%. During the first year, one of every seven buyers ordered seat belts.

Bob got the last word in, but the whole episode nearly cost him his job and his career at Ford.

THE
WHIZ
KIDS

The planning for Jack Reith's 1957 Mercury launch became such an obsession that Reith built a prototype platform in the parking lot outside his office. The reason: He wanted to insure that every dealer had a clear view of the stage for the extravagant show he was planning at the Dinner Key Auditorium in Florida where all the seating had to be constructed from scratch. Reith is the last person sitting in the row.

George Hackett, Reith's promotions manager, going over the final details of the 1957 Mercury launch.

An artist's rendering of how clay models were made in the 1950s.

Chapter 18

STEEL CARTOONS

■

"A super car, the very top of Mercury's dream-car fleet. Everything is different: the beauty you see, the magic you feel, the features you command. A brand new world of luxury awaits you. Nothing is wanting, except you at the wheel."

—1957 MERCURY ADVERTISEMENT

*M*cNamara was ahead of his time.

In the 1950s, a good set of wheels was the American male's freedom, his power, his superiority and virility. For them, the more horsepower under the hood, the more appeal the product held.

To a rationalist, this was all very irrational. But what McNamara failed to comprehend, Jack Reith seemed to embrace. The two Whiz Kids were on the fast track, racing forward at different trajectories. Ambition was pulling them apart from the single vision they had shared in the early days to remake Ford into a strong, profitable car company. Bob and Jack were positioning themselves on opposite ends of business strategy. The fact that these opposite ends of the earth met in Dearborn meant that something, and just as likely someone, would have to give.

WHEN TEX AND his men first arrived at Ford, the company employed more people to polish the floor in the Administration Building than to design cars. But now Jack and Crusoe's new $11.5 million design studios overflowed with 650 artists, draftsmen, modelers and engineers fulfilling their fantasies of what a car should be. It was where the men who loved the automobile made their home. They worked in near-nuclear-plant secrecy in an expanse of fountains and shimmering pools.

A security force of twenty guards run by an ex-FBI agent checked every employee's badge before they entered: Each badge was a different color so that no one from Bob's Ford Division could enter Jack's Mercury Division or Ben's Lincoln Division studios. Outside the center, the security patrol kept a 60-power telescope trained on a nearby grain elevator where rival spotters might lurk. All unused sketches were carefully burned; all experimental clay models smashed. The walls were hung with signs that read: "No matter where, talk with care" and "Don't foretell the future."

At least once a week, the divisional executives arrived in their well-tailored suits, trailed by small armies of product planners, men that the designers jokingly dubbed, "the walking file cabinets" or "book carriers." They'd follow the boss around in order, each a half step back from the other. They would jot down comments and promises, only to return to remind the designers what had been agreed to and when it had to be ready for inspection by the higher-ups. The stylists could tell when Henry came through with his entourage because everyone laughed harder when Henry cracked a joke. Some of his executives also came here, as a respite from the hours they spent in closed-door meetings around desks and conference tables, from shuffling paper from one office or division to another. It reminded them that they were still in the car business.

Jack Reith, however, treated the design studios as a home. Bob visited the center mainly for its official weekly presentations, but Jack came over to watch and guide every little detail. The designers were young, an average age of thirty-one, not fossilized executives with worn ideas biding time. George W. Walker, the company's chief of styling, sat in an office fit for a pasha—a spacious room done in creamy-white and mouton black, with raw silk draperies, leather couches, a huge black desk and inch-thick black lambskin carpeting.

Jack fit in not because he was as flamboyant as some of the men here, but because unlike the other walking file cabinets, including Bob, he loved cars—the faster, the more glamorous, the better. As a kid, Jack could identify every make and model car while it was still a full block away: a hulking 1930 Cadillac . . . a Stutz Bearcat . . . a 1929 Marmon Roosevelt . . . a J-series Duesenberg. In high school study hall, Jack spent too many hours dreaming and meditating on the kind of car he would own once he had one of those high-paying, fancy jobs. When he remembered the best times in his life—playing with his band or dating Maxine—a car was always there in the foreground.

Nothing was better than the gold Lincoln-Zephyr from his army days. Jack loved the car's styling: Fine horizontal bars, the raked front grill swept up from a slim bumper to match the vee'd alligator shape of the short hood. The headlights were snugly tucked into the top of the front fenders, like a pair of bulging eyes. It sported the same fastback roofline, rounded body contours and ovoid side windows as the 1934 Chrysler/ DeSoto Airflow. A critical success, the Zephyr sold in huge numbers for Lincoln and assured the marque's survival when most other luxury cars stumbled on hard times.

It was hard for Jack to believe that he now had the power to create and make a car that like the Zephyr might shape the dreams and experiences of a new generation of enthusiasts.

As soon as Reith took over as head of Mercury, he urged the men to scrap the standard Mercury models they were planning, and instead to bring out some of their flashiest sketches and to go to work styling an entirely new line for his Kill-GM program. It was a wild gamble. The long, painful passage from a dreamy sketch on a draftsman's table to a polished car in a dealer's showroom took three full years in the fifties. It gave meaning and frustration to tens of thousands of designers, modelers, engineers, factory workers, salesmen and dealers. It was as much a political journey as it was a business triumph. For as the project inched forward, there was always occasion for yet another person to make an imprint, often at the expense of someone else. It was a process filled with second-guessing and doubt.

A good corporate soldier in Detroit managed the journey, but spent many a night tossing in his sleep over it. Few, though, lived for it like Jack Reith, and he certainly did not try to shorten the perilous productive trip. There were too many things to go wrong, too many places for something to unravel. Even after a full-sized clay model of a new design was okayed, it took twenty-four months of engineering work and tooling up simply to begin production. Jack was now insisting that that schedule be compressed into only nineteen months—which was all the time they had to get four series of 1957 Mercurys on the market by the fall of 1956. Everyone thought Jack was crazy.

Walker assigned to Jack's styling team one of his top people, Elwood

P. Engle, a tall, lanky hawked-faced man with narrow features and jet black hair. Engle worked closely with Mercury's chief stylist, Don De-LaRossa, a dapper stout man with dark wavy hair. Alongside them were a cadre of other designers, specialists on interior and exterior sections, on advanced styling and body development.

Jack showed up daily at the design center at 7 a.m. and raced through hundreds of idea sketches, space-like renderings of sweeping bodies, fenders, intricate instrument panels and headlights. Each drawing, on eight-and-one-half-inch-by-eleven-inch velum paper, showed a car part from every angle. They were stapled on movable boards, seven feet high and twenty-five feet long. The wilder the idea, the more Jack liked it.

Car buyers, after all, did not dictate the design of the automobile, Jack thought. Nor did auto stylists try to mirror the tastes of the masses. Since car makers had to work two to three years in advance on designs, they had to gamble. "Who can say what a buyer really may want his car to look like three years from now?" Jack said. "His ideas get a lot of conditioning in that time."

Overstatement was the accepted idiom of the 1950s. The "highest," the "largest," the "biggest" translated into the best. The same held true for Jack's new line of cars. He wanted them lower, wider and longer than anything on the road. So the designers sketched out models with an extra three inches of leg and hip room and two more inches of head and shoulder room. And Jack insisted that the top-of-the-line model be feature-happy, overloaded with extra embellishments to make it extra special.

Free to let their imaginations roam, the designers devised some outlandish concepts. V-shaped tail lamps set into canted tail fins with gold-anodized strips running along the sides. Wrap-around windshields. Quad headlamps. Huge slit-like chrome bumpers. A deep-dish steering wheel. Art deco-inspired interior lights. Hood and trunk ornaments. Always, Jack prodded Engle for more ideas, often offering his own suggestions. For the top-of-the-line Merc, Jack suggested dual air pods above the windshield that would allow air to flow into the car over the heads of its passengers. The back window would retract at the push of a buttom to permit the air to flow out, allowing for what Reith called "breezeway ventilation." The designers and modelists loved the idea. It was oddly unique, a bit of eccentric folly that appealed to the more flamboyant spirits of the designers.

The evolving design was, to say the least, original and different. Still, Jack was intent with making it even more wild. Reith was trying to make a distinctive car in an era of excess, a goal that would only drive him overboard. He asked the men to attach two horizontal antenna-like steel rods to the front air pods to give the car a futuristic Buck Rogers look. With a small screen behind the rods to filter the air, the devices almost looked like microphones.

"Jack, you could keep the windows closed at the drive-in and order your hamburgers through them," laughed Eugene Bordinat, the director of Mercury stylists.

"It looks like a car that can break the sound barrier, Gene," Reith chuckled. "That's what we want."

At another session, he wanted "mouseholes" along the front sides of the top-of-the-line Mercury car, until the stylists convinced him it was too much. The idea was to punch holes in the side of the cars and fit them with small lights that would flash in sequence as the cylinders fired. It was a styling gimmick that Jack's hero, Harlow Curtice, summarily ordered for the Buick Super and Roadmaster in the Thirties. The holes served no functional purpose then, and Jack had no purpose for them now, other than to sell more cars.

Jack sailed through the ideas and the sketches with the designers, often refusing to break for lunch or for dinner. Instead, the men would send a couple of the younger product planners over to the Dearborn Inn to pick up some club sandwiches. Jack would slip off his jacket, loosen his tie and gather everyone around a massive round table to carry on business while eating: Reith and Bill Grimes, his product planner, with Bordinat, Engle, DeLaRossa and others. It would take most of them a half hour to get rid of a full club sandwich, taking bites in between rapid-fire discussions.

Jack was channeling everything into his work. Ideas spewed from him like molten lava from a volcano. Sometimes, he'd wake up in the morning only to realize that he had been at the styling studio all night in his dreams. Even before opening his eyes, Jack would have thought up some crazy concept to bring to work that day.

An aura of genius clung to him. A man who worked for him would be at the end of a stream of short notes on blue paper advising him to check into this or that. The ideas, some feasible yet many far-fetched, poured out. Radar-controlled brakes? A car radio that could receive not only FM signals but television audio. Record players in cars. Roof running lights. Bucket-type swivel seats. Sliding glass roofs. Disappearing sun visors. Telescoping head rests. Speed warning buzzers. Four-door convertibles. Some were original thoughts, others copies of what was coming out in the marketplace. Jack would read a small item in an obscure magazine and another idea would be hatched. After a chat with a Mercury car owner, he asked his advertising people to consider advertising station wagons in magazines like *Dog World, Popular Dogs* and *American Kennel Gazette* because, he figured, dog owners almost always bought station wagons. After a weekend visit to the Edison Institute, Jack came back with a bunch of suggestions for new car names drawn from earlier buggy makers: Buck Board, Irish Jaunting Car, Barouche, Hansom Cab, Opera Sedan.

When the styling ideas were agreed on, cars were blocked in full scale on enormous sheets of paper. A model three-eighths the full-sized car was made and changed dozens of times; then the men finally began to sculpt the full-scale clay model, complete down to the last chrome molding. Taking the specifications from the full-size drawings, fabricators would build a wooden frame, load it with Styrofoam, and put it atop a surface plate imbedded in the concrete floor. It was now ready for the studio men who would then sling the mud, or clay, over the model. The dull reddish clay arrived in twelve-pound packages which were put on aluminum trays and loaded into movable ovens. Heated at 120 degrees, the clay was reduced to the consistency of kneaded dough, then taken out of the oven drawers so the men could slap it on the three-dimensional model with gloved hands, over the Styrofoam. In some places, the mud would be slung eight-inches thick on the frame.

The model sat between two long metal tracks that supported a movable portal that helped the stylists shape the clay's dimensions. They'd slick the clay down with water, making the model shiny enough to show all its highlights, before sending it off to the paint shop for a surface coat of paint. Once returned to the studio, bright aluminum foil was molded over the model to represent the chrome trim. The entire process took between two and four weeks. The finished model weighed five thousand pounds and looked so astonishingly real that the suits would sometimes accidentally pull off a door handle, thinking that they could open a nonexistent door.

When Reith came in, the men set up the round table near the clay model and went over with him every feature of the car. Engle pointed out the items being developed, making fast graphite pencil drawings for Jack on a sketch pad to clarify a design or emphasize a point. Jack walked around the model, checking every detail as the men followed behind. There were numerous refinements, adjustments and revisions. The designers worked six to seven days a week, twelve hours a day for five weeks straight to make the deadline for Reith's major presentation to the Product Planning Committee in February of 1955. "Nine-tenths of the cars in the parking lot at 11 p.m. had to belong to people working for him," says Mercury stylist Leo Skidmore. Every Friday night, it seemed, they would get word that everyone had to come in on Saturday and Sunday because Jack wanted to see something on Monday morning.

They debated what to call the new cars. John Najjar, a young stylist who worked as Engle's assistant, suggested the name "Turnpike." Najjar added "Cruiser" to it, and mentioned it in a presentation before Jack. They rendered the name in color, mounted it on heavy stock cardboard, cut out the profile and placed it on the clay model.

Turnpike Cruiser: Jack immediately took to it. It conjured up images of traveling in comfort on the wide open highways, cruising in a Merc with "hair on its chest." It was as distinct a name as the new car itself was evolving to be, and it was completely separate from the names that had been chosen for the entry and mid-level Mercs for 1957: Monterey and Montclair. Jack immediately thought of including with the car a map showing all the turnpikes in the country. He adopted the name and also assigned it to the show car that would be built by Ghia in Italy.

When the clays went before Henry and Breech, Jack got the okay to scrap the other line of Mercs that had already been approved. Jack's designers then had to take the surface information off the clay model with templates down to fractions of inches so detailed drawings could be made of each section of the car to be sent to the engineers. After the prototypes of each part were hammered out in the fabrication shops, the designers would look them over with Jack, making sure the interpretations of their drawings were as accurate as possible.

There would be many more changes and many more decisions. Jack played a role in virtually all of them. No detail was too small or too dull for him. He seized an interest in everything, from the knobs on the instrument panel to the pin-hole headlining in the ceiling of the car. He wanted a push-button automatic transmission for the Turnpike Cruiser, and adjustable powered seats. This latter option allowed the driver to preset the front seat position on a pair of dials on the dash. When he switched off the ignition, the seat automatically sank all the way down to make it easier to enter and leave the car. When he turned the car on, the seat would assume the programmed setting. Jack dubbed it "Seat-O-Matic," and wanted to advertise it as the "seat that remembers."

He'd bring some of these decisions home with him. Not that he would heed Maxine's advice. But Jack was working so long and so hard that it only seemed natural to occasionally ask what she thought. One night he came home late, his briefcase filled with upholstery swatches for the

Cruiser. He laid them out on the table for Maxine to examine. Jack had already made up his mind. He loved the flashy upholstery with thick gold and silver thread shot through it. It seemed a good complement to the Cruiser's chrome and stainless-steel laden interior.

"What do you think of this?" Jack asked Maxine.

She thought it was horrible and didn't hesitate to tell him.

"Jack, I don't like it. It looks like cheap furniture. It looks like upholstery from Montgomery Ward!"

"Come on, Maxine," he protested.

"Those metal threads will rip women's hose and men's clothes," she told him. "They're no good to sit on."

Jack insisted she didn't know what people wanted, that it was different and it would sell. Another time, he showed her the sketches of the Turnpike Cruiser, with its horizontal aerials jutting out over the front windshield. They reminded her of antlers. They seemed too unique.

"Jack, that's awful. It makes the car look like something from Mars."

"Maxine," he said sternly, "they make the car look racier, more modern and advanced."

It got to the point where he would tell her, "Well, I'll show you this, but I don't want any editorializing."

He consumed and relished every element of the new cars, even helping to name the sixteen new model colors: among them Moonmist Yellow, Pacific Blue, Sherwood Green, Regency Gray; or the two-tones and flo-tones the Cruiser would come in: Pastel Peach, Brazilian Bronze, Tuxedo Black, Sunset Orchid.

So intense was Jack's participation that it riled some of the designers who felt he interfered too much. Not even Tex or Bob was more domineering than Jack—the early psychological exams the group took in 1946 confirmed it. The Ford psychologist, examining Jack's scores, thought that both his dominance and self-reliance suggested inflexibility and intolerance. Yet, none of the original ten scored higher than Jack in being socially extroverted. The charm would save his ass on many occasions.

Jack's enthusiasm too would sometimes get the best of him. Once he asked the designers for big leather saddle bags to hang off the back of the seats of the Cruiser. The stylists already were way over budget on the car's interior, yet had to run the entire project on overtime, developing several versions of these leather bags that had no chance of approval because they added too much to the cost of the car. Nothing seemed as if it could stop Jack.

Some thought the Cruiser excessive—even for the 1950s. Raymond Loewy, Studebaker's designer and stylist, had been publicly calling Detroit's cars loud and vulgar "jukeboxes on wheels." The cars that Detroit made did nothing, he said, to offset the impression that Americans were wasteful, swaggering, insensitive people. The American automobile, thought Loewy, had become "orgiastic chrome-plated brawl."

Bordinat, who was intimately involved in the car's development with Jack, would later joke that Ford and everyone was designing "cartoons of steel." Benson Ford, seeing the Cruiser model for the first time, said that it looked like a magnetized piece of steel driven through a hot rod shop, taking with it every gadget and gimmick in the place. Breech, too, was getting increasingly leery of Jack's emphasis on dream car design. He disliked a series of pastel sketches for future Mercurys, informing Walker in a letter that "if our stylists take time to make artists' renderings on anything it should be something that approaches realism and not fantasy. Save that for the magazine articles." On another of his trips to the design studio, Breech took more notice of the Turnpike Cruiser's fake aerials that stuck out of the air pods. He didn't like them.

"What the hell are they?" he asked Engle. "Pull those damn things out!"

The men complied with his order. Later in the day, when Jack came into the studio, he quickly insisted that the rods be put in again. And the men, more loyal to Jack than to anyone except perhaps Henry, reinstalled them. At a time when most design work had to meet committee approval, Reith exercised extraordinary influence and control.

Jack's fondness for daring design extended to the advertising and promotional campaigns for the 1957 Mercury line. The Italian-made Turnpike Cruiser showcar would debut at the Chicago Automobile Show in January. The car, with its twin-plastic butterfly roof panels, went on a coast-to-coast promotional tour in a custom-made, glass-sided, full-length trailer that cost $45,000. Although it had nothing to do with the production model, Jack would claim his 1957 models were direct derivatives from design—"from Dream Car to showroom in 10 months." It was a neat marketing gimmick—an acceptable Detroit deceit.

He urged his men to go all out for the big 1957 launch. After all, it was the first in many years to be built on its own body shell. Why shouldn't they celebrate in a big, splashy way?

"I want this show to be spectacular," said Jack. "It has to be the best ever done."

"Some of the things I'm going to tell you about are going to be pretty pricey," warned George Hackett, his balding and bubbly promotions manager.

"You can spoil us this one time," Jack laughed.

Hackett then laid out the plan: a musical extravaganza with entertainment headliners. Broadway actors and dancers. A large orchestra would be hired. All the dealers around the nation would be invited. Mercury would even put together two full-color movies of the new models in motion and flash them on two synchronized giant movie screens, each the size of the one at New York's Radio City Music Hall.

"It would be the most unusual car presentation ever attempted," assured Hackett.

Miami, he continued, would be the ideal location. In early October, the average temperature was 70 degrees, with the wind from the Northeast at 13.2 miles an hour. The weather would be perfect. Besides the Mercury launch, the dealers also would find plenty to do in sight-seeing, deep-sea fishing, golf, even a football game between Boston College and the University of Miami. Miami also was one of the few cities that could accommodate the more than five thousand people who might attend the celebration.

Jack loved the idea. And like everything else under his purview, he wouldn't let go of it. After Hackett found the ideal arena to stage the event, Jack even insisted that carpenters be hired to construct a model of the seating arrangements for the Miami dealer preview. For the show, the company would have to create an ideal football stadium inside the Dinner Key Auditorium. Jack wanted to make sure every dealer would have a good view of his new models from any seat in the house. The incline of the rows of seats had to be perfect, Jack said. Workmen spent days erecting a huge wooden model outside the Mercury Division's headquarters on Warren Avenue at Livernois. One afternoon, Jack and six colleagues traipsed out, climbed the rickety scaffolding, filled several rows of folding chairs and exercised their necks to get the views just right. After the trial, the men returned to ground level and huddled together until Jack decided he wanted a few more degrees added to the ramp. After the minor adjustments, Jack went through the seating ritual again and agreed, finally, that they had the right combination.

THE GROUP HAD given them strength, power and confidence in the early days. They had divided the labor: Bob in finance; Jack in budgeting; Jim in organization. Yet all the parts came together in the group, allowing them to bring something more to what each had discovered. The image of the Quiz Kids coalesced into reality and corporate legend, giving the group and each member in it more power and authority. "We looked after each other," Jim Wright later recalled. "We supported each other, helped each other—from personal to professional things. I could always go to Bob and discuss problems with him and get his opinion of my approach and whether he thought it was practical or not. And I feel he did the same with me on occasion, and the others did too."

Now, they were largely spread throughout the company.

And their own success had made them rivals. Each division competed with the other for the same financial resources, the same talent and the same attention from Henry and Breech and Crusoe. Each division prepared its cars for 1957. Outside of work, they no longer lived in the foundation apartments that originally bonded their lives and families together.

A space had opened up between them. If they did not talk about it, for friends do not always want to confront the unpleasant, they could sense it. The widest space, broad enough for a chill wind to blow through, seemed to be opening between Jack and Bob.

Jack did not share Bob's concern over safety. While Bob was plotting his safety campaign, Jack was deciding which stock car races Mercury should enter. Neither did Bob share Jack's penchant for the flamboyant, the need for the biggest and the best. Bob favored function over form, utility over style. He was already planning Ford's first compact car—just as Reith was building one of the company's biggest. He recalled that in the early times after the war, the first Plymouth was marketed by a president who was an engineer and who advertised the car as having more space on the inside and less on the outside. Bob loved it. In the same year, in 1948, Cadillac introduced the first upswept fin, inspired by the Lockheed P-38 Lightning fighter. It surprised and galled him. He didn't know what to make of it. It was, he thought, the beginning of the nonfunctional in automotive design. But it sold and sold, while the Plymouth hung around on the lot.

Henry, too, had made them rivals for something bigger, perhaps the presidency, if Breech would ever relinquish it. "It was pretty visible to all of us," says Robert J. Eggert, who was brought to Ford in 1950 by Jack and who later worked for Bob. "Bob was not comfortable with the success that Jack had demonstrated in France. They both had a strong aim to be number two in the company under Henry Ford II."

Sometimes Crusoe, who treated Jack as the Messiah, deliberately fueled the rivalry. One time, he pointedly asked Jim Wright why the Ford Division couldn't have advertising campaigns as exciting and dynamic as Jack's programs at Mercury. Jack loudly trumpeted "The Big M" and

"Dream Car Design," while Ford plugged the relatively subdued "It's Fun to Drive a Ford" theme. Jim and Bob thought Jack's approach was "bombastic."

Their differences, though, did not always rise to the surface. When the group gathered again in February of 1956 for a tenth anniversary party at Arjay's home in Ann Arbor, it seemed like old times. Bob and Ben came decked out in their old dark-green Air Force jackets and pinks. Jim filled the bill by wearing a sandwich board photo of himself in military uniform because it was impossible to squeeze into the old war outfit. Charlie Bosworth would have worn his except that his uniform, and everything else, was destroyed in a fire shortly before his discharge. Arjay dished out cheap anniversary watches to the men, and had a photographer take snapshots. If the celebration of old times seemed a little forced, a little strained, it was hard to tell if the friendship had run its course or if these rising executives had simply forgotten how to cut loose.

THE FIRST 1957 prototypes were ready in April of 1956, though it wasn't until a month later that Jack would get to drive the prototype of the Turnpike Cruiser. If the cars had followed the normal schedule, Mercury would have begun production on March 1. Instead, Jack would have to start producing the basic models seven months later on October 1, while the Cruiser wouldn't move on the assembly lines until November 1 at the earliest. Still, a special thrill awaited Jack one early morning in May. His men had driven the prototype of the Cruiser a quarter of a mile from the fabrication shop to the Ford test track across from the Dearborn Inn on Oakwood Boulevard. It was a strange sight: The car was covered with a dark green stretch cloth with a hole through the windshield so it could be driven down the open street. Wheel covers even hid the hubcaps. Once the car was behind the serpentine brick wall, the cover was removed for Jack to see the prototype.

He popped the hood to gaze at the huge engine under it: a 368 cubic inch monster, one of the largest V8 engines ever built for a production car. It was a machine that pumped and fired and exploded with power. An engine that pushed you back in the seat which was, after all, the real thrill of acceleration. As Jack instructed, the men had dressed up the engine by chrome-plating the valve covers and exhaust manifolds—anything and everything to make it special.

Jack slipped behind the deep-dish steering wheel and hit the accelerator. The car shot down the track, 975 feet forward in ten seconds after kickdown at fifty miles per hour. He drove the car over the simulated railroad tracks, down the macadam stretches, over the soft shoulders and the fade-away highways. The Cruiser took the 32-degree angle hill without a grunt.

More changes were made—some willingly, some not. When Henry grabbed the wheel, he didn't like the way it felt. Jack, of course, had revised everything, including the feel of the steering wheel. Instead of having the company's typically smooth, widely-spaced finger grips, the wheel had vertical parallel-ribbed grips. Jack had to change them.

By early October, the days of reckoning had arrived. Jack had talked Ford into a huge gamble, an investment of more than $500 million in development, engineering, manufacturing and marketing for Mercury's new 1957 models. A huge assembly plant had been built in California to increase Mercury production on the West Coast. More than $10 million was spent on improvements at Mercury's assembly plants in St. Louis and Metuchen, N.J. A new stamping plant in Chicago was expected to devote most of its capacity to Mercurys. Another new plant to make Mercury station wagons was being put up in Wayne, Mich.

It was an extraordinary bet at a time when Ford also was laying out substantial sums to bring out the Edsel the following year. Jack had large expectations for the 1957 cars, expecting to sell at least 100,000 more units in the first year, an unprecedented 45 percent increase in sales. Now he hoped the dealers who had to sell the cars would be as enthusiastic as he was.

With a couple of key aides, Jack left for Miami on Wednesday, October 3. He had a full agenda: On Thursday, Jack would oversee a complete dress rehearsal of the show, personally inspect all the show cars, visit with Miami dealers and arrange a golf outing with George Moore who would be flying in from Washington with Mimi. Maxine would travel closer to the main event with some of the other wives.

More than five thousand dealers, reporters, executives and their wives converged on Miami for the event. The formal show would be held twice because the auditorium could only accommodate 2,500 people. Mercury had reserved virtually every room in twenty-three hotels and fifteen motels for the party. The festivities began Saturday, October 6, with a 9:30 a.m. show in the Dinner Key Auditorium. As the dealers filed into the auditorium, a twenty-five piece orchestra played Broadway tunes. The band soared into an overture at showtime as the lights came down slowly and the chorus started off the revue with "On With The Show."

Adlai Stevenson was battling President Eisenhower for space on the nation's front-pages in a presidential campaign. So it only seemed appropriate to stage a goofy political convention titled: "Mercury—The People's Choice!" Flags from each of the forty-eight states were hung throughout the auditorium. A Broadway cast of fifty, a dancing chorus of leggy girls and two dozen university students who carried signs representing each state ran through the politico-theatrical sketch. The mustachioed comedian Jerry Colonna was cast in the role of a candidate, while Mildred Hughes, the Mello Larks and the Sportsmen moved through the play crooning campaign tunes. Jack's men had even arranged to rent an elephant and donkey for the sketch, but the elephant wasn't housetrained and had to be sent back to the zoo. It was pure corn, the kind of stuff that would have caused McNamara to wince. Yet it delighted the dealers.

When each state was to vote in favor of the Mercury, a person yelled, "I don't see anyone here from Texas! Is there anybody from Texas?" A midget donned in cowboy gear raced out onto the stage and fired a pair of pistols into the air. "I'm from Texas!" he shouted.

It was unbearably hot in the non-air-conditioned arena. And the audience was growing edgy with the heat and the length of the musical extravaganza. After the stage show, Breech, Crusoe and Benson Ford took to the stage to deliver short welcome speeches.

"This is a hot day in more than one way," Breech told the sweltering crowd. "You are about to see the hottest cars ever presented to a dealer body. I believe these new Mercurys will make automobile history."

Four motion pictures, two flashed on huge screens at a time, showed the new Mercurys in action, while the hand-built prototypes rolled out across the 250-foot wide stage. Model after model parked on three turntables where they spun around before the dealers. Back stage, Jack paced like a nervous father outside a hospital delivery room until it was finally his turn to climb aboard the stage. The dealers burst into applause.

"These new Mercurys introduce a new concept of motoring," he said, "with bold, new styling and many mechanical advances destined to influence the shape of cars for years to come. Designed to provide unequalled driving ease, comfort, safety and performance for motorists on America's turnpikes and freeways as well as on rutty, rural roads or city streets, they represent one of the most extensive model changes in the history of the automotive industry."

Outside the auditorium, a fleet of sixty buses waited to transport the dealers and their wives to Hialeah Race Course for lunch and an elaborate reception. The well-manicured grounds and the bougainvillea-covered grandstand made it an elegant showcase for a party. Dozens of pink flamingos danced on the man-made lake in the infield, and a bright pink Mercury convertible ran around in a circle, without a driver, its steering wheel taped down.

The Hialeah show began when the University of Miami Marching Band took to the field, forming a human M—Jack's "Big M"—in the front of the Mediterranean-style grandstand. Overhead a prop plane soared in the clear blue sky, sent by Ben Mills. Trailing behind it was a flapping banner that read: "Good luck Mercury! From Lincoln." A parade of Mercury cars moved round the smooth dirt track, beginning with the 1939 Merc, the first ever made, and followed by a Mercury representing each year. A Buick, Oldsmobile and Pontiac rolled out with "Going Out of Business Sale" signs attached to their sides.

Finally, Jack's 1957 models hit the track. When the top-of-the-line $3,758 Cruiser sailed into view, the band played a rousing crescendo. (It cost over $1,600 more than a basic Ford and about $1,100 more than the Mercury Monterey.) The car sped down the track with its back window down, and the dealers roared their approval. "They were like high school kids at a football game when their team scores the winning touchdown," recalled Robert R. Nadal, a Mercury man. "They were waving and cheering as the car went around the track."

When the show ended, the new models were parked in the paddock under the palm trees for inspection by the dealers. They surrounded an ebullient Jack, in his full-moon sunglasses and shirtsleeves. They lined up to shake his hand and give him a vigorous pat on his back. What the dealers thought of the new cars was crucial. They placed the orders, and they could make or break Jack at this critical time. Five men from marketing, equipped with hidden wire recorders, mingled through the crowd, informally interviewing dealers for their reactions. There were few criticisms.

"Mercury has been telling us for five years we would have something like this, but I never believed you could do it," one dealer said. "I just can't stop looking at these cars. Boy, am I going to make money off of these."

"Jack, if we can't sell this, we can't sell anything," chimed in another dealer.

Even the Cruiser air pods with the queer antlers—the same ones that Breech ordered removed—got rave reviews. "They look modern, like radar or something," laughed one dealer. "Shades of Buck Rogers," joked another man, "but I think they are good. They're flashy and nobody else has them so I like them."

A wide grin flashed across Jack's face. They were not just applauding the car; they were applauding him. The Cruiser was a part of his personality and his ambition. It was the car you could identify from a block away—just what the little kids in Des Moines would do to pass the time on a summer afternoon.

It was a triumph, all right. The *Detroit News* gave greater page-one prominence to the Mercury debut than it did to President Eisenhower's opposition to Stevenson's proposal for a ban on atomic bomb testing. Though Don Larsen was pitching a perfect World Series game against the Brooklyn Dodgers at Yankee Stadium that afternoon, the dealers riveted all their attention on Jack and his new cars. He had gotten the nearly impossible done while so many around him pleaded for more time. More time to design the cars; more time to engineer them; more time to enlist more dealers; more time to tool up the plants; more time for everything. He had pushed and shoved and moved them ahead and now all he had to do was to wait for the success he so clearly saw in front of him. It was a marvellous year. To Reith, it might have seemed as if no one, not even old Henry himself and certainly not Alfred Sloan, had accomplished so much in so little time.

THE

WHIZ

KIDS

In 1957, Tex Thornton's fast-growing Litton Industries is listed on the New York Stock Exchange. Tex is shown with G. Keith Funston, then head of the Exchange.

Tex reads the first ticker tape listing Litton on the exchange with Funston and an unknown person who was the market specialist for the stock.

THE BIRTH
OF A
NEW ERA

■

"Tell me I'm wrong."

—TEX THORNTON

Throughout the 1950s, the two overriding features of life in America were "affluence and anxiety." Never had Americans been so generally and spectacularly prosperous. Never before had they lived in constant threat of nuclear annihilation. Air raid drills forced children to crawl under their desks at school. The fallout shelter became the newest addition to a suburban home.

In the midst of these two defining attributes, Jack Reith was building dream boats for the affluent society while Tex Thornton was managing the creation of products central to the confrontations of a Cold War. It was not the first time that Thornton was a beneficiary of military conflict. He had risen to power in war-time Washington, found his way to Ford because of World War Two, and had prospered at Hughes Aircraft because of the Korean War. In the final months of 1953, as he sought to raise money for his own company, he would again benefit from these edgy years when the arms race was grimly pursued by the U.S. and the Soviet Union.

In severing his links to Howard Hughes, Thornton saw the path to a successful escape in a small supplier to Hughes Aircraft. The California firm owned by engineer Charles V. Litton produced a vital component of the fighter jets which defended the U.S. from a nuclear attack. The esoteric product, a magnetron tube, helped to guide the aircraft's deadly missiles to their targets. If he bought the company, Thornton could use it as the base to build a larger corporation.

All the out-of-work executive needed was a bundle of money he didn't have. With two Hughes colleagues, Roy Ash and "Bill" Jamieson, Tex Thornton could probably scrape together about $75,000 in cash. If the three toted up the value of their wives' jewelry, their houses and some investments, they might have been able to put together some $200,000. The sum was not nearly enough to meet the $1 million price tag Litton had placed on his microwave tube business.

On a chance, Tex approached Joseph P. Kennedy, who in those days always seemed ready for a good deal. Thornton didn't know Kennedy, who commanded a vast financial fortune, but Kennedy was interested enough to begin negotiations with Thornton. Already looking to his sons to fulfill his own political aspirations, however, he wanted Tex to steer clear of government contracts.

"But that's where I'd have to break in," Tex replied. "I don't follow you."

"I have my reasons," Kennedy told him. "Defense work creates a problem, and I just don't want there to be any complications."

The talks came to an abrupt end when Kennedy wanted full control of Tex's company in return for his money. Tex had learned his lesson at both Ford and Hughes. He could not work for someone else again. He had to run his own show, and he wasn't about to strike a deal in which he wouldn't have complete control.

So Thornton trekked to the richly furnished offices on Wall Street where the wheelers and dealers found him to be another brash entrepreneur with oversized objectives and too many demands. In the early 1950s, Wall Street was a closed, privileged club of gentlemen bankers. It raised capital not so much for financial speculation but for investment in American industry. They doled out money cautiously and conservatively, usually to their advantage.

In this atmosphere came Thornton openly predicting that he could convert Litton, with only $3 million in sales and 250 employees, into a

$100 million corporation within five years. If that wasn't too much to swallow, he also insisted that he and his management team get 60 percent to 70 percent of the company—even though they weren't going to ante up any of their own money in the deal.

If not for his publicized success at Hughes and his links with Robert Lovett, then an investment banker at Brown Brothers Harriman, Thornton would have been dismissed as a shrill promoter. Instead, he and Ash made the rounds from the small investment bankers such as Allen & Co. to the more prestigious firms of Clark Dodge and Lehman Brothers. Charles Allen, of Allen & Co., nearly laughed the pair away upon hearing Tex's insistence on controlling the company. "I'll bet you'll never get any more than 50 percent for management," Allen told him.

The pair heard the same reply elsewhere. "No one wanted to give us the 60 or 70 percent of the company," recalls Ash. "We fought for it on the theory that we were delivering more than just management. We were delivering up a particular kind of management that had proven it could achieve incredible numbers. We were also putting in the financial equivalent of a good buy and we wanted credit for that."

Eventually, Thornton met with Joe Thomas, a fellow Texan, of Lehman Brothers. Thomas was a key aide of Robert Lehman, grandson of the founder, and took an instant liking to Tex. He had followed Thornton's career closely since meeting him a year earlier when Tex was attempting to gain commitments for $30 million in loans to buy Hughes Aircraft. What's more, both Lehman and Thomas shared Thornton's enthusiasm for a broad-based company involved in advanced technology.

Some of Lehman's people were skeptical. The question was: Could Thornton deliver on his exaggerated promise? One prominent partner, Paul Mazur, doubted that Tex could reach even a tenth of his $100 million revenue target and felt that Lehman's clients would probably get stuck for the $1.5 million that Tex wanted to do the deal. After all, how could a tiny $3 million company compete in a new electronics field with the likes of Hughes, General Electric and R.C.A.?

Thornton, of course, had ready answers. He maintained that advanced electronics was still a young, fledgling field. Size and capital were less crucial to success than brain power. Competition in electronics was basically a competition for brains. Thornton maintained that many of the best scientists and engineers prefer to work in the intimate environment of a small company. With Ash as secretary-treasurer and with Jamieson as executive staff engineer, he had the nucleus of a management team to pull it off.

The deal sputtered along, with Tex spending much of his time during October and November of 1953 on overnight airplanes winging from one coast to another. To assist him in the negotiations, he had enlisted Glen McDaniel, a Wall Street lawyer whom he had met while at Hughes Aircraft. McDaniel had drafted the paperwork for a company charter and bylaws soon after Tex had gotten Charlie Litton to sign a contract granting him the option to buy his company. It was then that McDaniel had realized that Tex had not even decided what he would name the corporation.

"What do you want it to be called?"

"Gee whiz, I don't know," Tex replied.

"Why don't you call it Thornton Industries?" suggested McDaniel.

Tex wasn't keen on the idea. He believed that central to the company's success was its ability to lure and motivate superb managers. If one man's name was on the company, he reasoned, that would work against his belief. Thornton, the great populist, was staying true to his habit of viewing life through the lens of a group.

They drew up a long list of names, borrowing bits and pieces from electronics and technology, until finally settling on Electro Dynamics Corp. It was a clumsy name, but Tex liked it because anyone hearing the name would instantly know it was involved in technology. So for a fee of $1,000, Electro Dynamics was incorporated in Delaware on October 2, 1953, only a day after the effective date of Tex's resignation from Hughes. It was nothing more than a shell company, waiting for the acquisition of Charlie Litton's business to be completed.

The promising talks with Lehman Brothers began to lapse, especially after the firm's partners discovered that Tex's option to acquire Litton's business expired in sixty days. The closer they pushed the deal to the option deadline, the more likely they could extract greater concessions from Thornton and retain a larger share of the company for themselves —or so they thought. "Suddenly, everything was becoming more difficult," recalls McDaniel. "More issues started to come up, and the closer we came to our deadline, the tougher the negotiation became. As they dragged on, we were losing the time to get other financing."

Growing impatient, Tex decided to temporarily quit the negotiating table, fly back to California and visit with Charlie Litton yet again. Litton was having his own doubts. With the deadline for the option rapidly approaching, ITT was increasing its pressure on the entrepreneur to sell his firm to the New York company. "The deal almost came apart," recalls Roy Ash. "Tex went back to resell Litton and close the deal. Tex turned him around because that was his style. He convinced people of his own commitment, plans, intentions and drive. He got attention focused on what could be: lifting people from their daily preoccupations, the mundane chores, and forcing them to focus on the bigger vision down the road.

"In our hands," Thornton told the entrepreneur, "your company will go on to be great. All of your people will fare well, and a number of them will become millionaires. At ITT, you'll be just another cog in a big wheel."

Not only did Thornton talk him out of thinking about ITT, he also persuaded him to alter their contract. He got him to accept payment for his business in installments so Litton would be able to postpone part of his taxes on the transaction. The change meant that Tex now only needed $300,000 upfront to buy Litton's company—not the $1.5 million he sought from Lehman Brothers. Thornton then rushed to see Ransom Cook, president of the American Trust Company, who agreed to loan him the $300,000 based on the cash flow of Litton's business.

With these details tied up, Tex finally flew back to New York to finish his negotiations with Lehman Brothers. The first time he ran into another obstacle Thornton asked the firm's lawyers to step aside in another room.

"Look," he said, "if we can't wind this up, I'm going to have to see someone else. I've already exercised the option, anyway."

It was a brilliant stroke. The deal was done. Tex and his partners did not put any money into the venture, yet he retained full control of the management. For Thornton, the coup de grace was his ability to get not 60 percent or 70 percent of the company reserved for management, but roughly 80 percent of it. Lehman Brothers would raise the money in a private placement by selling fifty-two units of Tex's company for a cash investment of $29,200 each. Each unit would be composed of a package of convertible bonds and stock.

On a cold December night under a clear wintry sky, Thornton left Lehman Brothers' elegant, Italian Renaissance-style building at One William Street with the largest check he had ever seen in his life: $1.5 million. With his lawyer, McDaniel, he walked a couple of blocks through the narrow canyons of Wall Street to a branch of the National City Bank where they had arranged to deposit the money. Then they hopped into a taxi and headed straight to Longchamps restaurant, where Tex ordered a thick liver steak smothered with onions to celebrate.

Now, he finally had his own company and his freedom, too.

TEX NEVER HAD any intention of directly managing Litton's business. Instead, he wanted to build upon it, to use the company's cash flow to pursue other areas of technology. Besides, the company had strong managers already in place. So Thornton believed there was no reason to establish Electro Dynamics' headquarters in San Francisco, not far from San Carlos where Litton was based. Instead, he moved out of a rented garage in Venice on Montana Avenue, where they first hatched their plans for the company, into a 70,000 square foot sewing machine factory on Foothill Road in Beverly Hills in early 1954. Next store to the factory was the city dump and incinerator. Only a bakery up the street gave the area a better smell.

Within months, McDaniel, who was among the first to join Tex in his new venture, had received a call from the president of General Dynamics who complained about the use of the Electro Dynamics name. The company had an obscure division in New Jersey making electric motors with the identical name for over thirty years. "When I called Tex about it, he said, 'you know there was just a study issued by the British government which compares the magnetron tubes available in the world and comes to the conclusion that Litton's is the best. I think we could hardly do better than to use Litton's name." Tex rushed back to Charlie Litton, paid him a small fee and got him to agree to release his name. Electro Dynamics Corp. became Litton Industries Inc. on August 16, 1954.

More importantly, though, Thornton did what he had done before: He began to build a team of sharp executives, engineers and scientists. Once again, he used his past to bring together a nucleus of young, smart talent, reaching out to past colleagues from his days at Stat Control, Ford and Hughes Aircraft. He enticed Myles L. Mace, the young Harvard Business School instructor who had first met him in Dean Donham's office, to become a Litton vice-president. He brought aboard McDaniel as the company's counsel. He convinced a brilliant former MIT professor whom he had first met at Hughes, Dr. Henry Singleton, to leave a job at North American Aviation. He lured George Kozmetsky, who had been in the same Harvard Business School class as Ash, to join Litton from Hughes where he had been assistant controller. Also arriving later to join the top management team was Harry Gray, a savvy executive recruited from Greyhound.

Over them all, Thornton was the undisputed boss. Ash and Jamieson were deferential to him as the leader who put together the opportunity and cut the deal with Litton and Lehman Brothers. And he did not take advantage of the relationship. If Tex, with his soft drawl and ready smile, assumed the role of an ebullient salesman, the balding Ash was his alter ego. Cool and logical, he was a McNamara clone when it came to all things quantifiable and financial. Tex would often tell friends he knew only two geniuses in his life: one was Bob McNamara, the other Roy Ash. If he couldn't work with Bob, then Ash was more than a competent stand-in.

The tiny group of insiders would gather in his corner office, where Tex sketched out ideas on three-foot-wide pads of paper—ideas on organization or product lines or acquisitions. "We had no strategic plan," recalls Mace. "It was a plan in *his* head. He would draw these things out on this pad and then we would react to them. He was a dreamer, a concept fellow who could take a concept and support it with a bunch of persuasive words."

From his inner circle, Tex encouraged dissent. He claimed an aversion to management by committee, which he thought only protected weak executives from risk. "I once had a boss," he said, "who made the wrong decision and I told him so. He said he judges the loyalty of subordinates by how well they carry out his wrong decisions. I judge their loyalty by how well they tell me I'm wrong."

He also judged them by the pure sweat and time they put into his dream. "They work unconscionably long hours, they are gregarious, they dream in a disciplined sort of way, and they want to be rich," is the way a *Fortune* writer summed up the trio. Indeed, Tex had warned his associates when they got started that the pace would be feverish. "You think you know what work is?" he asked. "You think you know all about long hours and putting out a maximum effort? Well, you haven't seen anything yet. Forget it. We're going to get in shape. We're going to fight a war in peacetime."

Tex and Ash, who had worked closely together at Hughes, spent hours wildly dreaming of the kind of company Litton would become. "There was no limit to what we wanted to be and do," remembers Ash. "We were still brash enough to say there was nothing that was going to stop us."

Charlie Litton's company was the perfect base to build upon and capitalize on the surge in military spending fueled by a mortal enemy called Communism. More than half the total national budget would go toward defense in each year of Eisenhower's presidency, and Litton was in an advantageous position to benefit from it. Every military contractor would negotiate their profits on the sum total of the business. Before taxes and renegotiation, Litton made $1.2 million on $3 million in sales. After the payment of taxes and the renegotiation over excess profits, however, Litton's after-tax income was only about $100,000. For Tex, the challenge of managing Litton was to figure out how to keep the profits that Charlie Litton was paying back to the government each year.

The team gambled on five research and development projects, hoping that if one or two of them could ever be realized they would have it made. Instead of handing money back to the government, Tex plowed the excess profits into R&D. Charlie Litton's microwave tube business formed the center of what would become an electronics components business under Harry Gray. Kozmetsky headed up an R&D effort in defense computers. Singleton led a team of six scientists and engineers in laboratory research work on an inertial guidance device for airborne navigation systems, another war toy to feed the anxiety caused by the Cold War.

Singleton already had been engaged in such research at North American Aviation, and all the men knew of its importance to the military because of their experience at Hughes Aircraft. The device would allow a missile to approach a target "silently" without radiation from directional radar systems that would disclose its whereabouts. Singleton's team had to meet three revolutionary requirements: In contrast with radar systems, it had to be free of any need for contact with ground stations; it had to be small, and it had to be light.

His efforts became controversial when he began to pursue a technology that was considered less than valid by Douglas Draper, then the world's foremost expert on inertial navigation. Singleton, however, insisted his approach was right. "We came to the point where we didn't have much to show for shoveling millions of dollars into it," remembers Ash. "It was worrisome." At a board meeting in 1958, Jamieson, the only board member with a technological background, voted to terminate funding of the project. Both Tex and Ash insisted that Singleton keep at it. Not long after the vote, Thornton won a development contract for more than $1 million from the Defense Department that required Litton to place Singleton's theory into practice within a year. (Litton would deliver the product; it would work and because the device was rooted in radically different technology, it gave Litton a huge lead over every potential competitor.)

Myles Mace, along with the team that negotiated the deal with the Defense Department, recalls flying into Tex's office to give him the good news early on a Monday morning. "We'd been sitting up all night in an airliner from Washington, and we were bleary-eyed, unshaven, and thoroughly bushed after little or no sleep for three days," recalls Mace. "Tex was delighted, of course, but we were all in for a rude shock when I made a move to leave.

" 'Where do you think you're going, Myles?' Tex asked me. I reminded him politely that none of us had had breakfast, that we could use a hot shower, about twenty-four hours sleep, and a chance to become reacquainted with our families. Tex stared at me as though I were out of my mind. 'Do you think this is any time to take a day off?' he scolded me. 'Now's the very time to get this thing rolling! Nobody's ever built one of these things, including us, and we've got only a year.' For a few seconds, I guess we all hated Tex's guts, but you can't hate a man like him much longer than it takes to realize that he's being twice as hard on himself."

Besides the R&D money he poured into key areas, Thornton immediately began buying up a series of little-known outfits that made printed circuits, transformers and servomechanisms, or companies that had key patents on electronic digital computers. There were two acquisitions in 1954; three in 1955; two in 1956; and three in 1957. All of them were friendly deals, often done on a handshake, and Tex was in the middle of every one of them. The first acquisition was of a small, nearly defunct business operation owned by one of Tex's old personal friends from the Army Air Force days. The business was composed of three companies involved in making and selling wire resistors. It was hardly a glamorous operation, and it was on the verge of collapse. Thornton's friend did not want to suffer the ignominy of defaulting on his debt, so Tex was able to buy his three companies for a total price of $163.60 plus their liabilities.

From the start, Thornton believed that Litton had to grow fast—before larger companies could move into the markets of the future. In his first annual report to Litton stockholders—scarcely more than a band of insiders in those days—Tex said his goal was to make Litton "a major company in military, industrial and commercial electronics." His plan to do it was through acquisition. He didn't have the time to learn a new business, train people and develop markets. Acquisitions helped to shortcut the process. As he saw it, Litton didn't acquire companies so much as it acquired time, markets, product lines, plants, researchers and salesmen.

Thornton was creating a new model of business. He was buying one company after another, parlaying what had been a relatively small investment into something much bigger. In these early days, Tex bought businesses that he believed could be integrated into a greater whole. "High technology was the common denominator of all that we did," recalls Harry Gray. In time, acquisitions would come to mesmerize a generation of corporate strategists.

In a single deal, he gained Litton factory space and a workforce. With another acquisition, he brought to Litton a computer genius, George Steel, who had tired of his role as president of a small company called Digital Controls and yearned to return to the research lab. An absolute mad man and raving maniac, Steel would walk the beaches all night, not turning up at work for three days in a row. Yet, he had vividly laid out in his mind the future of digital computing and invented several products that allowed Litton to gain key contracts with the military.

The dealmaking also was a reflection of Thornton's own restless drive. He was wrapped up in the business—just as Jack Reith had been caught up in it at Ford. For Tex, though, there seemed more to prove, not only to himself but to Henry Ford and Howard Hughes. For years his mother had drilled into his head that he was special, capable of great things, and he was intent on proving it. Growth became an obsession. "He was terribly frustrated in those days by the company's smallness, like a symphony conductor with the full original score for an eighty-piece orchestra, but with only seven musicians on hand," recalls Crosby Kelly, one of Thornton's early Litton associates.

Thornton spoke about Litton with the zeal of an astronomer who dreams of new galaxies waiting to be discovered. Litton had to be big, he said, because "only big companies have the strength and vigor to take America into the new technological era. If we are to progress, tomorrow and the tomorrows after will have to be different from today and yesterday."

In less than four full years, Litton's sales approached $100 million, and Tex was well on his way toward getting rave reviews from Wall Street and the financial press. By early 1958, in a celebratory article entitled "Litton Shoots for the Moon," *Fortune* magazine would note that the average age of the more than one hundred managers in the company's incentive stock plan was less than thirty-seven years. "Youth should, of course, be encouraged in corporate affairs, but isn't this pretty darned young?" asked a *Fortune* writer.

Thornton—for so long in the shadows of other men like Ford and Hughes—now delighted in every role and every challenge, doing more than any of them had planned, going further than even he had intended. Ash, Jamieson and Mace sometimes thought he was pushing too hard, too fast. In his biggest coup to date, Litton had just acquired the Monroe Calculating Machine Company in early 1958. A maker of mechanical adding machines and calculators, Monroe was marking time, failing to update versions of its products by using electronic technology. It was a private company owned by members of the Monroe family, who wanted to sell out.

Thornton invited the family out to the West Coast. Then he, Ash, Jamieson and Mace divided them up so that each of the Litton executives would spend three to five days entertaining a specific member of the family, working him over, telling him about the great plans Litton had for Monroe's future. To Tex, who was quick to charm the family, the Monroe calculator itself was a masterpiece of carefully designed parts, a complex machine that was a tribute to the family. The addition of Litton's electronic know-how, he said, would insure that the Monroe name would be around for decades to come. When the wining and dining was over, the deal was in the bag—and what a deal it was.

In return for Litton stock worth about $17 million in market value but only $1.4 million in book value, Thornton gobbled up a company whose conservatively stated net worth came to some $16 million. For this, he bought a company that had earned as much as $2 million in a year and was nearly twice as large in sales as Litton itself. The deal helped to boost Litton's 1958 revenues to $83 million, up from $28 million in 1957. It was the classic case of a small, glamorous firm gobbling up a much larger, though somewhat troubled, business.

The Monroe deal also would become a harbinger of Litton's future direction. It was Tex's first truly large acquisition; it was bought not with cash but with Litton stock; and it was unrelated to the military electronics business he had been building. The message it sent to other company-hungry entrepreneurs was that still bigger deals were possible. Indeed, the market was willing to allow smaller companies to gobble up larger ones.

Yet the deal also raised doubts about Litton's overall goal to become a major player in advanced electronics. What did Tex want with a rather dull maker of mechanical adding machines? Some viewed the acquisition as opportunistic, made simply in the interests of empire building to quickly acquire growth, profits and sales. "We got calls from people saying, 'We thought you were in the electronics business,'" Thornton conceded at the time. " 'What are you doing with an office machine company?' You wanted to say, 'What the hell do you think electronics is? We don't sell electrons. We sell products.'"

To Thornton's thinking, Litton brought its knowledge of electronics to an era where nearly all things run by mechanical means would be replaced by faster, more efficient electronic versions. It would become a key part of Litton's strategy: Determine where the new technologies would have their biggest impact and buy a good market position in the business before technology changes shifted the industry. "The idea was to preside over the confusion by introducing your new technology," says Ash. "The prevailing logic was to build a better mousetrap and the world will beat a path to your door. We did just the opposite. The important part was to buy the market first, and then provide the product."

The marriage of Monroe and Litton was greater than the simple sum of the two because each company brought something special to the party. Monroe gave Litton the market; Litton would now give Monroe the means to lead the market with new, improved products. At least, that's how Thornton viewed the combination. In the days immediately following the 1958 buyout of Monroe, however, Tex's team was growing jittery. They had been working at a maddening pace for years, and they were worried that it would only get worse with the acquisition of a company larger than Litton. They believed Thornton should devote more time and energy to consolidate Litton's existing companies rather than establishing new ones. To them, it only made sense for Tex to slow down before Litton spun completely out of control. "Bill, Roy and I had the uncomfortable feeling that we were buying too many companies too fast," recalls Mace. So three of Tex's most senior lieutenants decided to walk into Tex's office and try to get him to agree to a respite.

"I think we ought to just stop buying companies for a while," said Mace. "We've doubled our revenues, and we've got to make damn sure we integrate that company well. Let's hold up on the buying."

Thornton leaned forward, over his desk, recalls Mace, obviously in disagreement with his three vice presidents. It would have been impossible to have come so far in so short a time without acquisitions. Tex wasn't about to give up on a strategy that had worked so well.

"You guys are crazy as hell," laughed Tex. "Now is not the time to slow up the process. Now's the time to buy these companies faster than ever and that's what we're going to do!"

THE
WHIZ
KIDS

Most of the men worked extremely long hours, often neglecting their families. But when it came time to celebrate, they did with gusto. A decade after joining Ford, the group reassembles for a ten-year anniversary party at Arjay Miller's home in Ann Arbor. Each Whiz Kid was to come dressed in his Army Air Force duds, but only Bob McNamara showed up in full dress uniform.

The entire gang, with wives, at the ten-year anniversary party.

Chapter 20

THE
IMPOSSIBLE
TAKES A
LITTLE
LONGER

■

"These men of the technostruc-
ture are the new and universal
priesthood. Their religion is business success; their test of virtue is
growth and profit."

—JOHN KENNETH GALBRAITH

"These men are monks, monks who've traded in their prayer books for a production line," a clergyman told a *Fortune* magazine reporter. "From the way they work, I sometimes think they want to overwhelm God with their cars. It may sound odd for me to say this, but I don't give as much of myself to my church as many of them do to General Motors and Ford and the rest."

Executives on the fast track in Detroit in the 1950s shared a slavish devotion to work. If they felt they were supermen, Ford only reinforced the belief. They were paid handsomely, set up in expansive offices, given new cars and stock options, and put in charge of thousands of people. Families nearly became subsidiaries of the company, called upon to attend Ford social events and to support their husbands' workaholic schedules.

The industry even dictated where you should live—more often than not in a Tudor mansion, a French chateau or a Colonial manor house in

Bloomfield Hills. Some twenty miles from the city, the high-income enclave is reached by ascending what are in effect a series of suburban steps populated by the junior executives—Ferndale, Berkley, Royal Oak and Birmingham. Each "waiting town" symbolized the auto man's success on the ladder. When you moved into one of the homes in Bloomfield Hills, you presumably had made it—like Jack Reith, Jim Wright and Ben Mills who all now lived in the settlement.

Fortune concluded in 1961—long after the victims in most executive families had discovered it—that the U.S. auto executive may be the hardest-working manager on earth. "To tell them to slow down," a Bloomfield Hills physician added, "is just like telling a dog he shouldn't raise his leg at a fire hydrant. When they're racing that model deadline, the new model becomes God. All these people stop being human beings. They exist for that deadline."

For the wives and families, one deadline always seemed to collide with another, and another one after that. Horrendously long hours, millions of dollars spent and untold neglect of families were often explained by little details that few ever noticed. Arriving home late, Jack explained to his visiting father-in-law that he had spent most of the day trying to decide where to place the ignition switch on the Cruiser. "Well, I can save you a lot of time and money," laughed Maxine's father. "Put it on the right side." On another occasion, Jack said that his men had spent four days figuring out how to take thirty cents off the cost of the mat in the trunk of the car. Maxine's father was incredulous, until Jack explained that thirty cents times a million cars would amount to huge savings.

Consuming little details made Detroit both a car town and a cardiac town. "It's said that many funerals take place late in the morning so the grieving friends can attend them and have their lunch without making more than one trip out of the office," wrote a *Business Week* reporter in 1953. "It's a town where men are still trying to live by such hackneyed mottos as 'the difficult we do at once; the impossible takes a little longer.' "

The higher they rose in the hierarchy, the more they became detached from ordinary people living ordinary lives. Caught up in the details of the business, some of them became detached from the emotions of real life. After a decade of marriage, Jack and Maxine Reith may have had only two things in common: their children and the Ford Motor Company. In other ways, they seemed virtual strangers. She could not relate to Reith's obsessive devotion to work nor to his neglect of family.

"I could understand if you're making military equipment if we were at war," Maxine complained, "but I can't understand how you can spend so much time on a car. You get home so late we can't ever do anything."

"You've got to get out during the day and do everything you want to do because I'm too tired to go out at night," he told her. "If you can't make dinner, I'd be happy to eat corn flakes every day. Go get yourself help and go out and do what you want during the day, but I want to stay home."

Jack's colleagues believed he loved his work far better than he did his family, and that if he had been forced to choose between one and the other, there might not have been the slightest doubt in his mind. The company served dinner in the management dining room every night, and a disproportionate share of Jack's men always seemed to be at the tables. "You'd meet him at 8 p.m. and that was a standard way of life with Jack, not an emergency," recalls Fred Secrest, one of Ed Lundy's deputies in finance. You were routinely expected to work fourteen hours a day for Jack."

At times, Maxine frankly envied Helen Mills because Ben somehow managed to keep far more reasonable hours than Jack.

"How is it that you and Ben Mills have the same job and he gets home at 6:30?" Maxine would ask Jack.

Ben wasn't so focused on moving ahead at nearly any cost as Jack. Ben was not only happy to delegate his responsibilities to the men who reported to him, he thought it was essential to get the best out of them. Ben would rarely work at night or on the weekends. He would only take home work if he faced a key deadline or a real crisis. He took his vacations, and he insisted that the people who worked for him do the same. He slashed their overtime pay, insisting that they try to get their work done in the allotted hours. "You can't work all day and all night without losing your effectiveness," he said. "Hours won't do it. It's how effectively your brain works. And if you lose it beyond its fatigue point, then you think you're working but what you're really doing is confusing things. You're not thinking straight anymore."

In the mania to produce a car, many couldn't think straight—especially when it came to family life. There were times when Jack could have shared a good moment with Maxine, but instead chose to keep it to himself. One day, Maxine's mother called from Oklahoma, wanting to talk to Jack. Her parents were retired and she was immediately concerned that something was wrong with one of them.

"What's the matter?" asked Maxine.

"Nothing is wrong," she insisted. "I just wanted to speak to Jack."

"Well, he's not here right now. You've scared me. Something's wrong."

"Don't you know?" Maxine's mother asked.

"No, I don't know!"

"He had a new car delivered to me today as a gift. Didn't he tell you?"

"No, mother, he didn't tell me."

"Well, the local dealer came out and told us we've got a new car and to pick it up."

Maxine then remembered that only a few days earlier she had mentioned in passing that her mother was driving around an old, beat-up car. There was no discussion about it. But Jack obviously picked up on it and arranged for her to have a new Mercury. He could do things like that, and it only made it harder for Maxine to fuss about how neglectful he was of the family. When she asked him why he didn't cue her in on the decision, he simply replied, "Well, I didn't want you to spoil the surprise, and frankly, I just didn't think about telling you."

IN THE ABSENCE of their husbands, the wives found each other. They were all on the threshold of building a life after the war, all strangers to Detroit and all married to men who worked for Ford. Those commonalities brought them together, forging strong friendships in the process. They would get together often for games of charades and poker. Helen and Maxine would drive into Detroit once a week for a long, leisurely lunch at the Statler. Maxine would get a babysitter for Donna and they'd go in for the hotel's fashion show on Wednesday. "We mostly talked about our lives, and what was expected of us," recalled Maxine. "We were all getting into a life that appeared pretty exotic compared to what we had been living. And we were expected to play a supportive role and to relieve our husbands of any problems at home so they could concentrate on work."

As the men achieved greater success and status, the roles of the wives also grew. They were expected to lend greater support to their executive husbands. There were rules of the game, too, that defined the role of the good corporate wife. As spelled out by William H. Whyte, author of *The Organization Man,* the tenets were second nature to the seasoned wife of the 1950s:

- Don't talk shop gossip with the Girls, particularly those who have husbands in the same department.

- Don't invite superiors in rank; let them make the first bid.
- Don't turn up at the office unless you absolutely have to.
- Don't get too chummy with the wives of associates your husband might soon pass on the way up.
- Don't be disagreeable to any company people you meet. You never know. . . .
- Be attractive. There is a strong correlation between executive success and the wife's appearance.
- Be a phone pal of your husband's secretary.
- Never—repeat, never—get tight at a company party (it may go down in a dossier).

At social events, some of the Ford wives would refuse to be photographed at their tables until they were able to snuff out their cigarettes and hide their cocktails behind the chairs so they would be out of the camera's lens. The new model launchings, trade show car promotions and dealer meetings demanded a stream of social obligations for the women of the Organization Men. There were receptions and cocktail parties, luncheons and black-tie banquets.

Oftentimes, the divisional general managers would talk business with the dealers and their wives would be expected to entertain the ladies at fashion shows and luncheons and little trips over to Greenfield Village. Jack would sometimes call Maxine on the phone and say, "I need a wife tonight." It meant another business/social engagement where everyone talked cars, the company and the competition. He would bring home pictures of the executives Maxine would meet, and she would sit and study the photographs, trying to memorize the faces with the names. Ben Mills would heavily rely on Helen, who readily matched faces and names, to whisper the names of dealers and other associates at social functions. She saved him from many an embarrassment.

For some women, these business engagements induced as much anxiety as a boardroom presentation would for their executive husbands. A corporate wife would be terrified of doing something that might humiliate her husband and possibly hinder his chances for success. At the Mercury car launch at Hialeah, Maxine swept past a cocktail table in a gray bouffant dress with a horsehair petticoat and knocked off four glasses, half of them falling on Crusoe. She was speechless, though Crusoe laughed it off.

MARGY MCNAMARA, OUT of the immediate Detroit spotlight in Ann Arbor, was the closest thing Ford had to a renegade wife. She did not play golf, as a good many of the corporate wives did, nor did she involve herself in women's clubs and organizations that did not have a serious social purpose. She refused to show up at the Bloomfield Center's fourteen-lane bowling alley where one day every week a large group of exquisitely coiffured, impeccably dressed auto wives tossed balls, drank cokes, and giggled. When the other Ford women would host local fashion shows for visiting wives, Margy would bring them on a tour of the University of Michigan cyclotron—the Physics Department's massive device to accelerate atomic particles. She was a member of the local UN group and the League of Women Voters. And she worshiped her three children, Margaret, Kathleen and Craig, creating a family where one might not have existed.

Bob, too, became in many ways a stranger to his children. He always left the house early, often before dawn, for the drive to Dearborn, only to return when it was dark. Years later his son, Craig, told an interviewer: "My father never shared his real life with us."

Fran Miller's escape came in the form of the only organization to which she belonged: the Ann Arbor Monday Club, a group of some twenty women who congregated every Monday at an alternating home to talk about servant trouble or husband trouble or to play a game of bridge. Otherwise, Fran's life revolved almost entirely around Arjay and their two children, Kenneth and Ann. It was a rare evening when Arjay didn't pull some work out of his ubiquitous briefcase, which his daughter Ann took to calling "daddy's purse." "The wives were neglected," Miller says, "and the children were neglected. It's true. But she understood that. She was very supportive. My wife never went back to work. I didn't want her to."

Their marriages were in many ways like the stereotypical Victorian marriage. The responsibility for the success of the relationship, in all its emotional, psychological and executive complexity, fell nearly entirely on the wife. "You didn't call your husband at work," says Maxine, "to tell him there was something wrong with the plumbing. You took care of it yourself." The corporate wife was required to do whatever it took to make their life together a contented one. She lived completely for her husband. Her interests and hobbies, under this rule, were often secondary.

Did they live full lives, or shadows? To a large extent, the wives were co-conspirators. When Flora married Tex during the war, she had not really known him. "I had signed up for better or worse," she says. "I would have felt a failure if I didn't make it work. I can remember thinking there are going to be times when your husband will be tempted by another woman. And I said to myself, 'I will be able to handle that. Tex turned out to be a one-woman man. But his mistress was his work and that was harder to deal with than another woman might have been."

Like Maxine, Flora would have preferred to participate a little more in her husband's career. But Tex, so thoroughly taken with all his jobs, could not bring himself to share them with her. He said he was sparing her the details of the tension he was under, but it would have been much easier for her to know the details because she imbibed the pressure. "If he was under stress," she says, "I was under stress. Yet he thought he was being very protective. Or maybe he wished that was the way he felt."

Andy and Jane Andreson went to a session called "The Art of Listening." The seminar warned wives that their executive husbands would have little time for them and coached husbands to demonstrate an interest in the events of their partner's lives.

"I want you to get into the practice of talking to your wife when you get home from work," Jane recalled the instructor telling the men. "Ask her how her day has been. It may not be as exciting as yours. But to her it was exciting or it had its problems. Communicate with her about what your day has been like."

The session sparked an interesting routine in their household. When Andy came home, he would fix a couple of drinks and the two of them would sit alone for a short time to compare days. "It was a great thing for us," recalls Jane. "I would have dinner all made when he came home. Sally was usually doing homework or playing. If I was in the kitchen he would come in and we'd chat there with our drinks. It was good for me because he would tell me what he was doing. And he used to tell me that it helped him because he used me as a sounding board. 'When I start telling you what happened, it becomes clear in my mind what I should do,' he said."

Little more than a year after joining Bekins, Andy came home with the news that he would be given the job of comptroller though not the title or pay until he had proven himself. "I'm going to have to completely rearrange the accounting systems in the company," he told Jane. "So be prepared not to see me too much for two years."

"I understood him," says Jane. "I knew this was the way it had to be and I appreciated that he told me what to expect. People in those days were all for their guys and did everything they could to help them. We were not ERA ladies. We shared in their achievements, and he always made me feel a part of it."

When Andy became a vice president, Jane was asked to help plan the social amenities for one of the Bekins family reunions. She wanted to have flowers and a basket of fruit in all the rooms for the arriving guests. It was just one of those things expected of a corporate wife.

Andy was a sensitive man. When their daughter married in June of 1952, they sponsored a large reception at the country club. Afterwards, Andy and Jane invited thirty of their closest friends to the house. The party was folding at 2:30 a.m. but picked up when all of Sally's friends arrived to keep it alive. They lingered until 5 a.m., playing records and musical instruments and dancing. "Andy said to me, 'You know, as long as we've stayed up this late and now that we have to start our lives all over, I think you and I should go down to the beach and watch the sun come up and start our new lives together,' " recalled Jane. So that's what they did.

The greater balance that Andreson was able to obtain at Bekins was not possible for Bob, Jack or Arjay at Ford or for Thornton at Litton. In the early days, Flora often worried whether Tex would die prematurely because he worked so hard and was under so much stress. Later, as she met more of Tex's business colleagues in groups like the Business Council, she saw something quite different. It seemed that the wives would die before their over-active husbands who, of course, would quickly remarry. She surmised that the wives probably died under the stress of being married to men who worked at a furious pace.

The overworked monks of business—whether in Detroit or elsewhere—seemed to extend their lives, not shorten them. In some queer way, there seemed little justice to the irony.

THE
WHIZ
KIDS

Jack Reith in sunglasses and a smile at the Indy 500 racetrack in 1956, posing with race car drivers. His oldest son, Fritz, is at left.

How much genius and how much folly was in Jack Reith's 1957 Mercury Turnpike Cruiser shown here? The public thought more of the latter. The Cruiser bombed and so did Reith's career at Ford.

If the Cruiser was Jack Reith in steel, his dreams and his ambitions, then the Ford Falcon was Bob McNamara. The McNamara-championed Falcon (above) was as utilitarian a car as the Cruiser was flamboyant. Unlike the Cruiser, it was also a huge success.

Chapter 21

THE INDY 500

■

"It is a piece of exotica . . . the
epitome of poor taste."

—Eugene Bordinat

*A*fter his flamboyant product launch in Miami, Jack
Reith walked headlong into a series of problems.
Within a week of Jack's return to Dearborn, Breech announced that
an outsider and friend, James J. Nance, former president of Studebaker-
Packard Corporation, would join the company as vice president of overall marketing. None of the Whiz Kids greeted the news with enthusiasm. It was an odd and curious development, for it only put another
body between them and Breech. Two weeks later, Jack found himself in
a heated meeting at the Mercury assembly plant in Wayne, Mich. A
somber Crusoe was there, crowded into the conference room with thirty
other executives and managers, to sort out massive quality problems with
the new cars.

Jack's new models required sharply sculptured sheet metal that
wrapped around a bulky Mercury frame. The doors made by the company's metal stamping division wouldn't fit the cars. Neither would

many of the other parts. You could fit your hand between some of the closed doors and the center pillars. At the Chicago stamping plant, some 13,500 Mercury doors that needed repairs had piled up in inventory. At an assembly plant in St. Louis, nearly two hundred employees were doing off-the-line rework operations, fixing what had just been manufactured.

There were quality problems with instrument panels, fenders, deck lids, lower and upper panels, pillars, doors and even the push-button transmission. The latter innovation, an internal Ford study would soon show, suffered a 50 percent failure rate during the first three months of customer use. The new models were coming off the assembly lines and being driven onto repair lines. Accusations were flung across the table. The engineers claimed their specifications were correct. The fabricators claimed they weren't. The assembly plant managers claimed they couldn't get the sheet metal to fit properly.

The quality problems were nothing new and not unique to Ford. But in the 1950s, a buyer couldn't defect to Honda. Every customer lost by Ford due to quality problems was picked up by GM, Chrysler or American Motors. Every customer lost by GM was picked up by Ford or the other firms. They traded the same disappointed customers again and again. Even Tex Thornton had reason to be disenchanted by the quality problems. At Thornton's request, Jack had earmarked a new 1956 Mercury Montclair for Flora soon after he took over the division. But Flora immediately discovered a spate of problems, even with a car specially flagged by a division's general manager. "It seems that the motor was not properly lubricated and after two hundred miles it sounded like a siren when running," Tex wrote Jack. "Also, the right rear door is too small for the opening. I think the dealer has taken care of all the problems she has had except the right rear door. Evidently there is no way to make the door opening smaller, or an automobile door larger. We don't mind so long as the door doesn't come open and we lose one of our boys." More than 10 percent of Mercury's 1956 models, at one point, had transmission troubles, forcing the division to process 13,500 warranty claims at a cost of nearly half a million dollars.

Car quality had become nearly unmanageable. One California dealer took delivery of a Mercury with a misspelled nameplate that read: Meccury. The quality of the cars was so bad that the plants could not even produce defective-free models for its own executives, including Ernie Breech or Bob McNamara. When Breech drove one of Ben's new Lincolns on a San Francisco business trip, the seat springs squeaked. A full investigation followed. Memos flew across several departments. The culprit: a jute insulating pad slipped out of position, causing the spring to rub against the seat frame. Breech also complained that the seat contour in the Turnpike Cruiser was uncomfortable. Another investigation ensued, and the engineers put through changes to fix it. The roof of a Mercury convertible sent to Dykstra leaked water. Bob's assigned Mercury also had problems.

It was not that Jack hadn't paid sufficient attention to quality. He would attach notes to his men on stationery headed with the phrase, "Operation Leadership." He hammered on them constantly to improve quality, ordering them to concentrate on such things as "door fits" because, Jack preached, customers determined a car's quality by whether the door opened quietly, closed easily and sized up perfectly against the car's body. He asked them to consider General Electric's market research when it developed a new combination washer and dryer. GE found that if an appliance lacked the "feeling or appearance of quality when controls are operated or doors are closed the customer will think the mechanical quality is poor also." Taking a leaf from GE, Jack insisted that special attention be paid to anything the consumer can see, feel and operate himself, from pull-out ash trays to glove compartment doors. Each item, Jack said, had to be "styled to give the appearance of strength, durability and quality."

It was a different definition of a quality product: Not absolute quality, but the "appearance" or the veneer of it—a problem that would severely cost Detroit years later when American consumers increasingly turned to Japan-made cars. It turned out, however, that Jack couldn't even gain the appearance of quality. The timing of Jack's 1957 program was widely believed to be the culprit. The men insisted they had to cram too much work into too little time because Reith refused to accept any delays in his grand plan to challenge GM.

Jack was caught in the sinking middle of the fight. As a division head, he had responsibility for assembly. But the manufacture of all the car's components largely came outside his purview. An engine and foundry division produced the engines. A metal stamping division turned out the deck lids, doors, trunks and fenders. Outside vendors supplied other parts. Even worse, by the end of October, 1956, the company's metal stamping division had delivered only three of twenty-six sheet metal samples for the Turnpike Cruiser, and two of the three parts had been rejected for poor quality. They were badly behind schedule on the Cruiser and nearly everything they were producing for Jack's other cars was of questionable quality. Alarmed by the extent of the problems, Jack wondered if the division should buy sheet metal parts on the outside for the Turnpike Cruiser and the Convertible Cruiser.

Bob's Ford division, the company's mainstay, seemed to be in much better shape than Jack and Ben's side of the business. It helped that the Ford division wasn't going through the dramatic changes Reith imposed in the Mercury line.

Earlier the day of the crisis meeting in Wayne, Crusoe received a startling memo from an increasingly frustrated Ben Mills, whose Lincoln Division already was off to an agonizingly slow start. The four-page, typewritten letter was astonishing for its candor and its criticism, however indirect, of Reith's splashy Mercury launch. Though he headed a separate division, Mills had to rely on the manufacturing plants of other divisions for his Lincoln models. His division also had to compete for corporate resources with Ford, Mercury, and now Edsel. Ben spent days working on the memorandum and then vacillated between forwarding it to Crusoe or sticking it into his files. Finally, he decided to put the message in the interoffice mail on October 25.

"In the last few weeks," Ben wrote, "the top management of the Ford Motor Co. has faced the realization that the launching of its 1957 models has been unsuccessful and extremely costly. Naturally, members of management have asked very pointed, but nonetheless very fair, questions as to what happened. Why did we miss schedules so badly? Why was management not informed by people who certainly must have known that the programs were unsound?"

After his dramatic opening, Ben said he lacked full authority to fulfill his job as a division head. Nearly eight years had lapsed since the company dedicated itself to the principles of decentralization advocated by Jim, Jack and Charlie. But Ford still hadn't reached it. Ben told Crusoe the company was "on a middle of the road course, halfway between decentralization and centralization. This results in divided responsibility and conflicting authority, which inevitably lends to the blaming of others in case of a showdown."

It was demoralizing to be held accountable for a business's results when you failed to have full control over it. Ben conceded that his passion and motivation to work for Ford was waning.

Pride of achievement is the strongest single motivation. A man will realize this pride of achievement if 1) he is given full authority to accomplish the job and 2) he is held strictly accountable for his results, be they good or bad . . . My mind is driven to thoughts of "rolling along with the tide," "hoping that in an enterprise this big any blame for failure can be steered to some other quarter," "computing my rate of income and finding solace in the realization that the pay is good" and other similar thoughts, none of which has anything but a deteriorating effect on the basic "pride of achievement" which is of dominant importance. It not only disturbs me to have such extraneous thoughts going through my head, but it also leads me to the conclusion that people in my organization are subject even more to an uninspired "I work for a pay check" attitude . . .

If I have any reputation at all, I believe it is based on my ability to organize people into a dedicated and effective team. They are dedicated because they are free to do their jobs in their own way and held account-able for the results they achieve. This philosophy is, in my honest opinion, being violated in portions of the Ford Motor Co. in such a manner as to preclude a flow of accurate information to top management; to preclude the holding of key executives accountable for their results, since the essen-tial authority is partially lacking; to preclude the dedicated attention of key executives to the single purpose of the Ford Motor Co. as opposed to the partisan protection of one division to the detriment of company objec-tives and other divisions.

Mills apparently never received a response to his memo. The com-pany's quality troubles and the lack of enthusiasm for Reith's new cars weighed heavily on Crusoe, who had been showing severe strain at work in recent days. The day after receiving Ben's memo Crusoe suffered a massive heart attack and was rushed to the Henry Ford Hospital.

If Jack was beginning to panic over his trouble at work, he didn't show it. On Saturday morning, October 27, he and Maxine went with friends to South Bend, Indiana, for the Oklahoma-Notre Dame football game. It was a typical Jack performance: irrepressible and agonizingly precise.

Every event, from the 8:12 a.m. pick-up of their friends in a hand-built prototype of the Turnpike Cruiser to their expected arrival time in South Bend was dutifully noted on a two-page schedule Jack carried with him. Once in the imposing car, Jack flew down the side roads from Birmingham to the Ann Arbor train station so that few people would notice the Cruiser. It wasn't scheduled to debut in dealer showrooms until several weeks later. He had arranged to put the car in a bonded garage in Ann Arbor before boarding the Alfred E. Smith car on the old Michigan Central Railroad. At the game, in a box of seats next to Notre Dame's president, the Fighting Irish left the Oklahoma Sooners for dead, beating them as one sports reporter later put it, "coolly, methodically, dispassionately as though they were meeting the junior varsity of Mrs. Featherington's finishing school for girls." The 40–0 rout left Oklahoma-born Maxine little to cheer about. But it was still a beautiful fall day and a memorable outing.

Instead of returning home after the game, the party traveled to the Oakland Hills Country Club, which they closed at 2 a.m. When Jack finally arrived home that evening, an urgent message was waiting for him. As soon as he read the note about Crusoe's heart attack, he turned to Maxine and said, "This is going to mean trouble for us." In one fell swoop, he lost his "twelfth floor protection"—a supporter with power in Ford's new headquarters, where Ford, Breech and McNamara had offices.

The problems quickly surfaced in the ten-day sales reports that the men of the automobile industry lived and died by. They were the most immediate barometer of success, a legacy of Alfred Sloan who began asking GM distributors for ten-day sales figures in the mid-1920s.

They caused tremendous anxiety. Every period, the reports filed in from each district sales office into each division. The numbers would get tallied up and the reports, each individually stamped with the word CONFIDENTIAL in red, would be analyzed by Arjay's men in the controller's office and delivered by hand to every member of the Administration Committee. And the second they arrived, secretaries would interrupt the business of the moment to give each executive the score for the latest ten days, confirming or denying the scuttlebutt in the halls. A quick scan would prompt a gloat or a shudder. A single percentage point change on this card would ripple through the organization, affecting hundreds of decisions and adjustments, changing steel orders and production schedules, scheduling overtime in the plants or temporarily laying workers off. For a single percentage point on the card could mean the difference between millions of dollars in profits and revenues for the company. "Beauty," it was said in the halls, "is a good ten-day sales report." A series of bad ones could mean dismissal.

What the reports showed was that Bob's Ford Division, chastised only a year earlier for over-emphasizing safety, was having one of its most successful years ever while Jack's Mercury Division was failing to deliver on his promises. On an average October day, the Ford Division was selling 54 percent more cars than it sold in September. Mercury was down 25 percent in the same period. By early November, Mercury sales were 55 percent below the previous year. Consumers were rejecting

Reith's cars because they were too extreme, and because the economy was beginning to slip into a recession. McNamara's 1957 Fairlane was stealing sales in the medium-priced market.

By the middle of the month, with Crusoe out of the picture, Jack walked into a buzzsaw. At a key executive committee session, Breech expressed far less enthusiasm for the program that he and the others had approved little more than eighteen months earlier. Yet, there were key elements of the plan that had to be implemented now. One of the most controversial aspects was the division of the Lincoln-Mercury dealerships. The plan required that dealers give up the Lincoln marque in favor of Mercury to allow Reith to more quickly expand his network of dealers and to make them more exclusive. If a dealer wanted to continue to sell Lincoln cars, he would have to gain the company's approval and build a separate outlet for Lincoln product. The plan anticipated that Ben would be able to sign up one hundred new Lincoln dealers and that the new Edsel Division would bring in a significant number of other dealers who would sell Lincoln cars along with the new Edsels. That way, Ben's Lincoln Division would largely have its own network of dealers, completely separate from Mercury.

It was an issue that was also creating tension between Jack and Ben. Mills could not come up with the new outlets as quickly as his current dealerships dropped Lincoln, and he worried that Edsel might not come through with its dual dealerships. Maroni, drafted as Crusoe's assistant before his heart attack, was in the uncomfortable position of having to mediate the details. One night, he recalled, the two friends thrashed it out for hours, unable to come up with a plan acceptable to both of them. All three of them were in Maroni's office in the company's headquarters building. The differences of opinion were sharp, and both men's reputations and futures were on the line.

"Look," Jack said, "this is what we've agreed to and this is what we have to do. We can't give up on it now. If it hurts your sales next year, that's the price we have to pay."

"There's no way we can reach our sales targets if this goes through," Ben argued. "We can't get the one hundred new dealers for Lincoln, and who knows whether Edsel is going to come through on the dual dealerships."

Each executive was pleading his case. Reith knew that if he failed to get his way, he would have no chance of ever meeting his goal of gaining 7.7 percent of the car market. Mills realized that if he couldn't delay the plan, his huge investment in a new 1958 Lincoln could prove a total waste. He wouldn't have enough dealers to market and sell the car. "From 7 p.m. to 1 a.m., I had Reith and Mills in a zoom, at each other's throat on the franchising issue," wrote Maroni to his father in a November 11, 1956, letter. "It will be hard to work out a compromise to keep them on the same side. At stake are hundreds of millions of dollars and the fate of thousands of dealers from coast to coast."

"I don't think you boys can pull this off," Breech told Jack. "If I were a dealer and you brought this thing to me, I'd kick you out." Henry sat in on the meeting, a silent Buddha. His face betrayed boredom, annoyance and skepticism. Breech began to distance himself from Jack's plan.

A WEEK BEFORE the Indy 500 race of 1957 where Jack would pace the event in a Turnpike Cruiser, Henry put McNamara into Crusoe's job and moved Jim Wright up the ladder as head of the Ford Division. It was apparent that Crusoe would not return to the company. It also became apparent that Reith was hanging onto his job by a thread. Now Jack, as well as Ben and Jim, would directly report to Bob.

Mercury problems increasingly crowded Bob's calendar: In his first month as group vice president, McNamara held meetings with Arjay about Mercury sales and the possible closure of a Mercury plant; meetings with Henry over the division's manufacturing troubles; endless sessions with Jack over quality, cost reduction, a profit improvement program, the dealer reorganization plan, advertising and styling. Bob was taking control, reviewing every detail and every aspect of Jack's plan. And now he was asking tough questions, too, the kind of questions that made it clear that business had become more important than their friendship, which had never really been tested before. Jack maintained his respect for Bob, but he also realized the threat he posed. "We have to watch out for him," he told Maroni, "he'll shoot us down."

If Bob had been completely candid with Jack, he might have confessed that from the beginning he had not been very fond of Reith personally nor impressed with him professionally. The group had not been there for six months when Bob was writing memos to Tex about the flamboyance of Jack's first reports. Instead of a simple binder for a company manual, he arranged for gold-lettered covers on an eighteen-ring binder with three-colored charts and gray backgrounds on printed pages. Breech cussed out Crusoe for the expense, and now Jack was planning another pricey presentation for the company's budgets which, Bob wrote to Tex, "had not been cleared by either you or me, and it was obvious that the printing bill would run into several thousands; my guess was $7,000 or $8,000."

It was a trifling matter given all the waste at Ford at the time, but it annoyed Bob because it was a sign that Reith was playing by his own rules. From the start, he badly wanted to impress people, and he didn't sense the need to report every detail to his superiors. Over the years, as the issues grew more substantial, Jack showed the same tendency to go overboard. When Jack worked alongside Crusoe in the Ford Division, he always campaigned to build greater production capacity than Bob and the rest of the finance department thought prudent. Henry wanted to beat Chevrolet, and Jack and Crusoe needed the extra capacity to do it. McNamara and Miller, however, were cautious: An asset was profitable only if it was employed; why pour money into assets that might be idle? Jack was more willing to have the extra capacity to meet peak demand.

Neither did Bob or the others share his conviction or passion for the great expansion plan he pushed through upon his return from Paris. It was, they all thought, too much, too soon. And then Jack lavished huge expense to launch the 1957 line, much more than Bob or Ben, who wrote Crusoe about it, thought necessary. Mercury's troubles, if anything, seemed to prove them right.

Bob would privately tell others that Jack only skimmed the surface of things, when Bob would demand and expect a broader, deeper level of analysis. He was not enough of the professional manager, the man who made decisions on facts, not opinion or gut. Jack's ambitions and his optimism got in the way. They had become an obsession for him. The workaholic had worked himself deeper and deeper into a fortress of his own making, further and further away from reality.

Like too much booze, too much ambition could weaken or destroy you. Reith had been drunk on ambition, losing the cautious perspective that had been the hallmark of his Whiz Kid colleagues. He always seemed to be over-promising. He had been off the target as soon as he took over Mercury. Jack kept claiming that the division would boost sales by 8.4 percent in 1956. Instead, sales plummeted 21 percent in the first seven months and never recovered to come anywhere close to his prediction.

He convinced Breech to pour huge investments into Mercury on the faulty basis that the division would be able to sell 423,000 units, that it would be able to capture 7.7 percent of the market from only 5 percent a year earlier. Now everyone was questioning the possibility and for good reason. It wasn't happening.

Maroni, Jack's good friend from their days together in Paris, would get called into meetings with Arjay and Ed.

"Why do we need all these extra dealers?" they asked.

"If we're going to sell 7.7 percent of the market, we need more capacity," Maroni replied.

"Well, how are we going to get a 54 percent improvement in market share in one year?"

Maroni, though he hardly believed it himself, repeated Jack's line.

"It's a unique line. We have broader coverage of the market. More at the top, more in the middle and the bottom. And we're no longer sharing body types with the Ford Division. So it's a better value."

When they suggested a revision in the numbers, Maroni argued it was premature to revise the targets.

"We were supposed to have three thousand dealers by Christmas and we did it," he told them. "We were supposed to have these new models with important market potential and we did it. We're still confident we can make the 7.7 percent target."

Around and around the questions would go. At the office, Jack's mood turned somber. He seemed, if possible, even more tightly-wound. His colleagues noticed that he seemed more tense, more impatient than usual. He returned to his old habit of chewing the ends of his pencils, leaving a trail of eraser bits and No. 2 wood splints on desks and conference tables behind him.

As he perused the sales reports, he must have felt like the helpless manager of a last-place team, sitting on the bench and watching the score worsen. Jack was still selling his plan, but no longer with the charm that he could so easily muster in the beginning. The strain was mounting. Jack's men, too, became tarnished, falling out of the charmed circle, while the men on Bob's team now came closer to the center, closer to Henry.

Breech began to turn up the heat, questioning everything—down to which magazines Jack should select for Mercury advertising. He didn't think Reith should advertise in *The New Yorker* because Breech felt its readership wasn't broad enough. Because Jack sometimes talked about the 1957 Mercury as being a "fashion car," Breech felt his advertising campaign should give more attention to women and fashion appeal.

He flew into a rage one Sunday night when he heard Mercury promoting its keyboard control as an industry first on the Ed Sullivan show —which was sponsored by Lincoln and Mercury. Chrysler had installed the same feature in its cars a year earlier. Breech, who had recently decried misleading advertising in a public speech, dashed off a quick memo on Monday morning, chiding Jack for the commercial. "My face was a little red when I heard us misrepresenting a gadget used in advertising," he wrote. "It seems to me that your air cushion springs; your larger cars; your motors; the Mercomatic transmission, and your performance should be played up strongly, rather than playing up some gadget such as 'keyboard control.' "

He even put pressure on Jack to cancel Elvis Presley's appearances on Ed Sullivan's show. Some dealers had sent telegrams to Ford headquarters to complain about the singer's risqué performance. "Because the situation is so serious and because of the adverse criticism coming from substantial organizations in New England, your Lincoln Mercury Dealers Association requests in the strongest terms that you cancel the appearance of Elvis Presley," wrote Frank Owen, head of the New England group. "Criticism of his performances is snowballing and may well create a situation that would be detrimental to the name of the Ford Motor Co." Cancel, Breech insisted, even if it meant paying Presley not to perform.

Jack, however, knew that trying to tell Sullivan how to run his show was hopeless. No one told Sullivan what to do, and now Breech was being a pain in the ass by forcing him to do the impossible if not the ridiculous. Sullivan's show was gaining record audience levels, thanks to Elvis.

Besides, Jack personally enjoyed Elvis. It was not because he loved his music, he didn't. But he was fascinated because he considered Elvis a true marketing phenomenon. Though he was no movie lover, Jack would drag Maxine, Donna and Fritz to the Birmingham Theater to see Elvis in *Love Me Tender, Loving You* and *Jailhouse Rock*. Elvis, Jack told Maxine, was the Al Jolson of the 1950s. Elvis's thrusting pelvis was the equivalent of Jolson's black face.

To placate Breech, he told him that the move would almost surely backfire on Ford. It was unlikely that Presley's manager, Colonel Tom Parker, would agree to a cancellation anyway. "According to Mr. Sullivan," Jack wrote, "Colonel Parker is a carnival-type promoter. It is quite possible that if a serious attempt were made to break the contract, Parker would exploit this fact through the press." It was enough to quiet Breech, but Jack still feared his grousing.

Breech was second-guessing almost all of Jack's plans. When Jack sought approval for more powerful engines, Breech complained that they would result in excessive noise and a rise in warranty claims. Breech expressed dismay when he spotted a new Mercury with red carpeting in the executive garage. He thought it was ugly and vulgar. Jack dashed off a memo saying that the carpeting was installed by mistake. It wasn't.

Increasingly, Breech and Reith engaged in a battle of reprimanding memos and dissembling replies. Breech shot them off in a stream, like volleys from a gun. They would burst in and around Jack and his men, who scurried to answer them. It was, of course, a one-sided battle, for Jack could not afford to alienate nor offend Henry's right-hand man. So his replies did not return the fire; they merely tried to deflect and shield it. Against the mounting criticism, Jack struggled to emphasize the positive.

He was guarded about his future with the company. News that went to the top had to be good news. That was a lesson taught him by Crusoe in the early days, and it was a lesson that stuck with him. If he had doubts and fears, he appeared to bury and suppress them. The bunker mentality was taking hold. When Ford initially tested the group for its "objective tendency," no one scored lower than Jack. "There is the suggestion of relative lack of ability to view himself objectively," was the way the psychologist described it more than a decade earlier.

All around him, the problems mounted along with the concern that he was reckless and too bold. Yet for the next model launch, Jack was devising yet another true spectacular. He thought up the idea to race a jet plane with one of his new Mercury cars on the company's test track in Romeo, Mich. "Our new car will out-accelerate any airplane in the country," Jack told promotion manager Hackett. "We'll line them up on the straightaway and have them take off at the same time. Our car will be out of sight by the bend!" It was as if he was in his own little world, blind to the deteriorating reality around him.

When he gazed outside the window of his new office in the old Administration Building, the view could only accentuate the positive, especially to the optimist in him. The large plate-glass window framed a spectacular picture of industrial might—the looming Rouge and its environs. It made the nearly impossible seem at least plausible. Shortly after the Miami debut, Jack had moved into this office—the same one that had belonged to old Henry Ford and to his grandson after that. Ford had by that time moved into the twelfth floor of the new glass-and-chrome headquarters building dubbed the "Glass House." But frugal old Henry would not have recognized his former office. It was draped in gold fabric, floored with soft sea-foam carpeting and outfitted with white-leather chairs and sofas. One wall was given over to a large map of the world, with plastic buttons marking the major installations of the Ford empire. It was a room that would nearly have fit Louis XIV, the Sun King.

Everything about Jack seemed incessantly ostentatious, hopeful and out of touch. Swathed in a lambswool Chesterfield with a velvet collar, he drove around town in a Convertible Cruiser in its standard Moonmist Yellow. For Maxine, he had ordered a two-door Cruiser in French beige with white and gold vinyl trim and a slew of options: from power windows to a glove box vanity mirror. Jack specifically asked that his men not install seat belts in the car—despite all of McNamara's mania for safety.

So even in the face of mounting trouble, the memos that flew from Jack's office were decidedly upbeat. Attaching a list of car registrations for nineteen states in a memo to Bob, Jack noted that in six of the states Mercury outsold all of its competition. "In thirteen states we outsold Buick, eleven states Oldsmobile and seven states Pontiac. This is by far the best market performance that Mercury has ever shown before in a fully competitive market," contended Jack. It was, however, only a small view of a big picture. Reith was carefully picking and choosing his facts, evading all the bad ones to serve up what was a misleading measure of the business.

When he could not write with enthusiasm about Mercury's sales, he wrote about the division's production. "Mercury is up 39 percent over the same period a year ago," he told Breech in late January. "All of General Motors' medium-priced car lines registered declines." But Jack was only building inventory in the face of a major recession in 1957, while GM executives had the foresight to cut production because sales were so bad.

For even in the midst of the Fifties boom, the economic system still was not able to maintain unbroken prosperity. A sharp recession had followed the end of the Korean War in 1953, and now a more severe recession was bearing down on the economy in the same year in which Reith had placed all his bets. The cars that continued to sell tended not to be the big, deluxe models like Mercury but the low-priced cars that McNamara was producing at Ford. Indeed, when *Business Week* surveyed auto dealerships during the slump, the magazine turned up only one dealer with what it dubbed "a boom on his hands." The automobile he sold: Volkswagen. "If you walked in today and laid cash on the table you'd have to wait sixty days for delivery," the dealer proudly declared, adding, "Detroit has gone the wrong way." Though no one knew it at the time, it was one of the earliest signals that Motor City wasn't producing all that the American public wanted. Reith had not envisioned a scenario that would make it impossible to achieve his overly optimistic projections, nor did he see the start of an important shift in the marketplace toward smaller autos. In the meantime, Jack's starry-eyed appraisals only provoked Breech.

For all the bombast and glamor, Jack's Turnpike Cruiser was proving a dud. By the end of the year's first quarter, Jack produced 101,322 Mercury cars, nearly double the division's output of 63,848 cars a year earlier. But while sales at Bob's Ford Division were way up (eventually allowing Ford to overtake Chevrolet for the first time since the introduction of the Model A), Mercury sales were flat. Jack was building massive inventory on little more than his own optimism. By late March, he put some plants on four-day work weeks and laid off 1,700 employees in St. Louis.

But all the bad news would not prevent Jack Reith from realizing one of his biggest dreams: driving a version of his dream boat as the Pace Car —the auto chosen to start the first lap of the race—in the Indy 500. It had to be the ultimate distraction from worsening problems at Mercury, further evidence that Reith was driving himself deeper into some fantasy detached from the real world.

THE GATES OPENED at dawn on a warm and mildly hazy morning. Car fans dashed onto the infield of the Indianapolis Motor Speedway, capturing the choice locations for the 500-Mile Race. Jack was still in bed, his sleep disturbed by a horrible nightmare on the eve of what would be the biggest thrill of his life.

In the dream, which Reith would later describe to friends, he heard the crowd cheer as he led the drivers around the track in formation in a gleaming, sun-glittered yellow Convertible Cruiser. He was driving the chosen Pace Car of the Year in 1957. Suddenly, as the Cruiser gathered speed for the flying send-off, his car stalled on the backstretch. The men in the racing cars behind him hit their brakes, fouling up the track in a huge tie-up. Worst of all, the Buick people at the race began laughing their heads off at Jack's predicament. Reith wasn't apprehensive about his own safety; he worried about embarrassing Henry and the company.

It was, of course, only a nightmare, and an unlikely one at that. For Jack had practiced and practiced the routine for weeks before the event. He and his son, Fritz, flew in the company plane to Indianapolis on the weekends so Jack could rehearse his laps on the track. It was a promotional coup for Mercury to start the race, a chance to grab the attention of people who loved cars like himself. Reith spent days in the pit, engaging the drivers in conversation about racing, lap times, automotive technology and car design. He had gotten tips from some of the best, Sam Hanks and Jimmy Bryan. Hanks had been at Wright Field with Jack in the Army Air Force during the war. Bryan had been cleaning up in stock car races with a Mercury.

They'd watch over Fritz, then not much more than nine years old, while Jack climbed into the Cruiser, flying down the track, looking for the right groove, feathering into and drifting out of the sharp turns. He careened around the asphalt ovals, as the speedometer needle on the dash touched 112 miles per hour. He had pushed the Convertible Cruiser, in his words "the most powerful car ever used to lead the Memorial Day classic," to 130 on a straightaway.

On the morning of the race, he was ready. The black top on the Convertible Cruiser was down. Jack could see his face in the polished chrome fenders. Fifteen minutes before race time, the Metropolitan Opera basso, Jerome Hines, sang the traditional "Back Home Again in Indiana." Then Speedway President Anton Hulman Jr., announced: "Gentlemen, start your engines." As the roar of the engines mounted, thousands of colored balloons soared from the Tower Terrace, a new stand behind the pits.

One could imagine Jack tightening his hands on the wheel. The thirty-three race cars noisily filed out of the pits and moved onto the track behind Jack's Mercury for the slow parade lap. When that lap was finished, Jack picked up the pace. But on the first line-up lap, a rookie driver ran into the rear end of one car and crashed its fuel tank, putting two cars out of the race and forcing Jack to take a third and final trip around the two and one-half mile track. He sped through the south turn, up the long backstretch past the golf course, through the north turn and down along the hallowed bricks of the homestretch, maintaining a steady advantage. He gunned the convertible to 100 mph and swerved smartly onto the pit apron as the green starting flag came down and the race was on.

Jack had come as close as any non-professional driver does to the sensation of actually driving a racing car in the Indy 500. It was a searing experience, one of the most exhilarating of his entire life. It was *the* event in car racing. Reith stepped out of the car all smiles. When he joined Maxine in Stand B, he shook with excitement, unable to control his trembling hands. Ben Mills offered encouragement as did many Ford men in their block of eighty seats. Three hours and forty-one minutes later, Sam Hanks sped past the grandstand to win the race.

Jack waited in line to congratulate Hanks as movie star Cyd Charisse kissed the driver's cheek. Jack had taken Charisse for a whirl around the track in the Pace Car a day before the race. The next evening Jack presented the keys to Hanks at the Winner's Banquet. Then he and Maxine left at 10 p.m. on the company's DC-3 for the one-and-a-half-hour flight to Des Moines, where Jack received the distinguished service award from Drake University.

Basking in the glory of piloting the Pace Car and acknowledging his business triumphs at his alma mater, Jack was trying desperately to distance himself from the more disturbing developments in Dearborn. In the past when Ford supplied the race with the Pace Car, the company would sponsor a private train from Dearborn to Indianapolis and back so that hundreds of executives and managers could attend the event with their families. This year, the train had to be cancelled because the Mercury Division financing was falling far short of Jack's expectations.

WHEN ALL THE Mercury registrations would finally come in for the 1957 model year, they would show that Jack only sold 136,162 cars, a far cry from the 423,000 he initially predicted and the weakest showing for the division since 1947. Mercury, the finance staff would later show, was losing $726 on every two-door Cruiser it sold. The car that Jack had thought of as a swan was increasingly being regarded as an ugly duckling. Henry and Breech viewed the car as a defect-prone, vulgar-looking product, laden with gimmickry. Bordinat, Jack's friend in the design studio, would later describe the car as "a piece of exotica which is probably the epitome of poor taste."

The car meant to be a recreation of "Gary Cooper on wheels" would become the "jukebox on wheels" that Lowry railed against, a symbol of ridicule and excess. Decades later, when *Life* magazine assembled a panel of car experts to choose the ten best and ten worst creations of American automotive ingenuity, the Cruiser would firmly secure a spot as the sixth biggest failure in the industry's history. "A clumsy car with a particularly unlovely quirk: its slant-back rear window," wrote *Life*'s editors. "What's worse, with rambunctious kids in back, it rolls down." The car to top the list of autodom's most infamous blunders was the Edsel, the product of Jack's ambitious plan to take on General Motors. McNamara, in the dispassionate prose of his corporate memos, would only refer to

Jack's styling as "controversial." But he would soon begin monthly reviews of all the Mercurys in the styling studio to insure that it would
never get out of hand again.

Breech was the kind of executive who would come to dislike anyone
who coaxed him into a wrong decision. "Jack was very good at what he
did," Bordinat would later say, "but he did tend to rig numbers to get his
own way. Jack was so sure that everything that he did would be right
that he didn't hesitate to warp the truth a little bit in order to make it
happen because he thought he'd be vindicated in the final analysis. It's
sort of like a guy in the service that disobeys an order and then captures a
hill. He receives a hero's badge. On the other hand, the guy that disobeys
an order and doesn't capture the hill is shot. Well, Jack got shot. It blew
back in his face, [and] that was the thing that Breech would hang onto:
'I, Breech, did not make a mistake in judgment. I, Breech, was given a
royal shafting by this son of a bitch that gave me the bad information.'
He said, 'I can't trust him.' "

Neither could Bob McNamara. By the end of June, Bob had gotten
Jack to agree to cancel the 1959 Turnpike Cruiser. It was already too late
to axe the 1958 version. By mid-July, Bob imposed the Ford Division's
quality audit system on Mercury plants to help solve the quality problems. In a confidential memo, he also asked Ben to personally review
Jack's future product programs at Mercury. By August 1, Mercury's
quality control manager was axed. Two weeks later, McNamara clamped
down still further, ordering Jack, Ben and Jim to get his written approval before assembling any car for which the company did not have a
firm dealer order.

As he pored over the numbers, Bob became convinced that Jack had
done a miserable job at managing his division. He calculated that Mercury could cut $20 million a year from its manufacturing costs if its
expenses were brought to the levels of the profitable Ford Division. By
putting back together the Lincoln and Mercury divisions that Jack had
taken apart, Bob estimated that the company could save another $6 to $8
million a year. He also noted that Jack had added $125 per unit to the
designed cost of the Mercury car since he took over the division. "Much
of the increase in the designed cost, moreover, has gone into features
which probably have little or no selling appeal," he wrote in a memo.

McNamara began taking a stronger hold on Jack's division, insisting
upon weekly meetings with him and key members of his staff to go over
every minute detail. That Bob felt differently toward Jack was even
reflected on his personal calendar. Whenever he had scheduled a meeting

with his friend, he would scribble "1:30 Jack Reith" into one of the daily slots on a monthly schedule. As the problems escalated, Bob would simply jot down, "F.C. Reith." It was a way to distance himself from someone who no longer was a friend.

At one point, Breech telephoned Bill Grimes, Jack's product manager, and began quizzing him about Mercury's products and quality.

"What do you think about the design of the Turnpike Cruiser?" Breech asked Grimes.

"Look, it seems strange to be asking me about this. Don't you really want to talk with Mr. Reith?"

"I don't want to know what Mr. Reith has to say," retorted Breech.

"I'd rather that you talk to him," said Grimes, not wanting to betray his boss.

"Meet us over at the styling studio in ten minutes," Breech said, hanging up the phone.

Grimes rushed into Jack's office to tell him about the strange telephone call.

"What the hell is going on?" asked Grimes. "I'm not going over there."

"Look, you better go," Jack said.

Grimes reported to the studio and dodged a barrage of questions from Breech. But it was clear to him and everyone else that Jack was in deep trouble. Some began to whisper that Jim Nance, the outsider who had become head of marketing, might take over Mercury. In fact, Breech had approached Nance about the possibility in mid-July. He told Nance that the company might consolidate Lincoln and Mercury again because the costs of supporting separate divisions could not be sustained by the current market.

"Jim," Breech told him, "I don't want your answer for a couple of days, but Henry concurs in something I want to ask you: would you undertake the consolidation?" A week later, after attending church on a Sunday morning, Breech visited with Nance at his home. Nance agreed to take the assignment. Bob would execute the changes as group vice president of Ford's car and truck divisions.

Jack did not hear the news until Friday, August 23. He was sitting in one of the black leather chairs in the basement barber shop, his hair being clipped by Edsel Beaty, the company's long-time affable barber. For years, Beaty had kept the hair of Ford executives neatly trimmed for $1.50 a cut and 75 cents a shave, while a porter polished their shoes. Jack was half way through his haircut when a message arrived that he was to see Henry immediately.

Jack left the chair and drove himself to the Glass House, took the elevator in the underground executive garage to the twelfth floor and made his way into Henry's office. It was a brief meeting. Henry simply told Jack what he had told so many executives over the years: "Things aren't working out." He told Jack they had decided to put back together the Lincoln and Mercury divisions and install Nance as its new boss. The debut of the company's Edsel car was only a few days away so there would be no official announcement of the change until a week later.

There could not have been much more to say.

Jack returned to his office mortified. He was asked to write a long memo for Nance and Bob on the current status of all of his division's major projects. Not only was he fired: he had to help his successor in the transition. In the hallways, the men of the corporation would piece together the facts from hints and snippets of gossip. Their knowledge was partial and second-hand, yet what little they knew captured the drift. "You'd hear around the watercooler that Jack was summoned to world headquarters and you knew the son-of-a-bitch would probably get fired," recalled one.

Jack, alone and depressed, confided in no one, his isolation growing by the day. "I could see how he couldn't talk to anyone then," said Maroni. "No one was his friend. If he approached anyone, they probably all ran away. They saw him as poison. He was now known as the loser. Who would want to be seen with him? Who was standing around Neville Chamberlain during the Battle of Britain? They were all blaming him for Munich. It was the same thing."

On his way home that night, Jack stopped off alone at the Fox and Hound, a tony restaurant on Woodward Avenue in Birmingham. Once there, he sought the security of a corner and a pinball machine. With a drink on the machine's glass top, he played and played and played. A couple of Ford men spotted him and wondered why Jack would be wasting his time playing a silly game. They preferred not to disturb him. He was alone with his thoughts, facing the flickering lights and bells of a novelty machine. "He played that machine throughout the time we were having dinner," recalled Gayle Warnock, whose own mind was fully engaged by the upcoming launch of the Edsel. "He was fixated by it."

When Jack finally reached home, he said nothing about his predicament to Maxine. Over the weekend, however, a friend called to tell her that her husband might no longer work at Ford. It was not the first time that something like that occurred. Obsession is the most selfish emotion, and Jack's emotions were all obsessive, all consuming. He closed himself off from his wife. A friend had told her earlier that Mercury was having problems.

"You know that, don't you?" the friend asked.

"No, I didn't know it," she replied.

"Well, there are some real problems in the division."

She finally asked him about it. "When haven't there been problems?" he retorted. "There's nothing for you to worry about."

"I hear that you're leaving the company," she told him.

"Where did you hear that?"

"I promised I wouldn't tell. Is it true?"

"Yes, it is."

Jack said he had lost his job as the head of Mercury, but he refused to be drawn into an explanation of what had happened to him. All that Maxine could think of was a social obligation she had two days later for the press launch of the Edsel. Every wife of a Ford vice president was expected to host a table for the introduction, herself included. Frankly, she couldn't imagine having to be the all-smiling Ford wife after her husband had just been gunned down by the company.

"I don't have to go down there to preside at that table for the press, do I?" she asked him.

"I sure hope you will."

On the morning of Tuesday, August 27, the Edsel introduction party began with a 7:30 a.m. breakfast for the media, followed by the car unveiling at the Styling Rotunda and a press conference. While Jack's dismissal was not yet official, the word was out among company insiders. At least six different Ford wives called Maxine to ask if they could drive her into Dearborn for the event. Jack, meanwhile, had left on a New York business trip on Monday to meet with a couple of Mercury dealers for a previously scheduled meeting. He wouldn't return until late Tuesday.

Maxine went to the luncheon for the wives of the newsmen that day and pretended that it was like any other day because that was what everyone expected of a good corporate wife. The Ford Rotunda's center court had been transformed into an outdoor garden for the event, with round tables topped with white linen arranged around a reflecting pool. An ensemble of violins entertained the 240 guests, and slim models pranced down an all-white runway in the latest fashion designs from New York.

While Maxine sat through the masquerade, Bob walked into a 2:30 p.m. executive committee meeting in the soaring Glass House with a twenty-six-page confidential report of recommendations, memos, press releases and organization charts. Bob was a masterful writer of the corporate memo. He was facile, brief and dull. His memos never volunteered more information than was necessary to gain a decision in his favor. They were devoid of all emotion and passion. In this latest batch, Bob urged the committee to relieve Jack and Ben of their duties as divisional general managers.

In a memo accompanying the report, Bob stated:

> Recent studies strongly indicate that the consolidation of the Lincoln and Mercury Divisions is in the Company's best interest. Such a consolidation would result in important cost savings, a simplified organizational structure and more effective administration of Lincoln and Mercury dealers . . .
>
> I request committee approval of the following:
> 1. The consolidation of the Lincoln and Mercury Divisions into one division, to be named the Lincoln and Mercury Division.
> 2. The appointment of Mr. J.J. Nance as General Manager and of Mr. Ben D. Mills as Assistant General Manager of the Lincoln and Mercury Division.
> 3. The assignment of Mr. F.C. Reith to my office.
> 4. The assignment of Mr. V.Z. Brink to the Central Finance Staff.

The report included an innocuous two-sentence resignation assembled by Bob for Jack to sign. The letter, to Henry and Breech, was bland and succinct: "Consistent with the organizational changes that are being made involving the Lincoln and Mercury Divisions and my consequent change in assignment, I hereby resign as Vice President of the Company. I also resign from the Administration, Product Planning, Technical Evaluation and Scheduling Committees."

The memo didn't simply strip Jack of his duties; the punishment lay in depriving Jack of his status as a vice president of the company, removing him from all those committee assignments, from having any substantial say in any of the company's business.

The committee, however, refused to go that far. Even Henry apparently couldn't go as far as Bob. The blow of losing the Mercury job was enough. In the lower right hand corner of the proposed letter, Bob scrawled the panel's decision in his handwriting: "Defer resign as VP. Others not req'd."

Three days later, on Friday, after the media had left Dearborn in their Edsel loaners, the memo went out making the changes official. That weekend, the janitors moved Jack's belongings out of Henry Ford's old office and into a smaller room in the Glass House.

Henry finally offered Jack a job as head of Ford of Canada, but it was nothing compared to what he had had. The Canadian company was little more than a sales arm with no manufacturing facilities of any kind. Jack thought he should leave the company. He and Tex Thornton had begun to discuss the possibility of Litton acquiring troubled American Motors Corp. Litton was becoming a raging success; its revenues would soon jump to $100 million in 1958 from only $3 million less than four years earlier. Thornton was casting about for ever-larger opportunities to satisfy his expansionist ambitions. At the time, he had no idea that Mercury was a disaster and that Reith was responsible for the mess. If Litton took over AMC, thought Jack, Thornton could give him the job of trying to turn the loss-plagued company around.

For a few days in September, there were a flurry of phone calls, telegrams and letters to discuss the potential deal. Jack arranged to contact George Romney, AMC president, about the possibility and then flew off to New York to meet with Tex about the plan. Thornton even privately mused that American might become immediately profitable if all of Litton's subsidiaries purchased its cars so that AMC would have a captive market. Nothing would come of it, however, because Romney had little interest in a merger. After several years of losses, he expected AMC to move into the black in 1958. He had no intention to sell out now.

There were other promising possibilities for Jack. An old friend from Des Moines called him as soon as he read of Jack's demotion in the newspapers. The call led to an offer from Avco Manufacturing, a diversified company with $315 million in revenues.

Avco wanted him to become president of its Crosley Division in Cincinnati, one of seven company divisions. The job lacked the allure and glamor of the auto business. The Crosley Division had helped make Avco one of the leading appliance makers in the country in the early 1950s. But a dizzying decline had caused its refrigerators, television sets, ranges and freezers to be hopeless also-rans. So Avco pulled out of appliances and the Crosley Division became a defense contractor, producing fire-control systems, aircraft components and radar equipment. Jack's assignment would be to broaden the division's commercial and industrial work. If he could succeed, he would have a chance to become president of the overall company.

It was not an easy decision because some of his friends were pressing him to accept the demotion and remain at Ford in the token job that

Henry had offered him. They thought he could ride out the problems and make a comeback. John Bugas, the man who had once grilled the Whiz Kids after their first meeting with Henry, and William Gossett, Ford's general counsel, even called Maxine on the telephone to ask her to convince Jack to stay.

"Don't let Jack quit," Bugas told her. "This is just a slap on the wrist. Tell him to take the job in Canada and everything will work out."

Maxine tried to persuade Jack to take the Ford job.

"Oh please, why don't you do it," she pleaded one evening. "I've always wanted to live in Canada anyway."

"Look," Jack said, "I'm 42 and this is my last chance. I've only worked for two companies in my entire life. And this is the last chance I'll ever have to change jobs again."

Maxine did not look forward to the move, and neither did their children. Fritz was ten and Donna was eight, both old enough to object to an uprooting. Charles had turned three only three months earlier. They had lived comfortably in the area, enjoyed the company of many friends and didn't really want to start all over again. Not knowing of Breech's role in the dismissal of Jack, Maxine wrote him in longhand a letter filled with affection for the company on October 30, 1957.

Dear Mr. Breech:

I can't stop being one of the "Ford Motor Co. wives" without telling you how much I have enjoyed every minute of it.

I'm absolutely convinced Ford must inspire more loyalty to the company in their employee's wives than any other company in the U.S.

In spite of being terribly thrilled with Jack's new job, I hate to think of us (is that being presumptuous?) no longer being affiliated with the Ford Motor Co.

Whatever the vague relationship is between a wife and her husband's company, I feel sad in breaking it. Jack and I have decided I must have a father image or something where the company is concerned—and if I do, it's because of the consideration and thoughtfulness I have always felt the company showed the wife.

It's been a thrill and an inspiration to me, knowing you and Mrs. Breech. My own personal thanks to you—and also—I'll never drive anything but a Ford product.

Sincerely,
Maxine Reith

A week later, she received a typewritten letter from Breech who clearly seemed surprised by Maxine's letter.

I have already told Jack, and I will tell you, that it is a matter of great sadness to me that things did not work out the way that I had dreamed of and planned for them to work out in Jack's case, and I think it is so nice of both of you not to hold rancor in your systems against us or the company. These things are bound to happen, and one must be broad-minded and philosophical enough to accept them.

I know that I and Jack's other friends at the Ford Motor Company wish him complete success in his new venture, and we wish both you and Jack complete happiness.

THE
WHIZ
KIDS

Accounted Profits at Ford Motor Co.

	1955	1956	1957	1958	1959	1960	1961
Ford Car	$253	$248	$230	$289	$385	$326	$367
Thunderbird	(155)	(723)	(508)	162	374	398	470
Falcon						209	310
Mercury	69	8	(369)	(395)	(129)	(63)	174
Edsel				(1,117)	(156)		
Lincoln	(298)	(1,051)	(1,525)	(920)	(464)	99	(35)

Whiz Kid Ben Mills, who was demoted with Jack Reith, is later assigned the task of cleaning up the Edsel mess.

Bob McNamara's Ford Division was keeping the company in the money through the late 1950s. His decision to redesign the Thunderbird turned a car that was bleeding money into a winner. Reith lost, on average, $369 for every 1957 Mercury his division sold, while McNamara's Ford Division booked $230 in profit for every 1957 Ford sold. Ben Mill's Lincoln Division was bad news, too: It lost $1,525 for every car it sold in the 1957 model year.

Data: A confidential analysis by the finance staff's cost department in 1960. The 1960 and 1961 model years were estimates.

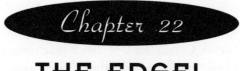

THE EDSEL
FIASCO

■

"This is the Edsel . . . Never
before a car like it . . . The one
car that can look you in the eye
and say you never had it like this
before."

—FORD ADVERTISEMENT, 1958

*G*one but hardly forgotten: Jack would long be remembered as the executive who sold Ford on the plan for the Edsel Division. Not even the headlines about the Soviet Union's threatening rain of nuclear bombs on the United States could dampen Detroit's paranoia over the Edsel.

On August 28, 1957, the Detroit *Free Press* reported this global news in a banner headline along with another local disaster in the making: the introduction of the Edsel—the first new nameplate launched by Ford in nineteen years. The car, named for the son of the original Henry Ford, made its debut in an orgy of hype—a two-day, all-expenses-paid junket for six hundred reporters and their wives, daughters and fiancees. Bountiful luncheons, fashion shows, a grand dinner-dance with the Glenn Miller orchestra—no expense was spared.

Bob and Margy McNamara sat at a ring-side table at the dance. It was just the sort of vaporous hoopla that flashed red ink before Bob's eyes—

just the sort of extravagance that would have been planned by Jack. Fairfax Cone, head of the advertising agency Foote, Cone & Belding which was awarded the Edsel account, sat at the table with the McNamaras. He spoke glowingly about the new car, though Bob seemed unimpressed. When Cone asked McNamara for his opinion, he said flatly: "I've got plans for phasing it out." Cone's face froze as he waited for an explanation that McNamara was not about to give. He hadn't known that Bob never supported Reith's plans, or that McNamara believed he could extend the Ford line upward to satisfy different customers.

But his off-handed remark was a harbinger of trouble for a car that was to become an embarrassing failure fast. In the first ten days, only 683 Edsels were sold each day—a dismal showing for a new auto given the vast promotional efforts of the time. Sales slumped to 440 cars in the second ten-day report. To reach the company's minimum expectations of a 200,000-car year, between 600 and 700 cars had to be sold every day.

By the end of September, when sales had fallen to little more than 350 units a day, McNamara gathered Richard E. Krafve, head of the Edsel Division, and nearly a dozen of Krafve's key executives to his office. He was not in a good mood. He testily handed each man around the conference table a piece of paper.

"I want you to put down what you think the Edsel Division will lose this year," he said.

The men pulled out their pens and made their estimates in silence as McNamara looked on. Finally, he collected the papers and read them all off. The numbers varied greatly, but each executive predicted a financial disaster—just what Bob had expected.

McNamara declared that he wouldn't put up with any more substantial losses. He began to pick the car apart, grousing that the push-button transmission—the feature that Jack had installed in his Turnpike Cruiser —was a meaningless gadget. So were other "trinkets and gadgets" of the car, he said, from its toggle switches to a dashboard compass. He ridiculed the car's styling, too. The car's front grille was likened by one writer to a toilet seat because of its shape. *Time* magazine said that the front of the Edsel looked like "an Olds sucking a lemon."

"He used our loss estimates as his platform to explain why the program should be stopped," recalls Emmett Judge, Edsel's product planning manager. "Some of us, including myself, pleaded that the program might have been developed improperly in some respects. We probably made a lot of mistakes. The premise of needing another car in the medium-price range was wrong, and the name was wrong. But I was still in favor of retrenching and then plodding ahead with a slow-growth approach. Bob wouldn't listen. He did that at times. It was evidence of the strong conviction he had. You'd go to a meeting in his office and it was fun and amusing. We'd sit down to ostensibly have a meeting and he would start off by saying here's what we're going to do. Thanks for coming. The meeting is over."

As group vp of cars and trucks, McNamara hit the road on a personal fact-finding tour to visit Edsel dealers griping about the sloppy workmanship on the car. The Ford Division accomplished the task of making Edsels by simply speeding up its assembly line. A huge plant in Mahwah, N.J., that built sixty Ford cars per hour would now produce sixty-one cars on the first day of Edsel production. On the second day, Ford would squeeze still another Edsel on the line every hour. The speed-up forced huge compromises in quality and sparked much friction between McNamara and Krafve.

Fairly quickly, McNamara developed a quality control system that tallied car defects by number. The idea: no car could be delivered to a dealer if it had more than thirty-five defect points. A missing part was equal to twenty points, a chip in the paint cost a tenth of a point. Auditors would examine a sample of the cars coming off the line. If the sample of six to eight cars averaged more than thirty-five points each, they were rejected and shunted to the "boneyard" for repair before they could be sent to dealers. That meant, however, that some cars could far exceed the arbitrary point total as long as the sum total of all the cars in the sample stayed within the average target. It was a system that condoned defects by allowing the shipment of cars with problems. When the cars finally were driven off the lots of dealers, other surprises often awaited the new owners of the Edsel: Just as the owners of the Turnpike Cruiser discovered, Edsel's push-button transmission also had a 50 percent failure rate within its first three months of use. Some cars were shipped with upholstery that didn't match or with loose nuts and bolts in hubcaps and door panels—the result of frustration by the workers over a speeded-up assembly line. In some cases, dealers received cars with repair instructions tied to the steering wheels.

The mediocre quality of the car could not have helped its sales, which were still trending lower and lower. Even a network television show for Edsel on October 13, featuring Bing Crosby and Frank Sinatra, failed to generate an uptick in sales. In November, 1957, two months after the car's release, when sales fell to only 222 autos a day, panic began to spread. (Sales would bottom out to a disastrous 113 units per day in the final ten-day period of the year.) Krafve put together a program to boost sales, hoping to present it before the company's Planning Committee. But when McNamara learned of his plans, he insisted on getting an advance peek at what the Edsel chief had in mind.

As soon as McNamara arrived for the meeting, he removed his jacket and sat at the end of the long conference table. It was as if he was ready for a brawl. "First of all, I want you to forget who I am," he said. "I want you to tell me if you think the Edsel has a chance with the program you're working on. I'm going 'round the table and will give each of you an opportunity to speak your mind. I want all of you to be candid."

McNamara began with Krafve, who believed his plan could save the car if its quality problems could be eliminated. "The Ford plants have built thousands of them now and the last one off the line is not much better assembled than the first," griped Larry Doyle, Edsel's marketing manager.

Immediately, McNamara buzzed his secretary and asked her to retrieve his report file from one of the dealer trips he made. As soon as his secretary handed him the file, he began to read aloud his notes. After completing one dealer report, McNamara slapped it on the table with a bang. Then he would reach into his folder and pull out another note to read, going through each one faster and faster. Not one of the dealers, according to McNamara's interview notes, mentioned quality problems with the car. Instead, several of them groused about the Edsel's advertising and promotion campaign.

Doyle mounted a feeble effort to convince McNamara otherwise, but he received little support from his colleagues around the table. Like many of the company's other executives, they did not want to face McNamara's bitter wrath. Though they were fearful of saying so, several of the Edsel executives believed that McNamara was unwilling to hear that his former Ford Division, now run by his friend Jim Wright, was turning out shabby product.

It was not the first time that McNamara focused on the Edsel advertising campaign. At an earlier session, Bob astounded the division's marketing managers when they arrived for a meeting at a headquarters' conference room only to find newspaper and magazine advertisements for Edsel and its competition taped to the walls. McNamara arrived for the early morning session wearing his galoshes and quickly launched into a harangue on the ineffectiveness of the Edsel advertising campaign. The men were stunned when McNamara, still in his wet galoshes, raced atop the white leather chairs placed against the walls to single out the ads mounted too high for him to reach from the floor.

If he disliked an ad, he ripped it from the wall, leaving tears in the wallpaper from the tape used to hang the advertisement. When the session ended, "It looked like a band of vandals had just left the room," recalls C. Gayle Warnock, Edsel's publicity manager. Said another executive who watched the spectacle: "That was the most incredible performance by a Ford executive I'd ever seen."

Yet, within Ford, they all knew how tough McNamara could be, even with his Whiz Kid friends. When Ben Mills had to go before Bob to present an advertising budget at one meeting, McNamara quickly interrupted him to get in the first word.

"Now Ben," he said, "I know that you're going to present a $29 million advertising program. But we can't afford it. There's no way that I can support that program. Our comparison studies show that it is much too expensive."

"Well, now, Bob . . ." Ben interjected.

"Ben, I'm just telling you. I am here today to tell you that I will authorize a $22.4 million program. I think that's within reason. So I don't think you should waste my time going through this. There's no way it can happen. Now I will say this: If there's any point in time that you'd like to talk about this again fine. But I think it's a waste of time. Let's go on to item number two."

And everyone would move on. "So the eyes would fall around the table after the weeks of work that went into the presentation," recalls Robert Jenkins, a Ford executive who attended the meeting. "And that was it. He was pretty cold about it."

Roy Brown, the Edsel's head designer, was trying to salvage the marque, hoping that the next year's models would prove more popular. But no one—not Breech or McNamara or Ford—had any interest in truly saving the car. Their dislike was apparent at a presentation by Brown of the proposed 1959 and 1960 models. "Roy was making a speech . . . and nobody was responding to Roy's marvelous words," recalls Kenneth Spencer, a fellow stylist at Ford. "Then one by one the executives got up with tape, and pencils, and knives, and were hacking up the clay models. And Roy continued his speech, and then he finally just stopped and walked away. It was terrible. The only word I heard out of the darkness was, 'Looks like a goddamn circus wagon!' I wanted to crawl into a hole because I knew it was bad—it was junk."

Market research showed that it would take a long time for Edsel to overcome its poor image. Besides, the economic recession that had settled in by August of 1957 would not end until April of 1958, bringing auto sales to their lowest levels in six years. On December 4, little more than three months after the Edsel launch, McNamara prepared a confidential memo urging the company's Operating Committee to abandon the car at the earliest opportunity. On January 15, Edsel was absorbed into the newly-created Lincoln-Mercury Division under Jim Nance, the Studebaker-Packard outsider brought into the company as vice president of marketing. He came to Ford with the understanding that he would have a shot at the presidency if he performed well as a vp—and that immediately made him a rival of McNamara's to whom he now had to report.

Under considerable pressure, Nance went about dismantling the Edsel Division and laying off three thousand employees. Warm and enthusiastic, Nance was a meticulous planner but an indecisive manager. A car and driver picked him up for work every day, and by the time he arrived at headquarters, he had his day planned—hour by hour—and had dozens of notes to distribute to his underlings. "Damn near every day, there would be ten to fifteen notes asking you to look into this or that," recalls Ben Mills, whose demotion made him Nance's assistant. "The decisions just kept getting put off with more and more notes. A week would go by and we would still ask questions when we should have made a decision. He really was afraid to take a firm stand."

He quickly got the nickname "Jungle Jim"—partly because he was wild and was preoccupied with his own image, so much so that he hired an outside public relations firm to help give him greater prominence at Ford. It was something that made Ed Lundy, who disliked the press anyway, especially critical of him. Nance worried how others, particularly his superiors, viewed him, often asking his assistant Mills how he looked after a meeting or presentation.

Sometimes he exercised bad judgment. On a business trip to New York, he told newspaper reporters that Ford would not be interested in getting into the small car business unless sales reached a certain volume. He had not been cleared to say anything to the press. McNamara and Wright had been quietly working on a small car at Ford for months, but no one at the company wanted the competition to know of the plans. The next day the papers reported his remarks, and Ford, Breech and McNamara were enraged that he violated company policy.

Besides, the trio of car lines under his purview—Mercury, Edsel and Lincoln—failed to show any marked improvement. When the consolidation of the divisions was largely completed by mid-summer, Nance took off to his cabin on Torch Lake in northern Michigan. It wasn't long before friends called to warn that McNamara was out to get him. The rumor spreading in Dearborn was that Bob had delivered an ultimatum to Henry Ford II: Dump Nance or McNamara and the other Whiz Kids would leave. The rumor was nonsense, but it underscored the mythical power that evolved around the group.

Even so, Nance's time was limited. While he was still away on vacation, Ford and Breech called Ben Mills to headquarters and asked him to assume the responsibility for the Mercury-Edsel-Lincoln Division.

"What about Jim Nance?" asked Mills innocently.

"We're going to fire Jim," answered Ford. "What in the hell has been going on over there?"

"Well," said Mills, "Jim did have trouble reaching decisions, and he wasn't very well liked." Mills embellished his remarks until Breech finally asked him, "Why didn't you tell us about it before?"

"Mr. Breech, you asked me to be Jim Nance's assistant. My loyalty was to Jim Nance and there was no way I was going to go around him. I disagreed with a lot of things he did, but was his assistant."

"Well, we're going to fire him and want you to take over the division," said Breech.

Mills agreed, but not before insisting on two conditions, which was pretty presumptuous.

"I want to be sure that both of you think that I am the best guy in this company for that job because, if I'm not, you get the best man and put him in there.

"Second, I want five years guaranteed because there is no way that anyone can turn a division around in less than five years."

Ford and Breech agreed to Mills's conditions and the Whiz Kid who had been demoted along with Jack now found himself in a new and better job than the one he had lost. Unlike Reith, Mills didn't allow failure to destroy him. His expectations were more realistic, and he never isolated himself from the support of his friends or of his family. He understood that success demanded a high tolerance for failure. When he lost his job, he didn't brood over the circumstances. It was just one of life's setbacks that he would have to ride out.

And while he waited, he focused on little else but his new job. "The job I have today is the best job in the world," he told himself. "No questions asked. No comparisons. The reason is because it's the job I have. If I'm going to sit around and waste time worrying about what's next, I'll never understand the fundamentals myself." More than a simplistic approach to work, it lent a neat balance to his life. Mills wasn't going to be one of Henry's presidents, but he was going to make time for other things in his life—from running the choir at the local church to spending time with his wife. He wasn't all work. "There were any number of occasions during my career when things didn't go exactly as I had hoped or planned," he recalled years later. "But I figured that I couldn't possibly expect to get my way all the time. There were bound to be setbacks, and in a big corporation survival is the first thing on your list. So I simply rolled with it. I said to myself, 'I will survive and I just may turn out to be this guy's boss someday.' And by God, it happened."

When Nance finally returned in early September of 1958, he, too, was summoned to Henry's office. Breech, still chairman of the board, was not in the room, though McNamara was sitting in a chair expressionless and silent.

"Sorry, Jim, it isn't working," Ford told Nance.

Ford never explained why he had failed in the job. Nor did he explain why Breech, who had brought Nance to the company, wasn't at the meeting. Nance hardly needed an explanation, though. Henry no longer needed Breech, who would soon leave the company himself. The same day of the meeting, Ford reported that Nance had resigned. Ben would take his place and have to confront the nagging problem of the Edsel.

BEN KNEW THAT Bob considered the Edsel just another Turnpike Cruiser —a big, clumsy blunder. When McNamara discovered that one of his neighbors, Robert Angell, was about to buy a new car, he was interested in knowing what it would be. Angell, a member of McNamara's book group and head of the University of Michigan's sociology department, told him he had always driven Pontiacs. But this time he was going to buy a Chevy because the Pontiac had become so large that he couldn't squeeze it into his garage. McNamara, Angell recalls, seemed alarmed by the remark. He wondered whether a Ford would fit and asked his friend if he could drive his own car over and try it. In fact, some of the Fords had become bloated boats.

McNamara was growing concerned by the swelling size of Detroit's cars—especially because each year the German company Volkswagen was increasing its market penetration with a tiny beetle-shaped auto. In the early 1950s, Volkswagen was shipping nearly 20,000 of the cars into the U.S. a year. The conventional wisdom in Detroit was that only damn fools who couldn't afford to buy Fords or Chevrolets would purchase the cheap, ugly car. Not so sure, McNamara asked his small market research group in the Ford Division to find out who was buying the cars.

The results, McNamara recalls, "scared the hell out of me." Lawyers, doctors and professors were buying the cars, not people who didn't know any better. Bob tried the Beetle out himself and liked it enough to ask Jim Wright and other Ford executives to test drive the car. They did so but to McNamara's chagrin did not share his enthusiasm. Still, Bob believed the success of Volkswagen could be attributed to the German company's ability to find a new, untapped car market instead of following the strategy of competing in the well-established one, the tactic employed by Reith in convincing Ford to make a bigger go of it in the medium-sized market.

In 1958, the German car maker sold 104,000 of the odd-looking bugs in North America, while Toyota was making its first foray into the U.S. The same year an internal study by Ford forecast that by 1961 "foreign economy car" sales could, if uncontested by Detroit, rise to 360,000, roughly 6 percent of the industry total. There were other ominous trends. From 1954 to 1959, the price of the basic Ford car had risen by $450. Foreign automakers, however, had been able to hold the line on prices, because of their lower wage costs and growing sales along with a strategy of fewer model changes. The price gap between the popular-priced U.S. car and a typical small import grew sharply, and economy-minded buyers began to swing to imports in growing numbers.

For more than a year, Bob McNamara and Jim Wright had been campaigning for a small car but had run into considerable opposition. Crusoe used to insist that Ford couldn't make money on a smaller car. But McNamara ordered up fourteen separate marketing research projects over a four-year period until finally gathering the facts and figures to make a convincing case. He and Wright finally gained approval to build an economy car on March 19, 1958. If the Cruiser was a car that personified Reith's reckless optimism, the Falcon—McNamara's economy compact—was a completely utilitarian vehicle that embodied McNamara's more cautionary beliefs. It was an idea car, the ideas being largely derived from his market studies of foreign car owners and dealers and potential car buyers. Around Ford, in fact, they called it a "paper car" because the car took shape in the printouts of McNamara's planners who had surveyed thousands of Americans—asking their preferences on the number of cylinders in the car, its length, weight, passenger capacity and gas mileage. The research took intuition out of the decision-making, but its results also appealed to McNamara's sense of economy.

He believed that the purpose of a car was to get a person from one point to another as cheaply as possible—no-frills economy transportation. The Falcon put his ideas into practice. Bob wanted something austere and clean, pragmatic and economical. It had to fit into the market below the typical Ford and above the used-car market. And it had to sell for less than $2,000. In other words, the car had to be the antithesis of Jack's steel cartoon.

It was not the kind of car that would appeal to an automotive purist, nor was it a car that Henry Ford could ever get excited over. "I don't think he ever liked the Falcon," believes Wright, who with Bob, was involved in every step of the car's development. "Henry thought it wasn't a Ford. We had a helluva time getting across the idea that any vehicle we produced in the division was a Ford." And many of the car designers actively despised the idea of a completely functional car. "At that time, all the stylists were telling us they couldn't make a good looking car out of a little thing," recalls Wright.

Throughout the process, McNamara and Wright fought and struggled to keep it under the $2,000 price tag. McNamara watched that level like a hawk, determined to keep the car light and free of gadgets, without the fins and the flash of the era's clunkers. He decreed that it would come in only solid colors, not any of those ghastly two- or three-tone jobs. He insisted that there not be any superfluous trim on the car, not even a single strip of chrome. It had to have simple body lines and a plain grill. Its gasoline mileage had to be at least 50 percent better than standard cars, and its mechanical components had to be designed so a competent backyard mechanic could take the car apart with hand tools. "Maximum function for minimum cost," as Bob put it.

When the car came to market in the fall of 1959, it weighed in at 2,366 pounds, about three-quarters of a ton less than the standard Ford. And at more than a foot shorter than the full-sized Ford, it could fit in anyone's garage. Bob held the line on the pricing, too, allowing the two-door sedan to list at just $1,912. The Falcon became immensely popular, the best-selling of the new economy cars introduced by the Big Three in 1959. In the first year alone, it sold 417,000 units, earning Ford a tidy $209 in profit per car.

For a short while at least, the Falcon's success helped to turn back the tide against the imports. Its popularity was in marked contrast to Jack's Turnpike Cruisers which cost Ford more than $700 in losses for each car sold in 1957, or the Edsel which piled up $1,117 in losses per car in 1958. Even Henry could not argue with that kind of success.

McNamara finally halted all Edsel production on November 19, 1959, discontinuing the car that would become known as the industry's most infamous blunder. The Edsel was dead. Between 1957 and 1960, only 109,466 Edsels were sold. Falcons would now run off the same assembly lines that had been producing Edsels. When Arjay Miller and Ed Lundy toted up the numbers, they discovered that the Edsel cost the company $250 million in losses—at that time one of the biggest commercial failures in the history of American business—not including the huge investments lost by the car's 1,200 dealers.

Bob McNamara was conquering Detroit. In 1957, when Reith's Mercurys were a failure, his Ford Division had beaten Chevrolet in total car sales for the first time since the introduction of the Model A, a victory repeated in 1959. He had put an end to the disaster Reith started and, even though no one considered him a car man, he now had a wildly successful automobile in the marketplace that he could call his own. McNamara's only public flop was a retractable hardtop convertible which turned out to be too complicated and too expensive and was quietly abandoned when the 1960 models were introduced.

Bob's success had to gall Jack, the Whiz Kid outcast who was trying to make another go of it elsewhere.

Jack Reith with his dream car, the Mercury Turnpike Cruiser. Not long after the car's debut, he lost his job, left Ford and the group in search of a second chance to rise to the top of another company. He didn't make it.

A BIRTHDAY

■

"An act like this is prepared
within the silence of the heart, as
is a great work of art."
—ALBERT CAMUS

*W*hen Jack Reith arrived at Avco, his task was to rebuild
the Crosley Division and to supplement its defense work
with commercial and industrial business. The company assumed that
Jack's connections in Detroit might make that goal easier to accomplish.
But that assumption proved wrong.

Reith came to Cincinnati not as a failed executive from Ford, but in
the words of a misinformed local reporter, as "one of the nation's top
sick-industry fixer-uppers." "This offered another challenge for me," he
told the journalist. "It was a company with a problem, but with good
opportunities. I just couldn't resist it. Age was a consideration, too. I can
handle the job now, but in ten more years I probably couldn't. It seemed
like my last chance to pick up a company and grow with it."

He accepted the work, though he continued to show signs that he was
still detached. He arranged to have a barber shop set up in the company
headquarters—not unlike the one at Ford from which Henry had sum-

moned him to the Glass House—so he and his top executives could save time. He prepared unrestrained and impressive presentations of his plans to the board and military procurement agencies. Jack had been on the payroll little more than three months when he was publicly announcing plans to double production and employment in five years and to move Crosley into the commercial field within sixty days.

Crosley, however, lacked the glamor and the scale of the car business. In the auto industry, if you move one decimal point in marketshare, profits soar. If you can take a few dollars out of the design cost of a car, the savings go right to the bottom line. At Crosley, Jack was mainly dealing with cost-plus contracts for the military. There was virtually no reward for squeezing the costs out of production. Instead of dealing with people who loved cars, who talked about cars as if they were strikingly beautiful women, he more often found himself with Ph.d. scientists working on Crosley's military contracts.

He sorely missed the passion of a business he loved. If Jack had not been a Catholic and rejected reincarnation, he would have wanted to come back to life as a race car driver. He loved the thrill of racing. Indeed, when he was trying to convince his young daughter, Donna, to give up jumping hurdles on horses for fear she could get hurt, she threw his love of race cars back at him.

"Donna," he told her, "why don't you find something to do that isn't so dangerous. It's not a social thing to do like playing golf. You're not going to say, 'Let's all get horses and jump fences.' "

"Daddy," she replied, "you know you would have given anything in the world to be a race car driver. You didn't get to be one, but you sure would like to have been, wouldn't you? Well, that's dangerous and you would have given anything in the world to do it. That's the way I feel about horses."

It shut Jack up. He told Maxine he could never say another word to Donna about it. Driving the Pace Car was the thrill of his life. Every new friend he met in Cincinnati was told the story of how he sped the Cruiser around the track to set up the Indy 500 race. He still dragged a very bored and fidgety Fritz, his oldest son, to one stock car event after another.

But in Cincinnati, business wasn't clicking. Jack found it difficult to gain the commercial work to keep his division busy. Competition was severe, the recession was still holding back the economy, and some of his plants lacked the flexibility to do a wide range of work. By late 1959, some two years after he joined the company, it had also become clear to

Jack that he had lost the race for the presidency. Victor Emanuel, Avco's chairman and chief executive, was sixty-two years old and near retirement. President Kendrick R. Wilson would likely succeed him, opening up the presidency Jack coveted. By late 1959, however, another divisional vice president, James R. Kerr, who headed Avco's highly profitable Lycoming Division, had won a seat on the board of directors. Kerr's division had been Avco's saving grace when the appliance business was bleeding the company dry. It specialized in sophisticated defense work and showed enormous promise producing military and civilian aircraft engines.

When the company awarded Kerr a directorship, it was the tip-off that Jack had lost out. Some of Jack's plants kept from the old Crosley appliance days were still only partly busy because he was less than successful in gaining the other commercial business to keep them active. Even worse, a decline in defense orders forced Jack to lay off three hundred employees in mid-April. "We knew he was under a lot of pressure at the time, but I don't think anyone thought it was that bad," recalled Gordon Tuttle, who served as general counsel in Avco's New York City headquarters. "It was clear that things weren't going well."

JUST HOW BADLY things were going would become evident to all on the birthday of Charles Crusoe Reith, the boy named after Jack's old boss at Ford. On July 3, 1960, there was supposed to be a grand party at Jack Reith's house. There was an oversized turkey ready for basting, a cake with seven candles to blow out, and gifts galore.

"Jack! It's time to wake up," cried out Maxine, clattering up the stairs to the main bedroom. "C'mon, you're sleeping the day away!"

Maxine waited for her husband's voice. It was late. But Jack had fallen into the habit of staying in bed long after sunrise on Sundays, recharging his batteries after a week of work at Avco. Even away from Ford, he remained a man who worked hard and played hard. One of the boys checked in on him earlier in the morning, only to report that dad was still sound asleep.

But now, at two o'clock in the afternoon, Maxine was anxious to rouse him from bed. She opened the door to the master bedroom and couldn't believe what she saw. Jack was sprawled over the bed, still clad in his pajamas. He was laying on his back, with his legs hung over the side. A pool of blood covered his chest and the clean snow-white linen on the bed. A .38 caliber Colt revolver lay near his left elbow. Two spent cartridges were in the cylinder. His dark-rimmed glasses were still on his head. A wedding band and a gold, black stone ring were on his fingers. It was a horror in a residential area of tall trees, sprawling homes and quiet streets.

Maxine reached for the telephone, frantically dialing Edmund Schweitzer, a neighboring doctor and family friend. Within minutes, he arrived with his wife, who swept the three children out of the chaotic house on West Rookwood Drive in Cincinnati. When the physician grasped Jack's hand, it was cold and failed to deliver a pulse. Sometime during the night, Jack sat up in bed, pointed the gun to his upper left chest just above the heart and pulled the trigger. Traces of gun powder were on his right hand. Jack was only forty-five years old. There was no birthday celebration that day. Betty Schweitzer kept the children away from the radio for most of the afternoon so that they would not be able to hear news reports of their father's death.

Maxine had not heard a gunshot. The night's quiet had been disturbed by severe thunderstorms, and she had a bad cold and a hacking cough that caused her to sleep in the guest room. She wished him good night just around 11 p.m., not long after he had been entertaining the kids in the backyard. He was setting off firecrackers, placing them under cans that shot into the sky. When the police the next day pulled in front of the mammoth stone house at the top of a hill, some neighbors thought that someone had complained about the noise Jack's celebration caused.

There was no suicide note. Maxine felt sure that if Jack really killed himself he was the kind of man who would leave a note, with precise instructions on what she should do. She searched the room for some sign, some clue to the terrible tragedy. There was nothing, only a copy of *Time* magazine on the bedside table. Someone once said that when you don't know what to do with your hands you light a cigarette, and when you don't know what to do with your mind you read *Time* magazine.

Jack had owned the gun for only a few months. Avco's security department had given it to him, Maxine would later remember, after he had received threats on his life from someone he fired at the company.

"I'm going to get you," the man taunted. "I'm going to kill you and your family," recalled Maxine years later.

Security was called to Jack's office to escort the man out. Maxine had to warn the school not to allow the children to leave without her or Jack. She even tacked up a quilt over the glass doors by the library so no one could peer into their house. Jack carried the gun to work everyday in his briefcase, though he never expressed much worry about the threat.

Jack could be moody, thought Maxine, but no more so than anyone else. Sometimes, though, he could become temperamental. Earlier in the year, the day before Easter, Jack had argued with Maxine over her reluctance to accompany him on a business trip to Florida. She felt that since the children were home for spring vacation she should stay with them. In a fit of anger, Jack took his gun out and squeezed the trigger "I'll show you what this gun will do," he said.

It was not meant as a threat, no more so than someone who grabs an ash tray, or anything else within reach, and flings it across the room in an emotional outburst. Moments later, you feel foolish and guilty for your childish behavior. It was like that with the gun, except of course it was far more serious to shoot a pistol in one's home. The bullet ricochetted off the tile in the bathroom and soared harmlessly out the window. If anything, it revealed Jack's high-strung fragility.

Still, Maxine could not bring herself to believe that her husband deliberately killed himself. He never spoke of suicide. He showed no outright signs of depression before his death. He was under no medical care. His only outward worry was some slight concern that his eyesight, which required that he wear glasses all the time, could weaken further. Obviously, it was not a grave concern. He had even begun to talk, perhaps half-jokingly, about a dream to own a hardware store when he retired. Jack said he would have his two sons and Donna's husband work in the store with him. He would locate the business in La Jolla so he could play lots of golf.

Only the day earlier, on Saturday, he had been out with friends on the greens at the Hyde Park Country Club. No one noticed anything terribly unusual about him, certainly nothing that would have suggested he was getting ready to take his own life. On Friday afternoon at work, he was laying plans for a business trip to Philadelphia, meticulously going over exactly what kind of room he wanted to stay in at the old Warwick Hotel.

Since they had moved from Dearborn, he had led a different life. Jack even announced the change to her after they settled into their new home. "You know," he said casually one day, "I could never again work as hard as I worked at Ford." For Reith, who was not openly introspective, it was something of a confession, a remark she would remember for years. He could not completely change, of course. Jack still was not always willing to share his thoughts with her. One time she was harmlessly complaining about a Crosley appliance that had been giving her trouble.

"Just throw the damn thing out and get what you want," he shouted.

Maxine was taken aback by his tense response. Only later in the evening did she discover that a union had called for a strike at his Avco plants. People called the house all through the night about it. The strikers also got their personal phone number and pestered him with an endless string of phone calls. Even when Jack took the phone off the hook, they were able to break through with the help of the operator. Finally, Jack covered the phones with pillows and blankets and went to sleep. "If you had just told me about the strikers," Maxine told him, "I wouldn't have complained about the refrigerator." Her concern seemed so trivial next to his strike, but he hadn't spoken a word about it until the phone began ringing off the hook. It was the same old Jack Reith, closed off and detached.

At times, he would seem happy, even content in Cincinnati. Maxine believed that Jack survived in this changed life, with different satisfactions and motives. Less a workaholic, more a family man, he was achieving, she thought, a more balanced lifestyle. They did something as a family that they had never done before: they took family vacations together. While at Ford, Jack either didn't have the time or the inclination to bring the children on vacations with him and Maxine. They were always left with baby-sitters and nannies. But in the nearly three years since he had left Ford, he and the family went to Disneyland and elsewhere.

There was too much holding Jack to life. He adored his children, and they adored him. It fell to Maxine to discipline the children because he was so lenient with them. After dinner, he would shoot baskets with Fritz or go out in the street to toss a football with him. Charles would play soldier with Jack's medal from France. How could he have killed himself on the day of his youngest son's birthday? A Catholic, how could he have chosen an alternative that his faith recognized as the most deadly of mortal sins?

These were questions that nagged and shocked his friends. When Maxine called Ed Lundy to tell him of her husband's death, she could hardly force out the words. She asked him to pass the word to the others. George, who had kept in close touch with Jack, was heartbroken. So was Tex, who had spoken with Jack on the telephone only days earlier. He was trying, once again, to bring him to Litton in a top job. "Jack's spirits seemed to be high and apparently things were going well with him at Crosley," Tex later wrote a friend.

Reith had kept in touch with his friends at Ford. Breech had even paid off on a bet the pair had made in better times. Jack wagered Breech

$200 that General Motors would not have a new body shell in 1959 and that GM's new 1959 model would not boast the compound windshield that Jack had put on the Turnpike Cruiser. He also would pay occasional visits to Dearborn and talk with members of the old group on the telephone.

To the outside world, Reith was hiding his failure again. On the inside, he must have begun to doubt his relevance. He reached that time of the soul when Scott Fitzgerald said it was always three o'clock in the morning. Few have any idea of the inner torture that precedes suicide. But Jack held himself to an exceptionally high standard of accomplishment, along with unreasonable ambition, and finally he was plagued by a great sense of disappointment and despair.

His dream car was no more. His dramatic reorganization of one of America's industrial giants was undone. His rivals—once friends and comrades—had leaped over him in their own achievements. And now he could not even win the contest at Avco, a company only a fraction of the size of Ford. For someone who once glimpsed the presidency of the second largest industrial corporation in America, it was a crushing defeat. He had aggressively pursued the promise of business; began to realize and appreciate its power at Ford, only to lose it more quickly than he thought possible. Somehow, the promise failed him.

The cover of the *Time* magazine Jack had at his bedside contained a story on the dramatic success of the compact car. Detroit had turned out its millionth compact in June, two weeks ahead of schedule because of the unexpected demand for smaller cars. Bob McNamara's Falcon—many of them produced in factories that had been geared up and built to make Jack's Mercurys and the new Edsels—was a huge success. All of Jack's predictions about the importance of the medium-sized car market proved dead wrong.

Back in Dearborn, Jack's friends and foes read the story under the Detroit *Free Press* headline: "F.C. Reith, 45, Ex-Ford Ace, Commits Suicide." They would whisper about the news for weeks. Some feigned no surprise that Jack could kill himself. He was, the Ford men surmised, unaccustomed to adversity so he couldn't cope with it.

Only in retrospect would Jim Wright think back to his telephone calls to Jack. He and Jack shared the same birth date, September 4, which also happened to be Henry Ford's birthday: so every fourth of September, like clockwork, Jim would call Jack and they would gossip about things. The last time they spoke, there was something in his voice, Jim thought later. It wasn't something that he could really put a finger on at the time.

But after Jack's death he knew what it was: he never sounded more vulnerable, more wounded than he did on that phone. "He just didn't talk like the old Reith, with the enthusiasm he used to show," recalled Jim. "I didn't think he wanted to be what he was."

Jack may well have regretted his decision not to accept the demotion and stay at Ford. A few months before his death, he had telephoned Bill Gossett, the general counsel of Ford who had tried to convince him to take the job in Canada. "He was unhappy, very unhappy," said Gossett. "He called me up and asked me to talk to Henry to see if he could come back. He was sick and tired of what he was dealing with over there. I told him I didn't think it was possible. There would be powerful opposition to it."

Some of Jack's other friends from Ford also saw the difference. He had gained weight and it showed in his face. It appeared puffy and there was a fold under his chin. He also lacked the spark they had come to recognize whenever he walked into a room. He seemed a man riven by internal tensions that he did his best to conceal. John Cuccio, one of the stylists in the Mercury design studio, had lunch with Jack three days before his death. "He introduced me to his managers in Cincinnati," recalls Cuccio, "and I remember that he was quiet. He didn't have much to say about the plans of Avco. It was not exciting or glamorous like the car thing. When you're into automotive, everything else is nothing. The stature, the size, the money can't be beat. He wasn't the same."

With his new-found neighbors and friends in Hyde Park, Jack seemed to spend a lot of time in the past, conversing as much or more about his days in Detroit than about his new life in Cincinnati. "He talked about being the Pace Car driver in the Indy 500," recalled Mrs. Schweitzer. "He said it was great and he would talk about it like a kid." Indeed, Jack missed at least one large, neighborhood party on a Memorial Day, preferring instead to attend the Indianapolis 500.

They were, however, only pieces of the puzzle, pieces that failed to complete the picture. The unequivocal motives that drive a man to take his own life are hidden, far from public view. Jack may have measured his worth in the eyes of others. His life, by the standards he set up himself, no longer made sense. Having left a world he loved, a part of his identity was eroded, his self-esteem injured. He faced a future unable to satisfy his once great ambitions.

If it was a telegram that led to their journey to Detroit together, there was oddly enough another telegram that conveyed with finality the dreadful news of Jack's death. It was as simple and direct as the one

George and Tex had drafted to Henry Ford fourteen years earlier. The men received the message from Avco's president the day after Jack died: "It is with deep regret that we inform you and your associates of the death on Sunday of F.C. Reith . . . Requiem High Mass will be at St. Mary's Church, 2851 Erie Ave., in Cincinnati, at 10:30 a.m., Wednesday, July sixth."

It was a grim group of tired men who went to pay their final respects that morning. Wright marshalled the team together, arranging for a company plane to fly himself, Bob, Ben, Arjay, Ed, Charlie and a couple of other friends to Cincinnati for the funeral. It was a morgue-quiet trip. Few people said much of anything on the plane. "We were all in a state of shock," recalled Chase Morsey, one of Jack's friends. George Moore flew in from Washington. Thornton and Andreson, unable to shake their business commitments in California, could not make the funeral and church service.

That there was a Mass for Jack was itself something of a victory for Maxine, for the Catholic Church does not honor suicide victims with a service in church. Initially, the church refused to hold a Mass for Jack. It was not until a neighbor of the Reiths, Thomas H. Clark, prevailed upon the parish priest, that the church consented to the service. Clark had told the priest that none of them could know for sure whether or not it was suicide and that the benefit of the doubt should be given to Jack. By the day of the funeral, however, the city's Violent Crimes Squad and the Hamilton County coroner already had determined that it was a suicide. The fact that Jack had not left a note, the coroner said, was not unusual. Only one in five suicides ever do.

Ford also dispatched a public relations man to Cincinnati, presumably so no one would connect the suicide to Jack's treatment by the auto company. As a former senior executive at Ford, Jack was still covered by a generous life insurance policy that provided for double indemnity in the event of an accidental death. So Ford also sent to Cincinnati its own investigator to examine the details of Jack's death. The man reported back to Robert Dunham, who had sponsored the joyous celebration for Jack and his fellow Whiz Kids when they got their promotions as general managers. Like the coroner, the investigator ruled it a suicide. He discovered that Jack could not have been cleaning his gun at the time because no cleaning solvents or rags had been found in his bedroom.

The men grimly filed into St. Mary's Church after watching the funeral home's pallbearers lift Jack's casket from the black Ford hearse, carry it up the seven stone steps and down the aisle of the English Gothic church. It was one of those terribly hot summer days when the last place you'd want to be is in church. On this July day, the place promised no relief from the heat nor much relief from the pain. The group had gathered for what might have seemed the last time. They had shared many triumphs and many defeats through the years. They had come to know each other's strengths and deficiencies. Maybe that's what made it so hard to understand. How so sensitive and bright a man as Jack had moved to such frightening extremes, how a life so full of great promise could end in self-destruction.

No one was more shocked by the news of his death than Charlie Bosworth, who had been the first of them to really know Jack as a friend and colleague. Gentle and engaging, he had at one time been closest to Jack of the ten in the group. They had worked together during the war, played out some typical wartime poses in New York and remained good friends during the early Ford days. Their friendship drifted apart when Jack left for Paris and when he returned only to busy himself with the Mercury job. Charlie had spoken to him a few times since he joined Crosley and had never detected anything unusual. Like virtually all his friends, Bosworth tried to convince himself that it wasn't a suicide, but something deep inside him made him fear the worst.

The flag-draped casket was laid before the pure white marble altar in St. Mary's. A heavy silence hung in the air, broken only by the words of the liturgy or the grand organ loudly playing "Dies Irae." The words and psalms bounced off the oak-beamed ceiling, echoing through the cavernous space. There was no eulogy for Jack. The Mass was in Latin, and the heat together with the indecipherable language made it seem as if the formal ceremony would never end. Some began to dab with handkerchiefs at their sweaty foreheads. George Moore was beginning to fidget in the church, and so was everyone else.

IF BOB HAD ever regretted his competition with Jack, he hardly showed it. Throughout the Mass, he was leafing through a pack of three-by-five note cards, ostensibly rehearsing for a business meeting the next day. He was not far behind the pew containing Maxine and her children. Years later, Bob conceded it was one of the toughest things he ever had to do— to fire a friend from his job; he would think of Jack as one of the casualties of the failed business plan to take on General Motors. Yet, when interviewed years later by another journalist for a book on Henry Ford, McNamara suddenly asked, "How is Jack Reith doing these days?" The question shocked the reporter. Bob had attended his funeral, yet years later he had put it all out of his mind. And in the English oak pew of the church, as he breezed through his cards, he showed little sympathy or remorse.

At Gate of Heaven Cemetery, after a brief graveside ceremony, the men sadly walked to the procession of parked cars on the nearby road. The workmen waited for all the mourners to leave the area before they would lower Jack's raised casket into a gaping hole dug in the ground. The cemetery's lush grounds were monotonously flat and surrounded by strong tall trees. Each grave was marked, not by an upright tombstone, but by a small two-foot-by-one-foot bronze marker that was flush with the ground. As the limousines drove off, Bosworth turned his head to peer out the back window for a final glimpse. "I'll never forget the very sad sight of driving away from the cemetery and seeing just that lonely casket all by itself," he recalled years later. "It didn't seem right."

They drove the five miles to Maxine's house to pay their respects to her. They grieved for Maxine and especially for her three children. She was composed when they arrived and they embraced her, each friend telling her how deeply sorry they felt for her and the children. "Is there anything I can do for you?" She heard the question dozens of times. Maxine listened quietly, exchanged a few nods and a few words. The men, of course, were polite enough to ask no questions, though she did offer an explanation. To protect Jack from the shame of suicide, Maxine told his friends that his death was an accident, that he was cleaning the gun when it went off unexpectedly. "I don't think even she believed it," said Morsey, one of Jack's Ford colleagues. "But that's how great a lady she was. She wouldn't want to say anything against Jack."

When the men returned to Dearborn, not all of them could put Jack out of their minds. If they had the chance to see someone who knew Jack in Cincinnati, some of them would gently inquire about his state of mind there. None of the visitors could provide any clear answers. In truth, no one knew with absolute certainty why Jack drove a bullet into his chest. But they did know that he was high strung. When he had a drink in his hand, you would notice it. The ice in the glass would sometimes clink. His handwriting, too, displayed a slight tremor. And when Jack tired, they remembered, he could drag his leg a little—a lingering sign of an earlier bout with polio. But it all seemed just a tense nervousness that was a part of his character. "I had never known Jack to be depressed," said Charlie. "During the entire war period, despite enormous problems and desperate situations, Jack was never depressed. He was always the optimist."

He was, thought some of his other friends, outwardly optimistic. But

he also was the kind of man who was stingy in expressing his own
personal thoughts. He was certainly that way with his wife, even re-
sisting the need to tell her that he had lost his job or that he had
arranged to send her mother a new car as a gift. Few people, if anyone,
really knew what thoughts coursed through his mind that night. One of
the more penetrating views of suicide came from the Soviet writer and
Nobel Prize winner Boris Pasternak. "A man who decides to commit
suicide puts a full stop to his being," he explained, "he turns his back on
his past, he declares himself a bankrupt and his memories to be unreal.
They can no longer help or save him, he has put himself beyond their
reach. The continuity of his inner life is broken, his personality is at an
end. And perhaps what finally makes him kill himself is not the firmness
of his resolve but the unbearable quality of this anguish which belongs to
no one, of this suffering in the absence of the sufferer, of this waiting
which is empty because life has stopped and can no longer fill it."

Like the true victims of suicide, Maxine mulled over the excuses and
the rationalizations but could never find a tidy answer to satisfy the
mystery of Jack's death. Neither could anyone else. In the end, the tragedy was not so much that he took his life, but that he lived so totally for
business that when he lost his ambition, there was nothing left. Not even
a birthday for a young son.

THE
WHIZ
KIDS

Bob McNamara (left) and Henry Ford II on November 9, 1960, shortly after Ford announced that Bob was named president of the company.

Bob with his new boss, President John F. Kennedy, in the White House.

Chapter 24

PRINCIPLE
VERSUS
EXPEDIENCY

■

"Just as the student now feels
technique more vital than content, so the trainee believes managing an end in itself, an expertise relatively independent of the
content of what is being managed."

—WILLIAM H. WHYTE

Two new presidents took stock of their faithful on November 9, 1960. They were kindred souls in a way, seizing different pieces of the world stage, one corporate, the other public.

In the tightest election in nearly half a century, the forty-three-year-
old John F. Kennedy had just gathered his political supporters in Hyan-
nis to thank them for helping to elect him president of the United
States, the first Roman Catholic and the youngest man to win that
office.

At the same time in the Ford Rotunda, Henry Ford II and Robert S.
McNamara took over a pair of seats at a turquoise velour-draped table
on a small auditorium stage. Henry announced forty-four-year-old Bob
McNamara as his new president. Jim Wright was named Bob's successor
as vice president of cars and trucks.

Ever since Ernie Breech had resigned as chairman of the board in
July, the consensus was that Bob would somehow succeed him. Now

Henry was making it official. McNamara had cast his rationalist spell on Ford. He had proven that he knew how to make money for the company when every other division was bleeding cash, and this promotion was his reward. Ford assumed the titles of chairman and chief executive, while McNamara became the first non-Ford to occupy the presidency since 1906.

"Mr. McNamara," Ford explained to the Detroit press corps, "is the kind of fellow who has facts and figures in his head that other people have to look up."

Less than two weeks later, McNamara provided a stunning display of his managerial brilliance at an internal conference for the company's senior executives at the Greenbrier Hotel in West Virginia. Chartered trains hauled hundreds of Ford managers from Dearborn to the annual corporate retreat, where the top officers engaged in reflective speechmaking.

Bob was at the top of his form, every bit the visionary that Ford could ever have hoped for. His two-hour presentation, with help from both Jim Wright and Ben Mills, warned that rising prices and wages in the U.S. would invite greater competition from foreign companies. He articulated the idea of a world car, an auto whose parts would be made in different countries around the world to take advantage of their lower costs of production—a breakthrough in thinking at a time when no one in Detroit had even begun to acknowledge foreign competition or to foresee its coming impact.

It was McNamara at his sublimely confident best. Quoting Harvard Business School scholar Theodore Levitt and a foreign competitor, the head of Volkswagen, he zipped through a commanding and remarkably forward-thinking analysis of the car business. His views were startlingly prescient, if foreboding, and they would cause many Ford executives— even decades later—to wonder just how differently Ford would be today if McNamara had stayed in the job.

Fittingly, like all McNamara sessions, the presentation overflowed with facts, figures and charts. unit labor costs, output per man-hour, indices of industrial production and prices. Every figure was compared with its equivalent not in Japan, but in West Germany. Indeed, not a single word was spoken about the threat of Japan, which had made little progress in the U.S. market. Toyota, for example, had first entered the American market in the mid-1950s, but its cars were poorly designed and lackluster in performance. Instead, McNamara foresaw a greater threat from European carmakers who he believed would be "larger, more aggressive, and more efficient than most of the present overseas companies."

What seemed to cause McNamara the most concern was the lower costs of labor outside the U.S. In 1952, West Germany's labor costs were a third higher. Due to vast improvements in productivity and relatively stable wage rates, however, West Germany by 1959 had achieved an 18 percent advantage. McNamara was predicting that West German labor costs would be 30 percent lower than U.S. rates by 1970.

"Should the trends continue," McNamara warned, "our domestic passenger car market will be invaded a second time by foreign producers and the second invasion will not be limited to VW-type products." To prevent greater losses in marketshare, McNamara urged Ford to push the bottom of its product line down to meet foreign competition. His own Falcon was one example, although the Volkswagen Beetle was selling for $300 less than the Falcon. He also believed the industry would have to consider sourcing selected components abroad where they were significantly cheaper. To this end, McNamara was planning a smaller and less expensive car, then called the Cardinal, which would rely on a West German-made engine and transmission to compete more directly with the VW.

McNamara sensed, too, that Ford had to reexamine not only its selling prices, but also to reevaluate how it measured the total cost of car ownership to consumers—a cost which included, McNamara believed, the cost of service and repairs. "With the prospect of further service cost increases, it is doubly important to hold total ownership costs down through increased reliability and durability, designed into the product and built into the product by the manufacturer," he argued. In the years to come, of course, Japanese automakers would learn this lesson better than anyone in the world. Though McNamara was among the first in Detroit to express it, his almost fanatical assault on costs—even those necessary to assure the basic quality of Ford cars—was a blatant contradiction.

In a final attack on Reith's failed plan, he declared that the car had declined in importance as a status symbol. It was what he had always considered it: a means of personal transportation and nothing more. "The consumer has become more critical in determining the amount of money he is willing to expend, both for his transportation, as such, and for nonfunctional values. His primary requirements at the present time appear to place increasing emphasis on true functional value, product reliability and durability, economy of operation, and convenience."

IT WAS AN astonishing performance. Indeed, anyone reading Bob's twenty-three-page-long analysis could not be anything other than taken aback by the warning it sounded. McNamara wasn't only a bean counter; he was a fortune teller. His foreboding prophecy of the industry's troubles was made possible not because he especially understood the business. It was because he stood apart from it, because he was going against the grain, building small cars when Jack and the others were pouring on the chrome. At this moment, the times were on his side. His prescriptions, surfacing from the total faith he had in the meaning of figures, were the right ones—or at least they seemed to be.

In choosing McNamara as president, Henry Ford might have thought he selected an executive who could protect his future and his company. No one was more elated by the news than Tex Thornton, the person who brought McNamara to Ford in the first place. "Bob's election as president of Ford Motor Co. is not only something that he well deserves, but is also great for that company," wrote Tex in a letter to George Moore on December 2, 1960. "I am confident that Ford in the future under Bob's leadership will become the standard of industrial management efficiency that General Motors was in the past under Mr. Alfred P. Sloan."

Sloan, however, he was not. McNamara's ascendance at Ford was symptomatic of a new trend overtaking Corporate America. At one company after another, the men of finance began a stampede into the top positions of many of the country's largest corporations. Only two years earlier, Frederic G. Donner, a reserved, thin-lipped accountant, had been chosen to head General Motors after the retirement of Harlow Curtice, Jack Reith's proclaimed hero. Curtice would become GM's last dynamic leader. The shift later prompted renegade John DeLorean into noting that Curtice was "the last guy who was president of GM who really ran it."

Like Donner at General Motors or Thornton at Litton, McNamara was one of a new breed of executives, more comfortable with balance sheets than blueprints, more likely to know the cost of a unit of production rather than engineering details, and inherently more interested in market projections than in product quality. The rise of the Ford accountant with the computer mind confirmed that the managers with finance backgrounds, the MBAs so diligently recruited by Ed Lundy and Arjay Miller over the past fifteen years, had seized control of the company. McNamara was, as one automan observed, the kind of executive that

HFII's grandfather would have thought "bookish and rather impractical."

Yet, in the early 1960s, McNamara and his fellow Whiz Kids had become prototypes of a new managerial thinking that favored credentialed professionals who put their trust in facts and figures over intuition and personal judgment. This new generation of executives rarely came out of manufacturing, but instead graduated out of the ranks of finance where they pored over the numbers of the corporation, not its products. For despite Bob's grand vision expressed at Greenbrier, the McNamara most people at Ford knew was the one who reduced costs, regardless of its impact on quality or people.

Within Ford, the change was real and palpable—a reality of corporate life that kicked in when Jack Reith and the Edsel were kicked out. Personally hurt by the failure of the car named for his father, Henry Ford had become more hesitant to risk money or to spend it. And in this new conservative environment, the naysayers in finance saw their power and their resolve strengthen.

To get ahead at Ford now, you had to be in or have come from McNamara's old stomping grounds in finance. The discipline of numbers had become the new center of power at Ford, a super corporate training ground. Under Arjay Miller, controller and vice president, the financial organization was described as like three legs of a stool: accounting; financial analysis and planning; and personnel and administration. This three-fold division was an early conception of the Whiz Kids and one way in which Ford's finance greatly differed from the finance staffs at other corporations.

By far, the most omnipotent area was financial analysis, the group formed and headed by Bob McNamara and now under the firm control of Whiz Kid cohort Ed Lundy. The department had a looming omnipresence, routinely interpreting, evaluating and often criticizing every activity within the company. The group was redefining the role of a corporate financial department from that of counting beans to the heady realm of total governance. Lundy himself said the function was concerned less with traditional areas such as auditing, accounting and managing the company's cash than with the continuous evaluation of Ford's costs, prices and profits. Finance ranged into long-term planning, major capital investments and mathematical simulations of Ford's distribution and maintenance systems. One New York *Times* reporter, employing a bit of hype, wrote of the "space-age management methods" of Lundy's men.

For years, Lundy oversaw the hiring, training, paying and moving of hundreds of college graduates with accounting and financial degrees, building in the process his own empire with a wealth of brainpower. Now, with one of their own as president of Ford, this carefully cultivated group was assuming dominant control of the corporation.

The kind of men Lundy lured to Ford were the same men William H. Whyte wrote of in his classic book, *The Organization Man,* published in 1956. They were young, educated men who completely dedicated themselves to Lundy's organization. They believed, as Tex himself believed in forming the archetypal managerial group, that men existed as a unit of society. "Of himself, he is isolated, meaningless," lectured Whyte. "Only as he collaborates with others does he become worthwhile, for by sublimating himself in the group, he helps produce a whole that is greater than the sum of its parts."

All the Whiz Kids disavowed Whyte's conclusions, which they deemed offensive, though most of them were very much like the men the author was describing. Arjay Miller derided the book and the emerging literature on the white-collar professional as a travesty. "It is a caricature, with a caricature's shade of perceptive wit," Miller once claimed in a speech. "It does not, however, constitute a reasonable generalization of how people really act in a large organization."

Yet the corporate whole created by McNamara and sustained by Miller and Lundy often seemed a whole unto itself, less individuals and more a company of men within a company. The managers in Ford's design studios, in its marketing and sales departments, and in its many factories were very different from those in finance. They could tell stories of how their fathers had dumped the disassembled parts of a Chevy in the driveway and challenged them to put a car together. They could talk about the industry's tough pioneers and how they gathered at the Pontchartrain Hotel bar to argue—sometimes with their fists—over parts and orders and franchises. They had a passion for the car, just as Reith had in fulfilling his childhood dream of creating an automobile himself.

Like McNamara, the young men in finance felt no overriding devotion toward the product. True, some of them enjoyed the notion that they worked for a car company, rather than one that made guns or cornflakes. But unlike so many of the oldtimers without MBAs or even undergraduate degrees, they didn't love the automobile. If it suddenly stopped dead on the road, they wouldn't know what to look for under the hood. None could duplicate the legendary World War Two feat of K.T. Keller who scrambled up the production ladder to become chairman of Chrysler. Walking along a board displaying sorely needed parts for the defense buildup during the war, it took him just fifteen minutes to select four out of several hundred parts that could be produced by one of his plants using a specialized process. "I'll be darned," said the plant's manager. "I spent the whole next day studying that board; I found we could do those four parts—and no others."

No, the men in finance could not understand the nuts and bolts of a nuts-and-bolts industry. Lundy himself conceded he was "hopelessly confused" when he stepped into Ford's styling studios. The men he brought to Ford came to "manage" and to analyze. Whyte aptly described them in *The Organization Man*. "Just as the student now feels technique more vital than content," he wrote, "so the trainee believes managing an end in itself, an expertise relatively independent of the content of what is being managed."

Lundy's recruits were products of the middle class with graduate degrees from prestigious universities. If they were, as one Ford man contended, "bloodless, colorless nonentities," they were also smart and articulate men who knew how to forcefully argue a point and win. "They had the best and brightest people in the company," recalls Donald Frey, a Ford engineer who later became chief executive of Bell & Howell. "With few exceptions, operational types—the people in sales, manufacturing and engineering—were considered dummies, inarticulate and not very bright. In terms of IQ points, I suppose every member of the finance staff had at least five points over everyone else in the company. Lundy was very fussy about that."

They knew they were strong, and they knew they were special, members of the "Lundy School of Economics" as some quipped. Toward the end of the 1960s, some 1,200 MBAs would work at Ford and 2,000 more would boast undergraduate degrees in business. The MBAs were hired at pay levels 25 percent more than the undergrads and, more significantly, their salary progress was 50 percent higher. "Working for the controller's office at Ford was like playing on the Dallas Cowboys," recalls James Kerley, who was brought to Ford after earning a master's degree in economic theory from the University of Pennsylvania. "There was an all-star at every position."

They were most adept at blocking. Every request for money had to gain approval from finance, whether it was to improve a car part or a factory. Again and again, the men who built the product would get turned down. The financial discipline imposed by the Quiz Kids helped to save Ford from complete ruin. But what was urgently needed to

resuscitate the company in the immediate postwar years was now beginning to smother it. Not only was finance killing many good product
ideas, it more importantly was creating a culture in which many people
simply gave up. The brighter lights in finance used their intellect and
their controls, much like McNamara at Ford, to beat up and to wear
down the engineers and the marketers.

The penny-pinching led to numerous compromises in the quality of
Ford's products, from door knobs to the finish of paint on its cars. In the
late 1950s, the managers of one of Ford's large manufacturing plants in
Chester, Pa., tried to convince to no avail central finance of the necessity
for new paint booths and drying ovens. The plant was antiquated and
the equipment was largely obsolete. The ovens were so old and dry that
the insulation in them had turned to dust which continually sprinkled
down on the vehicles before a new coat of paint could dry on the car. For
years, the plant shipped cars with patches of dirt imbedded under the
surface of the paint job.

"We had all the quality slogans and logos, but it was physically impossible to build a quality paint job," says Donald Lennox, who had been
controller of the assembly plant. "Still, we could not prove by the numbers that the investment in a new paint system could be justified so we
could never get the investment approved."

For three straight years, Lennox was turned down again and again.
What was all the more surprising was that Lennox, a former Arthur
Andersen & Co. accountant, had risen through the finance ranks. Lennox
moved over to manufacturing partly because the competition for advancement among Lundy's financial geniuses was so great, especially
compared to manufacturing. So Lennox knew how to play the game, yet
even he couldn't gain approval for the badly needed investment. Finance
insisted that the investment show an internal rate of return of 40 percent.
His estimates of lost sales and warranty costs were not enough to prove
that a new paint system was required for the plant. "The finance organization was the judge and the jury in deciding whether the numbers were
credible or not," recalls Lennox. When McNamara—not yet president—
visited the plant, he appealed to him directly. "McNamara listened,"
recalled Lennox. "He was sympathetic, but told us we had to spend
money only on a rational basis."

It reached the point where many men joked, half seriously, that Ford
was liquidating itself. That could be the only reason, they figured, that
finance turned down so many crucial investments with long-term impli-
cations. Donald Frey, the Ford engineer who fought and won more
battles than most, would often tell his people in disgust: "We must be

going out of business guys. This has got to be the last run! Throw it together. Who gives a shit?"

It was the beginning of the end, a sea change that eventually would open the gates to a flood of foreign imports. All the facts and all the figures that Bob could quote to Ford executives at their annual conference failed to acknowledge another critical insight about the coming competition: the rise in influence of Ford finance had tipped the company out of balance, making it more difficult for it to survive attacks by others who fully appreciated the need for good engineering, marketing and production—not only finance. But none of this would become the worry of President Robert S. McNamara.

BOB WOULD NOT get to pursue his vision for Ford, largely because of Tex Thornton's old World War Two mentor and father-figure, Robert Lovett. The man whose recommendation to Henry Ford II sealed the deal that brought McNamara and Thornton to Ford in 1946 now would pave the way for Bob's abrupt departure. When John F. Kennedy sought to fill the three most important appointments of his new administration —the Secretaries of Treasury, Defense and State—the first name that came to mind was Lovett.

Meeting with him on December 1, Kennedy offered Lovett his choice of the three key cabinet posts. Lovett turned him down because of health problems, but among the three or four names he suggested for defense was none other than Bob McNamara. From the earliest Stat Control days, Lovett had been impressed with Bob and had watched him progress at Ford in Thornton's absence. He also thought highly of Tex, of course, but believed that Litton's presence in the defense business created potential conflicts of interest that would hinder Thornton's ability to serve.

Kennedy's conversation with Lovett was soon followed up by Sargent Shriver, Kennedy's brother-in-law and a key aide, who came to New York to meet with him. Again, Lovett told Shriver he thought McNamara was the most outstanding from an expanded list of some ten people. "McNamara's virtues included an almost iconoclastic approach to any organization," Lovett recalled telling Shriver. "I suggested that this was a virtue only if it was under control, but that his eagerness for facts could be turned to great advantage in the department and that he was well equipped to do the analytical work which would necessarily follow this."

Barely five weeks into his new job, McNamara returned one day from lunch and went through his customary routine, asking his secretary, "Let's go down the list of the calls. What looks really important?"

"There's one here from a Mr. Kennedy," she said.

McNamara did not know a Mr. Kennedy, but dialed the number anyway and Bobby came on the line.

"My brother, the President-elect, would like you to see our brother-in-law, Sargent Shriver."

He did not explain the purpose of the call, insisting that he preferred to have Shriver discuss it with him in person.

"All right," McNamara said, "let's set up something next week."

"No, I mean this afternoon," Kennedy said. "He will fly out to Detroit today. He can be there in three hours. What would be convenient for you?"

At about 4 o'clock that afternoon, Sargent Shriver sat in McNamara's office and stated that he had been authorized by the President-elect to offer him an appointment in Kennedy's new Cabinet.

McNamara said he'd just taken on the presidency of the company. He was worried about deserting Henry who had just given him the top job. He was surprised at the offer because, although he had voted for Kennedy and contributed financially to his election campaign, McNamara was thought to be a Republican.

Still, Shriver felt the man out. He and Kennedy were intrigued by Bob because several other contacts confirmed Lovett's impressions of him. By most outside accounts, McNamara was an exceptionally brilliant manager, a Harvard MBA, a true Whiz Kid and the model of the rational modern executive in the early 1960s. No less, he boasted some refreshing eccentricities—shunning Bloomfield Hills to live in Ann Arbor with the university eggheads, getting along with labor leaders who traditionally despised the leadership of the auto companies, even supporting the American Civil Liberties Union.

Did he have any interest in being Secretary of the Treasury? asked Shriver.

"Not interested and not qualified," McNamara said.

"We thought that might be the response," Shriver said. "In that case, we are prepared to offer you Secretary of Defense."

McNamara laughed. Shriver recalled that he didn't seem surprised or arrogant about the offer. Indeed, he began to matter-of-factly discuss the jobs as if he were addressing a business issue at Ford. McNamara rattled off three or four main problems at the Treasury and then three or four main problems at Defense. At one point, McNamara leaned back in his chair and told Shriver that, of course, he would have to give up any stock or options in Ford and that it would cost him several million dollars. McNamara also would have to give up a salary that paid him $410,833 in 1959—before he became president—for a government job that would pay all of $25,000 a year.

"You know," he added, "I've got more money than I'm ever going to need or use."

It was Bob's way of saying he really didn't care about the money. Indeed, he didn't. He was already a millionaire several times over, thanks to Ford's generous salary and stock benefits.

Yet for all his musings, McNamara turned Shriver down, maintaining that he had no government experience that would have made him a viable candidate for the job. Shriver coolly responded that he had been authorized to accept a favorable reply, but in the event the reply was unfavorable, he had been instructed to ask Bob to meet with the President-elect. McNamara had no intention of changing his mind, but agreed to meet Kennedy as a matter of courtesy.

After Shriver left, Bob walked into Henry's office. But Ford had just left for the East Coast. McNamara called flight service and told them to get him a plane. He caught up with Ford in the East and asked him to ignore whatever news reports he might hear over the next few days because he categorically was not going to join John Kennedy's New Frontier. He was flattered, but he was uninterested.

The very next day, however, he was on his way to Washington to quietly meet with Kennedy. McNamara was still resolute about not leaving the company, citing his lack of experience. "President Kennedy said to me he wasn't aware of any school for either cabinet members or presidents and that the excuse of lack of experience was not an adequate one," remembers McNamara. "I then shifted my ground somewhat to say that I recognized there were few men who had served as Secretary of Defense, and few who could be considered experienced in that sense, but I was certain there were many more experienced than I. I listed several possibilities, each one of whom he disposed of with reasons that I was forced to accept."

So used to battering people at Ford with rapid-fire questions, McNamara asked the President-elect only one question at that first meeting: whether Kennedy had really written *Profiles in Courage*. It was, McNamara thought later, a rather presumptuous thing to ask. Yet what appeared little more than a social gaffe was an honest question. Bob had met his share of superficial people in Detroit. He wanted to make sure he wasn't meeting another one in Washington. McNamara had read the book when it was first published in 1956 and was impressed by both the substance of the work and by what he called "the beauty of the writing." He had heard numerous stories that it was ghost written and remained curious about it. "The book impressed me as no other book that I read in the 1950s did," recalls McNamara. "It impressed me because it dealt with one of our major problems—the problem of principle versus expediency, and he dealt with it beautifully, I felt."

Surprised by the question, Kennedy answered that of course he had written the book. And as the two spoke about the possibilities of McNamara joining his Cabinet, Bob found himself becoming mesmerized by what everyone would soon be calling the Kennedy "charisma."

"Wouldn't you think it over on the weekend and talk to me Monday?" Kennedy said. "We'll meet again Monday."

McNamara again warned Kennedy he would be making a mistake to put a person as inexperienced as he was into the Defense Department and went home to Ann Arbor, agreeing to reconsider his decision. That Friday evening, he stood in the study of his home, peering outside the window at a heavy snow.

"I think I'll call the President-elect," he told Margy. "I'll tell him that I'm writing a letter and that the letter stipulates that the only possible way I could be interested was if I could appoint all the senior people in my department solely on the basis of merit. And that I would have to be a working secretary, not a social secretary."

If McNamara took the job, he had no interest in managing the status quo, of being what most defense secretaries had been—controlled by the military. No, he would establish the same top-down approach he had at Ford, bringing a hand-picked cadre of smart, rational civilians like himself to control the military just as his financially trained analysts had gained power over the engineers and marketers of Ford. Only if Kennedy stood behind him to effect real change would it make sense to leave Ford.

Bob called Washington, but Kennedy had left for his family's estate in Palm Beach. He tried Florida and finally got JFK on the telephone.

"Mr. President-elect," he said, "I've been thinking and I want to write this letter and I can have it there Monday."

"Hell, Bob," JFK said. "If it's snowing in Michigan, it's probably snowing in Washington, too. I probably won't be able to get back there till Tuesday myself. Just bring the letter with you Tuesday."

Fascinated with the idea of going to Washington, McNamara could not put it out of his head. During World War Two, when he worked at the Pentagon with Tex and the others, he had begun to install the controls and techniques of management; but they hadn't taken hold because of interservice rivalries and pork barrel politics. Here was his chance to go back to Washington to complete the job of systemizing the entire Department of Defense and instituting a rational approach to everything from nuclear arms to future weapons systems.

Besides, for all his success at Ford, McNamara had abstracted the company into some kind of intellectual puzzle that intrigued him. He never felt any passion for the cars Ford produced nor did he share any great kinship with the people who worked in the business—other than some of his fellow Whiz Kids. Even though he rose to the top of the Ford empire, he remained an anomaly in Detroit. Yet, he also had clearly won the battle within Ford. The bean counters now ruled the empire, and his own victory at Ford in becoming president may have been enough to make him itchy for a whole new series of challenges.

Over the weekend and on Monday, he began talking about the offer with several of his Ann Arbor friends. One evening, he went to see Bob Dunham, who had been as much a part of the group as any of the Whiz Kids. Bob was in the mood to talk. He had two or three Johnny Walkers and the two of them sat in Dunham's living room and chatted until 2 a.m. Dunham was shocked that McNamara was seriously considering the post.

"Bob, look, you've just become president of the Ford Motor Company, one of the biggest companies in the world," Dunham told him. "You're just exactly what this company needs!

"You go down there to Washington and those goddamn politicians. . . . You'll be called in front of all these committees and they aren't half as smart as you but they will cut you to ribbons. Because they know the inside of Washington and you don't. You won't be able to hold your own."

"That may be what you think Bob but I think I can hold my own there," McNamara said.

"Well, I think you'd be making a bad mistake if you take this assignment."

"How do you say no to the President of the United States?"

"Just like you say no to anybody else," Dunham said, "just say no."

McNamara, however, didn't want to say no. He also discussed the offer with Neil Staebler, then Democratic National Committeeman in Michigan. "It was as if McNamara was asking the question: 'Why should I hire McNamara for the job?' " recalls Staebler, "as if McNamara were trying to see McNamara as the President saw him. It was as if he were trying to write a report on himself to himself. Could the job be done? Could you get all the people involved at the Pentagon to agree? Could the thing truly be unified? McNamara had seen enough throat-cutting at Ford Motor to prepare anybody for the Pentagon, but did anybody have the power to unify the Pentagon? And then, finally, I can't remember the words, there was this phrase: that maybe nobody could do the job; that maybe he couldn't last six months; maybe nobody was qualified; but that after all, he had been asked and therefore he would try."

At work, McNamara told Arjay Miller and Jim Wright about the offer. McNamara initially told Wright about it because he asked him to fulfill a scheduled speaking engagement for him at MIT's business school in Cambridge.

"My God, Bob, it's only two days away," said Wright.

"Oh, you can do it," McNamara told him.

"Where are you going, anyway?"

"I've got to go to Washington."

The rest of the story followed. "It was a terrible shock," recalled Wright. "I didn't see how he could turn it down. It was his decision and I could understand why he wanted to do it. And once he made up his mind, there was no sense in talking about it. He could be stubborn."

Wright, who had succeeded McNamara as group vice president, was understandably concerned about his own future at Ford. "I knew it was going to be a shock to Henry Ford and to the organization and it was. And I knew it was going to make life more difficult for me. In the first place, I was reasonably sure I wasn't going to succeed him. I had just been in the job a month-and-a-half myself. He had been group vp for quite a while, so he had a step ahead of me. It would have been very strange to pick me to succeed McNamara when I had only been in this job for a month-and-a-half. So I wondered who would be picked. His successor, of course, would mean a great deal to me in terms of what I would do."

Wright temporarily put his own concerns aside and flew to Boston to do the speech on the same Tuesday that McNamara flew back to Washington. The Secret Service picked Bob up at the airport and spirited him around through the back of the Kennedy home on N Street in George-town. Out front a pack of reporters, already mad with the rumor that McNamara had accepted, waited. The Secret Service let him out of the car and he scrambled up the narrow back steps and there was JFK and Bobby sitting next to each other on a small sofa.

"Mr. President, I've written this letter," he said. He reiterated he didn't think he was qualified but that he was ready to accept if the conditions in the letter could be met.

"Let's have a look," Kennedy said.

The President-elect read the letter. If he harbored any doubts about McNamara, he held them no longer. He was impressed with how strong and stalwart McNamara's position on the issue was. Here was a man who did not want political interests or favors to play any role in the operation of the Defense Department. In his earlier conversation, Kennedy had told him they were thinking of appointing Franklin Roosevelt, Jr., as Secretary of the Navy. McNamara had opposed the appointment.

Kennedy passed the letter to his brother. Bobby gave it a cursory read, and handed it back.

"What do you think, Bobby?" asked the older brother.

"Fine," answered his younger one.

"Well, then, what the hell, let's go out front and announce it," Jack said.

McNamara left for Ann Arbor that same day to pack his bags, his mission in Detroit complete as far as he was concerned. To Detroit's automen, Bob's sudden departure seemed erratic, even strange. His friends had barely congratulated him on becoming president when he moved on to another, perhaps larger triumph. It seemed so bizarre to men who ate and slept the car business. Bob had won the dream job at Ford. A Cabinet post in a new administration was all very fine, the thinking went, though considerably less so in a Democratic Administration. But in Detroit, the consensus was that no completely sane man would pass up the presidency of Ford for it.

Henry was angered and upset by Bob's decision. In some way, he also felt embarrassed that the man he honored with the presidency of his company would up and leave so abruptly. Ford had asked Sidney Weinberg, one of his directors, to meet with McNamara to help change his mind. But Bob's decision had been made and it was final. He had made more money than all the McNamaras before him, Bob said, and now he owed his country something in return.

The day McNamara's resignation was made public, Ford sat depressed in the study of his home. A friend of the family had been over to the house and noticed that Henry had been weeping and drinking. "This may be one of the worst days of my life," Ford told the guest. "I can't believe it happened. You've heard the news about Bob, haven't you? Well, I spent years training him. He's the first president outside the family. After all those years of training, he's leaving. I can't believe it. Now what do I do?"

Part Three

TWILIGHT OF HONOR

Tex hits the cover of *Business Week*, with his McNamara-clone Roy Ash, both in the Litton boardroom. The magazine marvels at how Litton is not just a successful company, but supposedly the successful model of the modern corporation, personifying the highest form of creative capitalism.

Tex Thornton with Roy Ash in the mid-1960s showing members of the Beverly Hills City Council a model of Litton's new headquarters complex.

Tex becomes one of the few businessmen to make the cover of *Time*. The magazine champions him as the manager of the 1960s for founding and running the go-go conglomerate of the go-go era.

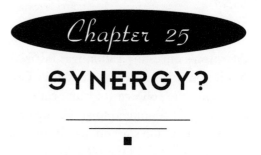

Chapter 25

SYNERGY?

∎

"Synergy: The only way
$2 + 2 = 5$."

—*Business Week*

Robert S. McNamara and Charles Bates Thornton were reaching the pinnacle of their destiny at roughly the same time. The two friends who would become the most famous Whiz Kids had been running on a parallel course, recreating the Stat Control formula of building teams of bright, like-minded people to apply numbers and facts to business. McNamara's ascent at Ford was founded on his ability to control costs and make decisions based on rational analysis. Thornton's success at Litton Industries was grounded in those precepts as well, but also had to do with a different set of qualities—his vision and his leadership.

Tex had spent two decades of his life preparing for Litton, surviving a series of personal setbacks at Ford and Hughes Aircraft. Finally, he had become a winner, and he wasn't about to let it go. His emergence as a modern-day business leader had everything to do with how to grow big quick. Just as Detroit's cars grew heavier and larger through the 1950s,

America's most successful companies were literally defined by bigness. Thornton's once-tiny Litton was fast becoming a giant, and few worried that it could bomb like Jack Reith's Cruiser.

Despite the concerns of some colleagues that he was moving too fast, too soon, Tex continued to gobble up one company after another. He had become the nation's grand acquisitor, making Litton the fastest-growing corporation listed on the New York Stock Exchange. By the end of 1961, after twenty-five mergers, Litton boasted forty-eight plants in nine countries, annual sales of $245 million and common stock worth $140 a share.

Thornton was making a business out of science, using technology to create products for "niche markets," long before anyone used that term. At his best, he was an intellectual broker. Tex spent hours with the scientists and engineers to gain a sense of what they could do. Then he peered into the marketplace to determine what it wanted. "Tex stood there and brokered this whole thing to build a business, based on his understanding of what the market wanted and the scientists' understanding of what could be done," said his partner, Roy Ash.

In the weeks before Bob began his brief stint as president of Ford, Thornton had pulled off yet another remarkable acquisition. He bought himself a shipyard in Pascagoula, Miss. Like many of his other acquisitions, Ingalls Shipbuilding Corp. was losing money in a tired industry—a reason why Tex was able to buy the company with $60 million in sales, by assuming $9 million of its debt and handing over $8 million of Litton stock.

What Thornton envisioned at Ingalls, however, was another beneficiary of the Cold War. On the ways of the nation's third-largest shipyard were attack submarines. They were being constructed for the Navy, anxious to buy more of them to answer the Soviet Union's new emphasis on undersea warfare. As Thornton mulled over the deal, he noted that each submarine was loaded with tons of sophisticated electronic gear, some of it already produced by other Litton companies. If the Navy began to contract entire weapons systems to private industry, Litton would be superbly placed to capture the bulk of the business.

THORNTON AND ASH would soon call it synergy—and the word would assume nearly magical proportions in the lexicon of business. Ash had heard the term from the chemist and inventor Arnold Beckman while visiting him in his laboratory. Synergy occurred when the additive properties of two components were much greater than the sum of the effects of the two separately. Or as translated by Tex and Ash, it meant that the whole of Litton was somehow worth more than its individual parts. And it was true that many of Litton's early acquisitions meshed well enough with one another to allow the company to bid on ever larger government defense contracts. Eventually, however, Thornton would bring the word "synergy" into public use to justify many more deals— far outside the technology core that unified his earlier conquests.

The concept fueled the conglomerate movement. Like other con-glomerateurs of the era, Tex argued that diversified companies could more easily ride out the dips in the business cycle that wreak havoc on industries vulnerable to economic downturns. When Wall Street bought into this logic, the shares of the conglomerates began to sell at higher prices than those of more typical industrial companies. Those overpriced shares were then used to buy still more companies.

Diversification was not an entirely novel idea. It had become popular in the 1930s when several specialized firms, particularly those making capital goods, found themselves vulnerable to the Depression. Still, in the 1950s, most industrial companies were largely focused around single pur-suits. They rarely diversified into unknown and unrelated businesses. Oil companies did not acquire department stores. Consumer goods compa-nies did not buy television networks or Wall Street brokerages.

Tex Thornton's Litton was another corporate creature altogether. He was using his early success as an electronics contractor for the military to enter fields now far removed from defense or electronics. In shopping for candidates, Thornton held to a few general guidelines. He tried to steer clear of companies or industries whose future growth was dependent on the growth of the economy. Each opportunity had to have a growth potential in its own right. He claimed to seek companies with a certain critical mass, not too large so that it would be affected by the ups and downs of the economy and not too small so that it would have to struggle to survive. Mostly, however, he bought opportunities, as he had when he acquired Ingalls shipyard.

His imagination soared freely over the possibilities—some mundane, some rather fantastic. He seriously considered buying Westinghouse, Tappan, and Lockheed—the company that had tried to buy Hughes Aircraft when he was there. But of all the potential deals, the most unusual had to be one in which Thornton would acquire Walt Disney's entertainment company. Disney apparently needed financing in the early 1960s when Litton stock was riding high. Tex had come to know and admire the entrepreneur. "They became good friends," recalls Harry

Gray, then a Litton executive. "Tex liked the market and Walt's creativity. But Walt couldn't visualize how he could sell the Litton stock to get the money he needed for his business." The deal never came off, and Disney died in 1966.

But Thornton's interest in doing the deal in the early 1960s was evidence that he was no longer building a technology company; he was intent on creating a conglomerate. To this day, it's not known who invented the term to describe corporations with widely diversified businesses. But the word began to creep into popular usage in the mid-1960s when high-flying Litton would emerge as the archetype of the conglomerate.

Whatever the term's origins, Litton was among the first companies to receive the tag, making the company and Thornton a much-studied model of the movement. At the Harvard Business School, Litton was the conglomerate held out as the swinging model of the era. For years, sections of MBAs—including Tex's own two sons who went to Harvard —routinely dissected and debated a trio of case studies on Thornton's corporate creations, and these cases led to four more studies on a single division in the Litton empire. For Thornton, who failed to gain a college diploma and had reached out to Harvard in the 1940s to gain legitimacy for his Air Force officers, it was the finest possible accolade.

Yet both Thornton and Ash initially protested the idea that Litton was a conglomerate. They pleaded for the term "multi-company industry" to describe Litton. Ash griped that the word "conglomerate" implied "a mess." It was really something else altogether: the ultimate numbers company. It had to be, because it owed its creation to a mindset in which the buying and selling of businesses was largely predicated on a number: price-to-earnings ratios. The only linkage its disparate parts shared was financial. Typewriters had little to do with cash registers. Nuclear-powered submarines had no connection with business stationery. Calculators bore little relationship to microwave tubes, or to amplifiers or radar antennas—not to mention Disney cartoons and movies.

What linked the oddly different pieces together were the numbers: return on gross assets, operating profit and revenues. The managers of the companies Thornton captured quickly found that they were not allowed to believe in anything beyond measurable "bottom line" efficiency. All behavior had to come under the technocratic control of the rules and the analyses. All the cash that was generated in the divisions was wire-transferred on a daily basis to headquarters which maintained strict controls on every dollar. Salaries greater than $30,000 had to be approved by Thornton or Ash, who generally demanded a 20 percent return on a division's gross assets. The division managers, who were supposed to be looking down to manage their own businesses, always felt the gaze from above. What each piece of Litton had in common with another was the need to satisfy someone who often failed to see beyond the bottom line—a reality lost in the glittering press clippings of the era.

Litton Industries became the first conglomerate to preach the gospel of management controls. Lacking either the experience or training to evaluate the performance of so many different businesses, Tex increasingly relied on financial data, reports from the field, and organized information. Each division put together a detailed financial plan each year. Then its managers would fly to Litton headquarters in Los Angeles to defend it in front of a chain-smoking, Coca-Cola-sipping Thornton. Every plan included projections for twelve months on a monthly basis, for twenty-four months on a quarterly basis and for thirty-six months on an annual basis. Every month, Thornton received a monthly report comparing the division's actual performance against its projections. When a gap appeared, he or Ash were on the telephone, asking questions and demanding answers. They spent so much time on the phone that the annual telephone bill for corporate headquarters was $7 million in the mid-1960s.

It was not possible for any single manager to know a business deeply in a conglomerate. In his distant headquarters in California, Thornton could not know the intricacies of the business at Monroe Calculating Machines in New Jersey nor could he understand the ins-and-outs of his shipbuilding yard in Pascagoula. The conglomerateur was even more removed from his company's products and services than the financial types at Ford and at so many other American companies.

For Tex Thornton, the non-technologist, professional manager, it was the perfect business form. Thornton didn't know much about the potentometers, barratons and duplexers made by his company, but he understood the more universal language of numbers. The conglomerate form allowed him to apply figures in the purest way, reviewing operations objectively and dispassionately, just as McNamara would now use the numbers in transforming the culture of the Department of Defense.

The downside, though less clear in these early enthusiastic days when generations of managers embraced the management controls touted by Thornton and McNamara, was real and dangerous. At Litton and other conglomerates, in the words of business professor Henry Mintzberg, management "remained distant from the subject of its efforts, acting as if it moved pieces on a chessboard, making little effort to influence what those pieces really do, even how they relate to each other in any but the most superficial ways. It did not involve getting deeply inside a business, coming to know its needs and its processes and its people well enough to weld them all together into a smoothly functioning entity that serves its markets with care and understanding."

None of this diminished the spell that Litton had cast over Wall Street because the company's fast growth blinded investors to the inherent weaknesses of a conglomerate. At the same time as American businesses badly needed to reinvest in new equipment and processes, Wall Street was turning away from the corporate blue chips. The people on the street were mesmerized instead by the wonder companies of the age. To qualify, a company had to dazzle investors with a hot new growth product, such as Polaroid or Xerox, or it had to dazzle by its expansionist ambitions, like Litton or ITT.

Thornton even managed to turn the negative connotations of running a conglomerate to his advantage by claiming that only the best managers could successfully manage such a complex corporation. He, of course, boasted the best and the brightest businessmen. Many traditional managers found the idea of running a huge, diverse empire of companies a daunting task. When Lammont duPont Copeland, president of Du Pont, said that "running a conglomerate is a job for management geniuses, not for ordinary mortals like us at Du Pont," the first genius who came to mind was Tex Thornton.

He was transforming Litton into a glamorous pioneer of the conglomerate movement—a movement which included such well-known names as Textron, ITT and Gulf & Western. By the mid-1960s, Litton would distinguish itself from the crowd because of Tex's ebullient manner and vivid rhetoric. The result was that Wall Street valued Litton's stock more highly than any other conglomerate: It sold for thirty-three times its annual earnings, while Textron's rate was only eleven, Gulf & Western sixteen, LTV thirteen and ITT was slightly below seventeen, or half that of high-flying Litton.

LITTON WAS NOT just another successful company. It was fast becoming the successful prototype of *the* corporation, personifying the highest form of creative capitalism. Success itself was a powerful magnet, drawing exceptionally talented people to the company. So were the stock options that Thornton doled out to his key people. Harry Gray, who would become one of Litton's most prominent executives, sought out the company expressly for the options Tex put on the table. He quit a $20,000-a-year job as an executive vice president of a Greyhound subsidiary in 1954 to take a $12,000 position at Litton with a pile of options that eventually made him a millionaire.

As Litton's stock skyrocketed and the media produced an endless stream of positive reviews on Thornton and his latest group of Whiz Kids, others wanted to become a part of the Litton success story. "In the sixties, Litton was magic and everyone felt it," recalls Fred O'Green, who was headhunted from Lockheed in 1962 as a divisional manager. "We were growing by leaps and bounds. It was a free-flowing environment. You could walk down the production line and talk to workers who had degrees in philosophy and everything else. It was a very enlightened group of people. They were attracted because of the magic of Litton."

Litton's success owed as much to Tex Thornton's salesmanship as it did to the timely deals he hatched. From his days in Texas, Thornton's goal was to be somebody and to do something big, and his rhetoric was shaped by that. He would sometimes speak glowingly about business's possibilities. "Only one-quarter of the surface of the earth is land, and yet look at all the people crowded there with their growing needs," he told a *Fortune* writer after acquiring the Ingalls shipyard. "Oceanography is as challenging as space, and has a tremendous potential. As far away in time as we can imagine, space has nothing for us in the way of food or minerals or other resources that we need; the ocean has."

Dreamy theories and arcane incantations became as much a part of the Litton mythology as dealmaking. Bringing "synergy" into popular use was but one example. Litton executives routinely spoke the magical words of new business thinking, introducing such terms as "entrepreneurship" and "cross-fertilization" into the vocabularies of a generation of managers. Litton, it was said, boasted a "free-form management." Once a year, executives generated new ideas and products at "opportunity reviews." Ash said Litton boasted "a creative culture" long before the phrase had become popular. "We had to have a nonbureaucratic, noninstitutional setting, so creative people would have headroom to do their thing," he proclaimed. The company's own press releases promoted the notion that Litton was populated by a "new breed" of business leader, evidence that a professional manager could manage anything.

Indeed, like corporate giants General Electric or Procter & Gamble, Litton was becoming a farm club for American business. The executives who left Thornton's employ even adopted a playful name in tribute of their former company. They called themselves LIDOs, an acronym for Litton Industries Dropouts. Some of the executives departed for key positions at other companies. Others left to start their own firms. Many of them launched conglomerates themselves. They included engineer Hugh Jamieson who quit in 1958 partly because of Thornton's refusal to slow down and consolidate, and scientist Henry Singleton and George Kozmetsky who left in 1960 to launch their own company, Teledyne, Inc. So many key people dropped out that *Business Week* magazine would call Litton a "B-school for conglomerates" and highlight nearly a dozen executives who "learned their Ps & Ls at 'Litton U.'" At most companies, the rapid turnover of top managers would have been a bad sign. Thornton turned it into a positive, suggesting that it was a way of "revitalizing the organization" because the turnover created greater opportunities for younger people to move up.

In truth, Litton was losing some of its most valuable people because Tex was failing to deliver on his promises to many executives and was becoming increasingly stingy with the company's stock. He had told Singleton and Kozmetsky they could run their own divisions when sales of their units hit $5 million. Singleton, a scientist from Hughes Aircraft with a Ph.D. from MIT, and Kozmetsky, a Harvard Ph.D. also initially recruited at Hughes, had been responsible for a couple of Litton's most important success stories: inertial guidance systems and digital computers for navigation. The revenue goals were met and surpassed, but Thornton was unwilling to grant them either greater independence or the stock options the pair believed they deserved. When they finally told Thornton they were going to start their own company, his first reaction was: "Damn it, you're going to drive the stock price down!" recalls Kozmetsky. "You'll hire the same people, use the same technology and go after the same contracts."

They assured him it wasn't true, that they wouldn't do anything to destroy what they had created at Litton. Thornton, who at his most Napoleonic could seem like anything but an enlightened leader, wasn't about to sanction their departures. "He sent us threatening letters after we left," says Kozmetsky. "He hired people to pick up our garbage. He tapped our telephones. We wondered what the hell was the matter with him. We hadn't even planned Teledyne as employees of Litton. We waited until we left."

Another top Litton executive, invited to Thornton's newly purchased ranch in Southern California, went horseback riding with him in the hills. They spent a pleasant afternoon together, with Tex gamely challenging the visitor to a race back to the ranch. After the executive beat Thornton, however, he noticed that Tex had suddenly become brusque and cool. He was never invited back.

For all his talk of creating a new business culture, Thornton also could be uncomfortably shy in the company of strangers. He preferred small meetings where he could engage people one-on-one to large staff sessions. And he could be painfully awkward in trying to express a thought. Thornton often would stumble over his own ideas, not knowing how to make them entirely convincing to the public. Crosby M. Kelly, a PR man Tex initially met at Ford and later brought to Litton, became his translator. "He spoke with great conviction," Kelly said, "but Tex couldn't verbalize. So I had to understand him and help to communicate his thoughts. There were people who credited me with the philosophy of the company. 'Litton was a figment in Crosby Kelly's imagination,' some said. But I knew Tex so well I could speak for him."

Kelly was the antithesis of Thornton. As Kelly insisted, "Facts never made a man. It's men that make the facts. Facts won't do it. It's people who do it, and unless you can reach the minds of people, don't bother me with the facts." A master image maker, he had planned the launch of the 1949 Ford at the Waldorf Astoria, and he was as much a creator of the Litton mystique as Thornton or Ash. He was the driving force behind the prodigious wave of positive publicity, whether generated by business reporters or Wall Streeters eager to write the company up.

When Wall Street analysts visited the company in Beverly Hills, Kelly would personally pick them up at the airport. After a full day of interviews with Litton executives, he'd invite them to his home for dinner, introduce them to his wife and children and swim with them in his pool before returning them to the airport. The wooing was no inconvenience to him or his family, just part of the job.

"I tell people I'm a confidence man, and I make no apologies for it," Kelly said unabashedly. "It's my business to get your confidence. That's my game. You have to see past the facts and past the logic of the CEO to get acceptance because people respond to non-logical things. Yet it's almost impossible to get the CEO to understand that."

If Thornton didn't entirely understand it, he knew it was important because he allowed Kelly much leeway in cultivating the aura about Litton that allowed Tex to clinch one deal after another. It was Kelly who convinced him to sink so much money into the company's slick annual reports which, as one critic noted, "bore a greater resemblance to

first-rate auction gallery catalogues than the accountings of major corporations." Each year, the report evolved around a different theme. In 1965,
full color reproductions of classical works of art graced its pages. A
portrait by the great painter Hans Holbein of a sixteenth-century entrepreneur adorned the cover because, it was explained, he represented the
"spirit which is important to the development of Litton Industries." A
year later, Litton's annual included an essay on "Managing Ideas" by
Allan Nevins, the American scholar and Pulitzer Prize-winner, along
with a photographic interpretation of the theme by one of the country's
top photographers. The theme of the report in 1967 was built around the
artistry and techniques of stained glass, with full-plate color illustrations.

Thornton believed that the impression made by Litton's annuals was
far more important than what the documents said. The report's paper
weight and printing quality were more critical than its content. Kelly
would tell the story of his first visit to the plant of a newly-acquired
company by Litton. Soon after his arrival, he groused to the general
manager that the lawn was overgrown. " 'Before I talk with you one
little minute,' Kelly said, 'I want you and me to go into the back and find
the lawn mower and together we'll go out and cut the goddamn grass.'
How could you have any confidence in the product or the people if the
grass is too high?"

SALESMANSHIP. TIMELY DEAL making. Clever image making. They all had
a crucial role in making Thornton a modern-day alchemist, seemingly
capable of transforming junk into gold and of turning himself into a
huge financial success. He and Flora had purchased from Frank Sinatra's
first wife Nancy a $250,000 ranch in the fashionable Holmby Hills sec-
tion of Los Angeles. It was in an area in which tourists rode in buses to
gawk at the homes of such Hollywood names as Walt Disney, Bing
Crosby and Claudette Colbert. Yet Thornton drove around town in a
Ford Falcon and a three-year-old Lincoln.

He also bought a twin-engine Aero Commander and learned to fly.
Thornton would take off from Van Nuys Airport and race out over the
desert in the pre-dawn, waiting for the sky to turn red with the morning
sun. "I like to see the sun come up," Thornton told a reporter. "Being up
there in that beautiful, clear air and watching the earth come to life early
in the morning is the most exciting thing I've ever seen. The excitement
doesn't let up. Each time it's like my first flight. It's a wonderful place to
think about things."

Still, he returned to Texas through the years, often going back to Haskell for his high school reunions to remember who he was and where he came from. And his childhood friends who remained in Texas believed that Bates Thornton, the scrawny but fiery kid now worth millions, hadn't changed at all.

In addition to the Holmby Hills house, he acquired a 230-acre ranch in Southern California where he bred thoroughbred horses, raised cattle and escaped for weekends. It was his way of "getting away from it all, getting out where I can clear my head of the traffic of everyday business. Here we don't watch the clock, we watch the sunsets."

He had a heroic quality about him, partly because he was achieving his dream and partly because he cultivated that image in what little time he left for leisure. Stories told how before daybreak Tex would climb atop Prince, a Tennessee Walker, and head into the mountains with a packed lunch, water and a first-aid kit. He'd carry a revolver to deal with rattlesnakes that could frighten the horse.

The cowboy capitalist was scaling the heights of American industry. His rise to power gained widespread exposure when he became the subject of a glowing story in *Time* magazine on October 4, 1963. Under the headline, "The Technology Industry: How a Whiz Kid Makes It Pay," an artist's portrait of him graced the magazine's cover—a color painting that prompted a fast letter from Ed Lundy who jokingly told Thornton he should sue Henry Luce for the rendering. "Even with the chicken pox, you never looked that bad," Lundy quipped.

If Tex didn't fancy his cover portrait, he could not have griped about the magazine's lustrous prose. *Time* called him "one of the most remarkable executives in the world . . . a dreamer and a visionary . . . the boss of a huge and exciting corporation that is dedicated to a relentless pursuit of the future." Concluded *Time:* "Many men in both business and government consider Thornton to be the best executive in the U.S. today." (It was no accident that the journalist who put Thornton on the cover had known Bob McNamara when he was *Time*'s Detroit bureau chief. Before moving to the magazine's Los Angeles office, he had visited with Bob and asked, "Who are the brightest men in California?" Replied McNamara instantaneously: "Way up at the top of your list you'd better put Tex Thornton.")

He had worked for two giants of American capitalism, Henry Ford II and Howard Hughes, and now Tex Thornton was becoming one himself. In the decade since he took over Charlie Litton's little company, he had created one of the most remarkable growth machines of the era. He had gobbled up some forty companies, increasing Litton's sales by 18,570 percent and its earnings 10,175 percent. The acquisition spree allowed Litton, with sales of more than half a billion in 1963, to rank as the country's hundredth largest corporation.

The stock market's love affair with his company had made Tex Thornton a millionaire forty times over. It also made millionaires out of twenty other Litton executives. Befitting his company's new stature in American business, Thornton would soon move the company from its modest headquarters adjacent to the city dump to a rambling mansion built by Hollywood agent Jules Stein on Santa Monica Boulevard in Beverly Hills. It was an elegant building, with a spiral staircase, where some scenes from *Gone With the Wind* were filmed.

As founder, salesman and grand strategist for the company, Tex Thornton was fast emerging as one of the golden boys of the golden age for conglomerates in the go-go 1960s. And, across the country, in his own inimitable way, Robert McNamara was setting the stage for a different type of revolution.

THE
WHIZ
KIDS

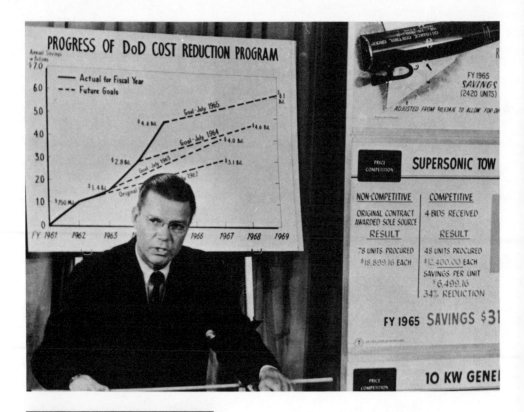

Bob McNamara, the cost-cutter extraordinaire, details how he has slashed costs in defense spending at a Pentagon press conference in 1965.

Not long after becoming Secretary of Defense, McNamara's management revolution hits the government and attracts widespread publicity, including these two covers in the major newsweeklies.

Chapter 26

"ADDING MACHINE WARRIORS"

■

"Statistics are the triumph of the quantitative method, and the quantitative method is the victory of sterility and death."

—HILAIRE BELLOC

O n January 21, 1961, the former president of the Ford Motor Company stood in a semicircle of eleven men in the gold-draped East Room of the White House. A crowd of friends and relatives, including Margy and the McNamara children, watched them simultaneously take their oaths of office in the presence of Chief Justice Earl Warren.

Wedged between Bob Kennedy and Douglas Dillon, McNamara repeated the words: "I swear that I will support and defend the Constitution of the United States against all enemies, foreign and domestic, that I will bear true faith and allegiance to the Constitution, that I take this oath freely, without any mental reservations or purpose of evasion, that I will well and faithfully discharge the duties of the office on which I am about to enter."

When the ceremony ended, the crowd broke into applause. President Kennedy suggested that all the children join the Cabinet for a picture, and then Jackie Kennedy shook hands with guests and members of the families of the new Cabinet. Robert S. McNamara was the new Secretary of Defense.

THE DAY AFTER accepting Kennedy's offer, Bob McNamara had moved into the Ford suite at Washington's Shoreham Hotel where he spent the three weeks prior to Christmas and the two weeks after the holiday on the telephone twelve to fourteen hours a day. He called acquaintances and friends, asking for names and ideas, cramming for his new test. He spent time with outgoing Secretary of Defense Thomas S. Gates. He visited with Lovett at his apartment in New York's Hotel Pierre and, with a notebook on his knee, asked what Lovett recalled were a series of "searching questions" on defense and staffing.

McNamara adopted Thornton's redoubtable game plan, assembling his own group of Whiz Kids—a team of loyal, like-minded, rational men of superior intelligence whom he could trust. The military top brass called them "wooly-headed academics." *Time* magazine dubbed them the "brains behind the muscle." Senator Barry Goldwater would derisively call them "the adding machine warriors."

His very first recruit was Roswell L. Gilpatric, a Yale-educated lawyer with a previous stint in the Pentagon as an under secretary. He had been recommended by President Kennedy who believed that McNamara needed a deputy who knew the Pentagon well enough to guide Bob through the politics of the place. Fittingly, McNamara called him from the Shoreham on a Saturday morning, waking his wife at 6:15 a.m. and talking Gilpatric into an interview later that day. They met at the Baltimore airport, sitting in a car in the snow to discuss the job.

Even before the session, Bob had concluded after what he called "a very intensive investigation" that Gilpatric was the best man qualified for the post. It was less than a week after Kennedy announced Bob's appointment, but already McNamara had done his homework, reading the right books and position papers, interviewing the key people, so that he knew more than anyone could have expected. Gilpatric, nine years older than McNamara, was astounded. He told Gilpatric that he wanted to run the Pentagon with a very small top group of people who would make all the critical decisions in a rational and analytical way through a system of planning and control.

"In the two hours that we spent together," recalls Gilpatric, "I was tremendously struck by the grasp he already had of the job and what it entailed. I found myself in complete sympathy with how he envisaged our relationship. And here I was an older person than he was; I'd been in the Defense Department twice before; I obviously had some pretty definite ideas myself, and to have been in a position where I was completely subordinated to somebody with very strong ideas of his own would have presented some problems. Well, that was all worked out right at the go-off."

The next time Gilpatric saw him, only four days later, McNamara had as many as eighty three-by-five file cards stuffed in the pocket of his shirt. On each card was scribbled the name of a job candidate, his background and the pros and cons of his appointment. Of all the people that McNamara would bring to the Pentagon, however, there were two mathematical minds that would help him bring the numbers revolution to the Department of Defense: Charles J. Hitch and Alain C. Enthoven, intellectual clones of Arjay Miller and Ed Lundy.

A former Rhodes Scholar at Oxford, Hitch, fifty, was chief economist of the Air Force-sponsored Rand Corporation in California. Only a year earlier, he had published a book called *The Economics of Defense in the Nuclear Age,* a mind-numbing tome filled with such esoteric concepts as isoquants, exchange curves and minimax—the latter a Hitchian term for how to minimize the enemy's maximum performance. As Bob's comptroller, Hitch would become the architect of a Planning-Programming-Budgeting System in the Pentagon that would dramatically shape all military decisions. Enthoven, a thirty-year-old Rand economist whose resumé included degrees from Stanford, Oxford, and MIT, had joined the Pentagon in a peripheral job the previous spring. Hitch immediately put him on his own staff, though Enthoven would soon become chief of a newly created Office of Systems Analysis, a civilian brain trust in the Pentagon that provided independent analysis of weapons programs and strategies and that was in some ways an updated version of Tex Thornton's old Stat Control group.

Enthoven first came to work for McNamara when Hitch was hospitalized with pneumonia. "It was love at first sight," he recalls. "We hit it off very well. Of course, you'd expect a fairly rugged interrogation, but if you brought good ideas and conclusions to him and could defend them, you would quickly gain his respect. I had done my homework."

He had just written a top secret book at Rand on thermonuclear war and strategy. Like McNamara, he was intellectually sharp, intense and abrasive. "His brilliance," noted Paul H. Nitze whom McNamara tapped as an Assistant Secretary of Defense, "was exceeded only by his arrogance, as he brought one general or admiral after another to the threshold of humiliation and quite often despair."

FROM THE ONSET, Secretary McNamara had a disconcerting habit of remaining behind the massive General Pershing desk, his eyes focused on the document before him as a subordinate was summoned to his office. Not until the visitor was nearly upon him would he look up to greet him, lest he waste a couple of seconds. Similarly, the caller was dismissed when Bob lowered his head to scan the document again. People soon came to call the eerie time it took to go from door to desk or vice versa "the walk."

The silent stroll was taken in an imposing office in the E Ring of the Pentagon. On the General Sherman table behind him were four telephones, a white one for calls to the President, plus a call director with twenty-nine buttons for his assistants. To the cavernous room, McNamara added only a few personal touches, replacing the battle paintings that once hung on the walls with color posters of the High Sierras and a black-and-white Rouault print. Behind his desk was a large oil portrait of the first Secretary of Defense, James Forrestal, who after taking office in 1947 was said to remark of the job's pressure and responsibility: "This office will probably be the greatest cemetery for dead cats in history." Forrestal's comment was ironically prophetic for shortly after resigning due to illness he took his own life. Not long after settling into the office, McNamara was said to have told an associate: "This place is a jungle, a jungle." As a complete newcomer at the top of a huge organization, he didn't know whom he could trust.

Yet nearly everyone was surprised by the speed and sureness the newcomer brought to this new job in the jungle. They had to agree it was not because of his knowledge of defense issues, no more than the people at Ford thought he was knowledgeable about cars. Instead, it was because the military couldn't satisfy him. Their positions could not stand up to his test of logic. "The reasoning wasn't sound, and too many times when they ran out of reasons, they used the phrase 'pure military requirements,'" recalls Eugene M. Zuckert, who served as McNamara's Secretary of the Air Force. "They couldn't satisfy McNamara intellectually."

So his confidence soared, not necessarily by experience or even by knowledge, but by his ability to strike fear into those around him who failed to think in a rational, fact-filled way. When a new Secretary of

Defense took office, it was customary for each branch of the military to put on elaborate presentations to familiarize the newcomer with key issues. McNamara, however, was not about to sit quiet in a room for anyone. "He wouldn't listen to briefings," says Gilpatric. "He didn't like flip charts, didn't like men in uniform with pointers reading off things. He wanted to ask his own questions, and he wanted unstereotyped answers, and that threw them off. And also, he was not very much on tact and diplomacy in the way he handled them."

The military chiefs quickly realized—as all the people at Ford knew so well—that they were dealing with a different kind of animal. He asked tough, penetrating questions. He demanded rigorous analysis. And he, Robert S. McNamara, was going to make the major program and budget decisions. He was not going to allow the Joint Chiefs of Staff and the services to divvy up the budget through horsetrading and politicking. He was going to do the carving up, and he was going to do it in the most rational, cost-effective way possible.

Within weeks of being sworn in, McNamara had developed a list of ninety-six questions to pose to the Joint Chiefs of Staff in a major review of defense needs. He also created four task groups to investigate the military's strategic nuclear capabilities and its ability to mount conventional war. This latter issue was central because the Eisenhower strategy had been based on a total reliance upon nuclear weapons. It was a bankrupt strategy because the Soviets did not believe the U.S. would respond to minor acts of aggression with a nuclear response. Kennedy and McNamara wanted a shift in strategy from sole reliance on massive retaliation with nuclear weapons to a controlled, flexible response. He set deadlines for the answers, sometimes demanding responses within thirty days, but in no case longer than three months.

The demands set off a scramble. The Joint Chiefs lacked the staff to get all the answers on McNamara's desk in time. They brought in planning officers from Europe, the Pacific and elsewhere to do the studies. "My people were working sixteen, in some cases eighteen hours a day, seven days a week in order to turn out this information," recalls Earle Wheeler, then director of the Joint Staff. Unaccustomed to delivering the kind of analysis McNamara expected, many staffers failed to satisfy him, and he increasingly turned to his handpicked civilian team for the answers.

As he dug deeper and deeper, McNamara found what Thornton and the original team had discovered first in the Army Air Force and then at Ford: disorganization and chaos. Decisions were largely made not on what was in the best interests of defending the country, but instead because of the parochial interests of the Army, the Navy and the Air Force, or because of the political interests of congressmen eager to get defense business in their own backyards. McNamara's audits found an utter lack of balance between men and equipment, ordnance supplies and requirements. Oddly enough, they were the kinds of things Stat Control brought to order during World War Two. The Air Force had only a fourth of the required number of Sidewinder missiles. Most of its air-to-ground weapons were so old they were not suitable for the aircraft in inventory. In effect, McNamara discovered that the Air Force would not have been able to provide meaningful tactical air support for the Army in the event of a non-nuclear limited war. Indeed, McNamara discovered that the Air Force actually had to borrow ordnance from the Navy to carry out a demonstration for him of tactical air power to support combat troops.

Shortly after taking over, officials of the supply corps from the separate services arrived in his office with a bewildering array of belt buckles and butchers' smocks. They asked Bob if he would decide for them which belt buckle and which smock they all should buy. McNamara could hardly believe that they would come to the Secretary of Defense for such a decision. But the buying authority was so fragmented among the Army, Navy and Air Force that they could not agree on a single standard for even a belt buckle. More than anything else, believes Solis Horwitz, then an assistant secretary, the incident convinced McNamara to centralize far greater authority in his office at the Pentagon.

And he did, hiring greater numbers of analysts and planners. He created the Defense Intelligence Agency to get top secret advice independent of the individual services and the CIA. He established a Defense Supply Agency to centralize control over the tens of thousands of purchases required by all the services.

Centralization, of course, translated into a huge buildup in staff. By mid-1965, there would be twenty-seven men in the Pentagon with the title of Deputy Assistant Secretary of Defense, instead of the seven in 1960. All together, the size of the office of the Secretary of Defense had risen by a third to over 2,300 people, accounting for one of every ten employees in the Pentagon. Enthoven's Systems Analysis unit alone boasted about two hundred analysts, 120 of them with MBAs or Ph.D.s.

They were sharply different from the senior military officers who had dominated defense thinking. This new group of Whiz Kids were often young, frequently skeptical of authority and generally lacked military experience. Vice-Admiral Hyman G. Rickover compared them to "spiritualists" and "sociologists" and accused them of "playing God while neglecting the responsibility of being human. Their studies are, in general, abstractions. They read more like the rules of a game of classroom logic than a prognosis of real events in the real world." General Thomas D. White, former chief of staff of the Air Force, did not believe that these "over-confident, sometimes arrogant young professors, mathematicians and other theorists have sufficient worldliness or motivation to stand up to the kind of enemy we face." General Curtis E. LeMay called them "armchair strategists."

To the Pentagon, they brought the kind of analysis Ford's central finance staff imposed on the company's managers before they could build or expand a plant, buy a new machine tool or replace antiquated paint ovens. What made McNamara's insistence on such analysis nearly unique at the time was that he was setting quantitative objectives in a non-profit organization. In government agencies, there was no broadly accepted numerical measure of benefit, no return on investment, no profit. It made cost-benefit analysis less useful and harder to apply in non-profit organizations. Even so, McNamara insisted that every project meet the test of rational analysis.

When the Army wanted to buy new helicopters to support ground combat troops, it had to guarantee the investment would provide at least the same degree of support at a cost no greater than the Tactical Air Force, or the Army tanks and artillery batteries already used to support troops on the ground. If it could not meet that test, McNamara believed he had no reason to even consider the proposal. Impassioned, but unsubstantiated, pleas for projects by the chiefs no longer carried weight in McNamara's new Pentagon.

There were numerous battles, and one of the most heated concerned the Navy's request for nuclear-powered aircraft carriers. In the early 1960s, many military officials believed it was an obvious decision. The Navy had already underway a nuclear-powered submarine fleet as well as a carrier, a cruiser and a frigate that used nuclear energy. The Navy, the Atomic Energy Commission and a Joint Congressional Committee on Atomic Energy unanimously supported the building of a nuclear-powered carrier. But McNamara remained unimpressed, arguing that the facts did not support the higher costs.

When Navy Secretary Fred Korth submitted his study recommending the nuclear carrier, he received a terse note in reply. Retorted McNamara: "You state that nuclear propulsion permits a significant increase in beneficial military results for a given expenditure and you note that the benefits may be taken in the form of either reductions in carrier task forces or increased effectiveness, but you have failed to identify the magnitude of the increase in effectiveness or the possible reduction in force. Thus, I am asked to consider a course of action which would, among other things, add at least $600 million to the five-year shipbuilding program without knowledge of the ultimate effect of these outlays." Korth failed to convince McNamara, and within days of Bob's decision in late 1963 to begin construction on a conventionally-powered carrier, Korth resigned his post. Adjectives were no substitute for numbers, not in McNamara's rational world.

Nearly every decision was made on the "facts" tallied up by the Pentagon's back-room analysts. They became disciples who brought the phrase "systems analysis" into vogue, elevating it into a new religion. The words became magic words, power words, for the better part of a decade. And those who invoked the words did so with spiritual zeal, as if pursuing a truth others could not comprehend. "It was a missionary job," recalled Ivan Selin, who as a twenty-eight-year-old analyst brought two Ph.D.s to the task. "You have to be somewhat overzealous when you're starting a new religion." No one could advance a simple definition of what systems analysis meant, in part because it drew upon theory from several academic disciplines like economics, mathematics and statistics, and because it was akin to operations research, another rational tool embraced by the business world in the early 1950s to help solve complex problems.

Some critics equated systems analysis with an occult art, often because the staff papers and analyses in which it was used were filled with technical terms and jargon that made them incomprehensible to the nonexpert. Generally, though, systems thinking argued that every decision should be considered in as broad a context as necessary. The strategic bomber, the airfield, the pilot, the fuel and the bombs are all parts of a single weapons system. "One cannot make sense out of requirements for any one part without looking at the whole system of interrelated parts," explained Enthoven. Analysis emphasized the need to reduce a complex problem to its component parts to gain better understanding. Questions of fact had to be tested against factual evidence, using quantitative economic analysis to root out the answers.

To McNamara, systems analysis was little more than "quantitative common sense." But it made little sense to military officers. They believed that abstract analysis made it impossible to consider many intangible factors vital in war: morale, discipline, leadership, integrity and courage. The old culture of the Pentagon, a culture that attached significance to such things as rank, experience and intuition, was being supplanted by a new one that made facts and figures all-important.

McNamara's cultural transformation brought a new set of acronyms and a new lingo to the Pentagon—the jargon of rationality: PPBS (Planning-Programming-Budgeting-System); FYDP (Five-Year Defense Plan); diminishing marginal utility; incommensurables; tradeoffs; suboptimization; criteria and upset points. The latter were targets that brought to McNamara's attention a potential problem with the quality, delivery or cost estimate of a weapons contract. If a new aircraft was to have a range of two thousand miles, for example, the analysts might set an upset point of 5 percent. The moment there was any indication that the aircraft's range would fall to 1,900 or fewer miles, the red lights would go off and management was all over the problem. The idea was to catch problems early and to prevent them from spinning out of control.

Central to it all was a planning process devised by Charles Hitch that forced the military to issue concise, detailed five-year plans. Hitch used the idea of "programming" to bridge the gap between planning and budgeting. The Joint Chiefs created "program packages" to deal with potential international crises from which all planning and budgeting flowed. The result was a fact-laden looseleaf folder containing the defense plans of the U.S. for the next five years. The pages detailed more than one hundred thousand items, each with its estimated cost under nine major defense programs, covering everything from nuclear war to a small conflict fought by conventional means. All the figures were not schemes, or desires, or dreams or propaganda, as one analyst pointed out. They reflected real decisions that McNamara would hold everyone to. For the first time, the Defense Department had a systematic procedure for translating strategic requirements into budget requests.

There were other key ideas, including what the young analysts called "McNamara's First Law of Analysis." It held that you should always start by looking at the grand totals of a proposal. "Whatever problem you are studying," counseled Enthoven, "back off and look at it in the large. Don't start with a small piece and work up; look at the total and then break it down into its parts. One can simply not make sense out of costs without looking at totals."

When the analysts studied the military's proposals, they would screen the papers for what McNamara called "slashing the gold watches." Once while at Ford, after reducing a department's budget, he got a howl of protest by cutting out the customary presentation of gold watches to men who retired after forty years or more of service. So McNamara men labelled all proposals that involved false economies or superficial actions as "gold-watch proposals" that should be rejected.

McNamara was clinical in the way he went about the job, believing that emotion destroyed the clarity of his rational approach on which he prided himself. "He doesn't care what your problems are," said Zuckert, who battled with him over Air Force issues. "Organization and administration relationships are pretty cold-blooded. His concern with human considerations is limited pretty much to after-office hours or on Sunday."

It did not take the apprehensive men of the military long before they, too, would be dazzled by Bob's mastery of the facts. For the more he learned, the more formidable and scintillating his performances became. At a meeting at President Kennedy's vacation home in Palm Beach, Florida, to review the defense budget, General Curtis E. LeMay appealed to Kennedy to restore an Air Force project that he said McNamara had deleted from the budget. Bob calmly explained that the general was wrong and that he had not cut the item. General LeMay sat in embarrassed silence as his aides fumbled through the huge budget document to locate the item. McNamara immediately gave them the number of the page.

Years later he would do the same for President Johnson. At a White House conference on an impending railway strike, Johnson asked for the cost to the industry of one of the union's wage demands. McNamara calculated in his head and spat out an answer in less than five seconds. It took several Department of Labor experts another five minutes to work out the same numbers on paper, only to confirm Bob's calculations.

Of all the occasions that helped to cultivate his image as a master of facts, none was more compelling than the time Bob sat for eight hours watching hundreds of slides showing what supplies were already in Vietnam and what was on the way. After seven hours, McNamara commanded: "Stop the projector. This slide, number 869, contradicts slide eleven." The aide operating the projector went back to slide eleven, and sure enough, McNamara was right. Everyone was overwhelmed.

Facts tumbled out of him as if stored on dozens of whirling computer tapes. Not only could he recite them, however. He somehow made sense of them, at least insofar as they proved his point. McNamara, recalls Robert N. Anthony, a Harvard Business School professor who worked under him at the Pentagon, was able to "take all the facts and figures that pour through his eyes and ears from a wide variety of sources, put them in juxtaposition with one another, and come up with relationships, weak spots, inconsistencies, and new insights that even the experts who are intimately acquainted with the details had never even thought of." One observer called him "the leading specimen of *homo mathematicus.*"

He was an intellectual bully. He exercised intimidating power through his mastery of facts. His mental capacity blinded admirers and muzzled potential critics. George W. Ball, then Under Secretary of State, was impressed with what he called McNamara's "extraordinary self-confidence based not on bluster but on a detailed knowledge of objective facts. He gave the impression of knowing every detail of the Defense Department's vast operations and had concise and impressive views on any subject that arose, reinforcing his opinions with huge verbal foot-notes of statistics. He quoted precise figures, not mere orders of magni-tude."

Even members of Congress were awestruck. Defense Secretary Gates's final annual statement to Congress ran thirty-three double-spaced pages. After zipping through it and answering a few questions, the secretary would leave and the technical experts would take over. McNamara's first presentation ran 122 pages single-spaced plus forty-four pages of detailed tables; his last would run 256 single-spaced pages, not counting the twenty-four pages of detailed tables or the supplemental information which filled five one-inch-thick notebooks. One staffer always had the job of rifling through the documents to hand the secretary the relevant page when asked a question. "I did indeed start out to do this," recalls Anthony, "but I gave it up after the first year. The plain fact was that he didn't need my help in finding the answers."

His stamina equally amazed people. One congressional hearing went from 10 a.m. until 1 p.m. and then from 2 p.m. to 6 p.m. with only a one-hour break for lunch. The senators were, as usual, coming and going as they wished. But McNamara sat there in the witness chair, effortlessly fielding question after question without let-up for seven hours without a single bead of sweat forming on his forehead.

WITHIN TWO YEARS, McNamara had radically transformed the Pentagon. And like the Ford Motor Company, it was badly in need of the planning, budgeting and efficiency he brought to it. In a paean to his accomplish-ments, *Fortune* magazine extolled the changes in a major story titled "McNamara's Management Revolution." "McNamaraism is plainly spreading beyond the Defense Department," concluded *Fortune.* "Some of the Pentagon's bright young men have already moved from the De-

fense Department to the Budget Bureau and the Treasury. Many of
McNamara's assistants believe they are involved in a management
revolution that will eventually transform the way the U.S. Government
does business."

They were—but it was a revolution begun long ago by Tex Thornton
and now only beginning to gain widespread public acceptance and acclaim. McNamara was doing at the Pentagon what Thornton was doing
at Litton and what Arjay Miller and Ed Lundy were still doing at Ford.
At each institution, the numbers they pored over were different but they
accomplished the same thing. They made Ford's cars, Litton's
potentometers and the Department of Defense's massive resources more
manageable abstractions to professionals who didn't or couldn't have
firsthand experience with a car, an electronic device or troops and missiles. The numbers were complex, yet subtle; illuminating, but often
deceptive; suggestive and always powerful.

Without them, McNamara could not have so quickly taken charge at
Ford or the Pentagon. Despite the controversy that swirled around him,
he won great admiration for leading the revolution—not only from the
media but also from the President. McNamara had comfortably made
the transition from Detroit to Washington, all right. Henry Ford II, after
witnessing one of McNamara's private performances in front of a room
full of defense contractors, concluded that Bob had caught "Potomac
Fever." McNamara was among the more vocal members of the Hickory
Hill Seminars, the freewheeling discussion groups named after the home
of Bob Kennedy, who initiated them. Bob Kennedy called McNamara
"the most dangerous man in the Cabinet because he is so persuasive and
articulate." And at the White House, he danced the twist with Jackie.
The gossip columnists had written that Mrs. Kennedy thought McNamara one of the sexiest men in the Cabinet.

The President had become so enamored with Bob McNamara that he
had begun to think about how he could advance him, and not his Vice
President, for the Democratic nomination for President in 1968. It was
not because McNamara had always served him well. Bob had been enthusiastically in favor of the Bay of Pigs invasion, the CIA-directed effort
of Cuban exiles to overthrow Fidel Castro. It was Kennedy's most painful blunder. Though the President assumed full responsibility for the
incident, McNamara was quick to say that the fault did not lay with
Kennedy but mainly with his three senior advisers, particularly himself.

Along with Secretary of State Dean Rusk and CIA Director John
McCone, he had accepted too readily the recommendations on the Bay of

Pigs from the Joint Chiefs of Staff and the Central Intelligence Agency. The whole affair, coming within ninety days of Kennedy's Inaugural, reinforced a lesson for McNamara: Do your own work, your own analysis. "I relearned a lesson I had learned many times before," McNamara said, "and that was never to rely on the advice anybody gives me on anything."

Bob applied that logic when the second Cuban crisis occurred in October of 1962. When Kennedy's military leaders advocated that the U.S. attack Cuba by air to knock out the Soviet missiles there, McNamara forcefully argued in favor of a naval blockade and moved other key advisers to his way of thinking. "He never changed his position," recalled Gilpatric. "He never indicated he had reservations about it, and I think that tended to pull people back from some of the extreme positions they'd taken."

When the crisis passed and Kennedy could savor his most important triumph, the President was especially impressed by McNamara's cool, dispassionate performance. "He thought most highly of McNamara and thought—particularly after Cuba, where you can see what can happen to a country and how much depends on a particular individual—that [the country] should be placed in the best possible hands," Robert Kennedy later said in an interview. "And we thought that McNamara was that individual."

Even more than that, however, the President was taken with McNamara because, as Thornton had learned many years earlier, he could completely trust Bob. They did not see eye-to-eye on every issue, but not once did anyone hear McNamara criticize or even imply a criticism of any decision made by the President—not only in staff meetings, but also in private conversations. Indeed, he would not allow anyone to criticize Kennedy in private. Once the President had made a decision, McNamara would fall in line and carry it out, even if he opposed it.

ON FRIDAY, NOVEMBER 22, 1963, Bob McNamara was in the E ring of the Pentagon, working on details of the $50 billion budget with McGeorge Bundy, Kermit Gordon of the Budget Bureau, and Jerry Wiesner, the President's scientist-in-residence. It had been a long week for the Secretary of Defense. On Wednesday, he had been in Honolulu for a strategy conference on Vietnam, where 16,500 U.S. military advisers were then stationed. After the meetings at the Pacific Military Headquarters, McNamara said that the war against the Communists had taken a decided turn for the better, so much so that he reaffirmed the withdrawal of one thousand U.S. advisers by the end of 1963. Bob had flown back to Washington in the early hours on Thursday.

Now, in the midst of the budget meeting, a McNamara aide abruptly rushed into his office only a few minutes past 1:30 p.m. His face drained of color, he rushed to Bob in silence, handing him a yellow strip of paper torn from the United Press International ticker in the Pentagon's communications center. Wiesner's first thought, as McNamara read the bulletin, was that "the bomb's been dropped."

It stated: "Dallas, Nov. 22 (UPI)—Three shots were fired at President Kennedy's motorcade today in downtown Dallas." McNamara remained composed and silent. He quietly handed the paper around and adjourned the session.

Within half an hour, Bob was among the first in Washington to be told, through the Defense Intelligence Agency, that the President was dead, assassinated in a custom-built blue Lincoln, one of Ben Mills's cars. Later that afternoon, McNamara had received word from Johnson that he was to be on the tarmac upon his arrival at Andrews Air Force base. Not long after twilight had settled on Washington, Robert Kennedy met McNamara at his Pentagon office and, along with Maxwell Taylor, the three men walked out to the Pentagon's south helipad, boarded a helicopter and flew to Andrews. The plane touched down at 6:05 p.m. After the casket was removed, Johnson slowly emerged and walked down the airplane ramp. McNamara was the first Cabinet officer to greet the new President. He did not know Johnson well, and had no idea how his work habits would compare with Kennedy's. He didn't even know if Johnson would want him to stay on as Secretary of Defense.

Johnson, however, was touched by McNamara's welcome, and asked him to accompany him back to the White House with Bundy and George Ball. In the helicopter ride to the White House, McNamara sat next to Johnson who seemed near a state of shock. Afterward, Ball recalled that Johnson moved erratically and his face twitched from the emotional strain. During the ten-minute trip, Johnson told the men that Mrs. Kennedy had been incredibly brave. Although her stockings were covered with blood, she refused to change them—since it was her husband's blood—even as she stood by Johnson as he was sworn into office.

Johnson then turned to McNamara, Bundy and Ball: "You're men I trust the most. You must stay with me. I'll need you. President Kennedy gathered about him extraordinary people I could never have reached for. You're the ablest men I've ever seen. It's not just that you're President

Kennedy's friends, but you are the best anywhere and you must stay. I want you to stand with me."

When the helicopter landed on the south grounds of the White House, a few yards from the Oval Office, everything seemed to have a different, sad, almost macabre appearance, recalled Ball. He and McNamara entered through the Cabinet Room and sat together for the next twenty minutes talking of the meaning of everything that had occurred in the last few hours as well as the significance of the Kennedy Presidency. They agreed how unfortunate it had been that JFK had felt his freedom of action limited because he had been elected by such a narrow margin. With a new election and a new mandate in 1964, they believed he would have led the country through the most innovative years it had ever known. Some insiders believed that in Kennedy's second term, McNamara would have led the President's Cabinet as Secretary of State.

They separated, and McNamara went home where he soon received a call from Robert Kennedy. Within minutes, he was off again, now with Margy, to Bethesda Naval Hospital where Kennedy's body had been taken. To the consternation of military officials, who thought McNamara should travel in an escorted limousine, he drove himself in the dark blue Ford Galaxie that had been shipped from Dearborn after he resigned the Ford presidency.

McNamara, only expecting to stay for a few moments, left Margy in the front seat and went upstairs to a hospital VIP suite where the Kennedys had gathered. And soon, just as he had dominated every business meeting at Ford or every Cabinet meeting in the White House, his presence in the suite was felt by all, especially Mrs. Kennedy who was still dressed in the same pink wool suit she had worn in Dallas, with dried blood all over her stockings. "I felt I had to be calm for her and listen to her," McNamara told author William Manchester. "We were in the kitchen, Jackie sitting on the stool and me on the floor. It went on for hours. I was concentrating entirely upon her, because she needed me and I felt, the hell with the others; let them take care of themselves."

Mrs. Kennedy recalled the day's horrifying details, talking them out little by little until it finally dawned on her: where would she live now that she was no longer the First Lady. The Kennedys had sold their Georgetown house after moving into the White House so she had no home of her own to go to. She thought it would be nice to move back to Georgetown, maybe even back to the same address.

"I'll buy it back for you," McNamara volunteered.

As the evening wore on, Bob—ever the man in charge—even became involved in the most intimate details of the slain President's funeral. When a discussion ensued over the burial site for the slain President, McNamara insisted that Kennedy be buried in a national cemetery and not in Massachusetts where several of Kennedy's Boston friends thought he should be laid to rest. Later, he argued that the President's casket should be open while Mrs. Kennedy strongly maintained that she wanted it closed to preserve the memory of her husband alive. "It can't be done, Jackie," McNamara said. "Everybody wants to see a Head of State."

They talked in the kitchen of the suite—Bob sitting on the sink and Mrs. Kennedy on the floor and Robert Kennedy on top of a small refrigerator—until after 3:30 a.m. when it was time to transport Kennedy's body back to the White House. With Robert Kennedy's wife, Ethel, McNamara followed in a car just behind the ambulance. And after the casket was placed on a catafalque in the East Room of the White House, Bob was one of only eight persons to peek inside it in efforts to finally decide whether the coffin should be closed. McNamara lost the argument.

He left at dawn to return home for little more than a cat nap, a shower and a change of clothes before arriving in his Pentagon office on Saturday at 8 a.m., studying the details of burials at national cemeteries and arranging to meet the superintendent of Arlington Cemetery. It did not take McNamara long to pick out a grave site from the three recommended by the superintendent, for he was able to race back for the 10 a.m. mass for family and friends in the dining room of the White House.

After the service, he and Margy approached the coffin with their son, Craig, to say a prayer. This was all on the same cold and gray day in which he attended Johnson's first Cabinet meeting, conferred with the new President in the middle of the afternoon, and posed with Johnson for one of several still photographs taken to show the new President at work. And in a torrential downpour he went to the cemetery three times during the day to show the Kennedy family and aides the slope of land he preferred until finally supervising the demarcation of the grave site himself at dusk. Then, with little more than an hour or two of rest in the last thirty-eight hours, McNamara and his wife joined the President's relatives and close friends for a small dinner at the White House, dining not far from where the body lay in state in what would be President Kennedy's last night in the mansion.

Wearing a blotched pink complexion from being out in the rain so much during his trips to Arlington that day, the indefatigable McNamara even engaged in a bit of horseplay to relieve the day's tension. Ethel

Kennedy had worn a wig to dinner because she didn't have the time for a hairdresser during the day. It was snatched off by one guest and passed from head to head until it finally covered Bob's trademark slicked-down hair. There the former president of Ford whom nearly everyone feared, one of the most powerful men in the world, sat with a wig atop his head.

This was the other McNamara, the warm and witty man who gave unsparingly of himself, who could console a grieving widow at her moment of despair, who could become the best possible friend anyone could hope for in a time of need. This was the man that Tex Thornton and Ed Lundy and Arjay Miller and Ben Mills knew because they had socialized with the man who so readily barked orders. It was not the McNamara familiar to most of his colleagues at either Ford or the Pentagon. But to his friends, it again showed that he was much more than the human IBM machine that he was so often accused of being.

Arjay Miller (right) lacked the cool confidence of McNamara, but he nonetheless became the second Whiz Kid to serve Henry Ford II as president. (Ford with Miller shortly after Arjay's promotion to the presidency of Ford).

Whiz Kid J. Edward Lundy always stood in the background, shunning the limelight. But he was a powerful figure at Ford who recruited thousands of MBAs and trained them to be tight-fisted financial controllers.

While Bob McNamara and Tex Thornton were making the covers of the major magazines, Arjay Miller appears on the cover of *Automotive Industries* in 1965.

A CHILTON PUBLICATION   APRIL 15, 1965

AUTOMOTIVE
INDUSTRIES

ENGINEERING · MANAGEMENT · PRODUCTION · DESIGN

ARJAY MILLER
President
Ford Motor Company

FRIDEN
BRAINS

■

"So much of what we call management consists in making it
difficult for people to work."

—PETER DRUCKER

*I*t was a scene oddly reminiscent of the November day in 1960
when Bob McNamara assumed the presidency of Ford. The
setting at the company's ultra-modern headquarters was identical and so
was the purpose: to introduce a new Ford president at an early morning
press conference.

There was Henry Ford II again, exuding cheer and confidence, just as
he had two-and-one-half years earlier. The executive sitting next to him
boasted the familiar slicked-down hair and gold-rimmed spectacles that
had become McNamara's trademark. The new man of the hour on this
April day in 1963 was the folksy and homespun Arjay Miller—the second of the Whiz Kids to gain the presidency.

He accepted the position with humility, not fully expecting the job nor
believing that he especially deserved it. But then, Miller, all of forty-
seven years old, never seemed ambitious and never really sought advancement. He had been in a quiet competition for the top job with John

Bugas, the man who had grilled the group after their very first meeting with Henry in 1945, and with his Whiz Kid cohort Jim Wright, who sincerely believed he deserved the job over his friend. The tipoff came about a month earlier when Arjay received $5,000 more in bonus money than Wright. Arjay then knew he had the edge, although Henry didn't tell him until five days before the actual announcement.

It was an awkward situation. Miller was fond of Wright and admired his skills as a general manager. He also thought him a better executive than Jack Reith ever was. "He was a lawyer, more gentlemanly and thoughtful and logical," Miller would say years later. "Wright was a better man than Jack. Jim would not have brought the Edsel through like Jack. Jim Wright would have coordinated with everybody and it would not have happened the way it did."

Wright, then fifty, deeply felt it was *his* time. As head of the Ford Division, he had taken pride in Ford beating Chevrolet in 1957 for the first time since the introduction of the Model-A. And he had done it again in 1959—something he considered his most important accomplishment at Ford. It was why Arjay, who held a succession of staff jobs, honestly believed that Wright earned the presidency more than he had. Wright had shadowed Bob McNamara's rise, moving up behind him with every promotion until Bob left for the Pentagon. He understood that Henry could not possibly name him president upon McNamara's departure. He had only been vice president of the car and truck group for a few weeks. (A young marketing ace, Lee Iacocca, had taken over Wright's old job as vice president of the Ford Division.) So the job went to John Dykstra. But as Dykstra's retirement approached, Wright was looking forward to what would have been the capstone of his career at Ford—being the second of the Whiz Kids to have made the climb to the top. After all, he was the No. 3 executive in the company, after Henry and Dykstra. And he had already turned down an opportunity to become president of Chrysler only a couple of years earlier.

When Henry chose, of all people, Arjay, he was devastated. He spent a couple of days in a fog, morosely thinking about his future and blaming Dykstra for the unexpected turn of events. If only Bob had stayed at Ford, he thought. Ever since McNamara left and was replaced by Dykstra, nothing seemed to go right for him. Dykstra was the extreme opposite of McNamara. He was an old-timer, a tough-talking, street-fighter without a college diploma. Son of a master coppersmith, he came to Detroit from the Netherlands at the age of four. He became an apprentice diemaker when he turned sixteen and spent the rest of his life in the auto industry, beginning with the old Hudson Motor Car Company and then with GM's Oldsmobile Division until joining Ford in 1947 as a general production assistant. He worked his way up through the production ranks, rising to the presidency on the basis of a campaign to build better quality into Ford's products. Wright surmised that McNamara's sudden resignation caused Ford to pick Dykstra partly because he was on an opposite pole. Maybe Henry had had enough of the intellectuals, he thought.

From the start, Jim harbored a vehement dislike of Dykstra. "I have absolutely no regard for the man, none," he said. "He would cover up the truth, butter up his superiors, and damn the people under him. You either agreed with him or you were his enemy. If you toed the line you would get along pretty well." He considered him a fraud and a consummate liar, a man who capitalized too much on opportunity. He picked up the baton to lead the band against defects, but the defects were seldom his own. They always seemed to fall under the domain of the other guy. Dykstra, in turn, viewed Wright as a hothead. They had argued and fought even before Ford made him president. Indeed, Ford came to Wright and told him of his decision, saying it wouldn't work unless Wright could make up with Dykstra. He assured Henry that he would.

But trouble began when Dykstra came to him, complaining about the quality of the cars. Trying not to be defensive, Wright attempted to explain that you couldn't just wave a wand and sweep away defects. But Dykstra wouldn't hear of it. Wright resented Dykstra's attempts to make decisions in areas such as sales or planning where he had little knowledge. And Wright was particularly incensed when Dykstra wanted the company to give up the Falcon, Bob McNamara's utilitarian car.

"He didn't like the damn car, and didn't consider it a Ford," recalls Wright.

"Why don't we make the Ford better?" asked Dykstra. "Why aren't we selling more standard Fords?"

"How the hell do you expect us to sell a big car to a man who doesn't want one?" retorted Wright. "Have you ever tried it?"

There were long sessions of disagreements between the men, and Jim did not disguise his dislike.

"We crossed swords," says Wright. "I did the job as best I could, but he didn't know a damn thing about dealers or sales or planning, and he attempted to run all that."

The dispute over McNamara's Falcon, however, spilled out into the open in front of product planners and members of the finance staff. The

car was a product of unitized construction under which its key components were welded together to create a uniform cabin. The change led to
major savings in production costs over the more typical system of building a car from a frame up. But Dykstra believed the Falcon would be
sturdier if it were built the old way. Wright argued it would only increase costs.

"I thought it was crazy," remembered Wright. " 'Look, John,' I said,
'GM has three car lines on this one frame. We have the one car. You're
going to add quite a few dollars to the cost of that thing and we're
winning because we've kept the costs down.' It was impossible to talk to
him. It's possible that things would have been different for me if I went
along, but I wasn't made that way. I just couldn't stand it."

His disagreements with Dykstra reached the breaking point, causing
Wright to consider resigning his job if Ford extended Dykstra's term as
president. When Henry failed to keep Dykstra any longer, the outgoing
president, thought Wright, made sure that Jim had no chance to succeed
him. "He fixed me but good," insists Wright. "I know that. He just
blackened me so I wouldn't have a future there. He bad-mouthed me to
Henry Ford, mostly because I didn't agree with him."

He had noticed a change in Henry's behavior toward him. "He was
on the muscle in those days, still smarting, I thought from McNamara's
leaving," said Wright. "He was grouchy and growly all the time, at least
with me." Ford was placing distance between himself and Wright,
readying himself for the decision not to give Wright the job he so badly
wanted and thought he deserved.

Wright, too, had never really known Henry. When he was a group
vice president, he would report through Bob and later through Dykstra
—always a step removed. He would see Ford, who was becoming more
remote, in the executive dining room and at the key executive meetings
—but that was all. Henry was never fond of the man and never associated the gains of the Ford Division with him but with McNamara.

Besides suffering the indignity of being passed over, Wright's current
job as group executive of cars and trucks was abolished and he was
effectively demoted to vice president of the credit and insurance group. It
was quite a come-down for someone who had expected the ultimate
promotion, and it left him numb with disappointment. Arjay came to
him and said he hoped he would stay on. A couple of days after the
announcement, Wright was brought a pile of folders and books for the
new job. "I looked at it and said, that's not for me. I could handle
the numbers, but that wasn't something I wanted to do."

"That's when I decided I had it. I went home, got out my papers and figured my own financial situation, and I wrote up my resignation. I was hurt. Alice went along with me every step of the way. Alice was highly in favor of my quitting. 'If you stay here another two or three years we'll probably have to bury you,' she said. She was right. The pressure was awful."

The next day, less than a week after Henry and Arjay Miller smiled for the cameras at the press conference, Wright marched into Henry's twelfth-floor office and handed him the resignation letter. He had been a loyal manager and executive to Henry Ford for seventeen years. It was Wright who became the first head of the company's organization office. He had laid the blueprints for the creation of the Ford Division in 1949, and he had been involved in many of the company's most important decisions in the postwar period. Yet Henry offered no explanations nor apologies for passing him over.

"I didn't think you would quit," Ford told him.

The response stunned him. Years later, the words would still remain in his head. "That's exactly what he said. I was disappointed. Mad is not a very good reason for leaving. I was quite disappointed and really hurt to be treated that way. I was quite hurt. There was no way I could talk to Arjay. He was just being named president. I didn't talk to any of the other guys. Mind you, just a year before Arjay had said to me, 'Jim, we all know that you're the next in line.' He said that and I'm sure he would tell you that to this day. It was Henry's decision, though. And no one ever knew what Henry would decide. We all lived with that problem."

When news of his resignation made the rounds, many of his old friends were jolted. John Bugas rushed into Wright's office, pacing the floor. He was shocked by the turn of events himself. "What a waste!" he muttered. "What a goddamn waste!"

Tex Thornton called Wright the same day his resignation was reported in the papers. Of all the men Tex originally brought to Ford, he had known Wright the longest and considered him one of his best friends.

"Don't do a thing until you talk to me!" Tex said.

"I'm not about to do anything anytime soon," Wright told him.

"I want you to come out here and talk to me about a job at Litton," Thornton commanded.

So Wright flew out to Los Angeles to meet with his old pal. They chatted about old times, Ford and Wright's uncertain plans for the future. "I sensed that he might have wanted me to join Litton," Wright recalls, "and I said, 'Look, you've built this company. Roy Ash has helped you build it. I don't know where I would fit in so let's not talk about it.' "

Tex, forever wheeling and dealing, wasn't about to be put off. "You shouldn't be roaming around," he lectured Wright.

Before he left to return to Detroit, Wright had been signed up by Tex as a consultant to review the marketing plans of Litton's Monroe Division. At least for a temporary period, Tex managed to get one of his men back. Wright's departure left only four of the original ten men at Ford: Ben Mills, who remained general manager of the Lincoln-Mercury Division, Charlie Bosworth, still purchasing director of the Ford Division, and Arjay and Ed Lundy, now the two most powerful executives at the company.

HENRY'S DECISION TO pick Arjay Miller over Wright ultimately came down to simple chemistry: Henry liked Arjay. He enjoyed his company and his advice. He respected his intellectually rationalist approach, like McNamara's in its technical efficiency but, unlike Bob, brought off with unassuming charm. That was one of the reasons why Ford involved Miller in several international assignments—then considered Henry's baby—and why Ford, watching in amazement at Tex's increasing success with Litton, put him in charge of diversifying the company. Henry was interested in expanding the company into areas outside of the automobile business. "Look what Tex is doing," he told Charles E. Beck, a Miller associate. "Boy, Tex is going to own everything one of these days."

Ford's fascination with Litton's growth by diversification had led in 1961 to Ford's $83 million takeover of Philco, with its interests in aerospace and radios and televisions. On the very day of the acquisition, Thornton rang Miller on the phone.

"Arjay," he said, "what the hell did you buy that damn company for? I didn't think any son of a bitch was stupid enough to buy that thing."

"Tex, I didn't want to buy it," Miller retorted. He explained that Ford and Breech wanted the company for its aerospace operations.

Tex quickly offered to buy from Ford all of Philco's white goods business. Though Miller was happy to sell it to him, Henry begged to differ. GM was making lots of money in white goods with its Frigidaire subsidiary and Henry thought that Ford could do the same. "What is Thornton offering us, only money. We have plenty of money," said

Ford. "Let's see if we can make a go of it." (Ford would lose several hundred million dollars on this business, however, prompting Arjay to later say: "We should have given it to Tex.")

But Arjay, ever the faithful servant to the Prince of Ford, did not argue the point. He accepted the fact that he was merely an agent for Henry, who made all the ultimate decisions. Indeed, he was willing to admit that no idea existed at Ford until Henry had thought of it or at least accepted it. In that way, he lacked the force of personality shared by Thornton, McNamara or Reith. "Henry was the boss," says Miller. "Even though he said, 'You're the boss, Arjay, you make the decision,' Henry didn't mean it. You could tell."

In all the years that Arjay worked at Ford, Henry was critical of him only once. At the time Miller was controller of the company. Ford summoned him to his office one day and much to Miller's surprise, he found his personal expense reports spread across the desk.

"Arjay," Ford said sternly, "I want to talk to you about your expense reports."

Miller froze, thinking he had made an innocent mistake in calculating his expenses, something that Ford was going to seize upon to embarrass him.

"You're too low," Henry said. "You're making the rest of us look lousy. And you haven't picked up a third car."

So Arjay signed out another Ford auto for his family and began to spend more of the company's money.

There was another reason why Arjay won Henry's faith. The reason was J. Edward Lundy. Just as Wright followed McNamara up the corporate ladder, Lundy followed in the footsteps of Arjay Miller, always supporting his close friend and always promoting him to others. It was an odd turn of events because it was Lundy who had originally brought Arjay to Tex's Stat Control group in Washington during the war. But through their years at Ford, Lundy often reported directly to Miller.

They had much in common: Miller was born in Nebraska; Lundy in Iowa. Like McNamara, both Miller and Lundy had begun careers as college instructors. At Ford, they were allies together in finance, handy at operating the old Friden calculators to crunch numbers. They always held staff jobs, never venturing out into operations like Bob, Jack, Ben or Jim. Their friendship would be the most intimate and most enduring of all the men in the group. And in his quiet way, Lundy, even though he would never rise as high as Miller at Ford, would eventually leave a more enduring imprint on the company and on American industry.

PEOPLE SAY LUNDY had only two loves in his life: the Ford Motor Company and the Roman Catholic Church. What many did not say was that he combined his two passions and nearly made them one. His parishioners were his men at Ford. He visited with them in their homes, conferred with them about their problems, even absolved them for their mistakes. And he made rationalism and quantification a secular religion at Ford, preaching its importance as if delivering a sermon from a pulpit.

As his finance department gained greater power and control, Lundy would become a legendary figure inside the company. And more than any of the other Whiz Kids, he would become a true confidant of Henry Ford II. What one man said of Lundy was true: "He was God in his area and a little bit of God outside it." There was nothing that went on at the Ford Motor Company that Lundy didn't know about.

The rise of finance at Ford began under McNamara in the early 1950s. It continued under Arjay in the latter 1950s. And now, in the early 1960s and beyond, Lundy would make finance nearly omnipotent. For decades, he had brought to finance the best and the brightest college graduates he could find. The result was that the financial people were the most talented managers in the company. There was no Lundy in marketing or sales, engineering or manufacturing, who methodically recruited year-after-year the best possible people in the market. Nor was there an equivalent god who served as mentor to so many people. And even if other functions within Ford had been more conscious of the need to buy the best talent, they still would have had to compete in a culture in which the ground rules were all financial.

Years later in the 1970s when other functions began to recruit MBAs, a Ford marketing executive went on a recruiting trip to Stanford University's business school. Arjay Miller was then the school's dean. "He was amazed that we would recruit MBAs for sales and marketing," the executive recalls. " 'What do you want MBAs for?' Miller asked. 'You could get high school girls to do that.' "

So when the engineers and the marketeers came up against Lundy's legions of arrogant financial wizards, they inevitably failed to impress. The result was an excessive attention to cost control above anything else, including the quality of the product. Shaving a nickel or a dime off the cost of a part was a victory and a triumph because savings immediately fell to the bottom line. Adding to the cost of a car—even to address key quality concerns—became verboten. Alarmed by piles of consumer complaints, one manager in the early 1960s urged that the Lincoln Division switch to an electronic voltage regulator from the mechanical one plagued by poor reliability. His plea was rejected because the change would have added $4 to the cost of the car. The electronic version was superior in every way, yet the cost-control demons in finance carried the day.

Much of this mindset, of course, had been established by McNamara, who once wondered if he could get rid of the spare tire in every car. "How many of you have changed your tire in the past year?" Bob once asked a meeting of Ford executives. They all replied that none of them did, and McNamara quickly thought of a way to increase the company's profits by hundreds of thousands of dollars. The idea didn't die until one of the managers reminded him that the executives never required spares because they seldom used their cars for longer than six months and because their tires were changed in the executive garage anyway.

The waves of Lundy men also had another impact on Ford: They represented layers of staff people whose energies were devoted not to the task of producing better products but to policing, bullying and manipulating the organization—a circumstance that began to occur in one American company after another. By 1979, when Lundy would retire, the size of Ford's financial staff rivaled the total employment of many American companies: more than 11,300 people, spending much of their time erecting barriers to new projects and ideas.

The only men who made a difference at Ford were those who immersed themselves in quantitative analysis. The successful managers rushed to put into practice systems thinking and operations research, a field that begat a series of unintelligible acronyms and buzzwords and an avalanche of charts, curves and diagrams. They pursued an array of intellectual puzzles in one assignment after another. A group of men worked on the idea of transfer prices, how much one division of Ford should charge another for an assembly or a part. In product planning, PERT charts became the rage. They were spiderweb-like diagrams to ensure that projects would be completed on time. Program Evaluation and Review Technique forced product planners to draw precise plans in advance, detailing every step required to reach a given objective. PERT charts compelled managers to sketch how each step affected the overall goal, how much each step would cost and how quickly it should be completed. As Secretary of Defense, McNamara also was making them *de rigeur* in the Defense Department.

As a young manager at Ford, Donald Frey recalls going to Wright

Patterson Air Force base where the military ostensibly had PERT chart-ing down to a science. "They had more guys working on PERT charts than they had doing the job," he says. "It was an enormous overhead cost just to allow the generals to show visitors their PERT charts. It took so much effort to get the charts done, you might as well have spent the time getting the job done."

Unlike Lundy's financial wizards, the men at Ford who loved the automobile could not comprehend the near fanatical emphasis placed on numbers. Ford was now a car company, as one designer put it, "con-trolled by bean counters and not by car people. A car person knows what he wants to end up with and somehow he gets there," explained Kenneth Spencer, who worked in Ford's design studio for more than twenty-five years. "But the bean counter wants to know all along the way how much is this, how much is that—and before you even get the genesis of the thing organized, they want to know the exact cost of each part. And you can't think that way so what you do is lie, fake, hide things behind the blackboard, whatever you can do. And it's really counterproductive. And another thing about a bean counter, they can always prove they are right. They've got it on paper. They are right, but they are wrong. You can't take creativity and put a quantitative analysis to it and that's what they kept on trying to do."

The systems ethos informed every major and minor decision in the company, down to the intricacies of a new car's design. The company even began to hold focus groups with consumers, asking them to react to new cars barely on the drawing boards. If a consumer rated a bumper highly, it could be the approved bumper for another car and so on. "They'd take all the good parts and put them on one car and wonder why it's ugly," recalls Spencer. "There is a time when a professional has to say, that's right and we ought to do this. You know if the guy is pitching a baseball game, and he looks into the dugout for every pitch, and then the manager looks up into the crowd and says, 'What'll we throw?'—it gets stupid. But the analogy is perfect. They don't use [mar-ket] surveys as tools . . . they believe in 'em. And I don't like it because I know more than a housewife in Anaheim. In the first place, when you get a respondent to a survey like that, they think now, they don't think four years from now. They think about what they're comfortable with, what they are used to and they are thinking of a car designed for today's prices. You can't plan like that. It's just awful. They act like they can't make a decision unless 187 wives in Toledo tell them what to do."

Though the rationalist approach invaded all functional boundaries at

Ford, the greatest passion for it lay in Lundy's financial area. His finance men were spread throughout the organization, omniscient naysayers who watched every dollar and how it was spent. On Ford's organization charts, the box containing the controller of each division was linked by a solid line to the box containing the division's general manager. A dotted line connected each controller to Lundy's office at Ford headquarters. There is both a philosophical and a pragmatic difference between a solid and a dotted line on an organization chart. The solid line links you to your boss, the person who can hire, fire, promote and hand out job assignments. The dotted line indicates a less powerful relationship, giving that person some unspecified say over your work.

The lines drawn on the charts made it appear that Lundy's men were completely beholden to the general managers. In practice, however, information often flowed up to Lundy through the alternate chain of command faster than through the operating channel. A Ford finance man who later went to ITT to work under Geneen marveled at the system. Geneen, an autocrat who micromanaged the financial details of his company, had the opposite relationship under which all financial men were linked by a solid line to corporate finance. "At ITT, the difference was clear and in the open," he says. "If you were in finance, you were clearly on the other side, responsible only to the men in New York who concerned themselves with all things financial. At Ford, you still reported to the operating head, but that dotted line to Lundy was a far stronger link than Geneen ever got in the solid line. Therefore, finance's role in the company was far more subtle and far more powerful."

Through these dotted-line relationships passed a spate of unofficial communication that gave Lundy and his men tremendous leverage over others in the corporation. "That dotted line," recalls another prominent Ford executive at the time, "had very few breaks in it." The group executives were virtually dependent on Lundy's finance operation because he often had more inside knowledge of what went on in the divisions than they possessed. "Your whole game on American Road (Ford headquarters) was to find out problems rather than to create solutions," explained a finance man. "What you were trying to do is to sell or defend to your audience. A lot of projects were killed because they didn't fit the financial format. The actual economics or market forces didn't count as much."

On a regular basis, the field controllers served up numbers on inventory control, scrappage, obsolescence and expenses. All of them had to meet targets and projections to the satisfaction of Lundy's men in Dearborn. Donald Lennox, having made the transition from finance to manufacturing, could understand the widespread frustrations in the field that led many to fudge the numbers. "We learned in manufacturing that reasoning didn't matter—only the numbers did. We were being controlled by the numbers. So you made sure your actual performance met or exceeded the numbers established by the central finance staff, even if it meant that you looked at a nut and said, 'Gee, that looks like a bolt to me.' You wanted all of your numerical performance by line item to conform to the objectives. Then, you were a good boy."

This was why many of Lundy's detractors thought him a bland, careful and legalistic man. Through his own beliefs and his recruitment of finance people, he had elevated corporate numerical goals into the commandments of Ford. Even men outside the realm of Ford could not help but notice how strong the finance men were becoming inside the company. One Wall Street executive, a man of finance who knew Ed Lundy, Arjay Miller and Tex Thornton, was nearly taken aback by their dominance in the company and their total obsession with the numbers. "I found them not totally human," he said. "They were all early quants. Numbers meant everything. At Ford, you didn't have a workforce. You had a payroll. There was very little discussion about people, and you never discussed the design of a car. If Ford was as good at making autos as they were at controlling costs, Ford would have been the best company in America."

Still, he found Lundy to be an engaging, likable man who had built the most impressive finance staff in corporate America. "It was so far superior to General Motors and many other large corporations," he says. "You could ask Lundy about raw material costs or the impact of labor contracts on Ford and he could give you chapter and verse on it. You had a sense that these guys were absolutely on top of things."

Lundy's role in creating and nurturing the financial empire assumed mythical proportions. "Sitting down with Lundy was like having an audience with the Pope," recalled one man who knew him well. He was not especially handsome. He was a solidly built man, with the broad shoulders of a football player, though he had no athletic ability. He kept his hair in a flattop, always cropped closely enough to give the appearance of a man in the military. Resting on a hawk-like nose were a pair of glasses in dark plastic frames that lent him a severe look. His conservatively cut suits were meticulously crafted by the same tailor in London who fitted Prince Philip. His shirts were custom-made in Paris. They were not, he insisted, bought at Brooks Brothers as some surmised. Still, they were clothes suited to his quiet style and his behind-the-scenes personality. For Lundy and his protégés were never to call attention to themselves.

He enjoyed fine things of exceptional value: books, clothes, exotic vacations and good meals. But he had no interest in things that were ostentatious. Lundy was the last of the men to move out of the Foundation Apartments. And when he left, he moved just across the street to a modern brick house on a quiet cul-de-sac in the Fairlane East development. Unlike the homes of most auto men, it was not a home of massive architecture situated on acres of property. It did not have a swimming pool or a putting green. It was as austere as his lifestyle.

Yet, by the mid-1960s, he was one of Detroit's most highly compensated executives, earning $400,000 a year as Ford's vice president of finance. Like McNamara and Miller, he didn't fit the Detroit corporate image. He didn't play golf. He was not a big drinker. He never played cards, either bridge or poker. Outside of Ford, his interests included gardening, the theater, movies and gourmet food. (Years later, he and Arjay Miller's wife became investors in a critically acclaimed restaurant called Les Auteurs in Royal Oak, about a half hour from Detroit.) He rather grudgingly followed football and basketball, particularly rooting for any team that played against Michigan.

Far more important to him was the church. Lundy had studied Latin through college because he seriously entertained the idea of becoming a priest. His best friend was Father Gerard S. Brennan, the pastor of St. Joseph's Church in Dearborn. St. Joseph's on Rotunda Drive was a small, modest church of cinderblock and brick, with an exposed beam ceiling— only a ten-minute walk from Lundy's home. He had known Brennan since the priest had started the parish in 1952, and often went to the rectory of the church for a pasta dinner with him. Lundy helped to plant and to tend the garden at St. Joseph's.

Some men at Ford took to calling him the "Civilian Pope" because Lundy not only attended mass every Sunday but was frequently in church on several weekdays, too. He generously donated money to many church-related causes. And he was instrumental in providing a new Lincoln limo to the cardinal every year for his personal use. When Robert Dunham, who was nearly a member of the Whiz Kid group himself, had a problem with the Catholic school his daughter attended, he went straight to Lundy with the dilemma. Dunham wanted to take his nine-year-old daughter out of class one year five days before the summer break so he could bring his family to South Dakota where he was going to give a commencement address. The priest in charge of the school refused to excuse his daughter. " 'If she doesn't finish, she'll flunk the grade,' he said. It burned me up. So I spoke to Ed about it. And of course he thought it was silly and asinine. And just as offhand as saying I'll call the weather bureau to get the weather forecast, he said, 'I'll call the cardinal.' Within days, the good father let her go but he was just fit to be tied that anybody would do this to him."

His interest and his influence within the church only added to the aura that surrounded him at Ford. Asked for his opinion of Lundy, one finance man who had only worked outside of Dearborn couldn't give one. "He was sufficiently next to God that I didn't allow myself an opinion in my own head," he said. Lundy was a benevolent God. He genuinely cared about his people. For the men and women who proved loyal to him, he would always go out of his way to prove his appreciation. He gave scholarships to the grandchildren of some of the help in the company's executive dining room. And he dispensed lots of money and advice to his own employees through the years. James Kerley worked under Lundy in the 1950s when Lundy was assistant controller of financial analysis. When Kerley discovered that his thirty-year-old wife had cancer, Lundy called him into the office. "Jim, I understand unfortunately that a radical mastectomy is going to be required," he told a heartbroken Kerley. "Well, there are surgeons and there are surgeons."

Lundy handed the man a blank check.

"You should put in any numbers you want to make sure she gets the best treatment," Lundy told him.

Then Lundy spoke to McNamara who arranged for the chairman of the radiology department at the University of Michigan to give Kerley's wife the six weeks of cobalt treatments required after surgery. McNamara summoned Kerley into his office not long after his chat with Lundy, and Bob insisted that Kerley take his wife to Ann Arbor for the treatments every afternoon. "It will be a lot easier on her if you go out and do that," McNamara said. "It will be the six most important weeks in your married life. That's your assignment for the next six weeks." It was one of the few times that McNamara, who was incapable of making the smallest gestures of tenderness to his own people, seemed human, and the episode occurred because Ed Lundy arranged it. It was what made the men so loyal to Lundy. He took care of you and your family as if it were his own. "If you ever worked for him he considered you one of his boys," recalls Kerley.

Lundy often would make a point of personally handing out a newcomer's first assignment, making sure that as they progressed in finance they were given more challenging jobs with greater visibility. Says Robert Masson, an ex-Lundy man, the message was: "While we are a big company, I want you to know from day one that you are a name and a face to me."

But if he was crossed, his sword was swift. It was part of the fear as well as the power of being part of the group. The men who failed to understand which side they were on suddenly found their careers truncated and blown up. "You had to be very, very bright and facile, and you had to be very loyal to him," recalls one foot soldier. "You could not be an extrovert. He wasn't and most of the people who moved up were fairly disciplined. It wasn't that they lacked a sense of humor, but there was a conformity that was required, from dress to all the rest. Family and lifestyle were important to him even though he was a bachelor. If you had a difficult marriage or a divorce that was a negative."

And Lundy was more than likely to know. His men would often invite him to their homes for quiet family dinners, where Lundy would get to meet their wives and children, many of whom called him "Uncle Ed." Even in this, there was a precise ritual involved. Lundy would arrive and leave at designated times. He would have exactly one drink of a rich scotch, like a twelve-year-old Ballantine. "We all had one bottle of good scotch, and we put it out when Ed was there," recalls Kerley. During one visit, Lundy noticed that Kerley's five-year-old son was playing with a car model of a Pontiac.

"Jimmy," Lundy asked the boy, "do you have any other automotive toys?"

The little boy went into his room to fetch a miniature model of an International Harvester tractor.

The next morning when Lundy saw Kerley, he thanked him for the invitation to dinner and then surprised him by bringing up the conversation with his son.

"Jim," Lundy lectured Kerley, "if you're going to work for Ford, your kids should at least play with cars with the Ford name on them."

Lundy adopted in his finance group a compulsive order and discipline. There was a wrong way and a right way to do things at Ford, and Lundy often decided which way was right—even down to keeping the point of a pencil sharp. Gerry Meyers, who would later become president of American Motors but spent a year in Ford finance, remembers the time when Lundy came by his desk to lecture him on how to use a pencil. "He continually rolled it in his fingers every few words so that you would only write with a sharp point," Meyers says.

Most of all, Lundy insisted that presentations be done a certain way:

Every backup book for every presentation would be bound in black with three rings. Paper reinforcing doughnuts had to be pasted over the top and bottom holes. A red tab had to be used to separate a major section of a presentation, while a pink tab was used for an important subsection. Only clear tabs could be employed for supporting documents. Each presentation was a carefully scripted show, with the most minute details worked out in advance and often rehearsed before Lundy himself, including the ad libs which also were structured and reviewed with him. Even the operation of the slide projector was critical to Lundy. He refused to trust just anyone with the job. He demanded that only one of his brilliant MBAs should be assigned the task to change the slides and work the arrow on the screen to point to the relevant numbers. Indeed, some thirty years after a key presentation, Lundy would still recall the name of a deputy who ran the projector for him and still make a point of mentioning it in conversation.

No presentation was more important than the Ford financial review— what Arjay Miller once said was the direct descendant of his progress analysis reports to General Arnold during Stat Control days. Each month, Lundy's brightest lights would give a review first to the inside management group composed of the top fifty or sixty men at Ford and then to the company's board of directors. There was a set pattern to each presentation, run and dominated completely by finance. First, there would be an economics overview, followed by reviews of the market, profits and the company's cash plans. Some found it peculiar that Lundy's finance group, rather than Ford's marketing department, made the presentation on market performance, but that, too, was a sign of finance's strength. When his men delivered the latest numbers on profitability, they had to be compared to all of Ford's major competitors and every change in every number had to be explained in detail.

For years, Lundy wrote the reviews and gave them himself. Then he began to delegate parts of the presentation to his men, until finally getting out of it entirely. But he always retained clear responsibility for the content and style of each presentation. A team of men did little else except work on the review and an accompanying backup book which had the heft of a Ph.D. dissertation. When a slide flashed on the screen, two facing pages in the book held the answers to every conceivable question the slide might provoke. The purpose was to never allow Lundy to be caught off guard.

Each review, he also insisted, had to be perceived as fair and unbiased. If a finance man was going to attack a division, he would be required to show the divisional managers the review in advance so they at least had the right of reply. And each review, Lundy demanded, had to be the archetypal business presentation, succinct and to the point. Most finance men who left to join other companies would agree that they had never participated in a financial presentation that was better organized or more thoroughly informed.

Lundy could not abide long, boring meetings or speeches. "He liked conciseness," recalls Fred Secrest, one of his officers. "I would pride myself on my ability to answer questions from the outside board members without spending too much time rushing through the backup book. I usually liked to answer right off the bat. On more than one occasion, they would ask questions and I would go on and on, thinking I was succeeding. Then, I'd see Mr. Lundy on the other side of the table making a motion to shut me up."

Like a stiff-necked schoolmaster, he particularly paid attention to a man's grammar and syntax. Since his men were giving presentations for which he was ultimately responsible, he insisted on correct grammar as he defined it. Sentences could never start with the word "however." The word "employee" was always to be spelled with a single "e" at the end. It was something drilled into him by a couple of strict grammarians in elementary school. The second edition of Webster's dictionary was a constant presence on his desk (he refused to rely on the latest edition because he felt the editors had become too liberal with the language). " 'If you'd say to him, the data is imperfect,' " recalls one Ford manager, "he'd say, 'You mean the data are imperfect.' " One time, when Kerley came to his office to report on the position of the Ford Division, Kerley made the mistake of saying, "The Ford Division feels . . ."

Leaping up from his chair, Lundy abruptly stopped Kerley in mid-sentence. He reached across his desk, grabbing the lapel of Kerley's jacket.

"Jim," he said, "I'm feeling this lapel. The word that goes in there is believes. Not feels!"

Then Lundy would walk the man out of his office, his arm around his shoulder.

His purview knew few boundaries—even down to his insistence that his men dress in a manner that commanded respect. There was a uniform at Ford, and it was conservative. Dark clothing, nothing to make you stand out. And he would always keep a stash of ties in his desk, just in case one of his recruits came in with a tie that was too flashy or wild for his taste. When one of Lundy's young cohorts walked into a presen-

tation wearing a blue blazer and a pair of gray slacks, Lundy sneered at
him: "Starting the weekend a little early, aren't we?"

On another occasion, a finance man had been called off his vacation in
Florida for an important meeting in Dearborn. He left his family and
literally rushed to work from the airport for the session, not having time
to change out of his sports coat. Lundy would have none of it. "Why
don't you go home and change," he said, with a look of disdain. "This is
serious!"

For Lundy's men, there was a code of behavior and no one, at least in
his presence, violated its tenets. One outside executive who did much
business with Ford recalls meeting Lundy and a few of his colleagues for
dinner at the Dearborn Inn. The executive had just flown into Detroit on
a white-knuckle flight in terrible weather. "We sat down for dinner and
the waiter asked if I would like a drink," he recalled. "I said, 'Boy would
I ever.' I had a double scotch and soda, but then no one else drank. Boy,
did I feel it was a boo-boo."

His men were under constant evaluation, even at breakfast in the
main executive dining room. Each morning at precisely 7:30, Lundy
would gather an informal breakfast club of twenty or so men. There was
casual and fun conversation, and reading of the morning newspapers.
But as all the men knew, it was also true that Lundy placed great
reliance on how the men handled themselves in small-talk situations. He
judged their competence on how they spoke and what they said. "If you
were the kind of person who didn't wake up until after your third cup of
coffee," says a finance man, "it was not a good idea to trade your quips
and observations with Ed at the breakfast table."

What his men did outside, however, was of no compelling interest to
him unless it was sufficiently controversial to attract too much attention.
It was one important way in which Lundy's rules differed from those of
several other large corporations. At other white-collar factories, the up-
wardly mobile manager might have to work for the Republican Party or
at least contribute a proportion of his income to it. His wife would be
required to join the junior symphony committee because it could make
or break a man's career. At General Motors, it was important for an
aspiring manager to apply for membership in the Bloomfield Hills
Country Club. But this was not the case at Lundy's Ford. "Lundy
couldn't care less about your politics," recalls Secrest. "Nor was he interested in what country clubs you joined, what charities you or your wife
supported. Your time outside the office was entirely your own."

FOR ALL HIS power at Ford, Lundy always seemed to be content to remain in the background. He declined invitations to give speeches, thinking them a waste of time. Of all the Whiz Kids who were interviewed by either Allan Nevins or Frank Hill for their commissioned biography of the Ford Motor Company, Lundy had the least to say. Hill's interview notes with Lundy ran only three pages, only a third of the length of his notes on Ben Mills and Jim Wright. To numerous reporters, he would boast that he never consented to an interview, which was not really true. But his distrust of the media ran so deep even Lundy believed he had never consented to an interview. In fact, he had once been interviewed by a reporter from the New York *Times*. On another occasion, he agreed to an interview by a reporter from *Forbes* magazine. But when the reporter arrived to meet him, Lundy refused to allow the man to use a tape recorder or to even take notes. The "interview" lasted all of five minutes before Lundy dismissed the startled reporter. His only message: It was Ernie Breech, not the Whiz Kids, who had turned Ford Motor around in the postwar period.

The only time he read something of any value in a newspaper or magazine, he said, was when as a newly drafted private at Fort Dix, N.J., he picked up a copy of the December 28, 1942, edition of *Life* magazine. In the midst of a cold winter, he was sitting in an outdoor latrine, thumbing through the oversized pages when his eyes focused on an article and photo essay. The story told how the resort hotels of Miami Beach had been transformed into a vast Army Air Force training center. The pictures showed the men in officer candidate school on the sandy beaches, in the odd-shaped pools of lavish hotels and in the surf. Yes, Lundy was going to Miami. It was the hook that brought him to Tex Thornton's Stat Control group.

When an article in *Time* magazine once called Lundy "publicity shy," Lundy recalled that Breech rang his office to tell him, "Now that's an appellation I'd love to have." Lundy tells this story with a sparkle in his eyes, for he also blamed the press for not giving Henry enough credit for the success of the company. The press, thought Lundy, was too interested in selling papers to care about the truth. It was more interested in Henry's three wives and in his drinking, than in his accomplishments. Indeed Lundy, in agreeing to an interview for this book, would talk with pride of how he convinced Henry in his later years not to speak to the press as often as he had.

Though he rivaled McNamara in analytic ability, Lundy never possessed Bob's overriding ambition. He surely relished the power he had at Ford, but he also disliked the spotlight and never sought the company's presidency. Indeed, when McNamara was named president in 1960, Bob tried to move Lundy out of his staff job in finance and into the field, perhaps as a divisional general manager, to allow Lundy to gain line experience. "It was a developmental move, not one of being sent to Siberia," recalled a Ford executive. "Bob only wanted to send him out to make him one day qualified to be president. Well that was the last thing Lundy wanted: he wanted to stay where he was. Bob was pushing this and finally Arjay told him that if you persist in this I'm going to quit. And I can tell you Lundy will quit. It was an ultimatum and Bob certainly didn't want that so he gave up on it."

Others surmised that Lundy himself didn't think he could make it in the field. It was one thing to stay at headquarters and second-guess everyone. It was another to be on the frontlines where you had to make tough decisions that made you more vulnerable. Like the other Whiz Kids, Lundy had never been on the battlefield, not during World War Two and not during his entire career at Ford. As the manufacturing people would say, he never got his hands dirty.

Lee Iacocca, the great product man of Ford whom Henry would later fire, would chide Lundy about this. "Ed," he told him, "the great thing about being in finance is, you don't have to worry about ten-day reports, you don't have to worry about sales, you don't have to worry about design, you don't have to worry about manufacturing breakdowns—just what is it you guys do for a living?"

Lundy knew the numbers and found great comfort in them, but he knew little else. "Numbers add up or they don't," as one of his friends put it. "But there is a kind of certainty to numbers. People like Lundy who are obsessive love things that add up. They find protection in it. It was freedom from ambiguity. And the consequences of being wrong were too great when life was ambiguous." In the plants, where the blue collars stamped out the sheet metal and tightened the lug nuts, there was considerable ambiguity.

Lundy's rise to great power at Ford also corresponded with his growing relationship to Henry Ford II. In the early days, Ford never really liked Ed. Though Lundy boasted as much brainpower as any of the men, with the exception of McNamara, he was something of a laggard in the early days. Indeed, Ford once asked one of his top executives if Lundy was a homosexual. "I told him no. I never observed anything like that about him. He never had girl friends as far as I know. Yet, women would enjoy his company. He would often escort or take to dinner somebody's wife if the man was out of town."

Lundy himself believes the turning point in his relationship with Ford came in 1960 when as treasurer of Ford, he was called upon to be the keynote speaker at a conference in Paris. "It was a great success," remembers Lundy. "HFII came up to me and said, 'You know that was the best presentation I've ever seen.' After that, Henry and I became good friends."

More than that, Lundy would become one of Henry's favorites. Within a year, Ford named him a vice president of the company and controller, and during the 1960s and 1970s he would gain new and rather heady power. In 1962, he became vice president of finance and three years later was given a seat on the company's board of directors. By 1967, Lundy would become an executive vice president. The very same characteristics that separated him from McNamara and even Miller were what made him so valuable to Henry. Lundy was the complete loyalist. He was never a threat to Ford for he was never a contender for the top job. Henry could trust his judgment because Lundy was unbiased in his opinions—at least so far as ambitions were concerned.

It was said that Lundy protected Henry's money as if it were his own. It was also said that Henry would not make a major decision without asking for Ed's advice and counsel. They became good personal friends, and Lundy often was asked to do things for Ford that went well beyond their professional relationship. One Tuesday, Lundy called one of his main contacts on Wall Street and asked that the man fly out to Dearborn for an important meeting on Thursday. The Wall Street man could think of no reason why Lundy would demand a meeting so quickly and feared that he was going to lose the Ford account.

Over lunch, they casually talked about the usual things: the economy, Wall Street, Ford's prospects, Lundy's affection for growing roses. They chatted about everything except something that would have explained the urgency for an immediate meeting. Finally, the two men ordered their coffee and the Wall Street man waited even more nervously for Lundy to fire him.

"I suppose you're wondering why I asked you here," Lundy finally said. "Well, Henry asked me to have you out because Tony Forstmann wants to marry Henry's daughter Charlotte. You're here to give me ten good reasons why Tony shouldn't marry her."

The man, who knew Forstmann, was taken aback but relieved because he was not losing the precious Ford account.

Over the years, Lundy and Ford would differ on only one issue: personnel. When a manager left Ford for a better position elsewhere,

Henry believed the person was disloyal and unappreciative. Lundy saw it differently. If you hired good people, he thought, they would be desired by others. In fact, he wanted to hire people whom competitors would find valuable and attractive. Otherwise, he reasoned, Ford was hiring the wrong kind of talent. "He felt that if someone left Ford and couldn't find a job elsewhere, it was an indication that we weren't doing a bang-up job ourselves," says Alan Gilmour, one of his prized hires.

"We run a high power business school, and from the jobs our alumni get, I believe a first-rate one," Lundy said. At times, he appeared as proud of the accomplishments of his "graduates" as he was of anything else. He had made finance an academy within a company that had gained a reputation for supplying the best financial executives in business. With the possible exception of General Electric, no other American corporation—not General Motors or IBM or Procter & Gamble or Coca-Cola—could boast a more stellar reputation for attracting and training men of finance than Ford. Decades later, in 1991, *CFO* magazine would ask more than two hundred observers of the financial scene which companies did the best job of preparing finance managers for the role of chief financial officer. The business publication found that "practically everyone" named Ford Motor and General Electric. It was part of the Lundy legacy.

Some of his dropouts became professors and bankers, but most of them moved into key jobs in other industries. By the early 1980s, Lundy estimated that more than 250 Ford alums held the positions of vice president or above at other American companies. As many as sixteen executives were lured directly from Ford into the presidencies of other corporations between the early 1950s and the early 1980s. At one point, the chairmen of Firestone, Rockwell International, Prudential Insurance Company of America, Zenith, Reynolds Metals, Navistar International and Bell & Howell all listed finance jobs at Ford on their resumés.

They spread Lundy's influence well beyond the confines of Ford, casting his shadow over the country's corporate landscape. His men would help to change the corporate cultures of Xerox, Zenith and Fire-stone—companies that would one day be devastated by Japanese competition in part because, like Ford, they became dominated by numbers men who had little sense of the copiers, televisions and tires those companies churned out. For wherever Lundy's men went, they propagated a devotion to numbers and analysis, spreading the revolution the Whiz Kids brought to Ford.

IN THE MID-TO-LATE 1960s so many of Lundy's finance men left Ford for Xerox that Lundy reportedly forbade his staff from using Xerox copying machines. Like Litton, Xerox was one of the "wonder shares" of the 1960s. After spending the first seventeen years of his career at Ford, Archie McCardell left Lundy and the company in 1966 to become Xerox's group vice president of finance and control. Melvin Howard joined as chief financial officer; Gerry Bennett as another key financial executive; Jim O'Neill, an intimidating and acerbic McNamara clone, was placed in charge of sales. Within five years, the cigar-smoking McCardell was named chief operating officer.

Xerox veterans derisively dubbed the new managers "the Ford Men," and McCardell and his band quickly went about remaking the culture of what was a hugely successful corporation, growing at breakneck speed. "The old-timers didn't feel the auto people shared the same values," recalls David Kearns, who would one day become chief executive of Xerox. "The eager Ford Men had manifest ambition, but they were not copier men. Their knowledge was about systems that they felt could govern any company—whether it made cars, bottle caps, or copying machines. Their language was the peculiar mumbo-jumbo of financial wizards."

The Ford Men did to Xerox what the Whiz Kids did to Ford: they imposed order on the company, introduced rigid financial controls, stripped power from operations and marketing and transformed Xerox into a company driven by cost savings. "At one point," recalls Kearns, "Jim O'Neill suggested that we begin using plastic hinges on the copiers to save some money. He looked at things the way auto people did—a penny here, a penny there. But it made no sense. The plastic literally fell off the machines and had to be changed back to the old material.

"Another time, we were going to build a second factory for one of our new copiers. All the financial analyses showed that we needed the plant. But everyone in marketing knew we didn't. I told O'Neill that we would never fully use the factory we already had, but he brushed that off and snorted, 'No, the numbers show it. Where's your proof statement?'

" 'Jim, we don't need any proof statement,' I replied. 'We can't sell that many machines.'

"In the end, the factory wasn't built and the one Xerox had was pretty empty for years. We were able to hold the annual meeting in it one year because it was never being used."

More than anything else, however, a computer model developed by the Ford Men came to symbolize the shift in management thinking at Xerox. Christened Shazam, it was used to calculate the impact of price changes or new product introductions. If Xerox's marketing department wanted to change the price of a product, it had to supply finance with as many as 3,500 facts and assumptions so the computer could forecast, to the third decimal point, the impact on sales and profits of a given price hike. "Eventually the finance department began to distrust the assumptions offered up by marketing," recalls Kearns. "It would run the model inputting the numbers from marketing and then run it again using its own assumptions—all to debate how many angels could dance on the head of a pin. To many it seemed like highly manipulated nonsense, and to some extent it was. Who, after all, knew these unknowable underlying assumptions on which everything was based."

Just as at Ford, the managers in marketing who best knew the customers lost the battles to the finance men with all the numbers. Now you had to arrive for meetings with computer printouts tucked under your arm. Xerox marketeers became more embattled with the finance department than with the marketplace. "The place changed from being market-focused and natural to highly complex and financial," says Kearns.

Like Ford itself, Xerox lost touch with its customers and fell into a dramatic decline. The company, which owned more than 80 percent of the market for copiers in the early 1970s, saw its market share tumble to less than 50 percent and its very existence placed into question—the handiwork of the men of finance from Ford.

THE WHIZ KIDS, whether Thornton at Litton or McNamara at Defense or Miller and Lundy at Ford, had unwittingly become ministers of a management theology that would dominate business thinking. The full ramifications of the transformation were not apparent in the early 1960s. America was still riding that huge wave of postwar prosperity, and there were only the beginning signs that something was wrong.

One of them occurred on a weekday morning in May of 1962. Lundy sat in the executive dining room at the Glass Palace, ready to breakfast with the other early-risers. If he had picked up a copy of the Detroit Free Press, he would have read like the rest of the nation of Bob McNamara's first trip to a place called Vietnam.

After touring the war-torn jungles for two days, Bob had held a press conference in the living room of the American ambassador's residence in Saigon. McNamara was unshaven that morning, in a creased khaki shirt and trousers and dusty hiking boots. "I've seen nothing but progress and hopeful indications of further progress in the future," he told the skeptical reporters, incredulous at his upbeat assessment. A journalist for the New York *Times,* unable to believe McNamara's optimism, rushed outside the house when the press conference broke up and buttonholed the Secretary of Defense just as he was ducking into his car.

"I'm not going to quote you," he said. "The question is off-the-record because I want to know the truth. How could you be so optimistic about a war we've barely begun to fight?"

Without a trace of doubt and without a moment's hesitation, Bob turned to the man and issued a variation of what he had told many of his adversaries at Ford a few years earlier. "Every quantitative measurement we have shows that we're winning this war."

Before the reporter could challenge his remark, McNamara quickly jumped into the sedan's backseat. The door slammed shut and the car rushed off to the airport where a four-engine jet would transport him back to Washington. Bob was falling victim to the same kind of hubris, the same self-confidence, the same supreme optimism that he had quietly abhorred in Jack Reith.

Bob McNamara, tears in his eyes, shakes hands with President Johnson after the President presented him with the Medal of Freedom in February, 1968, when Bob lost his job as Secretary of Defense.

Bob McNamara holds a Vietnamese flag given to him by a boy during one of his many visits to South Vietnam.

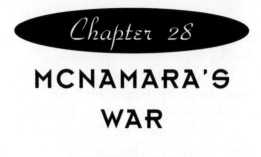

MCNAMARA'S WAR

■

"McNamara Get Human"

—A Placard
at an Anti-War March

The trees already were bare in Harvard Square, the ground littered with leaves, their lively reds and yellows faded into dull browns. The frisbees and footballs had disappeared from campus, casualties of the cold. This Monday, November 7, 1966, would have been like any other day of classes at Harvard College, except that Robert S. McNamara had come to visit the campus.

He had returned to Harvard as one of the first honorary associates of the new Kennedy Institute of Politics, and his day was largely filled with seminars and speeches. Earlier, in the morning, the Secretary of Defense had strolled through the square and into a Brattle Street bookshop to purchase a book of poetry—just as he had thirty years earlier as an instructor at the business school. He drew a polite crowd there, but nothing like the one that was now gathered outside Quincy House, a tall Georgian brick undergraduate dormitory where he had addressed a group of fifty handpicked students over lunch. On this cool November day, his presence generated some heat.

Throughout his session at Quincy, he could hear the protests rising from the street. Strains of Bobby Darin's "Mack the Knife" drifted through one of the windows. Draped from the windows of the dormitory buildings were white sheets with black or red lettering. Some expressed support; others opposition to American involvement in the Vietnam War.

"VIETNAM: EDSEL OF FOREIGN POLICY"

"KILL FOR PEACE"

"KILL THE CONG, BACK MAC"

"NAPALM SDS!"

McNamara had reason to think his trip to Harvard could be marred by an incident. More than a week earlier, he had received a telegram from the Students for a Democratic Society inviting him to debate Robert Scheer, editor of the pacifist magazine *Ramparts*. The group believed that McNamara should not be allowed to use Harvard as a forum to promote the government line on Vietnam without facing a challenge from the opposing camp. After word had arrived from Washington that McNamara declined the invitation, SDS leaders called for a "disruptive demonstration" during his visit. The plan was to capture McNamara outside Quincy using a throng of students and to confront him with Scheer, forcing an informal debate. When McNamara arrived in Boston in a cold drizzle on Sunday evening, he had his first confrontation when a group presented him with a petition signed by 1,600 students calling for the debate he declined to participate in.

The next day a group of young people outside Quincy House numbered three hundred. They were young, fresh faces with closely-cropped hair. They could not have looked much different from McNamara when he was a student. These were still the very early days of the anti-war movement, the nonviolent days, before the protests became more angry and vehement. McNamara was not even given Secret Service protection yet, and the Harvard crowd contained nearly as many supporters of the war as it did protesters. The atmosphere of the demonstration was, as one student recalled, congenial, "rather like a Yale-game rally."

Still, the organizers of McNamara's visit did not want a confrontation. The police set up two diversionary departures of other persons while McNamara was led through the Quincy basement to Mill Street and was spirited into a university police car that was to take him to the Harvard Business School. But the car traveled little more than a few feet before twenty-five demonstrators flung themselves under the front and rear wheels, forcing it to come to a halt.

More demonstrators converged on the car in a stampede. Some beat their clenched fists on the windows, while Bob sat inside with a single policeman, the windows up and the doors locked. They began to rock the car, trying to get McNamara to come out. Fist fights erupted around him as the Hawks tried to drag the Doves away. At first, Bob tried not to look outside the car window but then he couldn't help it. The shouts, the obscenities, the bodies over and under the car forced him to peer out and absorb the horrible scene. They were taunting him, these sons and daughters of the upper and middle class, clawing at the car, urging him to come out and debate.

Finally, after a long five minutes that must have seemed like a life-time, Bob abruptly pushed open the door and jumped outside amid the uproar, like a jack-in-the-box jolted out of hiding. One of the students, Harold Benenson, coaxed him to jump atop the hood of a convertible parked at the curb in front of McKinlock Hall. McNamara, his face visibly tightening and grim, took a microphone hooked to a portable PA system.

"I spent four of the happiest years at the Berkeley campus doing some of the same things you're doing here," he said, fighting back the crowd. "But there was one important difference. I was tougher and more cour-teous."

Catcalls erupted from the mass of bodies pressing forward.

"Murderer!"

"Fascist!"

"And I was tougher then," shouted McNamara above the protests, "and I'm tougher now!"

The remark drew only more harassment, even outright laughter. It was as if the revolt flipped a switch in McNamara's brain, exposing a bizarre macho streak in his otherwise cool, rationalist manner. He seemed to feel some queer need to defend his honor, to return the taunts. The IBM on legs, as one observer dubbed him, overheated—and over-stated. For when he was at Berkeley he was hardly engaged in anything that resembled a demonstration. Some U Cal classmates volunteered in soup kitchens to help demonstrators during the great general strike in San Francisco. But McNamara was not among them.

Now blood streamed into his face, turning it vibrant red. Many of the students had seen his taut features, with rimless glasses and swept-back hair, on television at Pentagon press conferences. They had heard his gravelly, assertive voice on TV as he would stiffly stand behind a Department of Defense podium, gesturing with a long wooden pointer at maps of Hanoi and Haiphong. Some students thought his face seemed "meatier and beefier" than they had noticed on the television news shows. McNamara was beside himself, shocked at both the intensity and anger of the demonstration.

"Listen," he said, "you organize a meeting that will be non-violent, and I'll come. I have a meeting across the river now and can't stay."

The raucous crowd, however, closed tighter and tighter. The area surrounding the car was so choked with demonstrators that it was impossible for McNamara to leave. The police were virtually helpless. The patrol car McNamara had left was being jostled by the screaming crowd. Unable to reach the Secretary of Defense, one policeman yelled, "We have to stay near you." McNamara was trapped, swallowed by a mob.

"Okay, fellas," he said in an effort to appease the group, "I'll answer one or two of your questions. But remember two things: First, we're in a mob and someone might get hurt and I don't want anyone to get hurt. I also have an appointment on the other side of the river in five minutes."

The chairman of the university's Students for a Democratic Society, Michael S. Ansara, grabbed the mike and called for a couple of questions from the crowd.

"Why did you not tell the American people that the war started in 1957 and 1958 as an internal revolution?" shouted a voice.

"The war didn't begin in 1957, it started in '54–'55 when a million North Vietnamese flooded South Vietnam," said McNamara, who was quickly drowned out by the mob.

"Yeah, and they were all Catholics!" screamed a demonstrator.

"A report from the International Control Commission states that it was aggression," McNamara countered, oddly trying to engage in serious debate. "I didn't write it. All you have to do is read it. You haven't read it and if you have, you obviously didn't understand it!"

"We've seen it," another voice cried.

McNamara, flushed with anger, shouted back.

"Why don't you guys get up here since you already seem to have all the answers."

Others shot still more questions at him until one reached his ears.

"How many innocent women and children have been killed?" demanded one student.

Bob repeated the query, which he called a "fair question," rephrasing it as, "How many South Vietnamese casualties have there been? We don't know."

"Why don't you know?" shouted another voice from the crowd. "Don't you care?"

By now, a wedge of ten policemen had pushed their way through and formed a protective cordon around McNamara. They cleared a path for him as he rushed off to Leverett House dining hall. Two policemen blocked the door of the house as students pushed from behind, trying to follow McNamara inside. The Secretary of Defense, however, was led through the university's network of underground steam tunnels to a Harvard police car and his escape from the chaos.

It was a harrowing experience for McNamara, especially because he had long fancied himself a progressive man and especially because this was Harvard. He had joined a union at the age of sixteen when he sailed on a freighter. It probably made him the first former union member to be on the Harvard Business School faculty. In 1940, the year of the Wilkie-Roosevelt race, the school's *Harbus News* launched a poll to determine how the faculty would vote in the presidential election. The only surprise in the outcome was that two of some one hundred professors actually had the gall to favor Roosevelt.

Eugene Zuckert, then on the Harvard faculty with McNamara, remembered the poll because it sparked an odd guessing game at the faculty club. "The senior profs were sitting in the big chairs as usual having their demitasse," he said. " 'Well, did you notice the poll in the *Harbus News,* ninety-eight to two?' one of them said.

" 'Who do you suppose the two were?'

"I said, 'Well, there's Edgar Haas.' 'He's a damn fool!,' one of them barked. 'He would certainly vote for Roosevelt. But who was the second one?'

Suddenly they looked at Zuckert because he had just come out of a New Deal agency, the Securities & Exchange Commission.

" 'Zuckert, it must have been you,' one accused.

"I said it wasn't me. I knew it wasn't a secret ballot, but I found out later it was Bob McNamara. We always had the feeling he was a little different."

McNamara had thought that, too. He had been a favorite of the students then, a well-liked teacher who could enter a Harvard classroom and command everyone's attention by his brilliance. He had kept, the story goes, a stack of jokes suitable for every teaching situation. In typical McNamara fashion, he would jot on three-by-five file cards the date the joke was tried along with the reaction it provoked, things like "Goats— Ghosts. Laughter." The students loved him then; Harvard loved him.

He had been picketed earlier in the year by students at Amherst and at New York University, but what did it matter? On both occasions, McNamara had gone to commencement exercises in June to pick up honorary degrees. About twenty students booed him at Amherst. Five days later at NYU, 130 students and faculty staged a protest walk-out.

Unlike Amherst or NYU, Harvard meant something to him. When he came to the campus, it was as if he had returned home. It was where he and Margy had begun their life in a cheap, sparse place in Cambridge. It was where he would have come after the war to make his life if Margy had been well. It was where he wanted to go had Tex Thornton not convinced him otherwise. Sadly, McNamara discovered that he was no longer welcome there.

In the protest's aftermath, Dr. John U. Monro, Dean of Harvard College, sent a written apology to McNamara. The Secretary of Defense told him no apology was necessary. "Occasionally all of us allow our zeal to exceed our judgment," wrote McNamara, "but such behavioral aberrations should not be a basis for curbing dissent—dissent is both the prerogative and the preservative of free men everywhere." But privately, McNamara's friends recall, the man was deeply hurt and embarrassed by the incident. Years later, during a public reemergence in the mid-1980s, McNamara would travel to eight or nine college campuses. "There wasn't one demonstration against me," he told a reporter.

On Saturday, November 12, just five days after Bob's visit to Harvard, some of his old buddies from the car business paraded into Boston for the annual automobile show. Some two thousand dealers and their wives opened the event with an evening reception at which nearly one thousand bottles of champagne and several hundred pounds of canapés were consumed. *Playboy* magazine's "Miss November," outfitted in a skin-tight black sweater with a white Playboy bunny emblazoned across her chest, was the official hostess. No demonstrators showed up.

WHAT THE STUDENTS at Harvard did not know was that their demonstration only underlined the many doubts, fears and frustrations that McNamara privately held about the war. As he would later testify in a libel case against CBS brought by General William C. Westmoreland, he had reached the view "no later than mid-1966" or "as early as the latter part of 1965" that the war could not militarily be won. Publicly, McNamara did not acknowledge such doubts. Privately in President Johnson's company, he still remained a hawk. Less than a month before the Harvard confrontation, he had made a generally optimistic appraisal of the war after yet another visit to South Vietnam.

The same day, October 14, 1966, he had also written a sobering memo for President Johnson: "The prognosis is bad that the war can be brought to a satisfactory conclusion within the next two years. The large-unit operations probably will not do it; negotiations probably will not do it. While we should continue to pursue both of these routes in trying for a solution in the short run, we should recognize that success from them is a mere possibility, not a probability.

"The solution lies in girding, openly, for a longer war and in taking actions immediately which will in 12 to 18 months give clear evidence that the continuing costs and risks to the American people are acceptably limited, that the formula for success has been found, and that the end of the war is merely a matter of time."

Vietnam had become an agonizing embarrassment to him. In the beginning in 1961, the problems of the Southeast Asian country were obviously a low priority. McNamara had, in fact, assigned Vietnam to one of his deputies, Roswell Gilpatric. But as the crisis in Vietnam deepened throughout that first year, the Joint Chiefs of Staff began urging the Defense Secretary to commit combat troops there. By October, President Kennedy sent several military advisers there on a fact-finding mission.

The trip resulted in a report from Maxwell Taylor, Kennedy's special military representative, that would change the course of American involvement. Taylor recommended on November 3, 1961, that up to eight thousand troops be sent. "I do not believe that our program to save South Vietnam will succeed without it," he wrote. Secretary of State Dean Rusk warned against troop commitment without reforms by the South Vietnamese government. Five days later, McNamara sent Kennedy his first key memo on Vietnam. The document reflected his belief in the "domino theory" of the Eisenhower era—that the fall of South Vietnam would lead to serious deterioration throughout Southeast Asia and that the U.S. was unlikely to prevent the fall without sending U.S. combat forces. He clearly envisioned a far larger commitment than the initial eight thousand troops. "I believe we can safely assume the maximum U.S. forces required on the ground in Southeast Asia will not exceed six divisions, or about 205,000 men," wrote McNamara.

President Kennedy, fearing a long-term commitment of U.S. soldiers in what he called the Vietnamese's war, rejected the proposal. Three days later, McNamara, with Secretary of State Dean Rusk, sent in another memo which reflected Kennedy's wishes. It committed the U.S. to add fifteen thousand support personnel and advisers to Vietnam to the small advisory commitment of personnel already made in the Eisenhower years. But the President stopped short of sending American soldiers to South Vietnam to wage war.

From then on, however, Bob quickly took the lead on Vietnam, volunteering to Kennedy that he would make it his special project. Suddenly, the key formulation of the country's policy on Vietnam was pretty much left to him, not Secretary of State Dean Rusk.

As was his nature, McNamara took charge, becoming the dominant member of the team whenever Vietnam came up. "If he was in something, he either was in charge of it or he'd turn it over to somebody else," says Gilpatric. "He didn't take kindly to being just a sort of junior member of any team. And the first time McNamara went out [to Vietnam], he spent a lot of time with Diem himself and came back with very positive impressions."

Vietnam became a subject that McNamara was totally confident about. "He felt very sure of himself," recalls Gilpatric. "He felt it was a very heavy responsibility because he knew the President's reluctance about the whole operation. When you add him and Taylor together, that was a pretty strong combination against which nobody in State really had the stomach or the capacity to stand up."

It wasn't until 1965, after Kennedy's assassination, that it became clear that the Vietcong were annihilating South Vietnamese troops. In January, McNamara told Johnson the war was going poorly and argued for a much stronger use of American power to force a change of Communist policy or to gain a negotiated withdrawal. After the Vietcong killed seven Americans in a February 7, 1965, attack at a U.S. installation in Pleiku, the President ordered retaliatory air attacks against North Vietnam and soon after that regular bombing raids. Two battalions of U.S. Marines splashed ashore the beaches south of Da Nang in early March ostensibly to defend the air base there.

As the conflict heated up, General Westmoreland asked for two hundred thousand additional U.S. soldiers. Paul Nitze, then Secretary of the Navy, visited Vietnam and returned to Washington highly doubtful about the U.S. situation. Nitze thought it would take far more than two hundred thousand men to accomplish the U.S. mission in Vietnam. He told McNamara he was skeptical that the country was worth the cost to the U.S. in men and resources.

"He looked at me with surprise and asked me whether I was recommending that we withdraw from Vietnam," recalled Nitze of the conversation. "I responded that I certainly didn't believe that we should send in two hundred thousand reinforcements, so I was indeed recommending that we withdraw.

"He bore down on me with his piercing black eyes, and asked: 'If we withdraw from Vietnam, do you believe the Communists will test us in another location?'

" 'Yes,' I replied.

" 'Can you predict where?'

" 'No, I can't,' I responded reluctantly.

" 'Well,' he said, 'under those circumstances, I take it you can't be at all certain that the difficulties of stopping them in the next area they may choose won't be greater than the difficulties of stopping them in South Vietnam.'

" 'No, I can't,' I said gloomily.

"With that his eyes glazed over as he lost interest. 'You offer no alternative,' he said, and I could tell that as far as he was concerned the subject was closed."

With Westmoreland's request still on the table, McNamara chose to go to Vietnam for five days in mid-July of 1965 to make another personal assessment. His return on July 21, a Wednesday, would mark the beginning of a long, tortuous debate in the White House, arguably the most important dialogue in all the discussions over Vietnam. In a memo he composed on the way home from Saigon, McNamara endorsed Westmoreland's request. He wrote: "United States public opinion will support the course of action because it is a sensible and courageous military-political program designed and likely to bring about a success in Vietnam."

In the Cabinet Room that afternoon, McNamara was urging the President to move ahead. Gloomy over the war's progress, he recommended that Johnson deploy an extra 100,000 troops by October 1 and prepare for another 100,000 in 1966. He advised the President to seek congressional approval to call up 235,000 reserves, to increase the regular armed forces by 375,000 and to increase air raids over North Vietnam to 4,000 a month from 2,500.

McNamara's position did not go unchallenged. George Ball, who had waged a lonely, protracted fight against U.S. involvement in Vietnam as Under-Secretary of State in both the Johnson and Kennedy Administrations, forcefully argued against the commitment. "We can't win," he told the group. "The most we can hope for is a messy conclusion."

He had taken on McNamara before, sending him nine months earlier a long memo that challenged every major assumption of Bob's Vietnam policies. McNamara was shocked that anyone would so abruptly challenge his position and implied that Ball was imprudent in putting such doubts on paper. It went no further until Ball put it in the President's own hands in early February. Gaining an audience of the President and McNamara, Ball outlined his position again. But McNamara, he recalled, responded with "a pyrotechnic display of facts and statistics to prove that I had overstated the difficulties we were now encountering, suggesting, at least by nuance, that I was not only prejudiced but ill-informed." Bob prevailed. The session ended without the reexamination Ball had hoped his memo would provoke.

Now in the Cabinet Room, one by one, Johnson's key advisers disputed Ball's pessimistic appraisal of the war: McGeorge Bundy, Dean Rusk, Henry Cabot Lodge and then Bob McNamara. "Our national honor is at stake," insisted McNamara. "Our withdrawal would start further probing by the Communists. We would lose all of Southeast Asia. I feel that the risks of following my program have been vastly overstated by George Ball."

The next day, the debate resumed with the Joint Chiefs of Staff who favored Westmoreland's request. Johnson, clearly tormented by the choices, turned to his Secretary of Defense at one point.

"Westmoreland's request means that we are in a new war," he said. "This is going off the diving board."

McNamara quickly responded with what Clark Clifford, in the meeting as an informal adviser to Johnson, thought was the most extreme version of the domino theory he had ever heard.

"Laos, Cambodia, Thailand, Burma, Malaysia are all at immediate risk," McNamara stated. "For two or three years, Communist domination would stop there, but the ripple effect would be great—in Japan, and India. We would have to give up some of our bases. Ayub Khan [of Pakistan] would move closer to China. Greece and Turkey would move to neutralist positions. Communist agitation would increase in Africa."

Clifford, a long-time Washington adviser to presidents, was incredulous at McNamara's aggressive stand. He had deep doubts about the war at the time, and was waiting for the proper time to mount his own offensive against McNamara. It would come on the weekend when he and his wife were invited to meet with the President at Camp David. On Saturday afternoon of July 25, the Cliffords shared a helicopter with Bob and Margy McNamara and their son Craig for the five-minute flight to the presidential retreat.

Vietnam would not come up until late Sunday when Clifford joined

Johnson and McNamara in the living room at Aspen Lodge, one of the many buildings at Camp David. The men sat around a rectangular dining-room table as two Filipino stewards served a round of drinks. Slowly, diplomatically, Clifford began to make his case against Vietnam.

"I do not believe we can win," he said. "If we send in one hundred thousand more men, the North Vietnamese will match us. If we won, we would face a long occupation with constant trouble. And if we don't win after a big buildup, it will be a huge catastrophe. We could lose more than fifty thousand men in Vietnam. It will ruin us . . . I can't see anything but catastrophe for my country."

Johnson turned to McNamara once again. McNamara forcefully retorted that he did not agree with Clifford nor his assessment of the chances for success in Vietnam. Without more American troops, he argued, South Vietnam would fall, and this would hurt the U.S. throughout the world. The extra troops, maintained Bob, were essential if the U.S. wanted to prevent a rapid defeat.

The arguments apparently were all too familiar to Johnson who put an end to further discussion without disclosing his own position. After the weekend, the meetings continued at the White House but the debate changed from Vietnam policy to the details of the exact numbers of soldiers to be sent and the public aspects of the announcement. President Johnson had ostensibly made up his mind. The week of tormenting and serious debate ended on July 28 when Johnson disclosed the buildup at a press conference. Though he had secretly approved the increase of one hundred thousand troops by the end of the year with the possibility of another one hundred thousand in 1966, Johnson only referred to an increase of fifty thousand men. He insisted the additional troops did "not imply any change in policy whatsoever."

IN FACT, THE decision would become the turning point in U.S. involvement. Vietnam would now become an American war, and the supremely confident McNamara would lead it. On October 3, 1964, when the U.S. had less than twenty thousand military advisers in South Vietnam, he had publicly predicted that the major part of the nation's military task in Vietnam could be completed by the end of 1965. The massive escalation he advocated in 1965, however, would eventually bring U.S. fighting forces to nearly four hundred thousand troops. Still, he forecast that greater numbers of men would be sent, ruefully confessing that "I have not proven the most reliable forecaster in the past."

As Secretary of Defense, McNamara had presided over and endorsed a huge military commitment to a distant land. McNamara had become the leading figure on Vietnam in Washington, the referee between the military and the President. His frequent trips to Vietnam received widespread attention on television. Always, the military brass would lead him along a controlled itinerary, putting well-rehearsed young officers with upbeat assessments in front of him for briefings. On those trips, McNamara saw what they wanted him to see, and presumably what he wanted to see because he never made any great effort to break the pattern of the trips and seek out the most informed people in Vietnam.

Every month, the war's progress would be measured by statistics: body counts, kill rates, weapons captured, miles of waterways and roads opened, villages pacified, percentage of population under government control, logistical installations completed, proficiency ratings of ARVN units. When McNamara was asked to appraise the success of a given military operation in Vietnam, recalled George Ball, he would answer with incredible precision, not mere orders of magnitude: one operation would have a 65 percent chance, another a 30 percent chance. "Once I tried to tease him, suggesting that perhaps the chances were 64 percent and 29 percent," said Ball, "but the joke was not well taken."

His desire to bring a measuring stick to the war was well known and openly attacked. "McNamara Get Human" read a placard in one of the early anti-war marches. "Statistics," McNamara would later explain, "are nothing other than the means of conveying information and recognizing that information is frequently imprecise; it is better to have as much coverage as one can get."

McNamara and his assistants, says General Westmoreland, "constantly prodded for more and more statistics." Dean Rusk, then Secretary of State, was often incredulous at the faith that McNamara placed in numbers. "One area where McNamara and I never saw eye to eye was in his heavy reliance on statistical methodology," recalled Rusk in his memoirs. "Sometimes he tried to reduce to numbers certain factors and values that I believed could not be quantified."

One of McNamara's men would return to the Harvard Business School and in his classes he would explain the concept of "funds flow" by drawing upon a similar Defense Department tool. To help determine what was happening in Vietnam, someone at the Pentagon had used a scheme called a "people flow." The scheme had a column, "Sources of People," listing where the soldiers had come from, and a column, "Applications of People," listing where they had gone. When the "Applications" exceeded the "Sources," the department had to ask for more soldiers to make up the difference. The whole idea horrified some of his students. "There was this feeling of bewilderment that the lives of so many men should add up to no more than two simple columns," recalls Peter Cohen, who sat through the classes at Harvard in the late 1960s.

LBJ himself would take to carrying around in his coat pocket statistics showing that the U.S. was winning the war: figures on tonnage, bombage, defections and the body count—obviously the most controversial of all the numbers to flow out of the war. In Vietnam, the Pentagon could not measure the war's progress by battles won and territory gained. So body counts became a queer benchmark, a statistic to measure a conflict characterized as a "war of attrition." Every night, the figure would become, like McNamara himself, an enduring television image of the era: Walter Cronkite and the body count.

The tallies would originate in the field at the squad or platoon level and work their way up the bureaucracy, often increasing in number at each step until they hit McNamara's desk in Washington. There he pored over the tabulations for hours, trying to use the statistics to quantify the war. The data, however, was what Henry Mintzberg, a management professor, would call "thin" information, numbers which were aggregated, analytical and detached. They lacked the far more valuable properties of "thick" information which is rich in detail and color and is far beyond what can be quantified. That kind of detail had to be dug out, on site, by people intimately involved with a problem. "In Vietnam," wrote Mintzberg, "it was the look on the peasant's face; in business, the will of a customer, the mood of the factory, the intricacies of a technological change."

McNamara tried to make body counts as reliable as possible. His regulations stipulated that only "males of fighting age and others, male or female, known to have carried arms" be included in the count. Every enemy corpse, however, did not have to be viewed by a foot patrol at close range to get recorded nor was every corpse marked to prevent recounting. The rules allowed "body counts made from the air" if they met his criteria "beyond reasonable doubt."

Ultimately, where the tallies originated didn't matter much anyway. Battalions routinely inflated the figures coming from the companies, and brigades hiked the numbers from the battalions. Then the figures would be upped again, to account for estimates of deaths caused by artillery and air support. Errors were common through double-counting, counting civilians, counting graves or by ignoring McNamara's precise regulations altogether because of the pressure in the field to exaggerate enemy losses.

After all, padded claims kept everyone happy. There were no penalties for overstating enemy losses, but understating could lead to sharp questions.

If you believed the official figures, they showed a "kill ratio" of one American or Vietnamese soldier for every 2.6 Viet Cong or North Vietnamese killed. General Westmoreland's intelligence chief reported in mid-1967 that his search of seventy captured enemy documents confirmed the 1966 body count to within 1.8 percent. A review of the same documents by McNamara's Systems Analysis office suggested that the enemy body count was overstated by at least 30 percent.

Even if the accuracy of the numbers were assured, it still would have made little difference. In 1966, the enemy's losses had been estimated at fifty-five thousand to seventy-five thousand men, losses the military believed the enemy could not possibly sustain. The following year, the estimated enemy losses doubled with no apparent decline in enemy aggression. By late 1968, it had become clear that the North Vietnamese could sustain annual losses as high as two hundred thousand men for years because the enemy could control losses by choosing to fight only at times and places favorable to him. The U.S. could never win a war of attrition.

Slowly, McNamara would become increasingly disenchanted with the military reporting—just as he had with many of the numbers that flowed in from the field at Ford. He began to realize that the mountain of statistics had marginal relevance to a jungle guerrilla war against a fanatic enemy. "You couldn't reconcile the number of the enemy, the level of infiltration, the body count and the resultant figures," he later conceded. "It just didn't add up. I never did get the answer because there weren't any answers."

Outside a small inner circle of associates, many of McNamara's own whiz kids at the Pentagon had no idea what he really thought about the war. They would often hear a story about one of them who felt ill at ease over McNamara's Vietnam policy and decided to let him know. " 'Mr. Secretary, I'd just like to give you a personal feel for this,' " he told McNamara. After the man spoke about his qualms over the war, McNamara thanked him. "They parted and that was the last time the man ever briefed him," says Colin C. Blaydon, who served on the Systems Analysis staff under McNamara. "It was the kind of story that floated around the Pentagon, the popular image of a man caught in his own analytical framework. He kept his counsel so much that no one ever really knew what he thought. He was very private. He was feared."

OUTSIDE WASHINGTON, MCNAMARA'S conservative Whiz Kids friends were generally supportive of the war and of his efforts. Only Thornton would somehow be officially drawn into it. For an independent view on Vietnam, McNamara called up Tex and asked him if he would be willing to visit the country on a special mission just before Christmas in 1965. An important part of the U.S. effort in Vietnam was a massive civilian pacification program designed to enlist the support of the country's peasants. Under the auspices of the Department of State's Agency for International Development (AID), the program built hamlet schools and clinics for the peasants, restored sabotaged roads and railways and imported sorely needed crops and construction materials. The goal of the program was to pacify guerrilla sympathizers by support of land reform as well as social and economic benefits. Like just about everything having to do with Vietnam, it was a miserable failure. Widespread corruption undermined the program, along with the misplaced idealism of U.S. officials showing peasants the great potential of living in a free world. President Johnson had expressed concern about the program's progress and had asked McNamara for an independent assessment on it. Tex went with Emerson Itschner, a Portland, Oregon, businessman who had spent thirty-seven years as an officer in the Army Corps of Engineers.

Before his departure to Asia, Tex came to Washington for a series of briefings and appointments at the State Department and the White House. At the time, opposition to the war was only beginning to emerge. Polls failed to show any widespread dissatisfaction. Most Americans believed that anti-war groups were mainly composed of draft dodgers or discontents carrying out Communist plans. Only one in five Americans thought the U.S. should have pulled out before fighting units became involved.

Thornton and Itschner landed in Nha Trang on December 17, 1965, for a one-week visit that started with a briefing in Saigon in the ambassador's office. They quickly got a glimpse of misplaced priorities even at the highest levels when the ambassador took a social telephone call from a local French woman who was inviting him to a society function. He conversed with her in French about nothing for five minutes, not knowing that Itschner understood the language. The two visitors waited and steamed.

What they saw in Vietnam was a poor, pitiful country populated by largely indifferent peasants. They flew south to Can Tho on the Hau Giang River, the center of a rich rice-growing region, to visit small schools built by the program. As they were driven past a group of farmers in a large rice paddy, the State Department guide said, "Look at them, planting rice during the day and planting mines at night."

By the time Thornton returned home, he had bad feelings about the war. He believed that once the U.S. had made the decision to support the South Vietnamese government, it should have rushed into the country with an overwhelming force to put a quick end to the conflict. Thornton told his oldest son, Chuck, that the war was hopeless. It took his son aback because Thornton had always been the complete patriot, strongly supporting the war. "He had maps which showed that only 15 percent of the territory was liberated," recalls Thornton Jr. "As soon as U.S. troops left an area, the VC would take it over again. He said, '15 percent of the people believe the war could be won, 15 percent don't, and the rest don't give a damn. That's Vietnam.' He believed you couldn't fight a limited war so the strategy was hopeless."

Thornton was particularly struck by the low morale of the men he met and how misguided they were in pursuing the goals of pacification. "A surprising number were, without encouragement, severely critical of their own organization, indicating an absence of the esprit de corps without which no organization can be fully successful," he wrote in a report on the trip. One senior official told him that a proposed model city near Cam Ranh Bay was justified as a demonstration of how America lived and that it should serve as incentive for the Vietnamese to adopt the American way of life. Similarly, a program to install generators in remote hamlets was defended by AID officials because the peasants wanted electricity and because it would demonstrate to them how America lived. The remarks shocked Thornton who found it odd that we were trying to impose our standards of life on a very different culture. He believed that AID activities should serve only one purpose: "to establish security and win the war first. All programs must be consistent with this objective," he said.

Thornton thought that the agency's massive Rural Electrification Program—an idea apparently hatched in Washington and imposed on AID officials in Vietnam—was a complete waste. The $5 million plan, he noted, would hook up electricity to only two thousand people at a cost of $2,500 per customer. If anything, he thought, the plan would provide just enough light to allow the Vietcong to more easily identify and attack its targets. "The average customer in the first year will consume the amount of electricity represented by three 60 watt bulbs burning less than four hours a night," Thornton wrote. "The benefit to the war effort would be much less than zero."

Tex spoke to McNamara about his thoughts, and quickly followed up with a letter to McGeorge Bundy, then special assistant to the President. "Mac, it seems that in winning the people, we make the job difficult, if not impossible, by trying to apply American standards to their needs. We overorganize, overplan and feel anything short of accomplishment in a big way belittles our effort. To understand the 'grass roots' of the Vietnamese is to help them in their environment and give them confidence of our understanding."

Thornton also played a role in another key decision of the period. At roughly the same time as Tex made his journey to Vietnam, he was also a member of the Defense Industry Advisory Council, a group of twenty-seven men that included the chieftains of principal defense contractors. The war was creating havoc with McNamara's efforts to keep a tight lid on the military budget. In figuring the military budget for fiscal 1967 in late 1965, McNamara estimated that the cost of the conflict was between $15 billion and $17 billion. (The cost, in fact, would rise to $21 billion in that period.) To fund the war, the President's Council of Economic Advisors pressed for a modest tax increase of 3 to 4 percent. McNamara and Paul Nitze both believed that to offset inflationary pressures, the increased defense costs brought about by our Vietnamese involvement should be offset by an increase in taxes. Obviously, it was not a politically attractive idea. McNamara tried it out first on the Defense Industry Advisory Council. Tex strongly opposed the idea, recalled Nitze. "He thought a little inflation would be good for everyone," he says. "When a vote was taken, all the members of the group but three sided with Tex. McNamara concluded the attempt would be politically hopeless and did not press it with the President." The decision against a tax rise in early 1966 eventually led to runaway inflation and a $9.8 billion deficit for fiscal 1967 that grew to $27 billion the following year.

Despite McNamara's arduous work pace, he still kept in touch with several members of the group. Indeed, at one dinner party at the Moores' he seemed in a playful mood. Maxine Reith was in Washington for the party, visiting from Michigan. Tex was there with Flora; Bob with Margy, and so was Eugene Zuckert, then Secretary of the Air Force, and his wife. Over dinner, Gene and Bob were laughing, making jokes, planning a game of squash where the wager would be several thousand extra troops wanted by Zuckert. Bob joked that if he could beat him, Zuckert could have the additional men. It was only table talk, a wisecrack exchanged in relaxed conversation, but it bothered Maxine. In fact, Zuckert could not play the game because of McNamara. During their early days at the Pentagon, the two would meet to play vigorous games of the sport. But McNamara, knowing only one ferocious speed, had collided with him and snapped Zuckert's ankle. The man limped around on crutches for twelve weeks and could never play again. The gentle sparring, however, was a clue to McNamara's non-public voice of restraint on the Indochina war.

Still, Maxine could not disguise her disapproval. She opposed American involvement in the conflict, had considered herself a pacifist and her eldest son, Fritz, would soon become a conscientious objector. Later, she would remember hearing his typewriter going for three nights as he worked on the papers to declare CO status. Fritz would end up working in a mental hospital for two years with some of the toughest and most difficult patients in the institution. The dinner-table banter frankly sickened her.

EVEN AS THE tragedy of Vietnam engulfed him and the country, McNamara's generation of business leaders still held the Secretary of Defense in high esteem. More than any other executive in America, he epitomized the professional modern manager. A University of Michigan poll of more than four hundred executives in 1967 found McNamara among the "greatest living businessmen in America" along with Henry Ford II, J. Paul Getty, David Sarnoff of RCA and magnate Howard Hughes.

But something else was happening that McNamara and many of those men in the Establishment could not plainly see. Slowly, the lyrical innocence and optimism that had characterized the postwar period was slipping away. Over the radio and on the record players, the spirited music of their generation had given way to what virtually all the original Whiz Kids considered noise—not such celebratory tunes as the "Casa Loma Stomp" or "All That Glitters," but angry songs of social relevance, songs against the Establishment. Bob even found himself in the title of one protest song by the folk-rock duo Simon and Garfunkel: "How I Was Robert McNamara'd Into Submission."

Not only was Vietnam beginning to rip apart the fabric of our society, it was also beginning to invade the personal life of Robert McNamara. From the beginning, it was really his war. Supporters of it referred to the draft as a "McNamara fellowship." As early as March of 1964, five months before the Gulf of Tonkin incident which led to the Congressional resolution authorizing the President to deploy soldiers in Vietnam, Senator Wayne Morse of Oregon had begun calling Vietnam "McNamara's War." As the conflict dragged on, many in the press and on Capitol Hill had picked up Morse's term. Disturbed by it, President

Johnson told domestic adviser Joseph A. Califano in early 1966: "They'll destroy that man. This isn't his war. If it belongs to anybody, it's my war. Let's stop him from talking about it so much, and I'll defend it. Make it the President's war, not McNamara's War."

In public, McNamara insisted the sobriquet didn't bother him and, at first, he even tried to use a bit of humor to ease the burden it imposed on him. He showed up at a costume party in Washington in a suit of armor, suggesting he could deflect the continuing criticism he was under. In his Pentagon office, he hung on the wall a framed copy of a quotation from Abraham Lincoln: "If I were to read, much less answer, all the attacks on me, this shop might as well be closed for other business. I do the best I know how—the very best—and I mean to keep on doing so until the end."

For McNamara, however, the end was coming closer and closer. At times, he seemed so consumed with Vietnam that he was incapable of thinking about anything else. "The death, destruction, and misery of Vietnam just ate away at him," recalls Dean Rusk, Secretary of State. "He agonized over that war." The agonizing affected his wife, Margy, whose health began to deteriorate. "It was very hard on Margy and the kids," recalls Robert Anthony, who had taught with McNamara at Harvard and worked with him at Defense. "One day he actually told a Congressional committee that criticism of him from several of the committee's members hurt his family. 'I went home last night and my son was crying over this.' " His son, Craig, would soon hang the American flag upside down in his room. One day he would confess to feeling greatly embarrassed when his father caught him reading David Halberstam's *The Best and the Brightest,* the highly critical account of McNamara's role in the Vietnam War. In the '70s, Craig would emerge as one of the leaders of the California peace movement.

The pressure on McNamara was building. He was jeered on the floor of the House of Representatives as "Robert S. (I've Got All the Answers) McNamara." One of his assistant secretaries and close friends, John McNaughton, tragically died in an airplane accident with his wife and child. Margy's bleeding ulcers had gotten so bad she had to be hospitalized. (McNamara told the press that Margy got *his* ulcer.) At a dedication ceremony on May 27, 1967, for the *John F. Kennedy* aircraft carrier, McNamara had barely made it through his brief speech before being overwhelmed by emotion. In the presence of President Kennedy's widow and daughter, McNamara's voice faltered and his words were slurred before he turned away from the microphone.

Plagued with doubts, the rationalist was close to cracking. Johnson, who was beginning to distrust McNamara, was concerned about his morale. After Johnson called Margy in the hospital to convey his best wishes one night during the summer of 1967, he hung up and peered at the ceiling.

"Johnny," he told John P. Roche, an aide, "we can't have another Forrestal."

Johnson's reference was to the first Secretary of Defense, James V. Forrestal, who committed suicide shortly after leaving office in 1949. At one point, McNamara even considered a return to Ford, possibly as head of the Ford Foundation. Ford chief counsel William Gossett had been at a White House dinner when McNamara approached him about a job. McNamara asked Gossett, who never really liked him, if he could give him a ride home after dinner.

"Bob, I already have a car and driver to take me home," Gossett recalls telling him. "But I'll see you tomorrow."

"No, I can't do that," replied McNamara. "But I do want to see you. Can't you dismiss your car and driver and ride with me?"

Gossett acquiesced. Later that evening, in the privacy of a black government limo, McNamara told him that he was thinking of leaving the Defense Department and wondered if Henry would have him back.

"What happened?" asked Gossett.

"Nothing," retorted McNamara, "except I've made recommendations that didn't work out. I can't give you the details, but they're there."

Gossett, who personally opposed the idea, returned to Dearborn with the news.

"That's very interesting," Ford told him. "But I don't know that we could find a place *worthy* of him." Gossett asked what Ford meant by the ironic remark. Ford simply said that Bob had been away from the auto business too long to be effective. "I could make him president of the Ford Foundation," he said, "but then it wouldn't be the Ford Foundation any longer; it would be the McNamara Foundation." With that, an easy escape from the rising troubles in Washington had been closed.

McNamara was turning against the war. Only a few months earlier, in May, 1967, he had told the President that the U.S. could not win the war in Vietnam and proposed that he negotiate peace. As General Westmoreland clamored for still more troops, McNamara urged holding him to no more than thirty thousand extra men and to limit bombing of North Vietnam to infiltration routes to the south. In August of 1967, McNamara testified so candidly before a subcommittee of the Senate Armed Services Committee that Senator Strom Thurmond called him a "Communist appeaser" for making a "no-win statement" and suggested in anger that the only conclusion to be drawn from McNamara's appraisal was that the U.S. should "get out . . . at once." The hearing, however, was behind closed doors.

Yet at another Congressional hearing the same month, McNamara publicly broke with the advocates of an escalation in bombing. He said that the U.S. was not bombing steel mills in North Vietnam, as the military generals had contended earlier. The U.S. had instead bombed iron ore foundaries and as president of Ford he had more foundaries at his disposal than existed in all of North Vietnam. President Johnson was enraged, though McNamara could have gone farther. McNamara was already telling others in private that the U.S. had simply run out of targets and that continued bombing would result in massive civilian casualties. Still, it represented the first time that McNamara, who had been associated with and who had defended every escalation of the war, publicly differed with the military.

Two months later, on October 21, 1967, McNamara's worst nightmare came true. Some fifty thousand anti-war protesters marched on the Pentagon, including several of the sons and daughters of his own men. The press captured a glum, sulking McNamara peering out the windows of his Pentagon office at the huge demonstration. Little work was done on that day. McNamara, with Deputy Secretary of Defense Nitze, watched the angry mob from his office, from a command post on the roof of the Pentagon and from just behind the troops standing shoulder-to-shoulder in a defensive line in front of the Mall entrance.

Some ten days later, McNamara again tried to convince the President to stabilize the country's military operations in South Vietnam and to turn over more responsibility for the war to the Vietnamese government. He also urged a complete halt in the bombing of North Vietnam— hoping to get the North Vietnamese to negotiate a settlement. He told Johnson that up to thirty thousand Americans would be killed by the end of the President's term in January of 1969. Already, some fifteen thousand U.S. servicemen had died in the jungles of Vietnam, more than half a million American troops were fighting there and more than one and a half million tons of bombs had been dropped on both the North and the South. Still, there was no significant progress, no end in sight.

The President, who took McNamara's advice in escalating the war, could not easily accommodate his change of heart. Johnson, who had described Bob as "brilliant, intensely energetic, publicly tough but privately sensitive, a man with great love for his country [who] carried more information around in his head than the average encyclopedia," now was overheard telling some of his advisers about McNamara: "I forgot he had been president of Ford for only one week."

Toward the end of November, Johnson felt that McNamara had become a liability and was quietly arranging his appointment to be president of the World Bank. Ever since Margy became ill in late 1966, he had made little secret of his desire to be relieved of the job's heavy burdens. He had vaguely spoken to Johnson about a casual interest in the World Bank, though he also had made it clear that he would stay for another year until the end of the presidential term if that is what Johnson wanted. When the appointment finally came, however, McNamara heard about it not from the President but through a press leak on November 27. The McNamara era was about to end.

His friends cast him as a loyal hero; his critics, a morally irresponsible weakling. If McNamara, as most of his friends suggest, allowed his loyalty to the President to silence his opposition to the war, he could hardly be a hero. In seven years of association with the Kennedy and Johnson administrations, McNamara had not uttered a public word of criticism or doubt about the Vietnam War. Slowly, gradually, he began to urge restraint behind closed doors. Only many years later would he finally concede his doubts. It was a contradiction that McNamara would have to live with for the rest of his life.

JUST HOW FAR McNamara had turned on the war shocked many of the President's closest advisers. On February 27, 1968, only two days before he was to leave Johnson's Cabinet, McNamara went to a luncheon in the Secretary of State's private dining room. The President's top people were there to discuss a speech Johnson planned to give on Vietnam at the end of March. The military had submitted yet another request for more troops, 205,000 men on top of the half million already there. McNamara was now beyond pessimism, terming the latest request "madness."

"The goddamned Air Force," he shouted, "they're dropping more on North Vietnam than we dropped on Germany in the last year of World War Two, and it's not doing anything! We simply have to end this thing. It is out of control."

The usually cool and precise Bob McNamara was cracking. Everyone was astounded at his display of emotion. Clark Clifford, who would soon take over his job, recalled that McNamara's "voice faltered, and for a moment he had difficulty speaking between suppressed sobs. We were all stunned, but out of a shared pain and sense of embarrassment, we went on with the discussion as though nothing out of the ordinary had occurred." Joseph Califano would recall it as "the most depressing three hours in my years of public service."

The very next day, Bob would break down in public when the President awarded him the Medal of Freedom at the White House. After Johnson turned the podium over to McNamara, the retiring secretary was overcome by emotion. "Mr. President," he said in a halting voice, "I cannot find words to express what lies in my heart today. I think I had better respond on another occasion." Johnson moved toward him, put his arm around McNamara, and led him out of the room.

Secretary McNamara was leaving the Pentagon just in time. There would be, however, one final, brief ceremony to formally end his seven-year reign as Secretary of Defense. On February 29, President Johnson left the White House just a few minutes before noon for the brief limo ride to the Pentagon. McNamara was waiting when the President's car, its windows spotted with rain, pulled into the Pentagon garage almost exactly at noon. He greeted Johnson and then escorted him, a handful of aides and Secret Service men to the river entrance one floor above for the ceremony. The contingent filed into the executive elevator. Shortly after the doors drew shut, elevator No. 13 abruptly stopped, jammed between the first and second floors.

Trying to make light of the situation, McNamara turned to Johnson and joked, "This is what's wrong with there being twenty-nine days in February. We didn't program the computer for Leap Year."

"I never knew it took so long to get to the top of the Pentagon," quipped Johnson.

But the President was losing his patience. An elevator operator struggled with the mechanism and the elevator overshot twice before jolting to a permanent stop two feet below the fourth floor. Harry McPherson, who had written the President's short, farewell address, reached up to push open the exit hatch in the elevator's roof to reassure Johnson. Instead, he somehow took out the lights. Some twelve minutes passed in the dark before someone pried open the doors and the entourage climbed out and walked downstairs. The President was furious.

After the strange episode, Johnson combed his hair, straightened his tie and made his way onto the Pentagon steps where an aide helped him don a topcoat and hat in a heavy, pelting rain. The U.S. Army band plugged away at an uninspired "Hail to the Chief," as Johnson, McNamara, Paul Nitze and the Joint Chiefs of Staff made their way to the parade ground. The President reached into his suit jacket for the speech but then the public address system went dead. General Earle Wheeler, chairman of the Joint Chiefs, tried to shake the microphone into operation to no avail.

Finally, in the wet and cold, Johnson began his short speech. But with the public address system out and the constant noise of jets from nearby Washington National Airport, the troops and dignitaries could barely hear a word he said. The rain was so bad the Air Force and Navy had to scratch a flypast of twenty military jets.

It would remind Roche, a Johnson aide who had long been critical of McNamara, of "a Greek drama written jointly by Euripides and Aristophanes." The President had invited him to the ceremony, he suspected, because of Johnson's perverse sense of humor. For nearly two years, Roche had been sending his boss "Eyes Only" memoranda suggesting that McNamara's Vietnam strategy was disastrous. "Nothing better symbolized the nature of the McNamara era at Defense than its eerie end," says Roche.

Most of the guests would only get to know what Johnson said when they picked up the Washington *Post* the following morning. "I have heard this place here at the Pentagon referred to as the puzzle palace," the newspaper quoted the President as saying. "Bob McNamara may be the only man who ever found the solution to the puzzle, and he is taking it with him."

After the ceremony, the men strode back to the Pentagon where the President's limousine was waiting. He turned, shook hands warmly with McNamara, and said:

"Thanks a lot, Bob."

"Thank you, Mr. President," McNamara replied. And the President drove off.

McNAMARA LEFT THE Pentagon exhausted and dishonored, attacked by the right for holding the military back and vilified by the left as a warmonger. Even some of his associates at the Pentagon wondered about him, including men who shared with him a belief in the invincibility of logic.

Like McNamara, Daniel Ellsberg was a numbers man. Another of the Rand Corporation recruits to the Defense Department, Ellsberg's Ph.D. thesis delved into subjective probability and statistical inference. It was Ellsberg who helped to draft McNamara's speech and press release in

July of 1965 to announce the major escalation of the war. It was also
Ellsberg who two years later began work on the historical study of U.S.
involvement in Vietnam that became known as the Pentagon Papers. He
read through seven thousand pages of cables and papers McNamara had
gathered in a single room near his office. And in 1971 he leaked many of
those papers to the media.

By and large, however, he was a McNamara admirer. He had been
inspired by Bob's efforts to gradually control the forces within the military that pressed for the threat and use of nuclear weapons. But when
Ellsberg broke with the Johnson administration on the war and began to
speak out publicly on the issue, he could not help but think of McNamara and the other men in the inner circle of decision-making as war
criminals—even comparing the man for whom he once worked to Albert Speer, one of the most powerful men in the Nazi regime.

In his memoirs, Speer quotes a 1944 article in the London *Observer*
that portrayed the Nazi as many have described McNamara over the
years, "a type which is becoming increasingly important in all belligerent
countries: the pure technician, the classless bright young man without
background, with no other original aim than to make his way in the
world, and no other means than his technical and managerial ability. It is
the lack of psychological and spiritual ballast, and the ease with which he
handles the terrifying technical and organizational machinery of our age,
which makes this type go far nowadays. This is their age; the Hitlers and
Himmlers we may get rid of, but the Speers, whatever happens to this
particular special man, will long be with us."

McNamara was an updated 1960s version of Speer, Ellsberg thought.
They were men with technical backgrounds. Speer had left architecture
to become Hitler's Minister of Armaments. McNamara left business to
become Secretary of Defense. Both transposed the techniques and philos-
ophies of industry to wage war, and both shared a commitment to efficiency and productivity that placed them beyond the reach of moral
dilemma. Like Speer, McNamara also privately expressed growing
doubts about the war.

Also like Speer, thought Ellsberg, McNamara seemed to lack any
strong sense of personal responsibility. It was a moral failure that Ellsberg could not excuse. Even as the conflict continued to drag on through
the Nixon years until its official humiliating end on April 30, 1975,
McNamara would refuse to speak out against the war. Indeed, he would
decline every opportunity to speak about Vietnam at all—even though he
may have been able to influence an earlier end to the conflict, to save

thousands of lives that still were being sacrificed to a failed crusade of his making. It was as if McNamara, whose friends now knew of his opposition, could not bring himself to admit his mistakes. To Ellsberg and other anti-war protesters, McNamara's self-imposed silence only compounded his evil. His crime lay less in being the principal architect of a human tragedy of appalling proportions than in his years of silence about a war he acknowledged was "out of control."

To others, like Alain Enthoven, his intellectual chief of Systems Analysis, McNamara was a hero of the first order, the best Secretary of Defense the nation ever had. "I feel great pride whenever I hear that magical name or when I am introduced as having been associated with him," says Enthoven, now a professor at Stanford University's School of Business. "It's like saying, 'He was with King Henry at Agincourt.' "

Enthoven looked beyond the horrors of Vietnam, beyond some of McNamara's military procurement gaffes like the F-111, Bob's money-saving effort to force the Navy and Air Force to use the same aircraft. (The result was an ill-fated, highly expensive aircraft that often crashed during tests.) He came to the conclusion that McNamara brought common sense to a Pentagon which for too long was run by the parochial interests of the armed forces and Congress.

Enthoven thought that Bob's single most overpowering achievement was in cutting the military's dependence on the use of nuclear weapons. "It could have gotten us into a nuclear war in which tens of millions of people would have been killed," believes Enthoven. By diversifying our nuclear capability, assuring the survival of our weapons so that the U.S could unleash a devastating second strike against the Soviet Union, Enthoven believed that McNamara may have saved the country from a nuclear holocaust.

Whatever his legacy, few would dispute that during his seven years as Secretary of Defense Robert McNamara was the dominant figure in the nation's capital after the President. For days and weeks after his farewell, the media which had been so quick to criticize him over the years generally showered praise on his tenure. "For Washington last week," wrote political commentator Hugh Sidey in *Life* magazine, "waking up to the fact that Robert McNamara was leaving the Cabinet was like finding the Washington Monument missing one morning." Columnist Joseph Alsop thought him "the greatest public servant to enter the Executive branch of the U.S. government since this Republic began."

If McNamara was a dismal Secretary of War, he may have been a superb Secretary of Defense, the most effective the country had ever known. It was his virtuosity with numbers and his fascination with facts that at once made him such a success and such a failure. His quantitative skills granted him unprecedented control over an ungainly bureaucratic defense establishment, just as those same skills blinded him to the real, unquantifiable issues in Vietnam. Bob McNamara failed to recognize that the numbers could carry him only so far—and his old employer was discovering that same simple truth.

George and Mimi Moore in Scottsdale, Arizona, at the Camel Back Inn.

George Moore, already visibly deteriorating, at the Homestead in 1966 with his family.

Chapter 29

DEATH OF A
WHIZ KID

■

"Men are disturbed not by things,
but by the views they take of
them."

—EPICTETUS

For Robert McNamara, the months and years as Secretary of
Defense had drifted by as quickly as a large cloud on a windy
day. It seemed like yesterday when he and Margy were riding down
Pennsylvania Avenue in an open car, waving to thousands of people who
came to Washington for the Kennedy inaugural parade. The troops had
swept the avenue clear of snow on the frigid, windy day.

Shivering together in the reviewing stands across from the White
House, wildly waving back to Bob and Margy, were George and Mimi
Moore. The President's bubble-top Lincoln had just passed and the procession of cars containing his Cabinet officers and their wives trailed not
far behind. The Moores cheered lustily at the first sight of their friends in
a car marked by a big sign: Secretary of Defense, Robert S. McNamara.
Unlike the other wives, Margy was hatless, her hair flying in the bitter
wind. Even in the President's parade she set her own pace, thought
Mimi.

The Moores had watched Kennedy's inaugural address on television at George's nearby office before coming down to the reviewing stand. The McNamaras' son, Craig, was sprawled on the floor before a portable TV watching the spectacle at George's home with the Moores' son, Doug. Bob McNamara had stayed with George and Mimi when he snuck into town for his first interview with Kennedy.

As Kennedy was forming his Cabinet, Mimi had a strange telephone call at the house.

"This is the FBI," a voice solemnly announced. "Do you know a Robert Strange McNamara?"

"Of course we know Bob!" she retorted.

"Well, what do you know about him?" the voice asked tersely.

"He's a good friend and we were all together in Detroit."

Then George came on the telephone and attested to the soundness and integrity of McNamara's character. So pleased at the prospect of having two good friends with prominent positions in the Kennedy administration—Bob at Defense and Eugene M. Zuckert as Air Force Secretary—that Moore had suddenly become a Democrat. The night before the inaugural the Moores and the Zuckerts had made the rounds from one gilt-edged ball to another, munching on rum cake and sipping champagne. The McNamaras traveled with the other members of the Kennedy Cabinet in heated red carpet buses, made gay with music by Lester Lanin.

It was Camelot all right. Or so it seemed back then. After glimpsing their friends in the parade, George and Mimi trudged through the snow back to his office on Connecticut Avenue to celebrate. Dozens of friends and workers had gathered at the place, made over in red, white and blue for an inaugural celebration of their own. Caterers were hired to bring in mountains of food. Bartenders generously poured the booze. George wandered through his dressed-up showroom entertaining guests.

But the grand party and the trappings were the realm of fantasy. Moore's auto dealership chain was in complete disarray. His partnership with his long-time friend James Grear had blown up. A new business venture Moore started was starved for capital. He was heavily in debt and his personal health was in jeopardy. Like a lot of things in his life, the opulent party was part of a grand illusion.

George had known tough times before. He had been near bankruptcy not long after he started his dealership and managed to survive and prosper. But the economic slump that helped push Reith over the edge at Ford in 1957 had severe consequences for the car business. Moore-

Grear's earnings fell nearly 20 percent to $163,000 in that year. When Reith's new line of Mercurys failed to sell, the dealership chain was stuck with $1 million of wholesale 1957 inventory on its lots as the new 1958 models were coming out. Moore scrambled to get rid of the cars, selling the last Lincoln for all of $6 in profit. But the firm's income collapsed to only $64,500 in 1958.

What had been one of the ten largest Lincoln-Mercury dealerships in the world, a precursor to the mega-dealers of today, was fast becoming a shadow of itself. George folded up five dealerships, cutting back to twelve in 1959. The downturn took a severe personal toll as well. To sustain his lush lifestyle, George borrowed cash on his life insurance policies and found himself with two mortgages on his own home. "It took a lot more effort and more control to survive and the firm had gotten a little soft," says George W. Thomassen, who joined Moore-Grear in 1951 as a controller. "The lines of communication got to be too much. There were more managers between Moore and the dealerships than they needed."

Desperate for cash, George sought help from Thornton. When the auto business was in rough shape in 1958, Tex had told George he could help him out. Now, six months before McNamara arrived in Washington as Secretary of Defense, George told Tex that Moore-Grear was breaking up as a partnership. "The underlying cause of the split between Jim Grear, his brother and myself is primarily organizational, but to some degree personalities are involved," George wrote Thornton. "It is my firm conviction that no organization can be run by the casting of three votes or committee action."

Besides, at least two dealerships in New Haven and Baltimore were still losing considerable money and several others badly needed capital to keep them running. George offered to flip a coin or draw straws—anything to decide who would remain as the surviving partner to run the firm. But Jim Grear would have none of it. He wanted out of the business. So George decided to buy his partners out. George asked Tex for $600,000—an investment that would make Thornton a 40 percent owner of the company. He forecast that the auto dealership chain could produce $250,000 of net profits a year and that Tex would be entitled to $100,000 of the income as the main minority shareholder.

What he failed to tell Tex was that his partnership with Jim Grear had blown up for more severe reasons. Grear had always played conservative bookkeeper to George's more flamboyant role. When he first arrived at the dealership, Grear actually brought the company checkbook home with him—so neither George nor his earlier partner, Mark Day, could continue to spend money they didn't have. He preached fiscal austerity as frequently as George went off on various spending binges. Through most of the years, one partner balanced the other. George sold and promoted; Grear pored over the books. Jim's brother Dan, a lawyer, was brought into the business as the third partner in 1955 when the chain recorded its most profitable year.

Unlike Grear, George was beginning to become ambivalent about the car business. He had enjoyed the challenge of success, of expanding the business into becoming one of the largest dealerships in the country. It had made him lots of money and that was important to him. "But intellectually it was always beneath him," says Zuckert. "It's kind of a schlock business. There were a lot of schlocky dealers and a lot of schlocky cars, and he sold me some of the worst. But he had more responsibility in Stat Control than he did running all those dealerships."

Zuckert had met George in Stat Control, but they had not become close friends until after the war when George returned to Washington. Their friendship grew during long afternoons on the links at the Congressional Country Club. After hours playing golf, they'd down a few at the club's bar and engage in card games of gin rummy. They became drinking buddies, too, as close as brothers. Zuckert had just left as chairman of the Atomic Energy Commission in July of 1954 and was looking for something to do. George was tiring of selling cars and was seeking his own escape from it.

"Look," he told Zuckert, "I'd like to do something else besides the automobile business. I'll pay you to look for opportunities for me."

There were only a few conditions he put on the search: that the business have nothing to do with cars and that it have something to do with technology. George also had no intention of moving from Lowell Lane. He loved the house and the area, and so whatever new business Zuckert could find would have to be based in or around Washington, D.C.

Zuckert pursued a spate of opportunities but eventually found a small, private company that captured George's interest. It was an unusual business that published an index of all U.S. chemical patents since 1950, selling it to large corporations like DuPont, Eastman Kodak and General Electric. It was basic stuff: not much different than a telephone directory that listed one hundred thousand patents instead of names, addresses and phone numbers. What intrigued George most was a project inside the company to build an electronic document storage system to be used for all the data the company compiled. George anted up the money with his old Stat Control pals, Lynn Bartlett and Zuckert. Jack Reith ended up with a 15 percent in the company. They called the company "Information for Industry."

From the start, George's new business interest began to strain further his relationship with Jim Grear, who unwittingly found himself partially underwriting the deal. To get cash for Information for Industry, George sold his half interest in their dealership in Yonkers, N.Y., to Grear. After selling out, George wrote out a $25,000 check drawn on the Yonkers dealership he no longer owned to pay Zuckert a finder's fee. The money came directly out of Grear's pocket.

It was innocently if naively done, Grear thought. But then George's new business interest began to siphon off the dealership's best people while they were still on the Moore-Grear payroll. Some of them, Grear thought, were now spending four-fifths of their time on Information for Industry. Dealers who had management contracts with Moore-Grear were less inclined to renew them once they learned that George had lost interest in his auto business. "Some dealers questioned whether they should pay George a management fee when it became harder to sell cars," recalls Philip L. Fitts, a Moore friend and colleague. "They were looking for ways to get out of the contracts. At one meeting, George got the drift that this was coming about and said, 'Hey, you guys want out? You can get out right now.' That upset Jim Grear who thought George should have enforced the contracts because some of the dealers walked out."

But what finally severed the relationship were George's long, martini luncheons. They had become less an occasion and more a habit that Grear believed was affecting the performance of the company's top four or five people. They wouldn't drink at work, but nearly every day George would lead a group of them to one of the city's most expensive restaurants. Once there, George would toss down as many as a half dozen stiff martinis. Sometimes no one would return to work after lunch.

George had always enjoyed a good drink, and he often spoke of drinking as if it were a hobby. During the war, his love letters carried his fantasies: a flask filled with Scotch on a brisk November day at a Redskins game, beer and oysters at the Shoreham and a return to what he called "pass-out nights at gay parties." Through his business years, there had always been many late-night meetings when he would go out for a few drinks. It brought him out. Moore was inherently a reserved man, less certain of himself and of his future than the rest of the men. When George's youngest daughter was born, George arrived at Zuckert's house completely smashed in celebration of her birth. He drank to free himself from his shyness until he began to drink to render himself unconscious. His friends believe he crossed the line from being a heavy drinker to becoming an alcoholic in the late 1950s.

Grear grew increasingly concerned over it, no less so because the luncheon drinking crew even included his own brother, Dan. Finally, he decided to confront both of them with the issue. "I told them they were alcoholics and they were encouraging others in the place to be drunks," Grear recalls. The place nearly exploded. They were outraged and indignant, glaring at him like a pair of angry dogs. "They were both mad enough to kill me," says Grear. "George was as angry as I ever saw him. My brother was ready to tear my head off. We had never had words until then, but this was gut check time. I could see the business collapsing. I could see Information for Industry bleeding us to death. The business was stripped."

Grear had enough. The break became so irrevocable that he hardly saw or spoke to either George or his brother after the screaming match. Indeed, some thirty years later Grear didn't know where his brother lived or whether he was alive. "I was sick and hurt," he says. "I couldn't stomach this and I certainly didn't want any part of the company. If I had known now what I didn't know then, I would have thanked George for the plane ride and gone back to Chicago."

Although Tex knew none of this, he politely declined the invitation to save the business even though he was willing to help in other ways. "George," he wrote, "I am very pleased that you thought of me, both as a friend and as a potential business partner. It would be a pleasure to be closely associated with you again. I would like it both from a personal point of view as well as from the business relationship. At the present time I am heavily committed, both as to my time and financially. I have put everything I could get my hands on into Litton Industries."

To make the investment, Tex would have had to sell Litton stock. There was no way that Tex would sell. The sale of stock by a corporate officer would be made public. "It would be very unpopular with members of my board, employees in the company, and our stockholders if I were to do any liquidating," Tex told George. He was right. Shareholders would think he was dumping the stock and assume that he was unsure of Litton's future. It was also a shrewd and diplomatic way to turn his friend down.

For even amid the troubles and the distractions, George was telling Tex he wanted to underwrite a major expansion again, adding twenty new dealerships. He talked of adding to his chain competing lines from General Motors—even though at the time it was unheard of that a single chain would sell cars from different manufacturers. As if he weren't already stretched too thin, Moore even thought of writing a book on the management of the retail auto business. His plans were competely unrealistic. "He didn't want to see the truth," says Grear. "He didn't want to face reality. It made no difference whether he was insolvent or not. He never really grew up."

After visiting with Tex in California, however, George was dissuaded from his plans of expansion. Tex told Moore that he had first to face up to the problems in the chain. Tex also wanted McNamara involved in George's plans to revive the company. After all, Bob knew the business in a way that Tex never did. When George returned from his West Coast visit with Tex in November of 1960, he quickly called McNamara to tell him of Tex's agreement to help—but only subject to Bob's recommendations. Tex wanted to make sure that his friend took advantage of Bob's counsel. McNamara dispatched a member of his staff and an independent business consultant from Detroit to see George and go over the dealership's finances and his business proposition with Tex. Only a few weeks later, on December 15, Tex discussed George's troubles with McNamara when the two of them met in New York at a dinner for Sidney Weinberg, the Wall Street executive and Ford board member who helped Henry Ford bring his company public.

The end result of it all was an extraordinary promise of help from Tex. He agreed to personally guarantee a $250,000 line of credit for George at Riggs National Bank in Washington. The deal required that Tex deposit half a million dollars of his Litton stock in the bank as collateral. This way, he could get George some money without having to sell his stock on the open market. The largest chunk of the money would be devoted to losses George expected from closing down several dealerships. The cash also would allow George to buy out Jim Grear, pay off a few outstanding loans and gain a shot at a comeback.

It was not to occur. Little by little, George sold off his dealerships and closed down his main dealership in Washington to focus on Information for Industry. He put his money and himself into the company, thinking that he could do with it what he had done with the car business in the early days. And there were glimmers of promise in the venture. During the decline of his car business in 1961, George also accomplished what only Tex had done. He brought his new company public, raising $300,000 in an equity offering and gaining more than five hundred shareholders in the process. The stock went public at $5 a share and within six months zoomed to $34.

He and the company's other insiders still retained nearly half the company's shares, but George believed he needed the extra cash to plow into the development of his electronic retrieval system. Information for Industry was still a small, fledgling company with net profits of only $57,400 on $221,770 in sales. But George had a grandiose vision of its future—a vision as unrealistic as his earlier plans to expand the auto dealership just as it was falling apart.

Long before computer visionaries would speak of an Information Age, George began to proselytize about the "explosive expansion of published scientific literature." The number of scientific papers—which could someday be catalogued and indexed on his pseudo-computer—had doubled every fifteen years. The facts would tumble out of his mouth as if they were the selling points of a Mercury on one of his car lots. Some ten thousand papers were printed in 1800; one hundred twenty thousand were published in 1900; over three million found their way into the world in 1960. Aside from scientific literature, every employee in American industry produced an average of twenty-five thousand pieces of paper a year at a clerical cost of $100 billion.

In the company's first annual report, George detailed the growing amount of information in what he called "logarithmic charts"—nothing more than simple bar charts that illustrated the growth in information. The obvious answer to the explosion was some kind of sophisticated means to analyze, sort, index and store this information, and George thought he had it in his Command Retrieval Information System, dubbed CRIS. The machine would spin a 400-foot-long microfilm copy of the company's patent data so that a customer could retrieve the requested information and within seconds gain a hard copy printout at the push of a button.

For all of George's promotional rhetoric, however, the device would become the beginning of his eventual financial ruin. He had sunk tens of thousands of dollars into the development of the quirky machine, and Thornton arranged for a Litton subsidiary to build it under contract. But there was no demand for the product. The machine scrolled the microfilm so quickly that the heat and pressure it generated gradually destroyed the film. Besides, his customers could just as easily access the patent information out of a printed manual than from a machine. The company sold only one retrieval system: to the U.S. Army Corps of Engineers at Fort Belvedere in Virginia.

When the money began to run out, George moved the offices for his machine subsidiary from Farragut Square into the car dealership head-quarters on Connecticut Avenue. The company's elaborate suite on the eleventh floor of that building was then swapped with Eastman Kodak for a much smaller one on the same floor. Information for Industry exhausted its letters of credit until George managed to pile on more loans against the company's accounts receivables. He even borrowed against the firm's future profits. One salesman, Harry M. Allcock, recalls having to rush around to customers to collect payments to help pay the com-pany's employees their weekly salaries. By 1964, George had to fire staff and take himself off the payroll.

George somehow thought he could sell five hundred of the machines over the next five years instead of the two thousand he had once pro-jected. But even that reduced number was optimistic thinking at best. His company and himself heavily in debt, he tried to sell the machine to another firm. Everywhere he went, he was turned down—Xerox, A.B. Dick, 3M, U.S. Industries, Singer and Remington Arms. Attempts to seek outside financing also failed. Litton estimated it would suffer a loss of $430,000 alone, based on its involvement in building the prototype and tooling up to mass produce the machines.

Again, George quietly sought Tex's help. He asked that Litton invest more money to help market the machine. It was a hopeless cause. One Litton manager reported that the product was three years ahead of the market and far too expensive. So no more money would be forthcoming from Litton.

It was a sad and depressing turn of events. "He called me into his office at the time and said we might have to file for Chapter 11," recalls David C. Weeks, a salesman who was among the last of a handful of employees still left. George had become a defeated man, with a haunted look. "He was badly shaken. He was hesitant. He spoke in a low and slow voice. I recall that he looked rather strange—awfully flushed."

In the midst of the turmoil, George remained a soft touch, generous to a fault. When Allcock discovered that his thirty-three-year-old wife had terminal cancer, he asked George if he could take time off. Hopeless for a medical remedy, he wanted to bring his wife to Lourdes, the Marian shrine in southern France, where he hoped she could be cured by a miracle. Though his company was virtually bankrupt in early 1967, George immediately suggested that he take a business trip with his wife to England and France at the company's expense. Allcock's wife died later that year, but not until after George bankrolled a last attempt to heal her at Lourdes.

The company managed to crawl along largely because of the basic patent indexing business. But George's grand ambitions were dead. "George was pretty black," says Lynn Bartlett. "He became morose. He was used to everything going up and getting higher."

At times, George would become desperately insecure in his private conversations with Bartlett.

"I just don't know what I'm going to do," he told Bartlett. Moore was severely in debt, yet continued to live as if he weren't.

"George," Bartlett said, "I don't know. All you have to do is keep trying and look around."

At home, life had become a disaster as well. George tried to hide his financial troubles from his wife, but as the bills began to pile up on his desk her concern understandably grew.

"Please let me know what's going on," she insisted. "Let me handle the finances and the money at home."

George had seldom discussed business with Mimi. She had never interfered with his work or volunteered advice on his decisions. That was his expectation as well. When the auto business fell apart in 1958, things had gotten so bad that he actually went house-hunting with his twelve-year-old daughter, Marika, unbeknownst to his wife. He wanted to sell their large, beautiful home on Lowell Lane and move into a more modest, less expensive place. He couldn't bring himself to do it, though he kept his wife in the dark about it. Indeed, Mimi would not learn of his trips to buy a new house until thirty years later when her daughter mentioned it in a casual conversation.

The deeper George and his business sank, the greater the strain on his family life. Though he had often spoken of his marriage as a partnership, it lacked the appearance of one. George's ebullient personality allowed him to dominate Mimi from the start of their relationship. He personally attended to all financial matters in the house. Mimi didn't even know how to balance the family checkbook. So her concern over the family's declining fortunes was viewed by him as something of a meddling threat. Her sudden worry injured his pride and jeopardized his role as the family provider. More than that, however, Mimi's interest in the details he had long excluded her from was a constant reminder of his failure. He saw it as an issue of trust.

"Don't you love me?" he asked. "Don't you trust me? Don't you believe in me?"

"Of course I love you and trust you and believe in you. But I'd like to know what's going on."

"Well, don't worry," insisted George, "I'll take care of things."

Of course, he couldn't take care of anything. The usually jovial Moore was plunging into a long, bitter period of depression. His optimism and idealism were falling away, replaced by a somber, less hopeful sense of his uneasy world. He became less communicative in the office. And he increasingly retreated into alcohol. Bartlett, who now served as president of Information for Industry, became so alarmed by it that he began to refuse to go out with him. He had met George in 1941 at Keesler Field in Biloxi, Mississippi, as the two of them raced to fetch the same cigarette butt on the ground. He had been a Stat Control buddy of Moore's through the war and a friend since joining his auto dealership as a tire salesman in 1948. But he couldn't believe the deterioration in his friend.

"I'm not going out to lunch with you if you're going to drink," Bartlett insisted.

"All right," George said grudgingly, "I won't order anything."

The two would disappear to Rive Gauche, and at first Moore would be true to his word. Eventually, however, he would begin to order just a single martini that always seemed to lead to another and another. It reached the point that George would outright refuse Bartlett's request that he not drink at lunch.

"Well, I'm going to lunch and I'm going to have some drinks whether you like it or not," he shot back.

His friend felt at a loss in trying to help. "Sometimes, I got blamed for the fact that he was off drinking," said Bartlett. "So you thought he was better off with someone else. George didn't like to think that people were trying to help him. He had to solve it himself. But he couldn't do it. Finally, he gave up. It just got worse."

His business reversals were made all the more difficult by a deterioration in his health. In the late 1950s, he developed harsh abdominal pains and nausea caused by pancreatitis, an ailment common to alcoholics. By 1957, the disease had progressed into diabetes, requiring daily shots of insulin. There were persistent stomach disorders and heart problems, a spate of various illnesses off and on. Still, despite the insistence of his doctors that he eschew alcohol, he drank more and more.

Bartlett was not alone in trying to get George to clean up his act. All his friends would plead with him to stop, but he often denied he had any problem with alcohol at all. "He laughed at you when you mentioned it," recalls Zuckert. "George really didn't respond. I think he knew he had a problem, but he denied it. George was pretty unhappy when he messed up his life. He didn't have finite ambitions. He wanted to do a lot, but I don't think he ever envisioned how he would make his ambitions come true. He didn't have an objective. He knew he wanted to be something, but he never knew what he wanted to be. George was torn between the desire to do something worthwhile and the need to make money to support a rich lifestyle."

A few of his friends, including Bartlett and Zuckert, suggested that they all take a cottage at his favorite vacation spot, the Homestead, where all of them would go on the wagon. They'd play lots of golf and cards and stay off drink together. But George was too proud and too depressed to agree to the plan. It only made him feel worse.

When he stopped drawing a salary from Information for Industry, no money came into the house. Mimi Moore had to go to the private schools in which her children were enrolled to tell them that her husband was in financial trouble and that they couldn't afford to pay the tuition. She managed to get scholarships for them, and when Marika went to college, she waited on tables to pay her way. It was an embarrassing decline for all of them. To gain school scholarships, the family had to give up what was left of its club memberships. School officials asked whether her daughter would have a debutante party? Of course not. They barely had enough money to pay the utility bills.

Growing increasingly worried, Tex talked to Ed Lundy at Ford about their fast-deteriorating friend. Their friendship ran deep. Lundy and George had burned the Pentagon lights all night long during the war. It was an enduring friendship. Lundy had asked Ford's marketing people to canvass some job opportunities for George in dealer and dealer relations. George told Lundy he had a possibility of getting a job at Western Union in the District; but it didn't happen. Jim Wright also was in contact with George, trying to help from afar. Eventually, things got so bad that McNamara gave him a job as a consultant in the Department of Defense.

Sometimes, he couldn't get out of bed to show up for work. When his wife brought up the possibility of getting a job, George exploded. She was offered a job selling wallpaper at a Washington store. It was nothing special, just a way to get some cash flowing into the house. But George felt complete humiliation at the prospect of his wife's employment. "He was personally offended," recalls his youngest daughter, Laura. "He thought that Mom was making a statement on his inability to be a provider."

They left the dinner table to argue the issue in the kitchen out of earshot. But Laura pressed an ear against the kitchen door to hear their quarrel. What she heard terrified her for it only confirmed the growing rupture in their family life.

"Well, do you want a divorce?" asked Mimi.

"No, of course not," he said. "Making money for you and the rest of the family is important. It's how I maintain my self-respect."

For all his promise, George Moore had turned out to be a rather small man: resentful of a wife and friends who sought to help him, ashamed of his sorry predicament yet unable or unwilling to change it. The innocence and love captured in his wartime letters had long since vanished. "To me, it was like an idol falling," says Mimi Moore. "Here was this wonderful man who was falling, a man who had been everything to me, a father, a husband, a lover, a romantic hero. To see him disintegrate was too painful and it was too difficult for him to talk about it to me. He felt he failed me. He would not discuss our finances and we were just in limbo."

For years, George would take the family to the Homestead for the Christmas holidays. It was a fixture of their family life. Their son, Doug, learned to ski at the resort. Laura Moore learned to ice skate on the Homestead rink and trained for years to become an Olympic skater, placing second in the national championships one year. Laura could recall going to the vacation spot and being able to charge anything she wanted. One year, she bought every Superman and Archie comic book in the place. Her father did not discover the extravagance until a month after they returned home when the bill arrived in the mail. He did not get angry, but he didn't hesitate to express his disappointment in her.

But those were luxuries he could ill afford now. "I remember Daddy sitting us all down in the Sun Room and saying there were financial problems," says Laura Moore. "If we really wanted to go to the Homestead for Christmas, we would go but it would be difficult. The next year, he sat us down in the Sun Room and said we couldn't go at all."

A comfortable space with a bar overlooking the patio, it was his favorite room in the house. When friends came to visit, they would always adjourn to the Sun Room. When Bob first came to Washington, they sat together in the room. McNamara settled into George's preferred chair and asked which school they favored for the children. George and Mimi enthusiastically endorsed the Sidwell Friends School.

"Is that a private school?" asked Bob.

"Yes," said Mimi, "but we call it an independent school because there are a lot of different ethnic groups there."

McNamara liked the distinction. He didn't want to send his children to an all-white elite school. So two of his three children, Kathleen and Craig, followed the Moores to Sidwell Friends.

Laura had spent hours with her father in this room. He would sit in an overstuffed chair in the corner, giving her rides on his bouncing legs. The hi-fi console would sound a scratchy and goofy recording of "Waltzing Matilda," a favorite tune of George's that rekindled the memories of his days in Australia during the war. A lamp on the left of the chair lit the newspaper or book he was reading. A side table had always held his drink. If the tumbler held a brown liquid, it was probably a diet cola and he was likely to be grumpy and on a diet. If it were something stronger, as it often was, he was likely to be cheerful and festive. Increasingly, though, he would hide out in his bedroom and Laura would be told that "Daddy is sick today."

The baronial house on Lowell Lane was his pride and joy, the most tangible symbol of the comfortable life he had sought for himself and his family after the war. And now even the ownership of their home was in jeopardy. As George's creditors began to close in on him, Tex stepped in to take care of his friend once again. He arranged to buy the house with his own money and take title to the property. Tex would assume the housing expenses, until George landed on his feet again. Then George could simply buy it back from his friend.

"Had our positions been reversed, George would have helped me," Tex told Mimi. "George taught me that. He said when you're able to do something for somebody you do it. You don't expect thank you's. You just do it."

So touched was George's mother by Tex's generosity that she wrote him a personal letter of thanks. Just a few days before Christmas in 1966, Tex responded with a poignant, though overly optimistic, letter of his own.

"I am confident that George is going to make a comeback, just as his father did. My only concern has been that George not try to do it overnight or ruin his health by worrying about it. Since the worst part is over with, I am now sure that George's spirits will continue to get better and better as things steadily improve for him."

On Christmas Eve of 1966, thirteen-year-old Laura sat with her father in front of the fireplace and a decorated tree in the living room. The house was quiet. Her mother had gone to bed in the guest room. Her older sister was out with a boyfriend, while her brother, Doug, was off with his girlfriend. George tried to comfort her as she cried over the absence of the family on Christmas Eve.

It frustrated his friends to see him go to waste. But no matter how hard they tried to get him help, he would refuse it. George badly wanted to assert control over his life. But no matter how he tried, he failed. He grew frustrated, worried and deeply despondent. He began to lose weight and his financial troubles brought him to the verge of personal bankruptcy.

One late afternoon, just before Memorial Day in 1967, George and Zuckert drove out to an overlook above the Potomac. The two of them got out of the car and sat on a bench there waiting for the sun to retire. Moore reminded Zuckert of something his mentor once told him at the Harvard Business School many years earlier. He said that one of the worst tragedies in life is the bright young man who stays the bright young man too long. That may have happened to George, thought Zuckert. In many ways, his friend might have peaked during the war in Stat Control when he was all of twenty-five. The happy-go-lucky George had gone from a buck private to the youngest non-flying Lieutenant Colonel in the Air Force—and then from a success to a bankrupt and broken man.

As they sat together above the Potomac, Zuckert again tried to talk some sense into his pale, sickly friend. "God knows I tried to stop him drinking," he says. "I was also trying to get him squared away financially. He was in bad shape. He promised me that he would do something, get the figures together."

George went home and straight to bed. Early in the evening, his young daughter caught a glimpse of him in a large mirror on one wall of his bedroom. "I looked in and his dinner tray was on his vanity chest and he was hunched over in bed with his face in his hands," Laura recalls. "He seemed to have the weight of the world on his shoulders. He had just given up."

It was the last time she saw her father alive. She awoke at 2 a.m. startled by her mother's scream. Doug came clattering up the stairs to his father's bedroom and began a futile attempt to revive him with mouth-to-mouth resuscitation. But it was no use. He was gone at the age of forty-seven. The combination of diabetes and drinking was a potent poison. The cause of death was officially listed as "insulin shock reaction," though there are fewer than a half dozen deaths in any given year attributed to an overdose of insulin.

McNamara, depressed himself over the course of the Vietnam War, told Mimi that George died of a broken heart. "He couldn't cope," Mimi said. "He was so depressed. And after he died we discovered he was a couple of hundred thousand dollars in debt. So not only was there no money, we were deeply in debt." Tex openly sobbed at the funeral of his friend. If not for bubbly George, who had the connections that led them to Ford, there might never have been the Whiz Kids. Tex, Jack, George and Ben Mills could have purchased a car dealership together after the war—as they had initially explored—and that would have been that. They would not have known of the great promise at Ford. Who knows what would have become of them?

THE
WHIZ
KIDS

On December 1, 1969, *Forbes* magazine published a cover story that helped to burst the Litton bubble.

Tex Thornton at a Litton annual meeting where he won widespread praise and adulation from his shareholders—until things went wrong.

Chapter 30

THE
SHATTERED
IMAGE

■

> "Success is never merely final or terminal. Something else succeeds it. . . . The world does not stop when the successful person pulls out his plum; nor does he stop, and the kind of success he obtains, and his attitude towards it, is a factor in what comes afterwards."
>
> —JOHN DEWEY

The annual meeting of a public corporation is typically a tame, if not an excruciatingly dull affair. The shareholders gather to see the chief executive give a perfunctory speech that often says nothing. They ask him questions yet never seem to get answers. If the company's size warrants the presence of a corporate gadfly, a few moments of interest might erupt. But even that is rare.

Litton's great fortunes, however, made its yearly rituals love fests. At them, Thornton was celebrated, showered with cheers and applause by shareholders who saw their personal wealth climb with every uptick in Litton stock. They had come to believe in Tex Thornton more than some of his own people inside Litton did. Investors saw in him a man of almost mythical proportions, the visionary manager of a forward-looking form of enterprise. He was a self-made man who spoke grandly of concepts and systems and of the technologies of tomorrow. As Litton became the fastest-growing corporation in business history, reaching $1

billion in revenues in twelve years, Thornton was canonized by the press
and adored by his shareholders.

The shareholders who swarmed into the cavernous Santa Monica
Civic Auditorium on December 2, 1967, for Litton's annual meeting
were thoroughly charmed by the magic. Their mood equaled the height
of the company's stock, which had soared to a high of $120 a share in
1967, nearly fifty times earnings. The company's premium price gave
Litton a market value of $2.7 billion that placed it in the company of far
older and larger corporations such as Chrysler, Westinghouse, Union
Carbide and Goodyear Tire. "By 1967," wrote John Brooks in *The Go-
Go Years,* "Litton had become a gray eminence among conglomerates, its
reputation impeccable, its stock soaring, its earnings rising steadily as
they had been doing for a decade, its self-image so assured that it could
decorate its annual report for that year with pictures of medieval stained
glass 'so that we may signify our respect and responsibility toward the
achievements of the past.' "

It was in that atmosphere of enchantment and adoration that a small
twelve-year-old boy named Gary Brewer had come to the 1967 annual
meeting. His parents refused his request for a suit to wear to Tex's
session, so he showed up in slacks, a sport shirt and sweater to let Thornton know that he was "very satisfied" with the single share of stock he
owned. Full of confidence, Tex would again report record first quarter
earnings and predict the nation's Gross National Product and even its
population in the years ahead.

If there was any cause for concern, it was not because of any suspicion
over the company's future. It was due to rumors that Thornton might
leave Litton to become Bob McNamara's successor as Secretary of Defense. The newspapers were speculating that Thornton was a candidate
for the job and few people could hardly imagine a successful Litton
without the ruddy-faced man at the top.

But at the 1967 annual meeting, Tex told an applauding audience that
"there is no foundation to rumors" that he might resign. "I have no plans
to leave Litton as long as you shareholders don't urge me to, or put me
out," quipped Tex.

Less than two months later, some shareholders would be doing just
that. The jokes and the euphoria turned to dismay on January 22 when
Thornton and Ash sent a letter to their stockholders reporting that Litton's profits for the fiscal quarter ending January 31 would be "substan-
tially lower than planned." The announcement ended fifty-seven consecutive quarters of earnings gains, the first reversal since Thornton formed

the company fifteen years earlier. The stock market greeted the news in complete shock. As one Wall Street pundit put it, "It was the day the cake of Ivory soap sank." Litton stock plunged eighteen points in a week. Within a month or so it lost almost half of its peak 1967 value.

Litton's collapse marked the start of the decline of the conglomerate era. It also occurred in the year in which the fabric of American life unravelled. In the month of Litton's sorry surprise, McNamara's last full month as Secretary of Defense, the *U.S.S. Pueblo* was seized by North Koreans, a humiliating event for what was the mightiest nation in the world. Vietnam protests grew larger and turned more violent. McNamara's departure from the White House would be followed by President Johnson's announcement only a month later that he would not run for re-election. Martin Luther King, Jr., would be murdered in April. Senator Robert Kennedy would be assassinated in June. Violence would mar the national convention of the Democratic Party in Chicago in August.

Amid the societal delusion, the glamour conglomerate would prove not so glamorous after all. For all the pretentious claims of management superiority, Tex Thornton failed to see the disaster coming. Management control—what Thornton had staked his very success on from Stat Control days—had been lost. The management of the company was part of the magic of Litton. Yet in Tex's letter to the shareholders, he abstractly blamed "certain earlier deficiencies of management personnel."

Tex and Ash had debated for hours on whether to issue the letter. "It was an attempt to plead guilty," remembers Ash. "Everyone thought we couldn't do wrong, but we did. We didn't want to be too crass about it, but we wanted to say we were not infallible. We had to say it, and maybe it was a weak way of saying, 'the buck stops here.' " Yet by not assigning blame directly to themselves, both Tex and Ash appeared to be placing the blame on others. Indeed, many Litton executives whose operations were still performing well were angered by the letter.

The problems cropped up in two key areas: business equipment and shipbuilding. Earnings on the business equipment hodgepodge of Royal typewriters, Royfax copying machines, Monroe calculators and Sweda cash registers had never been truly impressive. In a business where IBM earned 12.6 percent on sales and the industry average was 7 percent, Litton scraped to earn just 3 percent. Losses on its copiers alone clipped ten cents off per-share profits in the latest quarter, while the red ink from typewriters would total $6.5 million for the year.

The surprise in that business erupted because the numbers being reported to Beverly Hills disguised some real and basic problems. Harry

Gray, sent in to fix the operation after the debacle, recalls that the business equipment group had been forecasting a profit of $50 million for the year. It actually made all of $1 million, after a tremendous amount of work by him—a profit swing of $49 million that was completely unexpected by Thornton.

His strategy of buying ailing companies at bargain prices and trying to nurse them back to health had significant drawbacks—especially in hotly competitive markets. Such companies sorely needed heavy investment to develop new products, investments that Litton wasn't always willing to make. That was partly why Litton's marketshare in copy machines was all of 1 percent, compared to Xerox's 60 percent. And it was also a reason why Litton was failing in the electric typewriter market.

The statement that shocked Wall Street also would include an $8 million write-off to cover the unexpected costs of a contract to build commercial cargo ships at the Ingalls shipbuilding yard. The loss revealed that professional managers could not manage everything as Tex had long asserted, especially when they began to own operations they knew nothing about. Indeed, Litton took the write-off because it failed to correctly estimate its own costs in pricing the commercial contract.

The blow on Wall Street was so severe not because of the earnings setback caused by these problems. It was deep because Litton's stock was vastly overvalued. Six months before the crash, says Ash, he had made the calculations to show that the high price accorded Litton stock was completely without foundation. "It was in orbit and no matter what we did, there was no possible way to get the earnings to justify the price," he recalls. "People were buying at a huge multiple because they assumed a level of sales and earnings that were impossible to obtain. The question at the time was are we obligated to tell our shareholders that the price of the stock was totally unjustified. We decided against it."

Some nine months after the bad news, Thornton and Ash saw a chance to regain some of their mystique when *Forbes* magazine requested interviews for a cover story. What they didn't know is that the article was initiated by a principal at the State Street Bank in Boston. The man had just sold his Litton holdings after discovering some gimmicky accounting in Litton's financial reports. He had tipped off James W. Michaels, the magazine's editor, that he believed Litton was deliberately misleading investors by some rather fanciful bookkeeping. Michaels flew from New York to meet Tex Thornton in his Beverly Hills headquarters with James Flanigan, the *Forbes* Los Angeles bureau chief.

It was the typical Thornton session, with Tex waxing hyperbolic on

synergy and technology, mixing microwave ovens and frozen TV dinners together to talk about how Litton would "help to advance the
frontiers of technology and be able to bring that technology to a useful
product." He foresaw vast frontiers in an era when housewives would
supposedly shun the drudgery of preparing meals. As the reporters left
Tex's office, Michaels turned to Flanigan and asked, "What do you
think, Jim?"

"He doesn't venture an opinion on himself," Flanigan replied.

"Yeah," said Michaels, "but he's got a damn oven. Why does he have
to talk about changing the nature of the kitchen?"

Flanigan then spent weeks touring Litton's facilities around the country. The result of his trip would astonish both Thornton and Ash, and
the cover in *Forbes* would become a classic. Over a rendering of cracked
plate glass, the headline read: "The Shattered Image of Litton Industries." If any of the Litton mystique still existed after its surprising earnings reversal a year earlier, the story helped to finally put it to rest.
"Litton had woven a magic spell that convinced many people that its
growth could go on almost forever, that every $1 of its earnings was
worth more, much more, than that of more conventional companies,"
wrote Flanigan. "Suddenly, the spell was broken, the legend shattered
. . . Looked at up close—rather than through a glamorous prism of
Litton rhetoric—this huge company looks a good deal more like a collection of nuts and bolts, and less like a marvelous pattern of synergy."

What the *Forbes* reporter had finally discovered was what those inside
of Litton knew all along: that at least part of the company's mystique
was due to little more than sophisticated bookkeeping. After its fall from
grace in 1968, Litton was reporting in 1969 a 35 percent increase in
earnings as sales surpassed the $2 billion mark. Within the fine print of
the earnings statements, Litton revealed its income included a $23.2 mil-
lion capital gain from the sale of a company. The gain, however, was not
realized because it was used to offset losses on two shipbuilding contracts. In effect, the company was taking a write-off that it did not
acknowledge in its financial statements.

The financial reporting was not illegal, but it was ambiguous enough
to hide the company's continuing troubles. Few analysts and investors,
moreover, expected this behavior from Tex Thornton. The image of the
company was too pristine for that. Litton helped define the conglomerate
movement; Litton made the movement respectable. And Tex and his
fellow Whiz Kids had staked their careers on the truth in the numbers.

Even some of the company's former executives who conceded they owed much to what they learned at Litton began to turn on Tex and Ash. "The trouble with Litton today," one former executive said then, "is that they are singing the same old song that once was very popular. But they forgot that the new sounds now aren't from the Beatles, but from Arlo Guthrie."

Thornton and Ash were incensed by the story. Ash penned an angry letter to Malcolm Forbes, the magazine's publisher, but decided not to send it because it was so venomous. But even some insiders knew the magazine's critique to be the truth. "They were master image creators," recalls William W. George, who ran Litton's microwave oven division. "That's why they were so upset when the stock cratered."

WILLIAM GEORGE HIMSELF was central to some of the image making. A Harvard MBA, he came to Tex after a stint with McNamara in the Department of Defense. George joined Litton in 1969 at the young age of twenty-seven as director of long-range planning. He would soon become one of Litton's most celebrated executives, hailed in a series of Harvard Business School case studies as the "driving force" of the company's microwave division.

Raytheon had developed the first microwave oven in 1946, using a magnetron vacuum tube to cook food. Combining its own knowledge of making magnetron tubes with the acquisition of a small oven company in Cleveland, Litton introduced its first microwave oven in 1965. It looked like an ugly, oversized bread box, but because it was priced at $1,000, only half of what existing models cost, the company captured 80 percent of the commercial market within a year. The problem was that the market, mainly hospitals, schools and restaurants, only amounted to some nine thousand microwave ovens.

With costs likely to decline further, Tex foresaw a huge market for the devices in the home. He also thought that the way to create the market was to complement his microwave operation with a company that made frozen foods. He found one in Stouffer Foods. Founded by Vernon Stouffer, the company boasted a network of so-so restaurants and motor inns along with a strong brand name in frozen prepared foods. Stouffer's income was only $1.4 million a year on sales of about $95 million. Stouffer rejected Tex's initial bids for the company, holding out for a higher price. Eventually, Tex got what he wanted in 1967; but Stouffer became his most expensive acquisition, costing nearly $100 million in Litton stock.

From then on, with every mention of synergy, microwave ovens and frozen prepared foods became the example that Tex and Ash would trot out. To the outside world, Thornton spoke endlessly about providing microwave ovens and frozen food to workers on oil drilling platforms, to astronauts in space and to servicemen abroad who missed American food. Inside his company, however, his own executives harbored strong doubts and refused even the slightest amount of cooperation with each other. "Ash felt it was like a Gillette razor and a razor blade," recalls James Biggar, then vice president of Stouffer's frozen foods division. "It was more like an automobile and gas. Anybody's gasoline could go into the gas tank. What difference did it make? There was no synergy in that. And after the acquisition, there weren't many serious attempts at trying to gain some synergies."

When George, head of the microwave division, tried to convince Stouffer's executives to package their frozen foods in paper containers so they could be used in microwaves, they resisted. "There was no way Stouffer would convert from aluminum containers," says George. "Stouffer told me that 'when 50 percent of my customers have microwave ovens, then I'll change.' It was hopeless."

Within three years of its acquisition, Stouffer was trying to convince Tex to sell the company. The same man who had been talked into selling his company by Thornton had become disillusioned with him. Stouffer was flattered by Tex's visions of what Litton and his company could do together. When it became clear that the vision was just mere talk, he became frustrated. Besides, Vernon Stouffer had used Litton stock as collateral for a huge loan to acquire the Cleveland Indians baseball team. As Litton stock lost its value, he had to ante up more and more of his holdings to satisfy his bankers. When he signed his deal with Tex, Litton's stock was worth $106 a share. When Stouffer eventually unloaded the investment, it had dropped to $38. In 1973, little more than five years after the acquisition, Litton finally sold Stouffer to Nestlé Foods. "Vernon got the satisfaction of at last seeing some kind of relationship between the purchaser and his company," says Biggar, Stouffer's son-in-law. So much for synergy.

CURIOUSLY, MANY LITTON insiders placed most of the blame for the fall not on Tex, who had woven his own magic spell over them, but largely on Ash who was not nearly as well liked. What the critics failed to say was that Thornton had in recent years for the most part taken a more passive role in the management of Litton. The earlier rumors of his becoming Secretary of Defense were more than mere rumors. Tex himself had toyed with the idea, of course, and what his shareholders may not have clearly known was that Thornton had largely become a disengaged caretaker. He had joined the boards of directors of at least eight other companies and two colleges. He privately talked with friends about gaining a post as ambassador somewhere. And thanks partly to McNamara, he also found himself on a variety of government panels and groups.

Thornton had made the special mission to Vietnam, investigated a cheating scandal at the Air Force Academy and was a member of President Johnson's National Advisory Commission on Civil Disorders—a job that consumed many months full time and many hours on airplanes between Los Angeles and Washington. Unlike many executives who simply lent their names to various causes, Tex attended forty-four out of the forty-five meetings of the commission.

"His work in Washington really separated him from the business," recalls Harry Gray. "He was trying to do it by telephone and Roy was doing the best he could to keep things going. Some guys get taken up with yacht racing, and the business goes to hell. Some guys get taken up with women, and the business goes to hell. Tex did the honorable thing in working in Washington, but it had the same impact."

Success made Thornton a larger-than-life figure; it also distracted him from his family and his company. He had made the cover of *Time* magazine, along with every major American business magazine. His notoriety gained him only more distractions. With every ceremonial trip and every outside board meeting, Tex had slowly been giving up more and more power to Roy Ash—something that was not at all easy for him. "Dad once told me," recalls his son, Chuck, " 'You know, I had planned to turn over the operation to Roy. But as the phones stopped ringing for me and rang more for him, it troubled me a bit. But that's what I needed to do.' "

The sudden collapse of the company, however, forced him out of a semi-retirement and quickly put an end to his ambitions for a government post. It also dealt a severe blow to Tex's pride. "He was under great stress, and he blamed himself a lot," recalls his wife, Flora. He had delegated more and more responsibility in the company to Roy and he was more active on other national boards. He was enjoying that span of his life and it was really the best period in our marriage. He was finally relaxed about himself and was finally enjoying the fruits of his labor. I was thinking at that time that we would be able to do more things together that we never had time to do. And then this thing hit. Tex's reputation was on the line and so he got back in the saddle and said, 'I'll never retire until I get this company back.' He worked like a dog again. He kept at it. It was very strenuous and very hard on me. There's something about tension—it affected my health to some extent—just the stress. I didn't expect to be under such pressure again. It really took a toll."

The collapse dramatically changed the mood both inside and outside Litton. Many of the owners of the companies acquired by Tex were now retired, and they watched helpless and enraged when their Litton stock plummeted. Only a few years earlier, they had given up their own firms in exchange for some of the Litton magic. Now it was gone. "The age of magic numbers," as *Forbes* magazine put it, "of blind faith in corporate rhetoric, is over, and the time has returned when investors are going to ask about typewriters and machine tools and frozen dinners instead of simply being mesmerized by earnings curves."

BEYOND THE DISASTER at Litton, Tex was deeply troubled by other things in his life. Even as he was being celebrated on the cover of *Time* magazine as the best manager in American business, Thornton's reputation was being severely questioned in a bizarre court battle in Los Angeles. Emmett T. Steele, one of Litton's earliest employees, sued Thornton on October 21, 1959, claiming that he was a founder of the company and entitled to as much as $10 million worth of Litton stock. Steele insisted that he was instrumental in convincing Charles Litton to sell his business to Thornton. But Thornton's lawyers called Steele nothing more than a "martini pourer" at business parties given by the firm.

The litigation would only confirm and add to Tex's fundamental mistrust of the law, a mistrust which had developed years earlier when he saw his father's murderers set free. His father's trial would inspire a best-selling novel by Texan Al Dewlen as well as a forgettable movie, both entitled *Twilight of Honor*. The phrase itself reflected the dilemma faced by the attorney who defended the guilty by destroying the crime's victim. When Dewlen's book appeared in 1961, chronicling the crime in barely disguised form, the phrase would come to haunt him. Years later, William A. Masterson, one of Thornton's attorneys in the Steele litigation, recalled riding the escalator in a Los Angeles courthouse and having a conversation with him about the law.

"When you try lawsuits it's all shades of gray," Masterson told Thornton. "It's a helluva way to make a living. Sometimes you find yourself in the twilight of honor."

At the mention of the words, Masterson says, Thornton glanced up at him and glared in silence. "His face just paled, and I said, 'Oh, Jesus, Tex, I'm sorry. I forgot there for a minute. I didn't mean to remind you of anything.' He had a fundamental mistrust for the law and the jury system."

What happened to his father would soon happen to him. Among other things, Steele's attorneys dug through Thornton's past to publicly embarrass him. They found a willing witness in Noah Dietrich, Howard Hughes's now-retired henchman. Dietrich, by then seventy-three years old, testified in late 1962 that Thornton made an improper $5 million offer to him in the hope that Dietrich would help Thornton buy out Hughes Aircraft. He also told the court that Thornton was ordered to resign from Hughes Aircraft after overcharging the Air Force several million dollars on contracts.

"He offered me $5 million if I would induce Howard Hughes to sell the aircraft operation," claimed Dietrich. "I told him that as an associate and employee of Hughes, it was a very improper suggestion on his part and I couldn't consider it." Dietrich said Thornton made an initial offer of $85 million for the aircraft company after obtaining financial backing from Lehman Brothers, the New York investment banker.

But by then, Dietrich asserted, a group of certified public accountants had threatened to resign unless Thornton's accounting methods at Hughes were changed. Dietrich claimed the accounting system had resulted in profit margins of about 30 percent when the government contracts allowed a profit of only 11 percent. "I instructed him to immediately issue a check for $5 million and send it to the Air Force," said Dietrich. "I was dissatisfied and put him on notice that he was to be terminated."

When Thornton's eyes pierced the headline over Dietrich's charges in the Los Angeles *Times* on December 20, 1962, he exploded. Thornton promptly issued a press release denying the charges and calling Dietrich a malicious liar. The very same day, against the advice of some of his attorneys, he also filed a $40 million libel suit against Dietrich, Steele and Steele's attorney, Harold Rhoden. Thornton charged that the statements were "false and defamatory." Less than a week later, in a sarcastic rejoinder to Thornton, the three men filed a nuisance suit seeking forty cents in actual damages and $1 million in punitive damages. "Dietrich suffered a certain amount of concern and anxiety," the suit claimed, "and in view of the personal character, personal reputation and social and business position of the source of said libel, counter-claimant Dietrich estimates that the damages caused by this concern are in the amount of 40 cents." Thornton's libel suit would ultimately be dismissed because Dietrich's statements were made in the course of a judicial proceeding and were therefore considered privileged. Still, Thornton appealed the decision to both the District Court of Appeal and the State Supreme Court, which both refused to hear it.

It took five long years to bring Steele's original charges to a jury trial. For Thornton, it was painful to go to a Los Angeles County courtroom each day to hear his reputation maligned. He sat in the court on North Hill Street, in Department 21, full of gloom, alternately feeling either sorry for himself or angry. His lawyers had pleaded with him to settle the case out of court, but he refused, demanding that they become more aggressive on his behalf. "He was a tyrant in a way," recalls Gordon F. Hampton, a lawyer who first took the case. Hampton had gained a favorable out-of-court settlement on a similar claim against Thornton by Hugh Jamieson, but Thornton removed him from the Steele case. "Tex didn't think I was aggressive enough," says Hampton. "He wanted me to make these charges of libel and slander." The lawyer insisted that a libel suit would only escalate the legal battle and would ultimately be dismissed because the statements were protected by the court. But a furious Tex prevailed. "You couldn't cross him in any respect," recalls Hampton. "He had always dominated the business scene and he thought he could do the same in law. The litigation wasn't legitimate, but Tex didn't sense the danger in the lawsuits. He didn't face up to the realities of street-fighting litigation."

The legal battle would become an unending drain on him. After years of success, it challenged Thornton in a way that no business problem ever had. He had long held a desperate hunger for validation. It was what made him push too hard at Ford and at Hughes. With Litton, he finally achieved the validation that comes with wealth and power, and now Steele and Dietrich were threatening his name with a lawsuit he could neither control nor win. He felt as helpless now as he did a decade earlier in the Amarillo courtroom.

Thornton demanded that the law function as precisely as statistics or mathematics. He knew and understood the numbers. He could exercise control over them. But he had no hold over the law. Indeed, his attorneys were pitted against a legal anarchist in Harold Rhoden who took advantage of the law's every fallibility. Rhoden represented both Steele and Dietrich, and the trio became litigation regulars. One writer, checking the court records in Los Angeles County at the time, claimed that Dietrich had been party to twenty-three lawsuits in those years, while Steele had been involved in a dozen cases.

The trial itself became so drawn out that Thornton could no longer afford to attend it. Instead, each day he dispatched to the courtroom a Litton representative who would write a brief summary of each day's proceedings. Much of Thornton's surplus energy was expended on the charges and the lawsuits. "It was a very emotionally troubled thing for my father," recalls Chuck Thornton, his eldest son who was then a student at the Harvard Business School. "They really said things that slammed my father's integrity, and it was very painful for me to hear. I sat back there and said this was nonsense and bullshit, but Dad was very troubled by it. His reputation with the Air Force was very important to him. My dad was extremely angry and felt persecuted by some slime-bag."

The charges and counter-charges were making Thornton's life difficult in other ways. Having turned down a job in Kennedy's Administration, he was now giving thought to a possible post under President Johnson. "I feel I have to get the Dietrich-Steele thing over with and buried so that some political capital cannot be made of it," he wrote to a friend in early 1965, "or try to embarrass the Administration with some of the absurd statements which Dietrich has made concerning the Hughes Aircraft days. It is unbelievable that even Dietrich would so fantastically lie and perjure himself. Since California doesn't bring perjury action in civil suits, it leaves the barn door wide open for these kinds of attacks—[the] object being, of course, money."

Finally, on April 19, 1965, a jury returned a judgment in Steele's favor by a nine-to-three vote, awarding him $7.5 million. For Thornton, it was a devastating defeat and an illogical one. Obviously, the claims were ridiculous. Steele had no basis for claiming to be a founder of Litton. But when the jury looked at Thornton, they only saw a man with deep pockets who headed up a huge corporation. Two days after the verdict, Thornton wrote of his disappointment in a letter to his old friend at Hughes Aircraft, General Ira C. Eaker, who had testified in his behalf. "General, it is unbelievable—and it makes one lose faith in our jury system—that a claim which has absolutely no basis can reach this point," he wrote. "Such unfounded suits and such tactics, I am sorry to say, are on the increase, making a mockery of our court system by using them as tools for unmerited, selfish gain."

By early 1967, Steele, Dietrich and Rhoden had filed yet another suit against Thornton seeking nearly $90 million in damages for malicious prosecution over Thornton's dismissed libel suit. When Dietrich's libel claims finally went to trial in 1968, a jury awarded him $6.1 million. But the judge again said, as in the Steele case, that he did not believe the eleven-to-one jury verdict was supported by the evidence. He dismissed the jury and announced yet another trial. The judge found that Dietrich's testimony was in several instances at odds with the facts in the case. Dietrich claimed that Breech at Ford had given Thornton a bad recommendation, saying that Tex was "overly ambitious and untrustworthy." Breech, the judge noted, never had any contact with Dietrich whatsoever.

Still, the litigation dragged on so long that a court clerk destroyed seven hundred documentary exhibits in the case, mistakenly thinking that it was already over. The legal feud outlasted Steele, who suffered a heart attack while swimming in his Beverly Hills pool and died on September 7, 1971. The original Superior Court judge who had heard the early claims also died. Finally, in January 1973, Thornton reluctantly agreed to settle the original dispute out of court by paying $2.4 million to Steele's estate. It took Thornton's attorneys nine separate conferences with yet another judge to hammer out the settlement. Through it all, Thornton insisted that it make clear he wasn't conceding anything to Steele. "This agreement is not to be construed as an admission of the contentions of any party . . . but is rather entered into for the purpose of avoiding long and costly litigation," the settlement stated.

Still remaining, however, was the libel suit brought against Thornton by Dietrich. After a third jury trial, Dietrich won a $100,000 judgment against Thornton on March 20, 1974. It was another bitter fight. Harold Rhoden, Dietrich's attorney, was particularly harsh. At one point, he ridiculed Thornton for wearing a rosette in the lapel of his suit jacket, claiming that Thornton should have won the Distinguished Service Cross during World War Two to wear the rosette, not merely the Distinguished Service Medal which Thornton had won. The cross was given to military men who were under enemy fire. Beaten and frustrated, Thornton had no intention of settling this one—especially with Dietrich. His attorneys, then led by William Masterson, had been summoned to a conference room at Litton headquarters where Thornton was refusing to accept the latest $100,000 judgment against him.

"Pay the damn thing!" advised Masterson. "Get it over. Get it behind you."

Through nearly fifteen years of legal wrangling, Thornton had spent millions of dollars in legal fees and exhausted at least a half dozen attorneys in three separate jury trials. Masterson himself had been twenty-seven years old when he first became involved in the case as a newly-minted junior lawyer who mostly carried the bags of the lead attorney. Now he was forty-two, a seasoned trial lawyer, and had handled the third jury trial himself; and still Thornton wanted to file yet another appeal.

"You don't know what this has done to me and my family," Thornton muttered. "You don't know."

"I know exactly what it's done to you and your family because I know what it's done to my own family," Masterson replied. "I'm sensitive about it."

During the course of the litigation, the attorney had divorced his wife and remarried but had had to postpone his honeymoon because of the trial. He had developed a tic in his left eye over the pressure. He believed the trial judge would set aside even the $100,000 award, but he didn't think it was worth still more litigation. He told Thornton that he had discovered Flora sobbing in the hallway of the courtroom during a break in the closing arguments of the trial.

"Goddammit!" shouted Thornton. "We hired every goddamn lawyer in the United States and Rhoden has kicked the shit out of every goddamn one of them!"

Masterson, who considered the $100,000 verdict a victory since the previous trial resulted in a $6.1 million judgment against Thornton, stood up from the conference table and walked out. "I went downstairs at Litton headquarters, smoked a couple of cigarettes, kicked a few stones and went back and finished the conference," he recalled. "But that was the end of it for me and Tex, and I never saw any business from Litton again. You just didn't walk out on him, no matter what."

Thornton finally agreed to pay the $100,000 judgment to the eighty-five-year-old Dietrich ending the long ordeal in 1974. But the litigation took its toll. "These cases almost killed him," says Masterson, now a Superior Court Judge. "He bore them personally."

AT LITTON, THE problems continued to mount. In fiscal 1972, Litton barely eked out a profit of $1.1 million on more than $2 billion of sales. The company took $70 million in write-offs for consolidations, relocations and special expenses due partly to the shipbuilding problems. An acrimonious dispute emerged with the U.S. Navy over a contract to build amphibious assault ships. There were huge cost overruns and long delays on the contract and Litton fell years behind schedule. The Navy ordered costly changes in the ship's design that contributed to the problems, but Litton also had failed to account for the high rate of inflation in the years after the contract was signed.

Years later, as Ash reviewed his times with Tex, he acknowledged that the shipbuilding business was more than they had bargained for. "The shipbuilding problems dragged on and on," he said. "In retrospect, it was absolutely a mistake to have bought the shipyard. It was the biggest single mistake Litton made. Once we were in it, we learned you can't close down a shipyard very easily because of the diseconomies that come from building ships. You have to keep a crew around. It kills you. We had to learn about shipbuilding and we didn't learn what we should have at the time."

Some of the outside directors urged Tex to move Ash aside. But Tex couldn't do it. He blamed himself as much as anyone for Litton's troubles. He had become distracted enough to allow Ash to run the company virtually on his own. Years later, Tex's friends would dismiss Ash as little more than a numbers cruncher, an inferior clone of Bob McNamara. But Tex understandably felt a strong bond with the man who had worked by his side for more than twenty years. They had been loyal to each other through the problems at Hughes and through all the ups-and-downs at Litton.

To Thornton, loyalty was as much if not more important than talent. "Everything about his personality was based on loyalty," says William George, who spent nine years at Litton. "To quit the company was a personal thing with Tex, not a business decision. It was like a son leaving home. You abandoned the family." In the years that George ran Litton's microwave oven division, Tex only visited the facility twice. Once was to convince George not to leave the company. "Tex was personally hurt when I left," adds George. " 'How could you leave without talking to me?' he asked. 'How could you do this?' You could see the hurt in his eyes."

Tex was not about to boot out Ash. "It was one of those areas where Tex's loyalty to somebody caused a problem," believes Robert Lentz, a Litton vice president. "Had he moved a number of years earlier to replace Roy as chief operating officer, I think some of these problems could have been avoided. Yet, I never heard Tex blame Roy for the company's troubles."

Ash, however, must have sensed the growing tension enough to accept an offer from President Nixon to become the new director of the Office of Management and Budget. And Thornton, the college dropout who displayed little but awe for the educated people who always surrounded him, came to realize that education could not guarantee success nor prevent failure. Ash, thought to be the only MBA from the Harvard Business School without a single day of undergraduate study to his credit, seemed the source of Tex's disillusioning realization. "Tex always felt sorry for me because I never had an education," recalls his step-brother John Lewis, who successfully pursued a business career without a college diploma. "As he got older, he pulled away from it. He'd say Harvard was too liberal and wasn't teaching people the facts of life. He became extremely proud of my own success and he became very disappointed in some others who were highly educated but didn't produce for him."

Tex would pick Fred O'Green, an extreme opposite of Ash, to succeed his friend. Where O'Green had gotten his hands dirty in operations, Ash was largely a financial analyst. Where O'Green had a no-nonsense personality, Ash was cerebral.

When Tex tapped O'Green, Thornton insisted on establishing the man's loyalty and dedication to him and the company.

"You can't have one foot in and one foot out," Tex told him. "There's no such thing as half way. You've got to put both feet in or out."

He asked what O'Green might do if other opportunities came his way.

"Tex, I'm not going to sit here and tell you I'm not going to talk to anybody if they call," O'Green told him. "What the hell! If somebody down the street offers me twice as much to do the same thing and live in the same house, do you think I'm going to sit here? First of all, you wouldn't want me to do this if you really want to give me this job. You wouldn't take it under those circumstances. But there's one thing I would never do: I won't hang you out to die."

O'Green was named president. Ash was out, his escape made respectable by President Nixon. Litton's stock climbed steadily following his departure. Ash's last official appearance as president was at the company's shareholders meeting on December 10, 1972. Compared to previous sessions, it was a gathering marked by gloom. There were no cheers and no applause. A somber Thornton told the audience that the company posted $22 million in profits in the last two quarters and that that "is some indication that we are moving in the right direction."

He promised still further acquisitions that would fit into the company's mainstream product lines. "Those of you who have known Litton for many years will recognize that this statement sounds familiar and you are exactly right," Tex said. "Our basic plan is not cheating, but based on our broad expertise during the years, we are evaluating all areas of our business and taking action where indicated to further strengthen the company. During the next eighteen months you will see the evidence and results of this action—we believe you will approve."

One shareholder who had been promised a chance to be heard when the previous year's annual meeting was adjourned stepped up to a microphone after Thornton had picked her out of the crowd. The woman said that if she had been recognized a year earlier she would have suggested that Litton sell some unprofitable companies. "Well," she said, "you've done that and this year things are so bad that I have nothing further to say."

That said it all. As the size of Litton grew, Thornton needed to find more and more deals just to maintain growth. His efforts to extend the Litton magic only brought him into companies and markets further afield from his early technological core. Tex did not understand that every time you buy a business, you also buy a set of problems. The more you buy, the more problems you acquire. The sheer complexity of managing all these problems and the distractions of a host of outside commitments ultimately defeated him.

Shortly before his death in 1981, Tex rides his favorite horse on one of his two ranches. By now, Litton is thoroughly discredited as little more than a numbers game, and conglomerates are out of favor. The weekend rides through the hills of his property ultimately became his only release from the building pressure on him and his company.

Bob McNamara with his wife, Margy, in the garden of their Washington, D.C., home, after Bob became head of the World Bank.

Chapter 31

A REUNION

■

"Men of the very highest distinction are dependent upon their
times. Not all of them have lived
in the age which they deserved;
and, many, even though they did
so, failed to take advantage of it."
—BALTASAR GRACIÁN

*M*ore than three decades had passed since the men
had met Henry Ford. Yet a sense of fraternity
among them persisted through the years. Informed by long-distance conversation and letters, they remained close, particularly a core of them:
Thornton, McNamara, Miller, Lundy and Wright.

The others had either drifted to the edges of the group or died. Charlie Bosworth had gone his own way, living in Santa Barbara after his
retirement from Ford in 1965. Tex would hear of him only through the
tailor in Los Angeles the two shared. Ben Mills, who left Ford in 1971,
would stay in touch with Wright, his neighbor in Sea Island, but otherwise led the typical life of retirement in both isolation and contentment.
With the exception of Tex, who still ruled Litton, and Bob, who remained president of the World Bank, they had all retired from their full-
time jobs, though Ed and Arjay now served on Litton's board of directors. The three remaining original members of the group—Reith, Moore

and Andreson—had become life's casualties. Andreson died in 1979 from cancer.

In late 1980, Tex Thornton had been talking with several of his friends about a reunion. No final decision had been made on where it would be held: maybe Washington, where the partnership was forged so many years ago; maybe Detroit, where they had become the Quiz Kids and the Whiz Kids. In any case, Thornton was hoping to bring the men and their wives together for a celebration. It would be just another grand party, like the good old days when the group gathered in the Foundation apartments for fun and drinks.

Tex exchanged letters and phone calls with Ed and Arjay and Jim about the event. "Arjay, I mentioned to Ed that January 30, 1981, is the thirty-fifth anniversary when the ten of us went to Detroit," wrote Tex in a letter to Miller. "In one way, it seems that it was only yesterday. Our lives and careers were certainly influenced by that association." He wrote about the possibility of flying all of them to Los Angeles for the gathering, and he talked about tracking down Charlie.

But the planning came to an abrupt halt when he spoke to Bob McNamara in Washington. Margy lay in a hospital bed dying of cancer. He knew that she had not been well. But he did not know that her time was running out. It happened suddenly. She and Bob were going to ski at Aspen the previous February. Margy flew out on a Monday, and McNamara was to follow her two days later. She called him and said, "Bob, I don't think I can ski." She was in terrible pain, and her doctor already had urged her to rush home immediately. "No way," she said, "Bob is coming out."

But she returned home, was later diagnosed as having cancer and underwent surgery for the removal of her lung. When Tex was planning the event, Bob sadly told him the doctors predicted that Margy had only thirty days, perhaps less, to live. McNamara, disgusted at the insensitive treatment accorded terminal cancer patients, had signed her out of the hospital and set up a makeshift hospital room on the second floor of their home. He hired nurses to care for his wife twenty-four hours a day. They pumped two hundred milligrams of Demerol in her daily to ease the pain.

Still, Margy told him that he should go to the reunion, no matter what. "Even if I die that day, you're going," she told him. But Thornton knew that the group could never meet under that shadow so he decided to postpone the reunion until the summer when McNamara's ordeal would likely be past. And then, Tex thought: no, he couldn't do that.

There was magic and importance in the date. January 29 was the start of that long and wonderful partnership, so a reunion would have to wait for another year.

Margaret Craig McNamara died on February 3, 1981, at home. Only two weeks earlier, the President awarded her the Medal of Freedom, the country's highest civilian honor, for her work with Reading Is Fundamental, the nonprofit group that encourages underprivileged children to read. At first, Bob did not want her to attend the ceremony. "I said, 'Marg, you can't go to the White House,'" McNamara later recalled. "And she said, 'Oh, yes, I can and oh, yes, I am.' Well, goddamn, she did lovely. I had this seven-passenger caddy limousine and we got her into that thing, just rolled the damn wheelchair right up, and all of us piled in and went down there to Mr. Reagan's White House. Of course she looked like death's own self. She used to hallucinate from the medicine, and on the way down she said, 'Bob, what is that camel doing out there?' I said, 'Oh, honey, he's just out there.' Isn't that something? A goddamn camel."

Nine months after Margy's death, Thornton brought the group together one last time. It was not, however, a reunion they would celebrate.

TEX THORNTON FIRST began to feel some discomfort in his left shoulder in late April only two or three months after Margy's funeral. At first, he thought it was a simple sprain from lifting a heavy suitcase on a business trip. But when he went to the Ingalls shipyard for the dedication of the Litton-built *U.S.S. Ticonderoga* in mid-May, the pain had not gone away. Indeed, just as he rose from a chair to introduce Nancy Reagan, there to christen the ship, the pain was so great he nearly fainted. What he thought was a sprain had escalated into "bursitis" and then a "pinched nerve"—except the pain failed to disappear. He went to several doctors, including an orthopedic surgeon, who initially had trouble making a diagnosis until finally came the news that it was cancer.

Tex called Arjay Miller in June to tell him, though Miller had suspected something was wrong. When he last saw Tex in the spring at a board meeting, the man didn't seem right. "I remember always shaking his right hand," Miller says. "He had a strong, vigorous grip. When I reached out to grab it that time, he pulled his hand away because he said it hurt."

On the telephone, Miller could hear Tex's voice waver. "He was very distraught," he recalls. "He wanted to make some changes in the company, getting his son Chuck on the board of directors. He clearly was getting the company in shape to survive his death. He sobbed in the end and said he had planned to call Ed and Bob, but asked me to call for him."

By mid-July, some final tests at the M.D. Anderson Clinic in Houston confirmed that his bone cancer was invading the rest of his body. At first, Thornton seemed ready to overcome the disease, as if it were merely another obstacle. His mother had died of cancer, but Tex knew other friends who had beaten the disease and he thought he could do the same. He refused to speak of his illness as if it were fatal. He started chemotherapy treatments and gave up smoking. But his discipline lasted all of a month.

"Dad, why are you smoking again?" asked Laney, his youngest son. "I thought you were going to lick this."

"Ah, what's the use?" he said.

"He didn't want to die, but he became resigned to it," Laney recalls. "My brother and I went up to his room once because we had gotten the results of the latest scan. This was after he had some chemotherapy and it showed that the cancer had spread a whole bunch. His reaction was, 'Oh gee, I was afraid of that. Doggone it.' But he didn't start crying or throwing things across the room. He was being a big man about it, strong in the face of it, but also very human about it."

Not knowing how much time he had left, Thornton began to confront what he had put aside for years: his decision to relinquish his job. For Tex, whose identity was so intertwined with Litton, it was as difficult a task as any. Yet there was a time when a younger and bolder Thornton had talked up the virtues of youthful management. "I'm convinced that if all men fifty and over were eliminated as directors and top officers of companies, this country would have the biggest overnight economic boom in its history," he once told a journalist. "We need younger, more visionary men in industry. That's why I say get rid of everyone fifty and over. We might miss 20 percent of them, but the other 80 percent would be good riddance."

Yet he could never bring himself to take his own advice. He told his friends he would step down at the age of fifty-five, but when that deadline fast approached he couldn't let go. His own reluctance to make room for others resulted in the departure of scores of top Litton executives, including Harry Gray who had joined Litton in 1954. When Thornton turned fifty-eight years old in 1971, a frustrated Gray began to entertain an offer to join what would become United Technologies. "I had given him three years past his own self-proclaimed retirement age," says Gray.

"[Still] he was very upset about my job offer from United. He talked to me all day, from nine o'clock in the morning until just about supper. And I kept asking him, 'What are you going to do about your plan to retire?' And he kept not answering the question. I made the inquiry six times. I said, 'Just give me a time frame. I don't care if you're telling me it's going to be three to five years. But I've got to have one.' The key point was that he wouldn't. I came to the conclusion then that he would die in the job." After seventeen years at Litton, Gray finally quit the company in 1971.

Now, even while bedridden awaiting his death, he refused to yield full control to Fred O'Green, who had helped him turn around the company. He would make O'Green chief executive, but would hold on to the title of chairman until his death. Indeed, it was difficult to give up any role. Barney Oldfield, Litton's public relations chief at the time, recalls that he and George Fenimore, an old Stat Control hand, were asked to draft the announcement officially making O'Green chief.

"We're at about $5 billion in sales and $300,000 in earnings, and he had a lot to do with our being able to say that," Thornton told Oldfield. "I want that to be the tone of the release, upbeat; a dynamic company on the way to bigger things, and Fred the man to keep us rolling."

"Hasn't he been at least consulted?" Oldfield asked.

"Not today."

But as the three men began to draft the release, it became clear that Tex hadn't called Oldfield in for a simple story for the media. "It became the longest press release session we ever had," recalled Oldfield. "He really wanted to talk his life out, telling all the anecdotes he knew about the people in his life. He wanted to go through it one more time."

The meetings dragged on for three straight days, but Tex still could not bring himself to approve an acceptable version. "He'd say, 'Yeah, that's about right,' after reading the first paragraph, and then he'd say, 'but I think we can do it better.' Then, he would go off and tell story after story. I think we went through seventeen different versions of the press release before he finally settled on one."

Thornton called O'Green in to read him the statement, joking that it was too late to back out now. Then Thornton began telephoning the board members to gain their approval of the decision. It was his board, after all, and no one on it would disagree with the choice: not his Whiz Kids colleagues Ed Lundy, Arjay Miller, and Jim Wright or anyone else who sat on the Litton board. The announcement was made August 4; O'Green became CEO on October 1.

Tex's appearances at work became more infrequent. When he did show up, it was to set in place things for the continuance of the company. There were a few more assignments of people, a couple of board nominations, things like that. He worked with his son, Chuck, and his lawyer, Clarence Price, on estate details. Flora set him up in an upstairs bedroom at their home in the Los Angeles suburb of Holmby Hills. On September 1, the board of directors saw a worn, afflicted Thornton preside over his last board meeting. Ransom Cook did a humorous monologue about the Thornton he had known years earlier when he lent him the money to buy out Charlie Litton. Thornton was in a weepy, sentimental mood, asking that his son, Chuck, be named to the board. Chuck had more than fifty thousand shares of Litton stock and soon would be voting many times more.

Still, Tex felt pretty good that day, good enough to walk some four or five blocks to his barber for a haircut. But the next day the physical exertion of the outing put him in tremendous pain. After the meeting, Tex never had another business discussion with the man who would become his successor. He made another short appearance in the office on September 17, slowly walking across Litton Plaza and struggling up the steps to his office. He dictated a few letters to his secretary and left the office early, never to return. The cancer was spreading violently and swiftly, seeping into his bone marrow, causing the bones to crack until the pain became unbearable. To lessen it they filled him with morphine that made him delirious.

Two days later, Thornton received a call at home from Michael Deaver, President Reagan's assistant. Tex counted Ronald Reagan as a friend in California and had even contributed $10,000 to Nancy Reagan's project to redecorate the White House six months earlier. When he was told the White House was calling, Thornton painfully got out of bed and stood barefoot as Deaver invited him to the White House a week later to receive the Medal of Freedom from the President. It was the highest civilian honor given in the country—an honor given to the likes of Helen Keller, Walt Disney and Aaron Copeland and one that Margy McNamara had received only a year earlier before her death.

Deeply touched, Tex said bravely: "I'll be there!"

But it was impossible for Thornton, now a thin and withered man, to make the trip. So Flora and his two sons went to Washington to pick up the honor at a White House luncheon on October 9, 1981. It would have been an emotional day, whether or not Tex was about to die. His condition only heightened the award's impact.

Before Chuck went to the podium to receive the award for his father, the President read the citation: "To Charles B. "Tex" Thornton, industrialist, warrior and humanitarian. Tex Thornton's life has embodied all that is best in the worlds of commerce, military service and civic duty. In all three realms, he has never failed to give generously of his boundless energy, his unfailing courage and his deep love of country. In war and peace, in the public service and the private sector, Tex Thornton has earned the esteem of all Americans who value patriotism, enterprise and compassion as cornerstones of our nation's greatness."

Chuck went up, shook the President's hand and stood before the small crowd in the east room of the White House.

"Thank you, Mr. President," he said, his eyes misty. "I'm privileged to accept this award on behalf of my father who as you know could not be here today. He wanted very much to come, however. He asked me to tell you, though, that he feels very fortunate to have had the opportunities afforded by this great country of ours and to have been able to serve it and strive to contribute to its success. Perhaps only those who matured in the last Depression as he did can best appreciate just how far we as a nation have come in the last half century and the effort and sacrifice it took to get here.

"Even though his active role is drawing to a close, he is grateful to have played a part. He recognizes that the challenges before us remain enormous. Yet he is confident that this nation's new leadership will guide us on the proper course, a course which does not reject the past of which he has played a part but which lets us build on our accomplishments and learn from our mistakes. I can think of no one more respected by him than you, Mr. President. It is therefore deeply touching that you have honored him in this way. And that makes this award all the more meaningful to him, to our mother and to the two younger generations of our family here today. Thank you."

The family had asked the White House to tape the ceremony so that Tex could be shown it at home as he lay in his sick bed. When they returned to California and showed him what he missed, he was moved to cry. He watched it several times before he could no longer comprehend what it was that he watched. Indeed, when he slipped into a depression, Chuck would joke: "If you don't perk up, I'm gonna replay that tape of me accepting your medal!" Tex would smile and put his hands to his face to ward the sadness off.

His condition, however, swiftly deteriorated. He began to refuse all outside visitors, even long-time friends like George Fenimore, who had been with Tex through everything: Stat Control, Ford, Hughes and Litton. Thornton had fallen into a constant state of confusion, not knowing where he was nor whom he saw. And in his final month, he could barely recognize his own sons at his bedside who were sadly trying to evoke from him in his last few months a lifetime of wisdom and memory.

Their image of their father was largely of a man who had never felt pain or fear. Now they watched the image crumble and the strong man waste away. "My father and I talked a lot when he was dying and, literally, I was just pumping him," says Chuck. "It was more 'how did this happen? how did that happen?' And of course after he died I thought of a hundred things I forgot to ask him about. I remember once asking, 'Well what was Henry like. 'Henry was okay,' he said. 'He just always believed the last person he talked to.' I don't think he disliked Henry. Dad seemed willing to give him the preogative of ownership."

Laney, Tex's youngest son, sat next to his father, held his hand and listened to the stories pour out as well. Only weeks before the diagnosis of cancer, Laney had made peace with him. More than Chuck, who worked with Tex at Litton for several years, Laney had felt estranged from his father. Thornton would say how important it was for the family to be together. He would go on and on about it. Yet he was hardly ever around. He was distant and often disapproving—especially when Laney decided to launch, with a clothing designer, a women's apparel company in San Francisco that sold to upscale retailers like Bloomingdales and Nordstroms.

Thornton was skeptical of it just as he had been of his son's early jobs in small firms in Cambridge after Laney had gotten his Harvard MBA. "He just didn't see this business having much value," remembers Laney, "and compared to what he was doing it didn't have any value. He said, 'Just shut it down. Forget you ever started it, just shut it down.' I was offended and hurt. For whatever reason, this was available for me to do and it was manufacturing. It was what my dad did. I wanted to do it. I felt comfortable doing it. Yet this was something that he thought wasn't worthwhile. It was hard. He never shared his vision of business with me, with the exception that he told me what I was doing was wrong. I would ask him for advice, and he would ask me some pointed questions on something like insurance for garments in transit. I said, 'Well I think we're covered,' and he said, 'What, you don't know? Well you've got to have insurance. Why don't you just give up the business?' "

Laney had borrowed heavily from the bank. Then, when the company fell into the red, he borrowed more cash to fund the losses. Tex got wind of it and summoned him to Los Angeles over a weekend. He made a fuss over the situation and tried again to talk his son out of it; but when

Tex realized it wasn't possible, his attitude quickly changed. He ended up lending Laney the money he needed to sustain the company, and the two of them spent an entire day talking about every detail of Laney's business. The company's problems began to absorb Tex. He gave his son advice on getting expenses in line. He told him about the need to keep inventories low. Of course, the advice was not the most important thing. On that day, his son had finally established a relationship with his father. Not long after that weekend at home, Tex was diagnosed as having cancer.

"There are just all those things that we never talked about," says Laney, "that I wish I knew his point of view on. I always wished I had engaged him more." Laney can still vividly remember one of his last conversations with his father, when Tex was still lucid and upright in his bed. "I went to his room upstairs, and I said, 'Dad, I've always had a lot of respect for your values. Where do you get them? Where did they come from?' He said, 'Well you know it was living with my mother in a poor country town. We had to make everything that we lived on. Son, whatever you do, don't try to copy what I did. I was very lucky.'"

It was the last coherent conversation that Laney would have with his father. Just before midnight on November 24, 1981, Tex quietly died after having fallen in a final coma the previous day. If he taught them anything during the hours of conversation in his final weeks, he showed them how to face death.

FLORA HAD SPOKEN to him about a military funeral, but Thornton did not like the idea. Tex had a grave site picked out years earlier in Thousand Oaks. But the family decided that Tex deserved more than that. The Distinguished Service Medal he was given in 1946 for his work in Stat Control entitled him to internment at Arlington Cemetery. "We were really proud of him and wanted him to have a military funeral in Arlington," said Laney. "Washington D.C. was where my brother and I were born, where [my parents] were married, where I was married and where my wife was born." It was also where Tex had made a name for himself and had formed the partnership that brought him so many rewards throughout his life.

After a brief service at All Saints Episcopal Church in Beverly Hills on November 30, his body was flown to Washington on an American Airlines jet for burial on December 2. It was a cold and cloudy day—weather for overcoats.

Five of the six surviving Whiz Kids were there along with Mimi

Moore. Ben and Jim and their wives arrived in a car provided by Litton. As soon as Bob saw them, he rushed over to join his old friends. "It was an awfully sad trip," remembers Wright. "We were all shaken by Tex's death." Only Charlie Bosworth, who had long ago lost touch with the group, failed to show. There was George H. Mahon, the former congressman and long-time friend who had helped Tex get his first job in Washington. Nancy Reagan arrived in a small, unmarked car, and immediately went to Flora's side.

The funeral home attendants brought his flag-draped coffin to the spot where the cortege was forming. It was lifted from the hearse and transferred to the black artillery caisson behind six gray horses. A jet black caparisoned horse followed, wearing an empty saddle with a pair of boots reversed in the stirrups—a symbol of the fallen leader who will never ride again.

A commander and honor guards led the procession to the grave site, followed by a fifty-piece U.S. Army ceremonial band and two platoons of the Old Guard. The chaplain paced ahead of the riderless horse as the band played "Onward Christian Soldiers." The procession came to a halt at a high portion of the rolling grounds that Chuck had selected weeks earlier for his father's grave. The Pentagon could be viewed less than a half mile away. It was less than five miles from the place where Tex and Flora had first met and were later married.

The honor platoon and band set into position, and the men from several uniformed services carried Tex the last few steps. Family and friends then crowded under a tent erected at the grave site. Ben and Helen sat directly behind Mrs. Reagan. After a short service conducted by the military chaplain, the commander of the honor platoon shouted orders to a firing party of seven men. Three hollow shots rang out. A lone bugler sounded taps. After a brief silence, the soldiers marched to the casket, gently took the flag in their gloved hands and quickly folded it. A general presented the flag to Flora. In a quiet voice, almost a whisper, he told her it represented the nation's thanks for Thornton's services. Each calculated step of the funeral ritual had the same logic, consistency and orderliness that the men had sought in their lives.

There was a reception for the fifty or so people who had come to witness the funeral. Like most post-funeral receptions, it was an awkward, quiet and subdued affair. Friends and acquaintances whispered their condolences. Some of them wistfully reminisced about decades-old occurrences, events that caught the meaning of a person's life. Still, death can impose an odd silence in a room. "There wasn't a lot of talk," remembers Miller, who had flown in with Fran from California for the funeral. "Close friends didn't have to do a lot of talking. We had been so close for so long. We realized we lost a good friend and a great leader."

If many words didn't come out, the men traced memories that had surfaced from oblivion, the kinds of things you don't think about until you lose someone who meant so much to the path your life followed. Bob McNamara thought back to his first meeting with Tex in the dean's office at Harvard: how a young man spoke with such confidence and authority and vision. Ben Mills considered the time that Tex, fired from Ford, asked the men if they would one day join him elsewhere and there was silence. Jim Wright searched through all the contrasting pictures in his mind: one of a young Tex Thornton in Washington before the war without a job; another of him on the cover of *Time* magazine as one of the wealthiest men in America. Arjay Miller could still gleefully recall his very first encounter with Thornton, bumping into him on a volleyball court in war-torn Washington.

Imprinted in Ed Lundy's mind was the last time he saw Tex at his home, worn and in pain. It hurt him to see as strong a man as Tex in so weakened a state. A couple of years earlier, he had written Tex a letter that displayed his admiration for him. "Someone has said that a friend is a present you give to yourself," he wrote on May 23, 1979. "I think I was lavish with myself when I first met you at Harvard." To Mimi Moore, Tex had become more than a friend—something of a concerned older brother. Tex was there for her not only after George died, but also after her second husband passed away. She remembered how Tex conferred with her lawyers to make sure she could manage okay. He wanted to be sure that all her children got through college. He even hired her son at Litton, giving him a start after his graduation from college. "Tex was a giant, an inspiration and a good and kind man," she said. Mimi chatted with Chuck Thornton, who fondly recalled the day her husband George surprised Tex and his family with a new car on Christmas morning.

It was both fitting and ironic that Tex would end his journey in Washington. He had come to love the West, overwhelmed by its vastness and beauty. He spent hundreds of hours piloting his plane over the flatness of it and hundreds more atop his horse in the open land. But it was here in Washington where he had set the foundation blocks for his life. It was here that he showed he could lead; here that he married Flora and had his two sons; here that he formed the group that would so influence his life and the lives of nine other men. Washington closed the loop.

THEY WERE DIFFERENT men with common qualities and ambitions, all seeking to play important roles on the postwar stage. Would they have risen to achieve similar things without Tex Thornton? It was obviously possible, but it also was obviously unlikely. It took a war to break the pattern of their lives, to be fused into a team by a single man and to discover within themselves resources and abilities they had not known existed. Ten friends, cohorts on a unique journey, they had all the benefits of shared misery and joint effort, of how the group gave each of them a greater chance of making it than they had on their own.

There was a funny thing about their early friendship together, too. Even though they had grown and sought their own paths in the world, they still maintained their identification with the original group. Whenever an article was written on one of them it almost always noted that he was a member of the Whiz Kids at Ford. Every Thornton obituary prominently noted the appellation, and every person who ever worked for them considered himself or herself, in some way, a Whiz Kid, too. It was the root of both their successes and their failures.

They had come a long way from obscurity to prominence in America's golden age, its short-lived century of dominance in the world. Their wizardry had gained them worldwide fame and renown. Their unique story had become part of business lore. By any measure, they had been an extraordinary and unprecedented group. Six of them had become Ford vice presidents and two of them—McNamara and Miller—had served Henry Ford II as president before making waves in the worlds of government and academia. Three of the ten—Thornton, Andreson and Wright—moved on to become presidents and chief executives of other major American companies. Two of them—Tex Thornton and George Moore—brought public on the stock exchanges companies they founded and cultivated.

They came of age in a managerial time when business was the new professional frontier. And they became ministers of a management theology that sought numerative and analytical justification for all decisions Tex and his men did not originate rigorous and dispassionate analysis. They did not invent the rigid financial controls that would largely emerge as the basis for corporate decision-making. Indeed, not all of them completely subscribed to those key tenets of modern management. But they generally embraced those notions, perfected them and popularized them. The revolution they spawned in the Air Force and at Ford spread to all of government and American business.

Not all would have such an enthusiastic view of their contribution. Tom Peters and Robert Waterman, the authors of *In Search of Excellence*, decried what they called the rational model of management. "Its wizards," they wrote, "were the Ford Motor Company's whiz kids, and its grand panjandrum was Robert McNamara." The rational model was "dangerously wrong" and had led American business "seriously astray" in the 1970s and 1980s, aiding Japan in gaining a significant competitive advantage.

In 1980, the small nation that these ten men had fought to defeat became the world's largest producer of cars, trucks and buses. Slightly more than one of every four cars sold in the U.S. that year were foreign. Meanwhile, Ford Motor reported a loss of $1.5 billion in 1980, at the time setting a record for the largest loss in American corporate history. Like so many other U.S. companies, Ford had become a victim of the rational model propagated by the Whiz Kids and their powerful legend. Engineering and production—what had made U.S. industry and Ford a leader in the first place—had become secondary to finance. Too little attention was paid to innovation and superior products and too much to producing good-looking numbers. Senior management had become dominated by too many "financial types" who had little if any experience in running anything. Even among the Big Three in Detroit, Ford was rated dead last in the quality and styling of its cars. That would change, but only after the tight financial controls were renounced and put into balance with the engineering and manufacturing skills critical to producing quality products.

If Bob McNamara could have foreseen his future, he would have had to say how disillusioning it all was. He still generally refused to talk about Vietnam. It was a dark part of his life that he preferred not to openly confront. During the height of the conflict, Arlington averaged thirty-five military funerals a day. The sad truth was, there would be fewer names on the wall of the Vietnam Memorial in Washington if not for McNamara's early enthusiasm for the war. He had led the U.S. into a distant, horrifying war that divided a country, a war so painful and tragic that it clearly is one of the greatest blunders in the history of the U.S. government. Vietnam had become a metaphor for futility. The confidence in America's right and trust in America's power that were the legacy of World War Two collapsed in the face of ambiguity and defeat in Vietnam.

It was not unlike the symbolic impact of the Edsel, the ugly car that came out of Jack's overly ambitious plan at Ford. One anti-McNamara cartoon in 1964 featured the Edsel as the government's "Present U.S.

Policy in Vietnam." Bob was a passenger in the car, with President Johnson in the driver's seat. The caption: ". . . Bob, it'll never sell." If Vietnam had become a metaphor of futility, the Edsel had become the synonym for failure in the business world. The subtext of nearly every commercial catastrophe in the postwar era became the Edsel, whether it was the Susan B. Anthony dollar coin or New Coke.

At Thornton's death, Litton Industries was just another weary, out-of-fashion conglomerate. Tex was called an "illusionist," a financial conjurer whose temporary success was founded largely on the gullibility of Wall Street and its investors. Jack Reith, given to flashes of brilliance and poor judgment, had become a suicide victim. The youngest of them, George, who had scrambled to establish his own independence and fortune, virtually drank himself to death. Andy, who had suffered through a string of illnesses, had died as well, two years earlier. It was not long after he had been fired from the company he once called home. In retirement, Jim was still bitter that Henry chose Arjay over him. He still could not understand it. Charlie Bosworth, too, carried the injustice of being passed over in favor of Ben Mills. He did not attend the funeral because he no longer felt any kinship with the group.

THE IMPERFECT
WORLD THEY
LEFT US

■

*E*ven today, decades after the Whiz Kids reached the height of
their powers, we live in their shadows. We work in organizations they shaped; we made decisions based on the logic and reason they
preached. If our expectations differ, our ambitions and ideals do not. We
want to reinvent or reengineer the world into the same perfect place they
unsuccessfully sought to create.

Yet we're still battling the concepts and ideas of these earnest men of
the World War Two generation—the group that made dominant and
worldwide what Peter Drucker calls the Management Revolution from
1945 to 1990. Through legend and hype, they had become prototypes of
modern managers to hundreds of thousands of business executives. They
were emulated because they were perceived to be among the most successful business professionals of their era. The Whiz Kids became architects of a new economic order that valued analysis over experience, numbers over intuition, facts over emotion.

They were honorable, even heroic men who emerged from the war justly proud of what they had achieved. If the system they pioneered could crush the Axis, why not use it to defeat business rivals? That was the message Tex Thornton and his Army Air Force officers brought to Ford in their telegram in 1945, and that was the gospel spread by his Whiz Kids over decades. But with the system came this one killer side effect: managers became more responsible to each other than to customers.

Still, it worked well enough in a business world dominated by the U.S. But this model began to fail as American hegemony slipped away. Rapid change, not devotion to some internal order, is now the imperative. Old-style managers simply can't make the radical breaks needed to extend their success into the future. No wonder taps is being played in corporate corridors for this whole way of doing business that was modeled on the command-and-control procedures of the military. Nonetheless, the Whiz Kids' approach to business is still largely taught and practiced in most business schools and corporations.

Today's progressive managers are fighting the systems and attitudes put in place by the Whiz Kids and their stumbling descendants—from the belief that a good manager can manage anything to the notion that out of the numbers will come the answers. Our infatuation with those ideas led to the creation of massive staffs of detached professionals whose only job was to police the work of others. In some ways, we're unlearning what the Whiz Kids taught us.

Still, old habits die hard. It wasn't until late 1991 when Ford Motor abandoned the policy that all vice presidents send their memos on special blue paper while nearly everyone else use plain white. The practice—set in the 1940s by the Whiz Kids—was deemed pretentious and wasteful by an operating executive who beat out a lifelong finance man and Lundy protégé to become the most likely candidate to seize the next chairmanship of Ford. At the guys' old stomping grounds at least, experience in the trenches has won over dazzling analysis in the office.

A CYNIC MIGHT SAY that it was as if the Whiz Kids had taken a lifetime of learning, drive and ambition, only to become the modern-day goats of business. Why did it end this way? Why couldn't they have had it all? What do their mistakes teach us? In part, they failed because they were a little too confident, a little too brilliant. They began to believe what everyone said: that they were Whiz Kids. Whiz Kids didn't make mistakes. They have the answers and the unbridled confidence to believe in them. They could organize and run huge companies, build corporate empires and conquer government. They could, in short, forge a perfect world, based on logic, reason and rationalization.

No wonder so many of them fell short of their ambitions. It was because each man grew into a myth of himself. Bob McNamara, ever so cool, ever so tough, ended up shouting at the demonstrators at Harvard: "I was tougher than you . . ." Yet he wasn't tough enough to admit a mistake, or tough enough to encourage dissent from within. Tex Thornton, the ultimate empire builder, was strutting around Washington, in and out of briefings, meetings and White House dinners, thinking his success was assured and his work done at Litton. Jack Reith, a man of the 1950s, who measured his happiness with the singular goal of being on top, found that too much ambition can kill you. George Moore was always wanting more for himself, yet never quite measured up to either the myth or the reality of the group's superiority. And Arjay Miller and Ed Lundy, the Ford financial wizards, proved themselves to be so full of hubris and arrogance that they could never understand how the financial organization they built at Ford was destroying the company they loved. Their finance staff overwhelmed every other part of Ford, turning down badly needed investments to maintain quality, until the late 1980s when the company finally realized it was in the business of making cars, not merely money.

WHAT DO THEIR mistakes teach us? There are both simple and complex lessons to learn. These professionals found a pattern for success. Throughout their lives, they created groups of the best and brightest they could find, forced them to see business through a lens that captured little more than numbers, and then required that all decisions be based on those same figures. For a time, it worked. For a time, business and government badly needed rational organization and analysis. For a time, the Whiz Kids may have created a perfect world. What was right at one time, however, became overapplied, misused and advocated to an extreme. The solution for one day became the solution for many. Locked into this pattern, they kept reapplying the same techniques, unable to adapt, unable to admit mistakes—even when their world had changed.

Not only could they not adapt, but they were unaware that their ideas of how to manage large organizations had become self-sustaining, carried out to the extremes by people—like them—who wanted to get ahead. Each manager in every tiny box of the organization chart was reinforcing the behaviors of another, until the organization was more caught up by the process of the numbers than the end product. The upshot: the American corporation was wobbling out of balance, overwhelmed by a new professional ethic that made statistics all-important.

The Whiz Kids and the mythology they created led a generation of business professionals not only to put their faith in numbers, but to blindly follow the numbers as if they were commandments. At Ford Motor and many other companies, this new ethos came to life in the financial area. Other functions outside of finance which should have brought balance to rational application were smothered by it as well. For decades, the best and brightest produced by the business schools assumed jobs not in manufacturing or in engineering or anything even remotely linked to creating quality products, but rather in finance where they were more likely to command and control people and organizations.

In a way, the numbers became more important than judgment because many of the business professionals lacked the experience to bring wisdom to decision making. Like the Stat Control analyst in Washington, far removed from combat, the professional couldn't readily accept intuition because he had no experience to intuit from. The professional manager can manage anything, if it's from the abstract perspective of numbers on a sheet of paper or the screen of a computer. But it's a fool's paradise for sure.

The rules of equilibrium, however, don't only apply to organizations. They also apply to people. For the Whiz Kids, by and large, also allowed business to give them a false sense of themselves. Some of them became convinced they were infallible. McNamara could not admit that Vietnam was a mistake for so long not because of his loyalty to a President, but because he simply couldn't bring himself to concede that he could be wrong. Jack Reith was so convinced he was right that he created his own reality, desperately sifting through the numbers to select only those that fit with success, evading the overwhelming evidence that contradicted that image. Tex Thornton, so consumed by his triumph at Litton, began to believe the rah-rah press clippings that told only part of the story. Those clippings failed to capture Thornton's blind insistence that what worked once would work forever. His certainty distracted him and prevented him from relinquishing full control of his company until his death.

Why? Like so many of us, they wanted to put meaning into their lives. A friend of mine once said he wanted to accomplish three things in life: to have a child, write a book and plant a tree. The Whiz Kids wanted to father a movement, wield so much influence that hundreds of books would be written about them, and they wanted to plant forests. The end result of this additional burden was that they became obsessed with achievement, with the power to influence others. By investing so much of their identity in business, many of them severely neglected their families. Some of them became strangers to their wives and their children. Their personal lives were just as unbalanced as their professional belief in the numbers. There comes a time in everyone's life to work at different things, or along the way to not see yourself as the sum total of abstract success.

Perhaps, some might say, they bit off too much. Lesser men of their generation may have enjoyed greater success and happiness because they didn't aim nearly as high as the Whiz Kids. Nobody's hard work could have prevented Vietnam. Nobody's hard work could have prevented the Japanese from building better cars, and no one—not even Tex Thornton —could have made Litton defy gravity. Like a builder of a great cathedral, Thornton was a daring innovator pushing new ultimates of size and height. Building a business, however, is more like building a pyramid. You never see it done. You can't quite have it all.

In the end, they may have found that success, no matter how grand, had little permanence. It was only a temporary truce in the struggle to forge the perfect world so many of us try to create.

obert S. McNamara still rises early every morning and walks briskly in New Balance jogging shoes from his Georgetown home on Tracy Place to a cluttered office on Pennsylvania Avenue. In the large square room, he sits behind a massive ornate desk that once belonged to the first president of the World Bank. A conference table is covered with reports and papers, stacked high in separate piles. Inside the room, with his books and his family pictures, he seems relaxed—not nearly as intense as he has been.

From his office, he runs his life as a private though very active citizen, adviser, speechmaker and author of five books. His latest resumé explains that he is "associated with a number of non-profit organizations focusing on the issues of nuclear arms, population and development, world hunger and East-West relations." In fact, he has made nuclear weapons control his last crusade, strongly advocating that the superpowers adopt a doctrine of "no first use." He travels the world as a member of the International Advisory Committee of Goldman Sachs, and he sits on the National Commission on Public Service, the Urban Institute and the Trilateral Commission.

During his thirteen years as head of the World Bank, McNamara tried to bury the mistakes of his past through redemption. He dedicated himself to eliminating poverty, and he escalated lending to Third World countries to such an extent that many projects were poorly planned and many benefits flowed to those least in need. He testified against large-scale military action in the Gulf War, wrongly predicting from ten thousand to thirty thousand casualties among American-led forces if it occurred. Yet, wherever he goes, Vietnam seems to follow him like a cruel ghost seeking vengeance. At a conference in Japan in April 1991, he was brashly challenged to recall his role in Vietnam by a writer for a British newspaper. McNamara's face grew deadly pale and taut, until he momentarily lost all composure. "I was wrong! My God, I was wrong!" he exploded.

Sitting in his Washington office, he immediately tells you he's unlikely to recall much—then proceeds to recall the small and large details of his life, even from his early days in Tex's Stat Control group. He quotes facts and numbers at random, from casualty rates on Allied sorties over Germany to automobile accident figures from his days at Ford. To recollect, he occasionally covers his eyes with his hands and fiddles with a pen in his fingers. But McNamara's mind is sharp. His eyes, direct and hard, fix on you in a constant state of observation and evaluation.

In short, Bob McNamara—even at seventy-seven—lives an amazingly active life. Though he has not remarried, he has had a public relationship with Washington socialite Joan Braden that for years has kept the gossips buzzing. He has three grown children: Margaret and Kathleen, who live in the Washington area, and Craig, a walnut farmer in Solano County, California, who bears a striking resemblance to his father—replete with rimless glasses. He regularly jogs and plays tennis three times a week. And he continues to pursue with zest the sport that he has always loved—skiing. It is not out of the ordinary to see McNamara, stripped to the waist in mild winter weather, skiing in the Colorado high country where his family makes an annual pilgrimage to what is called "Margy's Hut."

In the early 1980s, McNamara and some of his friends had thought up the idea of building winter huts, spaced miles apart in the Colorado wilderness, for back-country skiers to enjoy as they made their way along the Tenth Mountain Trail linking Aspen and Vail. He convinced the

U.S. Forest Service to allow him to donate and build two huts in 1982 as memorials to Margy—who he confesses was the only person who knew the real Bob McNamara.

One of the ten shelters now along the trail, Margy's Hut has been described by *Town and Country* as the most beautifully sited and the most rustic. The modest structure, with a steep, sloped roof and walls of chinked spruce logs, is nestled between Bald Knob Mountain and Burnt Hole clearing. It is ringed by full-boughed spruce trees and set in a gentle slope against the north wind. Picture windows on three sides take in a majestic view of the Rockies. A wood-burning stove heats the hut, and solar panels power the lights.

It is where McNamara can find solitude, where he can escape far away from everything that may haunt him, where he can continue to explore his past and his future. As he once quoted T.S. Eliot in a revealing national television appearance:

> *We shall not cease from exploration,*
> *And the end of all our exploring*
> *Will be to arrive where we started,*
> *And know the place for the first time.*

He is still searching.

EVEN FRANK SINATRA could not get Flora Thornton to move out of the beautiful house she and Tex bought in 1961 in Beverly Hills. She had purchased the spacious Spanish Colonial mansion—built in 1937, the same year they were married—from Nancy Sinatra, the ex-wife of the singer. As Sinatra reached the October of his years, he instructed his agents to call her up. He wanted to buy the house back for sentimental reasons. Even though he had spent little time in the house, it was where his children had grown up. Flora named a price, even though she had no interest in selling, and the agent told her he would have the money in cash for her the next day. "No, no," she said.

Six months later, he tried again. "Do you think Mr. Sinatra could just walk through?" he asked.

She said she wouldn't mind if it were convenient, but still said she had no intention of selling. "I think maybe they thought that if Old Blue Eyes smiled at me I would sell my house to him," she laughed.

Flora Thornton, still slim and tall, continues to live in the house that

Tex died in; she never remarried. She involves herself in several charitable causes in Los Angeles.

She is estranged from her son, Charles Jr., who runs Thornton Corp., a private investment company that largely manages Tex's estate. Nine months after his father's death, he had two choices to meet the huge taxes on the estate: sell all of Tex's holdings of Litton stock or get rid of the T Lazy S ranch and its mineral leases in the wild sagebrush country of northeastern Nevada.

Charles Jr. decided on the latter. Large deposits of gold had been discovered on the property shortly after Tex and his long-time business partner Roy Ash bought the land in 1961. After a lengthy negotiation, he got Newmont Mining to pay $23.5 million for the ranch and another $10 million for 10 percent of the land's mineral rights. The company also agreed to royalty payments of 18 percent on the remaining rights—a deal worth as much as $600 million to both Ash and the family estate over the contract's ninety-nine-year term.

Charles Jr. is not unlike his father. A director of Litton, he's more conservative and more easily consumed by work, though he lacks his father's extroverted personality. He works out of a Los Angeles office building in a suite filled with heavy mahogany furniture. He's a dramatic contrast to Tex's younger son, Laney, who is more liberal and introspective. Laney Thornton wears bow ties and suspenders, drives a motorcycle, swims and runs in the mid-afternoons and listens to rock and roll. He is still chairman of the same business that his father once asked him to shut down. Today, however, Eileen West is an upscale lingerie company based in San Francisco with annual revenues of $20 million and 150 employees. It sells to premium department stores such as Nordstroms and Bloomingdales and specialty boutiques. The company is headquartered in a high-tech building, a loft-like space with exposed steel girders, brick walls and whitewashed plumbing and duct work.

Comparisons with Dad are inevitable. "I look at all he did, and what I've done compared to that is just laughable," says Laney. "But I've come to grips with this and feel comfortable doing what I do. He was a more intense person than I am. He was much more focused on business. I have a lot of other things that I do that re important to me. I think I have a more balanced life. I have a more developed peer relationship with my wife. I think I'm a little more involved with my children's growing up than he was. I think I'm more interested in culture—music and movies."

What he and Charles still marvel about was their father's ability to motivate people to accomplish things they could not have achieved on their own. "In the purest sense, that's what he was: a leader," believes Laney. "Other people were product or financial geniuses. But what skills did he master? The people who worked for my father always felt that he cared about them. He was as devoted to them as they were devoted to him. I've realized that being a leader isn't something you get. It's something you give."

Yet for all the lessons learned from Dad, there's a sense of disenchantment, too. "Even when you achieve everything you want, somehow the promise of life is never fulfilled," he believes. "You lose your youth or you lose your optimism or your loved ones. You never hold it all together at one time in your hand."

THE FIRST CHRISTMAS the Reith family spent without Jack was somber. Sitting around the table for dinner, Maxine recalls telling her three children that it would be the saddest Christmas they would ever spend together. She sold the house in Cincinnati and moved the family back to Bloomfield Hills in early August of 1961 to start a new life.

Little more than three weeks later, their fifteen-year-old daughter, Donna, died after her horse tripped over some low hurdles on the rolling acres of the Bloomfield Open Hunt. The horse rolled over the girl, breaking her neck and skull. And the group again rallied around Maxine.

Jim and Alice Wright rushed to her home to console her. Helen Mills and Fran Miller helped guide her through the tragedy. Helen tried to get her dates for parties, to put her life back together. She married again in 1968 to Clark Andraea who worked for Detroit Diesel, a unit of General Motors. But Andraea died in 1978, leaving her a widow for the third time in her life.

Still a lively and vivacious woman, with a wonderful sense of humor, she enjoys traveling—and has in recent years visited Mexico and the Soviet Union. And she still chats with Fran Miller by telephone from her home in West Bloomfield, Mich.

Her oldest son, Fritz, retains some attachments to his father—both warm and painful memories. He recalls some rough-house playing with his dad, tossing baseballs and footballs back and forth. "From time to time, he would let me sit in his lap and steer the car as we drove around the block," remembers Fritz. He also has a recurring nightmare of seeing an image of his father through a window. He repeatedly bangs on the glass with his fists, trying to get his father's attention. But Dad never seems to hear him. Fritz tried newspaper reporting for a while and disliked it. After working on a doctorate in anthropology at the University of California at Irvine, he began doing statistical analysis of all things on a freelance basis. He lives in Newport Beach.

Their youngest son, Charles, has only the faintest of memories of his father who died when he was seven years old. He has edited a couple of books on environmental issues. Married with children and living in New Orleans, where he works for an environmental concern, Charles has adopted a different lifestyle for himself and his family. "Charles is going to be home at 5:30 with his family or else," Maxine explains. "He says, 'My father worked himself to death, and I'm just not going to do that. My family is always going to come first.'"

THE PLACE IS a genuine dive. Tucked in one corner, a beat-up jukebox blares out Aretha Franklin's "Respect." Silver duct tape seals the gashes in the bar stools. Black-painted plywood protects the windows when the crowd becomes unruly. Neon beer signs light the outside sidewalk, flashing the names Strohs, Michelob, and Miller into the busy street.

Yet every Tuesday night, tomorrow's Whiz Kids in their button-down shirts and jeans gather at the Old Pro on El Camino Real. Once a week, the MBA students at Stanford University take over the place and call it Arjay's—one of many that Arjay Miller can claim from his long career. Indeed, when the students held a charity auction one year it was a "Fantasy Night" with Arjay Miller that closed with intensive bidding. Several students paid $300 to swill beer and shoot pool with him.

His Stanford deanship was an important detour from Ford because it was at the university where he gained greater affection and respect than he had at Ford. "In life," he joked, "your credibility goes up as your income goes down." It was under his watch that he built upon the earlier achievements of Dean Ernest Arbuckle, helping Stanford challenge Harvard and Chicago for the preeminent spot in graduate business school education. Miller hired faculty with government experience to create courses that dealt with consumer and environmental issues. He launched a public management program to give students an appreciation of working in the not-for-profit sectors of the economy. And when he ended his decade-long stint as dean in 1979, he had nearly quadrupled the business school's endowment from $6.4 million to $23.2 million.

Through the years, he has severed few ties. Federal Express packages from Ford still arrive on the doorstep of his contemporary ranch in

Woodside, California, the same home Miller and his wife, Frances, pur-chased when they returned to California in 1969. Miller still serves as an informal adviser to Ford, and he maintains informal links with Stanford. In a corner of his den sits a toilet-seat-shaped grill from the Edsel, a gag gift from the men in the finance department when he left as president of Ford. And on the wall there's a blown-up version of *the* Whiz Kid group picture taken shortly after their arrival at Ford in 1946, along with photographs of Miller with JFK, LBJ and Hubert Humphrey. All the stuff in the room, including the original three-by-five file cards he used to deliver the first cash forecast ever done at Ford on September 27, 1946, are reminders of a productive, if not always successful, past.

These days, Miller largely lives the life of a contented retiree. "I feel I've been extremely fortunate in my life," he says. "I don't feel unfulfilled in any way, and I've got nothing to prove to anybody."

He's right. He takes immense enjoyment in the company of his grand-children, and both his son, Kenneth, and his daughter, Anne, live nearby. Kenneth is an editor at the Peninsula *Times-Tribune*. Anne is a housewife in Palo Alto. Miller continues to share with his wife an enthusiasm for gardening, a hobby that is apparent to anyone who visits their home. He and Frances travel around the world—most often with Ed Lundy but also with Jim and Alice Wright—sampling the gourmet fare of the best restaurants. They've been to all the three-star restaurants in France; Mil-ler's personal favorite is Georges Blanc in Vonnas, north of Lyon, a comfy place in an old reconstructed mill with old timbers.

At age seventy, in 1986, he stepped off the boards of five corporations —including Litton and Ford, which held a retirement party for him at the Highlands Inn in Carmel. Henry Ford came out for the event and put on a big show for him. After an evening of toasts, Henry walked up to Miller and said: "Stay on an extra day. Let's you and I have our own retirement party."

So Arjay and Frances, and Henry and Kathy stayed, and Henry put his arms around Miller and cried. Ford would later tell Ed Lundy that his dismissal of Arjay was one of his greatest regrets. His faith in Miller was so complete that in 1986 Henry amended his private trust, directing that if he were kidnapped or held against his will Miller should "take charge" of efforts to secure his release. The last time Arjay saw the aging Prince alive was on April 9, 1987, less than six months before the death of the industrial patriarch at the age of seventy. Arjay had been invited back to Dearborn for a special board meeting at which Henry renamed the grounds around Glass House as "The Arjay Miller Michigan Arboretum." A large tombstone on the property reports that the arboretum was started by Miller in 1960 and opened to the public in 1966 when he was president of Ford to show the great variety of trees native to Michigan.

Miller felt somewhat embarrassed by the tribute, almost guilty to be singled out in such a public way among the hundreds of thousands of employees who had worked for Henry over the years. And years later, when he took his grandchildren there to look around for a few days, he was disappointed that the grounds weren't as well maintained as they should be. "I wished they would water those trees a little more," says Arjay. "Ed Lundy said he's going to get them on the stick and make them take care of that grove."

THE SWANKY RITZ-CARLTON in Dearborn had only opened its doors twomonths earlier, yet when the stocky, white-haired gentleman walked into its restaurant everyone already knew him by name. The general manager shuffles over to greet him. Every waitress winks and smiles a greeting.

J. Edward Lundy is still a very powerful figure in the land of Ford, and nearly everyone in these parts knows of the indelible imprint he made on the huge corporation. Lundy was an anonymous figure in the history of Ford—until the 1986 publication of David Halberstam's *The Reckoning* which included a chapter on him called "The Quiet Man." Shortly after the book hit the stores, he began receiving letters from old friends and colleagues with the salutation: "Dear Legendary."

Still, the book outraged Lundy, who repeatedly refused to be interviewed by Halberstam. What most offended him was the author's suggestion that he had asked to be invited to the homes of his protégés to size up their wives and families. "I never asked to be invited anywhere," he storms. Lundy tells you that three of his secretaries over the years called or wrote him to say they were shocked by it.

Retirement suits him well. It makes his quiet life even more private. He still lives in the Fairlane East development in Dearborn, only across the street from the Foundation Apartments where most of the men first moved after the war. He enjoys good food, traveling, the theater, movies and gardening, and roots for any football and basketball team that plays against Michigan. He is a witty conversationalist. He talks enthusiastically about Rosetta, his maid, who came to Dearborn in 1948, and how he recently arranged for one of the best surgeons in the area to remove a cyst from her eye. He recounts the story with the delivery and timing of a first-rate storyteller, down to imitating her southern drawl.

He acknowledges his role in building a powerful finance group within Ford, and he predictably pooh-poohs suggestions that it hurt the company. No sooner had he left Ford, however, than the company began downsizing its financial staff, reducing it by more than half the nearly fifteen thousand people who once tended the numbers. Thousands of the company's middle managers also have been sent back to school at the University of Michigan where the author of a book called *Beyond Rational Management* taught them about a very different way to manage. And Ford, better balanced than ever, has become one of the world's most efficient and productive carmakers.

Like Arjay, Ed remains an informal consultant to Ford, though he retired as executive vice president in charge of financial matters on June 1, 1979. Lundy left the Ford board in 1985 when he turned seventy.

Lundy stayed at Ford longer than any of the men, some thirty-three years of service. When he left, the stock he owned in Ford was worth about $2.7 million. Upon his retirement, Ford established a $1 million endowed chair in his name at the American Enterprise Institute. Henry wanted to surprise him, and he did, for if anyone bothered to ask Lundy, he would have preferred a chair at Princeton or a donation to the Henry Ford Hospital where he served on the board of trustees. Ford also wrote out a $100,000 check in Lundy's name and donated it to the Mercy nuns in Cedar Rapids, the same Catholic order which had taught Lundy in grammar school.

Lundy had never mentioned their influence on him nor his long-term devotion to them. "I had never discussed my early background with HFII," Lundy says. "My family likes to remain private, and I've kept it that way."

"I've heard about your gift to the Mercy nuns and I'm staggered," he told Ford. "How did you know about them?"

"Ed," Henry said with a smile, "you'd be surprised about the things I know about you."

THERE WAS NO gift for James Wright when he abruptly left Ford Motor in a huff in 1963 after being passed over for the presidency by Henry. He landed a job as president of Federal-Mogul Corp., a large automotive supplier, a position he held for five years.

James and Alice Wright left Detroit in 1968 and escaped to Sea Island,

Ga., the lush resort established in 1920 by auto magnate Howard Coffin. For years, they had vacationed on the golden isle until deciding to build a retirement home there. The gray brick ranch, which was finished in 1963, sits next to the Atlantic Ocean. Even inside the rambling home, ringed by swaying palm trees, you can hear the surf pounding the rocks. The ocean mist often clings to the picture window of the den.

It's a long distance from Detroit. When Jim, now a frail figure who walks slowly and deliberately, reminisces about the early days of the group, he does so with fondness and affection. "We looked after each other," he says. "We supported each other, helped each other from personal to professional things. And the casualty list of the ten was pretty small."

Jim still keeps in touch with most of the surviving members of the group. He and Alice have traveled to Mexico and to Alaska with Arjay and Frances. On October 22, 1988, they celebrated their fiftieth wedding anniversary by traveling to London. They have four grandchildren, a pair from each of their own children. Their daughter, Alice, is director of Creative Employment, a YWCA organization that helps to place disadvantaged women in jobs in Louisville, Ky. Their son, James, served a stint in the Peace Corps before earning a master's degree in economics from Georgetown. He now works for the World Bank in Washington, D.C., and lives in McLean, Va. ("McNamara," his father says, "didn't get him in there, but Jim did put him down as a reference. That raised some eyebrows.")

JUST A FEW blocks down the road lives Ben Mills. He and Helen moved to the island in 1971, buying a magnificent home on Sea Island Drive. He retired from Ford, after twenty-five years of service, when he was fifty-six years old. "I wanted to have time with my family," he says, "where we weren't tied down to a business or travel schedule with someone else dictating what my life would be."

For years, he and Helen traveled extensively and played lots of golf. He learned to fly an airplane, and they would do silly things, like young lovers, flying down to Jacksonville for a cup of coffee and then climbing back in the plane to return home. Both of them were active in civic affairs, involved with local schools, hospitals and a property owners association. Ben helped launch a hospice organization, while Helen kept busy with the local YWCA. On occasion, he played piano with a local band. Then, after a marriage that endured for forty-nine years, Helen died in

1986. Ben has two adopted children: Ben Jr. who heads a computer operation in Texas called "Fundsnet," and Robert, who with his wife owns a court reporting business in nearby Brunswick, Ga.

Though he failed to rise as high as several of his colleagues, he considers himself lucky beyond complaint. "We happened to be in the right place at the right time," says Mills. "There were damn few limitations. I've had more opportunity, met more wonderful people and made more money than I had ever believed would happen in my lifetime. Sure, I've had things happen that I'm sorry about. Helen died. When I say I wish it hadn't happened that's really dumb. I would have hoped it went on longer, but you can't change it. I've made some stupid mistakes, but I'm not going to parade them before you. Once in a while, you feel like a horse's butt. And if you don't learn from it you're dead. But if I had to do it over again, I wouldn't change anything. Regrets are worthless."

A DISENCHANTED CHARLES BOSWORTH left Ford on April 30, 1966, just three months shy of his fiftieth birthday, after being passed over for a promotion to a job gained instead by Ben Mills. "There was keen disappointment on my part," he says. "I was the only one who didn't attain VP-status with the company. Of those who stayed on, everyone else was a vice president or above. It was a disappointment, but I got over it pretty quickly."

Still, Bosworth has not worked a single day since he walked out of Ford as head of the purchasing operations of the Ford Division. He remained in Detroit for about a year to get his personal affairs in order and to find a place to live in retirement.

He had it with Detroit's sleet storms and freezing gales, and considered Florida and California his two top choices. He spent several days roaming around Fort Lauderdale and Palm Beach, but wrote Florida off because of the heat and humidity. He then turned to California and decided to scout out Santa Barbara—a small, clean town that he had visited a couple of times as a college student in the 1930s.

He liked it so much that he rented an apartment, skipped the rest of his tour of California and headed back to Detroit for a date with Bekins Van and Storage Co.—Andy Andreson's company. A year later, he bought a small, modern home perched on a bluff overlooking the bay. His home is lined with photographs—evidence of a hobby—and books —Dostoyevsky, Proust, D.H. Lawrence, Plato, James Baldwin and Tom

Wolfe. Magazines—*Scientific American, Natural History* and *National Geographic*—are stacked on a cocktail table as neatly as they would be in a dentist's office. There's a small garden with Valencia orange trees, and a Ford Thunderbird parked outside.

When Bosworth first came to California, he says he got a little carried away—drinking far too much for his own good. He has been "on the wagon" for some twenty years. He came close to getting married four times in his life, but always backed out of it, preferring to remain single and independent. Every morning, he walks the beach and listens to the surf. There are, he says, no regrets, no misgivings. If he could have changed anything, it would have been Tex. Somehow, he would have had Tex Thornton stay at Ford.

For a while, Charlie used to chat on the telephone and exchange Christmas notes with Jim Wright. But he did not really stay in touch with the other men in the group and several of them have no idea of what happened to him. Today, he lives a solitary life in Santa Barbara. Even among other Ford retirees in the town, he's something of a recluse. Asked if he would attend a reunion of the Whiz Kids, if one occurred, he says flatly he would not be interested. Too much time has passed by.

FOR SOME TIME after George Moore's death in 1967, his widow struggled to make ends meet. Marika married Gregory Aires four years after George's death, and he died of a stroke three years later. Today, she lives in a modest townhouse in the shadows of the Washington Cathedral in the District of Columbia.

She remembers the war years in Washington, when Tex and the group first got together, as a golden period of their lives. "At that time, we were all young," she says. "All the women were beautiful, and all the men were good-looking."

They had four children: Marika, whose godfather is Ed Lundy, is a psychiatric social worker at the National Medical Center; Doug works in computer programming in Bethesda, Md.; Jenny, a painter in South Keeport, Me., and Laura, a manager at a financial services company. Of all the children, George's death most affected their youngest daughter, Laura, who was only thirteen at the time. She became an alcoholic, drinking to feel more powerful and outgoing. Unlike her father, Laura managed to beat the disease. She views her life as fulfilling, in some way, the unfinished odyssey of her father. "I validated myself through my work for many years," she says. "I believe my work is an extension of my dad's career since he didn't have the chance to achieve as much."

JANE ANDRESON NEVER married again after the death of her husband in 1979. She and her daughter, Sally, who is also a widow, live in Los Angeles.

NOTES AND SOURCES

You can't research and write a book like this without getting obsessive about it. At least, I couldn't.

Over the last five years, I tracked down the six Whiz Kids who were still alive, searched out their friends and families in Santa Barbara, San Francisco, Los Angeles and Woodside, California; in Sea Island, Georgia, in Dearborn and Bloomfield Hills, Michigan, and in Washington, D.C. To talk with anyone who knew them, I crisscrossed the U.S. and stopped in remote towns and big cities from Chicago to Houston. I interviewed nearly five hundred people. There were times when the talk broke down into sentiment and tears.

I have read tens of thousands of personal letters and calendars, notes, memos and studies, piecing together their story from old newspapers and magazine clippings. I was astonished by the precise details of their lives that had been committed to paper—dates of meetings, diary jottings, even the agendas of their very first huddles together at Ford—records most businesspeople today would destroy.

I used these documents, my interviews and other source materials to construct the novelistic rendering of their story here. I took some fictional license to recreate a few scenes, but only when supported by interviews with direct participants. Sometimes, for example, a Whiz Kid could not recall the dialogue in a meeting, but could remember the tone or substance of the discussion. I created a few lines that would reflect the tone of the session as recalled by a key participant. Most of the events were corroborated by several witnesses. In every case, the book is based on the factual record of events and interviews that support that record.

The collection of documents at the following archives proved invaluable in my research: The Ford Motor Company Industrial Archives in Redford, Michigan; the Edison Institute at the Henry Ford Museum in Dearborn; The National Automotive History Collection at the Detroit Public Library; the Lyndon Baines Johnson Library at Austin, Texas; the John F. Kennedy Library in Boston, Massachusetts; and the letters, memos and press clippings maintained by Tex Thornton's son, Chuck, in Los Angeles, California.

A number of my interviews were off-the-record. Among the many interviews I conducted were those of: Marika Aires, Harry Allcock, Charles Anderson, Maxine Andraea, Jane Andreson, Sally Andreson, Robert Anthony, Roy Ash, Richard Ashpole, Lynn Bartlett, Charles Beck, Harold Benenson, James Biggar, Colin Blaydon, Charles Bosworth, Pat Brescia, George Brown, McGeorge Bundy, John Cadman, Phil Caldwell, Thomas Clark, Dr. Frank Cleveland, Buford Cox, Keith Crain, Richard Crane, Florence Crane, David Crippen, John Cuccio, Marika Moore Cutler, Mark Day, Donald DeLaRossa, Peter Drucker, Robert Dunham, Nora Dunning, Robert Eggert, Alain Enthoven, Lloyd Erxleben, George Fenimore, Philip Fitts, Donald Frey, William George, Alan Gornick, William Gossett, Ruth Graves, Harry Gray, James Grear, Bill Grimes, Bud Grissinger, Walter Haas, George Hackett, David Halberstam, Gordon Hampton, Richard Hanel, Evan Bond Hannay, Harry Hansen, Sally Hartmann, Patty Herrick, Richard Hodgson, Mrs. Milburn Hollengreen, E.C. Itschner, Allen Janger, Robert Jenkins, Elmo Jensen, Tom Johnston, Emmet Judge, Sandy Kaplan, Bud Kaufman, Matthew Kelly, James Kerley, John Kimbrough, Philip Klass, George Kosmetsky, Louis Lataif, Edmund Learned, Donald Lennox, Robert Lentz, John Lewis, Jan Lipkin, J. Sterling Livingston, Paul Lorenz, J. Edward Lundy, Frank Lynch, Gerry Lynch, Myles Mace, Robert Mace, Jacques Maroni, Lyonette Maroni, John Martin, William Masterson, Glenn McDaniel, Gene McKranzi, Robert McNamara, Claude Meconis, Gerry Meyers, Ruth Mihalic, Arjay Miller, Ben Mills, Laura Moore, Richard Moore, William Moriarty, A. Reynolds Morse, Chase Morsey, Robert Nadal, John Najar, John Nichols, Fred O'Green, Barney Oldfield, Joe Oros, Kenneth Otto, Frank Owen, Tom Peters, Jack Phillippe, Dusty Porterfield, Si Ramo, Charles Reith, Fritz Reith, Stephen Saltonstall, Wallace Sanders, Fred Secrest, Charles Sawyer, Mrs. Edmund Schweitzer, Leo Skidmore, Mrs. John Slavich, Bill Stack, Richard Stout, George Thomassen, Flora

Thornton, Chuck Thornton, Laney Thornton, Robert Throckmorton, Gordon Tuttle, Virginia Peyton Unger, Gordon Walker, Lois Walker, Gayle Warnock, Charles Watson, David Weeks, Lauran White, Robert Wieland, John Harvey Wills, Kendrick Wilson, Dean Wooldridge, James Wright, Alice Wright, Adam Yarmolinsky, Frank Yoakum, Eugene Zuckert.

INTRODUCTION: WHAT IT TAKES TO CHANGE THE WORLD

p. 9 "Gary Cooper on wheels . . ." Author's interview with Jacques Maroni.

p. 10 "We didn't want to rain . . ." Author's interview with Arjay Miller.

CHAPTER 1: INDUSTRIAL PRINCE

p. 13 Bob McNamara and Charlie . . . Author's interview with Charles Bosworth.

p. 14 the war had not been an interruption . . . Author's interview with Ben Mills.

p. 14 They matched planes to airfields . . . Statistical Control in the U.S. Army Air Forces, report by Charles B. Thornton, December 12, 1945.

p. 17 Ford losses nearly canceled out . . . *Life,* October 1, 1945.

p. 18 Yet Lieutenant Colonel McNamara was the only . . . Author's interview with Robert S. McNamara.

p. 18 But in Henry's aura, some of them felt small. Author's interview with Bosworth.

p. 20 "We ran our operations . . . Statistical Control in the U.S. Army Air Forces.

p. 20 "Well, Mr. Ford . . ." Nevins & Hill interview with John Bugas, Ford Archives.

p. 20 "The most gifted . . ." *The Best and The Brightest* by David Halberstam, pp. 281–282.

p. 21 On the way home . . . Author's interview with Bosworth.

CHAPTER 2: "YOUNG NAPOLEON"

p. 23 "Those figures of yours are wrong . . ." Author's interview with Dusty Porterfield.

p. 24 Young Napoleon's military . . . Statistical Control in the U.S. Army Air Forces.

p. 24 he heard Ian Fleming . . . Author's interview with Glenn McDaniel.

p. 26 Tex's father was a tough . . . Author's interview with John Lewis, George Fenimore, Chuck Thornton.

p. 26 Cash or clothing would sporadically . . . *Someone Has To Make It Happen* by Bernie Lay, p. 30.

p. 27 "Even before the Depression . . ." Ibid.

p. 27 Tex developed his sense of self . . . Author's interviews with Lewis, Fenimore, C. Thornton.

p. 28 "Bates wasn't any angel." Author's interview with John Kimbrough.

p. 28 "It made him mad as hell." Author's interview with Wallace Sanders.

p. 28 His mother would have a recurring dream . . . Author's interview with Lewis.

p. 29 he opened up a small Plymouth dealership . . . Author's interview with Buford Cox.

p. 29 With $50 borrowed . . . *Someone Has To Make It Happen* by Bernie Lay, p. 38.

p. 30 "See that bench . . ." Ibid. Author's interview with James Wright.

p. 30 Thornton had met a woman . . . Author's interview with Flora Thornton.

p. 31 "I saw this integrity . . ." Ibid.

p. 31 "Who said anything about marriage?" Ibid.

p. 32 Tex befriended . . . *Someone Has To Make It Happen* by Bernie Lay, p. 49.

p. 33 "Mr. Secretary . . ." Ibid.

p. 33 Almost every day . . . Statistical Control in the U.S. Army Air Forces.

p. 34 Flora, then pregnant . . . Author's interview with Flora Thornton.

p. 35 "Knowledge . . ." Statisical Control in the U.S. Army Air Forces.

p. 36 "Statistical Control" sounded innocuous . . . Author's interviews with James Wright, Roy Ash.

CHAPTER 3: OF RULERS & MEASURING STICKS

p. 39 Tex Thornton arrived on the doorstep . . . Author's interviews with Myles Mace, Ed Learned, Robert McNamara.

p. 40 They were an impressive . . . Author's interview with Myles Mace.

p. 40 Thornton began his animated pitch. Ibid.

p. 40 "The more Tex talked . . ." Author's interview with Myles Mace.

p. 41 The Harvard Business School . . . Author's interviews with Ed Learned, Myles Mace.

p. 42 Spurred by Thornton's enthusiastic appeal . . . Ibid.

p. 42 At the forefront . . . Author's interview with Ed Learned.

p. 42 Dull and tedious . . . *A Delicate Experiment: The Harvard Business School 1908–1945* by Jeffrey C. Cruikshank, pp. 240–248.

p. 43 At the half-way mark . . . Author's interviews with Roy Ash, Arjay Miller, James Wright.

p. 44 Most people read words . . . *Managing* by Harold Geneen with Alvin Moscow.

p. 45 "Staff policies and commands . . ." Statistical Control in the U.S. Army Air Forces.

p. 45 He relished the academic life. Author's interviews with Robert McNamara, Myles Mace, Eugene Zuckert.

p. 47 "He was so painfully good . . ." *Look,* April 23, 1963.

p. 47 "Parents of my classmates . . ." *Time,* February 11, 1991.

p. 47 "He liked to be in the spotlight." Author's interview with A. Reynolds Morse.

p. 48 "He started taking off . . ." Author's interview with Walter Haas.

p. 48 To celebrate . . . Author's interviews with John Martin, Richard Hodgson.

p. 49 McNamara and his Harvard colleague . . . Author's interview with Myles Mace.

p. 49 Each morning, McNamara and Mace . . . Ibid.

p. 50 It was analysis that led . . . Statistical Control in the U.S. Army Air Forces.

p. 51 Thornton's men acquired influence and lots of it . . . Author's interviews with Roy Ash, Dusty Porterfield, John Martin, George Fenimore.

CHAPTER 4: CARNIVAL MAN

p. 53 She had been refusing . . . Author's interview with Maxine Andreae.

p. 53 had become so unaccountably . . . *Someone Has To Make It Happen* by Bernie Lay, p. 65.

p. 54 "Now please don't hang up on me . . ." Author's interview with Maxine Andreae.

p. 55 "Well, you can let me take . . ." Ibid.

p. 55 Beneath his feet lay . . . Author's interviews with Charles Bosworth, Chase Morsey.

p. 56 At war's end . . . Reith's Legion of Merit citation.

p. 57 Everywhere you looked . . . Statistical Control in the U.S. Army Air Forces.

p. 58 Jack lived in "Little Woods" . . . Author's interview with Charles Bosworth.

p. 59 His mother . . . Author's interview with Robert Throckmorton.

p. 59 "If my dad had spent . . ." Author's interview with Maxine Andreae.

p. 60 sweet talked his way . . . Author's interview with Robert Throckmorton.

p. 60 One day, Major Barringer . . . Author's interview with James Wright.

p. 60 "What did he do before the war?" Author's interview with Maxine Andreae.

CHAPTER 5: GENTLE GEORGE

p. 66 One of Tex's early favorites . . . Author's interview with Marika Aires.

p. 67 Dearest Mims . . . This and all other letters are courtesy of Marika Aires.

p. 73 In Washington, Tex . . . Author's interview with Arjay Miller.

CHAPTER 6: THE TELEGRAM

p. 78 Before the war had disturbed . . . Author's interview with Flora Thornton, James Wright.

p. 79 He was drawn to Washington from Oklahoma . . . Author's interview with Ben Mills.

p. 79 The basic theme . . . Ibid.

p. 79 The mailing drew some . . . *Someone Has To Make It Happen* by Bernie Lay, p. 78.

p. 81 The group considered buying a dealership. Correspondence among Thornton, Reith, Mills and Moore. Chuck Thornton's archives.

p. 81 "We cased the joint . . ." Ibid.

p. 81 Then, good old George Moore . . . Author's interview with Marika Aires.

p. 82 Tex and George debated . . . Ibid.

p. 82 "bordered on impudence." Author's interview with Ben Mills.

p. 82 The telegram . . . *Someone Has To Make It Happen* by Bernie Lay, p. 78.

p. 82 "Cripes," he said . . . *Bob Considine's Firsthand Story of the Fabulous Henry Ford II*, p. 23.

p. 83 "I'll be having breakfast . . ." Ibid, p. 82.

p. 83 "We've got to have . . ." Author's interview with Marika Aires.

p. 84 At Tex's request . . . Author's interview with Ben Mills.

p. 84 Tex wanted him to consider . . . Ibid.

p. 85 Virtually everyone Tex spoke to . . . Ibid. Author's interviews with Dusty Porterfield, Myles Mace.

p. 85 With the Ford offer in hand . . . Author's interview with Robert McNamara.

p. 86 Before arranging the group's . . . Author's interview with Ben Mills.

p. 87 Ben was elated. Ibid.

p. 87 "Hell," he laughed . . . Author's interview with Arjay Miller.

CHAPTER 7: QUIZ KIDS

p. 91 Though they barely had . . . Author's interview with Charles Bosworth.

p. 92 Jack had typed up a fourteen-page agenda . . . Chuck Thornton's archives.

p. 92 "We'll no doubt be under some suspicion . . ." Notes of meeting. Thornton archives.

p. 92 Tex told the men. Ibid.

p. 92 "Four of you . . ." Ibid.

p. 92 This had already become . . . Author's interview with James Wright.

p. 95 They spent all that January afternoon . . . Notes of meeting. Thornton archives.

p. 95 A major shock . . . Author's interviews with James Wright, Ben Mills, Robert McNamara, Marika Aires.

p. 96 They settled into wooden . . . Author's interview with Robert Dunham.

p. 96 "Are you inclined to be moody?" Author's interview with Sally Hartmann.

p. 97 More than the others . . . Author's interview with Arjay Miller.

p. 99 He was Harry H. Bennett . . . *Ford: The Men and the Machine* by Robert Lacey, p. 198.

p. 100 A man in the Rouge . . . Author's interview with Arjay Miller.

p. 100 Among the several hundred . . . Author's interview with Robert McNamara.

pp. 100–1 As GM's vice chairman . . . *Adventures of a Bystander* by Peter F. Drucker, p. 259.

p. 101 "There is much that labor . . ." Letter from McNamara to Learned dated December 29, 1946, courtesy of Learned.

p. 101 The setup didn't allow for much privacy . . . Author's interview with Ben Mills.

p. 103 Every afternoon or night . . . Author's interviews with James Wright, Ben Mills, Charles Bosworth.

p. 103 "Say fella, who do you work for?" Author's interview with Arjay Miller.

p. 103 "Mr. Thornton . . ." Ibid.

p. 105 Near their desks . . . Ibid.

p. 107 For three straight months . . . Author's interviews with Ben Mills, James Wright, Charles Bosworth.

CHAPTER 8: ALL THAT GLITTERS

p. 111 "In this part of the country . . ." Thornton letter dated March 20, 1947. Thornton archives.

p. 113 Most of them lacked the money . . . Author's interviews with Ben Mills, Marika Aires.

p. 113 Jack and George were stuck . . . Author's interviews with Marika Aires and Maxine Andreae.

p. 114 Early on . . . Author's interview with Arjay Miller.

p. 114 Enthused by the purchase . . . Author's interview with Flora Thornton.

p. 115 They converged on each other's . . . Author's interviews with Jane Andreson, Marika Aires, Maxine Andreae.

p. 115 Several were real fans . . . Author's interviews with Charles Bosworth, Ben Mills, James Wright.

p. 117 "I am not a B student . . ." Author's interview with Arjay Miller.

p. 118 Andy knew . . . Author's interview with Jane Andreson.

p. 119 "Dear Mr. Thornton . . ." Resignation letter. Thornton archives.

p. 119 The excitement Andy . . . Author's interviews with Jane Andreson, James and Alice Wright.

CHAPTER 9: CLASH OF AMBITION

p. 123 The rumors . . . *Ford: The Men and the Machine* by Robert Lacey, p. 446.

p. 123 Thornton "wanted to be president . . ." Jack Davis interview, July 25–26, 1960, Ford Archives of the Edison Institute.

p. 124 In May, some five weeks . . . *Someone Has To Make It Happen.,* by Bernie Lay, pp. 86–87.

p. 125 "As you can imagine . . ." Letter to Lovett. Thornton archive.

p. 126 One of Arjay's . . . Author's interview with Arjay Miller.

p. 126 The car zipped down . . . Author's interviews with Nora Dunning, Arjay Miller.

p. 127 The company's inability . . . Author's interview with Ben Mills.

p. 127 "The part's not going to be there." Ibid.

p. 128 At Ford, there were loose ends. Author's interview with Arjay Miller.

p. 129 As soon as Breech arrived . . . Author's interviews with James Wright, Arjay Miller.

p. 130 In the old Administration Building. Interview by Michael Ciepley of Charles Thornton.

p. 130 "Would you take him in?" Ibid.

p. 131 "I don't need to know how . . ." Author's interview with James Wright

p. 132 In the early days, Crusoe . . . Ibid.

p. 133 The maxims gushed . . . Author's interviews with Chase Morsey, James Wright, Arjay Miller.

p. 133 One of his assistants . . . Author's interview with Robert Jenkins.

p. 134 They would argue over everything . . . Author's interview with James Wright.

p. 136 Tex believed that government . . . Interview by Ciepley of Charles Thornton.

p. 136 "There is a definite lack . . ." Thornton letter. Thornton archives.

p. 136 "At the moment I feel . . ." McNamara letter. Thornton archives.

p. 136 One day, Henry came to town . . . Interview by Ciepley of Charles Thornton.

p. 138 "I think Tex would be wiser . . ." Author's interview with Ben Mills.

p. 138 The same was true . . . Author's interviews with Marika Aires, James Wright.

p. 140 One friend relayed the rumor . . . Correspondence to Thornton. Thornton archives.

p. 141 "The Ford Motor Company . . ." Ibid.

CHAPTER 10: WASHOUT

p. 144 The gang had gathered . . . Author's interview with Robert Dunham.

p. 144 "Oh God!" Ibid.

p. 145 His feuds with Tex over everything . . . Nevins and Hill interviews with Lewis Crusoe. Ford Archives of the Edison Institute.

p. 145 "I've had it up to my eyeballs . . . Author's interview with Gerry Lynch.

p. 145 "I can't believe it . . ." Author's interview with Robert Dunham.

p. 145 Bob felt so concerned . . . Author's interview with Ed Learned.

p. 145 "I would again like . . ." Letter to Breech. Thornton archives.

p. 147 He explored the possibilities . . . Author's interview with Flora Thornton.

p. 147 On Monday morning . . . Author's interviews with Charles Bosworth, Ben Mills, James Wright.

p. 149 But that silence . . . Author's interviews with Charles Bosworth, Ben Mills.

p. 149 Ben Mills struggled . . . Author's interview with Ben Mills.

p. 150 "For two or three days . . ." Ben Mills letter to Thornton. Thornton archives.

CHAPTER 11: ANOTHER CHANCE

p. 155 Jane had just stepped . . . Author's interview with Jane Andreson.

pp. 156–57 The three of them . . . Ibid.

p. 158 As the two men sat . . . *Someone Has To Make It Happen* by Bernie Lay, p. 97.

p. 159 Thornton may have been disappointed . . . Author's interviews with Flora Thornton, George Fenimore.

p. 160 What Tex found here . . . Author's interviews with Simon Ramo, Dean Wooldridge.

p. 160 "My God," he told . . . Author's interview with Arjay Miller.

p. 160 Tex decided to ditch . . . Author's interviews with George Kosmetsky, Roy Ash.

p. 161 "That's not what I hired you to do . . ." Author's interview with George Fenimore.

p. 162 That fall, in 1948 . . . Author's interview with Simon Ramo.

pp. 162–63 When an item . . . Correspondence. Ford Industrial Archives.

p. 163 "Unless an entrepreneur . . ." Thornton speech. Thornton archives.

p. 164 "I do feel that you . . ." Correspondence. Thornton archives.

p. 165 "Henry, contrary to . . ." Ibid.

CHAPTER 12: THE CIRCUMFERENCE OF A BERRY

p. 167 Upwards of two thousand . . . The New York *Times,* June 11, 1948.

p. 170 GM invited Drucker . . . *Adventures of a Bystander* by Peter F. Drucker, pp. 256–93.

p. 170 "To my mind . . ." *My Life and Work* by Henry Ford with Samuel Crowther, p. 91.

p. 172 At one point . . . Author's interview with James Wright.

p. 172 Jim maintained in his report . . . Organizational Problems of the Ford Motor Co., Thornton archives.

p. 174 "Oh, I'm fine, fine . . ." Author's interview with Charles Bosworth.

p. 174 In the past . . . Author's interview with John Dearden.

p. 175 The new approach . . . Nevins and Hill interview notes with Robert S. McNamara. Ford Archives of the Edison Institute.

p. 175 The financial staff of the company . . . Author's interview with Arjay Miller.

p. 176 The way Lundy and his deputies . . . Ciepley interview with Tom Lilly.

p. 177 When Crusoe first joined . . . Author's interview with James Wright.

p. 178 Always, they kept in touch . . . Correspondence. Thornton archive.

p. 179 They worked well . . . Author's interviews with Chase Morsey, Robert Jenkins.

p. 180 But when one of Jack's . . . Author's interview with Chase Morsey.

p. 181 "If I were you I'd take this job for nothing . . ." Nevins & Hill interview notes. Ford Archives of the Edison Institute.

p. 182 "Can he handle the job?" Breech memoirs.

CHAPTER 13: MR. BLANDINGS' DREAM HOUSE

p. 186 George Moore didn't have his eye . . . Author's interview with Marika Aires.

p. 187 George was out suggesting . . . Washington *Post,* December 12, 1948.

p. 187 He and Day had capitalized . . . Author's interview with Mark Day.

p. 187 "This seems of particular . . ." Correspondence. Thornton archives.

p. 188 "He was a born salesman . . ." Author's interview with James Grear.

p. 189 "Look," he bravely said . . . Author's interview with Lynn Bartlett.

p. 189 Disheartened, he flew to Detroit . . . Author's interviews with Mark Day, James Grear, Lynn Bartlett.

p. 190 "The thing that thrills me . . ." Letter from Dobbs, courtesy of Marika Aires.

p. 191 Over this expanding empire . . . Author's interviews with Eugene Zuckert, Philip Fitts, Marika Aires.

p. 192 As soon as Grear joined . . . Author's interview with James Grear.

p. 193 "George, it's beautiful . . ." Author's interview with Eugene Zuckert.

p. 193 "She was treated like a doll . . ." Author's interview with Virginia Peyton Unger.

p. 194 George was smashed . . . Author's interview with Eugene Zuckert.

CHAPTER 14: AN AMERICAN IN PARIS

p. 197 Jack was vacationing on . . . Author's interview with Maxine Andreae.

p. 198 By late 1952 . . . Author's interview with Jacques Maroni.

p. 199 Jack returned to Dearborn . . . Author's interview with Alan Gornick.

p. 199 "Congratulations on your appointment . . ." Author's interview with Jacques Maroni.

p. 200 While Jack struggled . . . Author's interview with Jacques Maroni.

p. 201 "Tell him he's way out . . ." Ibid.

p. 202 It was sometimes difficult . . . Correspondence with Richard Hanel, author's interview with Jacques Maroni.

p. 203 "You must not go in the plant . . ." Author's interview with Jacques Maroni.

p. 205 Jack Reith and his men . . . Author's interviews with Jacques Maroni, Bill Grimes.

p. 205 One night, he joined . . . Author's interview with Jacques Maroni.

p. 209 When a last-minute hitch . . . Author's interview with Maxine Andreae.

p. 210 "Well," she said . . . Ibid.

CHAPTER 15: "GARY COOPER ON WHEELS"

p. 214 Black and white images . . . Author's interview with Jacques Maroni.

p. 217 At headquarters . . . Author's interview with Bill Grimes.

p. 218 Against this backdrop . . . Author's interviews with Chase Morsey, Robert Jenkins, Jacques Maroni, Bill Grimes.

p. 219 Behind the plan was a dream . . . Eugene Bordinat oral history. Ford Archives of the Edison Institute.

p. 221 Within days . . . Author's interview with Jacques Maroni.

p. 221 "Well boys," he said . . . *The Fords: An American Epic,* by Peter Collier and David Horowitz, p. 242.

p. 222 Jim immediately went to . . . Author's interview with James Wright.

p. 223 "Mr. Crusoe," Wright eventually . . . Ibid.

p. 224 "There comes a time . . ." Author's interview with Jacques Maroni.

p. 225 "The numbers were wild . . ." Author's interview with Emmett Judge.

p. 225 When Paul Lorenz . . . Author's interview with Paul Lorenz.

p. 226 He moved through the numbers first . . . Presentation documents, courtesy of Emmett Judge.

pp. 227–28 The news was worth a party . . . Author's interview with Robert Dunham.

p. 229 "The Whiz Kids exercised . . ." *The Managerial Mystique* by Abraham Zaleznik, p. 94.

p. 229 "They are not auto men . . ." *Business Week,* September, 1959.

CHAPTER 16: SHOWDOWN AT CULVER CITY

p. 232 Wolfe had his doubts . . . Deposition by Thornton. Thornton archives.

p. 233 Tex was recruiting . . . Author's interviews with Maxine Andreae, Jane Andreson, Nora Dunning.

p. 233 "the company's dress rehearsal . . ." *Someone Has To Make It Happen* by Bernie Lay.

p. 234 A unique culture evolved at Culver City . . . *Fortune,* February, 1954.

p. 235 "Do you think Shakespeare was . . ." Author's interview with Glenn McDaniel.

p. 235 It was a rare day . . . Author's interviews with Myles Mace, Roy Ash, George Fenimore, Simon Ramo, Dean Wooldridge.

p. 236 It was too bad that . . . Author's interview with Roy Ash.

p. 237 "I'm surprised you can sit here . . ." Author's interview with George Fenimore, Roy Ash, George Kosmetsky.

p. 238 . . . by June of 1952 . . . Thornton deposition. Thornton archives.

p. 239 Tex first met with Lovett in Washington . . . Correspondence. Thornton archives.

p. 240 "We really don't have a disagreement . . ." Author's interview with Simon Ramo.

p. 240 "I am disappointed . . ." Correspondence. Thornton archives.

p. 241 As relations worsened . . . Author's interview with Roy Ash; *Fortune,* February, 1954; *Business Week,* October 3, 1953.

p. 242 The four vice presidents . . . Author's interviews with Simon Ramo, Dean Wooldridge.

p. 243 Now the escape . . . Thornton deposition. Thornton archives.

p. 244 "You're a young man . . ." Ibid.

p. 244 Hughes phoned him . . . Author's interview with Laney Thornton.

CHAPTER 17: UNSAFE AT ANY SPEED

p. 248 "He didn't understand people . . ." Author's interview with Ben Mills.

p. 248 "He was one of the brightest men . . ." Author's interview with Charles Beck.

p. 249 "Bob is so smart . . ." Eugene Bordinat oral history. Ford Archives of the Edison Institute.

p. 249 When he was controller . . . Author's interview with Thomas C. Page.

p. 250 Bob told those . . . *Iacocca: An Autobiography* by Lee Iacocca with William Novak, p. 42.

p. 250 "Oh where does your husband work . . ." Author's interview with Robert Dunham.

p. 250 She raised hell . . . *Promise and Power* by Deborah Shapley, p. 51.

p. 250 Margy brought McNamara back . . . Author's interview with Emmett Judge.

p. 251 Unlike most auto men . . . Author's interview with Robert Dunham.

p. 251 When McNamara later gained . . . Author's interview with Charles Bosworth.

p. 252 He always read the book . . . *The Best and the Brightest* by David Halberstam, pp. 291–92.

p. 252 One time, Bob got together . . . Author's interview with Ben Mills.

p. 255 "I know what the capacity . . ." Author's interview with Jacques Maroni.

p. 256 "I think it would be even more in keeping . . ." McNamara memo. Ford Industrial Archives.

p. 256 He had worried about safety . . . Author's interview with Robert McNamara.

p. 258 In the Fifties . . . Ibid.

p. 262 Decades later . . . Ibid.

p. 262 Soon it got ugly . . . Cieply interview with Holmes Brown.

p. 262 Jim Wright also was called in . . . Author's interview with James Wright.

p. 264 "Since two of the five . . ." Ford press release. Ford Industrial Archives.

CHAPTER 18: STEEL CARTOONS

p. 268 As a kid . . . Detroit *Free Press,* April 2, 1957.

p. 270 Free to let their imaginations roam . . . Author's interview with Bill Grimes.

p. 271 The ideas, some feasible . . . Various memos from Reith. Ford Industrial Archives.

p. 272 When the styling ideas were agreed . . . Author's correspondence and interview with John Najar.

p. 273 "Nine-tenths of the cars . . ." Author's interview with Leo Skidmore.

p. 273 He'd bring some of these . . . Author's interview with Maxine Andreae.

p. 275 Bordinat, who was intimately . . . Eugene Bordinat oral history. Ford Archives of the Edison Institute.

p. 275 He urged his men to go all out . . . Author's interview with George Hackett.

p. 276 "We looked after each other . . ." Author's interview with James Wright.

p. 277 "It was pretty visible . . ." Author's interview with Robert Eggert.

p. 278 When the group . . . Author's interviews with Arjay Miller, Charles Bosworth.

p. 279 Adlai Stevenson was . . . Author's interview with George Hackett.

p. 280 "This is a hot day . . ." Miami *Herald,* October 7, 1956.

p. 280 "These new Mercurys . . ." Ibid.

p. 281 "Mercury has been telling us . . ." Report to Reith. Ford Industrial Archives.

CHAPTER 19: THE BIRTH OF A NEW ERA

p. 286 All the out-of-work . . . Author's interview with Roy Ash.

p. 286 If the three . . . *Fortune,* April 1958.

p. 286 On a chance . . . *Someone Has To Make It Happen* by Bernie Lay, pp. 127–28.

p. 287 "No one wanted to give . . ." Author's interview with Roy Ash.

p. 288 The deal sputtered along . . . Author's interview with Glenn Mc-Daniel.

p. 288 "In our hands . . ." Author's interviews with Roy Ash, George Fenimore.

p. 290 Within months, McDaniel . . . Author's interview with Glenn Mc-Daniel.

p. 291 "We had no strategic plan . . ." Author's interview with Myles Mace.

p. 292 "We came to the point . . ." Author's interview with Roy Ash.

p. 293 "We'd been sitting up . . ." Author's interview with Myles Mace.

p. 293 "High technology was the common . . ." Author's interview with Harry Gray.

p. 294 "He was terribly frustrated . . ." *Someone Has To Make It Happen* by Bernie Lay, p. 191.

p. 295 "We got calls from people saying . . ." Ibid.

p. 296 "I think we ought to . . ." Author's interview with Myles Mace.

p. 296 "You guys are crazy as hell . . ." Ibid.

CHAPTER 20: THE IMPOSSIBLE TAKES A LITTLE LONGER

p. 299 "These men are monks . . ." *Fortune,* July 1961.

p. 299 The industry even dictated . . . Ibid.

p. 300 "Well, I can save you . . ." Author's interview with Maxine Andreae.

p. 300 "It's said that many funerals . . ." *Business Week,* 1953.

p. 300 "I could understand if you're . . ." Author's interview with Maxine Andreae.

p. 301 "You'd meet him at 8 p.m. . . . ." Author's interview with Fred Secrest.

p. 301 "How is it that you and Ben . . ." Author's interview with Maxine Andreae.

p. 302 There were rules . . . *Fortune,* November 1951.

p. 304 Bob, too, became in many ways . . . *Promise and Power* by Deborah Shapley, p. 137.

p. 304 "The wives were neglected . . ." Author's interview with Arjay Miller.

p. 304 "You didn't call your husband at work . . ." Author's interview with Maxine Andreae.

p. 305 "I had signed up for better or worse . . ." Author's interview with Flora Thornton.

CHAPTER 21: THE INDY 500

p. 309 Jack's new models . . . Various corporate memos. Ford Industrial Archives.

p. 310 There were quality problems . . . Ibid.

p. 310 Even Tex Thornton had reason . . . Correspondence. Thornton archives.

p. 311 Jack was caught in the sinking middle of the fight . . . Author's interview with Robert Jenkins.

p. 312 "In the last few weeks . . ." Mills memo. Ford Industrial Archives.

p. 313 If Jack was beginning . . . Author's interview with Maxine Andreae.

p. 314 "This is going to mean trouble . . ." Ibid.

p. 315 It was an issue that was also creating . . . Author's interview with Jacques Maroni.

p. 316 "I don't think you boys can . . ." Ibid.

p. 316 Mercury problems increasingly crowded . . . McNamara's personal calendar. Ford Industrial Archives.

p. 316 The group had not been there . . . McNamara memo to Thornton. Thornton archives.

p. 318 "Why do we need all these . . ." Author's interview with Jacques Maroni.

p. 319 "My face was a little red . . ." Memo from Breech to Reith. Ford Industrial Archives.

p. 319 He even put pressure on Jack . . . Ibid.

p. 320 "Our new car will out-accelerate . . ." Author's interview with George Hackett.

p. 321 "In thirteen states we outsold . . ." Reith memo to McNamara. Ford Industrial Archives.

p. 322 In the dream . . . Indianapolis *News,* May 30, 1957.

p. 324 Bordinat, Jack's friend . . . Bordinat oral history. Ford Archives.

p. 325 "Jack was very good at what he did . . ." Ibid.

p. 325 By the end of June . . . Corporate memos, Ford Industrial Archives.

p. 326 At one point, Breech telephoned . . . Author's interview with Bill Grimes.

p. 326 Jack did not hear the news . . . Author's interview with George Hackett.

p. 327 "I could see how he couldn't . . ." Author's interview with Jacques Maroni.

p. 327 On his way home that night . . . Author's interview with Gayle Warnock.

p. 328 "You know that, don't you . . ." Author's interview with Maxine Andreae.

p. 328 Bob walked into a 2:30 p.m. . . . Corporate memos. Ford Industrial Archives.

p. 330 For a few days in September . . . Correspondence. Thornton archives.

p. 331 "Don't let Jack quit . . ." Author's interview with Maxine Andreae.

p. 331 "Dear Mr. Breech . . ." Letter from Maxine Andreae to Breech. Ford Industrial Archives.

p. 331 A week later . . . Letter from Breech to Maxine Andreae. Ford Industrial Archives.

CHAPTER 22: THE EDSEL FIASCO

p. 335 Bob and Margy . . . *The Edsel Affair* by C. Gayle Warnock, p. 207.

p. 336 "I want you to put down . . ." Author's interview with Emmett Judge.

p. 336 "He used our loss estimates . . ." Ibid.

p. 337 Fairly quickly, McNamara developed . . . *The Edsel Affair* by C. Gayle Warnock, pp. 214–16.

p. 338 As soon as McNamara arrived . . . Ibid.

p. 339 "Now Ben," he said . . . Author's interview with Robert Jenkins.

p. 339 Roy Brown, the Edsel's head designer . . . Kenneth Spencer oral history. Ford Archives of the Edison Institute.

p. 340 "Damn near every day . . ." Author's interview with Ben Mills.

p. 340 He quickly got the nickname . . . Author's interview with Richard Stout.

p. 341 "What about Jim Nance . . ." Author's interview with Ben Mills.

p. 342 When McNamara discovered that one . . . Cieply interview with Robert Angell.

p. 343 For more than a year . . . Author's interview with James Wright.

p. 344 "I don't think he ever liked . . ." Ibid.

CHAPTER 23: A BIRTHDAY

p. 347 ". . . one of the nation's top sick-industry . . ." Cincinnati *Enquirer,* February 7, 1958.

p. 347 He arranged to have a barber shop . . . Author's interview with Kendrick Wilson.

p. 348 "Donna," he told her . . . Author's interview with Maxine Andreae.

p. 349 "We knew he was under . . ." Author's interview with Gordon Tuttle.

p. 349 But now, at two o'clock . . . Cincinnati *Enquirer,* July 5, 1960.

p. 350 Maxine reached for the . . . Author's correspondence with Dr. Edmund Schweitzer.

p. 350 Traces of gun powder . . . Coroner's report.

p. 350 Maxine had not heard a gunshot. Author's interview with Maxine Andreae.

p. 350 Jack had owned the gun for only a few months . . . Ibid.

p. 351 Only the day earlier . . . Author's interview with James Kerley.

p. 352 "Jack's spirits seemed to be high . . ." Correspondence. Thornton archives.

p. 353 Only in retrospect would . . . Author's interview with James Wright.

p. 354 A few months before his death . . . Author's interview with Bill Gossett.

p. 354 "He introduced me to his managers . . ." Author's interview with John Cuccio.

p. 354 "He talked about being the Pace Car driver . . ." Author's interview with Mrs. Edmund Schweitzer.

p. 355 "We were all in a state of shock . . ." Author's interview with Chase Morsey.

p. 355 That there was a Mass . . . Author's interview with Thomas Clark.

p. 355 Ford also dispatched a public relations . . . Author's interview with Robert Dunham.

p. 356 No one was more shocked . . . Author's interview with Charles Bosworth.

p. 356 Throughout the Mass, he was leafing . . . Ibid.

p. 356 "How is Jack Reith doing these days?" Author's interview with David Horowitz.

p. 357 "I don't think even she believed it . . ." Author's interview with Chase Morsey.

p. 357 "I had never known Jack to be depressed . . ." Author's interview with Charles Bosworth.

CHAPTER 24: PRINCIPLE VERSUS EXPEDIENCY

p. 362 "Mr. McNamara," Ford explained . . . Detroit Free Press, November 10, 1960.

p. 362 Bob was at the top of his form . . . McNamara speech. Ford Industrial Archives.

p. 364 "Bob's election as president . . ." Thornton letter. Thornton archives.

p. 365 One New York Times reporter . . . The New York Times, February 5, 1967.

p. 366 All the Whiz Kids disavowed . . . Arjay Miller speech. Ford Industrial Archives.

p. 367 "Just as the student . . ." *The Organization Man* by William H. Whyte, Jr.

p. 367 "They had the best and brightest . . ." Author's interview with Donald Frey.

p. 367 "Working for the controller's office . . ." Author's interview with James Kerley.

p. 368 "We had all the quality slogans . . ." Author's interview with Donald Lennox.

pp. 368–69 "We must be going out of business . . ." Author's interview with Donald Frey.

p. 369 Kennedy's conversation with Lovett . . . Lovett oral history, JFK Library Archives.

p. 369 Barely five weeks into his new job . . . Washington *Post,* May 9, 1984.

p. 371 "President Kennedy said to me . . ." Robert McNamara oral history, JFK Library Archives.

p. 372 "I think I'll call the president-elect . . ." Washington *Post,* May 9, 1984.

p. 373 Over the weekend and on Monday . . . Author's interview with Robert Dunham.

p. 374 McNamara, however, didn't want to say no . . . Michael Ciepley interview with Neil Staebler.

p. 374 "My God, Bob, it's only two . . ." Author's interview with James Wright.

p. 375 "Mr. President, I've written this letter . . ." Washington *Post,* May 9, 1984.

p. 376 "This may be one of the worst days . . . *The Fords: An American Epic* by Peter Collier and David Horowitz, p. 292.

CHAPTER 25: SYNERGY?

p. 380 By the end of 1961 . . . Litton annual reports.

p. 380 "Tex stood there and brokered . . ." Author's interview with Roy Ash.

p. 381 His imagination roamed . . . Author's interview with Harry Gray.

p. 383 Litton Industries became the first conglomerate . . . *Management: Tasks, Responsibilities, Practices* by Peter Drucker, pp. 681–82.

p. 383 At Litton and other conglomerates . . . *Mintzberg on Management* by Henry Mintzberg, pp. 153–72.

p. 385 . . . sought out the company . . . Author's interview with Harry Gray.

p. 385 "In the sixties . . ." Author's interview with Fred O'Green.

p. 385 "We had to have a nonbureaucratic . . ." Author's interview with Roy Ash.

p. 386 He had told Singleton . . . Author's interview with George Kosmetsky.

p. 386 "He sent us threatening letters . . ." Ibid.

p. 387 Kelly was the antithesis of Thornton. Author's interview with Claude Meconis.

p. 387 "Facts never made a man." Tape of Kelly before class of students, courtesy of Claude Meconis.

p. 387 "I tell people I'm a confidence . . ." Ibid.

p. 388 He and Flora had purchased . . . Author's interview with Flora Thornton.

p. 389 . . . "one of the most remarkable executives in the world . . ." *Time,* October 4, 1963.

p. 389 "Who are the most brightest men in California?" Interview notes. Thornton archives.

CHAPTER 26: "ADDING MACHINE WARRIORS"

p. 394 His very first recruit . . . Gilpatric oral history. John F. Kennedy Library archives.

p. 394 "In the two hours . . ." Ibid.

p. 395 "It was love at first sight . . ." Author's interview with Alain Enthoven.

p. 395 "His brilliance . . ." *From Hiroshima to Glasnost* by Paul H. Nitze with Ann M. Smith and Steven L. Rearden, p. 243.

p. 396 "This place is a jungle . . ." *Look,* April 23, 1963.

p. 396 "The reasoning wasn't sound . . ." Author's interview with Eugene Zuckert.

p. 397 "He wouldn't listen . . ." Gilpatric oral history. John F. Kennedy Library archives.

p. 397 "My people were working . . ." Wheeler oral history. JFK Library archives.

p. 398 Enthoven's Systems Analysis . . . Author's interview with Alain Enthoven.

p. 400 "It was a missionary job . . ." Washington *Post,* January 16, 1981.

p. 400 "One cannot make sense . . ." *How Much Is Enough? Shaping the Defense Program, 1961–1969* by Alain C. Enthoven and K. Wayne Smith.

p. 401 There were other key ideas . . . Ibid.

p. 402 "He doesn't care what your problems are . . ." Author's interview with Eugene Zuckert.

p. 402 Of all the occasions . . . *The Best and the Brightest* by David Halberstam.

p. 402 McNamara, recalls . . . Author's interview with Robert N. Anthony.

p. 403 ". . . extraordinary self-confidence based . . ." *The Past Has Another Pattern: Memoirs* by George Ball.

p. 403 McNamara's first presentation . . . Author's interview with Robert N. Anthony.

p. 406 Now, in the midst . . . *The Death of a President* by William Manchester.

p. 406 Within half an hour . . . Ibid.

p. 406 The President then turned to . . . *The Past Has Another Pattern: Memoirs* by George Ball.

p. 407 They separated . . . *The Death of a President* by William Manchester.

pp. 407–8 As the evening wore on . . . Ibid.

p. 408 Wearing a blotched pink . . . Ibid.

CHAPTER 27: FRIDEN BRAINS

p. 411 He had been in a quiet competition . . . Author's interviews with Arjay Miller, James Wright.

p. 412 "He was a lawyer . . ." Author's interview with Arjay Miller.

p. 412 When Henry chose . . . Author's interview with James Wright.

p. 413 From the start, Jim . . . Ibid.

p. 415 "That's when I decided . . ." Ibid.

p. 415 "Don't do a thing . . ." Ibid.

p. 416 "Look what Tex is doing . . ." Author's interview with Charles E. Beck.

p. 416 "Arjay," he said . . . Author's interview with Arjay Miller.

p. 419 In product planning . . . Author's interview with Donald Frey.

p. 420 Ford was now a car company . . . Spencer oral history. Ford Archives.

p. 422 "We learned in manufacturing . . ." Author's interview with Donald Lennox.

p. 422 They were not, he insisted . . . Author's interview with J. Edward Lundy.

p. 423 Some men at Ford . . . Author's interview with Robert Dunham.

p. 424 "Jim, I understand unfortunately . . ." Author's interview with James Kerley.

p. 425 "While we are a big company . . ." *Automotive News,* June 27, 1988.

p. 425 "We all had one bottle . . ." Author's interview with James Kerley.

p. 425 Lundy adopted in his finance group . . . Author's interview with Gerry Meyers.

p. 426 Every backup book . . . *The Reckoning* by David Halberstam, pp. 253–54.

p. 427 "He liked conciseness . . ." Author's interview with Fred Secrest.

p. 428 His men were under constant . . . Author's interview with Robert Jenkins.

p. 429 The only time he read something . . . Author's interview with J. Edward Lundy.

p. 430 "Ed," he told him . . . *Iacocca* by Lee Iacocca with William Novak.

p. 430 Indeed, Ford once asked . . . Author's interview with Robert Dunham.

p. 431 Lundy himself believes . . . Author's interview with J. Edward Lundy.

p. 432 "He felt that if someone . . ." *Automotive News,* June 27, 1988.

p. 433 Xerox veterans . . . Author's interview with David Nadler.

p. 433 "The old-timers didn't . . ." *Prophets in the Dark: How Xerox Reinvented Itself and Beat Back the Japanese* by David Kearns and David Nadler, pp. 57–65.

p. 433 "Another time . . ." Ibid.

p. 435 "I'm not going to quote you . . ." *A Bright Shining Lie* by Neil Sheehan, pp. 289–90.

CHAPTER 28: MCNAMARA'S WAR

p. 437 He had returned to Harvard . . . *The Harvard Crimson,* November 8, 1966.

p. 438 McNamara had reason . . . Ibid.

p. 439 "I spent four of the . . ." Ibid.

p. 439 Now blood streamed . . . Author's correspondence with Stephen Saltonstall.

p. 440 "Okay, fellas," he said . . . *The Harvard Crimson,* November 8, 1966.

p. 441 It was a harrowing experience . . . Author's interview with Robert Anthony.

p. 441 " 'Who do you suppose . . .' " Author's interview with Eugene Zuckert.

p. 442 As he would later testify . . . McNamara testimony at Lyndon Baines Johnson Library archives.

p. 443 The same day . . . Memo in LBJ Library archives.

p. 444 "If he was in something . . ." Gilpatric oral history, JFK Library archives.

p. 444 "He looked at me . . ." *From Hiroshima to Glasnost* by Paul H. Nitze with Ann M. Smith and Steven L. Rearden, pp. 258–59.

p. 445 McNamara's position did not go unchallenged. *The Past Has Another Pattern: Memoirs* by George Ball.

p. 446 "Laos, Cambodia, Thailand . . ." *Counsel to the President* by Clark Clifford, with Richard Holbrooke, p. 414.

p. 447 "I do not believe we can win . . ." Ibid.

p. 448 McNamara and his assistants . . . *A Soldier Reports* by General William C. Westmoreland, p. 273.

p. 448 "One area where . . ." *As I Saw It* by Dean Rusk, p. 522.

p. 449 "There was this feeling . . ." Author's interview with Peter Cohen.

p. 449 "In Vietnam . . ." *Mintzberg on Management* by Henry Mintzberg, pp. 354–55.

p. 450 A review of the same documents . . . *How Much Is Enough? Shaping the Defense Program, 1961–1969* by Alain C. Enthoven and K. Wayne Smith.

p. 450 "You couldn't reconcile . . ." Washington *Post,* May 10, 1984.

p. 450 " 'Mr. Secretary, I'd just like to . . .' " Author's interview with Colin Blaydon.

p. 451 Tex went with . . . Author's correspondence with Emerso Itschner.

p. 452 "He had maps . . ." Author's interview with Chuck Thornton.

p. 452 "A surprising number were . . ." Thornton report. Thornton archives.

p. 453 Tex strongly opposed the idea . . . *From Hiroshima to Glasnost* by Paul H. Nitze with Ann M. Smith and Steven L. Rearden, p. 263.

p. 453 Over dinner, Gene and Bob . . . Author's interview with Maxine Andreae.

pp. 454–55 Disturbed by it, President Johnson . . . *The Triumph & Tragedy of Lyndon Johnson* by Joseph A. Califano, Jr., p. 249.

p. 455 "The death, destruction . . ." *As I Saw It* by Dean Rusk.

p. 456 "Johnny," he told . . . *National Review,* June 10, 1988, pp. 28–29.

p. 456 "Bob, I already have a car . . ." Author's interview with William Gossett.

p. 458 "The goddamned Air Force . . ." *Counsel to the President* by Clark Clifford, with Richard Holbrooke, pp. 456–59.

p. 460 It would remind . . . New York *Times,* July 1, 1971.

p. 462 To others, like Alain . . . Author's interview with Alain Enthoven.

CHAPTER 29: DEATH OF A WHIZ KID

p. 465 Shivering together . . . Author's interview with Marika Aires.

pp. 466–67 Moore-Grear's earnings . . . Financial report. Thornton archives.

p. 467 "It took a lot more effort . . ." Author's interview with George Thomassen.

p. 467 "The underlying cause . . ." Letter to Thornton. Thornton archives.

p. 467 He wanted out of the business. Author's interview with James Grear.

p. 468 "But intellectually, it was . . ." Author's interview with Eugene Zuckert.

p. 469 "Some dealers questioned . . ." Author's interview with Philip Fitts.

p. 470 "I told them they were . . ." Author's interview with James Grear.

p. 470 "George," he wrote . . . Letter from Thornton. Thornton archives.

p. 471 The end result . . . Correspondence. Thornton archives.

p. 472 George began to proselytize . . . Annual report.

p. 473 "He called me into his office . . ." Author's interview with David Weeks.

p. 473 In the midst of the turmoil . . . Author's interview with Harry Allcock.

p. 474 "George was pretty black . . ." Author's interview with Lynn Bartlett.

p. 474 When the auto business fell apart . . . Author's interviews with Marika Aires and Marika Moore Cutler.

p. 475 His friend felt at a loss . . . Author's interview with Lynn Bartlett.

p. 475 "He laughed at you when you . . ." Author's interview with Eugene Zuckert.

p. 476 "He was personally offended . . ." Author's interview with Laura Moore.

p. 478 Laura had spent . . . Ibid.

p. 478 "I am confident that . . ." Letter from Thornton. Thornton archives.

p. 479 One late afternoon . . . Author's interview with Eugene Zuckert.

p. 479 "I looked in . . ." Author's interview with Laura Moore.

p. 479 "He couldn't cope . . ." Author's interview with Marika Aires.

CHAPTER 30: THE SHATTERED IMAGE

p. 484 The shareholders . . . Los Angeles *Times,* December 3, 1967.

p. 484 "By 1967 . . ." *The Go-Go Years* by John Brooks, p. 180.

p. 484 "I have no plans to leave . . ." Ibid.

p. 485 "It was an attempt to plead . . ." Author's interview with Roy Ash.

p. 486 "It was in orbit . . ." Ibid.

p. 486 It was the typical . . . Author's interview with James Flanigan.

p. 488 "The trouble with Litton today . . ." *Forbes,* December 1, 1969.

p. 488 "They were master image creators . . ." Author's interview with William George.

p. 489 "Ash felt it was like . . ." Author's interview with James Biggar.

p. 490 "His work in Washington . . ." Author's interview with Harry Gray.

p. 490 "He was under great stress . . ." Author's interview with Flora Thornton.

p. 492 "When you try lawsuits . . ." Author's interview with William Masterson.

p. 492 "He offered me $5 million . . ." Court records, Los Angeles County Court.

p. 493 "He was a tyrant . . ." Author's interview with Gordon Hampton.

p. 494 "It was a very emotionally . . ." Author's interview with Chuck Thornton.

p. 497 "In retrospect . . ." Author's interview with Roy Ash.

p. 497 "Everything about his personality . . ." Author's interview with William George.

p. 497 "It was one of those areas . . ." Author's interview with Robert Lentz.

p. 498 "Tex always felt sorry . . ." Author's interview with John Lewis.

p. 498 "You can't have one foot out . . ." Author's interview with Fred O'Green.

CHAPTER 31: A REUNION

p. 502 In late 1980 . . . Ciepley interview with Charles Thornton.

p. 502 Tex exchanged letters . . . Correspondence. Thornton archives.

p. 502 But the planning . . . Ciepley interview with Charles Thornton.

p. 502 McNamara, disgusted at the . . . Washington *Post,* May 10, 1984.

p. 503 Tex Thornton first began . . . Author's interviews with George Fenimore, Barney Oldfield, Flora Thornton.

p. 503 Tex called Arjay . . . Author's interview with Arjay Miller.

p. 504 "Dad, why are you smoking . . ." Author's interview with Laney Thornton.

p. 504 "I had given him . . ." Author's interview with Harry Gray.

p. 505 "We're at about $5 billion . . ." Author's interview with Barney Oldfield.

p. 506 Two days later . . . Ibid.

p. 507 Indeed, when he slipped . . . Author's interview with Chuck Thornton.

p. 508 Only weeks before . . . Author's interview with Laney Thornton.

p. 509 Five of the six . . . Author's interview with Flora Thornton.

p. 510 "There wasn't a lot of talk . . ." Author's interview with Arjay Miller.

p. 513 "Its wizards . . ." *In Search of Excellence* by Tom Peters and Robert Waterman, p. 29.

PHOTOGRAPHS AND ILLUSTRATIONS

p. 12 Photo of River Rouge from the Detroit *Free Press;* pp. 22–23 Photo of Tex & Flora Thornton courtesy of Mrs. Flora L. Thornton, photos of Tex as a teen and with mother courtesy of John P. Lewis; p. 38 Photo of Stat Control staff in Washington and Tex at officers' club courtesy of Marika D. Aires, photo of Bob McNamara reprinted with permission of AP/Wide World Photos; p. 52 Photo of Reiths with Bosworth courtesy of Charles E. Bosworth; p. 64 Photos of George Moore and Stat Control officers and George and Mimi Moore courtesy of Marika D. Aires; p. 76 Photo of Tex with General Arnold courtesy of John P. Lewis, photo of cartoon-like portrait of Tex courtesy of Marika D. Aires; p. 90

Photo of Whiz Kids courtesy of Litton Industries Inc.; p. 110 Photos of "Andy" Andreson and family courtesy of Mrs. Jane Andreson; p. 122 Photo of Henry Ford II and Ernest Breech by Alfred Eisenstaedt, *Life* Magazine, © 1956 Time Warner Inc., portion of organization chart courtesy of James Wright; p. 142 Photo of magazine cover featuring Louis Crusoe reprinted from the November 13, 1954, issue of *Business Week* by special permission, © 1954 by McGraw-Hill, Inc., photo of Tex courtesy of James P. Lewis; p. 154 Photo of Howard Hughes reprinted with permission of AP/Wide World Photos; p. 166 Photo of Henry Ford reprinted with permission of AP/Wide World Photos; p. 184 Photos of Moore-Day Motors, George Moore and Mark Day, and George and Mimi Moore courtesy of Marika D. Aires; p. 212 Photo of magazine cover featuring Bob McNamara reprinted from the September 16, 1959, issue of *Business Week* by special permission, © 1959 by McGraw-Hill, Inc.; p. 230 Photo of Tex and Roy Ash courtesy of Litton Industries, Inc.; p. 246 Reproduction of Ford advertisement courtesy of the Henry Ford Museum, The Edison Institute; p. 266 Photos of Jack Reith on prototype platform and George Hackett courtesy of George Hackett, artist's rendering courtesy of John Najar; p. 284 Photos of Tex Thornton at New York Stock Exchange courtesy of Litton Industries, Inc.; p. 298 Photos of 10th anniversary party courtesy of Charles E. Bosworth; p. 308 Photos of Mercury Turnpike Cruiser and the Ford Falcon reprinted with permission of the National Automotive History Collection of the Detroit Public Library; p. 334 Photo of Ben Mills from the Detroit *Free Press,* profit table from the Ford Industrial Archives; p. 346 Photo of Jack Reith from the Detroit *Free Press*; p. 360 Photo of Bob McNamara and Henry Ford II from the Detroit *Free Press,* photo of McNamara and John F. Kennedy by Alfred Eisenstaedt, *Life* Magazine, © Time Warner Inc.; p. 378 Photo of Tex Thornton and Roy Ash courtesy of Litton Industries, Inc., magazine cover featuring Tex and Roy reprinted from the April 16, 1966, issue of *Business Week* by special permission, © 1966 by McGraw-Hill, Inc., reproduction of Thornton cover of *Time* magazine by permission of Time, Time Warner Inc.; p. 392 Photo of Bob McNamara reprinted with permission of AP/Wide World Photos, reproduction of cover of *Time* magazine by permission of Time, Time Warner Inc., reproduction of cover of *Newsweek* magazine by permission of Newsweek, Washington Post Co.; p. 410 Photos of Arjay Miller and Henry Ford II from Detroit *Free Press*, photo of J. Edward Lundy from NYT Pictures, reproduction of Automotive Industries cover courtesy of Chilton Publishing; p. 436, Photos of Bob McNamara in Vietnam and with Lyndon B. Johnson reprinted with permission of AP/Wide World Photos; p. 464 Photos of George Moore and family courtesy of Marika D. Aires; p. 482 Photo of Tex Thornton courtesy of Litton Industries, Inc., reproduction of *Forbes* cover reprinted by permission of *Forbes* magazine, © 1969 Forbes Inc.; p. 500 Photo of Tex Thornton by Richard Hewlett, photo of Bob and Margy McNamara by Alfred Eisenstaedt, *Life* magazine, © Time Warner, Inc.

Bibliography

Alvarez, A. *The Savage God.* New York: Random House, 1970.

Arbib, Robert S. *Here We Are Together.* London: Longmans, Green & Co., 1946.

Ball, George W. *The Past Has Another Pattern: Memoirs.* New York: W. W. Norton & Co., 1982.

Bradlee, Benjamin C. *Conversations with Kennedy.* New York: W. W. Norton & Co., 1975.

Brooks, John. *The Go-Go Years.* New York: Weybright & Talley, 1973.

Brough, James. *The Ford Dynasty: An American Story.* New York: Doubleday & Co., Inc., 1977.

Califano, Jr., Joseph A. *The Triumph & Tragedy of Lyndon Johnson.* New York: Simon and Schuster, 1991.

Callahan, David. *Dangerous Capabilities: Paul Nitze and the Cold War.* New York: Harper & Row, 1990.

Clifford, Clark, with Richard Holbrooke. *Counsel to the President.* New York: Random House, 1991.

Collier, Peter and Horowitz, David. *The Fords: An American Epic.* New York: Summit Books, 1987.

Cruikshank, Jeffrey L. *A Delicate Experiment: The Harvard Business School 1908–1945.* Boston: Harvard Business School Press, 1987.

Drucker, Peter F. *Adventures of a Bystander.* New York: Harper & Row, 1978.

———*Concept of the Corporation.* New York: John Day, 1946.

———*Management: Tasks, Responsibilities, Practices.* New York: Harper & Row, 1973.

Ellsberg, Daniel. *Papers on the War.* New York: Simon and Schuster, 1972.

Enthoven, Alain C. and Smith, K. Wayne. *How Much Is Enough? Shaping the Defense Program, 1961–1969.* New York: Harper & Row, 1971.

Ford, Henry, with Samuel Crowther. *My Life and Work.* New York: Garden City Publishing, 1922.

Geneen, Harold S., with Alvin Moscow. *Managing.* New York: Doubleday, 1984.

Goodwin, Richard N. *Remembering America.* Boston: Little, Brown & Co., 1988.

Guthman, Edwin O. and Shulman, Jeffrey, editors. *Robert Kennedy: In His Own Words.* New York: Bantam, 1988.

Halberstam, David. *The Best and the Brightest.* New York: Random House, 1972.

———*The Reckoning.* New York: William Morrow & Co., 1986.

Iacocca, Lee, with William Novak. *Iacocca: An Autobiography.* New York: Bantam, 1984.

Isaacson, Walter and Thomas, Evan. *The Wise Men.* Simon and Schuster Inc., 1986.

Karnow, Stanley. *Vietnam: A History.* New York: Viking Press, 1983.

Kearns, David and Nadler, David. *Prophets in the Dark: How Xerox Reinvented Itself and Beat Back the Japanese.* New York: HarperBusiness, 1992.

Lacey, Robert. *Ford: The Men and the Machine.* Boston: Little, Brown & Co., 1986.

Lay, Beirne. *Someone Has to Make It Happen.* Englewood Cliffs, NJ: Prentice-Hall, Inc., 1969.

McNamara, Robert S. *The Essence of Security, Reflections in Office.* New York: Harper & Row, 1968.

Manchester, William. *The Death of a President.* New York: Harper & Row, 1967.

Maurer, Herrymon. *In Quiet Ways.* Dayton, Ohio: The Mead Corporation, 1970.

Mills, C. Wright. *White Collar.* New York: Oxford University Press, 1951.

Mintzberg, Henry. *Mintzberg on Management: Inside Our Strange World of Organizations.* New York: The Free Press, 1989.

Nader, Ralph. *Unsafe at Any Speed.* New York: Grossman Publishers, 1965.

Nevins, Allan and Hill, Frank Ernest. *Ford: Decline and Rebirth, 1932–1962.* New York: Charles Scribner's Sons, 1963.

————*Ford: Expansion and Challenge 1915–1933.* New York: Charles Scribner's Sons, 1957.

Nitze, Paul H., with Ann M. Smith and Steven L. Rearden. *From Hiroshima to Glasnost.* New York: Grove Weidenfeld, 1989.

O'Donnell, Kenneth P. and Powers, David F. with Joe McCarthy. *Johnny We Hardly Knew Ye.* Boston: Little, Brown & Co., 1970.

Petersen, Donald E. and Hillkirk, John. *A Better Idea: Redefining the Way Americans Work.* Boston: Houghton Mifflin, 1991.

Rae, John B. *Henry Ford: Great Lives Observed.* Englewood Cliffs, NJ: Prentice-Hall, Inc., 1969.

Ramo, Simon. *The Business of Science.* New York: Hill & Wang, 1988.

Richards, William C. *The Last Billionaire.* New York: Charles Scribner's Sons, 1948.

Rusk, Dean. *As I Saw It.* New York: W. W. Norton & Co., 1990.

Shapley, Deborah. *Promise and Power: The Life and Times of Robert McNamara.* Boston: Little, Brown & Co., 1993.

Sheehan, Neil. *A Bright Shining Lie.* New York: Random House, 1988.

Sloan, Alfred P. *My Years with General Motors.* New York: Doubleday, 1963.

Snyder, William P. *Case Studies in Military Systems Analysis.* Washington, D.C.: Industrial College of the Armed Forces, 1967.

Sobel, Robert. *The Rise and Fall of the Conglomerate Kings.* New York: Stein & Day, 1984.

Stout, Richard H. *Make 'Em Shout Hooray!* New York: Vantage Press, 1988.

Trewhitt, Henry L. *McNamara: His Ordeal in the Pentagon.* New York: Harper & Row, 1971.

Warnock, C. Gayle. *The Edsel Affair.* Paradise Valley, AZ: Pro West, 1980.

Westmoreland, General William C. *A Soldier Reports.* New York: Doubleday, 1976.

Whyte, William H. *The Organization Man.* New York: Simon and Schuster, 1956.

Wright, J. Patrick. *On a Clear Day You Can See General Motors.* New York: Avon Books, 1979.

Zaleznik, Abraham. *The Managerial Mystique.* New York: Harper & Row, 1989.

Acknowledgements

I had stumbled upon the story of the Whiz Kids in 1984 as a curious staff writer for *Forbes* magazine in New York. Scanning the book titles in the magazine's library, I came across the authorized biography of the Ford Motor Company. Even in the few paragraphs of description I read of them in Allan Nevins' and Frank Hill's *Ford: Decline and Rebirth, 1933–1962*, the ten originals and their unique story fairly leaped off the page.

That early interest resulted in one of those whatever-happened-to stories for *Forbes* and eventually put me on a personal journey to find out much more about these Army Air Force officers and their odyssey through postwar America. Michael Ciepley, then a *Forbes* colleague who had been researching a book on Henry Ford II, had interviewed several of the Whiz Kids, including the late Charles Thornton. His notes, often rich in detail and candor, inspired me to think in book terms. Harriet Rubin, my editor at Doubleday/Currency, loved the idea from the start. She has been a supportive champion through the years I've worked on the book, an invaluable collaborator and intellectual companion who always challenged me to do more and to do better.

My wife, Sharon, and my children, Jonathan, Kathryn and Sarah, were supportive and tolerant of the many hours I dedicated to the project during vacations, weekends, nights and mornings. Steve Shepard and Mark Morrison, my editors at *Business Week,* were gracious enough to allow me two leaves of absence from the magazine. My agent, Martha Millard, prodded me along, always encouraging me to get it done. Catherine Phillips, a researcher in Michigan, helped to dig up a lot of basic material in the early days of the book.

Librarians in dozens of cities and towns greatly assisted my search for press clippings and materials on the men and the times. Darleen Flaherty, the archivist at the Ford Industrial Archives, could not have been more helpful. The same is true of David Crippen, who led me to the gold in the many documents and oral histories at the Ford Archives at the Henry Ford Museum.

Lastly, I'd like to thank the Whiz Kids and their families for opening their doors and allowing a stranger to examine their lives. I interviewed every surviving member of the group—often numerous times—as well as the widows and children of the four members who are no longer alive. Without their cooperation, this book would not have been possible.

Index

Accidents, auto, 256–57
Accountability, 164, 171, 313
A. C. Nielsen Co., 80
Advertising, 13, 77, 188, 247–64, 267, 277–78, 332, 337–38
  quantification, 255
  safety, 258–61
Agricultural Adjustment Administration, 29
Air Force. *See* Army Air Force
Air Policy Commission, 136
Air Transport Command, 161
Allegheny Corporation, 79, 83, 87
Allen & Co., 287
Alsop, Joseph, 462
Ambition, 98, 144–45, 267, 317, 429
American Civil Liberties Union, 251, 370
American Motors, 81, 330, 425–26
American Trust Company, 289
Analysis
  cost, 248
  economic, 126, 168
  financial, 365
  of market research, 80
  overvalued, 515
  quantitative, 8, 174, 419
  systems, 395, 398, 400
  of weapons programs, 395
Andreson, Andy ("Wilbur"), 17, 85,
  88, 90*il*, 98, 110*il*, 114, 118–20, 156, 305–6, 502
  at Ford Motor Company, 169
Angell, Robert, 252, 342
Anthony, Robert, 402–3, 455
Army Air Force, 7, 13, 18, 19, 20, 49
  Officer Candidate School, 43, 51
  organization, 33, 34, 35, 36
Arnold, Henry "Hap," 34, 35, 40, 61, 62
Arthur D. Little, 79
Ash, Roy, 241–42, 286, 287, 288, 290, 291, 292, 294, 295–96, 380, 382–83, 385, 416, 484, 485, 486, 488, 490–91, 497–98
Assembly line, 168–69, 178
Atomic bomb, 73, 233
Atomic Energy Commission, 399, 468
AT&T, 171
Audits, 104, 237–38
Authority, 170
  centralized, 8
  conflicting, 312
  in decentralization, 173
  delegation of, 125, 163–64
  lines of, 60, 169, 171
  and responsibility, 164, 169
Auto industry, 7, 16
  abuses, 186, 188
  bootlegging, 186

Auto industry *(cont.)*
Japanese, 311
postwar, 81, 186, 188
reconversion of plants, 105
social responsibility, 101, 256, 262
traditional management, 93, 99–101
treatment of workers, 95
Automation, 130
Automobile Manufacturers
Association, 261
Automobiles
compact, 277
part in American life, 112
postwar demand for, 186, 188
safety, 247
as status symbols, 112, 218
trade-ins, 190
Automotive News, 262
Avco Manufacturing, 330, 347–49

Balance, 6
Ball, George, 403, 406, 445, 446, 448
Barringer, Reau, 60
Bartlett, Lynn, 187, 190, 469, 474, 476
Bates, Sarah, 27–28
Bay of Pigs invasion, 404
"Beat GM," 214
Beck, Charles, 248, 249, 416
Beckman, Arnold, 380
Bekins Company, 119, 156, 305
Bell Laboratories, 160, 231
Bendix Aviation Corp., 123, 124, 130
Bennett, Gerry, 433
Bennett, Harry, 99–100, 102, 107
Bergbom, Warren, 223, 224
The Best and the Brightest
(Halberstam), 433
Biggar, James, 489
Blaydon, Colin, 450
"Blue Book," 172
Bordinat, Gene, 219, 271, 275, 324–25
Bosworth, Charles, 13, 16, 17, 21, 52*il*,
58, 59, 84, 88, 90*il*, 98, 103, 107,
116, 118, 251, 278,. 356, 357, 501,
510, 531–32

at Ford Motor Company, 132, 163,
169, 173, 174, 177
"Bow Legs," 232
Breech, Ernie, 122*il*, 123–25, 129–30,
138, 168, 180, 197, 199, 217, 240–
41, 259, 280, 281, 316, 318, 319–
20, 324–25, 326, 342
firing of Thornton, 144–45, 146–47
resignation from Ford Motor
Company, 361
as threat to Thornton, 124–26, 130–
31
Brennan, Father Gerard, 423
Brink, V., 329
Brooks, John, 484
Brown, Donaldson, 170
Brown, Holmes, 259, 262
Brown Brothers Harriman & Co., 125,
287
Bryan, Jimmy, 323
Budget, 168, 179
capital, 126
centers, 175
military, 397, 453
Bugas, John, 20, 100, 107, 331, 411–12,
415
Buick, 112, 215, 219, 227
Roadmaster, 271
Super, 271
Bundy, McGeorge, 405, 406, 446, 453
Bureaucracy, control over, 56
Burns, Arthur, 218
Business
application of military experience
to, 78–79
law of balance, 6
public responsibility, 101, 136, 137
traditional management, 93
Business Week (magazine), 112, 140,
218, 229, 300, 321, 386

Cadillac, 215, 227, 277
Califano, Joseph, 455, 459
California Institute of Technology, 160
Capitalism, 9
Carnegie, Andrew, 41

Castro, Fidel, 404
Central Intelligence Agency, 404–5
Centralization, 398
    of authority, 8
Chain of command, 100
Change, 175, 516
Chesapeake & Ohio Railway, 80
Chevrolet, 177, 180, 181, 215, 227, 258,
    262
Chicago Automobile Show, 275
Chrysler Corporation, 81, 171, 219,
    226, 258, 260, 318
    market share, 17
    Plymouth, 227
Citroen, 198, 207, 208
Clark Dodge, 287
Clifford, Clark, 446, 447, 458
Cold War, 232
Cole, Ed, 258, 260, 262
Colgate University, 68
Command Retrieval Information
    System, 472–73
Communism, 158, 200, 204, 291, 444–
    45
Competition, foreign, 260–61, 342,
    343–45, 362, 368, 432, 513
Computers, 292, 293
    digital, 386
Concept of the Corporation (Drucker),
    125, 170
Cone, Fairfax, 336
La Confédération Générale du Travail,
    200, 204
Conflict, line and staff, 179
Conglomerates, 381, 382, 383, 484
Contracts
    defense, 232
    government, 286
    management, 191
    military, 348, 381, 496
    union, 201
Control
    centralized, 172
    cost, 418–19
    financial, 168
    hierarchy in, 24

inventory, 61, 421
    management, 485
    organizational, 168
    politics of, 43
    systems, 18
Cook, Ransom, 289, 506
Copeland, Lammont, 384
Cordiner, Ralph, 171
Cornell University, 256–57, 258, 260
Corporation
    decentralization, 170–71
    divisions, 171
    growth of, 169
Corruption, 103
Costs
    analysis, 248
    centers, 175
    control, 175, 418–19
    cutting, 8
    estimates, 180–81
    isolating, 174
    labor, 362–63
    manufacturing, 175
    production, 348, 364
    reduction, 365
    of service, 363
Coulton, George, 83
Council of Economic Advisers, 218,
    453
Cox, Buford, 29
Craig, Burt, 81, 82
CRIS, 472–73
Crusoe, Lewis, 122*il*, 130, 177–81, 199,
    219–20, 227, 277, 280, 303, 309
    friction with Thornton, 131–38
    illness, 313, 314
    relations with Reith, 179–81
Cuccio, John, 354
Curtice, Harlow, 220, 271, 364
Customer, 420
    complaints, 418–19
    relations, 170
    respect for, 190
    satisfaction, 8

Dahlinger, Ray, 128–29

Dashboard, padded, 257, 259
David, Donald, 226
Davis, Jack, 123, 219
Day, Mark, 139, 184*il*, 187, 188, 191, 194
Dealers, 220–21
  abuses by, 186, 188
  bootlegging, 186
  consulted on changes, 180
  gray-market, 186
  Lincoln-Mercury, 314–16, 319, 467
Deaver, Michael, 506
Decentralization, 163, 170, 171, 172, 173, 177, 312
Decision-making, 8
  centralized, 8
  fact-based, 19, 35, 44, 56
  numbers in, 19
  planning in, 57
  processes, 171
  research in, 347
  use of figures in, 42–43
  wartime, 44
Defense Industry Advisory Council, 453
Defense Intelligence Agency, 398, 406
Defense Supply Agency, 398
DeLaRossa, Don, 270, 271
DeLorean, John, 364
Department of Defense, 8, 48, 292, 369–76, 393–409
  Office of Systems Analysis, 395
Department of State, 135, 137
  Agency for International Development, 451
Depression, Great, 14, 17, 18, 27, 29, 47, 220
Design, 268, 324
De Soto, 227
Detroit, 111–13
DeVore, Malcolm, 238
Dietrich, Noah, 158–59, 160–61, 162, 236, 237, 238, 239, 240, 242, 244, 492–93, 494, 495–96
Digital Controls, 294
Dillon, Douglas, 393

Distinguished Service Medal, 509
Diversification, 381
Dobbs, James, 189–90
Donham, Wallace, 39, 40, 41, 44
Donner, Frederic, 364
Doyle, Larry, 338
Drake University, 60
Draper, Douglas, 292
Drucker, Peter, 100, 125, 170, 171, 515
Dunham, Robert, 96, 227, 229, 250, 251, 258–59, 355, 423
Dunn, James, 208
DuPont, Pierre, 170
Durant, Billy, 131
Dykstra, John, 311, 412, 413, 414

Eaker, Ira, 157, 158, 161, 494
Earl, Harley, 220
Eastman Kodak, 79, 176
The Economics of Defense in the Nuclear Age (Hitch), 395
Economy
  postwar, 14, 169, 186, 188
  recessionary, 315, 321, 340, 348
  wartime, 30
Edsel, 9, 209, 215, 216, 279, 315, 324, 328, 335–42, 513–14
Efficiency, 8, 50
Eggert, Robert, 277–78
Eisenhower, Dwight, 202, 218, 279–80, 282, 291, 397
Electro Dynamics Corp., 288, 290
Electronics, 292, 293, 380
  fire-control systems, 160, 162, 232, 233, 243
  inertial guidance systems, 292
  military, 295
  radar, 160
Elliot, Nora, 126–27, 233
Ellsberg, Daniel, 460, 461
Emanuel, Victor, 349
Engineering, 106, 177, 180, 279, 513
  schedules, 127
Engle, Elwood, 269–70, 271, 272, 273, 275

Enthoven, Alain, 395, 398, 400, 401, 462
Entrepreneurship, 385

Fenimore, George, 162, 505, 507
Finance, 83, 94, 177, 179–80, 417–32
Fisher Body Company, 131, 135
Fitts, Philip, 191, 469
Five-Year Defense Plan, 401
Flanigan, James, 486, 487
Flying Boat. *See* Spruce Goose
Foote, Cone & Belding, 336
Forbes (magazine), 429, 486, 487, 491
Ford, Benson, 130, 133–34, 275, 280
Ford, Clara, 128
Ford, Edsel, 16, 114, 220
Ford, Henry, 8, 16, 17, 41, 99, 100, 128, 167, 170–71
Ford, Henry II, 7, 9, 13–14, 16, 18, 80–81, 94–95, 107, 108, 164–65, 197, 198–99, 206, 209, 279, 316, 342, 361, 365, 371, 375–76, 411–12, 414–15, 417, 430, 431–32, 527
    hiring of Ernie Breech, 123–25
    lack of interest in government, 135–37
    postwar activities, 81–83
    relations with unions, 101
Ford automobiles
    Cardinal, 363
    Deluxe 6, 112
    Fairlane, 223
    Falcon, 249, 343–45, 353, 363, 413, 414
Ford Foundation, 456
Ford Motor Company, 7–8, 12*il*, 81
    advertising, 13, 77, 247, 267, 335
    Cadillac Division, 227
    disorganization in, 103–7
    Edsel, 9, 209, 215, 216, 279, 315, 324, 328, 335–36
    Ford Division, 112–13, 172, 177, 179, 206, 218, 222, 248, 251, 255, 256, 262, 267–68, 337, 414–15
    and government contracts, 135–36
    hierarchy in, 103

    hiring of Thornton's group, 82–108
    lack of executive team, 124–25
    Lifeguard Design, 247, 260
    Lincoln Division, 187, 219, 226, 227, 268, 310, 312, 325, 329
    management role in policy formation, 125
    market share, 17
    Mercury Division, 9, 215–16, 219, 220–21, 222, 226–27, 260, 267–82, 310, 325, 329
    Operating Committee, 340
    Policy Committee, 126, 127
    pre-Thornton organization, 99–107
    production scheduling, 126, 127
    Product Planning Committee, 270–71
    profits, 124–25
    quality problems, 309–32
    recruitment, 175–76
    reorganization, 19, 172
    rivalries at, 134–35
    rivalry with General Motors, 9–10, 168, 213–14, 218–19, 344–45
    salaries, 85–88, 92–93
    security system, 99–100
    smoking in, 102
    traditional management, 99–101
    Vedette, 198, 208, 209, 219
Ford of Canada, 330
Ford of France, 9, 181, 197–210
Fortune (magazine), 291, 294, 299, 300, 385, 403–4
Frey, Donald, 367, 368–69, 419–20
FUBAR, 104
FYDP, 401

Gandelot, Howard, 261
Gates, Byron, 36
Gates, Thomas, 394, 403
Geneen, Harold, 44, 421
General Dynamics, 290
General Electric, 60, 61, 116, 160, 171, 233, 234, 287, 311, 432
General Motors, 9, 81, 100, 123, 131, 132, 171, 217, 314, 324, 364

General Motors *(cont.)*
  attitude toward safety, 257–58, 264
  Buick, 112, 215, 219, 227, 271
  Cadillac, 215, 277
  Chevrolet, 177, 180, 181, 215, 227,
     258, 262
  decentralized structure, 170
  market share, 17
  Oldsmobile, 112, 215, 219, 227
  Pontiac, 215, 219, 227
  profits, 101
  rivalry with Ford Motor Company,
     9–10, 168, 213–14, 218–19, 345
  strikes against, 111
George, Harold, 161, 162, 239–40
George, William, 488–89, 497
George Washington University, 32
GIGO, 105
Gilmour, Alan, 432
Gilpatric, Roswell, 394, 395, 397, 405,
     443, 444
Glass, safety, 257
The Go-Go Years (Brooks), 484
Goldwater, Barry, 394
Gornick, Alan, 199
Gossett, William, 138, 331, 353, 456
Gray, Harry, 290, 292, 294, 381–82,
     384–85, 485–86, 490, 504–5
Grear, James, 188, 189, 192, 194, 466,
     469, 471
Grimes, Bill, 271, 326
Gross, Robert, 240–41
Guadalcanal, 70

Hackett, George, 275, 276, 320
Halberstam, David, 455, 528
Hampton, Gordon, 493
Hanks, Sam, 323, 324
Harder, Del, 130
Harvard University, 14, 18, 24, 36,
     39–44, 45, 47, 51, 60, 85, 146,
     175, 176, 187–88, 193, 200, 252,
     362, 382
  antiwar protests, 437–42
  training in statistical control, 39–44
Haskins and Sells, 237, 238

Hatcher, Harlan, 251
Highways, interstate, 217
Hill, Frank, 429
Hiroshima, 73
Hitch, Charles, 395, 401
Hodgson, Richard, 48
Horwitz, Solis, 398
Howard, Melvin, 433
Hughes, Howard, 9, 155–58, 161, 162–
     63, 235, 239–40, 244, 286
  sense of patriotism, 158
Hughes Aircraft, 159–64, 231–44, 285–
     86, 287
Hughes Tool Company, 158, 235
Hull-Dobbs Company, 189
Hulman, Anton Jr., 323
Human relations, 43

Iacocca, Lee, 412, 430
IBM, 55–56
Infantile paralysis, 85, 115
Inflation, 453, 496
Information
  authority over, 35
  flow, 313
  gathering, 35
  and power, 36
Information for Industry, 468–74
Ingalls Shipbuilding Corp., 380, 385,
     486
In Search of Excellence (Peters/
     Waterman), 513
Internal Revenue Service, 105, 129
Inventory, 181, 190, 205, 207, 322
  control, 61, 422
  military, 56, 57
Investment, 9, 217, 317
Itschner, Emerson, 451
ITT, 44, 288, 289, 384, 421

Jamieson, Hugh ("Bill"), 286, 287, 290,
     292, 294–95, 386, 493
Japan
  auto industry, 311, 362, 363
  in World War Two, 67–68, 73
Johnson, Lyndon, 402, 406, 409, 442–

43, 444, 445, 447, 449, 455, 456, 457, 458, 459–60, 490, 494
Joint Chiefs of Staff, 397, 401, 405, 443, 446, 459–60
Judge, Emmett, 225, 336
J. Walter Thompson agency, 263

Kaiser-Fraser, 81
Kearns, David, 433, 434
Kelly, Crosby, 294, 387
Kennedy, Jacqueline, 406–9
Kennedy, John F., 361, 369–72, 393, 394, 397, 402, 404, 405, 406, 443, 443–44, 466
Kennedy, Joseph, 286
Kennedy, Robert, 370, 374–75, 404–5, 406, 408
Kennedy Institute of Politics, 438
Kerley, James, 367, 424, 425, 427
Kerr, James, 349
Kimbrough, John, 28
Korth, Fred, 399–400
Kozmetsky, George, 290, 292, 386
Krafve, Richard, 336, 337

Labor
    costs, 362
    management's role in problems with, 95, 101
    relations, 170
Layoffs, 101
Leadership, 98
Learned, Edmund, 42, 43, 101, 104, 146, 175
Legion of Honor, 256
Legion of Merit, 61
Lehideux, Francois, 181, 198, 199, 200, 201, 202, 203
Lehman Brothers, 244, 287, 288, 289, 492
LeMay, Curtis, 50, 399, 402
Lennox, Donald, 368, 422
Levitt, Theodore, 362
Leyte, 72
Life (magazine), 16, 17, 186, 324, 429
Lilly, Tom, 176, 252

Lincoln, 219, 226, 227, 310, 312, 315–16, 325, 329
    Cosmopolitan, 187
    Zephyr, 269
Lincoln Mercury Dealers Association, 319
Litton, Charles, 243, 244, 286, 288, 290
Litton Industries, Inc., 8, 290–96, 379–90
    acquisitions, 293–94
    stock collapse, 483–91
Lockheed, 237, 240, 385
Lodge, Henry Cabot, 446
Loewy, Raymond, 274–75
Lorenz, Paul, 225
Lovett, Robert, 32, 33, 35, 36, 80, 82, 83, 125, 135, 136, 137, 287, 369, 394
Lundy, Ed, 17, 64*il*, 84, 88, 90*il*, 97, 98, 102, 107, 114, 116, 127, 176, 199, 217, 340, 352, 364, 389, 476, 501, 511, 517, 527, 528–29
    at Ford Motor Company, 132, 163, 365–68, 417–32
Lynch, Gerry, 145

MacArthur, Douglas, 66, 71
McCardell, Archie, 433
McCone, John, 404
McCracken, Paul, 251
McDaniel, Glen, 234, 235, 288, 289, 290
McDonnell, James, 130
Mace, Myles, 49, 50, 85, 187, 188, 235, 290–91, 292, 293, 294, 295
McGee, William, 237
McNamara, Claranell, 46
McNamara, Margy, 85, 117, 250–51, 304, 502–3
McNamara, Robert, 7, 13, 16, 17–18, 19, 21, 38*il*, 45–50, 60, 65, 83, 85–86, 87, 88, 90*il*, 98, 101, 106, 116, 126–27, 143–44, 216, 225, 229, 501, 510, 517, 521–22
    and Ford Falcon, 342–45
    at Ford Motor Company, 133, 163,

McNamara, Robert *(cont.)*
    174–75, 222–23, 247–64, 316–17,
      325, 342–45, 361–65
    at Harvard, 40, 45, 47–48, 49
    head of Ford Division, 218
    involvement in Vietnam War, 437–
      42
    joining of Ford Motor Company,
      85–86
    as leader of Whiz Kids, 147–48
    personal style, 247–57
    receives Medal of Freedom, 459
    as Secretary of Defense, 8, 48, 369–
      76, 393–409, 437–63
    in Vietnam War, 8
    in World War Two, 49–51
McNaughton, John, 455
Mahon, George, 29, 510
Management
    contracts, 191
    control, 485
    cult of, 8, 20, 434
    flow of information to, 313
    free-form, 385
    military, 24
    modern, 515
    overall, 94
    professional, 8, 14–15, 19, 41, 169,
      170, 173, 229, 364–65, 516
    rational, 8, 513
    relations with unions, 95
    responsibility for labor problems,
      95, 101
    revolution in, 44, 50, 515
    role in policy formation, 125
    scientific, 41
    as separate discipline, 170
    techniques, 14
    traditional, 41, 93, 99–101, 516
    in World War Two, 14
Manchester, William, 407
Manufacturing, 279
Market
    niche, 380
    penetration, 342
    research, 311, 339–40

share, 216, 221, 362–63
    surveys, 420
    volume, 198
Marketing, 179, 217, 279, 281, 309,
      337, 339–40, 434–35
    quantification, 255
Maroni, Jacques, 199, 200, 201, 203,
      205, 206, 207, 208, 215, 216, 221,
      224, 315–16, 218, 327
Marshall, George C., 135, 136, 137
Masson, Robert, 425
Masterson, William, 491–92, 495, 496
Mazur, Paul, 287
MBAs, 175, 176, 200, 364, 367, 398,
      426
Mead, George, 58
Medal of Freedom, 459, 503, 506
Menger, Val, 199, 209
Mercury, 215–16, 219, 220–21, 223,
      226, 227, 260, 267–82, 325, 329
    Convertible Cruiser, 213, 323
    as Indy 500 Pace Car, 322–24
    Montclair, 273, 310
    Monterey, 219, 273
    quality problems, 313–22
    sales, 322, 324
    Turnpike Cruiser, 9, 10, 269–82,
      311–12, 322, 326
Mergers, 207–9
Meyers, Bennett E., 23–24, 25
Meyers, Gerry, 425
Michaels, James, 486, 487
Military
    Air Transport Command, 161
    Army Air Force, 13, 18, 19, 20, 33,
      49
    budget, 453
    contracts, 348, 381, 496–97
    disorganization in, 41, 397–98
    electronics, 295–96
    management, 24
    Officer Candidate School, 43, 51
    organization, 24, 57
    purchasing, 398
    Statistical Control group, 24, 35–36,
      40, 42–45, 49–51, 55–60, 66–68

Miller, Arjay, 10, 17, 84, 87, 88, 90*il*,
    97, 103, 105, 106, 114, 126, 127,
    128–29, 163, 249, 278, 364, 501,
    517, 526–28
    at Ford Motor Company, 132, 134–
    35, 136, 163, 172, 365, 411–12,
    416–17
Miller, Fran, 88, 114, 304
Mills, Ben, 17, 79, 84, 87, 88, 90*il*, 98,
    103, 114, 127, 149, 150–51, 216,
    278, 281 501, 510, 530–31
    devotion to work, 301
    at Ford Motor Company, 132, 163,
    181, 248–49, 312–13, 329, 340,
    341
    postwar activities, 81
Mills, Helen, 114, 117, 302, 303
Mintzberg, Henry, 383, 449
Missiles
    air-to-air, 160, 233
    air-to-ground, 397–98
    Falcon, 233
    guidance systems, 160
    intercontinental, 243
    Sidewinder, 398
Mitchell, Don, 234
Monroe Calculating Machine
    Company, 295–96
Moore, George, 7, 17, 64*il*, 65–74, 79,
    83, 88, 90*il*, 97, 107, 113, 114,
    118, 184*il*, 206–7, 279, 355, 356,
    501, 517
    auto dealerships, 139–40, 185–95
    death, 479–80
    financial ruin, 465–80
    at Ford Motor Company, 132–33,
    169
    in Information for Industry, 468–73
    leaves Ford Motor Company, 138–
    40
    postwar activities, 81, 82
    in World War Two, 66–74
Moore, John, 256–57, 260
Moore, Mimi, 64*il*, 67, 68, 70–71, 73–
    74, 113, 114, 116, 139, 184*il*, 191,

    193, 194, 474, 477, 479, 509–10,
    532–33
Moore-Day Motors, 187, 191, 192
Moore-Grear Motors, 191, 192, 466–67
Morse, Wayne, 454
Morsey, Chase, 180, 355
Munro, John, 442

NAACP, 251
Nadal, Robert, 281
Najjar, John, 273
Nance, James, 309, 326, 329, 340, 341,
    342
Nash Motor Company, 79, 81
National Advisory Council on Civil
    Disorders, 490
National Defense Mediation Board, 58
Nevins, Allan, 388, 429
New Deal, 25, 29
New Frontier, 371
Newsom, Earl, 130
New York Central Railroad, 80
New York Stock Exchange, 47, 380
Nitze, Paul, 395–96, 444–45, 453, 457,
    459
Nixon, Richard, 498
North American Aviation, 290, 292
Numbers
    belief in, 8
    in decision-making, 8, 19–20, 42–43,
    56
    measurement through, 41
    patterns in, 45
    power in, 49, 421–22
    trends in, 44
    use in Vietnam War, 447–50

O'Dwyer, Paul, 167
O'Green, Fred, 385, 498, 505
Oldfield, Barney, 505
Oldsmobile, 112, 215, 219, 227
O'Neill, Jim, 433
Organization, 20, 83
    blueprint for, 171–72
    charts, 100, 106, 113, 122*il*, 126, 168,
    178, 421

Organization *(cont.)*
  controlling, 168
  military, 24
  relation to the individual, 170
  and social responsibility, 170
  tables of, 169
The Organization Man (Whyte), 302–3,
    366, 367

Packard, 81
Paris Auto Show, 209, 220
Pearl Harbor, 34, 39, 57, 60, 65
Pentagon, 19, 78, 232, 394, 398, 403–4
Pentagon Papers, 460–61
Personnel, 96
PERT, 419–20
Peters, Tom, 513
Peugeot, 208
Planning, 83
  product, 271, 272–73
Planning-Programming-Budgeting
    System, 401
Plymouth, 227
Policy
  decisions, 93
  information in, 45
  making, 173
  management role in formation of,
    125
Pontiac, 215, 219, 227
Porterfield, Dusty, 85
Power
  and information, 36
  and knowledge, 45
  in numbers, 49, 174
  politics of, 43
  vacuums, 126
PPBS, 401
Price Waterhouse & Co., 48, 49, 117
Princeton University, 84, 97, 114
Product
  divisions, 171
  planning, 179–80, 271, 272–73
  quality, 106, 169, 171–72, 198–99,
    205–6, 309–13, 412–13
  sales, 172

warranty claims, 319–20
Production, 172–73, 321, 513
  costs, 348, 364
  increasing, 181
  lack of regard for people in, 20
  program, 127
  schedules, 126, 127, 168, 311
  units of, 168
Product Planning Committee, 273
Profit
  centers, 175, 177
  forecast, 105, 126, 127
  and loss, 104, 105, 106, 172–73
  before taxes, 223
  true, 174
Program Evaluation and Review
    Technique, 419–20
Protests, antiwar, 437–42, 451, 457
Public relations, 107, 130, 340
Purchasing, 106
  military, 398
  schedules, 127

Quality
  compromises, 368
  control, 337–38
  problems, 171–72, 337
  product, 106, 169, 171, 198, 205–6,
    309–13, 413
  warranty claims, 319–20

Radar, 231–44, 330
  airborne, 160
Radio-Television Manufacturers
    Association, 234
Ramo, Simon, 160, 162, 232, 233, 237,
    239, 242, 243, 244
Ramo-Wooldridge Corp., 243
Ramparts (magazine), 438
Rand Corporation, 395, 460
Reader's Digest (magazine), 255
Reagan, Nancy, 503, 510
Reagan, Ronald, 503
Recession, 321, 340, 348–49
Reith, Jack, 7, 18, 52*il*, 65, 68, 79, 86,

87, 88, 90*il*, 107, 112, 113, 196*il*,
  501, 517, 518
at Avco Manufacturing, 330–32,
  347–49
devotion to work, 300–1, 302
at Ford Motor Company, 163, 173,
  177, 213–27, 267–82
at Ford of France, 197–210
postwar activities, 81
problems at Ford Motor Company,
  309–32
relations with Crusoe, 179–80
suicide, 9, 349–58
termination at Ford Motor
  Company, 326–32
in World War Two, 53–62
Reith, Maxine, 42, 52*il*, 53–55, 60–62,
  113, 116, 198, 200, 210, 273–74,
  301, 302, 303, 327–28, 331–32,
  349–53, 525
Renault, 198, 208
Research
  contracts, 160
  and development, 292
  market, 80, 311, 339–40
Rhoden, Harold, 493–94, 495, 496
Rickover, Hyman, 399
Rivalry, Ford vs. General Motors, 9–
  10, 134–35, 168, 213–14, 218–19,
  344–45
RKO Studios, 157, 158
Robertson, Dale, 157
Romney, George, 330
Roosevelt, Franklin, 15, 25, 29, 30, 32,
  47
Roosevelt, Theodore, 225
Rusk, Dean, 404, 443, 444, 446, 448,
  455

Safety, auto, 256–64
Sales, 216
  by-product, 105
  divisions, 106
  Edsel, 336
  gray-market, 186
  new car, 94

premiums, 186
quantification, 255
reports, 318
staff, 177
used car, 94, 186
Sanders, Tom, 175
Sanders, Wallace, 28
Scheer, Robert, 438
Schweitzer, Edmund, 350
Searles, Ed, 55
Seat belts, 257, 259, 260, 261–62, 263–
  64
Secrest, Fred, 301, 427
Selin, Ivan, 400
Senate Armed Services Committee,
  456
Sharp, Jim, 194
Sheppard, Mervin, 135
Shortages, 106
Shriver, Sargent, 370, 371
Simca, 198, 208
"Singing Statisticians," 43
Singleton, Henry, 290, 292, 386
Size, corporate, 7
Skidmore, Leo, 273
Sloan, Alfred, 170, 171, 257, 282, 314
Smoking, 102
Social responsibility, 101, 112, 170, 256
Spencer, Kenneth, 420
Spruce Goose, 159, 160, 233
Standardization, 20
Standard of living, 8, 218
Standard Oil, 171
Stanford University, 125
Statistical Control group, 24, 35–36,
  40–41, 42–45, 49–51, 56–60, 66–
  67
Statistics, 42, 43
Steel, George, 294
Steele, Emmett, 491–95
Stratemeyer, George, 150
Strikes, 110, 111
Stromberg-Carlson, 234
Studebaker, 81, 274, 309, 340
Students for a Democratic Society,
  438, 440

Styling, 177, 268, 269–70, 272, 274–75, 325, 354
Suburbs, 217
Suicide, 9, 80, 349–58
Suttle, Harold, 68
Sylvania, 234
Symms, John, 85
Synergy, 380–81, 385, 487
Systems, 20
  analysis, 395, 398, 400
  control, 18
  fire-control, 160, 162, 232, 233, 243
  inertial guidance, 292, 386
  quality control, 337–38

Tait, Bob, 234
Tax increases, 453
Taylor, Frederick, 41
Taylor, Maxwell, 406, 443, 444
Technocracy, 176–77
Teledyne, Inc., 386
Texas Technological College, 29, 30
Thomas, Joe, 287
Thomassen, George, 467
Thompson Products Co., 243
Thornton, Charles "Tex," 17–18, 21, 22il, 38il, 62, 65, 82, 90il, 95–96, 225, 415–16, 476, 478, 501, 514, 517, 518, 524
  acquisition of Litton, 285–96
  ambition, 144–45
  childhood, 25–29
  death, 509–11
  disappointment in Henry Ford II, 145–46
  at Ford Motor Company, 123–38, 143–51
  friction with Crusoe, 131–38, 143
  at Harvard, 39–44
  hiring at Ford Motor Company, 82–108
  at Hughes Aircraft, 231–44
  illness, 503–9
  joins Hughes Aircraft, 158–65
  leaves Ford Motor Company, 144–49

leaves Litton, 496–99
at Litton Industries, Inc., 379–90
and Monroe Calculating Machine Company, 294–96
postwar activities, 78–88
receives Medal of Freedom, 506–7
role in Vietnam War, 450–54
stock collapse at Litton, 483–91
sued by Emmett Steele, 491–95
in World War Two, 32–36, 70
Thornton, Flora, 22il, 30–32, 34, 117–18, 305, 306, 490, 496, 506–7, 510, 523–24
Thornton, W. A. "Tex," 25–27
Thurmond, Strom, 456–57
Time (magazine), 107, 206, 262, 336, 350, 353, 389, 394, 429, 490, 491
Titles, 100, 164, 171
Toyota, 343, 362
Truman, Harry, 73, 77, 163, 233
TRW, 243
Tucker, Preston, 162–63
Tuttle, Gordon, 349

UCLA, 114, 117
Unions, labor, 201, 204, 352
  La Confédération Générale du Travail, 200, 204
  relations with management, 95, 101
  strikes, 101
University of California at Berkeley, 47, 117
University of Michigan, 251, 304, 424, 454
University of Notre Dame, 163
U.S. Housing Authority, 30, 32, 79
U.S. Steel, 79
U.S. Treasury, 47

Vedette, 198, 208, 209, 219
Vietnam War, 437–42, 522
  domino theory, 443–44
  protests against, 437–42, 451, 456–57
  use of statistics in, 447–50
Volkswagen, 321, 342, 343, 362, 363

Walker, George, 268, 269, 275
Walker, Russ, 175
Wall Street, 8, 17, 125, 286–87, 289, 294–95, 384
War Department, 14, 32, 33, 34, 35
    disorganization in, 40
Warnock, Gayle, 327, 339
Waterman, Robert, 513
Webber, Jimmy, 226
Weeks, David, 473
Weinberg, Sidney, 375, 471
Western Electric, 234
Westinghouse, 160, 233
Westmoreland, William, 442–43, 444, 445, 448, 450, 456
Wheeler, Earle, 397, 460
White, Thomas, 399
Whiz Kids
    devotion to work, 299–306
    effect on modern organizations, 515–19
    at Ford Motor Company, 123–38, 143–51, 168–82
    hiring by Henry Ford II, 13–21, 83–108
    personal lives, 299–306
    social relations, 111–20
    and Statistical Control unit, 35–74
    and World War Two, 23–74
Whyte, William, 302–3, 366, 367
Wiesner, Jerry, 405, 406
Williams, Walker, 261
Wilson, Charles, 123
Wolfe, Kenneth, 232

Wooldridge, Dean, 160, 162, 232, 233, 237, 239–40, 242, 243, 244
Workers, treatment by management, 95, 101
Works Progress Administration, 29
World Bank, 458, 501, 521–22
World War Two, 7, 13–15, 32–36, 49–51, 53–62, 66–74
    demobilization, 78
    management in, 24
    Statistical Control group in, 42–45, 56–60, 66–68
Wright, Alice, 103, 117, 415, 525
Wright, James, 18, 38*il*, 60, 84, 90*il*, 95–96, 102, 107, 114, 118, 148, 216, 277–78, 476, 501, 510, 525–26, 529–30
    at Ford Motor Company, 163, 169, 172–73, 177, 276–77, 316, 361, 362, 374–75
    with Ford of France, 181–82
    leaves Ford Motor Company, 411–16

Xerox, 433–34

Yntema, Ted, 224
Yonkers Ford, 190–91
Young, Robert, 79, 80, 83, 87
Youngren, Harold, 130

Zaleznik, Abraham, 229
Zuckert, Eugene, 193, 194, 195, 396, 402, 441, 468, 469, 475–76, 479